LIQUIDITY ANALYSIS AND MANAGEMENT

LIQUIDITY ANALYSIS AND MANAGEMENT

SECOND EDITION

George W. Gallinger
Arizona State University

P. Basil Healey
Wilfrid Laurier University

ADDISON-WESLEY PUBLISHING COMPANY

Reading, Massachusetts □ Menlo Park, California
New York □ Don Mills, Ontario □ Wokingham, England
Amsterdam □ Bonn □ Sydney □ Singapore □ Tokyo
Madrid □ San Juan

Library of Congress Cataloging-in-Publication

Gallinger, George W.
    Liquidity analysis and management / George W. Gallinger, P. Basil
Healey. — 2nd ed.
      p.   cm.
    Includes bibliographical references and index.
    ISBN 0-201-53533-5
    1. Cash management. 2. Corporations — Finance. I. Healey, P.
Basil. II. Title.
HG4028.C45G34 1991
658.15'244 — dc20   90-725
                                                   CIP

ISBN 0-201-53533-5
1 2 3 4 5 6 7 8 9 10-MA-95 94 93 92 91

Preface

Financial managers conduct their business in an environment that requires frequent decisions to be made to direct economic activities that create economic value for shareholders. The academic literature is replete with theoretical discussion and models pertaining to long-term value-enhancing decisions. Unfortunately, the same cannot be said for short-term financial decision management, more commonly referred to as working capital management. The purpose of this book is to make a small contribution to help alleviate this deficiency.

Short-term financial management has different focuses than those of long-term financial decision making. The first difference is the shorter time dimension. Short-term financial management is concerned with day-to-day operating decisions. The strategic issues of dividend policy, long-term investments, and capital structure are primarily the province of long-term financial management. A second difference is that short-term financial management has a stronger accounting orientation than does long-term financial management — an emphasis that is prevalent in this book.

Traditionally, short-term financial management has been referred to as (net) working capital management — the management of current assets and current liabilities. The duration of these assets and liabilities is considered to be a year or less. The objective when one is managing these short-lived assets and liabilities is the maintenance of adequate *liquidity* to meet obligations as they come due. Since the emphasis is on liquidity, we prefer to think of working capital management as *liquidity management*. Liquidity management is a more descriptive and accurate title of the responsibilities associated with short-term financial decisions.

Analysis of liquidity requires understanding of cash flows — both *to* the business and *from* the business. This chore may seem simple enough.

Unfortunately, these flows can become very difficult to understand under accrual accounting concepts. The primary purpose of accrual accounting is to match expenses with revenues generated in the normal operations of the business. The emphasis is on satisfactory estimation of profits, *not* cash flows. However, the accrual accounting exercise of determining profits affects the balance sheet and the overall financial condition of the firm. The opportunity for management to select from a number of generally accepted accounting principles for recording inventories, tax liabilities, and contra accounts, for example, requires financial statement analysts to conduct a thorough analysis if they are to understand the quality of the earnings and the true liquidity of the company. Unfortunately, most books in finance ignore many of the accounting issues that affect liquidity. Although no statement is made for the reason, the implication is that the untangling of anything other than the simplest accrual accounting complexities more properly belongs with the accountants.

We agree that the accounting functions should be left to the accountants. However, if you are to understand liquidity management, you must feel comfortable with accounting. When you do, you should have a better appreciation of the relationship between economic value and the accountant's historical cost value — and, subsequently, of corporate liquidity and the financial condition of the firm.

Objective

The objective of this book is to reconsider traditional analytical techniques and to investigate new approaches to the liquidity management decision process. The tools of analysis cross the disciplines of accounting, economics, finance, and mathematics. The emphasis is on everyday operations of the firm from a financial perspective. Long-term financial management topics such as dividend policy, optimal capital structure, and capital budgeting decisions are discussed only in terms of their significance to liquidity management. A number of topics discussed in various academic and practitioner journals, but not generally included in financial management books, are examined here. A partial list of these topics includes off-balance sheet financing, variance analysis models, improved liquidity indicators, and hedging techniques. The topics examined in this book should both broaden and deepen your understanding of liquidity management.

Coverage

The book is divided into four parts: (1) foundations, (2) financial analysis of liquidity, (3) cash and risk management, and (4) trade credit and inventory management.

Part I consists of the first two chapters. These chapters introduce two important concepts that must be understood: "How to go broke . . . while making a profit" and the importance of marginal analysis in financial decision making.

Part II includes Chapters 3 through 6. These chapters discuss financial statement analysis and closely related topics for understanding liquidity. Emphasis is on understanding cash flows and learning about liquidity measures that are better than those that have been traditionally used.

Part III covers Chapters 7 through 11. Coverage includes cash management, hedging, and asset-based financing. Each of these areas plays an important role in liquidity management.

Part IV consists of Chapters 12 through 17. Discussion pertains to management of credit and inventories.

Part V consists of a summary chapter.

Four end-of-book appendices, which pertain to forecasting accounts receivable flows and bankruptcy and reorganization, conclude the coverage. A bibliography of selected readings is found at the end of the book.

Several chapters have appendices. We have attempted to place involved mathematical material, or material that is important but can be ignored without affecting the continuity of the discussion, in appendices.

Features

The basic features of the first edition have been improved upon. However, the book still has:

- Several illustrations per chapter to clarify and summarize important concepts and techniques.
- Discussion of the shortcomings of traditional ratio analysis.
- Up-to-date coverage of all topics.
- A breadth and depth to topics not covered by competitors' books.
- Discussion that consistently relates liquidity management to the wealth-maximizing criteria.
- Extensive questions and problems in each chapter.
- W.T. Grant Company as a unifying example to show that management had very little understanding of liquidity management.

We have made a number of significant changes in this second edition. Suggestions we received from people who used the first edition, and from very conscientious reviewers of this edition, have been incorporated. We greatly appreciate the time they took to express their thoughts to us.

A very important change in this edition is a significant reorganization of chapters. This has been done to better integrate the material. The following discussion briefly summarizes chapter-by-chapter changes.

☐ *Chapter 1: Introduction to Liquidity Management.* The explanation of the residual income model has been greatly expanded. A detailed illustration shows the difference between accounting profit and economic profit, using residual income as a proxy for economic profit.

☐ *Chapter 2: Economic Fundamentals for Analysis of Liquidity.* Subtle changes have been made in an effort to clarify discussion and help tie economic profit and residual income together.

☐ *Chapter 3: Cash Flow Analysis.* This is a new chapter on cash flows. Some of the material was part of Chapter 6 in the first edition. Given the recent emphasis that the Financial Accounting Standards Board (FASB) has placed on cash flows, we felt it necessary to introduce the reader to this material earlier. Also, by placing the discussion of cash flows here a more natural transition is made from the economist's often abstract concept of profit to information that is available in accounting records.

☐ *Chapter 4: Traditional Financial Analysis: Some Shortcomings.* This was Chapter 3 in the first edition. It has undergone a major reorganization and has assimilated material about bankrupty warning signals previously included in Chapter 19.

☐ *Chapter 5: Off-Balance-Sheet Financing and Financial Analysis.* The discussion of off-balance-sheet financing (formerly Chapter 4) has been updated to incorporate the FASB's recent pronouncements. The discussion on project financing has been expanded to discuss R&D limited partnerships. Brief discussions about interest rates swaps and postemployment benefits are now included in this chapter.

☐ *Chapter 6: Indicators of Liquidity.* This was Chapter 5 in the first edition. The discussion of maximizing ROE with debt (along with the calculus) has been removed to an appendix. Discussion pertaining to sustainable growth and cash breakeven analysis has been improved.

☐ *Chapter 7: Overview of Cash Management.* A key change in this chapter is the inclusion of payment techniques from Chapter 16 of the first edition. This has allowed separate sections to be included on techniques for accelerating cash inflows and for decelerating cash outflows. A new section on international cash management is included.

☐ *Chapter 8: Minimizing Cash Balances.* This chapter has undergone a major reorganization. The discussion starts with new material on the motives for holding cash balances. This is followed by discussions of theoretical models for managing cash, practical cash management applications, and liquidity indices. Discussion of the liquidity flow index has been clarified.

□ *Chapter 9: Duration Analysis and Hedging with Futures.* This was Chapter 18 in the first edition. The discussion on options has been eliminated (and now included in the next chapter) and a discussion of duration analysis has been included.

□ *Chapter 10: Hedging with Options, Options on Futures, and Interest Rate Swaps.* This chapter includes the discussion of options from the first edition's Chapter 18 and adds interest rate swaps as a means of hedging. The discussion about options is greatly improved from the first edition.

□ *Chapter 11: Asset-Based Financing.* This was Chapter 17 in the first edition. Significant changes have been made. The discussion on factoring has been streamlined, whereas discussions about other forms of asset-based financing have been expanded. Asset securitization is a new topic discussed.

□ *Chapter 12: Credit Selection Models.* This was Chapter 11 in the first edition. Several changes have been made. A discussion of traditional sources of credit information is included and incorporated with the five C's of credit, which has been streamlined. The discussion on sequential decision models has been revised to sever its link to Chapter 10 in the first edition.

□ *Chapter 13: Analysis of Credit Policy.* This is the first edition's Chapter 9 with a slightly different title. Some aspects of the first edition's Chapter 16 on accounts payable management are incorporated here. However, the most notable change in this chapter is the inclusion of the derivation of the residual income model for analyzing credit decisions.

□ *Chapter 14: Monitoring Trade Credit.* This is Chapter 12 of the first edition with parts of Chapter 16 incorporated. The title has been changed to reflect the fact that the monitoring of outstanding receivables and payables is basically the same. Minor changes have been made to improve the discussion.

□ *Chapter 15: Inventory Accounting and Cash Flow Effects.* This was Chapter 13 in the first edition. Most changes in this chapter pertain to the discussion on variable versus absorption costing.

□ *Chapter 16: Inventory Investment: How Much?* This was Chapter 14 in the first edition. The chapter has an expanded discussion of just-in-time (JIT) inventory and how it relates to materials requirement planning and economic order quantity (EOQ) analysis.

☐ *Chapter 17: Monitoring Inventory Balances.* This chapter, which was formerly Chapter 15, received minor changes.

☐ *Chapter 18: A Summary.* This chapter is a carryover from the first edition.

☐ *Appendix 1: Forecasting Accounts Receivable Flows.* This was Chapter 10 in the first edition.

☐ *Appendix 2: Corporate Bankruptcy, Reorganization, and Liquidation.* This was Chapter 19 in the first edition. As mentioned above, part of the material is now included in Chapter 4.

The second edition also has some ancillary material. Included in the *Instructor's Manual* are 413 true-false questions and 397 multiple-choice questions that have been class tested. This represents about 22 true-false questions and 21 multiple-choice questions for each chapter, including the appendices.

Who Should Read This Book

This book is intended for both business students and business professionals. In the academic environment it is aimed at senior-level undergraduate and MBA students majoring in either finance or accounting. The book is appropriate either as a primary text for a lecture and problem-solving course or as a reference text in a case course. Students who study this book should be in a position to immediately contribute to the daily management of corporate liquidity. This book is also intended for treasurers, controllers, finance directors, budget analysts, and business consultants involved in liquidity analysis. People in these positions may learn new techniques as well as improve their understanding of existing techniques.

There are some minimum prerequisites if the reader is to enjoy the benefits we feel can be gained from this book. These prerequisites are as follows:

☐ An understanding of introductory finance and accounting. Knowledge of intermediate accounting will help in certain areas, although it is not necessary.

☐ A basic working knowledge of high school algebra. If you are willing to learn some matrix algebra and elementary calculus, you will obtain a better appreciation of some of the models we discuss.

☐ A willingness to have some of your preconceptions about finance challenged. We show that various ratios discussed in many finance books are questionable tools. We also show that to understand finance, at least as it pertains to liquidity management, you must have a better understanding of accounting.

Acknowledgments

Many people have been involved in this book. The first edition benefited from the encouragement and insightful criticisms of William Beranek of the University of Georgia, Russell P. Boisjoly of Fairfield University, Michael D. Carpenter of the University of Kentucky, Thomas E. Copeland of McKinsey & Co., Richard Norgaard of the University of Connecticut, Keith V. Smith of Purdue University, and John Stowe of the University of Missouri. Frank T. Griggs and Joo-hyun Kim, former doctoral students at Arizona State University, and Chris Maziarz, an MBA alumnus at Wilfrid Laurier University, made significant contributions.

The thoughtful reviewers of this second edition are Russell P. Boisjoly of Fairfield University, C. Steven Cole of the University of North Texas, Brian Kluger of the University of Cincinnati, James W. Pennington of Babson College, Alan Frankel of Boise State, and Philip Horvath of Bradley University.

Individuals at Addison-Wesley who deserve recognition are Barbara Rifkind, our editor, Kari Heen, her assistant, Kazia Navas, production supervisor, Barbara Pendergast, for production services, Cynthia Benn, for copy editing the manuscript, and Jason Jordan, production coordinator for the IM material.

Lastly, we thank our wives for their patience while we devoted the many hours it takes to see a project of this nature to completion.

Undoubtedly, there are still some errors that have not been eliminated (the fault lies with the coauthor). We encourage you to bring any errors, differences of opinion, or topics you feel should be included to our attention. We hope that our labors have minimized any serious distractions. We feel that the topics discussed in this book can be readily transferred to practice. This book is not meant to be one of those that is fine in theory but not in practice. Enjoy your reading!

Tempe, Arizona   G. W. G.
Waterloo, Ontario   P. B. H.

Contents

PART II ☐
Financial Analysis of Liquidity

CHAPTER 3 ☐
Cash Flow Analysis   41

CHAPTER 4 ☐
Traditional Financial Analysis: Some Shortcomings   68

Foundations of Liquidity Analysis

CHAPTER 1 □

Introduction to Liquidity Management

Liquidity management *is the allocation of liquid resources over time for payment of obligations due and for various investments that management undertakes to maximize shareholder wealth.* This definition emphasizes the dynamic nature of liquidity management, that is, the providing of resources at times when they are needed and the control of various financial risks, especially that of insolvency.

Liquidity management is frequently thought to be synonymous with **net working capital** *(NWC) management* — the management of current assets and current liabilities. Such a view fails to capture the true nature of liquidity management. NWC management (or as it is popularly known, short-term financial management) is a subset of liquidity management. It is through liquidity management that NWC management is linked with long-term financial management and **wealth maximization** for shareholders. This will become apparent as you learn about different profit concepts, cash flow analysis, techniques for evaluating liquidity, how to account for off-balance-sheet financing, and how to monetize assets, among other things.

History is replete with examples of good and bad management. Periods of economic recession are generally perceived to be times of liquidity problems. However, periods of economic prosperity have also proven to be burdens to prudent liquidity management. Economic growth, whether inflationary or real, drains cash. Participating in a strong market is exciting, but keeping up with the pace requires liquid resources. Even if real market growth is zero, inflation may consume limited financial resources almost as quickly as real growth. The failure of management to provide adequate liquid resources to finance growth objectives and meet liabilities as they come due has been as common a cause of business failure as have economic recessions. *Dun & Bradstreet,* in its periodic studies of the causes of business failures, reports that managerial incompetence is the primary reason for bankruptcy.

Perhaps the most fundamental change that has occurred in economies of the Western world since World War II is government legislation influencing the availability and cost of money. Government goals of reduced unemployment and a high standard of living with minimal inflation have produced such a strong consumer and social demand for goods and services that businesses and governments have been hard-pressed to satisfy it, even while utilizing all available credit.

Figure 1.1 indicates how the increased demands for credit have been reflected in the rising cost of money over the past 30 years. Formerly, increasing costs of money reduced the credit demand when growth and speculation became excessive. In recent years cost has been less significant than the availability of funds in controlling the demand for money, as evidenced

FIGURE 1.1
Supply and Cost of Funds

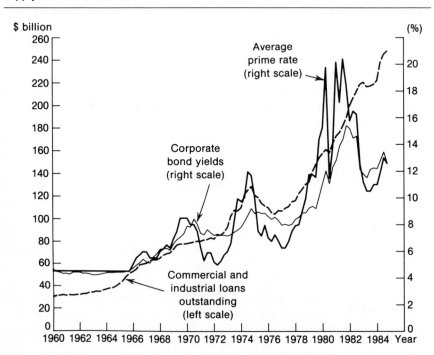

Source: Data from *Federal Bulletins* and issues of *Survey of Current Business.*

by credit restrictions in the mid-1960s and by a latent interest in the use of credit control in highly inflationary periods.

Corporate financial managers must learn to live with relatively expensive and limited supplies of money under various economic conditions. Their role has become more important in determining corporate policy and direction. It is the responsibility not only of the chief financial officer but also of the treasurer, controller, credit manager, and all other financial personnel to seek ways to make more effective use of corporate cash resources in order to satisfy the heavy cash demands of the corporation during growth periods as well as during recessions. Furthermore, financial personnel need to strive to improve the rate of return on corporate assets by recycling underutilized liquid resources into expanding assets or temporarily investing them in the money markets until they are needed to support corporate operations designed to satisfy company objectives.

Corporate Objectives

The discipline of economics defines the firm as an economic *profit-* or *wealth-maximizing entity* dealing in markets of varying degrees of competition. The definition has remained virtually unchanged for 200 years. Noticeably absent in most discussions of valuation of the firm is explicit discussion of how liquidity affects value by managers seeking to maximize shareholders' wealth.[1]

Given the dominant role that *agency theory* now plays in corporate finance, the importance of liquidity management to valuation of a firm may receive more attention. Under agency theory, management is generally considered to perform in a manner that will result in maximizing its utility, possibly at the expense of creditors (including employees) or shareholders or both.[2] This may be accomplished by following strategies that maximize sales or size, growth, or market share, or management's own survival, perquisites, and peace of mind.

Conflicting interests among parties to the firm — creditors, managers, and shareholders — may lead to suboptimal allocation of resources

---

[1]Examples of notable exceptions are R. A. Cohn and J. J. Pringle, "Steps Toward an Integration of Corporate Finance Theory," in *Readings on Short-Term Financial Management,* 3rd ed., edited by K. V. Smith and G. W. Gallinger (St. Paul, MN: West, 1988), pp. 10–16, and H. Bierman, K. Chopra and L. J. Thomas, "Ruin Considerations: Optimal Working Capital and Capital Structure," *Journal of Financial and Quantitative Analysis* (March 1975): 119–28.

[2]This is certainly evidenced by management's usage of golden parachutes, poison pills, and greenmail tactics to ward off unfriendly takeover attempts. Also management participation in leveraged buyouts (LBO) has frequently been at the expense of shareholders. For example, management involved in the LBO of Cone Mills attempted to have a low value placed on the firm prior to submitting an offer to buy it.

within the company. This productive inefficiency exhibits itself in the form of *agency problems*. The term derives from the fact that corporate decisions are delegated to agents (the managers) who perform on behalf of the other parties.

In an effort to minimize agency problems, creditors and shareholders cause the firm to incur *agency costs*, which are largely expenditures to monitor managerial actions. Failure of creditors and shareholders to exercise prudent control over management can result in serious financial problems. The financial press is replete with stories of management allegedly misappropriating funds for its own benefit (e.g., American Continental Corporation), using poor business judgment to satisfy management ego (e.g., Pinnacle West), fraudulently reporting financial results (e.g., MiniScribe), and so on. These stories suggest that breakdowns occur in the often invoked assumption that sufficient processes of control (e.g., the threat of proxy fights or takeovers) or motivation (e.g., alignment of management's incentive compensation with the stock price) exist to remove any conflicts between the individual and corporate functions of the managers.

However, in general, if complex legal contracts can be structured between management, creditors, and shareholders, then management, acting in its own best interests, will pursue goals that are basically consistent with wealth maximization for shareholders.[3] This also means that creditors are generally treated fairly; that is, shareholders do not make it a habit of expropriating wealth from the firm's creditors. If they did, management would eventually find access to suppliers, skilled labor, and capital markets difficult, if not impossible.

The Objective of Liquidity Management

From a liquidity perspective, value maximization is secondary to survival. The most fundamental objective of liquidity management is to ensure corporate solvency. **Solvency** is a dynamic task and is a function of the allocation of resources, the rate of conversion of assets into cash, the

[3]W. G. Lewellen, "Management and Ownership in a Large Firm," *Journal of Finance* (May 1969): 299–322, concluded that managers' decisions are consistent with the idea of stock price maximization. A. Coughlan and R. Schmidt, "Executive Compensation, Management Takeover, and Firm Performance: An Empirical Investigation," *Journal of Accounting and Economics* (April 1985): 43–66, find a significant positive relationship between executive compensation and changes in shareholder wealth. M. W. McDaniel, "Bondholders and Corporate Governance," *Business Lawyer* (February 1986): 413–460, concludes that maximization of the firm's valuation should be management's goal. Such a goal is consistent with maximization of shareholders' wealth only if bondholders' interests are protected.

profitability of the firm, and the firm's creditworthiness and debt-paying ability. The word *solvency* has two meanings: actual solvency and technical solvency. Actual solvency is important in a theoretical sense, whereas technical solvency is important in a practical sense.

In the theoretical sense, *actual solvency* is a state in which the market value of the assets of a firm exceeds its debts. Asset values must be sufficiently great to meet all creditors' claims. This notion of solvency, however, is of limited use. The fact that asset values exceed liabilities can be determined actually only by the sale of the assets. Such a means for testing solvency cannot be used by an ongoing business. No other means for estimating asset values is fully dependable, and hence none indicates with precision whether a firm is actually solvent. In practice, action is based on a condition of *technical solvency*.

It is this second meaning of the word that is operational and is used throughout the text. A business is said to be technically solvent if it pays its obligations as they fall due. In this sense determining whether the business is solvent is easy. Deciding whether there are obligations, whether they are due, and whether they are paid can be done with readily available facts. For example, the judicial tests for deciding whether a firm is bankrupt are based on this concept of technical solvency.

Resource allocation decisions are very important to liquidity management if insolvency risk is to be contained. The appetite for cash is voracious in even the most efficient firm, but management does not seek to hold cash, for idle cash is unprofitable cash. Hence as soon as cash is received, it should be committed elsewhere — for example, in the expansion of the firm, in its income-earning activities, in the distribution of dividends, and in the payment of creditors. Managers tend, however, to limit the outflow of cash to creditors for two reasons: First, they can use the cash more profitably within the business. Second, since short-term trade credit finance is usually considered interest free, they will not pay it off until it is due. Therefore, one would expect to see current liabilities maintained at the maximum level compatible with the firm's debt-paying ability and need for cash funds.

Since the ability to pay obligations in cash is the criterion of solvency, the manner in which a firm holds its assets may be more crucial than a favorable net working capital position — that is, the difference between current assets and current liabilities. At the extreme the conclusion is that with perfect conditions the firm will have no current assets on hand on any one day and will always be operating in part with resources supplied by creditors. Thus net working capital has little relevance to operating efficiency and liquidity management. The important question concerning liquidity is the ability of the firm to pay in the future, not how much net working capital, profit, or even cash it has at present.

Profits versus Cash Flows

The objective of the firm often mentions maximizing profits, whereas the objective of liquidity management emphasizes cash flows. Therefore you must be aware of the difference between profits, both accounting and economic, and cash flows.

The determination of profit would present no difficulties if it were measured from the beginning of the firm's life to the day the firm goes out of business. In this case the company's debts would be paid off, and the value remaining over the amount the owners had committed to the business would represent the profit for the period — assuming, of course, that no nonwage payments had been made to the owners.

But two things are wrong with this picture. First, most businesses do not begin with the idea of going out of business at the end of some definite period. Most are initiated with the hope of operating in perpetuity. Second, financial data must be current to be useful. Investors cannot wait until the firm goes out of business to know whether additions have been made to their wealth (the firm operated at a profit) or capital was consumed (the firm operated at a loss). For financial data to be used, estimates of additions or subtractions to wealth over a period shorter than the life of the business must be made annually, quarterly, monthly, or over some shorter period, depending on the needs of management and investors.

Accounting Profits

Since measuring true profit, with precision, over any period less than the life of the company is not possible, accountants are forced to estimate profit by applying a consistent, logical procedure in some arbitrarily chosen time period. For this period, they must, in effect, make assumptions about what the future will hold, assumptions that may or may not prove true.

In most businesses some assets will be used over a period greater than the arbitrary accounting period. The amount of revenues and the amount of costs that can properly be assigned to the period are a matter of judgment. Much of the technical logic of accounting is associated with rules for assigning revenues and costs to arbitrary accounting periods. In an accounting sense **profit** is defined as *the amount by which realized revenue for a period exceeds the historical cost of the assets used up to obtain the revenue.* This provisional concept of profit measurement allows periodic estimates to be made of the results of operations on the company's resources.

Even though the determination of profit for periods shorter than the life of the business enterprise involves judgments and cannot be accomplished with precision, the generally accepted accounting principles that guide this estimate still point toward the basic concept of profit as a surplus of, or accretion to, resources committed to the firm: an amount, in effect, that could be distributed as dividends without curtailing the earnings base on the firm (assuming no inflation). Hence profit, to the accountant, is a residual concept based on the identification of explicit costs. It is owner-oriented, static, and historical. It can be manipulated by using combinations of generally accepted accounting principles, which include, among others, methods of depreciation, inventory valuation, capitalization versus expensing techniques, and the use of acquisition accounting in mergers.

Cash Flows

Profit is generally perceived by most people as being the appropriate barometer for measuring a firm's success. Such a view often fails to ascertain the *quality of earnings* (a concept that is discussed further in Chapter 4). For example, if a credit sale is made, the accounting records will show a profit (assuming the selling price exceeds costs) and the creation of an account receivable. However, the profit is not recognized in a cash flow sense until the receivable is actually collected. However, to wait for the collection to record a profit is contrary to the accountant's matching and realization principles. This aspect of timing is the basis for the difference between profits and cash flows.

The concept of **cash flow** is vitally important in the management of a business. Managers are concerned with allocating resources in such a way that they are used optimally to maximize the long-run market value of the company. In the short run the timing and matching of inflows (conversion of noncash asset balances to cash) and outflows (payment of currently due liability balances with cash) of resources must be balanced so that sufficient liquid resources are on hand to meet demands by creditors. In this context the main interest centers on net liquid resources. In short, managing cash is more important than earning an adequate profit. Earning a good profit does not necessarily guarantee adequate cash flow when needed. *Waiting too long to turn profit into cash reduces the value of the profit.*

ILLUSTRATION 1.1

Several years ago *Business Week* magazine ran an article entitled "How to Go Broke While Making a Profit." It is summarized below to emphasize the significant difference between profits and cash flow.

How to Go Broke . . . While Making a Profit

As the year started, Mr. Jones of the ABC Co. was in fine shape. His company made widgets — just what the consumer wanted. He made them for $.75 each, sold them for $1. He kept a 30 day supply in inventory, *paid his bills promptly,* and billed his customers 30 days net. Sales were right on target, with the sales manager predicting a steady increase. It felt like his lucky year, and it began this way:

   □ Jan. 1: Cash $1000, inventory $750, receivables $1000, equity $2750.

In January, he sold 1000 widgets; shipped them at a cost of $750; collected his receivables — winding up with a tidy $250 profit and his books looked like this:

   □ Feb. 1: Cash $1250, inventory $750, receivables $1000, equity $3000.

This month sales jumped, as predicted, to 1500. With a corresponding step-up in production to maintain his 30 day inventory, he made 2000 units at a cost of $1500. All receivables from January sales were collected. Profit so far: $625. Now his books looked like this:

   □ Mar. 1: Cash $750, inventory $1125, receivables $1500, equity $3375.

March sales were even better: 2000 units.

Collections: on time. Production, to adhere to his inventory policy: 2500 units. Operating result for the month: $500 profit. Profit to date: $1125. His books:

   □ Apr. 1: Cash $375, inventory $1500, receivables $2000, equity $3875.

In April, sales jumped another 500 units to 2500 — and Jones patted his sales manager on the back. His customers were paying right on time. Production was pushed to 3000 units, and the month's business netted him $625 for a profit to date of $1750. He took off to Florida before he saw the accountant's report:

   □ May 1: Cash $125, inventory $1875, receivables $2500, equity $4500.

May saw Jones's company really hitting a stride — sales of 3000 widgets, production of 3500 and a five month profit of $2500. But suddenly, he got a phone call from his treasurer: "Come home! We need money!" His books had caught up with him:

   □ June 1: Cash $0, inventory $2250, receivables $3000, equity $5250.

He came home — and hollered for his banker.

Source: Reprinted from the April 28, 1956, issue of *Business Week* by special permission, © 1956 by McGraw-Hill, Inc.

   Table 1.1, which lists the sources and uses of resources, captures the critical interactions and relationships between accounting profits and cash flows.
   The message of this illustration is clear: Profits are wonderful, but liquidity is critical.   □

Economic Profits

The "How to Go Broke . . ." illustration provides an excellent bridge between accounting profits, cash flows, and economic profits. The derivation of accounting profit leaves much to be desired for financial decision making. **Economic costs** are vital considerations in this process. Economists and accountants use what appear to be identical definitions of profit. Profit is a firm's total revenues minus its total costs. However, economists think of

TABLE 1.1
How to Go Broke ... While Making a Profit
Sources and Uses of Resources

	Feb.	Mar.	Apr.	May	June	Total
			Beginning of			
Sources						
Profits	$ 250	$375	$500	$625	$750	$2500
Uses						
Receivables	$ 0	$500	$500	$500	$500	$2000
Inventories	0	375	375	375	375	1500
Total	$ 0	$875	$875	$875	$875	$3500
⟨Increase⟩/decrease						
in cash	⟨$ 250⟩	$500	$375	$250	$125	$1000
Cash balance	$1250	$750	$375	$125	$ 0	

profits in terms of cash flows and economic costs, or opportunity costs, which encompass both explicit and implicit costs. **Economic profits** *are a cash flow concept.* Accountants fail to include in total costs many of the implicit costs incurred by a business. Implicit costs are the opportunity costs of the resources the firm's owners make available for production without direct outlays of cash. Examples include the value of the entrepreneur's labor, the interest that could be earned on the owner's assets if they were not tied up in the business, and the cost of capital used to finance the business.

Residual Income

Rational decision making should be based on economic costs and profits. But to identify all implicit costs and assign a value to them is often difficult. So that we can operationalize the economist's definition of profit, the profit objective of the firm is defined here as being the maximization of **residual income**,[4] which is reconcilable to the net present value technique. And since the net present value model is equivalent to the economist's marginal revenue, marginal cost model the residual income approach is logically consistent with a wealth maximization objective.

The net present value (NPV) model is generally accepted as being

---

[4]Ezra Solomon was an early advocate of residual income in his book *The Theory of Financial Management* (New York: Columbia University Press, 1963). General Electric Company uses a residual income model to help determine executive incentive compensation bonuses.

appropriate for evaluating investment decisions. A general specification of the model is

$$\text{NPV} = -I_0 + \sum_{t=1}^{N} F_t \frac{(1 - \tau)}{(1 + k)^t} \geq 0, \tag{1.1}$$

where I_0 is the necessary incremental investment at time zero, F_t is the incremental pretax *cash flow from operations* occurring in period t, τ is the marginal corporate tax rate, and k is the appropriate risk-adjusted discount rate.[5] Management is willing to accept projects down to the point where the NPV is zero, for at this point marginal revenue from the project equals its marginal cost.

The NPV model can be readily converted to the *residual income model*. Assume that F_t is constant (thus the subscript can be dropped) and N approaches infinity; that is, the life of the project is infinite. Equation (1.1) can be rewritten as

$$\text{NPV} = -I_0 + F(1 - \tau)/k. \tag{1.2}$$

If both sides of the equation are multiplied by k, residual income (RI) can be stated as

$$\text{RI} = k(\text{NPV}) = F(1 - \tau) - kI_0. \tag{1.3}$$

Thus management is fulfilling the wealth maximization objective whenever it undertakes investments where after-tax cash flows from operations are greater than or equal to the opportunity cost of investment as measured in dollars; that is $F(1 - \tau) \geq kI_0$, or stated differently, when residual income is greater than or equal to zero.

Adjusting operating cash flows for a required dollar return on investment requires management to acknowledge that resources tied up in investments have an opportunity cost associated with them. Management must cover all costs, not just those costs that appear on the income statement, if investors are to be adequately compensated for risk. Unfortunately, investment opportunity costs are things accountants do not measure when they organize the firm's financial statements.

ILLUSTRATION 1.2

It is relatively easy to translate accounting income into residual income. Table 1.2 shows the accounting profits of Illustration 1.1 to be $2500. However, not all sales revenue has been collected nor has all inventory been

---

[5]Excellent discussions can be found in many corporate finance and investment books on how to calculate k. The firm's weighted average cost of capital can be used as an approximation of k.

TABLE 1.2
How to Go Broke ... While Making a Profit
Residual Income Calculation

	Jan.	Feb.	Mar.	Apr.	May	June	Total
			Beginning of				
Sales		$1000	$1500	$2000	$2500	$3000	$10,000
Cost of Sales		750	1125	1500	1875	2250	7500
Profit		$ 250	$ 375	$ 500	$ 625	$ 750	$ 2500

							Total change
Cash	$1000	$1250	$ 750	$ 375	$ 125	$ 0	($1000)
Receivables	1000	1000	1500	2000	2500	3000	2000
Inventory	750	750	1125	1500	1875	2250	1500
Equity	$2750	$3000	$3375	$3875	$4500	$5250	$2500

Sales minus increase in receivables: $10000 − $2000	=	$8000
Cost of sales plus increase in inventory: $7500 + $1500	=	9000
Cash flow from operations		($1000)
Opportunity cost of capital (kI_0): $0.10 \times \$3792$	=	379
Residual income		($1379)

Note: k is assumed to be 10 percent. I_0 is calculated as a six-point average of investment, January through June. If end-of-period investment is used to calculate I_0, the opportunity cost of capital is $525.

sold. Indeed, accounts receivable have been increased $2000 over the period. This represents an investment or use of resources and means that $2000 of recorded revenues have not been collected. Thus, cash sales were $8000 (that is, $10,000 − $2000).

Inventory increased $1500. This also represents a use of resources. It is beneficial to think of inventory as a deferred expense — not as an asset. The investment in inventory is made up of material, labor, and overhead, which get formally recognized as an expense when the inventory is sold. In the context of economic profit, the $1500 inventory increase represents an economic cost. Hence, the economic cost of sales is $9000 (that is, $7500 + $1500).

The subtraction of economic cost of sales from the economic revenues results in a loss of $1000 versus an accounting profit of $2500. When an adjustment[6] is made for the opportunity cost of capital, residual income (the proxy for economic profit) becomes a negative $1379. Although the

---

[6]Later chapters will introduce more complexity into the residual income calculation.

firm is profitable in an accounting sense, it is very unprofitable in an economic context.[7] Unfortunately, this is all too common. Management tends to stress accrual accounting profits when, to be realistic, the emphasis should be on cash flows and economic profits.   □

What Lies Ahead?

The preceding discussion has laid some important foundations for understanding liquidity analysis and management. The residual income model will reappear in a number of future chapters. Chapter 2 discusses liquidity in the framework of microeconomics in order to relate the subject to economic concepts you have previously studied. The importance of understanding cash flow is exemplified by the fact that Chapter 3 is devoted entirely to this topic. Chapters 4–6 pertain to the analysis of financial information. Some shortcomings of this information are examined and techniques are discussed to aid in the interpretation of financial performance.

The focus changes with Chapter 7 and continues throughout the next several chapters. The emphasis is on various aspects of risk management.[8] Cash management is examined in Chapters 7 and 8, hedging strategies in Chapters 9 and 10, and asset-based financing in Chapter 11. The remaining chapters discuss various aspects of trade credit, Chapters 12–14, and inventory management, Chapters 15–17.

A summary chapter is included (Chapter 18). For readers who are more mathematically inclined, Appendix 1 shows how Markov chain analysis can be used to forecast accounts receivable collections and bad debts. Appendix 2 provides an overview of bankruptcy, liquidation, and reorganization procedures. The remaining appendices include present-value tables and a table for areas under the normal curve. A glossary and answers to problems are also included at the end of the book.

Summary

The basic economic objective of managing a firm is generally accepted to be the maximization of shareholders' wealth. This objective requires management, as agents for creditors and shareholders, to act in the best interests of these parties. Implicit in the fulfillment of these duties is the

---

[7]This example does not recognize any balance sheet effects on income, such as depreciation or amortization, which would have an impact on both accounting and economic profits.

[8]Our discussion of risk management does not include insurance. An excellent book on this topic is by N. A. Doherty, *Corporate Risk Management: A Financial Exposition* (New York: McGraw-Hill, 1985).

requirement that management ensure adequate liquidity is available to satisfy financial obligations as they come due.

If management is to manage liquidity, it must understand the difference between profits and cash flows, and how accounting profits differ from economic profits. Rational resource allocation decisions must be made on a sound economic basis. This statement holds true whether the decision pertains to a short-term investment, such as investment in inventory, or to a long-term investment, such as investment in a new machine with an expected life of 15 years. Both investments consume scarce resources of the company.

A major theme of this book is shown by Illustration 1.1, with the quoted excerpt from "How to Go Broke . . . While Making a Profit,"and its extension in Illustration 1.2. Later chapters will make reference to this example since it exemplifies the mismanagement of liquidity that is found in many companies.

Key Concepts

Accounting profit
Cash flow
Economic costs
Economic profits
How to Go Broke . . .
   While Making a Profit

Liquidity management
Net working capital
Profit
Residual income
Solvency
Wealth maximization

Questions

1.   Discuss the objective of liquidity management.

2.   How is the objective of liquidity management related to the economist's concept of wealth maximization?

3.   What are the differences between economic profit, accounting profit, and residual income?

4.   What are the differences between funds and profits? Which is the treasurer of the company more concerned with? Why?

5.   What does the following statement mean? "You can't pay your bills with profit." Is it possible for a profitable firm to go broke? Explain.

6.   What is the difference between actual solvency and technical solvency? Relate this difference to the "How to Go Broke . . ." example.

7.   Johnson Company has been having problems paying debts as they come due. The company operates on a seasonal cycle, with production and sales at their peaks in the summer months. Inventory must be ordered four months before the beginning of summer to avoid a shortage in supplies. Management cannot understand why the company is experiencing payment difficulties since the income statement has shown profits increasing over the past few years. Analyze and discuss this problem.

Problems

1.   From the following information, determine the amount of residual income for the year. Explain why this figure is more appropriate than the net income amount. Assume net operating income is the same as operating cash flow.

Current assets	$220
Fixed assets	$400
Net operating income	$1500
Opportunity cost of capital	18 percent

2.   If the firm in Problem 1 sold 1750 shares of common stock at $1 per share, what would be the influence on residual income? Assume the amount received does not change cash flow from operations.

3.   If the opportunity cost of capital in Problem 2 was

    (a) 36 percent,

    (b) 9 percent,

what impact would this have on residual income?

4.   At what opportunity cost of capital would the investors, in Problem 2, be indifferent to the investment?

5.   Should a firm invest $10,000 in a project that has forecasted cash flows from operations of $2500 and an opportunity cost of capital of 20 percent? Explain. Assume all numbers are stated after tax (if applicable).

6.   A company has an expected net cash flow of $700 for each of the next three years based on an investment of $1250. The firm's opportunity cost of capital is 8 percent.

   (a) Find the net present value (NPV) of this investment.

   (b) Find the residual income (RI) of this investment.

   (c) What is the relationship between NPV and RI in perpetuity?

7.   Following Illustrations 1.1 and 1.2 and Tables 1.1 and 1.2, determine residual income if sales in January were 900 units and the following months' sales were expected to increase by 20 percent each month. Price per unit is $1.00 and cost per unit is $0.75. All other relationships existing as of January 1 and operating rules remain as given in Illustrations 1.1 and 1.2. (*Hint:* 30 days' supply of inventory is based on the current month's sales.)

8.   If the selling price in Problem 7 increased to $1.05, determine the residual income. Discuss the implications of this result.

CHAPTER 2 □
Economic Fundamentals for Analysis of Liquidity

From the economist's point of view *resource allocations take place until the marginal benefits of holding each asset just equal the marginal costs.* For instance, in the case of money or commodities the marginal benefits can come from lower transaction costs to the firm. For customer loans the benefit may arise because of lower transactions costs to the firm's customers. In either case the underlying unsynchronized cash flows must induce a demand for the financial liabilities and equity capital to finance both the fixed and working capital assets desired by the firm's managers.

Most treatments of economics fail to discuss liquidity management in a manner that allows the reader to relate the topic to the disciplines of accounting and finance. The purpose of this chapter is to relate liquidity management to the economist's profit maximization model. It does so by explaining economic costs, examining a number of constraints that affect managerial decisions, and relating economic concepts to financial statements.

Economic Costs

For most people, expenditures involve what are called outlay costs. These costs are the moneys expended in order to carry on a particular activity. Some examples of outlay costs to a business are wages and salaries of employees, expenditures on plant and equipment, payments for raw materials, power, and rent. Such costs are also called explicit costs, historical costs, or accounting costs, because they are the tangible items that an accountant records in the company's ledgers.

Whenever the inputs of an activity are scarce and have alternative uses, economists use a more basic concept of cost: economic, or **opportunity, cost**, defined as the value of the benefit that is foregone by choosing one alternative rather than another. This concept is extremely important because the real cost of any activity is measured by its opportunity cost, not by its outlay cost. The variable k (the opportunity cost of capital) in the residual income model, discussed in Chapter 1, attempts to capture opportunity costs related to financing.

The environment within which a business operates is imperfect, with the result that many opportunity costs are the result of **constraints**, or limitations. These constraints arise because of influences of time, production, factor and product markets, and cash flows.

Time Constraints

The traditional economic functions of business are the production of goods and services and the consequent generation of wealth. Production, production planning, and the sale and distribution of goods and services take time. Managers must acquire stocks of financial assets and commodities in order to offset costs associated with the unsynchronized revenue and expenditure flows caused by time-consuming production, distribution, collection, and payment processes.

For convenience we divide decision making into three different time dimensions: immediate, short run, and long run.

Immediate Time

Immediate time is the here and now. When a customer wishes to buy immediately, either the firm has the goods to sell or it does not. Similarly, when a creditor demands payment, either the firm has sufficient liquidity to honor the request or it does not. Each of these situations influences liquidity management. Can a firm afford to increase working capital investment in inventories to ensure that customers will always be satisfied? Should the firm carry large cash balances to reduce insolvency risk? Later chapters will discuss these and related issues in detail.

Clearly, the importance of the immediate market means that the firm must protect itself from the possibility of numerous influences. However, the protection against insolvency dominates other issues. The protection provided by cash or cash equivalents has virtually no perfect substitute. Insolvency risk is not lessened by high profitability but, rather, by sufficient liquidity. The degree of risk acceptable depends upon the forecasting ability of managers and the risk profile acceptable to them.

The Short Run

The **short-run time** is described as the time needed to change some of the conditions influencing the firm. These changes must occur in tune with certain other conditions. It is in this short-run framework that the concept of matching cash inflows and outflows and analyzing sources and uses of resources gains significant prominence.

The firm makes economic profits through involvement in production across time, but it survives day to day by having sufficient liquidity to honor ongoing and currently due obligations. Management needs sufficient time to extend accounts receivable, to build inventory, and to negotiate or re-negotiate a loan. Time is a necessary but not a sufficient condition for these actions. Unless the firm has liquid reserves, it will not survive to take the necessary actions.

The Long Run

Today's decisions commit the firm to a course through time. This **long-run time** path is interpreted to mean that the physical production conditions have the possibility of being expanded or contracted, along with financial balances. Only in this way can management take advantage of the potential variability of productive factors. Management must recognize the essential difference in the degree of variability in resources, the impact these differences have on possible actions, and the associated risk to the firm.

In summary, time constraints influence all management decisions. Many plans need to be completed in a relatively short period of time. Unfortunately, the current literature of economics and finance tends to ignore the importance of these daily or weekly recurring decisions. The development of good operating policies and the control of short-term operations should not be simply assumed to exist if management expects to achieve a long-run maximization position. John Maynard Keynes,[1] the noted British economist, once said, "In the long-run we shall all be dead," implying that short-run decisions take precedence over long-run concerns. Or in the context of this book, liquidity cannot be ignored. Understanding the time dimension, as it constrains the decision process, is essential for good management.

Physical Production Constraints

Even if adequate financial resources exist, technological constraints determine what can be produced and how long it takes to produce it (thus involving time constraints). The analysis of how to employ technology requires an understanding of the firm's production function. Although this analysis belongs properly with production managers, the impact that technology-related decisions have on the financial future of the firm is direct

---

[1]J. M. Keynes, *The General Equilibrium Theory of Employment, Interest and Money* (New York: Harcourt, Brace, 1936).

and compelling. It is the finance manager's responsibility to allocate the firm's scarce resources efficiently. Financial managers need to understand the relationship between physical production, production constraints, and monetary flows.[2]

Production efficiency directly influences cost and pricing decisions. If the rules that lead to production efficiency are known, then these rules can be employed for profit and cash flow analysis. The reason for examining this issue is that the concept of maximum production efficiency is frequently associated with maximum profitability in introductory finance and accounting texts and in financial newspapers. This association is a misconception, which is clarified later in this chapter.

Knowledge of the basic steps in combining factors in the most efficient physical input/output relationships is important to the financial manager. This person is responsible for ensuring efficient resource allocation within the firm. This task requires communication with nonfinancial personnel to convince them of the merits of making decisions consistent with wealth maximization.

Output capable of satisfying demand is the direct result of combining various productive factors (resources). These productive factors are relatively scarce, which makes them **economic goods**. This term is used to differentiate them from those factors that have no scarcity and therefore no economic cost.

For purpose of discussion, consider the treasury function of a company that has a fixed level of technology. If one employee is in the treasury department, that person must perform each of the numerous activities necessary to run the department. Productivity is going to be quite small.

As additional employees are added to the treasury system — holding constant the amount of fixed inputs (capital) — output expands rapidly. The improvement in capital utilization resulting from the specialization of increased labor employment means that the increase in output of each successive employee increases over some range of labor additions, and then decreases as too much labor is added. This increase is known as **marginal physical product**.

Table 2.1 illustrates a situation where the marginal product of an input changes. To relate this discussion to liquidity management, think of the variable input as being liquid resources being added to a fixed-investment production base. The first unit of variable input V results in 8 units of output. With 2 units of V, 24 units are produced; the marginal physical product of the second unit of V (16) exceeds that of the first unit (8). Sim-

---

[2]See E. W. Walker, "Toward a Theory of Working Capital," *Engineering Economist* (Winter 1964): 21–35, for an interesting discussion of how rates of return vary when working capital levels are varied for several technologically different industries.

TABLE 2.1
Physical Production Data

Units of variable factor V	Total output in units	Average physical product per variable input (APP$_V$)	Average physical product per fixed input (APP$_F$)	Average physical product per total input (APP$_T$)	Marginal physical product per variable input (MPP$_V$)
0	0				
1	8	8	0.8	0.73	8
2	24	12	2.4	2.00	16
3	42	14	4.2	3.23	18
4	64	16	6.4	4.57	22
5	85	17	8.5	5.67	21
6	96	16	9.6	6.00	11
7	105	15	10.5	6.18	9
8	112	14	11.2	6.22	7
9	117	13	11.7	6.16	5
10	120	12	12.0	6.00	3
11	121	11	12.1	5.76	1
12	120	10	12.0	5.45	−1
13	117	9	11.7	5.09	−3
14	98	7	9.8	4.08	−19

Note: APP$_V$ is total output divided by the number of V units; APP$_F$ is total output divided by the unit value of the fixed factors (which is assumed to be 10); APP$_T$ is total output divided by the sum of the fixed- and variable-factor inputs; MPP$_V$ is the change in total output divided by the change in the number of V units.

ilarly, addition of another unit of V results in output increasing to 42 units, indicating a marginal physical product of 18 for the third unit of V.

Eventually, enough variable input V is combined with the fixed input that the benefits of further V additions are not as large as the benefits achieved earlier. When this occurs, diminishing marginal productivity results. Finally, a point is reached where the quantity of V is so large that total output actually begins to decline with additional employment of that factor. This situation may occur when the variable input becomes so large that congestion occurs and hinders the process. In Table 2.1 this point is reached when more than 11 units of input V are combined with the fixed factor.

Figure 2.1 graphs the physical relationships of Table 2.1. It shows that total production goes through three stages — first rising rapidly, then tapering off until it reaches a maximum, and then declining. These stages are labeled stage I (OAB), stage II (BC), and stage III (CD).

Stage I represents production up to the point of maximum total **average physical product** (APP$_T$). Because APP$_T$ is increasing throughout this

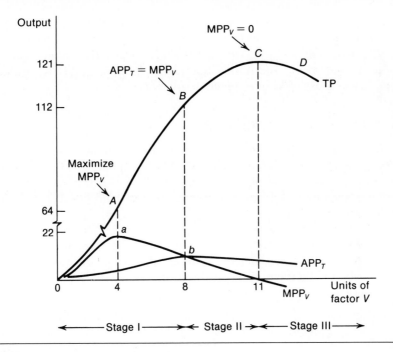

FIGURE 2.1
Graph of Physical Production

range, we say that production efficiency is also increasing. Fixed factors are underutilized in the initial phase of the production process.

Analysis of production efficiency in stage II is not as straightforward. At the beginning of stage II the marginal physical product of the variable factor, MPP_V, and the average total physical product, APP_T, are equal (that is, optimal production exists). As additional units of the variable factor are added to the fixed factor, production continues to increase at a declining rate until MPP_V is zero. When this happens, total output is maximized (point C).

Marketing and sales managers may desire to have the firm operate at point C, where the chance of product shortage is reduced. In contrast, production managers are most interested in achieving production efficiency, which occurs at point B, the start of stage II. However, the decision of how much to produce should not be solved simply by consideration of physical efficiency. Shareholder wealth maximization requires the additional consideration of consumer demand and the firm's financial capabilities. These topics are discussed later in this chapter.

Stage III is a particularly interesting area of production. In this range the efficiency of all factors falls, with the result that total output declines.

To improve efficiency, management should decrease the variable input, which is possible in the short run, or increase the fixed factor, which may only be possible in the long run. Both alternatives have implications for liquidity management. Continued operation within stage III is irrational and occurs because of poor management.

Integration of Output and Costs

The discussion of the physical production constraints indicated that *production efficiency occurs whenever* APP_T *equals* MPP_V (point *b* in Fig. 2.1). The assignment of costs to the productive factors allows for the connection between average physical product and **average cost**, and between marginal physical product and marginal cost.

The assumption regarding production was that all factors except factor *V* were fixed. Therefore *average variable cost* (AVC) equals per-unit cost (*c*) of the variable factor times the number of units of the variable factor (*V*) used, divided by the output produced (*Q*). Since the APP_V is *Q/V*, by a little algebraic manipulation we obtain

$$AVC = \frac{c}{APP_V}.$$ (2.1)

TABLE 2.2
Production and Cost Data

Units of V	Total output	Fixed costs	Average fixed cost	Variable costs	Average variable cost	Total costs	Average total cost	Marginal cost
0	0	$245				$245		
1	8	245	$30.63	$ 30	$3.75	275	$34.38	$ 3.75
2	24	245	10.21	60	2.50	305	12.71	1.88
3	42	245	5.83	90	2.14	335	7.97	1.67
4	64	245	3.83	120	1.88	365	5.71	1.36
5	85	245	2.88	150	1.77	395	4.65	1.43
6	96	245	2.55	180	1.88	425	4.43	2.73
7	105	245	2.33	210	2.00	455	4.33	3.33
8	112	245	2.19	240	2.14	485	4.33*	4.28
9	117	245	2.09	270	2.31	515	4.40	6.00
10	120	245	2.04	300	2.50	545	4.54	10.00
11	121	245	2.02	330	2.73	575	4.75	30.00
12	120	245	2.04	360	3.00	605	5.04	—
13	117	245	2.09	390	3.33	635	5.43	—
14	98	245	2.50	420	4.29	665	6.79	—

Note: The true minimum lies between 8 and 9 units at the point where average total cost (ATC) equals marginal cost (MC).

A similar algebraic exercise can be used to show that **marginal cost** (MC) is the cost of the variable factor divided by MPP_V:

$$MC = \frac{c}{MPP_V}. \qquad (2.2$$

Table 2.2 monetizes the unit production information of Table 2.1. Monetization is accomplished by using Eqs. (2.1) and (2.2) and assuming

FIGURE 2.2
Graphical Relationship Between Production and Costs

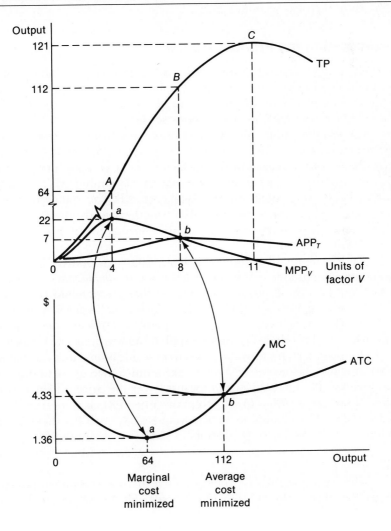

that the fixed-factor is cost is $245 and the variable-factor cost is $30 per unit.

Figure 2.2 summarizes Tables 2.1 and 2.2 to show the relationship between physical production and costs. *They are inverted images of each other.* The importance of this finding is that production management generally thinks in terms of physical output. Financial management, in contrast, thinks in monetary terms. Since the most efficient unit production level ($APP_T = MPP_V$) is also the **cost minimization** (lowest cost) level, financial managers who understand this concept should be able to communicate better with other managers about why the firm *should not* operate at this level. *Achieving a production optimum is not synonymous with achieving maximum profitability in an economic sense under conditions of imperfect competition.* This result is shown in the next section.

Incorporating the Product Market

Production management defines efficiency as maximizing the unit output per last dollar of expenditure. However, investors and creditors do not directly reward production efficiency; rather, they reward those producers who are most profitable in an economic sense.

The level of production should not rely solely on the production and cost structures unless the firm operates in perfect markets. If such markets exist, then cost minimization for all factor use is an appropriate strategy. This situation occurs when average total cost is minimized. At this point marginal cost (MC) equals average total cost (ATC) as well as average revenue (AR) and marginal revenue (MR). In other words, the firm operates at economic breakeven — it simply earns a normal profit. Figure 2.3 summarizes this situation.

If the firm operates under the more usually encountered imperfectly competitive conditions, *cost minimization is not an appropriate strategy.* In imperfect markets the *law of demand* implies that the demand curve — also called the **average revenue** (AR) curve — facing the firm will be downward sloping. Price (P) is inversely related to quantity (Q) demanded. Any extra units ($Q_2 - Q_1$) produced cannot be sold at the previous market price (P_1) because consumers are unwilling to purchase additional units at that price. When the price is lowered (P_2) to sell extra units, management must lower the price for all units sold. It cannot just lower the price for the extra customers to whom it wishes to sell. Total revenue (TR) changes from $P_1 \times Q_1$ to $P_2 \times Q_2$. The change in total revenue ($TR_2 - TR_1$) divided by the change in volume ($Q_2 - Q_1$) results in **marginal revenue** (MR) per unit. The MR curve also slopes downward to the right and falls faster than the AR curve.

Whenever marginal revenue equals zero, total revenue is maximized. Figure 2.4 depicts the relationships between demand, marginal revenue,

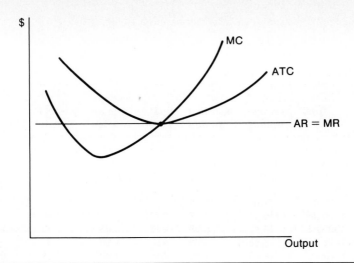

FIGURE 2.3
Profit Maximization in Perfect Product Markets

FIGURE 2.4
Demand, Marginal Revenue, and Total Revenue in Imperfect Product Markets

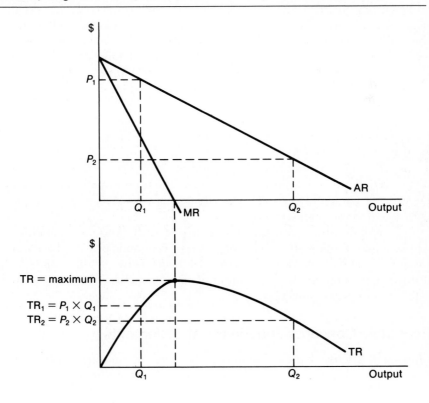

TABLE 2.3
Revenue-Cost-Profit Relationships

Total output	Total revenue	Average revenue	Marginal revenue	Total cost	Average total cost	Marginal cost	Profit
0				$245			− $245.00
8	$ 185.60	$23.20	$23.20	275	$34.38	$ 3.75	− 89.40
24	518.72	21.61	20.82	305	12.71	1.88	213.72
42	832.46	19.82	17.43	335	7.97	1.67	497.46
64	1128.36	17.63	13.45	365	5.71	1.36*	763.36
85	1320.93	15.54	9.17	395	4.65	1.43	925.93
96	1386.82	14.45	5.99	425	4.43	2.73	961.82
105	1422.82	13.55	4.00	455	4.33	3.33	967.82*
112	1439.69	12.85	2.41	485	4.33*	4.28	954.69
117	1445.74	12.36	1.21	515	4.40	6.00	930.74
120	1447.00	12.06	0.42	545	4.54	10.00	902.00
121	1447.22*	11.96	0.22	575	4.75	30.00	872.22

*A maximum or a minimum. Profit is actually maximized between 105 and 112 units at the point where marginal revenue (MR) equals marginal cost (MC).

and total revenue. However, analysis that concentrates solely on the revenue relationships is as faulty as analysis restricted to examination of cost relationships. *The optimal quantity to produce and sell is neither where costs are minimized nor where revenues are maximized.* This result is illustrated in Table 2.3.

Several important conclusions can be made. A production efficiency strategy results in minimizing average total cost ($4.33), that is, producing 112 units. If all of these units are sold, profits are about $954. Given a downward-sloping demand curve, total revenue is maximized when marginal revenue equals zero (121 units). It is more profitable for management to produce and sell a lesser quantity (105 units) and at a slightly higher average cost ($4.33), since economic profits ($967.82) are larger than can be realized at any other output level. Under the more usually encountered imperfectly competitive conditions, *whenever marginal revenue equals marginal cost, economic profits are maximized.*

Economic profits are maximized where cash flows are maximized. This statement follows from the definition of economic profits provided in Chapter 1, and it provides the critical linkage between the economist's profit-maximizing model and liquidity management. The next section elaborates on this connection.

Economic Concepts and Financial Statements

Chapter 1 discussed the relationships between accounting profits, cash flows, economic profits, and residual income. Based on these relationships it is possible to show how economic concepts relate to financial statements.

Income Statement and Economic Profit

The primary recording of cash flow is through the income statement. This statement presents the record of product revenues and factor costs. Since most businesses use an accrual accounting system, this statement neither reflects economic profit nor shows all the necessary information concerning cash flows. That is, accrual accounting recognizes revenues as goods are sold and as services are rendered, independent of the time when cash is received. Expenses are recognized in the period when the related revenue is recognized, independent of the time when cash is paid out.

Thus you must adjust sales for the change in the accounts receivable balance (since not all sales have been collected), adjust cost of sales for changes in inventory and accounts payable balances (since not all inventory has been sold nor purchases paid for), adjust operating expenses for accrued liabilities (since they have not been paid for), and add to net income any noncash expenses, such as depreciation, bad-debt expense, and deferred taxes, in order to convert the accrual accounting based income statement to a cash accounting based statement. By deducting an amount for the opportunity cost of capital, the cash-based income statement becomes a statement of residual income that reasonably represents economic profit in a practical sense.

ILLUSTRATION 2.1

Assume that the investment (I_0) supporting the production and sales figures captured in Table 2.3 amounts to $10,000. If the appropriate risk-adjusted cost of capital (k) for this investment is 10 percent, then the firm's after-tax cash flows from operations,[3] CFFO $(1 - \tau)$, is found by rearranging the residual income (RI) equation:

$$\begin{aligned} \text{CFFO } (1 - \tau) &= \text{RI} + k\,I_0 \\ &= \$967.82 + 0.10 \times \$10,000 \\ &= \$1967.82. \end{aligned} \tag{2.3}$$

Further, if investment in production/revenue related assets and liabilities (accounts receivable, inventories, accounts payable, accruals) resulted in a net increase, or use of resources, of $1200, then accounting income would be

$$\text{CFFO } (1 - \tau) + \$1200 = \$3167.82. \tag{2.4}$$

With these reasonable assumptions, accounting income is 3.27 times as great as residual income (economic income). This indicates that account-

---

[3]This was referred to as $F(1 - \tau)$ in Chapter 1, Eq. (1.1).

ing earnings are of low quality (a concept discussed in Chapter 4). Management can easily be lulled into a false sense of satisfaction and security by concentrating on the wrong standard of performance. Indeed, it is possible for accounting income to be positive but for economic income to be negative. This means that accounting profits are not sufficient to cover all costs — both implicit costs and explicit costs.   □

Balance Sheet and Economic Stocks and Flows

In the firm's balance sheet, factors of production do not appear, for example, as hours of potential service or acres of land but as obligations (liabilities), value potentials (assets), and created value (equity). The balance sheet is often used to identify the resources available and the resources used in the normal cycle of business activity. The sources of resources come about through the use of factors of production that are funded by the owners of these resources to the extent that these owners allow the firm time differences between the use of the factors and the payment for their use. The timing differences are partially recognized on the balance sheet by the segregation of assets and obligations into *current* and *fixed* categories. This division ignores the reality that part of the current assets and part of the current liabilities have a fixed nature. In most firms many current balances seldom drop below a certain amount. This part of the total is as fixed as any of the so-called fixed assets. What it means is that a certain part of the capital of the firm is used to finance the assets, and this investment is expected to continue. If part is fixed, then some part is variable, and these parts have entirely different liquidity demands and, consequently, present different management problems.

The same argument may be made for virtually all the accounts listed on the balance sheet. The balance sheet does not directly or completely indicate the timing nature of accounts nor the time constraint on factors. The liquidity component is virtually ignored in the balance sheet, and what is there is often the poorest of data. Additionally, any account changes need careful analysis.

To illustrate, assume that a bank extends a loan to the firm. The initial changes are to the cash account and to the notes payable account. It is expected that the firm will use these funds to facilitate its production and sales position but at the same time to prepare for the repayment of the loan. Management might use the funds to buy more factors and, one hopes, to increase the efficiency of factor use. In addition, part of the credit might go to fund an expansion in credit sales via an increase in accounts receivable. Both of these increases can be considered permanent investments. Since the change in current liabilities is matched by the change in current assets, it might be erroneously concluded that liquidity has not changed.

Economic Constraints

What might be perceived as having changed is the balance presented in the statements. The inventory and receivable changes are permanent, whereas the change in liabilities is not intended to be permanent. The creditor may be concerned with this situation and deem it wise to increase assurity of repayment by imposing a minimum cash balance constraint to be held at the bank. The minimum cash balance has the effect of increasing the cost of the loan and causes both the average and the marginal cost curves to shift upward. This shift will result in a new optimal output level.

From the perspective of liquidity management the effect of the cash constraint is to reduce the estimate of cash generation, since the firm has less of the loan to use productively. If noncash charges remain the same, the estimate of net cash generation should still increase relative to the pre-loan period. The creditors' concerns should be eased as they see that their short-term loan is replaced by cash generated through increased sales. The only remaining *concern of the creditors is whether or not the timing of the new cash flows matches the timing demands for repayment of the loan.*

As another example, suppose that creditors insist that management use the credit extended to the firm to employ a more capital-intensive, and more costly, production method, causing the average total cost curve and the marginal cost curve to shift upward. This request is not an unreasonable one, since the creditors might view the difficulties of securing equipment as a greater threat to the firm's success than the difficulty of obtaining labor.

Management may attempt to pass the cost changes on to its customers. This action may be possible if the cost changes are industrywide and not just associated with this firm. If only this firm experiences cost changes, and if this firm is selling in a competitive market, then the probability of shifting costs to the customers is low. If management shifts the additional costs, the consumer price must increase. If the product has competitive substitutes, management simply prices the firm out of the market. The only other solutions available to management are to have the initial constraint removed or to have the equity investors bear the burden of the increased costs.

If management is constrained in this way, *it should still follow the usual rules and expand production and sales until marginal revenue equals marginal cost.* The result would be higher fixed costs and lower profits. A positive influence may be that management now has reduced operating risk. The relatively small profit erosion is the cost for lowering the risk of operations. This decreased risk, at least as perceived by creditors, might be sufficient to encourage them to extend additional credits with no additional constraints. This argument is intended to illustrate that the firm's operations, while constrained by conditions of factor supply, time, and technology, may also be constrained by creditors' perception of risk. It also illustrates that *additional fixed costs may actually reduce operating risk* — a result contrary to general wisdom.

One of the most demanding constraints is the limitation of funding. The flow of resources from the cycle of production and sales and from the change in balance sheet accounts must all work smoothly. Otherwise, the firm is constrained to operate at a lower level of output, efficiency, and profit than that allowed by the market forces.

In the short-run situation the usual assumption is that the cycle of funds is sufficient to generate enough cash at the right time to service debts as they come due. This decision is important and should not be left to chance. Variability of some factor is the assumption of the short run, yet risk is present throughout this period. The risk involves all facets of the business, including the risk of technical insolvency — the risk of not having sufficient liquidity upon demand.

In the long run all costs must be recognized. Thus the demand for factors depends on both the total costs of production and the total revenues of sales, as well as on the resultant cash flows. Any long-term equilibrium depends on the ability of the firm to survive both the immediate and the short-run market conditions.

The firm might attempt to increase its resources by borrowing additional short-term funds or by not paying accounts either within the discount period or as these accounts come due. If borrowing is possible, one impact is to expand the resources available. Another impact is to increase the product cost by the addition of an interest charge or the loss of purchase discounts and to suffer the loss of credit availability through nonpayment of accounts due. In addition, the liquidity and leverage ratios change. Possibly, these changes may violate some constraint, such as an indenture constraint on the leverage ratio. Raising funds in this manner clearly can have other effects, any one of which can cause other constraints.

Summary

This chapter reviewed basic microeconomic concepts as they pertain to production and sale of products in an imperfect market environment. A major theme is the impact of timing of financial matters on the use of factors and the derived goods and services output. The concept of management means the firm is involved in a series of decisions, some immediate, others short term, and still others of a long-term nature. In the immediate time liquidity either exists or does not exist. If it exists, the firm is solvent; otherwise, it is either technically or actually insolvent. The long-term horizon allows management ample time to structure a liquidity strategy that is consistent with the objective of economic profit maximization. The difficulty in managing liquidity falls primarily within the short-term horizon. Cash balances, credit decisions, payable policies, investment decisions, including these pertaining to current assets — all must harmonize in order for the firm to maximize economic profit in the long run.

   Much discussion is found in the financial press about cost minimization efforts and productivity gains. These reports often leave the impression that cost minimization is the same as profit maximization. This equivalence is only the case under pure competition, a situation not faced by most firms. Management must determine the most profitable level of operations that is consistent with adequate cash flow generation. This level may satisfy neither the desires of marketing and sales personnel, who seek maximum product availability, nor the wishes of production management, who want the lowest per-unit cost the technology is capable of producing. Financial managers need to understand the different viewpoints and be able to convince managers of other functional areas of the relevance of marginal analysis for generating profits and cash flows. As will become apparent in future chapters, the economist's decision rule of continuing to operate until marginal revenue equals marginal cost is the only legitimate criterion for maximizing shareholder wealth.

Key Concepts

Average cost	Long-run time
Average physical product	Marginal cost
Average revenue	Marginal physical product
Constraint	Marginal revenue
Cost minimization	Opportunity cost
Economic goods	Economic profit maximization
Immediate time	Short-run time

Questions

1. Contrast the concepts of diminishing returns to scale and diminishing marginal productivity.

2. What is meant by economic profit? Is profit maximization an appropriate goal for owners? For managers? What tends to happen if owners are themselves managers?

3. Differentiate between immediate time, short-run time, and long-run time in their components as far as effects on the firm's liquidity strategies are concerned.

4. What is wrong with the following explanation by the production manager?

The plant is working at its most efficient output level. However, I could meet an increase in short-run demand by operating the machines a little faster and deferring maintenance. In the short run my marginal cost is zero.

5. For what reason(s) should managers not desire to operate the plant at a level where APP_T equals MPP_V? Under what circumstance(s) would it be an appropriate strategy to produce where APP_T equals MPP_V?

6. Starting from the following total revenue (TR) function, show how the average revenue and marginal revenue functions are derived.

$$TR = 50Q - 0.2Q^2$$

7. In terms of the general relationships among total, average, and marginal quantities, which of the following statements are true and which are false?

(a) When the average total cost function is rising, the marginal cost function is rising.

(b) When the total revenue function is rising, the marginal revenue function is positive.

(c) When the total cost (revenue) function is rising, the marginal cost (revenue) function lies above it.

(d) When the marginal cost function is rising, the average cost function is also rising.

(e) When the average revenue (cost) function is falling, the marginal revenue (cost) function lies below it.

(f) When the marginal cost function is neither rising nor falling, the average cost function is constant.

8. Why do we assume diminishing marginal returns in operations (whether it be in production, cash management, or whatever)?

9. Why is it important for the financial manager to argue against the production manager's insistence that the firm operate at a level that maximizes output?

10. Timing differences are only partially recognized on the balance sheet by the segregation of assets and liabilities into current and fixed (or long-term) categories. Explain why this practice can be misleading for the true timing of accounts.

11. Assume that a banker requires a firm seeking a loan to hold 5 percent of the loan in a cash account with the bank. Discuss what happens to the revenue and cost curves. Does the output level of profit maximization change?

Problems

1. Fill in the blanks in Table 2.4.

TABLE 2.4
Output and Input

	Units of variable factor	Total output in units	APP per variable input	MPP per variable input	APP per fixed input
(a)	1	6	6	___	0.3
(b)	2	___	10	14	___
(c)	3	48	___	___	2.4
(d)	4	___	___	8	___
(e)	5	40	___	___	___

2. Complete Table 2.5, a production and cost table, given fixed costs of $35 and variable costs of $15 per unit of V.

TABLE 2.5
Production and Costs

Unit of V	Total output	Average fixed cost	Average variable cost	Average total cost	Marginal cost
0	0				
1	2				
2	4				
3	8				
4	16				
5	32				
6	40				
7	45				
8	48				
9	50				
10	48				

3.   Complete Table 2.6, and show how total and marginal revenue curves are derived from the price equation AR = 15 − 0.1Q, where AR is average revenue and Q is the quantity sold. What is the profit-maximizing output level?

TABLE 2.6
Revenues and Costs

Q	TR	AR	MR	TC	AC	MC
0				150		
5				190		
15				230		
35				270		
55				310		
70				350		
80				390		
85				430		

4.   The Keem Company operates in a relatively competitive market. It is large enough to influence the product price but not factor prices. The average revenue (AR) curve is approximated by AR = 26 − 0.05Q, where Q represents the number of units offered for sale. Fixed costs of production are $285, and variable costs are $25 per unit of variable input. The variable inputs can vary between 0 and 11 units, in increments of 1. There are 10 units of the fixed factor. The relation of product output to variable input is as follows:

Input	0	1	2	3	4	5	6	7	8	9	10	11
Output	0	12	36	56	74	90	105	117	128	138	147	145

(a) Calculate the values for total product, variable and total average physical product, and variable marginal physical product. Determine the most efficient output level.

(b) Calculate the average and marginal curves for cost and revenue. Determine the least cost output. Calculate the approximate profit-maximization point.

(c) Determine the impact on output, profit, and factor use if the average revenue curve is AR = 24 − 0.1Q, fixed costs are $500, and variable costs are $35 per unit of variable input.

(d) Discuss the implications of your answer to parts (b) and (c) for managing liquidity.

(e) What are the implications for liquidity management, profit management, and production management if the firm has economic power to influence factor prices?

5.   Weber Carpet Company sells its products in a highly competitive market. The firm's current conditions are as follows:

Selling price per unit	$12.50
Variable costs per unit	$5.27
Fixed costs	$10,395
Units sold	1500

The balance sheet simply consists of cash and net worth, both equal to $8502.40. The treasurer has arranged a line of credit with the bank for $5000. If the line is used, the firm must maintain a current ratio of at least 3:1. Cash sales are 20 percent of total sales. Credit sales have terms of net 60 days. All resources employed must be paid for by the end of the month. Management expects that average total cost of production will be approximately the same for the next production period.

(a) How many units of production can the firm finance in the next period? Round your answer to a whole number. (*Hint:* Equate the funds available for production to the cost of production, which will give you an equation with Q, the production quantity, as the unknown.)

(b) Estimate the end-of-period balance sheet. What will the current ratio be at the end of the next period assuming the firm sold all it could finance?

(c) What adjustments must management make to its production plans in order not to violate the bank constraint?

PART II □
Financial Analysis of Liquidity

CHAPTER 3 □
Cash Flow Analysis

Companies with publically traded stock are required by the U.S. Securities and Exchange Commission to include in their annual reports a completed *Statement of Cash Flows*. This statement provides an excellent means of more fully examining the economic concepts discussed in the last chapter. Its importance was underscored in late 1987 when the Financial Accounting Standards Board (FASB) issued *SFAS 95, Statement of Cash Flows*, to replace the *Statement of Changes in Financial Position*. The new approach adopts a cash definition of funds and introduces substantial changes in the statement's reporting format. Under the revised approach, the working capital approach to funds flow, widely used since 1971, is no longer permitted. *SFAS 95* encourages, but does not require, restatement of financial statements for years before its adoption.

The importance of *SFAS 95* is that it moves the information provided by the annual reports a step closer to the economic cash flow concept. Cash flow information may bring to light problems that lead to business failure, may help identify overvalued or undervalued companies, and may improve assessments of the quality of earnings (discussed in the next chapter).

Many businesses have failed because they were unable to generate sufficient cash to meet their obligations. Presumably, if the financial statements had been designed to help businesses recognize that cash flow problems were occurring, many firms that ended in bankruptcy might be operating today.

Throughout this chapter reference will be made to W. T. Grant Company's financial statements (shown in the appendix to this chapter). W. T. Grant was chosen because prior to declaring bankruptcy in 1975, it was a major retailer in the United States, had a significant presence in Canada through a 50.2 percent wholly owned retail subsidiary called Zeller's Limited, and was looked upon favorably by the capital markets. Although modern finance theory strongly supports the concept of *efficient markets*, the assumption that the market is all-knowing, W. T. Grant appears to have fooled the capital markets. A major reason for this deception is that creditors and investors failed to understand the economic (cash) flows of the business.

We shall begin with a discussion of cash flow analysis and then examine funds flow analysis as it existed prior to 1988. The reason for examining pre-1988 funds flow is that many analysts use several years of company history in their analysis. Prior periods' funds flow statements, based on net working capital, will need to be restated to cash flow in order to be comparable.

Importance of Understanding Cash Flows

During the 1980s, and prior to adoption of *SFAS 95*, many managers began to place less emphasis on changes in net working capital and more on **cash flow**, the change in cash and near-cash balances, in an effort to better understand liquidity. In the final analysis, cash flows into and out of the business are the fundamental events upon which liquidity measurements are based. Cash is significant because it represents generalized purchasing power, which can be transferred readily to satisfy obligations.

The most visible and dramatic reason for the greater attention being paid to cash flow is the 1980s' increased use of takeovers and leveraged buyouts (LBO). Raiders and "buyout artists" gobbling up whole companies have paid huge premiums over current market prices based on earnings because they see a higher value based instead on cash flow — and, of course, they need their target companies' cash to service the debt they pile up to finance the deals.

Management can "massage" earnings numbers to achieve an attractive financial profile of the firm. It can defer discretionary expenses such as advertising or reduce last-in, first-out (LIFO) inventory. Firms can also count as income money that has been billed but not received. These examples do not mean that earnings figures are useless. But there are situations where the reported earnings can be misleading. In addition to providing a check on the quality of earnings, cash flow smooths the comparison of companies with different accounting methods. This will be elaborated on later in the book.

Erroneous Definition of Operating Cash Flow

It is often said that operating cash flow (generally called just *cash flow*) may be defined as net income plus depreciation and other noncash expenses. This definition is incorrect for a couple of reasons.

First, it is incorrect to say that cash flow consists of net income plus noncash expenses. A noncash expense does not generate cash flow; it provides a tax shield.[1] Some might argue that this definition is merely a play on words. However, the notion that the cash provided by operations consists of net income plus noncash expenses leads to the erroneous conclusion that there are two sources of cash: net income and noncash expenses, a fallacy that pervades much accounting, economics, and finance literature. To consider noncash expenses a source of cash is contradictory. For example, depreciation is the cost of fixed assets that has been assigned to the period under review — a cost, not a gain.

As a result of this erroneous concept, one sometimes hears comments such as that a certain corporation is obtaining sufficient cash from depreciation to finance its expansion plans. If this statement were true, it would follow that cash is obtained from bad debts and fire loss, the amortization of bond discounts and patents, and losses on sales of fixed assets. Obviously, all that is obtained is a tax savings, which indeed can be treated as a cash inflow. But this is distinctly different from saying that the total expense is synonymous with a cash inflow.

The second, and more serious, reason why operating cash flow should not be defined as net income plus noncash expenses is because this definition ignores many operating cash flows.

ILLUSTRATION 3.1

For example, when a company makes a credit sale the following entries are recorded:

Debit	Accounts receivable	$100	
Credit	Sales		$100
Debit	Cost of sales	75	
Credit	Inventory		75

The sale results in a $25 profit. And when noncash expenses, of say $5, are added to the profit, the traditional definition of operating cash flow results in $30 cash flow. It is obvious that there has not been $30 of cash flow. No cash was received from the sale, and if the inventory was already paid for, there was a cash outflow of $75 in an earlier period.   □

Illustration 3.1 shows that to determine **cash flow from operations** it is necessary to convert accrual accounting profits to cash accounting prof-

---

[1]Not all noncash expenses provide tax shields. For instance, amortized goodwill is not a tax deductible expense.

its. The fallacy of measuring cash flow as *net income plus noncash expenses* is captured in Fig. 3.1. The line labeled "Working capital provided by operations" is *net income plus noncash expenses*. Under this definition (also frequently called **funds flow**) W. T. Grant generated reasonably stable cash flows through 1974. However, W. T. Grant's subsequent bankruptcy in 1975 is not surprising when the true definition of operating cash flow — that is, cash accounting profit — is analyzed. Figure 3.1 shows Grant's inability to generate cash from operations.

Should Accrual Accounting Be Ignored?

Emphasizing the importance of cash flow does not mean that accrual accounting is inappropriate. Income statements and balance sheets prepared under accrual accounting concepts are accepted on the basis that they represent useful measurements of firm efficiency and provide relevant infor-

FIGURE 3.1
W. T. Grant's Financial Trends

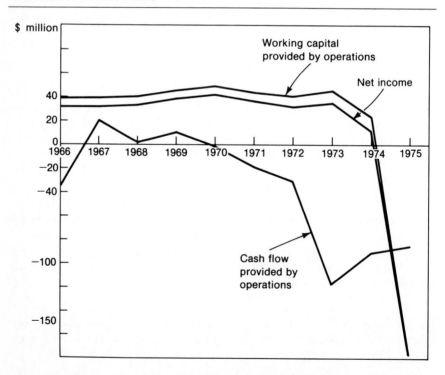

Source: From James Largay and Clyde Stickney, "Cash Flows, Ratio Analysis, and the W. T. Grant Company Bankruptcy," *Financial Analysts Journal* (July–August 1980): 54. Reprinted by permission.

mation for the prediction of future firm activity. Accrual accounting makes every effort to match revenues and expenses so as to provide a picture of the firm's efforts and accomplishments, regardless of whether payments have been made or receipts have been realized. However, because of problems created by the use of alternative allocation procedures (such as inventory valuation or depreciation approaches) and historical transactions prices, which fail to adjust for price changes, traditional accounting methods may not be adequate for reporting the complex economic activities of the firm. A means of minimizing these problems is to emphasize the reporting of cash flows.

It is important to realize that requiring most firms to use accrual accounting as dictated by generally accepted accounting principles leads to superior cash flow information. If management could use cash accounting, many abuses would be prevalent and it would be impossible to obtain a good understanding of the true cash flows. For example, in an effort to lower profits this year, management could delay recording receipts until after the ledger is closed. Obviously, many other courses of action are possible.

Overview of Calculating Cash Flow

A cash flow statement is superior to a funds flow statement that balances to changes in net working capital since it shows how the activities reported in the income statement were financed. It also summarizes the financial transactions that caused changes in the assets, the liabilities, and the capital, as shown in the related balance sheet. The cash flow statement summarizes the business transactions involving cash receipts and cash disbursements without considering their relationship to revenue-producing activities and the process of matching revenues and expenses.

Instead of lumping all current assets and current liabilities together as net working capital, a cash flow statement considers changes in some or all of these items separately. Cash flows are classified according to *operating, investing,* and *financing activities.* Explicit criteria exist for classification of cash flows as **investing** or **financing activities**. All other cash flows are considered **operating activities**. Table 3.1 outlines how cash flows are allocated to investing, financing, or operating activities.

Management can present operating cash flows either indirectly,[2] using a reconciliation format between net income and net cash flow from operating activities, or directly, by presenting major classes of *operating cash receipts* (such as those from customers) and cash payments (such as those to suppliers). The direct method effectively presents income statement infor-

---

[2]Table 3.5 uses this approach.

TABLE 3.1
Classification of Cash Flows

Investing activities

Cash paid to

Acquire property, plant and equipment and other productive assets (including capitalized interest), provided the cash is paid close to the time of purchase

Acquire a business

Purchase debt (other than cash equivalents) or equity securities (including investments accounted for by the equity method) of other entities

Make loans to another entity

Purchase loans from another entity

Cash received from

Sale of property, plant and equipment, and other productive assets

Sale of a business unit, such as a subsidiary or division

Sale of debt (other than cash equivalents) or equity securities of other entities

Collection of principal on loans made to another entity

Sale of loans made by the entity

Financing activities

Cash paid to

Owners in the form of dividends or other distributions

Repay amounts borrowed, including amounts related to short-term debt, long-term debt, capitalized lease obligations, and seller-financed debt

Reacquire treasury stock and other equity securities

Cash received from

Issuing equity securities, such as common stock

Issuing bonds, mortgages, notes, and other short- or long-term borrowings

Operating activities

Cash received from

Sale of goods or services, including receipts from the collection or sale of trade accounts and short- and long-term notes receivable (including sales-type leases)

Returns on loans (interest) and on equity securities (dividends), including dividends from equity-method investees

All others for transactions not defined as investing or financing activities. This includes amounts received to settle lawsuits, proceeds of insurance settlements not pertaining directly to investing or financing activities and cash refunds from suppliers.

Cash paid to

Acquire materials for manufacture or goods for resale, including principal payments on trade accounts and both short- and long-term notes payable to suppliers

Employees for compensation

TABLE 3.1 (Cont.)

Creditors for interest

Governments for taxes, duties, fines, and other fees or penalties

Other suppliers for other goods and services

All others for transactions not defined as investing or financing activities. This includes payments to settle lawsuits, cash contributions to charities, and cash refunds to customers.

mation on a cash basis rather than an accrual basis. This approach presents the income statement in a format that is closer to the economist's concept of revenue and expense.[3]

Table 3.2 outlines typical items for reconciling net income and net cash flow from operations.

Preparation of Cash Flow Statement

Cash flow analysis rests heavily on an understanding of commonly accepted accounting methods, since accounting statements serve as the basis for analysis. Frequently, two balance sheets are used to reflect the net effect of transactions from the beginning of an accounting interval to its end. The assets side shows the way in which resources have been used, and the liabilities and equities side shows the sources from which resources have been obtained.

Sources and Uses of Resources

Since balance sheets balance with total assets equaling total financing, analysis of changes in the balance sheet from one period to another results in an analysis of **sources and uses of resources**. Total sources of resources must equal total uses of resources. Table 3.3 summarizes the sources-and-uses approach for W. T. Grant's balance sheets.

Problems with Analyzing Balance Sheet Changes

A problem with simply finding differences in balance sheet accounts is that they do not provide a complete picture of major resource flows. The following major classes of adjustments are needed.

---

[3]Commercial lending officers suggested to the FASB that the direct method be required. Most companies prefer the indirect method. Whether the indirect method catches on will depend strongly on banking officials pushing corporate borrowers to use it.

TABLE 3.2
Reconciling Net Income and Cash Flow from Operations

Accruals of expected future operating cash receipts and disbursements

Accounts receivable

Notes receivable from customers arising from sales of goods or services

Interest receivable

Accounts payable

Notes payable to suppliers to acquire materials for manufacture or goods for resale

Interest payable

Income taxes payable

Excess of income of equity method investees over dividend received

Other accrued expenses

Deferrals of past operating cash receipts and disbursements

Inventory

Deferred income

Deferred expenses

Prepaid expenses

Noncash expenses/income

Depreciation

Depletion

Deferred income taxes

Amortization of intangible assets

Amortization of debt issuance costs

Amortization of discounts on securities

Provision for bad debts

Provision for losses on long-lived assets

Gains or losses from transactions where cash flows are investing or financing activities

Sale of property, plant and equipment and other productive assets

Sale of debt (other than cash equivalents) or equity securities of other entities

Sale of loans

Sale of business operations

Return of an investment, such as a liquidating dividend

Retirement of debt

▢ *Change in retained earnings.* There are two elements of interest. The first is net income or loss from operations, and the second is dividends paid to the various classes of shareholders.

▢ *Accounting entries that do not require cash.* Net income contains a number of transactions that have no cash flow consequences (undistributed earnings of affiliates, for example).

▢ *Change in net fixed assets.* This is a result of both cash and noncash movements. It consists of changes in gross fixed assets, changes in accumulated depreciation, and often the effect of nonrecurring adjustments for retirements of plant and equipment.

Changes in Retained Earnings

Changes in retained earnings can be analyzed by the following equation:

Ending retained earnings

= beginning retained earnings   (3.1)

+ net income for the period

− cash dividends declared for the period.

For example, for data for W. T. Grant (see the Appendix to this chapter, Tables A.1 and A.2), the equation is

$248,461 = $261,153 + $8429 − $21,122,

which balances.[4] However, if upon substituting the relevant information into the right-hand side of the equation, it did not equal ending retained earnings, you would need to look for clues in the published information accompanying the statements about adjustments made to retained earnings.

Stock dividends are a frequent reason that the equation does not balance. A stock dividend, which is defined as the distribution of additional shares of capital stock without cash payments to existing shareholders, requires a book adjustment to be made reducing retained earnings and increasing capital stock. Strictly speaking, no economic value has resulted, nor has liquidity been affected. Stock dividends are frequently given in lieu of cash dividends as a means of conserving liquidity while still allowing stockholders to feel that they are receiving something of value (albeit of questionable value).

Another prime candidate to consider if the equation does not balance is a change in a reserve account. For example, a reserve for self-insurance

---

[4]Dividends consist of $293 paid to preferred shareholders and $20,829 (see Table A.2, note 6) paid to common shareholders.

TABLE 3.3
W. T. Grant Company
Sources and Uses of Resources
For the Period Ended January 31, 1974
($000)

	1974	1973	Source	Use
Assets				
Current assets:				
Cash and marketable securities	$ 45,951	$ 30,943		$ 15,008
Accounts receivable (net)	598,799	542,752		56,047
Inventories (lower of cost or market)	450,637	399,533		51,104
Prepaid expenses	7,299	6,648		651
Total current assets	$1,102,686	$ 979,876		
Miscellaneous assets:				
Investment in subsidiaries	$ 32,600	$ 29,030		3,570
Investment in debentures of unconsolidated subsidiaries	11,651	5,951		5,700
Total miscellaneous assets	$ 44,251	$ 34,981		
Fixed assets:				
Building and equipment	$ 152,922	$ 138,607		14,315
Less accumulated depreciation	52,546	47,926	$ 4,620	
Net building and equipment	$ 100,376	$ 90,681		
Land	608	739	131	
Total fixed assets	$ 100,984	$ 91,420		
Other assets:				
Common stock of W. T. Grant held for deferred compensation plan	$ 2,500	$ 2,381		119
Other	1,200	600		600
Unamortized debt expenses	1,362	1,440	78	
Total assets	$1,252,983	$1,110,698		

or a contingency for a lawsuit may have been established. It can be argued that such items do not represent cash movement since no economic values were committed, and should therefore be excluded from the analysis. To do so, however, may be ignoring information extremely relevant to the long-term success of the business.

TABLE 3.3 (Cont.)

	1974	1973	Source	Use
Liabilities and equity				
Current liabilities:				
Trade accounts payable	$ 58,192	$ 60,973		2,781
Short-term commercial				
notes payable	453,097	380,034	73,063	
Bank loans payable	0	10,000		10,000
Accrued wages payable	14,678	19,000		4,322
Other miscellaneous	31,040	24,443	6,597	
Federal income taxes				
payable	0	8,480		8,480
Total current liabilities	$ 557,007	$ 502,930		
Long-term liabilities	$ 220,336	$ 126,672	93,664	
Indeterminant liabilities:				
Deferred contingent				
compensation	$ 2,396	$ 2,394	2	
Deferred income taxes	14,649	11,926	2,723	
Deferred credits, principally				
income taxes related to				
installment sales	133,057	130,137	2,920	
Other	1,800	2,300		500
Total indeterminate				
liabilities	$ 151,902	$ 146,757		
Shareholders' equity:				
Cumulative preferred				
stock —				
3¾% $100 par value;				
authorized 250,000				
shares	$ 7,465	$ 8,600		1,135
Common stock —				
22,500,000 shares of				
$1.25 par value				
authorized	18,599	18,588	11	
Capital surplus	84,271	84,718		447
Amounts paid by				
employees under				
purchase contracts for				
common stock	1,638	1,429	209	
Retained earnings	248,461	261,153		12,692
Less treasury stock	⟨36,696⟩	⟨40,149⟩	3,453	
Total shareholders'				
equity	$ 323,738	$ 334,339		
Total liabilities and				
equity	$1,252,983	$1,110,698		
Total sources and uses			$187,471	$187,471

Noncash Accounting Entries

Net income contains many accounting write-offs and adjustments intended to account properly for the effect of past or anticipated revenue and cost elements in the current period. Since analysis of cash flow is an attempt to recognize the impact of resource commitments, **nonmonetary write-offs** such as depreciation and amortization of past expenditures tend to obscure the picture. The true impact of net income on a company's resources is measured before any such items. Reported net income, however, is stated after write-offs and must therefore be adjusted if considered important enough.

Table 3.2 lists several transactions that affect net income but not net working capital. All the items listed enter into the calculation of net income as revenue, expense, or gain or loss.

Net income is often affected by gains and losses from the sale of capital assets. Since the resource allocation effect is normally tied to a combination of circumstances affecting the components of the net property account, the discussion is taken up next.

Changes in Fixed Assets

Analysis of fixed assets requires comparing the change in accumulated depreciation on the balance sheet against the depreciation expense charged to operations for the period. This comparison is made to determine whether any *sale or retirement* of fixed assets has occurred. If

Ending accumulated depreciation

= beginning accumulated depreciation   (3.2)

+ depreciation expense,

then no sales or retirements of assets have occurred. However, if the calculated accumulated depreciation exceeds the accumulated depreciation amount on the ending balance sheet, then a fixed asset(s) has been disposed of through a sale or a retirement. For example, the depreciation expense on W. T. Grant's income statement for the year ended January 1974 is $13.579 million, and the change in the accumulated depreciation account of the balance sheet is $4.62 million (see Table 3.3). Assets with accumulated depreciation of $8.959 million have been written off.

W. T. Grant's balance sheet, as of January 31, 1974, indicates that total gross fixed assets (including land) increased $14.184 million. Since the retired assets were fully depreciated (as was disclosed in the notes to the financial statements), the amount of new capital expenditures for the period is $23.143 million (= $14.184 million + $8.959 million). Also, since fully depreciated assets were disposed of, any cash received for them would represent a gain on disposal of assets. Notes to the financial statements reveal that it is company policy to report gains under other income and losses under selling, general, and administrative expenses. Since the notes indicate that $1.960 million of the 1974 gain of $2.027 million was from early retirement of debts, the remaining gain is possibly from the sale of fixed assets. Assuming that it is, the accounting entry is

Debit	Accumulated depreciation	$8,960,000	
Credit	Fixed assets		$8,960,000
Debit	Cash	67,000	
Credit	Gain on sale of assets		67,000

Statement of Changes in Financial Position

Prior to the FASB requiring firms to issue a Statement of Cash Flow, firms prepared a Statement of Changes in Financial Position. Table 3.4 shows such a statement for W. T. Grant as of January 1973 and 1974. The statement indicates that sources of funds ($125,826) exceed uses of funds ($57,093) for the year ended January 1974 by $68.733 million. Net operations contributed resources of $23.583 million. However, dividends ($21.122 million) and expanded facilities ($23.143 million) consumed $44.265 million of resources. Without the new bank debt of $100 million, uses of funds would have exceeded sources of funds by $31.267 million (= $100 million − $68.733 million). Although the uses of resources for fiscal year ended January 1974 are comparable to the previous year's expenditures, they put a strain on the company's liquidity because profits were down about $29.358 million.

The $68.733 million of surplus funds in 1974 means that investment in net working capital increased by this amount. This means that net working capital consumed $68.733 million of resources. This is shown in the bottom part of the table. Investment in accounts receivable and inventories increased $107.151 million. This follows a $166.284 million investment in these accounts in the previous year. Trade accounts payable used $2.781 million of resources (they used $15.147 in the previous year). To finance these investments, management relied heavily on the commercial paper market and short-term bank loans. Over $63 million was borrowed in the year ended January 31, 1974. The previous period saw the company utilize $152.293 million of financing from these sources.

One conclusion to draw from analysis of the funds statement is management's reliance on the debt markets, both short-term and long-term, to finance expansion and to make up for the inability to generate resources from operations. The severity of the problem can be appreciated even more by extending this analysis to cash flow analysis, which is done in the next section.

TABLE 3.4
W. T. Grant Company
Statement of Changes in Financial Position
For the Period Ended January 31
($000)

	1974	1973
Sources of funds		
From operations:		
Net income	$ 8,429	$ 37,787
Less increase in the undistributed equity in unconsolidated subsidiaries	3,570	3,403
	$ 4,859	$34,384
Plus charges to income not affecting working capital:		
Depreciation and amortization	13,579	12,004
Increase in deferred federal taxes	5,643	19,553
Decrease in other liabilities	⟨498⟩	⟨558⟩
Funds provided by operations	$ 23,583	$ 65,383
Notes payable to bank	100,00	0
Receipts from employees under stock purchase contracts	2,584	3,491
Common stock issued upon conversion of debentures	259	174
Decrease (increase) in other assets	⟨600⟩	2,229
Total sources of funds	$125,826	$ 71,277
Use of funds		
Dividends to stockholders	$ 21,122	$ 21,141
Investment in properties, fixtures and improvements	23,143	26,250
Investment in unconsolidated subsidiaries	5,700	2,040
Retirement of long-term debt	6,074	1,584
Purchase of preferred stock for cancellation	612	252
Purchase of treasury common stock	133	11,466
Conversion of convertible debentures	262	176
Increase ⟨decrease⟩ in sundry accounts	47	⟨79⟩
Total uses of funds	$ 57,093	$ 62,830
Increase of net working capital during the period	$ 68,733	$ 8,477
Increase ⟨decrease⟩ in net working capital		
Current assets:		
Cash and short-term securities	$ 15,008	$ ⟨18,908⟩
Accounts receivable	56,047	65,427
Inventories	51,104	100,857
Other current assets	651	1,271
Total assets	$122,810	$148,647

TABLE 3.4 (*Cont.*)

	1974	1973
Current liabilities		
Short-term commercial notes and bank loans	$(63,063)	$(152,293)
Accounts payable	2,781	15,147
Accrued wages payable	4,322	(3,325)
Federal income taxes payable	8,480	997
Other miscellaneous	(6,597)	(726)
Total liabilities	$(54,077)	$(140,200)
Working capital increase	$ 68,733	$ 8,447

Statement of Cash Flows

The major change required to convert the Statement of Changes in Financial Position to a Statement of Cash Flow is to incorporate the changes in net working capital, excluding cash and near cash, directly into the statement and rearrange the items into operating, investing, and financing categories. This is shown in Table 3.5.

The Statement of Cash Flow is an obvious improvement over the Statement of Changes in Financial Position. Net working capital, or rather the change in it, is a very poor indicator of the firm's ability to generate cash. For the two years ended January 1974, W. T. Grant's operations consumed over $205 million cash (= $92,554 + $112,994). And over this same period, investments consumed about $57 million (= $30,141 + $27,253). Banks and investors in the money markets were a major source of capital, as expressed by their willingness to lend to W. T. Grant and buy its commercial paper.

The knowledge that net working capital increased about $75.2 million over this same period means little in terms of understanding liquidity. Unfortunately, many people were not aware of this discrepancy. A Morgan Guaranty vice president who handled the W. T. Grant loan said, in an interview with *Business Week* magazine (July 19, 1976):

> The *first* (emphasis added) signs of trouble were apparent to us in the spring of 1974. We agreed to help because they looked sound if they received some bank help. . . . We never knew how bad their internal systems were.

The primary objective of the cash flow statement is to provide information that allows investors and creditors to forecast the amount of cash likely to be disbursed in the future to satisfy obligations and to evaluate the probable risk. The cash flow statement takes a narrow point of view. Its

TABLE 3.5
W. T. Grant Company
Statement of Cash Flows
For the Period Ended January 31
($000)

	1974	1973
Cash flows from operating activities		
Net income	$ 8,429	$ 37,787
Less increase in the undistributed equity in unconsolidated subsidiaries	3,570	3,403
	$ 4,859	$ 34,384
Plus charges to income not affecting cash flows:		
Depreciation and amortization	13,579	12,004
Increase in deferred federal taxes	5,643	19,553
Decrease in other liabilities	(498)	(558)
	$ 23,583	$ 65,383
Increase in accounts receivable	(56,047)	(65,427)
Increase in inventories	(51,104)	(100,857)
Decrease in accounts payable	(2,781)	(15,147)
Increase (decrease) in accrued wages	(4,322)	3,325
Decrease in federal income taxes payable	(8,480)	(997)
Increase in other miscellaneous payables	6,597	726
Net cash flow from operations	$(92,554)	$(112,994)
Cash flows from investing activities		
Increase in investment in properties, fixtures, and improvements	$(23,143)	$ (26,250)
Increase in investment in unconsolidated subsidiaries	(5,700)	2,040)
Increase in other current assets	(651)	(1,271)
Decrease (increase) in sundry accounts	(47)	79
Decrease (increase) in other assets	(600)	2,229
Net cash flow from investing	$(30,141)	$ (27,253)
Cash flows from financing activities		
Increase in notes payable to bank	$100,000	
Increase in short-term commercial notes and bank loans	63,063	$152,293
Retirement of long-term debt	(6,074)	(1,584)
Conversion of convertible debentures	(262)	(176)
Increase in common stock issued upon conversion of debentures	259	174
Increase in receipts from employees under stock purchase contracts	2,584	3,491
Purchase of treasury stock	(133)	(11,466)
Purchase of preferred stock for cancellation	(612)	(252)
Dividends paid to stockholders	(21,122)	(21,141)
Net cash flow from financing	$137,703	$121,339
Net increase (decrease) in cash and cash equivalents	$ 15,008	$ (18,908)
Cash and cash equivalents, beginning of year	30,943	49,851
Cash and cash equivalents, end of year	$ 45,951	$ 30,943

scope is limited to a summary of the cash transactions during a period, disregarding events that have occurred in prior periods or will occur in future periods but that have a bearing on the operations of the period under review.

Summary

This chapter discussed funds flow and cash flow analysis. An understanding and use of such analyses helps move the evaluation of the company closer to the economic concept of profit. Simple sources and uses analysis provides a gross indication of flows within the business. These flows involve the decisions made by management regarding movement of investment into and out of the firm by either creditors or investors.

The new Statement of Cash Flows provides information about the cash receipts and cash payments of a business during a time period. Such information should help analysts assess a firm's ability to generate future cash flows, assess the firm's ability to meet its obligations and pay dividends, and assess the effects of a firm's cash and noncash investing and financing activities during a time period.

Key Concepts

Cash flow
Cash flow from operations
Financing activities
Funds flow

Investing activities
Nonmonetary write-offs
Operating activities
Sources and uses of resources

Appendix

W. T. Grant Company's Financial Statements

The ratios discussed in this chapter have been calculated for W. T. Grant for two years. Table A.3 summarizes results for the years ended January 31, 1973 and 1974. Supporting calculations for the year 1974 follow. The financial statements for W. T. Grant are included as Tables A.1 and A.2.

TABLE A.1
W. T. Grant Company and Consolidated Subsidiaries
Consolidated Income Statement For the Year Ended January 31 ($000)

	1974	*1973*
Operating section:		
Net sales	$1,849,802	$1,644,747
Less cost of sales (1)	1,163,998	1,023,014
Gross profit	$ 685,804	$ 621,733
Less: Selling, general, and administrative (2)	518,279	442,211
Depreciation and amortization	13,579	12,004
Leasing	105,367	90,243
Net profit from operations	$ 48,579	$ 77,275
Nonoperating section:		
Income from concessions	3,971	3,753
Interest earned on installment sales	1,035	602
Miscellaneous (3)	2,027	586
Earnings before interest and taxes	$ 55,612	$ 82,216
Creditors' section:		
Interest expense	51,047	21,127
Owners' section:		
Earnings before taxes	$ 4,565	$ 61,089
Less taxes: Current	⟨6,020⟩	11,255
Deferred	6,807	17,163
Earnings before unconsolidated subsidiaries	$ 3,778	$ 32,671
Equity in net earnings of unconsolidated subsidiaries (4)	4,651	5,116
Total net earnings	$ 8,429	$ 37,787
Less dividends on preferred stock	293	335
Net earnings available to common stock	$ 8,136	$ 37,452

Notes:
1. Two percent of this expense is assumed to include fixed-overhead allocations.
2. Twenty-five percent of this expense is assumed to be variable.
3. Includes gains of $315,000 and $1,960,000 for the years ending January 31, 1973 and 1974, respectively, for the early extinguishment of long-term debt.
4. Represents the portion of subsidiaries' profits owned by W. T. Grant.

TABLE A.2
W. T. Grant Company and Consolidated Subsidiaries
Balance Sheet as of January 31 ($000)

	1974	1973
Assets		
Current assets:		
Cash and marketable securities	$ 45,951	$ 30,943
Accounts receivable (net) (1)	598,799	542,752
Inventories (lower of cost or market) (2)	450,637	399,533
Prepaid expenses	7,299	6,648
Total current assets	$1,102,686	$ 979,876
Miscellaneous assets:		
Investment in subsidiaries	$ 32,600	$ 29,030
Investment in debentures of unconsolidated subsidiaries	11,651	5,951
Total miscellaneous assets	$ 44,251	$ 34,981
Fixed assets:		
Building and equipment	$ 152,922	$ 138,607
Less accumulated depreciation	52,546	47,926
Net building and equipment	$ 100,376	$ 90,681
Land	608	739
Total fixed assets	$ 100,984	$ 91,420
Other assets:		
Common stock of W. T. Grant held for deferred compensation plan	$ 2,500	$ 2,381
Other	1,200	600
Unamortized debt expenses	1,362	1,440
Total assets	$1,252,983	$1,110,698
Liabilities and equity		
Current liabilities:		
Trade accounts payable	$ 58,192	$ 60,973
Short-term commercial notes payable (3)	453,097	380,034
Bank loans payable	0	10,000
Accrued wages payable	14,678	19,000
Other miscellaneous	31,040	24,443
Federal income taxes payable	0	8,480
Total current liabilities	$ 557,007	$ 502,930
Long-term liabilities	$ 220,336	$ 126,672
Indeterminate liabilities:		
Deferred contingent compensation	$ 2,396	$ 2,394
Deferred income taxes (4)	14,649	11,926
Deferred credits, principally income taxes related to installment sales (5)	133,057	130,137
Other	1,800	2,300
Total indeterminate liabilities	$ 151,902	$ 146,757

TABLE A.2 (*Cont.*)

	1974	1973
Shareholders' equity:		
Cumulative preferred stock — 3¾%, $100 par		
value; authorized 250,000 shares	$ 7,465	$ 8,600
Common stock — 22,500,000 shares of $1.25 par		
value authorized	18,599	18,588
Capital surplus	84,271	84,718
Amounts paid by employees under purchase		
contracts for common stock	1,638	1,429
Retained earnings (6)	248,461	261,153
Less treasury stock	(36,696)	(40,149)
Total shareholders' equity	$ 323,738	$ 334,339
Total liabilities and equity	$1,252,983	$1,110,698

Notes:

1. Over $2 million of loans to directors and officers were outstanding as of the end of the 1973 and 1974 fiscal years. In the fiscal year ended January 1973, $245,000 of loans to directors/officers were written off as uncollectible. In the following year $301,500 in loans were written off.

2. Inventories, as of January 31, 1974, increased 12.8 percent over the previous year's level. Since sales increased 12.5 percent during the same period, management stated in the annual report that the inventory increase was satisfactory.

3. Maturities ranged from 1 to 270 days from the date of issuance.

4. $30 million more depreciation was taken for tax purposes than for financial reporting purposes in the fiscal year ended January 31, 1974.

5. Revenues from installment sales were entered in the financial records on the date of sale but were entered in the tax returns for periods when payments were collected. This step allowed $133 million in taxes to be deferred for the year ended January 1974.

6. Common dividends of $20,829 were paid in 1974.

Questions

1.   Identify the major changes in the Financial Accounting Standards Board's Statement of Cash Flows, which replaced the FASB Statement of Changes in Financial Position.

2.   Discuss the primary objective of the cash flow statement.

3.   Explain what is meant by the assertion "Cash represents generalized purchasing power."

4.   Discuss the error in the assertion "Cash flows equal income plus depreciation and other noncash charges."

5.   Contrast the cash basis of accounting with the accrual basis of accounting.

6.   Discuss and illustrate cash flows of the investing activity.

7.   Discuss and illustrate cash flows of the financing activity.

8.   Discuss and illustrate cash flows of the operating activity.

9.   Changes in fixed assets, as reported on the balance sheet, often fail to identify completely the total changes in these resource flows. Discuss.

10.   Generally accepted accounting principles require the use of accruals and deferrals in the determination of income. How is income determined under the accrual basis of accounting? Include in your answer those factors that cause an item to be considered an accrual item or a deferred (prepaid) item, and give appropriate examples of each.

Problems

1.   Classify each of the items in the list below as an (1) investing, (2) financing, or (3) operating activity.

   (a) Payment of long-term debt
   (b) Purchase of equipment
   (c) Issuance of common stock for cash
   (d) Sale of marketable short-term equity securities
   (e) Cash dividends
   (f) Sale of bonds
   (g) Purchase of treasury stock
   (h) Payment of income taxes payable
   (i) Income from operations

     (j) Issuance of stock to acquire a productive asset

     (k) Collection of accounts receivable

     (l) Sale of a division of the company

2.   Using the following data, determine

     (a) the disposal of existing fixed assets;

     (b) the purchase of new fixed assets.

Assume that any assets disposed of were fully depreciated.

Beginning gross fixed assets	$ 5729
Ending gross fixed assets	6450
Depreciation expense for the year	1500
Beginning net fixed assets	3795
Ending net fixed assets	4975

3.   Use the data of Problem 2, but assume that ending gross fixed assets were $5729 and accumulated depreciation was $2434. Determine

     (a) the disposal of existing fixed assets (if any);

     (b) the purchase of new fixed assets (if any).

4.   Table 3.6 shows a balance sheet Cactus, Inc., has prepared comparing the past two years.

TABLE 3.6
Cactus, Inc., Balance Sheet

	This year	Last year
Cash	$ 97,500	$ 90,000
Receivables	102,000	105,000
Inventory	156,000	166,500
Prepaid expenses	15,000	13,500
Plant assets	457,500	330,000
Accumulated depreciation	(130,500)	(106,500)
Goodwill	48,000	55,500
	$745,500	$654,000
Accounts payable	$123,000	$135,500
Wages payable	120,000	105,000
Mortgage payable		150,000
Preferred stock	187,500	
Preferred paid-in capital	9,000	
Common stock	225,000	225,000
Retained earnings	81,000	37,500
	$745,500	$654,000

The accumulated depreciation account has been credited only for the depreciation expense for the period. The retained earnings account has been charged for dividends of $19,500 and credited for the net income for the year. The net income for the year is as follows:

Sales	$210,000
Cost of sales	117,000
Gross profit	$ 93,000
Operating expenses	30,000
Net income	$ 63,000

From the information above, prepare a statement of cash flows. It is not necessary to categorize according to SFAS 95, but identify cash flow from operations in the statement.

5.   Presented below is the income statement of F&R, Inc.

Sales	$360,000
Cost of sales	228,000
Gross profit	$132,000
Operating expenses	49,200
Income before taxes	$ 82,800
Income taxes	39,600
Net income	$ 43,200

In addition, the following information relating to changes in net working capital is presented:

	Debit	Credit
Cash	$18,000	
Receivables (net)		$3,600
Inventories	25,200	
Accrued expenses		6,000
Accounts payable	4,800	
Income tax payable	1,200	

The company indicates that depreciation expense for the year was $15,600 and that the deferred income tax account credit balance increased $1200.

Determine the cash flow from operations.

6.   A firm's account balances at the end of the year are shown in Table 3.7. Determine the net profit after taxes and the changes in the cash balance for the year.

TABLE 3.7
Account Balances For the Year Ending December 31

Sales		$6,500
Cost of sales*:		1,875
Materials	75%	
Direct labor	15%	
Direct overhead	10%	
Account balances as of January 1		
Accounts receivable		1,870
Inventory		2,690
Net fixed assets		10,500
Accrued direct labor wages		550
Accrued administrative expenses		2,600
Accrued rent		600
Accounts payable — material		400
Account balances as of December 31		
Net fixed assets		10,000
Accounts receivable		2,100
Inventory		2,010
Accrued direct labor wages		590
Accrued administrative expenses		2,950
Accrued rent		600
Accounts payable — material		700
Period expenses:		
Rent expense		450
Depreciation expense		1,250
Administrative expenses		1,770
Taxes at 40% on profit before taxes (paid)		

*Assume these proportions are constant from year to year. There were no outstanding overhead expenses at January 1 or December 31.

7.   STELCO, Inc., is a Canadian steelmaking company located in Ontario. Using the financial data supplied in its 1989 annual report (Tables 3.8 and 3.9), determine the statement of cash flows for the years 1988 and 1989.

TABLE 3.8
STELCO, Inc.
Consolidated Statement of Income and Retained Earnings
For the Year Ending December 31 ($000)

	1989	1988
Revenue		
Sales	$2,749,054	$2,711,491
Equity income	7,569	21,824
Income from short-term investments	3,312	5,469
Total revenue	$2,759,935	$2,738,784
Expense		
Cost of sales	$2,266,482	$2,253,696
Administrative and selling	138,108	132,363
Research and development	8,209	9,489
Depreciation	129,570	124,604
Interest on long-term debt	85,220	79,809
Other interest	5,303	1,912
Income tax — current	6,816	3,661
— deferred	26,358	34,879
Total expense	$2,666,066	$2,640,413
Income before extraordinary items	$ 93,869	$ 98,371
Extraordinary items net of tax		1,600
Net income	$ 93,869	$ 96,771
Retained earnings		
Balance at beginning of year	571,452	544,069
Premium on redemption of preferred stock		(5,750)
Dividends	(50,043)	(63,638)
Balance at end of year	$ 615,278	$ 571,452

TABLE 3.9
STELCO, Inc.
Consolidated Statement of Financial Position
For the Years Ending December 31 ($000)

	1989	1988
Current assets		
Cash	$ 5,431	$ 14,462
Short-term investments	6,996	6,039
Accounts receivable	361,312	354,625
Inventories	856,527	649,945
Prepaid expenses	4,761	4,703
Total current assets	$1,235,027	$1,029,774
Current liabilities		
Short-term notes payable	$ 67,957	$ 47,714
Accounts payable and accrued	442,500	347,327
Income and other taxes	50,895	43,704
Cash dividend payable	11,535	10,927
Long-term debt due within one year	76,252	19,419
Total current liabilities	$ 649,139	$ 469,091
Net working capital	$ 585,888	$ 560,683
Other assets		
Fixed assets	$1,624,523	$1,612,136
Long-term intercorporate investments	196,235	186,419
Deferred foreign exchange losses	9,808	14,915
Unamortized long-term debt issue expense	12,720	12,689
Total other assets	$1,843,286	$1,826,159
	$2,429,174	$2,386,842
Other liabilities		
Accrued pension obligation	$ 1,812	$ 13,850
Provision for blast furnace relines	60,945	112,467
Long-term debt	855,453	822,413
Deferred income taxes	282,359	259,208
Total other liabilities	$1,200,569	$1,207,938
Shareholders' equity	$1,228,605	$1,178,904

TABLE 3.9 (*Cont.*)

	1989	1988
Derived from:		
Capital stock		
Preferred stock	$ 189,146	$ 190,679
Common stock	424,181	416,773
Retained earnings	615,278	571,452
Total shareholders' equity	$1,228,605	$1,178,904

Notes:	1989	1988
[a]Net changes in:		
Accrued pension obligation		($1,292)
Provision for blast furnace —		$ 15,265
beyond one year		
Changes in operating elements of		
net working capital:		
Acccunts receivable		($10,094)
Inventories		(77,111)
Prepaid expenses		2,462
Accounts payable and accrued		14,696
Income and other taxes		(3,452)
Total changes in working capital		($73,499)
[b]Net proceeds from issue of:		
Long-term notes payable	$ 325	$ 23,157
Retractable debentures	123,813	
Convertible subordinate		145,567
debentures		
Common shares	5,937	5,163
[c]Purchase of preferred shares	1,534	196,671
[d]Reduction of long-term debt	33,040	35,459
Adjustment	788	0
Total	$ 33,828	$ 35,459
[e]Expenditures for fixed assets	$ 140,710	$ 116,391
[f]Long-term intercorporate	$ 18,823	$ 6,975
investment		
[g] Cash dividend paid	$ 47,963	$ 65,616

[h]The statement of cash flows defines beginning of year cash as cash plus short-term investments less short-term notes payable.

CHAPTER 4　□
Traditional Financial Analysis: Some Shortcomings

The complexity, continuity, and joint nature of economic activity creates problems in measuring the effects of these activities and associating them with specific processes, products, and time frames. Measuring the resources and obligations of a firm and measuring the changes in them are two aspects of the same problem. Management attempts to capture and understand these dynamics as they affect the firm through the use of financial statements and analysis of these statements.

Financial statements report for a specific time period where resources come from, where they are invested for the time being, and how often they turn over. These statements have the appearance of completeness, exactness, and finality. However, generally accepted accounting principles permit alternative treatments of many accrual accounting events. Which treatment management chooses will affect the balances and flows reported in the financial statements of the company and thus any subsequent financial analysis.

The analysis of financial statements is meant to result in the presentation of information that will aid decision making by managers in the financial status of the firm. Traditionally, these parties have relied on financial ratios to analyze a firm's performance. Ratios such as the current ratio, debt/equity ratio, and interest coverage ratio have been firmly entrenched in analysts' tool kits for decades. But do these ratios really provide a strong basis for drawing meaningful conclusions about a firm, particularly its liquidity?

The purpose of this chapter is to review the traditional financial ratios used in analyzing corporate liquidity and to highlight some of their limitations. The discussion purposely concentrates on negative aspects of the measurements since these aspects are generally not discussed in other books. This discussion may stimulate you to think critically when analyzing liquidity.

Traditional Financial Analysis

Financial ratios are usually categorized according to the rapidity with which assets can be turned into cash, the efficient management of assets, the degree of protection for creditors and investors, and the profitability of assets. The result is four categories corresponding to these descriptions: (1) liquidity, (2) activity, (3) coverage, and (4) profitability. Each category can be related (either directly or indirectly) to liquidity management. However, from the perspective of short-term financial management, these categories decline in relative importance as you go from category 1 to category 4. This decline should be apparent from the "How to Go Broke. . ." scenario examined in Chapter 1.

The following discussion of the ratios does not include any calculations. The appendix at the end of this chapter shows the calculations by using the financial statements of W. T. Grant Company. You are encouraged to refer to this appendix while reading the rest of this chapter.

Liquidity Ratios

Liquidity is defined as the ability to meet demands for cash as they occur. From early in this century to recent years the most widely used measure of the firm's liquidity position has been the *current ratio,* defined as the ratio of current assets to current liabilities:

$$\text{Current ratio} = \frac{\text{current assets}}{\text{current liabilities}}. \tag{4.1}$$

The current ratio is thought to be important because all current liabilities (liabilities that require cash during the current operating period) are usually paid with funds generated by the liquidation of current assets turned into cash within the current operating period.

The intent of the current ratio is to provide a measure of the margin of safety in meeting obligations that will mature during the current period. If a firm's current assets are large relative to the value of current liabilities, there is a high probability that the liabilities can be paid as they fall due. This probability is embodied in the widespread acceptance of a current ratio of 2:1 as the standard or norm for adequate liquidity. The standard current ratio should be viewed with some skepticism, for a high current ratio by itself does not guarantee adequate liquidity. A satisfactory current ratio does not disclose the fact that a portion of the current assets may be tied up in slow-moving inventories and prepaid expenses. With inventories, especially raw materials and work in process, there are questions of how long it will take to transform them into finished products and what ultimately will be realized on the sale of the merchandise.

In the absence of cash and near-cash holdings, liquidity depends entirely on the relationship between cash inflows and required cash outflows. What is appropriate liquidity for a firm varies widely, and no general standard can possibly be applicable to all firms under all circumstances. In a detailed study of bankrupt and nonbankrupt firms, Ohlson[1] found that the average current ratio of the failed firms was above the mystical 2:1 standard in all five years preceding the ultimate bankruptcy.

A test considered to be a more rigorous test of a firm's liquidity is the *quick ratio*, sometimes called the *acid test ratio*, which compares with current liabilities only those current assets that could be expected to produce relatively sure cash if the firm were to cease operation. For the quick ratio both inventory and prepaid items are deduced from current assets; prepaid expenses, of course, produce no cash, while the amount of cash that can be realized from inventory if the firm ceases operations is highly uncertain. Thus, the quick ratio is defined as follows:

$$\text{Quick ratio} = \frac{\text{cash} + \text{marketable securities} + \text{receivables}}{\text{current liabilities}}. \qquad (4.2)$$

The widely held rule of thumb for the quick ratio is 1:1. The quick ratio attempts to emphasize values at liquidation rather than going-concern values — thus eliminating differences in operating requirements. If a liquidation perspective is meaningful to the analysis, the 1:1 rule deserves somewhat more credence than the similar figure attached to the current ratio. However, it must be viewed with skepticism in analyzing a going concern.

The current and quick ratios are functions of many variables that affect liquidity differently. Recognition of the relevance of cash flow data to liquidity has led a number of analysts to question the traditional significance of the current and quick ratios. Some have explicitly censured the static character of these ratios as their fundamental shortcoming. Although the limitations have long been recognized, the customary directive is to allow for them in interpreting performance, which makes reliable interpretation a truly virtuoso performance.

The *defensive-interval ratio* has been proposed as an alternative to the current ratio. This ratio measures the time span during which a firm can

---

[1] J. A. Ohlson, "Financial Ratios and the Probabilistic Prediction of Bankruptcy," *Journal of Accounting Research* (Spring 1980): 109–31.

operate on present liquid assets without resorting to revenues from next year's income sources. The defensive-interval ratio is

$$\text{Defensive interval} = \frac{\text{quick assets}}{\text{daily cash operating expenses}}. \quad (4.3)$$

The statement of cash flows can be used to help calculate cash operating expenses. First, it is necessary to convert accrual sales on the income statement to *cash sales*,[2] and then to subtract from this amount the *cash flow from operations* (as given in the statement of cash flows) and divide the difference by 360 days.

Whether this ratio provides a better measure of liquidity than either the current ratio or the quick ratio is difficult to evaluate. It does depart from the strictly static analysis of the current and quick ratios and tries to focus attention directly upon the relationship between liquidity and the need for liquidity. However, the ratio is based on the stock level of defensive assets and not on the inflow of cash. Liquidity needs of the firm that is a going concern are settled with cash.

Another liquidity measure in popular use is the amount of net working capital of the firm. **Net working capital** is defined as the difference between current assets and current liabilities and should not be confused with *working capital*, which is often used as a substitute for current assets (although accountants usually define the difference between current assets and current liabilities as working capital).

Financial managers look at current assets as resources invested in assets that are closely linked to day-to-day operations. Any item included in current assets can be expected to turn into cash within the firm's operating cycle or one year, whichever is longer. These assets are arranged on the balance sheet in order of their nearness to cash, that is, in descending order of liquidity. In this context the term *liquidity* means flexibility and exchangeability of assets into cash.

Current liabilities are debts due to be paid within the firm's operating cycle or one year, whichever is longer. These debts are bona fide current debts owed outside the business and payable only with cash. Each current debt exposes the business to the risk of insolvency. The distinction between the insolvency risk of individual current liabilities is not as easily defined as the difference between the liquidity risks of individual current assets, and therefore they are not arranged on the balance sheet in terms of insolvency risk.

The interpretation placed on the calculation of net working capital is that if current assets exceed current liabilities, the firm is solvent. This

---

[2]Recall from Chapter 3 that this is done by adding (subtracting) the decrease (increase) in accounts receivable for the period to the reported sales amount.

interpretation is not necessarily true, because the *net working capital amount fails to indicate anything about liquidity*. Cash and near-cash assets are truly the only liquid assets. A high positive net working capital amount may arise from extraordinarily high investments in receivables and inventories. Thus one must analyze net working capital in conjunction with receivable and inventory management, which frequently rely on the use of turnover ratios. However, as will be discussed in Chapters 14 and 17, turnover ratios can lead to erroneous conclusions. They must be used with caution.

Net working capital is more informative when defined as follows:[3]

$$\text{Net working capital} = \text{[long-term and indeterminate debt]}$$
$$+ \text{[net worth]} \tag{4.4}$$
$$- \text{[fixed and other assets]},$$

where *indeterminate debt* is defined as deferred income taxes, pension liabilities, and minority interest claims (which arise from less than 100 percent ownership of subsidiaries). If current assets exceed current liabilities, this definition shows that *net working capital is permanent capital invested in current assets*. If current assets are less than current liabilities, the excess of current liabilities over current assets is helping finance fixed and other assets.

The only way that net working capital can change is as a result of a transaction that affects current assets or current liabilities as well as either net worth, debt other than short-term debt, or fixed and other assets. Thus net working capital has three sources: transactions that increase net worth, transactions that increase long-term and indeterminate debt, and transactions that reduce fixed and other assets. Conversely, there are three competing uses for the sources of net working capital: transactions that reduce net worth, payments or reductions of long-term and indeterminate debt, and increases of fixed and other assets.

Until 1988 the majority of accountants defined the change in net working capital as **funds**. This was a poor cash flow concept. Increases in receivables arising from the sale of goods and services were considered a constructive receipt of cash. Increases in accounts payable were considered to represent the constructive payment for goods and services received. This definition assumed that the collection of receivables and the actual payment of accounts payable simply represented conversions from one (quasi) monetary form into another.

Another troublesome feature of the net working capital concept of funds is that nonmonetary assets, such as inventories and prepaid expenses, and a few nonmonetary liabilities, such as advance receipts for ser-

---

[3]Equation (4.4) provides the same answer for net working capital as does taking the difference between current assets and current liabilities.

vices to be performed by the firm in the future, are included as if they were monetary items. The inclusion of these items is particularly disturbing if the information is to be relevant to investors and creditors in their predictions of future liquidity and funds flows. They are disturbing because the dollars assigned to inventories and prepaid expenses are the result of allocations of cost or other measurement over several periods. An increase in the reported amount of these items, for example, could not be interpreted as an increase in general purchasing power available for other uses. In addition, the realizable value of these items in a forced liquidation may be relatively low, compared to value received for other assets.

An interesting relationship between the current (or quick) ratio and net working capital can be illustrated to indicate the difficulty with using these techniques for evaluating liquidity. If current assets (CA) are $200 and current liabilities (CL) are $100, the current ratio (CR) is 2:1 and net working capital is $100. Now suppose that the firm increases both current assets and current liabilities by $50. This increase causes the current ratio to fall to 1.67:1, indicating a deteriorating liquidity position. The net working capital amount, however, does not change. Table 4.1 summarizes the relationship between the current ratio and net working capital under other assumed conditions. Obviously, great care must be exercised in interpreting these liquidity measures.

Activity Ratios

The *activity ratios,* also called turnover ratios are often cited as indirect measures of cash flow. Activity ratios attempt to reflect the relative efficiency of resources management by relating the level of investment in various asset categories to the level of operations.

TABLE 4.1
Relationship Between Current Ratio and Net Working Capital

Assumption	Current ratio	Net working capital
CR > 1:1		
Increase CA and CL equally	Decreases	No change
Decrease CA and CL equally	Increases	No change
CR < 1:1		
Increase CA and CL equally	Increases	No change
Decrease CA and CL equally	Decreases	No change

Figure 4.1 illustrates that the cash flows within a firm begin in a cash reservoir and move to raw materials (if the firm is a manufacturer) through purchases. Raw materials are placed into production, and the resources representing finished goods are accumulated through production costs and move on again to finished goods. Finally, as finished goods are sold, the resources return to the cash reservoir directly or via accounts receivable and collections. The resources flowing in this arrangement are expanded by a finished good markup so that an increment of profit is carried along with the flows on their return journey. The flow of resources, in financial statement analysis, usually faces an inspection at two critical points — finished goods and accounts receivable — to ascertain that they are flowing freely.

The commitment of resources to receivables is customarily examined by an *accounts receivable turnover* calculation:

$$\text{Accounts receivable turnover} = \frac{\text{credit sales}}{\text{accounts receivable}} . \quad (4.5)$$

Most analysts use year-end receivables in the denominator. However, some analysts prefer to use an average of beginning and closing receivables for the denominator. If seasonal factors are significant, the receivable turnover ratio will be distorted. In any case, receivables net of the allowance for doubtful accounts should be used for the computation. Frequently, net sales are used instead of credit sales since credit sales are not available. Net sales can be a poor substitute if cash sales are a significant proportion of total sales.

FIGURE 4.1
Flow of Net Working Capital

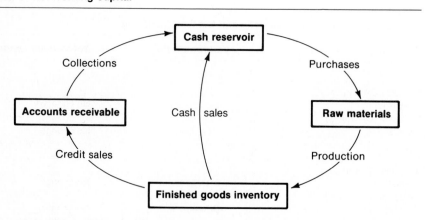

A closely related ratio is the number of *days sales outstanding* (also called the *average collection period*). It is calculated as

$$\text{Days sales outstanding} = \frac{\text{accounts receivable}}{(\text{credit sales})/360}. \qquad (4.6)$$

This ratio can be derived directly from the accounts receivable turnover ratio by dividing 360 (which represents the number of days in the year) by the turnover ratio.

Both the receivables turnover and the collection period are rough measures of cash flow. The information they provide supposedly gives some indication of the quality of the receivables and also an idea of how successful the firm is in collecting its outstanding receivables. The general rule credit managers often use is that the time allowed for payment by the selling terms should not be exceeded by more than 10 to 15 days. As will be explained in Chapter 14, these general rules can severely distort accounts receivable management.

An unusually high accounts receivable balance relative to sales may be indicative that the next period's sales have been pulled into the current period. Sales are moved in this way by overloading dealers, distributors, and customers. To hide a growth in receivables, companies can sell receivables, arrange customer financing with third parties to pay for orders shipped earlier than required by the customer, or sell on an operating lease rather than a capital lease basis. Therefore analysts should check the notes to annual reports to see whether receivables have been sold, contingent liabilities for customer obligations to third parties have been assumed, and the mix of capital and operating leases has shifted toward operating leases so that fewer lease payments receivable have to be shown in the balance sheet.

An unusually low receivable balance can also be bad. It may indicate that credit terms are too restrictive and the company is losing business. Credit terms are examined in Chapter 13.

Another measure of accounts receivable management is the *aging schedule*, which shows the proportion of receivables initiated in each month as a percentage of total sales. Chapter 14 discusses days sales outstanding, turnover calculations, and aging schedules in some detail and shows that they present problems for evaluating accounts receivable management when credit sales are not constant from period to period.

The commonly accepted measure of inventory utilization is *inventory turnover*. It attempts to measure how quickly inventory is sold. The accepted view is that the higher the inventory turnover ratio, the better the company is performing. Possibly, however, the firm is incurring high stockout costs because not enough inventory is available.

The inventory turnover ratio is customarily defined as the ratio of cost of goods sold to average inventory. The calculation is

$$\text{Inventory turnover} = \frac{\text{cost of goods sold}}{\text{average inventory}}. \tag{4.7}$$

As will be discussed in Chapter 16, sales may replace cost of sales in the numerator, and the denominator may be defined as either year-end inventory or a monthly average inventory. Some consider the use of sales a poor substitute since sales include the profit markup, with the result that the turnover is inflated. However, if consistency is maintained over time, this problem is not serious. Knowing the inventory valuation method used is often more important than the problem of inflated turnover. Different valuation methods may affect liquidity analysis more drastically than will the numerator of the inventory turnover ratio being stated by using cost or by using selling price.

Analysis of the efficiency of fixed-asset utilization can provide insights into liquidity management. A *fixed-asset turnover ratio* attempts to measure the intensity of utilization of fixed assets. It does so by relating sales to net fixed assets (after depreciation):

$$\text{Net fixed-asset turnover} = \frac{\text{sales}}{\text{average net fixed assets}}. \tag{4.8}$$

If the turnover ratio is high, the implication is that the company is using its fixed assets effectively to generate sales and, thereby, one hopes, cash flows. If the turnover ratio is low, the implication is that the company either has to use its assets more efficiently or dispose of some of them.

The turnover of net fixed assets can be relatively high for two reasons. A new plant may improve the quality of the product, leading to a high and rising sales volume. In this case the high ratio would be coveted by all. A heavily depreciated plant can also lead to a high turnover ratio, even when the firm's sales are low and falling, a condition that would not be envied. To determine which of these two possibilities is actually the case, one must consider other facts. For example, did the profit margin per item change? What is the trend in sales? What is the firm's depreciation policy?

Analysis of *total asset turnover* provides information of resource management efficiency at an aggregate level. This ratio provides a gross indication of asset utilization and is defined as follows:

$$\text{Total asset turnover} = \frac{\text{sales}}{\text{average total assets}}. \tag{4.9}$$

This ratio summarizes other turnover ratios, and thus it is an overall indication of productivity of invested funds. As such, it is susceptible to a couple of problems. First, the problems inherent in the individual ratios are embodied in the total turnover ratio. Second, the contribution of each asset to the total asset turnover cannot be measured directly. Chapter 6 presents a technique for overcoming this latter problem.

Coverage Ratios

The financial analyst computes *coverage ratios* in order to determine the long-run solvency of the firm. The issue of debt capacity is of critical importance because of its impact on margins of profitability and on solvency. If a firm wishes to reduce the risk of insolvency to a minimum, it would employ only equity capital. However, in so doing, management reduces the opportunity for higher gains (or losses) on equity capital, since it is not taking advantage of the leverage that results from *trading on the equity*. In other words, it is not fully utilizing the relatively cheap source of debt financing to earn project returns in excess of the cost of debt. Conversely, if management wishes to take advantage of leverage, it would increase the amount of debt capital employed in the financing of current assets; in so doing, it must be prepared to accept more risk.

When the word *risk* is applied to debt, it refers to the chance of running out of cash. This risk is inevitably increased by a legal contract requiring the business to pay fixed sums of cash at predetermined dates in the future, regardless of the financial condition at that time. Note that although debt necessarily increases the chance of cash insolvency, this risk exists whether the company has any debt or not. So the debt-equity choice is not between some risk and no risk, but between more and less.

The conventional form for expressing debt capacity rules is in terms of some *debt-to-capital ratio*:

$$\text{Debt/capital} = \frac{\text{debt}}{\text{capitalization}}. \tag{4.10}$$

The numerator of the ratio can include all liabilities, all but current liabilities, or only long-term, interest-bearing debt. The analyst must decide whether to include the indeterminate liabilities of deferred taxes, minority interest, and pension liability. The denominator of the ratio is similarly variable. It sometimes includes only owner's equity, sometimes only long-term sources of capital (long-term debt plus owners' equity), and sometimes all the items on the right-hand side of the balance sheet. A variation of this ratio is often found in debt contracts that limit new long-term borrowings to some percentage of net tangible assets.

Unfortunately, any of these debt-to-capital ratios can seriously mislead unwary analysts. In many cases adjustments for off-balance-sheet items (inventory profits, leases, pensions, deferred taxes, insubstance debt defeasance), which are the subject of Chapter 5, should be made to the ratio.

The ability to pay debts is a dynamic concept and is a function of the profitability of the enterprise, the rate of conversion of its assets into cash, and its creditworthiness. In the short-run a firm's debt capacity is predicated largely upon cash flow rather than earnings that are reported on the income statement.

Generally, the longer the maturity of the debt, the less refunding risk the firm assumes, since management has more opportunities to acquire resources from operations to satisfy the debt, or it will have sufficient opportunity to refinance the obligation. Conversely, the shorter the maturity, the greater the refunding risk is, since the firm will have less time to accumulate sufficient funds to liquidate the debt or have less time to refund the loan.[4]

There are obvious weaknesses of the long-term, debt-to-capital ratio as a way of looking at the chances of running out of cash (other than the fact that many off-balance-sheet items exist). First, there is a wide variation in the relation between the principal of the debt and the annual obligation for cash payments under the debt contract. The annual cash outflow associated with $10 million on the balance sheet may, for example, vary from $1,500,000 (interest only at 15 percent), to $1,523,000 (interest plus principal repayable over 30 years), to $1,992,494 (interest plus principal repayable over 10 years). Second, as loans are repaid by partial annual payments, as is customary, the principal amount declines and the percent-of-capitalization ratio improves, but the annual cash drain of repayments remains the same until maturity is reached. Third, there may be substantial changes in asset values, particularly in connection with inventory valuation and depreciation policies; and as a consequence, there will be changes in the percent-of-capitalization ratio that have no bearing on the capacity to meet fixed cash drains.

An alternative form in which to express the limits of long-term borrowing is income statement data. This form is the *fixed-charge coverage ratio* — the ratio of earnings available for servicing debt and other fixed charges to the total amount of these charges. The numerator is earnings before taxes increased for such fixed charges as interest and lease obligations (among others). The denominator can include tax-deductible interest, lease payments, and nondeductible dividends and sinking fund payments,

---

[4]The longer (shorter) the maturity of debt, the higher (lower) is the *interest rate risk.* The *refunding risk* for shorter maturities has been labeled "crisis-at-maturity" by R. E. Johnson, "Term Structures of Corporate Bond Yields as a Function of Risk of Default," *Journal of Finance* (May 1967): 318–21.

both grossed up (by dividing by 1 − tax rate) to show pretax cash amounts that are necessary to service them:

Fixed-charge coverage

$$= \frac{\text{adjusted earnings before taxes}}{\text{interest + leases} + \dfrac{\text{sinking fund charges + dividends}}{(1 - \text{tax rate})}}. \quad (4.11)$$

The *simple interest coverage ratio* is derived by defining the numerator as earnings before interest and taxes and the denominator as interest charges. Under a fixed-charge coverage rule no new long-term debt can be contemplated unless income available for servicing debt and other fixed charges is equal to or in excess of some multiple, say 3, of the debt-servicing and fixed charges. The reason for this rule is to allow a company to survive a period of decline in sales and earnings and still have enough earnings to cover the fixed charges.

The fixed-charge (or interest) coverage ratio is influenced by the *earning power* of the assets (*return on assets,* discussed later in this section), the debt/equity ratio, the fixed charges (such as interest and lease payments), and the proportion of debt repayment each period. Implicit in the coverage ratio is the idea of variability. The greater the variability in earning power of assets, the higher the required ratio is. Conversely, the lower the variability, the lower the required coverage standard must be — in other words, the more debt and other fixed obligations the firm can support.

The fixed-charge (or interest) coverage ratio has limitations as a basis for determination of debt capacity. First, it is a point-in-time measure, a measure that cannot adequately measure flows available to meet obligations because it is static. Second, the earnings figure found in the income statement is derived under normal accrual accounting procedures and is not the same as net cash inflow, an assumption that is implicit in the coverage ratio. Even when adjustments are made for the noncash items (such as depreciation), this equivalence cannot safely be assumed. Ideally, the analysis should be in terms of cash and not accrual accounting information. Third, the ratio fails to reflect the financial position of the firm under adversity when earnings may be down and interest up. Finally, nothing is reported about the state of the capital markets and the fact that financing capacity varies markedly for many firms over the business cycle.

The *degree of financial leverage* (DFL) is often employed to measure the extent of a firm's borrowings. The higher the degree of financial leverage, the higher is the risk of the firm's not being able to meet financial obligations. Financial leverage refers to the use of fixed-income securities — debt and preferred stock — in an effort to boost earnings per share. The calculation is as follows, where EBIT is earnings before interest and taxes:

$$\text{DFL} = \frac{\text{EBIT}}{\text{EBIT} - \text{interest} - \dfrac{\text{preferred dividends}}{(1 - \text{tax rate})}} . \qquad (4.12)$$

Financial leverage is frequently shown in graphical form, as in Fig. 4.2, to highlight the impact of additional debt on earnings per share. Favorable financial leverage results in higher earnings per share (EPS) and is thought to be good. Unfavorable leverage results if the EPS declines as more debt is added. In the first case, management is able to invest the debt funds and earn more on them than they cost. In the second case, it earns less on the funds than they cost.

Unfortunately, the *EPS–EBIT analysis* contributes little to an understanding of liquidity. Impact on earnings, and not cash flow, is the determining factor in the analysis. The model emphasizes maximization of earnings per share, which is not consistent with maximizing shareholder wealth, as discussed in Chapters 1 and 2. Management can always increase short-term earnings per share, usually at the expense of long-term value to the shareholder.[5]

Additionally, *earnings per share* is an unreliable standard for measuring economic value for shareholders. There are several important reasons why it is unreliable. First, earnings vary with the use of different accounting methods (for example, last-in, first-out inventory valuation vs. first-in, first-out inventory valuation). Second, earnings do not reflect differences in business and financial risk faced by various companies. Third, earnings do not account for relative rates of investment in net working capital and fixed capital needed to support sales growth. Finally, reported earnings do not incorporate changes in a company's cost of capital due to either shifts in inflationary expectations or changes in business or financial risk.

A much-used basis for evaluating the net worth and any changes in it from year to year is found in the *book value* or *equity value per share* of stock. Book value per share of stock is the amount each share would receive if the company were liquidated on the basis of amounts reported on the balance sheet. The figure loses much of its relevance since the valuations on the balance sheet (generally) do not approximate fair market value or even the liquidation value of the assets. It is computed by allocating the stockholders' equity items among the various classes of stock and then dividing

---

[5]Appendix B in Chapter 6 has an extensive discussion and illustration to underscore this statement.

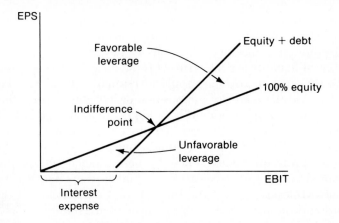

EPS

Favorable
leverage

Equity + debt

100% equity

Indifference
point

Unfavorable
leverage

EBIT

Interest
expense

FIGURE 4.2
Financial Leverage: The Debt/Equity Trade-off

the total so allocated to each class of stock by the number of shares outstanding:

$$\text{Book value per share} = \frac{\text{common shareholders' equity}}{\text{outstanding common shares}}. \qquad (4.13)$$

A popular, but poorly understood, measure is *cash flow,* or in ratio form, *cash flow per share.* This so-called cash flow figure is computed by adding noncash charges to net income. In the conversion to a ratio the cash flow is divided by the number of shares of common stock outstanding:

$$\text{Cash flow per share} = \frac{\text{net income} + \text{noncash adjustments}}{\text{outstanding common shares}}. \qquad (4.14)$$

This amount represents neither the flow of cash through the firm nor the residual of the cash received minus the cash disbursed divided by the outstanding shares of stock. It is frequently used to determine approximately the amount of resources generated internally. However, for this purpose changes in accounts receivable, accounts payable, inventory, accruals, and prepaids need to be factored into the numerator. These changes were shown in Chapter 3.

Profitability Ratios

Profitability is frequently used as the ultimate test of management's effectiveness in directing the firm and ensuring that its liquidity needs are satisfied. An amazing number of financial ratios are based on the idea that a period's earnings reveal a company's financial strength. However strong the profit motives of management may be, they can never wisely be permitted to take precedence over safety. Safety means solvency — the capacity of the corporation to meet its obligations as they become due. The appropriate levels of liquidity are the result of fundamental decisions concerning the firm's various net working capital investments, the firm's fixed-asset investments, and the maturity composition of its debt. In turn, these decisions are influenced by a trade-off between profitability and risk. The risk of running out of cash can be reduced or even eliminated, of course, by maintaining a high proportion of liquid assets. There is a cost, however: the foregone profit on the investment of these funds in other assets.

Ratios are often used to measure profitability, or effectiveness, at one or both of two levels: that of the fundamental profitability of the firm's operations and the profitability on the owner's investment, which reflects not only operating profitability but also capital structure.

As a measure of financial performance, profitability ratios inadequately incorporate timing effects, risk, and value. The timing problem pertains to the sacrifice of present earnings for future earnings, or vice versa. High returns usually entail high risk. Unfortunately, the profitability ratios are silent about risk. The value problem arises because historical book values are used in calculations and not market values.

A widely used measure of the basic profitability of the firm is *return on assets,* which is frequently defined as the ratio of net income to total assets. This ratio reflects the ability of management to generate income on a given amount of total assets. The return-on-assets concept is particularly useful because it can be broken down into various components to identify reasons for a change in earning power over time. The ratio is usually defined as the product of percentage return on sales (possibly adjusted to eliminate the interest charge) times asset turnover:

$$\text{Return on assets} = \underbrace{\frac{\text{net income}}{\text{sales}}}_{\substack{\text{return on} \\ \text{sales}}} \times \underbrace{\frac{\text{sales}}{\text{total assets}}}_{\substack{\text{asset} \\ \text{turnover}}}. \qquad (4.15)$$

The usefulness of this construct is that it helps the analyst integrate ratio analysis, because it shows that a change in return on assets may come about through a change in the profitability of sales or through more intensive utilization of the firm's assets by increasing asset turnover.

Earnings before interest and taxes (EBIT) rather than net income after taxes, can be used in order to eliminate the influence of differential tax treatment and different capital structure decisions on earnings performance. Any nonoperating income and expenses are also eliminated from EBIT.

If net income after tax is used, analysts *should* add back the after-tax interest charge [net income + interest (1 − tax rate)]. This procedure has the effect of eliminating the financing charge from the calculation but not the taxes. The rationale is that interest is a financing charge, not an operating expense, and should be eliminated from any evaluation of earning potential of the investment. On the other hand, taxes are an operating cost and should be included. Another adjustment many analysts make is to use only net operating assets in the denominator. This adjustment eliminates miscellaneous and intangible assets from the calculation.

Degree of operating leverage, breakeven, and margin-of-safety analyses are often used along with profitability ratios to show management how income and risk varies with changes in sales volumes, costs, or prices. From an examination of the relationship between costs, prices, and income, management attempts to gain insight about the operating risk (and indirectly about the liquidity risk) of the firm.

If a high percentage of a firm's total operating costs are fixed, then the firm is said to have a high degree of operating leverage. This implies that a relatively small increase (decrease) in sales results in a large increase (decrease) in operating income. Other things being held constant, the higher a firm's operating leverage, the higher is its operating risk. The *degree of operating leverage* (*DOL*) is defined as

$$
\begin{aligned}
\text{DOL} &= \frac{\text{sales} - \text{total variable costs}}{\text{sales} - \text{total variable costs} - \text{total fixed operating costs}} \\[2mm]
&= \frac{\text{percentage change in EBIT}}{\text{percentage change in sales}} \\[2mm]
&= \frac{\text{sales}}{\text{sales} - \text{breakeven sales}},
\end{aligned}
\tag{4.16}
$$

where fixed operating costs exclude interest expense.

The equation for calculating *operating breakeven sales dollars* is

$$
\text{Breakeven sales dollars} = \frac{\text{fixed operating costs}}{\text{contribution margin percent}},
\tag{4.17}
$$

where

$$
\text{Contribution margin percent} = 1 - \frac{\text{variable costs}}{\text{sales}}.
\tag{4.18}
$$

Margin of safety indicates the proportion that sales can decline (or need to increase) before operating breakeven profit is reached. It is calculated as

$$
\text{Margin of safety} = 1 - \frac{\text{breakeven sales}}{\text{actual sales}}.
\tag{4.19}
$$

The inverse of margin of safety is the degree of operating leverage in Eq. (4.16).

In terms of liquidity analysis a major concern with traditional break-even analysis and its associated margin-of-safety concept is that they fail to incorporate cash flows. This problem can be alleviated to some extent, as will be discussed in Chapter 6. Other problems usually associated with breakeven analysis are the following:

- □ The analysis is only appropriate for a single product or a constant mix of products.
- □ A distinction between fixed and variable costs is necessary.
- □ The analysis is only appropriate for a relevant range of production.
- □ All costs and prices must be known at each level of output.
- □ Costs are generally assumed to be linear (however, nonlinear costs can be easily introduced).

Another measure of profitability is *return on equity*. It indicates the success of management in generating earnings (*not* cash flow) for the firm's owners and is defined as the ratio of earnings available to the common stockholders' equity divided by equity:

$$\text{Return on equity} = \frac{\text{earnings available to equityholders}}{\text{total equity}}. \qquad (4.20)$$

If there is any preferred stock outstanding, the amount of the preferred stock dividends is deducted from net income after taxes. The par amount of preferred stock outstanding is deducted from net worth to obtain the common stockholders' equity. This ratio can be expanded to provide a broader perspective for analyzing profitability:

$$\text{Return on equity} = \underbrace{\frac{\text{net income}}{\text{sales}}}_{\substack{\text{return} \\ \text{on sales}}} \times \underbrace{\frac{\text{sales}}{\text{total assets}}}_{\substack{\text{asset} \\ \text{turnover}}} \times \underbrace{\frac{\text{total assets}}{\text{equity}}}_{\text{leverage}} \qquad (4.21)$$

The first and third ratios on the right-hand side of the equation relate to the income statement and balance sheet, respectively. The middle ratio combines information from these two statements. If preferred stock is outstanding, preferred dividends paid should be deducted from net income (that is, calculate earnings available to equityholders). The interest deduction paid to debtholders is included in the calculation of net income since return to common shareholders is being measured. The return-on-equity ratio encompasses all the problems inherent in the liquidity, activity, and coverage ratios, since these ratios are embedded here.

Standards of Financial Comparison

The previous discussion indicates that financial analysts must understand the shortcomings of financial ratios if meaningful conclusions are to be drawn. The next step is to compare the results to some standard. Three types of comparisons are frequently used to analyze financial data: industry, trend, and predictive models.

Industry Comparisons

Industry comparisons involve comparisons of a particular ratio within the firm with the same ratio for a representative number of other firms in the same industry line. This comparison indicates whether figures on the firm's balance sheet or income statement are out of line with the figures on financial statements of similar companies.

There are no standardized financial statement forms used by all businesses. Furthermore, the classification of some of the statement items varies widely. These variations are frequently a result of the following:

- Management's intention and the use that is to be made of the statements
- Differences of opinion among those who prepare the statements
- Differences in the accountants' knowledge, training, and experience
- Failure to adopt generally accepted current changes in terminology and classification

Standard ratios for various industry lines are available from a number of sources, including trade associations and regulatory agencies. Possibly the best known are the ratios published annually by Dun & Bradstreet, a nationwide credit-reporting firm, by Robert Morris Associations, an organization of bank credit officers, and by the *Almanac of Business and Industrial Financial Ratios* (shown as Table 4.2). The implicit assumption in making industry comparisons is that the consensus of other firms — as expressed in the standard ratio — represents a norm from which any significant deviation on the part of the firm would require explanation.

Great care must be exercised in defining industries since firms are very diverse. For example, if W. T. Grant was still in existence today in the form it was as of 1974, a comparison of it to Sears would be misleading. Although Sears is in the retail business, the majority of its revenues and profits today are from financial services — selling insurance, real estate, and securities.

TABLE 4.2
Retail Trade: General Merchandise Stores

		Size of assets in thousands of dollars (000 omitted)										
Item description for accounting period 7/73 through 6/74	A Total	B Under 100	C 100 to 250	D 250 to 500	E 500 to 1000	F 1000 to 5000	G 5000 to 10,000	H 10,000 to 25,000	I 25,000 to 50,000	J 50,000 to 100,000	K 100,000 to 250,000	L 250,000 and over
1. Number of establishments	24,524	11,555	6368	3110	1681	1365	133	134	59	50	24	45
2. Total receipts (in millions of dollars)	138,989.8	1899.7	2847.1	2709.7	2844.1	6543.7	2107.8	4783.0	5231.9	5921.5	6713.4	97,387.3
Selected operating factors in percent of net sales												
3. Cost of operations	63.6	69.0	69.2	68.3	68.9	66.8	69.0	69.0	68.3	66.8	67.1	61.8
4. Compensation of officers	—	4.1	2.7	2.7	1.9	1.7	1.1	0.6	—	—	—	—
5. Repairs	0.5	—	—	—	—	—	—	—	—	—	—	0.5
6. Bad debts	—	—	—	—	—	—	—	—	—	—	—	0.5
7. Rent on business property	2.6	3.9	2.9	2.9	2.1	2.8	2.6	3.3	3.5	2.9	2.2	2.5
8. Taxes (excl. federal tax)	2.5	2.2	1.8	1.7	1.8	2.0	2.1	1.9	2.2	2.2	3.0	2.7
9. Interest	2.2	—	0.5	—	0.5	0.7	0.7	1.0	0.9	1.6	1.4	2.7
10. Deprec./deplet./amortiz.†	1.5	1.1	0.8	0.7	0.8	1.1	1.0	1.1	1.0	1.6	1.7	1.6
11. Advertising	2.7	1.1	2.0	1.7	2.0	2.2	2.3	2.4	2.1	2.5	2.0	2.9
12. Pensions and other benefit plans	0.8	—	—	0.5	0.6	0.6	—	—	—	—	0.5	0.9
13. Other expenses	23.1	16.7	17.2	17.9	18.4	20.8	21.5	22.3	21.0	22.9	21.6	24.2
14. Net profit before tax	*	0.7	2.1	2.8	2.4	0.9	*	*	*	*	*	*

Selected financial ratios *(number of times ratio is to one)*

15. Current ratio	1.6	2.1	2.4	2.8	2.1	2.1	2.1	2.0	2.0	2.0	1.9	1.5
16. Quick ratio	0.8	0.5	0.6	1.0	0.7	0.8	0.9	0.6	0.7	0.7	0.9	0.9
17. Net sales to net working capital	6.0	8.9	5.6	5.2	5.6	5.5	5.1	5.8	6.5	5.0	6.7	6.1
18. Net sales to net worth	3.9	9.6	4.8	3.9	4.5	4.3	3.9	5.0	5.1	3.6	4.2	3.7
19. Inventory turnover	4.7	5.1	4.2	4.2	3.9	4.3	3.8	4.0	5.3	4.2	0.9	—
20. Total liabilities to net worth	1.5	1.6	0.8	0.5	0.9	0.9	0.9	1.2	1.2	1.2	1.2	1.7

Selected financial factors in percentages

21. Current liability to net worth	102.0	94.6	59.4	41.8	68.7	68.5	65.3	79.6	77.8	66.6	66.7	114.1
22. Inventory to current assets	41.5	71.1	69.1	62.7	64.6	56.1	52.8	64.8	56.9	58.6	48.8	36.5
23. Net income to net worth	15.1	48.9	21.4	21.9	23.5	19.8	14.9	24.9	22.5	12.1	11.9	13.8
24. Retained earnings to net income	69.7	96.6	91.3	89.7	87.2	92.8	89.4	93.9	89.0	76.9	72.9	60.9

Source: From the book *Almanac of Business and Industrial Financial Ratios*, 1977 edition, by Leo Troy. © 1977 by Prentice-Hall, Inc., Englewood Cliffs, NJ 07632. Used by permission of the publisher.

Note: Because the source deals with *all* returns, those with and without income, a loss before tax in any industry, or asset size within an industry, is shown by an asterisk (*) at number 14. This will explain those instances in which the sum of the operating factors exceeds 100 percent.

†Depreciation largest factor.

If standard ratios are to be meaningful and informative, they should be developed for the following types of companies of an industry:

□ Companies that use a uniform accounting system and accounting procedures, including a uniform classification of accounts and similar depreciation methods

□ Companies that follow a uniform accounting period, preferably on a natural business-year basis

□ Companies that follow similar asset valuation and amortization policies

□ Companies that represent a homogeneous product line

□ Companies that adopt and maintain somewhat uniform managerial policies

Because of diversity across firms in their access to product, factor, and financial markets, these points may not hold rigorously. Thus the analyst, when using either inter- or intraindustry comparisons, must constantly be aware of the limitations of the data in drawing meaningful conclusions. Table 4.3 summarizes some of the more obvious differences in financial and operating data of companies.

TABLE 4.3
Some Financial and Operating Differences of Companies

1. Wide separation geographically, with different price levels and costs of operations
2. Operation of owned or leased properties or a combination thereof
3. Ownership of large or small amounts of investments in properties that are not used in connection with regular operations
4. Different price levels reflected in noncurrent asset items
5. New rather than old properties
6. Manufacture of one or a large number of products
7. Utilization of a high or low percentage of maximum plant capacity
8. Purchase or production of raw materials or semifinished goods
9. Vertical or horizontal integration
10. Maintenance of large inventories or adoption of an informal policy of purchasing raw materials or merchandise
11. Valuation of inventories on FIFO, LIFO, moving average, or some other basis
12. Sale of merchandise largely on either short- or long-term credit or mainly for cash
13. Sale of entire product to a single purchaser or to a large number of wholesalers, retailers, or consumers
14. Dependence on creditors for financing to a greater extent than owners' equity financing, or vice versa
15. Different systems of accounting and accounting procedures including classification of financial statement items, accounting periods, and depreciation methods

Trend Analysis

Although intercompany and interindustry financial comparisons are difficult, evaluating the same firm over a period of time is less of a problem. However, even this seemingly simple comparative analysis can prove hazardous.

Trend ratios generally are not computed for all of the items on the financial statements, since the fundamental objective is to make comparisons between items having some logical relationship to one another. This type of presentation can be useful in discerning whether certain segments of a firm's financial picture are deteriorating or improving and what can be expected in the future. Many times, this presentation is accomplished by plotting trend lines of a company's ratios. However, no conclusions can be made about the operations of the firm as a whole by examining only a single measure, such as a trend in the current ratio. These trends, important as they may be, will not, for example, answer such questions as the following: How effectively is the firm utilizing its resources? How has its past growth been financed? Where are funds for future growth likely to come from? How well can the firm meet its current obligations? How soon can it collect its receivables? How rapidly can it convert its inventory into cash?

The analyst must keep in mind that ratios are never conclusive in and of themselves. The comparability of trend ratios is adversely affected by the extent to which accounting principles and policies reflected in the accounts have not been followed consistently throughout the periods being studied. Comparability of the data is also adversely affected when the price level has changed materially during the years under review. Some analysts deflate the statement data by dividing the dollar amounts by a related price index, thereby providing figures that will give a rough picture of changes exclusive of price changes. This technique is used in some later chapters.

Even if the analyst identifies an apparently deteriorating trend in some ratio or a significant deviation from published standards, these anomalies are merely circumstantial evidence of a financial defect. They should be taken as warning signals indicating that additional investigation is necessary and not as conclusive evidence of financial strength or weakness. It is in the interpretation and evaluation of these anomalies — and in the recognition of what constitutes an anomaly — that the judgment, skill, and experience of the analyst receives the most severe test.

There are no hard-and-fast rules to guide the analyst in this task of drawing meaningful information about the firm's financial condition from reported data. Instead, the analyst must use her or his accumulated skill and experience to frame conclusions. The numbers on the financial statements are merely representations of states (in the case of the balance sheet) or flows (for the income statement and cash flows statement) within the financial framework of the firm. With minor exceptions, they take on meaning and significance only in the light of a detailed understanding of the basic considerations used in the financial management of the firm. The analyst should carry this viewpoint into any discussion of financial analysis. There are no rules or shortcuts that will eliminate the need for seasoned judgment.

Warning Signals

History has proven that prevention of corporate failure requires constant attention to the firm's operations. Insolvency occurs when management cannot pay the firm's debts as they fall due. A firm must remember that insolvency and liquidation are the endpoints of the process of failure. Management must continually review how the company is operating to prevent any slide toward corporate collapse.

A model of the business failure succession is presented in Fig. 4.3. There are many causes and symptoms of corporate collapse.

Quantification of Warning Signals

Prior to the development of quantitative measures of performance, agencies were established to supply qualitative information to assess the creditworthiness of particular firms. From this information studies were developed that revealed that failing companies exhibited different financial performance than companies that did not fail. As a result of these studies, financial ratios eventually became widely used in predicting business failure.

Univariate Models

A study by Beaver[6] of failed and nonfailed firms found that an analyst, by comparing a number of seemingly independent ratios that measure profitability, liquidity, and solvency, could discriminate between the two types

---

[6]W. H. Beaver, "Financial Ratios as Predictors of Failure," *Empirical Research in Accounting: Selected Studies*, supplement to *Journal of Accounting Research* (1966): 77–111.

Minor/temporary ————————————→ Major/permanent

	Operating results below expectations	Nonpayment of dividends	Net loss and negative cash flow trends	Lowered bond rating	Deteriorating operation results year after year	Debt accommodation	Loan default	Bankruptcy	Liquidation
Alternatives available to the failing firm									
	Policy changes/operating reorganizations								
			Major reorganization						
					Discontinued operations				
					Merger with solvent corporation				
						Troubled debt restructuring			
								Bankruptcy petition	
									Cease operations
Alternatives available to creditors									
	Careful analysis of financial performance of failing firm								
							Receipt of cash under judicial provisions		
						Debt accommodation/exchange of debt for equity position			

FIGURE 4.3
Business Failure Events

Source: Gary Giroux and Casper E. Wiggins, Jr., "Chapter XI and Corporate Resuscitation," *Financial Executive* (December 1983), Table 2. Reprinted by permission from *Financial Executive*, December 1983, copyright 1983 by Financial Executives Institute.

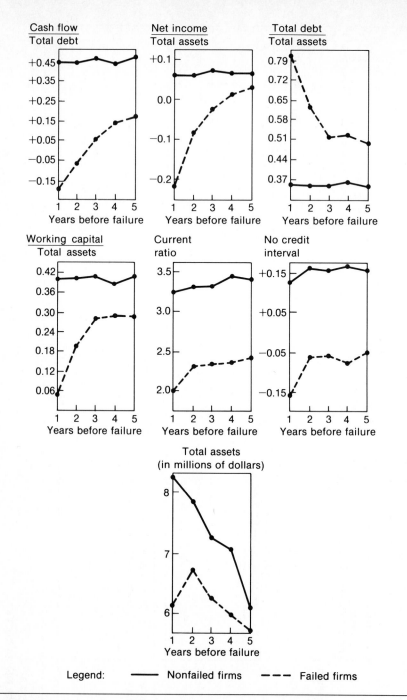

FIGURE 4.4
Profile Analysis of Failed and Nonfailed Firms

Source: William H. Beaver, "Financial Ratios as Predictors of Failure," Fig. 1. Reprinted by permission from the *Journal of Accounting Research* (Supplement 1966).

of firms for periods up to five years prior to failure. Figure 4.4 is a profile of mean values for failed and nonfailed types of firms. Although Beaver's results are impressive, this type of study, where emphasis is placed on individual signals of impending problems, is often questionable since the variables' interactions are not revealed.

Multivariate Models

More meaningful predictive models have been developed that operate in a multivariate prediction framework. A model that has received much exposure is Altman's *Z score model*.[7] The *Z* score model uses multiple discriminant analysis (MDA), which is discussed in Appendix A in Chapter 12. Basically, MDA is used to classify an observation into one of several groupings dependent upon the observation's individual characteristics.

Altman's *Z* score model is a method of linear analysis in that five measures are objectively weighted and summed to arrive at an overall score that then becomes the basis for classification of firms into one of two groupings: bankrupt or nonbankrupt. The five measures used are as follows:[8]

1. X_1 = working capital/total assets. This ratio supposedly indicates what the net liquid assets of a company are relative to its total capitalization.

2. X_2 = retained earnings/total assets. This ratio attempts to measure long-term profitability.

3. X_3 = earnings before interest and taxes/total assets. This ratio is meant to measure the real productivity of the assets.

4. X_4 = market value of equity/book value of total liabilities. This ratio tries to measure how much a company's assets can shrink before they are exceeded by liabilities.

5. X_5 = sales/total assets. This ratio attempts to measure how much revenue the company's assets can bring in.

The discriminant model selects the appropriate weights to use with these measures. The purpose of the weights is to separate, as much as possible, the average values of each group while at the same time to minimize

---

[7] E. I. Altman, "Financial Ratios, Discriminant Analysis, and the Prediction of Corporate Bankruptcy," *Journal of Finance* (September 1968): 589–610.

[8] Variables X_1 through X_4 must be calculated as decimal equivalents of percentage values (e.g., 0.10 instead of 10 percent). Variable X_5 is written in terms of number of times (e.g., 2 instead of 200 percent).

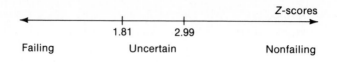

FIGURE 4.5
Altman's Z Score Cutoffs

the statistical distance of each observation and its own group mean. Altman's discriminate function was estimated as

$$Z = 1.2X_1 + 1.4X_2 + 3.3X_3 + 0.6X_4 + 1.0X_5. \tag{4.22}$$

He found (in order of importance) that variables X_3, X_5, and X_4 contributed most to differentiating between firms with liquidity problems and solvent firms. Altman's model classified firms with a discriminant Z score of greater than 2.99 as nonfailing and firms with a score of less than 1.81 as failing (see Fig. 4.5). The range 1.81 to 2.99 was considered a gray area or zone of ignorance where it was difficult to effectively discriminate.

ILLUSTRATION 4.1

The results of applying Altman's model to W. T. Grant for the period January 31, 1971, to January 31, 1975, are summarized in Table 4.4. Prior to the January 31, 1974, results, W. T. Grant was consistently classified as a nonfailing firm (although its Z score was steadily declining). Performance ending January 31, 1974, resulted in the model classifying W. T. Grant in the uncertain range. It was not until January 31, 1975, that W. T. Grant was clearly labeled a failing firm by the model. On October 2, 1975, W. T. Grant filed for bankruptcy protection under Chapter XI of the U.S. Bankruptcy Code.   □

TABLE 4.4
Classification of W. T. Grant, Using the Altman Model (Year Ended January 31)

Year	X_1	X_2	X_3	X_4	Z_5	Z score*	Classification
1971	0.44	0.29	0.11	1.10	1.55	3.51	Nonfailing
1972	0.50	0.26	0.08	1.26	1.46	3.44	Nonfailing
1973	0.43	0.24	0.08	0.75	1.48	3.05	Nonfailing
1974	0.44	0.20	0.05	0.38	1.48	2.68	Uncertain
1975	0.16	0.03	⟨0.07⟩	0.09	1.63	1.69	Failing

*Z scores were calculated by using Eq. (4.22).

Little satisfaction is derived from the fact that the model was able to predict W. T. Grant's demise. As discussed in Chapter 3, and later in Chapter 6, W. T. Grant had serious problems in its ability to sustain growth and was unable to generate a positive cash flow from operations in the six years prior to filing for bankruptcy in October 1975.

Although the Z-score model may be a useful technique for summarizing complex interrelationships among variables, it should be used with caution and only if there is reason to believe that it is appropriate for the task.[9] As Altman's sample companies were all U.S. manufacturers, one could hardly expect the formula to work accurately for companies outside that category, and this is borne out by experience. Another critique of the model is that no weight is given to concepts of risk or market conditions. Even if the model is thought to be acceptable, it must be reviewed periodically to ensure that the weights for the parameters (X_i's) have not changed or that different parameters might not be more appropriate for predicting problem firms.

Quality of Earnings

In order to place the discussion of liquidity analysis using financial ratios in proper perspective, this section focuses on quality of earnings. Understanding a company's quality of earnings is always a problem for creditors and investors alike, for **quality of earnings** is *relative,* not absolute. The relative quality of earnings is as important as the absolute level of earnings. Chapter 3 briefly touched on the extent to which W. T. Grant Company relied on noncash items to generate income (see Fig. 3.1). In this case failure of analysts to take quality of earnings into consideration led to the erroneous conclusion that the W. T. Grant Company was financially sound. On March 18, 1974, the accounting firm of Ernst and Ernst gave unqualified certification of W. T. Grant's financial statements for the fiscal year ended January 31, 1974. The stock market had assigned a higher price-earnings multiple to W. T. Grant than to all other variety retail stores in the industry with the exception of Kresge Company. W. T. Grant was also able to sell commercial paper (which is nothing more than an uncollateralized promissory note), thus convincing the debt markets that it had rela-

---

[9] I. G. Dambolena and J. M. Shulman, "A Primary Rule for Detecting Bankruptcy: Watch the Cash," *Financial Analysts Journal* (September–October 1988): 74–78, show Altman's model can be improved by including a variable that captures net liquid balances of the firm. E I. Altman, R. G. Haldeman, and P. Narayanan, "Zeta Analysis: A New Model to Identify Bankruptcy Risk of Corporations," *Journal of Banking and Finance* (June 1977): 29–54, have constructed a more comprehensive discriminant model (called ZETA). However, for proprietary reasons they have not revealed the discriminant function Z.

tively low default risk. About one year later, W. T. Grant declared bankruptcy.

The distinction between accrual income and cash flow causes difficulties in interpreting and analyzing financial statements. The concept of earnings quality arose from the need to compare the earnings of different companies and the need to recognize such differences in quality for valuation purposes. Although quality, as it is used here, has no single definition, it relates to a company's conservatism in calculating earnings, the variability or stability of the company's earnings, the relationship between the company's accrual income and its cash flows, and the degree to which the company's operations generate cash flow for the maintenance of assets and the enhancement of future earnings.

The discussion that follows reviews, through an examination of several sources of low earnings quality, the characteristics of these earnings and how analysts may detect a decline in earnings quality. *Failure to detect low earnings quality makes any form of ratio analysis suspect as a management tool.* Excerpts are taken from W. T. Grant and other companies' annual reports and 10-K statements submitted to the Securities and Exchange Commission of the United States to illustrate points in the discussion.

Fraudulent Actions

Low earnings quality due to fraudulent actions are difficult to detect. As the details of recession-induced bankruptcies seem to indicate, desperate managements sometimes engage in fraudulent activity as they try to stave off impending bankruptcy. An example is the deliberate misstatement of inventories and cost of sales in order to improve profits.

Was fraud present in the W. T. Grant case? It is difficult to say, but W. T. Grant's public accounting firm and its primary banker, Morgan Guaranty, both settled lawsuits out of court for failing to reveal the company's disastrous financial condition.

Above-Average Financial Risk

Earnings quality is influenced by a company's financial condition. Earnings accompanied by an increasing level of financial leverage begin to jeopardize their quality long before the liquidity crisis. Fixed-interest payments build greater volatility into the earnings figure. Analysts should keep track of the changing financial risk due to on- and off-balance-sheet financial obligations of companies, such as unfunded pension liabilities and leases (explored more fully in Chapter 5).

In the case of W. T. Grant, its 1973–74 commercial paper obligations exceeded the total equity of the company. Maturities ranged from 1 to 270 days and placed a considerable strain on liquidity, particularly since this was a time when the Nixon administration had imposed price controls on the economy in an attempt to slow the rate of inflation.

Less-Than-Conservative Accounting

The principal source of low-quality earnings during periods of waning customer demand and difficult financial times is the use of the following types of accounting practices:

- Practices that are less conservative than available alternatives
- Practices that fail to reflect the underlying economic reality of the transactions they represent
- Practices that are based on optimistic assumptions about future events

Most low-quality accounting practices are within the bounds of so-called *generally accepted accounting principles,* since no public company can afford to have anything less than a clean auditor's opinion if it wants its common stock to trade in the public markets. Consequently, *analysts should not assume that audit certification ensures acceptable earnings quality.* It simply indicates that in the auditor's opinion acceptable accounting standards have been met. In a study of bankrupt firms Ohlson[10] found that the majority of the firms had an unqualified auditor's opinion in the immediate years prior to filing for bankruptcy.

Some hints for detecting accounting-generated low-quality earnings follow.

- *Is there adequate disclosure in the notes to the financial statements?* These notes should describe how the company arrived at the dollar figures shown in the statements. For instance, readers of General Electric Corporation's annual report, prior to new consolidation reporting requirements, would have difficulty detecting that its unconsolidated subsidiary, General Electric Credit Corporation, has been a large contributor to cash flow over the years.
- *What alternative accounting practices might the company have used?* For example, if W. T. Grant had capitalized all financing leases, its accountants estimated that net earnings for the year ended January 31, 1974, would have been reduced by about $1.6 million, which would have resulted in earnings per share declining 20 percent.

---

[10]Ohlson, "Financial Ratios and the Probabilistic Prediction of Bankruptcy."

□ *What accounting practices does the so-called industry leader follow?* Use of less conservative practices may suggest that management is trying to hide a competitive weakness with accounting. For example, Sequent Computer Systems reported a 50 percent increase in per share profits for the first nine months of 1988 fiscal year. The entire gain was derived from management's decision to defer rather than expense about $2 million of software development costs.

□ *What is the earnings process of the company?* Low-quality income results when companies recognize income before all of the material uncertainties about whether the company is better off economically from its revenue-producing activities are resolved. For example, W. T. Grant, as of January 1974, was involved in legal proceedings in nine states that involved allegations that the company's finance charges on installment sales exceeded the maximum amounts permissible by law. In two states the court had handed down adverse decisions. Management felt unable to determine the ultimate obligations and had not allowed for any contingency reserves.

□ *Are there adequate reserves for future obligations?* If the company has obligations to perform future services to customers or employees after income is recognized, determine whether adequate provisions for the costs of these future services have been established. Managements trying to protect accounting profits tend to underestimate their future expenses that relate to income recognized currently. For example, in 1988, Regina Corporation, a manufacturer of vacuum cleaners, admitted to grossly understating customer returns. Management hid sales returns of at least $13 million of vacuums by not recording the correct accounting entry.

□ *Does the company make dubious claims that certain expenditures should be called assets because they create future benefits?* Maybe these expenditures should be called expenses. For example, in March 1989 CUC International admitted that its profits had been grossly inflated by deferring over several years the costs of attracting new customers. The *Generally Accepted Accounting Principles (GAAP)* allows either immediate recognition of the expense or deferral over the likely life of the membership contract. CUC International deferred the expense using an inflated estimate for membership life. The $51 million write-off wiped out profits of the last three years.

□ *Has the company changed accounting practices recently? Was a less conservative practice adopted?* For example, in 1974 management of W. T. Grant decided to change its accounting principle for finance charges on its customers' installment accounts. This change resulted in increased earnings per share for the financially depressed years 1973 and 1974. When reported net income was relatively good, prior to this period, management had seen no need to change.

☐ *Has the company changed auditors?* The change may have occurred because the previous auditor would not go along with management's decision to adopt a lower quality accounting practice. For example, American Continental Corporation (ACC) (the parent of the bankrupt Lincoln Savings and Loan) replaced its auditors when they would not agree to ACC's request to certify an accounting entry that would have increased income about $84 million, "earned" on an exchange of unlike property with another firm. There was no cash flow associated with the transaction. It was purely an attempt to increase accounting profits.

☐ *Is there a significant difference between tax and book (financial) accounting, as indicated by the size of the deferred tax expense?*[11] A material overstatement of net income compared to taxable income may reflect lower earnings quality, since liberal accounting policies may have been used for book reporting, while conservative ones were used for tax reporting. For example, W. T. Grant reported profit before taxes of $4.6 million for the year end January 31, 1974. Yet the provision for *current taxes* claimed a refund of $6.0 million, indicating that tax accounting profits were considerably less than financial accounting profits.

☐ *Is the company picking up liquidity through accounting practices that reflect the influence of the company over the dividend decision of the investee company?* For the year ended January 31, 1974, 55 percent of W. T. Grant's earnings per share was contributed by its unconsolidated subsidiaries. Interestingly, during the next fiscal year the chairman of the board of the major subsidiary (Zeller's Limited) became chairman of W. T. Grant, indicating that a close relationship existed between investor and investee.

☐ *Is there a significant difference between the reported income and inflation-adjusted income?* If so, reported income may be increased by under-depreciation and phantom inventory profits because of inflation. As you will see in Chapter 6, W. T. Grant's profits, when adjusted for inflation, became significant losses.

☐ *Are the interim accounting results in line with what would be expected given analysts' knowledge of the industry?* Pay attention to gross margin percentages, which may be estimated rather than based on actual

---

[11]This problem is examined in more detail later in this chapter.

physical inventory count. Bear in mind that quarterly reports are not audited.

□ *Does the company provide minimal data for analysis?* If there are not enough data for you to understand the figures, assume low quality.

Reported earnings that are a long way from turning into cash are a common form of low-quality earnings. Analysts can detect this situation by thoroughly analyzing the cash flow from operations and the cash conversion cycle. These techniques are discussed in Chapters 3 and 6, respectively. These approaches indicate how much and how fast cash is generated from the company's cycle of buying goods and services, creating inventories, selling for credit, and collecting payments from customers. Companies that have trouble turning sales into cash often have lengthening ages of receivables, inventories, and payables and declining cash flow from operations.

One-Time Transactions

A frequent source of low-quality earnings is one-time transactions. Analysts should discount these low-quality earnings heavily, since they do not represent recurring income. Common one-time transactions are sales of subsidiaries, of investments in various companies, and of corporate real estate. Debt-restructuring gains are another common source of one-time earnings. The gains generally occur in high-interest rate, low-bond-price environments. W. T. Grant participated in this tactic to some extent. It reported a miscellaneous gain of over $2 million for the fiscal year ended January 31, 1974, which is a period when a large tax loss was recorded. Evidently, management was looking for accounting profits wherever it could find them.[12]

Borrowing from the Future

Earnings included in current reports that represent deductions in future earnings should be considered low-quality because they are not indicative of future earnings levels. The most frequent practice is to accelerate sales to customers in advance of the normal delivery date. This procedure is usually done during the last weeks of the accounting period. The maneuver is difficult, however, during recessionary periods when customers are unwilling to build inventories and are actually trying to have suppliers hold

---

[12]About $1.8 billion of General Motors' $4.9 billion of profits in 1988 came courtesy of one-time transactions: $790 million by lengthening depreciation schedules, $480 million from a change in accounting for its pension plan, $217 million from changing inventory accounting, and $270 million from changing assumptions about the residual value of cars leased out by the company.

inventories longer. To convince customers during such periods to accept orders in advance, suppliers tend to provide generous direct or indirect financing at low interest or no interest. Usually, the disclosure of the customer financing arrangement or a substantial buildup of receivables (possibly before the subsequent sale of receivables) is a clue that customer shipments are being accelerated.

Reaching into the Past

Profits earned (and stored in the balance sheet) in past periods that are run through the current period's income are considered to be low quality. Typical ways to include past profits in current income are to reduce bad-debt reserves, warranty reserves, and other contingency type of reserves. In the past the charge to establish these reserves reduced income. The accounting entry in the current period to reverse the reserve improves income. *Cash flow, however, may not be improved.* For example, estimated warranty expense does not qualify as a tax deduction. The cost of providing the warranty service becomes a tax deduction when the actual repair is made.

When you encounter reserve reversals, you should determine whether the reversal was justified by a change in circumstances. If it was not, management is manipulating profits, which is a good indication that reported income may include other low-quality earnings. W. T. Grant's change in accounting practices for finance charges on installment sales, discussed earlier, is indicative of adjusting reserves to generate profits.

Riding the Depreciation Curve and Other Factors

Current earnings can be a misleading indicator of future earnings potential if management fails to make the technological, marketing, and fixed-asset investments necessary to maintain earnings. In addition, failure to make these investments may result in low-quality boosts to current earnings through reductions in managed costs, such as research and development or advertising expenses, and depreciation charges. This situation most frequently arises when companies run into operating difficulties. To detect this source of lower quality earnings, analysts can make the following types of calculations.

□ *Compute the estimated average age of a company's assets.* Estimated age is calculated as

$$\text{Estimated age} = \frac{\text{accumulated depreciation}}{\text{depreciation expense}}. \qquad (4.23)$$

A lengthening of the estimated age may indicate declining earnings quality due to inadequate replacement investments and a boosting of current earnings from lower depreciation charges relative to sales. This practice is called "riding the depreciation curve."[13]

□ *Compare the level of capital expenditures with inflation-adjusted depreciation expense.* Capital expenditures can be taken from the statement of cash flows. A ratio of less than 1.0 may indicate that management is not making the necessary capital investments required to effectively compete.

□ *Analyze research and development and marketing expenditures.* A down trend in these expenditures, either when adjusted for inflation or as percents of sales, may indicate lower earnings quality.

The relationship between reinvestment and earnings quality is a critical one. The ability of companies to compete effectively may be determined in large measure by their reinvestment practices.

Top Management

An examination of the board of directors can reveal whether all fundamental parts of the business are represented. Ideally, the broader the representation, the more efficiently projects will be analyzed. Obviously, a group with one specialty, say accounting, would not be effective in examining most manufacturing issues. Problems like these do in fact exist in major corporations.

Related to this problem is the one of the chief executive officer (CEO) who acts as if in a sole proprietorship. If the CEO tries to run an organization alone, there will be problems; there is a limit to the amount that any individual can do. The board that does not involve itself with collective decision making, or does not have a sense of collective responsibility, will not have the necessary powers to avoid insolvency when it threatens. Also, if a firm lacks good middle managers, decisions made by the board will not be implemented properly. Signs of poor management include too many layers of management, rapid personnel turnover, more competition directed internally than directed toward outside competitors, and incongruency among forecasted and actual corporate funds.

Deferred Taxes

Much insight into the quality of earnings can be obtained by understanding the deferred tax liability. Deferred taxes occur when the accounting meth-

---

[13]This calculation is only meaningful if the firm uses straight-line depreciation in determining accounting income (which most firms do use). If accelerated depreciation is used, the computed average age is meaningless.

ods used for financial reporting purposes differ from those used for tax purposes. This causes accounting income to be different than taxable income. The major differences can be classified as follows:

- Permanent differences arising from special legislative allowances or restrictions permitted or required for economic, political, or administrative reasons not related to the computation of accounting income
- Differences arising from the direct charges or credits to retained earnings of items included in the computation of taxable net income
- Differences in timing of charges and credits to income

Timing differences are by far the primary cause of differences between accounting and tax income. The causes are various.

- Revenues or gains that are taxable after they are recognized for accounting income. *Example:* In an installment sale, gross profit is recognized for accounting income at time of sale and for tax income when collected or deemed to be collected.
- Expenses or losses that are tax deductible after they are recognized for accounting income. *Example:* Warranty expense is recorded at time of sale for accounting purposes but deducted for tax purposes in a subsequent period when warranty expense is actually incurred to fix the product.
- Revenue or gains that are taxable before being recognized for accounting income. *Example:* Cash subscriptions are taxed when the fee is collected but recorded for accounting income calculations when earned.
- Expenses or losses that are tax deductible before they are expensed for calculating accounting income. *Example:* ACRS depreciation used for calculating tax income but straightline depreciation used for determining accounting income.

ILLUSTRATION 4.2

This hypothetical illustration highlights some of the differences between financial accounting and tax accounting. It is based on the following assumptions:

- 200,000 units were sold at a price of $115 each.
- Selling, general, and administrative expenses, excluding officers' salaries, are $2,250,000.

□ $250,000 was paid as salaries to officers, and options were awarded to purchase common stock in the company. The options have a market value of $120,000 and expire at the end of next year. For financial reporting purposes the option expense is amortized over the exercise period.

□ Depreciation for financial reporting purposes is $500,000; for tax purposes it is $1 million.

□ Inventory purchases for the year were as follows: January 1, 80,000 units @ $50/unit; May 1, 90,000 units @ $55/unit; September 1, 100,000 units @ $60/unit. The firm uses LIFO inventory accounting (that is, the last product purchased is the first product sold). Income tax regulations require a company to use LIFO in its financial statements if it uses LIFO for its tax return.

□ The income tax rate is 34 percent.

The income statement follows.

| | ($000) | |
	Financial	Tax
Sales	$23,000	$23,000
Expenses:		
Cost of sales	11,450	11,450
Depreciation	500	1,000
Officers' compensation:		
Salaries	250	250
Stock options	60	0
Selling, general, administrative	2,250	2,250
Total expenses	$14,510	$14,950
Income before taxes	$ 8,490	$ 8,050
Taxes	2,887	2,737
Net income	$ 5,603	$ 5,313

The journal entry follows.

Debit	Income tax expense	$2887	
Credit	Income tax payable		$2737
Credit	Deferred income tax payable		150

The debit appears on the income statement, whereas the credits are shown as liabilities on the balance sheet.   □

The Financial Accounting Standards Board (FASB) issued *SFAS 96, Accounting for Income Taxes* at the end of 1987. The new tax accounting standard presents many computational and recordkeeping problems for accountants. The fundamental change has been to focus the emphasis on the balance sheet and away from the income statement.[14] The primary goal of the new standards is to present the *estimated actual taxes to be payable in future periods* (deferred taxes) as the income tax liability on the balance sheet. The annual computation is considered a tentative estimate of the liability (or possibly an asset) which is subject to change as the statutory tax rate changes or as the taxpayer moves into other tax rate brackets.

Prior to the adoption of *SFAS 96*, deferred taxes were calculated at marginal tax rates much higher than those in existence today. This means that the deferred tax liability was overstated. Adoption of *SFAS 96* caused many firms to record a significant increase in profits (with no associated cash flow) as a result of having to restate the deferred tax liability to the amount expected to be owned in the future.

A publicly traded firm is required to show a tax reconciliation in its annual report. This report, when coupled with a close reading of the footnotes in the report, provides a wealth of information about the quality of earnings. Consider the following illustration.

ILLUSTRATION 4.3

The following information is representative of tax disclosure found in the notes to the annual report:

(In millions)	*1990*	*1989*	*1988*
Currently payable:			
Federal	$17.3	$ 1.0	$ 6.4
State	4.7	3.5	2.3
	$22.0	$ 4.5	$ 8.7
Deferred — principally federal	36.9	31.0	19.2
Total tax expense	$58.9	$35.5	$27.9

Principal items giving rise to deferred income taxes are:

(In millions)	*1990*	*1989*	*1988*
Customer lease transactions	$19.4	$25.3	$14.2
Spare parts	15.0		
Depreciation	7.6	9.1	3.8
Other, net	⟨5.1⟩	⟨3.4⟩	1.2
Total	$36.9	$31.0	$19.2

---

[14]Excellent discussions of the new rules are found in the following articles: N. R. Meonske and H. Sprohge, "How to Apply the New Accounting Rules for Deferred Taxes," *The Practical Accountant* (June 1988): 15–50; J. E. Stewart and A. A. Ripepi, "Financial Reporting of Income Taxes Is Altered by a New FASB Statement," *Taxation for Accountants* (September 1988): 182–7.

Under the assumption that the statutory tax rate for each year is 34 percent, pretax accounting income exceeds pretax tax income by $108.5 million in 1990 ($36.9/0.34 = $108.5) and by $256.2 million over the three years. In 1990 the higher accounting income results from recording the leasing of equipment to customers as revenue before payments are recognized for tax purposes, writing off spare parts inventory for tax purposes but not for accounting purposes, recording more depreciation for tax purposes than for accounting purposes, and incurring expenses (shown as "Other, net") for accounting purposes which are not deductible for tax purposes.   □

Analysis of deferred taxes can frequently uncover some aggressive accounting practices used by management in its efforts to maintain profits. Although there is not a wealth of information provided about deferred taxes, there is generally enough to allow the financial analyst to draw conclusions about the quality of earnings.[15]

Summary

This chapter examined some preconceived notions about financial analysis. The discussion highlighted inherent weaknesses in many of the traditional ratios. The intent was not to have you forgo using these ratios (although a strong argument can be made in several cases to do so), but to have you use the ratios more intelligently by understanding their weaknesses.

Probably the most often heard criticism of financial analysis is the difficulty of achieving comparability among firms in a given industry or access to sufficient internal information about the firm. Achieving comparability among firms that apply different accounting procedures is difficult and requires that the analyst identify basic differences existing in accounting and adjust the balances to achieve comparability. Even that may not be enough if the analyst relies too heavily on the generally accepted ratios.

Problems associated with the generally accepted ratios of liquidity, activity, coverage, and profitability were discussed in detail. A common theme throughout the discussion was the inability of any of the ratios to truly measure resource flows. This limitation is a serious one. Since the firm is a series of resource flows, analysts must provide a clear picture of past receipts, expenditures, and disbursements to debt and equity suppliers. This

---

[15]Section 6103 of the U.S. Internal Revenue Service's tax code allows shareholders who own at least 1 percent of a company's stock to ask for and receive a copy of IRS Form 1120, Schedule M-1, which shows a reconciliation of income per accounting books with income per tax return.

information is essential for assessing liquidity risk and prediction of future cash flows and profitability.

An important problem of financial analysis is ascertaining the quality of earnings of a firm. Management often stretches the interpretation of accounting principles or, less frequently, commits outright fraud in preparing financial statements.[16] The obvious purpose is to make the financial picture look better than it really is in order to attract capital and to bolster or support the price of firm's common stock. Failure to recognize the quality of earnings can lead to incorrect interpretations of financial ratios both within the company and across the industry.

Key Concepts

Activity ratios
Coverage ratios
Funds
Liquidity ratios
Net working capital

Profitability ratios
Quality of earnings
Trend analysis
Warning signals

---

[16]Warren Buffett observes in his 1988 Berkshire Hathaway annual report: Many managements view GAAP not as a standard to be met, but as an obstacle to overcome.

Appendix

Ratio Analysis for W. T. Grant Company

The ratios are calculated for years ended January 31, 1973 and 1974, with detailed calculations shown for 1974. The ratios are calculated from W. T Grant's financial statements, which are included in the appendix to Chapter 3.

TABLE A.1
W. T. Grant Company
Financial Ratios

	1974	1973	Traditional interpretation
Liquidity ratios			
Current ratio	1.98	1.95	It is apparent from these
Quick ratio	1.16	1.14	ratios that liquidity
Defensive interval (days)	123.0	122.0	has not changed
Net working capital ($000)	545,679	476,946	materially.
Activity ratios			
Receivables turnover	3.09	3.03	
Days sales in receivables	116.5	118.8	
Inventory turnover (cost)	2.58	2.56	Differences are
Inventory turnover (sales)	4.10	4.12	insignificant.
Net fixed-asset turnover	18.32	17.99	
Leverage			
Total debt/equity	2.87	2.32	Greater reliance on
Long-term deby/equity	1.15	0.82	long-term debt,
Total debt/capital	0.74	0.70	coupled with lower
Long-term debt/capital	0.30	0.25	operating earnings,
Fixed-charge coverage	0.88	0.88	has greatly decreased
Simple interest coverage	1.09	3.89	simple interest
Degree of financial leverage	13.21	1.36	coverage and degree
Book value per share ($)	21.26	21.91	of financial leverage.
Cash flow per share ($)	1.48	3.35	
Profitability			
Breakeven sales ($000)	1,518,846	1,217,650	Significant increase in
Margin of safety	0.18	0.26	breakeven sales;
Return on operating assets	0.04	0.01	profitability is down
Return on operating assets			considerably.
adjusted for interest	0.04	0.05	
Return on equity	0.01	0.12	

Keep in mind that the ratio can be computed a number of different ways by defining numerators and denominators differently from the definitions shown in our calculations.

The ratio calculations follow.

Liquidity Ratios

$$\text{Current ratio} = \frac{1,102,686}{557,007} = 1.98$$

$$\text{Quick ratio} = \frac{644,750}{557,007} = 1.16$$

$$\text{Defensive interval} = \frac{644,750 \times 360}{(1,849,802 - 56,047 + 92,554)}$$
$$= 123.0 \text{ days.}$$

The numbers in the denominator are sales, change in receivables, and cash flow from operations, respectively

$$\text{Net working capital} = 1,102,686 - 557,007 = 545,679$$

Activity Ratios

$$\text{Receivable turnover} = \frac{1,849,802}{598,799} = 3.09 \text{ times.}$$

Sometimes, this ratio uses average receivables in the denominator.

$$\text{Receivable days sales outstanding} = \frac{598,799}{1,849,802/360} = 116.5 \text{ days.}$$

This ratio can also be calculated by using average receivables.

$$\text{Inventory turnover} = \frac{1,163,998}{450,637} = 2.58 \text{ times} \quad \text{(using cost of sales).}$$

$$\text{Inventory turnover} = \frac{1,849,802}{450,637} = 4.10 \text{ times} \quad \text{(using sales).}$$

Average inventory can be used in the denominators.

$$\text{Net fixed-asset turnover} = \frac{1,849,802}{100,984} = 18.32 \text{ times.}$$

Average net fixed assets can be used in the denominator.

Leverage

$$\text{Total debt/equity} = \frac{929,245}{323,738} = 2.87$$

Long-term and indeterminate debt/equity $= \dfrac{372,238}{323,738} = 1.15$

Other debt/equity ratio calculations lie between these extremes.

$$\text{Total debt/capital} = \frac{929,245}{1,252,983} = 0.74$$

Long-term and indeterminate debt/capital $= \dfrac{372,238}{1,252,983} = 0.30$

Other calculations lie between these extremes.

Fixed-charge coverage

$$= \frac{4565 + 51,047 + 105,367}{51,047 + 105,367 + \dfrac{293 + 20,829}{1 - 0.172}} = 0.88 \text{ times.}$$

The numerator is earnings before tax adjusted to eliminate the effect of interest and lease expenses. The denominator is interest ($51,047) and lease payments ($105,367) plus after-tax dividend payments for preferred stock ($293) and common stock ($20,829) adjusted to the cash required before taxes.

$$\text{Simple interest coverage} = \frac{55,612}{51,047} = 1.09 \text{ times.}$$

$$\text{Degree of financial leverage} = \frac{55,612}{55,612 - 51,047 - \dfrac{293}{1 - 0.172}}$$

$$= 1.321$$

$$\text{Book value per share} = \frac{316,273}{14,879} = \$21.26$$

$$\text{Cash flow per share} = \frac{8429 + 13,579}{14,879} = \$1.48$$

Profitability

$$\text{Return on assets} = \frac{48,579}{1,849,802} \times \frac{1,849,802}{1,203,670} = 0.040$$

This calculation is based on net profit from operations before taxes and operating assets (i.e., total assets less miscellaneous assets and other assets), rather than as defined in the chapter. The reason for using this calculation basis is that significant nonoperating income/expense exists. Sometimes, current liabilities are subtracted from the operating assets.

$$\text{Return on assets} = \frac{[8429 + 51,047(1 - 0.172)]}{1,849,802} \times \frac{1,849,802}{1,203,670}$$

$$= 0.042$$

This calculation adjusts net income after taxes for interest expense (that is, it excludes the interest charge). Sometimes, total assets are used, and current liabilities may be subtracted from these assets.

$$\text{Breakeven sales} = \frac{581,982}{0.3833} = \$1,518,346$$

Sometimes, depreciation and amortization and interest payments are excluded from fixed costs for this calculation.

$$\text{Margin of safety} = 1 - \frac{1,518,346}{1,849,802} = 0.179$$

$$\text{Return on equity} = \frac{8136}{1,849,802} \times \frac{1,849,802}{1,252,983} \times \frac{1,252,983}{316,273} = 0.026$$

The $8136 amount is net income less preferred dividends, that is, earnings available to common. Sometimes, current liabilities are subtracted from total assets.

Questions

1. Of what significance is the current ratio? If this ratio is too low, what may it signify? Can this ratio be too high? Explain.

2. Is the defensive-interval measure any better than either the current ratio or the quick ratio? Explain.

3. Might there be a decrease in the amount of net working capital and at the same time an increase in the current ratio? Explain.

4. What are some limitations of ratio analysis?

5. What are the benefits and shortcomings of industry analysis?

6. "The significance of financial statement data is not in the amount alone." Discuss the meaning of this statement.

7. Comparative balance sheets and comparative income statements that show a firm's financial history for each of the past several years may be misleading. Discuss the factors or conditions that might contribute to misinterpretations. Include a discussion of the additional information and supplementary data that might be included in or provided with the statements to prevent misinterpretations.

8. The controller of your company has requested you to include in your report certain balance sheet and income statement ratios so that comparisons may be made. Indicate the types or categories of ratios that might be provided, and explain their significance.

9. Why should a firm strive to hold liquid balances, since it can earn a profit by drawing down its liquid balances and investing the funds that it frees?

10. On December 31, 1983, the book value per share of the common stock of the Eastern Company was $25. At the same time the price of the shares on the market was quoted at $38. What reasons might there be for this difference? If the market price was $18, what reasons might explain the difference?

11. Discuss the importance of financial statements in warning of financial problems.

12. Name five signals of potential insolvency.

13. What is a major problem with model like Altman's Z score model?

14. What is the significance of earnings quality to liquidity management? How can low-quality earnings be detected?

15. What does "riding the depreciation curve" mean?

Problems

The problems that follow use the financial data shown in Tables 4.5 and 4.6.

TABLE 4.5
Homeland Variety Corporation
Income Statements
For the Years 1988–90
($000)

	1990	1989	1988
Sales	$400	$302	$285
Cost of sales	170	121	108
Gross margin	$230	$181	$177
Expenses:			
Selling and administrative	120	93	82
Rent	20	20	20
Utilities	10	10	10
Earnings before interest and taxes	$ 80	$ 58	$ 65
Interest	18	15	14
Profit before taxes	$ 62	$ 43	$ 51
Taxes	19	13	15
Net income	$ 43	$ 30	$ 36

1. Calculate the liquidity, activity, leverage, and profitability ratios for the years 1988 through 1990.

2. Evaluate the financial performance of the company over the 1988–90 period. Pay careful attention to interpretation of these ratios and overall management of liquidity.

3. From your ratio analysis and financial evaluation in Problems 1 and 2, project Homeland Variety Corporation's financial statements for 1991.

4. Using the industry ratios that follow, project the financial statements for Homeland Variety Corporation for 1991. Use the common stock and paid-in capital of 1990 and estimate the retained earnings for 1991 in order to determine the equity amount for 1991.

Total debt/equity ratio	0.75
Current debt/equity ratio	0.43
Current ratio	1.96
Return-on-equity ratio	12.5%
Return-on-sales ratio	7.0%
Gross margin	58.0%
Days sales outstanding	82 days
Inventory turnover	6.0 based on sales
Fixed-assets/equity	0.91

TABLE 4.6
Homeland Variety Corporation
Balance Sheet
For the Years Ending December 31, 1988–90
($000)

	1990	1989	1988
Assets			
Current assets:			
Cash	$ 10	$ 15	$ 20
Net accounts receivable	90	95	96
Inventory	80	68	60
Total	$180	$178	$176
Net plant and equipment	200	176	172
Total assets	$380	$354	$348
Liabilities and capital			
Current liabilities:			
Accounts payable	$ 45	$ 48	$ 54
Notes payable	75	60	62
Total	$120	$108	$116
Long-term debt	60	50	40
Common stock ($1 par)	40	40	40
Paid-in capital	125	125	125
Retained earnings	35	31	27
Total liabilities and capital	$380	$354	$348

Note: Depreciation is $17,000, $18,000, and $20,000 for the years 1988, 1989, and 1990, respectively. It is charged to the cost of sales. Notes payable as of 1990 are a $20,000 demand note at 12.5 percent annual interest rate and a $55,000 line of credit at 13 percent annual interest rate. Long-term debt as of 1990 is as follows: $60,000 due in 1995 at 14 percent annual interest rate. Dividends in 1990 are $0.975 per share.

5. WLU Company provides the following data:

Net working capital	$ 250,000
Current assets	500,500
Current liabilities	250,500
Total assets	900,000
Total liabilities	300,000
Retained earnings	200,000
Sales	1,000,000
Operating income	150,000
Common stock	
Book value	210,000
Market value	300,000
Preferred stock	
Book value	190,000
Market value	160,000

Determine the Z score using Altman's model. Discuss whether or not the firm is near insolvency. Discuss possible limitations of the model.

6.   Assume the firm in Problem 5 suffered a major loss. The changes are as shown below. Assume the WLU stock values decreased in proportion to their adjusted book values. How do these changes influence the WLU Z-scores?

Net working capital	$ 75,000
Current assets	325,500
Current liabilities	250,500
Total assets	725,000
Total liabilities	300,000
Retained earnings	200,000
Sales	1,000,000
Operating income	150,000
Common stock	
Book value	35,000
Market value	50,000
Preferred stock	
Book value	190,000
Market value	95,000

7.   Schavo Corporation's latest annual report contained the data shown in Tables 4.7 and 4.8. Calculate the defensive interval and current ratio, and comment on the liquidity of the firm. Assume a 360-day year.

TABLE 4.7
Schavo Corporation
Balance Sheet
As of December 31
($000)

	19x1	19x0
Current assets:		
Cash	$ 14	$ 66
Accounts receivable	157	136
Inventory	139	121
Other	19	18
Total current assets	$329	$341
Fixed assets:		
Plant	$357	$276
Accumulated		
depreciation	132	112
Net fixed assets	$225	$164
Goodwill*	$ 50	$ 36
Total assets	$604	$541

TABLE 4.7 (*Cont.*)

	19x1	19x0
Current liabilities:		
Accounts payable	$115	$ 96
Taxes payable	2	10
Long-term debt due	5	3
Total current liabilities	$122	$109
Long-term debt	$148	$125
Total debt	$280	$234
Equity:		
Retained earnings	$170	$143
Preferred shares (7%)	60	60
Common shares	104	104
Total equity	$334	$307
Total debt and equity	$604	$541
*Amount amortized	$ 10	$ 10

TABLE 4.8
Schavo Corporation
Income Statement
for the Year Ending December 31
($000)

	19x1	19x0
Revenue:		
Sales	$1,087	$1,041
Cost of sales*	818	773
Gross profit	$ 269	$ 268
Expenses:		
Selling and administrative (60% variable)	169	168
Earnings before interest and taxes	$ 100	$ 100
Interest	13	10
Profit before taxes	$ 87	$ 90
Taxes (40%)	35	36
Profit after taxes	$ 52	$ 54
Earnings per share — common shares	$ 0.50	$ 0.51
*Includes depreciation expense	$ 20	$ 20

8. Using the financial data of Problem 7, calculate and discuss the degree of operating leverage and the degree of financial leverage for each year. What is the estimated age of the fixed assets in each year?

9.   Using the financial data in Problem 7, calculate the breakeven point and the margin of safety for each year. Include interest expense as a fixed cost.

10.   Using the following conditions determine the deferred income taxes payable for 1990.

- □ Sales in 1990 were $3,500,000.

- □ Cost of sales were 44 percent of sales.

- □ Selling and general administrative expenses were 11 percent of sales.

- □ Executive compensation, not included in selling and general administrative expenses, were $120,500 plus a stock option. The option was valued at $350,000 and will expire at the end of 1993. For financial reporting purposes the option expense is amortized over the exercise period.

- □ Depreciation for financial reporting purposes was $75,000 and for income tax purposes was $125,000.

- □ The firm will use an investment tax credit (ITC) of $300,000 to be taken in 1990 for tax purposes but amortized over the seven-year life of the investment.

- □ The effective income tax rate was 35.5 percent, while the effective reporting tax rate was 42 percent.

CHAPTER 5 ☐
Off-Balance-Sheet Financing and Financial Analysis

One of the most controversial issues in financial reporting today is what is called **off-balance-sheet financing**. This term refers to forms of financing that are not reported in the balance sheet, such as certain long-term lease commitments and other obligations. The main concern about off-balance-sheet financing activities is whether the information not reported on the financial statements lessens their usefulness. The financial theory of efficient capital markets[1] posits that it does not matter whether financing is off or on the balance sheet because accounting information cannot be used to fool or mislead investors.

However, the Financial Accounting Standards Board (FASB) believes that sufficient evidence exists to seriously question whether capital markets are as efficient as propounded by the theory. For example, consider the following case, which is but one of many that could be mentioned.[2] In 1982 Baldwin-United Corporation's stock was being touted as a "buy" by most

---

[1] The underpinning for efficient capital markets is the *efficient market hypothesis (EMH)*. It is predicated on the assumption that competent and well-informed analysts constantly evaluate and respond to an ever-changing stream of information. However, advocates of EMH claim that all known information is already instantly impounded in market prices. Such logic presents an unresolved paradox: How can intelligent, well-informed analysts be capable of keeping security markets efficient through their efforts, but not be intelligent enough to know that their efforts yield no individual gain? If the EMH is correct, do markets cease to be efficient when analysts realize their efforts are unrewarded?

[2] The following books by A. J. Briloff contain many examples: *Unaccountable Accounting* (New York: Harper & Row, 1972), *More Debits Than Credits* (New York: Harper & Row, 1976), and *The Truth about Corporate Accounting* (New York: Harper & Row, 1981).

of the major investment houses. But then James Chanos, an analyst with a small brokerage firm in Milwaukee, concluded from a detailed study of the financial statements that the accounting figures had been seriously misrepresented. Baldwin-United filed for bankruptcy shortly after this information was revealed.

Baldwin-United's management was acting in a manner similar to that of many managers (and bankers) who believe that by devoting substantial effort they can make the firm's balance sheet appear stronger than it really is.[3] It is this problem that led FASB to conclude that the amount of a company's debt could be reaching alarming proportions without users of financial statements, even sophisticated users, being aware of it.

The practice of off-balance-sheet financing became prevalent during the 1970s when inflation became a major concern of management, and it is still widely used today. The impetus for using off-balance-sheet financing arose because investors' expectations and concerns regarding inflation were reflected by a substantially reduced interest in the stock market. This reduced interest led to greater difficulty for management to provide funds by selling new equity. Inflation also made it difficult for management to turn to the debt markets because of the undesirability of bonds as a means of raising capital during inflationary periods. This undesirability occurred because the debt portion of the firm's capital structure kept increasing with inflation whenever new debt financing was undertaken, while equity remained measured on a historical cost basis. The result was a deterioration in the quality of the firm's debt-to-equity ratio.

Potential creditors, financial analysts, and investors all have vested interests in understanding the nature of off-balance-sheet financing. Once they understand the type of items that may be excluded from the balance sheet, they are better prepared to make the adjustments needed to arrive at the true economic position of the corporation. An analyst who carefully examines the 10-K report, annual report, and proxy statement can usually discover most of the hidden liabilities.

The focus of this chapter is on common types of off-balance-sheet financing and on what an analyst can do to overcome distortions caused by exclusions from the balance sheet. Thus this chapter, in a very particular way, continues the discussion of the previous chapter about the shortcomings of ratio analysis and how these unreported liabilities can affect the future liquidity condition of the corporation.

---

[3]W. A. MacPhee, a former banker with several major U.S. banks, reports in his book, *Short-Term Business Borrowing: Sources, Terms, and Techniques* (Homewood, Ill: Dow Jones–Irwin 1984), examples of off-balance-sheet financing banks willingly got involved with. He makes the point that severe legal and accounting conditions had to be circumvented in some cases.

Motivation for Off-Balance-Sheet Financing

Managers of many companies are strongly motivated to keep liabilities off their balance sheets, especially when they can do so and still accomplish their operating and financing objectives at little or no additional cost or even at a lower cost. Some of the apparent advantages of off-balance-sheet financing are

□ *Improvement in the firm's leverage ratios.* This is important not only for borrowing purposes, but also for reducing the perceived riskiness of the firm's stock, thus favorably affecting the market value of the stock.[4]

□ *Increase borrowing capacity.* Sometimes, preventing liabilities from appearing on the balance sheet will enable a company to borrow more than it otherwise could, especially if there are contractual debt limit restrictions related to what actually appears on the company's balance sheet.[5]

□ *Lower borrowing costs.* A more attractive looking financial statement may result in lower borrowing costs.

□ *Improve management compensation awards.* To the extent that management compensation plans are tied to ratios or reported earnings that are affected favorably by off-balance-sheet financing, management benefits directly from the use of these arrangements.[6]

□ *Risk sharing and tax management schemes.* The use of limited partnership arrangements and insubstance defeasance of debt provide means, respectively, for a company to spread the risk associated, for example, with research and development activities and to defer tax payments.

---

[4]Support for this can be found in the study by R. T. Ro, "The Disclosure of Capitalized Lease Information and Stock Prices," *Journal of Accounting Research* (Autumn 1978).

[5]A. Abdel-Khalik, R. Thompson, and R. Taylor, "The Impact of Reporting Leases Off the Balance Sheet on Bond Risk Premiums: Two Exploratory Studies," Accounting Research Center Working Paper No. 78-2, University of Florida, 1978, found that credit analysts penalize a firm's debt capacity if it capitalizes leases.

[6]A. Barnea, R. Haugen, and L. Senbet, *Agency Problems and Financial Contracting*, Prentice-Hall Foundations of Finance Series (Englewood Cliffs, N.J.: Prentice-Hall, 1985), p. 139, state that "[A]t least some studies report a significant effect of the compensation plan on management choices."

Significance of Off-Balance-Sheet Financing on Ratios

Obligations of a firm pose future cash outlay requirements that have significant effects on liquidity. If these economic liabilities are excluded from the balance sheet, the ratios are subject to further distortion. The exclusions may preclude the uncritical generation of ratios by computers that only have balance sheet data to use.

Table 5.1 provides a summary of why analysts must understand off-balance-sheet financing. It shows how the conventional debt-to-capital ratio compares with adjusted ratios for General Motors and J. C. Penney, during a time when off-balance-sheet financing was basically ignored. The table shows that by getting debt off the balance sheet, management improves the character, or quality, of its financial condition.

The most common types of off-balance-sheet financing consist of li-

TABLE 5.1
Conventional and Adjusted Debt/Equity Ratios for 1977 ($ millions)

	GM	J. C. Penney
From the balance sheet		
1. Long-term debt	$ 1,091.7	$ 415
2. Current deferred taxes	0	346
3. Long-term deferred taxes	104.6	111
4. Owner's equity	15,766.9	2,167
From notes to the statements		
5. Excess of FIFO value of ending inventory over reported LIFO value	697.3	122
6. Present value of noncapitalized financing leases	0	300
7. Present value of unrecognized pension cost	7,300.0	63
8. Long-term debt of unconsolidated subsidiaries	8,067.7	580
Conventional debt/capital ratio: $(1)/[(1) + (4)]$	6%	16%
Adjusted debt/capital ratio: $$\frac{(1) + (6) + (7) + (8)}{(1) + (2) + (3) + (4) + (5) + (6) + 0.48^*(7) + (8)}$$	56%	33%

*Assumes a 48 percent tax rate.

Source: Adapted from D.A. Lasman and R. L. Weil, "Adjusting the Debt-Equity Ratio," *Financial Analysts Journal* (September–October 1978): 50.

abilities that fall into the following categories: unfunded pension liabilities, postemployment benefits, leases, sale of receivables, product financing, in-substance defeasance of debt, unconsolidated subsidiary debt, uncondi-tional commitment agreements, and interest rate swaps.

Unfunded Pension Liabilities

There are two kinds of pension plans: defined-benefit plan and defined-contribution plan. In a **defined-benefit plan** the firm is obligated to pay a predetermined contractual benefit to retired employees vested in the plan. The company bears the investment risk. If the assets do not realize a large enough return, the firm will incur greater future cost to fund the plan. The alternative pension plan is referred to as a **defined-contribution plan**.[7] Retirement benefits are not predetermined in this plan. Retirees simply receive their portion of the market value of the assets when they retire. This type of plan shifts the investment risk from the firm to the employees and enables management to have better control over cash flows consumed by the pension plan.

A pension plan has separate legal and accounting identity for which a set of books is maintained and financial statements are prepared. The pension assets and liabilities do not show on the firm's financial statements. If pension liabilities exceed pension assets for defined-benefit pension plans, then the pension plan is not fully funded and off-balance-sheet fi-nancing exists. This is not the case for the defined-contribution plan, as should be obvious from the definition in the preceding paragraph.

Despite new accounting standards,[8] off-balance-sheet liabilities still exist for unfunded pension obligations. This liability can be staggering. For example, in 1982 General Motors Corporation had underfunded its pen-sion plan by $1.9 billion (10 percent of its net worth) and Chrysler was underfunded by $901 million (91 percent of its net worth).

Pension Put Option

Firms with underfunded defined-benefit pension plans possess a valuable *put option* in that they can put the assets of the pension plan (plus 30 percent of the market value of the corporate net worth) to the Pension Benefit

---

[7]The various types of defined-contribution plans include the following: profit-sharing plans, 401(K) plans, money-purchase plans, stock bonus plans, and employee stock own-ership plans (ESOP).

[8]They became effective after December 15, 1988, although firms had the option to adopt them earlier.

Guarantee Corporation in satisfaction of pension claims. This pension put is more valuable the greater the variance in the value of the underlying assets (the assets of the plan plus 30 percent of the net worth of the firm). This constitutes an incentive for low-level funding. If the firm has potential pension liabilities greater than 30 percent of its net worth, a maximizing strategy is to underfund to the greatest possible extent and invest pension assets in extremely high-risk assets. If the investments are profitable, the underfunded plan may become overfunded simply because of appreciation of the investments.

Financial Reporting Requirements

Although *SFAS 87 Employers' Accounting for Pensions* requires firms to record an additional pension liability they did not have to record before, much of the unfunded pension liability still remains off the balance sheet. The true (economic) unfunded liability is the difference between the *projected benefit obligations* and *pension plan assets,* concepts that are explained shortly. However, this difference is not the liability recognized by *SFAS 87.*

Illustration 5.1 is used to examine the problem. However, it is necessary first to explain some terminology:

□ *Projected benefit obligation (PBO).* This is an actuarially present value amount as of the date of all benefits attributed by the pension benefit formula (including expected future pay changes) to employee service rendered prior to that date.

□ *Pension plan assets (PPA).* The amount the pension plan could reasonably expect to receive for the assets in an orderly liquidation (not a forced sale).

□ *Prior service costs.* Costs of retroactive benefits granted in a plan amendment.

□ *Actuarial gain or loss.* The change in value of either the PBO or PPA resulting from experience different from that assumed or from a change in actuarial assumptions.

ILLUSTRATION 5.1

SFAS 87 requires that a schedule reconciling the pension plan's fund status be disclosed in the annual report. The following example is representative.

	Year 19x1	Year 19x2
Accumulated benefit obligation	$1500	$1550
Progression of salary and wages	400	456
Projected benefit obligation	$1900	$2006
Plan assets	1400	1543
Underfunded amount	$ 500	$ 463
Unamortized actuarial loss	210	177
Unamortized prior service cost	320	293
Unamortized net obligation ⟨asset⟩ existed at *SFAS 87* application	⟨30⟩	⟨27⟩
⟨Accrued⟩/prepaid pension cost	$ 0	$ ⟨20⟩

From an economic perspective, the unfunded liability in years 19x1 and 19x2 is $500 and $463, respectively. However, neither of these amounts gets recorded. In 19x1, *SFAS 87* requires a liability of $100 to be recorded — the difference between the accumulated benefit obligation ($1500) and plan assets ($1400). The entry to record this liability is

> Debit   Intangible asset $100
> Credit   Liability $100

In year 19x2, no additional liability is recorded since the accrued pension cost of $20 exceeds the difference between the accumulated benefit obligation ($1550) and plan assets ($1543). In fact, the pension liability recorded in 19x1 gets reversed:

> Debit   Liability $100
> Credit   Intangible asset $100

Neither entry has any effect on pension expense in the income statement. The net result is that in 19x1, only $100 of the true unfunded liability of $500 is recognized on the balance sheet, whereas in 19x2, none of the true unfunded liability is recorded.

From an economic perspective, it makes sense to record additional obligations before doing ratio analysis. In 19x1, liabilities should be increased $400; additional liabilities of $443 (= $463 − $20 accrued cost) should be recorded in 19x2. A contentious issue is what the offsetting (debit) entry should be. Should intangible assets be increased, or should retained earnings be decreased? If it makes more sense to charge retained earnings, then the $100 increase in 19x1 to intangible assets should be reversed and charged to retained earnings as well.[9]   □

It was mentioned earlier that actuarial gains or losses result from changing actuarial assumptions. An important assumption concerns what interest rate to use to determine the actuarial present value of benefits. It is estimated that a 0.25 percent change in the interest rate assumption generally affects the annual pension cost by 6 percent. For instance, in 1970 Penn-Dixie Cement Corporation disclosed in a footnote that an increase in the actuarial interest rate assumption (for the earning power of the pension assets) from 4 percent to 6 percent resulted in a decrease in pension expense for the year of approximately $665,000 and an increase in after-tax net income and cash flow of $338,000.

In the recessionary period of 1980–82 about 90 New York Stock Exchange firms each year raised their assumed pension asset earnings rate. Such an exercise causes profit and cash flow for the year(s) to improve because of this change in assumption. The question remains: Did portfolio return really improve, or did management simply borrow from later periods? This issue is one of quality of earnings and is indicative of how managers think they can fool the marketplace.

Postemployment Benefits

Many employers provide health benefits to employees that include life insurance and health care coverage after retirement. These benefits are earned by employees during the periods in which they work. Such benefits can represent a significant unreported liability for a firm. For the Fortune 500 companies, this liability has been estimated to be 150 percent of total assets.[10]

Under current accounting standards, the obligation related to these future postemployment benefits does not have to be reflected on an employer's balance sheet if they are accounted for on a *pay-as-you-go* (that is, cash) *basis* — which is the prevalent method used — as opposed to being accounted for using full accrual accounting standards. The FASB is currently studying this issue. The current suggestion is basically to follow the

---

[9]One of the original proposals advanced when this issue was being debated was to debit retained earnings and credit liabilities. Much lobbying pressure from industry resulted in FASB making the debit entry to an intangible asset account. Obviously, this results in less pressure on the debt/equity ratio.

[10]T. G. Nelson, "Post-Retirement Benefits: The Tip of a Financial Iceberg," *Management Accounting* (January 1987): 53.

framework used for unfunded pension liabilities as set forth in *SFAS 87*. If this becomes the required approach, then much of the unfunded liability will still remain off the balance sheet.

Leasing

From the perspective of the lessee a lease offers certain advantages over purchase of the asset. For instance, the lessee may not have sufficient resources or credit to purchase the asset but can lease it. If the firm has low profitability, it might not be able to take advantage of the tax benefits of accelerated depreciation associated with owning the asset. A lessor can take advantage of the tax implications and pass some of the savings along to the lessee by lowering the lease payments.

The conventional reasons for leasing are as follows:

□ Leases give firms with limited capital budgets alternative sources of obtaining resources.

□ The period of a lease for equipment is often longer than the repayment period allowed by conventional financing.

□ Leases are frequently tailored to meet the cash budget need of the lessee.

□ Leasing may be perceived as not affecting debt capacity of the company, primarily because of accounting conventions.

□ The entire lease payment is tax deductible.

□ Leasing avoids underwriting and flotation costs associated with new issues of capital.

The major disadvantage of leasing, as perceived by managers, is that the net present value cost of leasing generally exceeds the net present value of purchasing, since the lessor must earn a profit. Given all the advantages listed, though, this may be a small price to pay.

Financial Reporting Requirements

In December 1976 the FASB attempted to remedy the exclusion of leasing liabilities from the balance sheet by issuing *Accounting for Leases, SFAS 13*. In summary, *SFAS 13* says that if at the date of the lease agreement the lessee is party to a noncancelable lease that meets one or more of the following four criteria, the lessee shall classify and account for the arrangement as a **capital lease**.

1. The lease transfers ownership of the property to the lessee by the end of the lease.

2. The lease has a bargain purchase option.

3. The lease term is equal to 75 percent or more of the estimated economic life of the leased property.

4. The present value of the lease payments at the beginning of the lease is equal to or greater than 90 percent of the leased property's fair market value.

If a lease does not meet any of these requirements, it is classified as an **operating lease**.

Under the operating lease method the lease is simply treated as an expense. The leased asset does not appear within the body of the balance sheet, but the lessee discloses the minimum future rental payments, in total and for each of the next five years.

Capitalizing the Lease

Under the **capital lease** method the lessee treats the lease transaction as if an asset were being purchased on time, that is, as a financing transaction in which an asset is acquired and an obligation is created. The lessee records a capital lease as an asset and as a liability at the lower of the following two values:

☐ The present value of the minimum lease payments during the lease term.

☐ The fair market value of the leased asset at the inception of the lease.

Accounting rules require capitalized leases to be shown on the lessee's balance sheet. Both depreciation and the interest expense implicit in the lease payments are deductions from income. The criterion that causes the lease to be capitalized determines the depreciation method. If a bargain purchase option exists or if the lease transfers ownership, then the firm's normal depreciation policies apply. However, if neither of these criteria are satisfied, but if the lease term is equal to or greater than 75 percent of the leased asset's economic life, or if the present value of the lease payments is equal to or greater than 90 percent of the leased asset's original cost, then the asset is amortized over the life of the lease contract.

ILLUSTRATION 5.2

The terms of a noncancelable lease require payments of $103,762 at the beginning of each year for 5 years. The equipment has a fair value at the inception of the lease of $450,000, an economic life of 5 years, and no residual value. The lessee's borrowing rate is 15 percent per year. The amount to be capitalized as a leased asset is computed as follows:[11]

$$\$103,762 \times \begin{array}{c} \text{(present value of an annuity due} \\ \text{for 5 periods at 15 percent)} \end{array}$$

$$= \$103,762 \times 3.855 = \$400,000.$$

Thus reported assets and liabilities increase $400,000. Annual depreciation expense is $80,000 (assuming straight-line depreciation), and interest is based on an amortization schedule with the first period's expense being $60,000 (that is 0.15 × $400,000). Total charges against pretax income are $140,000. If this lease could be recorded as an operating lease, only $103,762 would be charged to operations.   □

Hence in management's quest for higher, short-term reported profits, it generally prefers to record leases as operating leases. Because of the "debt" amortization, later periods will result in higher profits for the capitalized lease whenever the imputed interest plus depreciation become less than the operating lease payment.

Circumventing Disclosure

The difficulty in enforcing *SFAS 13* is evidenced by the fact that it has been amended by nine more FASB Statements and explained further by six FASB Interpretations. The problem is that management would rather report leases as operating leases because they are not included in the balance sheet and imputed depreciation and interest expenses can be excluded from the income statement. Apparently, management feels that debt capacity is somehow not impaired if leases are omitted from the balance sheet. Implicit in this idea is that capital markets can be fooled if leases are not shown as liabilities.

Another reason for attempting to structure leases as operating leases is that management feels that return on equity will be impaired by structuring leases as capital leases. This impairment happens because of depreciation and capitalization requirements of the FASB, as shown above in Illustration 5.2.

Strategies used to avoid lease capitalization include:

□ Do not include a clause in the lease agreement that transfers title to the lessee.

---

[11]The annuity due factor can also be found by the formula (PVIFA 5 years, 15 percent) × (1 + 0.15), where PVIFA is the abbreviation for *present value interest factor for an annuity.*

□ Do not include a bargain purchase option in the lease agreement.

□ Identify the lease agreement as less than 75 percent of the true economic life of the leased property.

□ Establish a high incremental borrowing rate so that the present value of minimum lease payments will be less than 90 percent of the fair value of the leased property at the inception of the lease.

□ Lease property where the lease term begins during the last 25 percent of the economic life of the leased asset.

An additional strategy illustrates the ingenuity of those companies that wish to avoid capitalization. According to *SFAS 13,* "minimum lease payments" are defined as the payments made by the lessee and may include the guaranteed residual value of the leased property. However, when the residual value of leased property is guaranteed by a third party, the present value of the residual value is not included in the definition of "minimum lease payments." Using a third-party guarantor frequently results in the lessee not capitalizing the lease whether or not the lessor accounts for the lease as an insubstance sale of the leased property.

ILLUSTRATION 5.3

The information of Illustration 5.2 is used here to show how management can cause a capital lease to become an operating lease. Equipment with an economic life of 5 years is leased for a period of 3 years and 8 months, which means that requirement 3 is not met. The present value of lease payments can be as much as (90 percent × $450,000) − $1, which is just below the threshold of requirement 4. The only other requirements are to write the lease contract so that ownership is not transferred to the lessee by the end of the lease (which satisfies requirement 1) and to ensure that the lease does not have a bargain purchase option (which satisfies requirement 2). These actions result in off-balance-sheet financing since the lease does not have to be capitalized.   □

Liquidity Analysis

For purposes of liability analysis all leases should be included in the data that is used to assess liquidity. However, a problem exists in dealing with leases that are not capitalized on the balance sheet. Capital leases are disclosed on the balance sheet at their present values. Future payments for operating and capital leases are disclosed in the footnotes to the financial statements. The year-by-year minimum payments are shown for each type of lease for five years, and then the balance is shown for each lease as an aggregated amount.

Two approaches are available to estimate the present value of the operating leases. One approach attempts to estimate the net present value of
the operating leases by discounting the future operating lease payments at
the firm's cost of debt. The second technique provides a rough net present
value approximation. Both techniques are shown in Illustration 5.4. The
information shown for future lease payments is similar to that contained in
most annual reports.

ILLUSTRATION 5.4

Minimum future obligations on leases with an initial term greater than one
year for the fiscal years ending December 31:

Future periods	Capital leases	Operating leases
	(In millions)	
19x1	$ 15.7	$ 69.1
19x2	14.2	62.5
19x3	13.1	59.4
19x4	12.2	54.9
19x5	11.6	49.3
Later	71.8	488.9
Total minimum obligations	$138.6	$784.1
Less amount representing interest	61.4	
Present value of net minimum obligations	$ 77.2	

Net Present Value Approach

Assume the firm's average cost of debt is 12 percent as disclosed elsewhere
in the annual report.

$$\text{NPV} = \frac{69.1}{(1.12)} + \frac{62.5}{(1.12)^2} + \frac{59.4}{(1.12)^3}$$

$$+ \frac{54.9}{(1.12)^4} + \frac{49.3}{(1.12)^5}$$

$$+ \frac{(488.9)}{10} \times [\text{PVIFA (15 years, 12\%)}$$

$$- \text{PVIFA (5 years, 12\%)}]$$

$$= \$373.4 \text{ million.}$$

The "later" amount of $488.9 is estimated to extend as an annuity over 10
years. This is arrived at by dividing the "later" payment by year 5's pay-

ment: 488.9/49.3 = 9.9 or about 10 years. The present value interest factor for an annuity for 15 years is PVIFA (15 years, 12%) = 6.811; for 5 years it is PVIFA (5 years, 12%) = 3.605.

Capital Lease Ratio Approach

$$\text{NPV} = \frac{\text{present value of capital leases}}{\text{total capital lease payments}} \times \begin{array}{c} \text{total} \\ \text{operating lease} \\ \text{payments} \end{array}$$

$$= \frac{77.2}{138.6} \times 784.1 = \$436.7 \text{ million.}$$

As shown in Illustration 5.4 the two techniques can result in significantly different answers. Most likely the net present value technique provides the better answer, but you will have to decide which one is best. In some cases, the firm may have only operating leases. Thus the net present value approach will have to be used. In other cases, it may be too difficult to determine an appropriate rate for the firm's debt. Thus the ratio approach lends itself to use.

The significance of capitalizing operating leases is that it improves ratio analysis by stating both assets and debt more correctly by bringing the off-balance-sheet leases onto the balance sheet. By showing all leases (both capital and operating) on the balance sheet, comparability of ratio analysis is improved and promotes a more accurate picture of the reliance firms place on debt versus equity capital.

The importance of being able to keep leases off the balance sheet is that studies have revealed that accounting income figures and ratios are used extensively to evaluate risk. Bond rating studies show accounting ratios to be highly informative for determining bond risk. Similarly, bankruptcy studies show the predictive behavior of ratios in determining bankruptcy. Thus management's concern about keeping debt off the balance sheet may be legitimate.

Table 5.2 summarizes the effect of the omission of lease obligations on the financial statements and ratio analysis. The ability to keep the lease off the balance sheet results in significant improvement in ratios. Both profitability and asset management appear to be better, and financial leverage is less. This improvement is an illusion, though, since the lease payments represent a contractual obligation. Note, however, that this obligation is less burdensome on the firm in times of bankruptcy or reorganization than is debt. Although the lessor retains ownership of the asset in bankruptcy, it has a claim on only one year's lease payments. If the firm is in reorganization, the lessor has a claim on three years' lease payments. Further, in cases where the solvency of the firm is called into question, the operating leases are subordinate to the capital leases in their claim status.

TABLE 5.2
Effect of Leasing on Ratios

	Alternatives	
	Borrowing	Leasing
Balance sheet		
Current assets	$ 2,000	$ 2,000
Net fixed assets	5,000	3,600
Total assets	$ 7,000	$ 5,600
Current liabilities	$ 1,500	$ 1,500
Long-term debt	3,000	1,600
Total debt	$ 4,500	$ 3,100
Equity	2,500	2,500
Total liabilities and equity	$ 7,000	$ 5,600
Income statement		
Sales	$10,000	$10,000
Income before depreciation, interest, and lease payments	$ 3,000	$ 3,000
Depreciation	⟨1,000⟩	⟨800⟩
Interest on debt (15%)	⟨450⟩	⟨240⟩
Lease expense	0	⟨190⟩
Income before taxes	$ 1,550	$ 1,770
Taxes (40%)	620	708
Income after taxes	$ 930	$ 1,062
Ratios		
Asset turnover (times)	1.4	1.8
Return on assets	13.3%	19.0%
Debt to equity	1.8	1.2
Times interest coverage (before depreciation)	6.7	12.5

Note: This example assumes that management is able to circumvent having to capitalize the lease.

Sale of Accounts Receivable with Recourse

When a company sells its receivables,[12] and the buying company retains the right to hold the selling company responsible for paying accounts receivable that turn out to be bad debts, then that sale is *with recourse*. The accounting profession takes the position that the sale of receivables with recourse is, in substance, a financing transaction. The cost of financing

---

[12]Chapter 11 discusses the sale of receivables through the processes of asset securitization and factoring.

should be accounted for as an interest cost over the life of the receivables and a contingent liability should be reported in the balance sheet.

To circumvent treating the sale as a loan, all of the following conditions must exist:

☐ Control of the future economic benefits of the receivable is transferred to the buyer.

☐ Cost of the seller's obligations under the recourse provisions (collection and repossession costs, for example) is subject to reasonable estimation.

☐ The buyer cannot force the seller to purchase the receivable by means other than the recourse provisions.

Instances have been found where management was willing to offer the purchasing company a larger than normal discount so that the transaction was structured to appear as if it were without recourse — and hence would not have to be reported on the balance sheet. The usual approach to avoid the recourse provisions is to write a contract so that the selling company retains physical control of the assigned accounts, collects amounts remitted by customers, and then forwards the proceeds to the company that purchased the receivables. As the company makes collections and turns them over to the lender, it is really paying off an "unrecorded" note payable. But since the transaction was initially structured as a sale of receivables, with no new debt obligation recorded, management can use the proceeds for the sale to pay existing liabilities.

The result of this transaction is to lower leverage and improve the current ratio, assuming it was greater than 1:1 to begin with. The company is able to generate cash without reporting the corresponding liability. Liquidity appears improved, but in reality, it is not.

ILLUSTRATION 5.5

The following simplified balance sheets illustrate the significance of treating a sale of receivables with recourse but making it appear to be without recourse. It assumes that funds from the sales of receivables are used to pay off existing debt. In actuality, management is using the receivables as collateral for a loan, but it wants to give the impression that a sale of receivables has occurred and not a new debt obligation.

1. Before the Sale

Balance Sheet

Receivables	$ 80,000	Debt	$100,000
Other assets	200,000	Equity	180,000

Debt/equity ratio = 0.56:1

2. At the Time Receivables Are Sold

Debit	Cash	$76,000	
Debit	Loss on sale	4,000	
Credit	Accounts receivable		$80,000

Balance Sheet Reported

Cash	$ 76,000	Debt	$100,000
Other assets	200,000	Equity	176,000

Debt/equity ratio = 0.57:1

3. They Should Report

Debit	Cash	$76,000	
Debit	Unamortized debt discount	4,000	
Credit	Debt		$80,000

Balance Sheet That Should Be Reported

Cash	$ 76,000	Debt	$180,000
Receivables	80,000	Unamortized discount	⟨4,000⟩
Other assets	200,000	Equity	180,000

Debt/equity ratio = 0.98:1

4. Disbursement of Funds from Sale

Balance Sheet Reported

Other assets	$200,000	Debt	$ 24,000
		Equity	176,000

Debt/equity ratio = 0.14:1

Balance Sheet That Should Be Reported

Receivables	$ 80,000	Debt	$104,000
Other assets	200,000	Unamortized discount	⟨4,000⟩
		Equity	180,000

Debt/equity ratio = 0.56:1

The improved leverage ratios show why management is willing to pursue this tactic if it thinks it can deceive readers of its financial status. Management is able to significantly increase the firm's *apparent* debt capacity and present the firm as a relatively low-risk firm as measured by the debt/equity ratio. □

Product Financing

The impact of product financing on the firm's financial statements is similar to selling accounts receivable with recourse. With **product financing** one company sells an asset to another because it needs earnings and as a result improves its liquidity. What is not shown on the ledger is that the seller made a deal to buy back that asset at some point in the future, that deal being a liability of the firm. So earnings are improved and debt has been kept off the balance sheet. The transaction is treated as a sale rather than as a loan, and no recognition is made in the accounts of the agreement to purchase. Neither the loan nor the promise to buy back is reported in the balance sheet of the borrower.

The Securities and Exchange Commission issued a statement in late 1978 stating that sale of a product with an agreement to repurchase should be recognized as a loan and not as a sale. But frequently, the agreement to buy back the asset is hidden in legal contracts, and off-balance-sheet financing prevails.

ILLUSTRATION 5.6

In 1982 Datapoint Corporation was discovered to be using a variation of product financing. For some period of time prior to 1982, management had customers book millions of dollars of orders with payment to be made much later. On this basis, Datapoint recorded sales as revenue even though the product had not been manufactured in many cases. This allowed the company to meet sales and profit objectives. However, when the practice was discovered, Datapoint was required to reverse a significant amount of sales.   □

Insubstance Defeasance of Debt

In November 1983 the FASB decided to permit companies to consider their fixed-rate known maturity debt to be extinguished for financial reporting purposes when the company entered into an **insubstance defeasance of debt** transaction. This can be an attractive way for companies with low coupon debt outstanding to boost earnings and improve the debt/equity ratio.[13] Indeed, Standard & Poor's disregards any debt issue de-

---

[13]This reason has been suggested by G. Darrow in a Bear Stearns publication, Insubstance Defeasance: How to Do It, Who May Do It (December 14, 1983). Also see the article by D. Mielke and J. Seifert, "A Survey on the Effects of Defeasing Debt," *Journal of Accounting, Auditing, and Finance* (1988): 65–78.

feased, and its related interest and escrowed assets, when computing financial ratios for debt-rating purposes.

The following types of debt are not eligible for defeasance:

□ Debt with a floating interest rate

□ Debt that is payable on demand

□ Convertible debentures

□ Any kind of debt that does not permit advance determination of future debt service requirements

□ Issuance of new debt and its concurrent extinguishment through an insubstance defeasance

Arguments in favor of insubstance defeasance are that the reported gain may exceed the amount of any future gain that could be obtained if the debt were retired at a later date when different interest rates might be in effect. If creditors and investors are not aware of this situation, the removal of the debt may be perceived as a favorable development by creditors and investors.

How It Works

The debtor irrevocably segregates assets with a third party (that is, the debtor establishes an irrevocable trust); the third party invests them in direct obligations of the U.S. government, U.S. government guaranteed obligations, or securities backed by U.S. government obligations as collateral under which the interest and principal payments on the collateral generally flow immediately to the holder of the security. The Federal National Mortgage Association (Fannie Mae) and other government agencies are not adequate since they are not direct or guaranteed obligations of the U.S. government.

This investment, and the interest on it, is then used to satisfy scheduled payments of principal and interest on the outstanding debt. The outstanding debt has a lower coupon yield than the segregated assets, so less funds must be set aside to satisfy the outstanding lower coupon debt obligation than would be required if management just retired the debt. If management is virtually assured that no further funds will need to be transferred to the third party, the firm can account for the transaction as an extinguishment of the outstanding debt. The firm can then take any difference between the face value of the outstanding debt and the funds set aside as a gain, to be reported in the income statement. For tax purposes, the company continues to deduct interest expense but also pays tax on the income from the trust securities. The gain from defeasance is not taxed until the debt actually matures. Defeased debt must be disclosed in the annual report's footnotes through a description of the transaction as long as the debt is outstanding.

Two restrictions apply. First, the timing of the cash flows from the securities placed in trust must approximately coincide with the scheduled payments of debt principal and interest. Frequently zero coupon bonds are used with maturities matching debt service requirements. Second, the probability that a company will be required to make any future payments on the debt must be remote.

ILLUSTRATION 5.7

Assume that a company has $10,000,000 of debt outstanding, at book value, which has a fixed coupon rate of 5 percent and 10 years until maturity. Interest is paid annually. Management decides to segregate assets to defease this debt. It can earn 10 percent by investing in government securities. Therefore, it must segregate $6,927,680 of government securities in order to retire annual interest payments of $500,000 and the principal repayment in year 10 of $10,000,000:

$$\text{Segregated amount} = \$500,000(\text{PVIFA } 10\%, 10)$$
$$+ \$10,000,000(\text{PVIF } 10\%, 10)$$
$$= \$500,000(6.14457) + \$10,000,000(0.38554)$$
$$= \$6,927,680$$

where (PVIFA 10%, 10) is the present value interest factor of an annuity at 10 percent for 10 years, and (PVIF 10%, 10) is the present value interest factor at 10 percent in year 10.

TABLE 5.3
Insubstance Debt Defeasance

Year	Value of segregated funds at the beginning of the year	Annual payments to debtholders	Value of segregated assets at the end of the year before 10% interest is earned
0	$ 6,927,680		
1	7,620,450	$ 500,000	$7,120,450
2	7,832,490	500,000	7,332,490
3	8,065,740	500,000	7,565,740
4	8,322,320	500,000	7,822,320
5	8,604,550	500,000	8,104,550
6	8,915,000	500,000	8,415,000
7	9,256,500	500,000	8,756,500
8	9,632,150	500,000	9,132,150
9	10,045,370	500,000	9,545,370
10	10,500,000	10,500,000	0

Note: Beginning balances are grossed up to include the interest earned. For example, the balance starting in year 5 is $7,822,320 × 1.1 = $8,604,550.

Table 5.3 summarizes the annual transactions and confirms that $6,927,680 is needed to retire the $10,000,000 worth of bonds. The difference of $3,072,320 becomes an extraordinary pretax gain to the company in the year the funds are set aside.   □

The effect of defeasance on the company's capital structure can be shown by extending Illustration 5.7.

ILLUSTRATION 5.8

Assume the company has net income of $5,000,000 before defeasance and a tax rate of 40 percent. The after-tax gain from defeasance is $1,843,390.

1. Before Insubstance Debt Defeasance

Balance Sheet ($000)

Cash	$10,000	Debt	$20,000
Other assets	40,000	Equity	30,000

Debt/equity ratio = 0.67:1
ROE ratio = 0.17

2. After Debt Is Defeased

Balance Sheet ($000)

Cash*	$ 3,072.32	Debt	$10,000.00
Other assets	40,000.00	Deferred taxes	
		on gain	1,228.93
		Equity	31,843.39

Debt/equity ratio = 0.35:1
ROE ratio = 0.21

*Opening balance ($10,000) less amount segregated with a trustee ($6,927.68).

The firm has given up present liquidity to enhance profitability and lower perceived financial risk as measured by the debt/equity ratio. If the deferred taxes payable on the capital gain are eliminated from the leverage calculation, financial risk appears even lower.   □

Pros and Cons

Insubstance debt defeasance transactions have both advantages and disadvantages to the corporation over the more traditional ways of retiring debt before maturity.

Advantages

1. The use of defeasance circumvents dealing with individual bond-holders. It avoids paying redemption premiums, and the debt can be effectively retired without driving its price up through open-market, buy-back transactions.

2. Debt defeasance transactions can be attractive to the debtholders. Since the debt is now backed by government securities, rather than the general credit of the issuer company, its quality and price may rise. The establishment of an irrevocable trust may improve the debt rating of the extinguished debt issue since future payments are guaranteed.

3. Debt defeasance results in lower debt/equity and higher interest coverage ratios in future periods.

4. A current gain can result for accounting purposes, which, if material, may be classified as an extraordinary item in the income statement.

5. Any gain recognized ordinarily does not result in a current tax liability. Since the company is still legally obligated for the debt, no gain is recognized for tax purposes at the time of the transaction. At maturity a capital gain tax will be due on the government securities since they were bought at a discount.

6. A company with excess cash can be a target for acquisition. In some cases, one way to make the firm less attractive is to use such cash to effect an insubstance debt defeasance. The associated increase in profit may make shareholders less inclined to sell their shares in a takeover attempt.

Disadvantages

1. The company is not legally released from being the primary obligor under the debt instrument (for example, collateral is not released and debt covenants generally still apply).

2. The trust arrangement must be irrevocable. Management does not have access to future trust assets if it needs additional funds.

3. Yields on U.S. government securities typically are less than the returns available on other investments by the firm. Consequently, such investments cost more in relative terms.

4. In some cases the interest costs associated with financing the purchase of government securities may exceed the interest costs of the debt being extinguished.

5. Any income from the irrevocable trust, because there is not a perfect match between the cash flows of the government securities and the debt being defeased, may flow back to the company and be re-

corded as income from a nonexistent asset. Accounting principles do not allow such income on the company's financial statements. This problem can be avoided by using zero-coupon treasury bonds.

One can argue that insubstance defeasance of debt is a questionable practice on two counts, since liquidity analysis can be distorted.

First, defeasance amounts to balance sheet manipulation (as shown in Illustration 5.8) and a poor use of corporate cash, particularly for the shareholders. Since securities are placed in an irrevocable trust, management gives up current liquidity and is forced to forgo potentially higher yields available on other (riskier) investments that could be disposed of more readily. Debtholders, however, gain a reduction in risk (because the debt is defeased) without a loss in yield.

Second, insubstance debt defeasance may also be an indication that management is struggling to keep its earnings up. In this case the quality of earnings is suspect, which means that cash flow (liquidity) analysis requires careful study.

Related to the above two counts is that insubstance defeasance most likely leads to a decline in the firm's stock price. This can be due to redistribution of wealth from shareholders to bondholders and using resources to invest in lower earning opportunities.[14] If zero-coupon bonds are used to fund the trust, the company must pay a capital gains tax, at the maturity date of the defeased debt, on the difference between the face value of the zero-coupon bond and its discounted purchase price. This will cause the net present value of the decision to be negative, thereby lowering shareholder wealth.[15]

Debt of Unconsolidated Subsidiaries

In October 1987 the FASB published *SFAS 94, Consolidation of All Majority Owned Subsidiaries,* which set forth the procedures to be used to consolidate majority owned subsidiaries. The primary purpose of these new rules was to help resolve the perception that problems associated with off-balance-sheet financing were increasing. The FASB alleged this to be a problem because investors were fooled into underestimating the fixed claims in the firm's capital structure.[16] This was accomplished through the use of major-

---

[14]P. F. Roden, "The Financial Implications of Insubstance Defeasance," *Journal of Accounting, Auditing and Finance* (1988): 79–89, discusses this issue.

[15]This is shown by T. E. Copeland and J. F. Weston, *Financial Theory and Corporate Policy,* 3rd ed. (Reading, Mass.: Addison-Wesley, 1988): 533–4.

[16]E. E. Comiskey, R. A. McEwen, and C. W. Mulford, "A Test of Proforma Consolidation of Finance Subsidiaries," *Financial Management* (Winter 1987): 45–50, found that firms'

TABLE 5.4
Unconsolidated Debt as of 1986

	Total debt/equity ratio		Percent increase
	Sub-debt excluded	*Sub-debt included*	
Chrysler	0.5	3.8	660
Deere	0.8	1.9	138
Ford Motor	0.2	2.2	1000
General Motors	0.2	2.8	1300
Textron	1.3	3.3	154

ity or wholly owned leasing, factoring, or other financing subsidiaries which were then excluded from the parent's financial statements.[17] The actual justification given by management was that consolidation of such "nonhomogeneous" operations would distort the parent's key financial and operating statistics.[18] This was cited particularly as the rationale for excluding highly leveraged financing subsidiaries.[19]

Table 5.4 indicates the significant amount of debt some firms were hiding in their unconsolidated subsidiaries at the end of 1986.

Companies can avoid consolidating subsidiaries if

□ control is temporary, and

□ control does not reside with the majority owner.

Absence of control is likely to occur only when a domestic subsidiary is in bankruptcy proceedings or when a foreign subsidiary operates in an envi-

---

betas are more closely associated with financial leverage based on a proforma consolidation than on an unconsolidated basis. On the other hand, V. L. Andrews, "Captive Finance Companies," *Harvard Business Review* (July–August 1964): 80–92, discusses market inefficiencies.

[17]Memorex Corporation used a wholly owned unconsolidated leasing subsidiary for a very different purpose. In an effort to increase the parent's sales and profits, management treated the transfer of equipment to the subsidiary as an immediate sale, even though the accounting requirements to satisfy a genuine sale had not occurred.

[18]The FASB has received much criticism since issuing *SFAS 94*. Some accountants speculate that the ruling may get reversed in the future, which happened in Canada in 1979 after a six-year experiment with it.

[19]Shortly after *SFAS 94* was announced by FASB, Tenneco, Inc. called a special meeting of shareholders to approve a significant corporate reorganization. The announcement stated:

> indebtedness of the Company's finance subsidiaries will for the first time be included in consolidated debt for purposes of computing the Company's borrowing capacity. . . . This result, which was unforeseen and unintended at the time these debt instruments were originally created, will unacceptably restrict the ability of the Company and its subsidiaries to issue long-term debt and thus significantly impair the Company's future financing flexibility.

ronment of extreme exchange controls or restrictions on repatriation of earnings.

Majority-owned subsidiaries not consolidated will generally be accounted for by the **equity method of accounting**. Under the equity method a substantive economic relationship is acknowledged between the parent company and the subsidiary company. The investment is originally recorded as an asset at the cost of the shares acquired but is subsequently adjusted each period for changes in the net assets of the investee. That is, the investment (asset) carrying amount is periodically increased or decreased by the parent's proportionate share of the profit or loss of the subsidiary and decreased by all dividends received by the parent from the subsidiary:

Investment in subsidiary

= initial investment at cost   (5.1)
  + (−) proportioned share of subsidiary's profit (loss)
  − dividends received from subsidiary

With the equity method *none of the liabilities of the subsidiary are shown on the parent company's balance sheet.* Thus, off-balance-sheet liabilities are created.

Since most firms now have to consolidate their subsidiaries, future concerns about this form of structure to keep debt off the balance sheet should be minimal. However, implicit unconsolidated subsidiaries exist, which concerns FASB and the Securities and Exchange Commission. These implicit subsidiaries fall under the labels *nonsub subsidiary* and *project financing.*

Nonsub Subsidiary

This entity arises when another firm plays a major role in the creation and financing of a new business but does not take an equity position at the outset. For example, an established company might finance the **nonsub subsidiary** by means of convertible debt or debt with warrants for the later purchase of common shares. The original equity partner in such arrangements most often will be the creative or managerial talent (possibly of the firm providing the financing), which generally exchanges its talents for a stock interest. If the operation prospers, the investor company will exercise its rights to a majority voting stock position; if it fails, the investor company presumably avoids reflecting the losses in its statements.

While this strategy avoids the requirements of both equity accounting and consolidation, the economic substance clearly suggests that the operating results of the subsidiary should be reflected in the financial statements of the real parent, even absent stock ownership.

Project Financing

In the case of traditional financing for a project, the lender's security would be provided by the basic assets and financial strength of the project's sponsors. In **project financing**, lenders do not have direct recourse to the sponsor's assets or revenue but rely on the economics of the project, project assets, and the revenue stream generated by the project for their security. This is the basic difference between traditional financing and project financing.

Pure project financing based solely on a project's assets or revenue stream is extremely rare. Lenders are reluctant to rely solely on revenues generated by the project to service their debt. Therefore, they generally insist on backup credit support from a project's sponsors, other project participants, or third parties interested in the success of the project. This support is commonly provided through guarantees, contractual obligations, deficiency agreements, or other similar arrangements that are designed to ensure that debt will be serviced by some creditworthy party if the cash flow from project revenues is inadequate or interrupted.

In project financing the project is usually created as either a joint venture or a partnership, which is usually considered a separate legal entity with no one firm owning more than 50 percent of the project (company). The equity accounting method is used with the result that each company reports only its share of the investment (which incorporates the earnings of the venture) and none of the debt. In other words, consolidated statements are not required. The project is thinly capitalized and highly leveraged, generally with the debt guaranteed by the venturers. Also, no disclosure of the debt guarantee is made on the venturers' balance sheets.

An important benefit of this method of financing is that greater leverage can be achieved for projects employing these concepts than would be permissible if the projects were carried on the balance sheets of their equity sponsors. Debt leverage of up to 90 percent is not uncommon, depending on the creditworthiness of the backers.

When companies contribute noncash assets to the joint venture, they frequently transfer the assets at a fair market value and recognize the difference between historical cost and fair market value as either a profit or loss. If a very close economic relationship exists between the company and the joint venture, the appropriateness of recognizing a gain or loss seems questionable. It is not acceptable accounting to recognize a gain or loss on a contribution of capital to a related party.

Careful financial analysis is required of a firm involved in a joint venture. Before the financial ratios of a company and its joint venture are computed, additional steps and decisions are necessary. The first is to always eliminate the company's investment account in the joint venture with its share of joint-venture equity. If there are no other intercompany transactions, the analyst may simply elect to combine the company's share of joint-venture assets, liabilities, revenue, and expense accounts with the company's own accounts. However, if most of the joint venture's sales are to the company, the combining process would result in dubious figures, since total sales would be overstated in computing certain financial ratios.

Illustration 5.9 discusses a project financing method that has become popular with many high-technology firms.

ILLUSTRATION 5.9

Funding for an enterprise's research and development (R&D) costs can be arranged either through traditional debt or equity issues or through various arrangements with external parties. Although the form and legal structure of external arrangements can vary, one of the more popular arrangements is the *R&D limited partnership*. Firms most likely to form these partnerships are those in the pharmaceutical, drug, medical, electronic, and computer industries. Factors favoring use of a limited partnership (LP) include taxes,[20] shifting risk from the R&D firm onto other parties, and off-balance-sheet financing.

The details of such R&D partnerships can be elaborate, but the essential ingredients of the arrangement are shown in Fig. 5.1. A sponsoring corporation creates the off-balance-sheet financing of its R&D costs through the creation of a limited partnership in conjunction with a group of outside investors. The sponsor transfers rights to develop a certain "basic technology" to the partnership, but, as general partner, the sponsoring firms acts as manager for the partnership. Any successfully developed technology is purchased (or leased) by the sponsor from the partnership.

The R&D partnership generally contracts development work out to an R&D contractor (which can be, and often is, the sponsor firm itself). Payments to the R&D contractor generate tax losses by the partnership that are passed on to the partners. The partnership retains rights to any technology successfully developed by the contractor and generates income through the sale or lease of rights to any successfully developed technology. This income is subsequently passed through to the partners.

The R&D limited partnership form of funding avoids some of the financial statement effects of in-house funding. Because most sponsor

---

[20]T. Shevlin, "Taxes and Off-Balance Financing: Research and Development Limited Partnerships," *Accounting Review* (July 1987): 480–507, finds that low-marginal-tax-rate firms are more likely than high-marginal-tax-rate firms to fund their R&D through limited partnership.

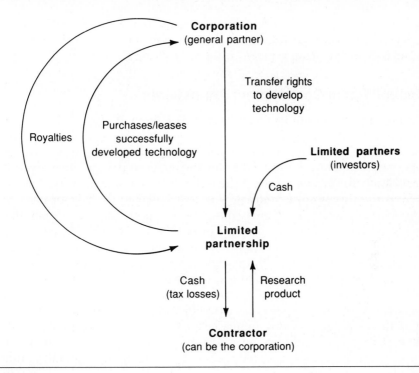

FIGURE 5.1
R&D Limited Partnership Structure

firms disclose limited partnership details only through notes to financial statements, funds raised through the partnership do not appear as debt on the balance sheet and R&D expenditures funded by the partnership do not appear as expenses on the income statement of the sponsoring firm. In the short run (specifically, until the sponsor must pick up expenses resulting from the purchase or lease of any successfully developed technology), the limited partnership may be used by the sponsor to avoid the negative effects of in-house funding on leverage, interest coverage, and the unrestricted pool of retained earnings.

The key issue with respect to a R&D limited partnership is whether or not a substantive and genuine transfer of financial risk from the sponsoring firm to the outside partners has occurred. If the sponsor is obligated to repay any of the funds provided by the outside sponsors, regardless of the outcome of the R&D, the financial risk is presumed not to have been transferred. In such case, the sponsor firm must estimate and recognize its liability to the outside partners. Thus, if properly structured (that is, the sponsor firm does not guarantee funds contributed by the outside partners to the partnership), an R&D partnership agreement can result in an off-balance-sheet financing activity for the sponsoring firm.   □

Unconditional Commitment Agreements

Unconditional commitment agreements, as a method of off-balance-sheet financing, relate mostly to capital-intensive industries such as mining and public utilities. One form is the **take-or-pay contract**, which is an agreement between a buyer and a seller for the buyer to pay specified amounts periodically for products even if the buyer does not take delivery. Another form is the **throughput contract**, which is similar to the take-or-pay contract except that it represents contracts to acquire services rather than goods. Payment is required whether or not the service is rendered.

There are many ways a take-or-pay arrangement can be structured. For instance, U.S. Steel (USS) financed a $690 million seamless steel plant this way. USS proposed to build a seamless-pipe plant since seamless pipe was in great demand by the oil companies. The oil companies, as customers, signed take-or-pay contracts with USS. These contracts provided more than enough cash flow to service the financing needed to pay for the plant. USS then found an investing group that was willing to accept the purchase agreements as credit support (as a form of collateral) to fund the plant. The plant operates under a sale-leaseback arrangement (a topic discussed in Chapter 11) between USS and the investment group. The result was that USS raised $690 million to build a steel plant. Because the lease is structured as an operating lease, its liabilities did not increase on the balance sheet and liquidity was not impaired.

Interest Rate Swaps

A type of financial transaction that may occur in virtually any type of business is an **interest rate swap**. The most basic type of interest rate swap involves two companies, both with outstanding debt. One has fixed rate of interest on its debt, and the other has a variable rate tied to some interest index such as the prime rate. For various reasons, these companies consider it beneficial to exchange interest rates. Almost always, these exchanges are made through a financial intermediary.

Sometimes one or both companies may find themselves obligated to pay amounts substantially in excess of the interest cost elements reflected in their balance sheets or in their notes to financial statements. The present value of these additional interest costs, especially if such amounts are not viewed as executory costs, are considered to be a form of debt whose omission from the balance sheet is a form of off-balance-sheet financing. Chapter 10 extends the discussion on how swaps work.

Summary

This chapter discussed several ways management can raise debt financing without having to report it in the balance sheet. Exclusion of these economic liabilities diminishes the credibility, completeness, and comparability of the balance sheet. Off-balance-sheet financing has the effect of making the liquidity of a firm look better than it really is. Incorporating off-balance-sheet information into financial ratios and other methods of assessment can have dramatic effects on the financial picture that the ratios portray. Financial positions are often not what they seem to be. For the average user of financial statements the credibility of the data conveyed will become increasingly poor.

Any prudent user of balance-sheet information should become acquainted with the nuances of off-balance-sheet methods. A careful and critical analysis of the footnotes to the financial statements must be made in order to assess correctly the economic reality of a firm's financial position. Important adjustments can be made by using footnote data in order to arrive at an accurate view of the total corporate liabilities. Financing methods are changing so fast that only personal vigilance can protect the analyst from being deceived or uninformed.

Key Concepts

Accounts receivable sale with
   recourse
Capital lease
Debt of unconsolidated subsidiaries
Defined-benefit pension plan
Equity method of accounting
Insubstance defeasance of debt
Interest rate swap
Nonsub subsidiary

Off-balance-sheet financing
Operating lease
Pension expense
Postemployment benefits
Product financing
Project financing
Take-or-pay contract
Throughput contract
Unfunded pension liability

Questions

1. What does the expression *off-balance-sheet financing* mean?

2. What are some reasons that managers desire to finance their firms using sources that do not directly appear on the financial statements?

3. How do unfunded pension liabilities arise?

4. What is the difference between defined-benefit pension plans and defined-contribution plans? Which plan provides management with more flexibility for financial reporting and liquidity management?

5. Describe the difference between an operating lease and a financial (capital) lease. Which type of lease would management rather report? Why?

6. What disclosures should be made by a lessee if the leased assets and the related obligations are not capitalized?

7. What is a sale of accounts receivable with recourse?

8. What are the necessary conditions for insubstance debt defeasance? How does debt defeasance work?

9. A company that owns less than 50 percent of another company is not required to report its financial statements on a consolidated basis. Which method is usually employed by these companies, and what impact does it have on the financial statements?

10. What is a nonsub-subsidiary, and how might it help disguise the nature of a subsidiary investment?

11. Identify and discuss a R&D limited partnership.

12. Describe take-or-pay and throughput contracts.

13. Discuss the basic arrangements of an interest rate swap.

Problems

1. The following financial conditions concerning the pension funds were reported:

Actual benefit obligation (ABO)	$29,650,341
Present market value of pension fund assets (PPA)	28,790,650
Progression of salary and wages	1,256,000

(a) Determine the unfunded liability of the pension fund from an economic perspective (as opposed to the accounting requirement).

(b) Determine the recorded funding obligation according to SFAS 87. How is it recorded?

(c) Assume that in the following year that ABO exceeds PBO by $500,000. What adjustment is made to the financial statements in the next year?

2.   Chandler Ballon, Inc., is expanding its operations and is in the process of selecting the method of financing this program. After careful investigation management determines that it may purchase the needed assets either by using the proceeds received from issuing bonds or by leasing the assets on a long-term basis. Without knowing the comparative costs, answer these questions.

(a) What might be the advantages of leasing the assets instead of owning them?

(b) What might be the disadvantages of leasing the assets instead of owning them?

(c) In what ways will the balance sheet be differently affected by leasing the assets as opposed to issuing bonds and purchasing the assets?

(d) Will liquidity be affected at all? Discuss.

3.   The Pacific South Company must install a new machine costing $30,000. The machine has an economic life of 12 years and is not expected to have any residual value. Straight-line depreciation will be used. Management has three options to acquire the machine:

☐ Option 1. It can borrow $30,000 from a local bank at 10 percent, with principal and interest amortized over the 12 years.

☐ Option 2. It can lease the asset with annual payments of $4438 (prepaid one period) for a 10-year term. The first payment will be strictly for reduction of principal. The asset will be amortized over the life of the lease.

☐ Option 3. It can lease for maximum allowable terms and payments to qualify as an operating lease. All payments will be annual, with a one-period prepayment.

The firm's most recent financial statements are given in Table 5.5.

(a) Assume that as a result of acquiring the new machine, Pacific's sales increase to $280,000, the cost of goods sold increases to $196,000, and operating expenses, excluding interest, depreciation, and lease expense, increase to $12,000. Calculate the net income for each of the first three years after the new machine became available for each financing option.

(b) Assume that depreciation on the old fixed assets is as shown on the income statement and that straight-line depreciation is used on all assets. Develop the balance sheet for the end of the first year after the new machine became available for each of the financing options. Use current assets as the balancing item. Separate liabilities into their short-term and long-term components.

TABLE 5.5
Pacific South Company, Inc.
Income Statement and Balance Sheet
For the Latest Year

Income statement		
Sales		$200,000
Cost of sales		140,000
Gross margin		$ 60,000
Less: Operating expenses	$10,000	
Depreciation	10,000	
Lease expense	0	
Interest expense	15,000	
		35,000
Profit before taxes		$ 25,000
Taxes		10,000
Net income		$ 15,000

Balance sheet				
Current assets	$ 30,000		Current liabilities	$ 20,000
Net fixed assets	120,000		Long-term debt	50,000
			Shareholders' equity	80,000
Total	$150,000		Total	$150,000

(c) From the income statements and balance sheets generated for the borrowing and leasing options, calculate the following ratios: debt/equity, times interest earned, total asset turnover, return on assets, and return on equity. Return on assets should be calculated as (profit after tax + interest (1 − tax))/net assets (that is, add back interest on debt and capital leases).

(d) Discuss the effects of the borrowing and leasing options on the firm's financial picture as indicated by the ratios calculated in part (c).

4.   Peacock Enterprises' annual report indicates financial leases of $10,000,000. These leases are noncancelable for a period of 10 years. The total minimum payments for these leases amount to $15,802,156, or $1,580,215.60 per year. The following is a schedule, by years, of future minimum rental payments required under noncancelable operating leases:

Next year	$ 2,552,628
2 years from now	2,552,628
3 years from now	2,552,628
4 years from now	2,533,506
5 years from now	2,437,896
Later years	35,090,315

Assume that all lease payments are made at the beginning of the period.

(a) What rate is used to capitalize the financial leases?

(b) What is the approximate present value of operating leases using the ratio approach? the net present-value approach?

(c) What effect would the capitalization of operating leases have on ratio analysis?

5. A corporation has a choice of either purchasing a machine or leasing it. The purchase price is $1,200,000, whereas the annual lease payment is $500,000 for five years. If the company leases, can it record the lease as an operating lease if the useful life is seven years and the purchase price at the end of the lease is $100,000? If the lease were capitalized at a 15 percent cost of capital, what would be the book value?

6. Calculate the conventional debt/capital and adjusted debt/capital ratios, using the following data, and discuss your findings.

Long-term debt	$ 1,500,000
Owners' equity	4,000,000
Current deferred taxes	250,000
Long-term deferred taxes	10,375,000
Present value of noncapitalized leases	750,000
Present value of unrecognized pension costs	3,429,000
Tax rate	40 percent

7. Determine the capitalized value of an operating lease if the lease requires annual payments of $87,492 at the beginning of each year for 7 years. The lessee's borrowing rate is 12 percent.

8. Determine the annual lease payments of a capitalized asset valued at $447,207.48. Lease payments are made at the end of each year for seven years, and the borrowing rate is 12 percent.

9. **(a)** If the lessee in Problems 7 and 8 has a choice of classifying the lease as either a financial lease or an operating lease, which alternative would he choose? Discuss in terms of the effect on both the income statement and liquidity for the life of the lease by calculating the net cash outflows and charges against operations for each alternative. Assume a tax rate of 40 percent.

(b) Which alternative causes net income to be lower in year 5, and by how much?

(c) Calculate the internal rate of return between the two alternatives.

10. Alpha Firm has reached the limit imposed on it by the bank of requiring its debt/equity ratio to be less than or equal to 1:1. Its balance sheet is shown below. The firm wishes to get additional short-term funds to pay the long-term bonds currently due through the use of the sale of accounts receivable. The buyer of these accounts demands full recourse.

(a) How can Alpha Firm accomplish its objective of raising funds while ignoring the full recourse provision if the buyer demands a 10 percent discount on the funds supplied? Show the correct ending balance sheet if recourse is not recognized.

(b) What is the correct debt/equity ratio of Alpha Firm? Show the correct ending balance sheet if recourse is recognized.

Alpha Firm
Balance Sheet
For the Year Ending December 31, 199x

Cash	$ 5,290	Trade payables	$ 6,870
Accounts			
receivable	32,730	Taxes payable	4,521
Inventory	42,871	Long-term bonds due	18,000
Total current assets	$ 80,891	Total current liabilities	$ 29,391
Net plant	217,891	Long-term bonds	120,000
		Common stock	125,000
		Retained earnings	24,391
		Total liabilities and	
Total assets	$298,782	equity	$298,782

11. Alpha Firm, of Problem 10, has the following income statement for the year ending 199x before taking the actions described below. The firm's management believes that its profit to sales ratio is too low and that its liquidity ratio should be improved. To correct these problems by the time of the shareholders meeting, management plans to employ "product financing" using the sale and repurchase of $4,000,000 of the firm's inventory (value is stated at selling price). It has found a partner who agrees to the arrangement if Alpha Firm will buy back the inventory early in the new fiscal year. The arrangement calls for a 10 percent selling discount on the inventory. Repurchase will be at full value.

(a) Determine the firm's current profit to sales ratio and quick ratio and indicate how these may be improved by using product financing.

(b) Show how the arrangement should be disclosed on the firm's statements.

Alpha Firm
Income Statement
For the Year Ending December 31, 199x ($000)

Revenues:	
Sales	$25,000
Cost of sales	11,400
Gross margin	$13,600
Expenses:	
Selling	6,000
Depreciation	4,250
Administration	2,400
Profit before taxes	$ 950
Taxes	380
Profit after taxes	$ 570

12.   York Enterprises has $20,000,000 of debt with a coupon rate of 7 percent. The debt matures in five years. The treasurer is considering insubstance debt defeasance as a means of improving this year's profit figure and lowering the debt/equity ratio. If government securities are yielding 10 percent, how much must the treasurer segregate with a trustee in order to use debt defeasance? How much will the gain be? Is liquidity of the firm improved?

CHAPTER 6 □
Indicators of Liquidity

Ratio analysis is a much-used technique for unraveling a firm's financial performance. Chapters 4 and 5 discussed many of the problems inherent in traditional ratio analysis. Those chapters were intended to stimulate you to question many commonly accepted notions about ratios and be more critical when conducting financial analysis.

Since many of the ratios discussed in Chapter 4 have been used for several decades, many managers, analysts, and students place more credence in them than they deserve. If these people are to discard old habits, they must be convinced that superior methods of liquidity analysis exist. It is the intent of this chapter to do so. Implicit in any discussion in this chapter is that *off-balance-sheet financing is not used by management.* This assumption is made to simplify the discussion. Obviously, if off-balance-sheet financing exists, proforma balance sheets must be prepared to capture it.

This chapter discusses a number of imperfect liquidity indicators. They are imperfect because they rely on some of the traditional ratios and provide but an overview of liquidity. The analysis that follows indicates important interrelationships between those areas normally considered in liquidity analysis and those areas commonly viewed to be outside the realm of managing liquidity. Included in this chapter is analysis of return on equity, sustainable growth, cash conversion cycle, cash breakeven sales level, and inflation-adjusted financial statements.

Return on Equity

Invariably, when inexperienced analysts are asked to conduct financial analysis, they calculate most of the traditional ratios before conducting any analysis. A more direct and productive approach is to start with the **return-**

on-equity (ROE) ratio, an accounting measure that serves as a proxy for maximizing shareholders' wealth.[1]

Maximization of ROE is consistent with maximization of residual income (net present value in perpetuity) when cash — not accrual — profits are calculated. A mathematical proof is shown in Appendix A of this chapter. Since ROE is seldom calculated using cash flows, the analyst must not lose sight of the *quality of earnings* issue and the many accounting-based problems associated with ROE calculations, discussed in Chapters 4 and 5. An analyst must avoid unequivocal acceptance of any conclusions drawn using this ratio.

In addition to the proof shown in Appendix A, another rationale exists for the use of return on equity as a surrogate for maximization of wealth. Consider the situation where all investments undertaken by management earn a net present value of zero. That is, all investors simply earn their minimum risk-adjusted required returns — debtholders earn the market cost of debt, and equityholders earn the market cost of equity. In this case, return on equity equals the cost of equity (k_e), and the market value of the stock equals its book value.[2] When management's investments generate positive net present values, the excess accrues to the equityholders. In this situation the market value of equity should exceed the book value of equity, and ROE should be greater than k_e.[3] This situation is desirable and is one that management strives for. Figure 6.1 summarizes the important relationship between ROE and k_e.

The remaining discussion in this chapter assumes that managers pursue wealth-maximizing decisions; that is, $ROE/k_e \geq 1$. If managers find that $ROE/k_e < 1$, even when ROE is maximized, they need to give serious consideration to reallocating resources more profitably. If reallocation is not possible, liquidation is most likely in shareholders' best interests.

---

[1] E. M. Lerner and W. T. Carleton, in *A Theory of Financial Analysis* (New York: Harcourt, Brace and World, 1966), W. E. Fruhan, Jr., in *Financial Strategy: Studies on the Creation, Transfer, and Destruction of Shareholder Value* (Homewood, Ill.: Irwin, 1979), and R. C. Higgins, in *Analysis for Financial Management* (Homewood, Ill.: Irwin, 1984) rely on return on equity as a meaningful proxy to capture the shareholder wealth objective.

[2] Management finds it difficult to determine the cost of equity. The academic literature favors the Gordon dividend growth model and the capital asset pricing model (CAPM) as being appropriate for calculating k_e. Theoretically, the CAPM is more appealing than the Gordon model.

[3] Alternative ways to state the wealth maximization objective are $Max[ROE - k_e]$ and $Max[NI_e - k_e E]$. NI_e is cash earnings available to common shareholders and E is shareholders' equity. See Appendix A for further details.

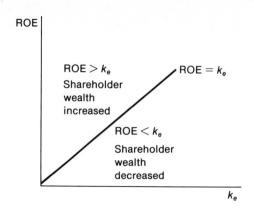

FIGURE 6.1
Relationship Between ROE and k_e.

ROE Model

Return on equity can be separated into the following three components:

$$\text{ROE} = \underbrace{\frac{\text{net income}}{\text{sales}}}_{\substack{\text{return on} \\ \text{sales}}} \times \underbrace{\frac{\text{sales}}{\text{total assets}}}_{\substack{\text{asset} \\ \text{turnover}}} \times \underbrace{\frac{\text{total assets}}{\text{equity}}}_{\substack{\text{financial} \\ \text{leverage}}} \qquad (6.1)$$

Analysis of each of these components against budget and/or prior years' performances (and maybe industry, although it is doubtful how beneficial this analysis will be) may well reveal patterns. If no problem exists with a particular component, there is little need to pursue further analysis of that component. When significant deviations exist, the component can be broken down to pinpoint problems.

Table 6.1 summarizes data for W. T. Grant during the period preceding its liquidity crisis and subsequent bankruptcy. The trend in ROE has been down and, surely as of 1974, is less than any reasonable estimate for the cost of equity. This trend was a signal that severe action was required to return the firm to a profitable and liquid state.

What has contributed to this dismal ROE performance for 1974? Table 6.1 indicates that each of the components should be analyzed to reveal the reasons. Although management of return on sales is the major deficiency, asset turnover is less efficient than in three of the four previous years. The leverage component needs analysis since it indicates that ROE has been supported through an ever-increasing debt component. However, what is not readily apparent is how the increased leverage has affected the other two components. The interactions are examined shortly.

TABLE 6.1
ROE for W. T. Grant Company for the Year Ended January 31

Year	ROE	Return on sales	Asset turnover	Financial leverage
1974	0.026	0.004	1.476	3.962
1973	0.115	0.023	1.481	3.410
1972	0.110	0.025	1.455	2.983
1971	0.134	0.031	1.553	2.762
1970	0.148	0.034	1.713	2.531

Note: Multiplication of the components results in a small rounding error for ROE.

Profitability

The return on sales (ROS) ratio can be further analyzed by using **common-size income statements** (see Table 6.2). These statements reflect each item on the statement as a percentage of net sales. By comparing each category of expense across years (or against budget), analysts can isolate problem areas. Answers to questions such as "What is the reason for the falling gross profit margin?" are revealed by such an analysis.

TABLE 6.2
W. T. Grant Company Common-Size Income Statements for the Year Ended January 31

	1974	1973	1972	1971	1970
Sales	100.0%	100.0%	100.0%	100.0%	100.0%
Cost of sales	62.9	62.2	61.6	61.4	62.4
Gross profit	37.1%	37.8%	38.4%	38.6%	37.6%
Period costs:					
Selling, general, and administrative	28.0	26.9	27.0	26.1	25.1
Depreciation and amortization	0.7	0.7	0.8	0.8	0.7
Leasing	5.7	5.5	5.4	5.0	4.4
Net profit from operations	2.7%	4.7%	5.2%	6.7%	7.4%
Other income	0.3	0.3	0.4	0.5	0.4
Earnings before interest and taxes	3.0%	5.0%	5.6%	7.2%	7.8%
Interest expense	2.8	1.3	1.2	1.5	1.2
Earnings before taxes	0.2%	3.7%	4.4%	5.7%	6.6%
Taxes: Current	⟨0.3⟩	0.7	1.0	1.8	2.3
Deferred	0.3	1.0	1.2	1.1	1.2
Earnings before unconsolidated subsidiaries	0.2%	2.0%	2.3%	2.9%	3.2%
Equity in net earnings of unconsolidated subsidiaries	0.2	0.3	0.3	0.3	0.3
Total net earnings	0.4%	2.3%	2.5%	3.1%	3.4%

For example, Table 6.2 indicates that W. T. Grant's gross profit margins declined steadily for four years. Is this decline a result of higher costs for merchandise, decline in selling prices, or a change in product mix? According to W. T. Grant's annual report, all three reasons contributed to the decline. Increased selling, general and administrative costs, and higher leverage continued over the period. These higher costs, coupled with lower margins, are the main reason for the decline in total net earnings.

A plot of return-on-sales (ROS) data is shown in Fig. 6.2. For the purpose of discussion, assume that management budgeted a -8.0 percent return for the year ended January 1974. Since actual performance was better than that budgeted, management possibly ignored any analysis of the variance. This procedure could be most unfortunate, particularly if the budget was based on a strategy to reverse or slow this declining trend. Possibly the better-than-budgeted performance was achieved by not implementing some strategic decisions. The result of such action may be to perpetuate factors that are detrimental to the long-run survival of the firm.

The list that follows outlines possible explanations for "beating a budget." Each reason results in either reduction of expenses or conversion of cash flow, or both, in the current period. These "savings" may imperil future growth and market position since a firm that grows less rapidly than competition (even though it is on trend) erodes its market position and profitability — and eventually liquidity — relative to its past performance and to the competition.

FIGURE 6.2
W. T. Grant Company's Trend in Return on Sales

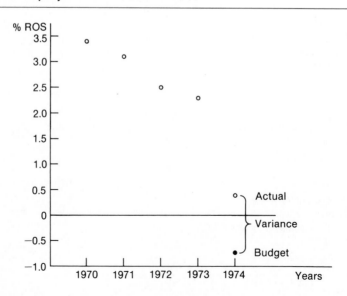

Causes of "Beating a Budget"

☐ Advertising and R&D expenses were slashed.

☐ Product planners/engineers were laid off in order to cut costs.

☐ Actuarial assumptions regarding the pension plan were changed.

☐ Selling prices increased, but sales volume decreased.

☐ Extraordinary gain occurred.

☐ Inventory valuation method was changed.

☐ Marketable securities were sold for a profit.

☐ Debt defeasance was used.

Asset Turnover

When a problem lies with the trend in the sales-to-asset ratio, called **asset turnover**, management's attention is directed to the balance sheet. It is seeking to determine the productivity of investments in current assets and fixed assets for supporting sales. The denominator of the ratio can be represented as

$$\text{Assets} = \text{current assets} + \text{fixed assets} + \text{other assets.} \qquad (6.2)$$

This denominator allows turnover ratios to be calculated for each component. However, once these calculations are made, they cannot be added to obtain the total asset turnover ratio since no common denominator exists. This result is unfortunate, since the relative contribution of each component cannot be readily assessed.

The problem can be overcome by inverting the individual asset turnover ratios. Since the common denominator is now sales, the turnover ratios are additive and equal to the total (inverted) turnover ratio. Table 6.3 summarizes the problem and the solution.

The traditional turnover statistics for 1974 indicate that total turnover is lower than in three of the four previous years. Each asset category contributed to this decline. However, the relative importance of each category to the total turnover ratio cannot be easily determined. Once the ratios are inverted, it becomes apparent that each asset category has maintained a fairly constant contribution to total asset turnover in each year. W. T. Grant's management appears to be following a policy of maintaining a constant mix of current, fixed, and other assets.

Even if the turnover ratios display an upward trend, the analyst must be aware of hidden future problems associated with favorable trends in turnover ratios. The following list outlines some of these problems.

TABLE 6.3
W. T. Grant Company Analysis of Asset Turnover for the Year Ended January 31
($000)

	1974		1973		1972		1971		1970	
Sales	$1,849,802		$1,644,747		$1,374,812		$1,254,131		$1,210,918	
Current assets	$1,102,686		$ 979,876		$ 831,229		$ 719,182		$ 628,409	
Fixed assets	100,984		91,420		77,173		61,832		55,311	
Miscellaneous and other assets	49,313		39,402		36,268		26,614		23,075	
Total	$1,252,983		$1,110,698		$ 944,670		$ 807,628		$ 706,795	
Traditional turnover ratios										
Current assets	1.678		1.679		1.654		1.744		1.927	
Fixed assets	18.318		17.991		17.815		20.283		21.893	
Miscellaneous and other assets	37.511		41.743		37.803		47.123		52.477	
Total	1.476		1.481		1.455		1.553		1.713	
Inverted turnover ratios and their contributions										
Current assets	0.596	88%	0.596	88%	0.605	88%	0.574	89%	0.519	89%
Fixed assets	0.054	8	0.055	8	0.056	9	0.049	8	0.046	8
Miscellaneous and other assets	0.027	4	0.024	4	0.026	3	0.021	3	0.019	3
Total	0.677	100%	0.675	100%	0.687	100%	0.644	100%	0.584	100%

Hidden Problems in Favorable Turnover Ratios

□ Equipment is old and nearly fully depreciated.

□ Receivables have been sold to a finance subsidiary or with recourse to an independent third party.

□ Inventories are too low.

□ Replacement cost greatly exceeds cost carried on the books.

□ LIFO (last-in, first-out) inventory valuation is used instead of FIFO (first-in, first-out).

□ Liquidity is dangerously low.

□ Fixed assets are misstated — some expenditures are expensed rather than capitalized.

□ Contra-accounts for receivables and inventories are too large.

□ Current liabilities are overstated.

Financial Leverage

The third component of the ROE ratio is the ratio of net assets to equity. This ratio measures **financial leverage**. If the leverage ratio equals 1, the firm has no debt.[4] As debt is added to the firm's capital structure, the ratio increases above 1. Although the absence of debt makes liquidity management easier, it is not in the firm's best interest to forgo debt financing whenever the firm is in a growth pattern. Growing less rapidly than competition erodes market position and profitability relative to competition.

If management chooses not to fully utilize its debt capacity, this choice may imply a high and increasing degree of business risk. The properly leverage competitor can grow faster than the more conservatively financed company and with a lower required rate of return, since its cost of capital will be lower. This argument is simply stating that by judiciously using debt to help compete for growth, management may be able to reduce its weighted average cost of capital relative to competitors. Hence, *the ultimate risk of overconservatism (the failure to utilize debt more) is increasing business risk if competition is aware.* On the other hand, the use of too much debt leads to higher financial risk and a higher cost of capital. Management must find some trade-off between too much debt and too little. Appendix B of this chapter discusses a model for determining the capital structure that maximizes ROE.

---

[4]The ratio can be less than 1.0. Such a ratio would signify that the firm has negative equity, which is frequently found with firms experiencing serious liquidity problems.

The conventional **debt capacity** rule that long-term debt should not exceed, say, 50 percent of total capitalization implies that debt in excess of this limit is too risky. Just what this phrase means is not always clear. The obvious inference is that if further additions are made to fixed-debt servicing charges, the time may come when the company does not have enough cash to go around. In the extreme case there may not be enough cash to meet legal commitments, and hence the company may become insolvent. In a less extreme form the drain of debt servicing may prevent management from covering expenditures it desires to preserve. This situation is called **cash inadequacy**.

Hindsight indicates that W. T. Grant was flirting with cash inadequacy as of January 1974. However, as Table 6.4 summarizes, diligent analysis would have revealed the debt problem confronting W. T. Grant prior to this period. Analysis of the leverage component of the ROE equation indicates the major reasons for the increase in financial leverage to be a continuing reliance on short-term debt (commercial paper) and a significant increase in long-term debt in the last period.

Analysis of Table 6.3 indicates that current assets comprised about 88 percent of total assets. The heavy reliance on short-term debt suggests that W. T. Grant was following a policy of financing short-term assets with short-term debt. On the surface this policy appears appropriate. However, note that most of the current assets are really *permanent*. There was about a 75 percent increase in current assets during the 1970–74 period. W. T. Grant's reliance on short-term debt to finance these current assets meant that it was constantly having to refinance them. That is, cash generated from operations was reinvested in additional current assets.

An even more striking aspect of W. T. Grant's financing policy is revealed by looking at investors' expectations for interest rates over the 1969–74 period. These expectations are captured in yield curves for U.S.

TABLE 6.4
W. T. Grant Company Analysis of Leverage for the Year Ended January 31

Year	$\dfrac{\text{Assets}}{\text{Equity}}$ =	$\dfrac{\text{Current liabilities}}{\text{Equity}}$ +	$\dfrac{\text{Long-term liabilities}}{\text{Equity}}$ +	$\dfrac{\text{Indeterminate liabilities}}{\text{Equity}}$ +	$\dfrac{\text{Preferred stock}}{\text{Equity}}$ +	$\dfrac{\text{Equity}}{\text{Equity}}$
1974	3.962	1.761	0.697	0.480	0.024	1.000
1973	3.410	1.544	0.389	0.451	0.026	1.000
1972	2.983	1.145	0.406	0.403	0.029	1.000
1971	2.762	1.246	0.110	0.373	0.033	1.000
1970	2.531	1.025	0.127	0.338	0.041	1.000

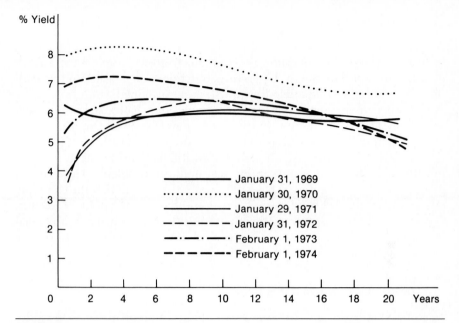

FIGURE 6.3
Yield Curves for U.S. Treasury Bonds

Source: Data from the *Wall Street Journal* for the dates shown.

government treasury bonds in Fig. 6.3. A **yield curve** depicts the relationship between the yield on debt securities (of constant default risk) and the maturity of the debt.

W. T. Grant's heavy reliance on issuing debt in the money market to finance growth suggests that either the firm did not understand what interest rates were expected to do or else thought it could forecast interest rates better than the financial markets. For instance, with the exception of the yield curves for January 31, 1969, and January 29, 1971, financing with long-term debt with a maturity of 15 years or more would have resulted in an interest rate not very different from that in the money market. If W. T. Grant had financed with long-term debt around the January 30, 1970, period, interest costs could have been reduced since long rates were more than 100 basis points lower than short rates.

Thus either asset expansion in W. T. Grant was not financed with a targeted debt/equity ratio in mind, or else the targeted ratio, in retrospect, was much higher than it should have been. Management did not have a clear understanding of the significance of debt servicing on cash flows.

Sustainable Growth

At various points in the discussion of ROE the importance of growth has been mentioned. The question is: How much growth can a firm afford, either real or inflationary?[5] Operating and financial policies and growth objectives must be compatible for growth to be sustained.

Earlier discussion in this book mentioned the change in strategy that management of W. T. Grant was pursuing, namely, making significant investments in new stores so as to become a more dominant firm in its product markets. Ratio analysis indicated that profitability problems developed, but the analysis failed to reveal any real liquidity problems. However, as investors in W. T. Grant were painfully aware, the growth that the company enjoyed over the 1970–74 period did not enhance shareholders' wealth. Growth was not managed in a manner consistent with prudent financial policies. In other words, corporate policy did not adequately address how sustainable growth could be achieved.

Definition of Sustainable Growth

Sustainable growth (g_s) can be expressed in a simple mathematical model as

$$g_s = \frac{R(1 - p)(1 + D/E)}{T - R(1 - p)(1 + D/E)} \tag{6.3}$$

where

$$R = \text{profit margin (return on sales)},$$
$$1 - p = \text{retention rate}; p \text{ is dividend payout},$$
$$D/E = \text{debt/equity ratio},$$
$$T = \text{asset/sales ratio (inverse of asset turnover)}.$$

An alternative specification of sustainable growth[6] that is entirely consistent with Eq. (6.3) is the following:

$$g_s = \frac{(1 - p)\,\text{ROE}}{1 - (1 - p)\,\text{ROE}}. \tag{6.4}$$

---

[5]Much of the discussion in this section is based on R. C. Higgins's article, "How Much Growth Can a Firm Afford?" *Financial Management* (Fall 1977): 7–16.

[6]A third definition of g_s is $(1 - p) \times \text{ROE}$, where ROE is calculated as net income divided by *beginning* (as opposed to *ending*) equity. Equations (6.3) and (6.4) use ending equity amounts. The amount calculated for sustainable growth will be the same regardless which formula is used.

These equations are derived in a *sources and uses of resources* framework (see Appendix C of this chapter) and include all the principal elements of a financial goals system. Management's demand for funds is balanced by the supply so that it will never be forced to default on expenditures essential to its competitive strategy. An implicit assumption is that management wishes to be independent and self-sufficient. As a result of this desire management trades off maximum economic scale for greater control of its resources. In other words, the firm *grows at a rate that can be sustained* into the future. Equity financing is relied upon as a last resort to support this growth.[7]

For a firm in *sustainable growth equilibrium,* in which it does not issue new equity (any equity growth is the result of retaining profits), the *ongoing annual growth in sales is equal to the growth in assets,*[8] *debt,*[9] *earnings, and equity.* However, if sales expand at a rate faster than the sustainable growth rate, something in the company's financial objectives has to give — usually to the detriment of financial soundness. Conversely, if sales grow at a rate less than the sustainable growth rate, a surplus of funds should exist.

A cautionary note is in order. The sustainable growth model is based on sources and uses of resources, as mentioned previously. The accounting ratios are only proxies for the actual inflows and outflows of resources that are central to the management of corporate wealth. To the extent that these accounting ratios do not properly capture resource flows because of accrual accounting principles, actual growth rates may deviate from sustainable growth rates somewhat from period to period without violating sustainable growth equilibrium.

Interpretation of Growth

A growth index can be constructed by subtracting sustainable growth from actual growth (that is, $g_a - g_s$). An index of zero means that actual growth is in equilibrium with sustainable growth. When the index is positive, the firm is growing faster than it can sustain under current financial policies. A negative index indicates that the firm can support higher sales growth.

---

[7]G. Donaldson, in *Managing Corporate Wealth* (New York: Praeger, 1984), greatly expands on this theme. The concept is consistent with the discussion of agency theory introduced in Chapter 1.

[8]The equation assumes that the growth rate of assets equals the growth rate of sales. Obviously this is not always the case, as companies may use assets more or less efficiently at different times and thereby alter the ratio. However, the use of a relatively stable ratio of sales to assets is an assumption that many managers use for planning purposes.

[9]The growth in sales equal to the growth in debt is consistent with the idea that most firms maintain a relatively constant debt/equity ratio.

The "How to Go Broke . . . While Making a Profit" scenario presented in Chapter 1 is an excellent example of a company growing too fast for its own good. Actual growth (g_a) far exceeded sustainable growth (g_s). Management failed to realize that rapid growth requires a large amount of cash. The cash needs can be met temporarily by taking advantage of leverage, but whenever the debt capacity is reached, management must turn to some other source of resources for sustaining growth.

ILLUSTRATION 6.1

Table 6.5 summarizes the liquidity problems of W. T. Grant that were surfacing during the early 1970s because sustainable growth and actual growth were not synchronized. The interpretation of W. T. Grant's sustainable growth is that as of January 1974, growth would decrease at a rate of 3.8 percent annually as long as there was no change in any of the four ratios $R, T, 1 - p,$ or D/E. In each of the last three years actual growth exceeded sustainable growth. This result signaled that changes were needed if the company was to avoid severe growth problems. When actual growth exceeds sustainable growth, the company is an absorber of cash. It is a generator of cash when the reverse situation exists.

Unfortunately, adjustments made by W. T. Grant's management after 1974 were insufficient, with the result that bankruptcy was declared, which led to subsequent liquidation of the firm. This situation was brought about by a management decision. The 1973 annual report states:

> The management of your company recognized . . . [the industry] shift from smaller, limited stores to larger, "full line" stores and committed itself to the complete restructuring of the Company.

The 10-K report indicates that during the five years ended January 31, 1974, this restructuring had resulted in 369 newer and larger stores opening and 272 smaller ones closing. It is evident from Table 6.5 that management's strategy did not adequately incorporate the sustainable growth formula and its implications for liquidity management.   □

Responses to Disequilibrium in Sustainable Growth

If actual sales growth (g_a) is at any rate other than the sustainable growth rate (g_s), then sales, $R, p, D/E,$ or T must change. For example, when actual growth exceeds sustainable growth, and management expects this situation to persist, the following alternatives are available.

TABLE 6.5
Sustainable Growth Calculation for W. T. Grant Company
for the Year Ended January 31

	1974	1973	1972	1971	1970
Return on sales (R)	0.004	0.023	0.025	0.031	0.034
Inverted asset turnover (T)	0.677	0.675	0.687	0.644	0.584
Retention rate ($1 - p$)	-1.542	0.444	0.402	0.477	0.532
Financial leverage (D/E)	2.962	2.410	1.983	1.762	1.531
Sustainable growth (g_s)	-0.038	0.054	0.046	0.068	0.085
Actual growth (g_a)	0.125	0.196	0.096	0.036	0.096
$g_a - g_s$	0.163	0.142	0.050	-0.032	0.011

New Financing

□ *Sell new equity.* New equity plus the additional borrowing capacity it creates provides sources of needed cash to finance further growth. In W. T. Grant's case the new equity could have been used to retire debt that was exceedingly high.

□ *Increase leverage.* This alternative utilizes the unused debt capacity and provides funds for further growth. It does not apply to W. T. Grant, as indicated above.

Increase Retentions

□ *Reduce the payout ratio.* This alternative increases the proportion of earnings available to finance growth opportunities. W. T. Grant's management used this technique in the following year. However, it should have done this much earlier.

□ *Change selling prices.* When actual growth is too high relative to financing capabilities, raising prices increases the profit margin and may increase sustainable growth. Of course, it may also cause market share to decline. W. T. Grant's management felt it was unable to increase prices. The Nixon administration had imposed price controls in an effort to slow the rate of increase in inflation. W. T. Grant's annual report states: "We felt compelled to lower our selling margins during the second half of 1973 in order to comply with government regulation; this involuntary action caused a substantial profit decrease."

Reduce Costs

□ *Cut operating costs.* Judicious cuts in operating costs should result in a more profitable firm both in the short term and in the long term. W. T. Grant's management was not effectively controlling costs.

□ *Prune product lines.* Firms can sell marginal businesses and commit resources to businesses with stronger market potential. This action generates cash and reduces sales growth for businesses that are poor at generating profits or sustaining cash flow. W. T. Grant was attempting to use this technique by closing older, smaller, and less profitable stores. Unfortunately, they were investing in larger stores too quickly.

When sales grow at a rate less than the sustainable growth rate, a surplus of funds should exist. If this situation is expected to be temporary, management can accumulate resources in anticipation of future growth. However, if slow growth is expected to persist, management must look at the following alternatives.

□ *Increase payouts.* The most direct response to idle resources is to increase dividend payout or repurchase shares from shareholders as a form of liquidating dividend.

□ *Purchase growth.* Acquire existing firms that offer growth prospects. It is necessary for management to understand the complexities of firms they consider acquiring, so that any acquisition will be successful.

Flows, Life Cycle, and Growth

The ROE model says nothing explicitly about cash flows. However, in the long run *sustainable growth implicitly incorporates the idea that adequate cash flows exist.* By definition, sustainable growth means prolonged growth. Such growth requires a business strategy that incorporates sufficient resources to support it. Thus the sustainable growth model captures the principal components of cash flow management and defines their basic relationships with one another. It defines key points within the financial goals that management must control, namely, return on sales, dividend payout, financial leverage, and the asset-to-sales ratio.

Accumulated evidence demonstrates that a business's competitive position, the growth rates of its markets, and its current strategic decisions have a predictable effect on cash flows. The most significant influences, derived from a study of interrelationships of ROE, cash flow, and market share, can be summarized as follows:

□ *Growth drains funds.* Participation in a strong market requires plenty of funds. Even if real market growth is minimal, inflation drains funds.

□ *Funds are generated by a relatively high market share.* And high ROE is associated with high market share. However, building a strong market position consumes large amounts of funds for new-product development, advertising, and promotion.

☐ *Sufficient funds can only be ensured through aggressive asset management.* Funds supply is strained by increasing investment-to-sales ratios.

The need for resources is dependent on the firm's position in its **life cycle**. The concept of life cycle is particularly important for financial managers because companies have different needs as they develop. Early recognition of these needs enables the financial manager to make better policy decisions.

The placement of a firm on the life cycle curve (see Fig. 6.4) is a matter of judgment, because no precise method exists for making that determination. Moreover, the phases of the life cycle are functional measures that do not represent time. For example, a firm could remain in the same position on the life cycle curve for many years.

Companies in the **pioneering phase** of the life cycle are heavy consumers of resources. Resources are needed to finance research and development and to market their products. During the **growth stage** of the cycle a strong demand for resources still exists. They are needed for investment in plant and equipment and working capital in order to increase market share. If management invested in efficient productive capacity in the pioneering stage, the firm may have a competitive advantage during the growth stage because of being a low-cost competitor.

During the growth stage of the life cycle prices fall rapidly and profits get squeezed. It follows that firms with low costs can tolerate declining prices better than those with high costs. In fact, the high-volume firm can drive prices down and force high-cost competitors out of the market. Therefore, the offensive strategy is to have sufficient resources to be

FIGURE 6.4
Life Cycle Curve

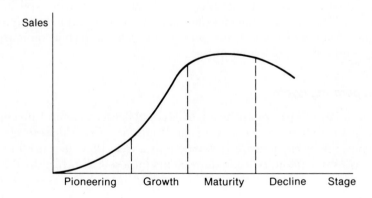

able to produce and sell a large volume quickly, thereby undercutting competition.

In the **mature stage** growth is minimal, and the demand for resources abates. The firm is established in its markets, and investments are made for purposes of product differentiation in order to protect market position. Some products of the firm in this stage are referred to as "cash cows." This term simply means that these products generate more cash than they need to support themselves. Management can use the excess cash to support new growth areas, to pay dividends, and to reduce debt.

In the **decline stage** negative growth exists. Management conserves resources in the sense that no investments are undertaken. The product is truly a "cash cow."

Cash Conversion Cycle

Cash is the net outcome of the activities of a business. When a firm functions efficiently, the operating cycle moves smoothly through its cash-to-inventory-to-receivables-to-cash stages, and final decisions are concerned with the distribution of residual cash. If this **cash conversion cycle** is interrupted or if the flow is distorted, financing problems ensue that may have grave consequences if they are not quickly worked out.

Management should focus its concern on avoiding default situations by emphasizing (1) the firm's ability to cover its obligations with cash flows from an employment of inventory and receivable investments within the normal course of the firm's operations, and (2) the sensitivity of these operating cash flows to changing sales and earnings during periods of economic hardship and growth. Operating cash flow coverage, rather than asset liquidation value, is the crucial element in liquidity analysis. It looks at the problem from the perspective of an ongoing entity.

Incorporating accounts receivable and inventory turnover measures into an operating cycle concept provides a more appropriate view of liquidity management than does reliance on the current or quick ratios as indicators of insolvency. These additional liquidity measures explicitly recognize that the life expectancies of some net working capital components depend upon the extent to which production, sales, and collections are neither instantaneous nor synchronized.

Operating Cycle

The cumulative days for turnover of accounts receivable and inventories provides a rough approximation of the length of a firm's **operating cycle**. The operating cycle concept is deficient as a cash flow measure in that it fails to consider the liquidity requirements imposed on a firm by the time

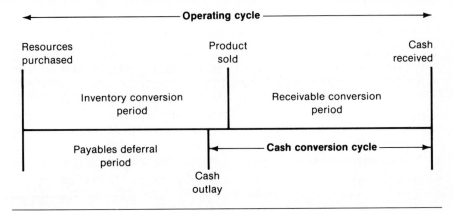

FIGURE 6.5
Operating and Cash Conversion Cycles

dimension of its current liquidity commitments. Integrating the time pattern of cash outflows required to satisfy current liabilities is as important for liquidity analysis as evaluating the time pattern of cash inflows generated by the conversion of its current asset investments. The outflow for current liabilities can be incorporated into the analysis by a payables turnover ratio. This ratio relates operating costs requiring current cash expenditures to the accounts payable and accrued payable liabilities created by the short-term deferral of these operating expenditures.

Definition of Cash Conversion Cycle

A simple extension of the operating cycle concept results in the cash conversion cycle.[10] The cash conversion cycle is defined as the time interval between actual cash expenditures for a firm's purchases of productive resources and the ultimate cash collection from the sale of the product. This integration of cash inflow and outflow patterns provides a fairly complete approach to liquidity analysis.

Figure 6.5 illustrates the cash conversion cycle. This diagram points out that a residual cash flow financing period (the cash conversion cycle) is influenced by both expansion and contraction in the three liquidity flow

---

[10]The cash conversion cycle was popularized by V. D. Richards and E. J. Laughlin in their article "A Cash Conversion Cycle Approach to Liquidity Analysis," *Financial Management* (Spring 1980): 32–38.

TABLE 6.6
W.T. Grant Company Cash Conversion Cycle for the Year Ended January 31
($ millions)

	1974	1973	1972	1971	1970
Sales	$1849	$1645	$1375	$1254	$1211
Cost of sales*	$1164	$1023	$ 846	$ 771	$ 756
Depreciation	13	12	11	10	9
Administration and other*	623	533	446	389	356
Total operating expenses	$1800	$1568	$1303	$1170	1121
Net operating income	$ 49	$ 77	$ 72	$ 84	$ 90
Cash and marketable securities	$ 46	$ 31	$ 50	$ 34	$ 33
Accounts receivable	599	543	477	420	368
Inventories	451	399	299	260	222
Other	7	7	5	5	5
Total current assets	$1103	$ 980	$ 831	$ 719	$ 628
Accounts payable and accrued expenses	$ 104	$ 104	$ 116	$ 105	$ 95
Taxes	0	8	9	14	10
Commercial paper	453	390	238	246	182
Total current liabilities	$ 557	$ 502	$ 363	$ 365	$ 287
Ratios					
Current ratio	1.98	1.95	2.29	1.97	2.19
Quick ratio	1.16	1.14	1.45	1.24	1.40
Current ratio excluding commercial paper	10.61	8.75	6.64	6.04	5.98
Quick ratio excluding commercial paper	6.20	5.13	4.22	3.82	3.82
Accounts receivable turnover	3.09	3.03	2.88	2.99	3.29
Inventory turnover (on cost)	2.58	2.56	2.83	2.97	3.41
Payables turnover (based on cost of sales and administration	17.18	13.89	10.34	9.75	10.59
Cash conversion cycle (days)					
Receivables	116.5	118.8	125.0	120.4	109.4
Inventory	139.5	140.6	127.2	127.2	105.6
Operating cycle	256.0	259.4	252.2	247.6	215.0
Less payables	21.0	25.9	34.8	36.9	34.0
Cash conversion cycle	235.0	233.5	217.4	210.7	181.0

*Assumed to be cash operating expenditures.

measures: the inventory conversion period, the receivables conversion period, and the payables deferral period. An increase in the length of the operating cycle without a concomitant lengthening of the payables deferral period creates additional liquidity management problems. Management will need to acquire additional *nonspontaneous* (negotiated) financing.

Mathematically, the cash conversion cycle is defined as follows:

$$
\begin{aligned}
\text{Cash conversion cycle} = 360 &\left[\frac{\text{inventory}}{\text{cost of sales}} + \frac{\text{receivables}}{\text{sales}} \right. \\
&\left. - \frac{(\text{accounts payable} + \text{other spontaneous current liabilities})}{\text{cash operating expenditures}} \right] \\
= 360 &\left(\frac{1}{\text{inventory turnover}} + \frac{1}{\text{accounts receivable turnover}} \right. \\
&\left. - \frac{1}{\text{accounts payable turnover}} \right).
\end{aligned}
\tag{6.5}
$$

Table 6.6 compares traditional ratios with the cash conversion cycle, using W. T. Grant's data. Although overall performance has deteriorated from levels attained in 1970, improvements have been made for the year ended January 31, 1974, relative to the previous year, as measured by the traditional ratios. However, the cash conversion cycle indicates continuing erosion in liquidity. The cash conversion cycle increased again in 1974, as it had in each of the previous years. This increase means that liquidity is worse, even though the traditional ratios signal improvement.

Cash Conversion Cycle versus Traditional Liquidity Ratios

In general, policies that result in a longer cash conversion cycle produce a larger commitment to cash and noncash current asset investments and a lesser ability to finance these investments with current liabilities. These policies can be expected to produce higher current and quick ratios. This result occurred for W. T. Grant (particularly when commercial paper obligations are excluded from the current and quick ratios). The implication is that higher values for the current and quick ratios are the result of a greater commitment of resources to less liquid forms of working capital. The inclusion of the commercial paper and the bank loans in the calculations causes the inverse relationship between the cash conversion cycle and traditional ratios to be blurred. In summary, trade creditors and the debt markets were apparently not aware of W. T. Grant's real and deteriorating liquidity position. Lenders felt secure in providing money to W. T. Grant.

Cash Conversion Cycle, ROE, and Growth

The cash conversion cycle should be inversely related to ROE and sustainable growth, as evidenced by the fact that the cash conversion cycle is a function of turnover ratios. As the turnover ratios for inventory and accounts receivable increase, and that for accounts payable decreases, *assuming all else remains constant,* ROE and sustainable growth increase while the cash conversion cycle decreases.

Thus the point made earlier that ROE management has little to say about cash flow can be relaxed. By optimizing the cash conversion cycle, management can improve ROE and sustainable growth. The better the cash conversion cycle, the greater is the availability of debt and equity capital that can be used to service maturing negotiated debt, to invest in new capacity or cost-saving equipment, and so on.

Cash Breakeven Analysis

Many of the traditional ratio techniques focus on analyzing profits and profitability with little direct concern about solvency. *Cash breakeven analysis* represents a useful first step toward analysis of solvency and is a logical extension to the cash conversion cycle. The **cash breakeven point** occurs when aggregate cash inflows just equal aggregate cash outflows.

Earning versus Cash Breakeven

Chapter 4 discussed traditional earnings breakeven. Generally, *earnings breakeven and cash breakeven do not coincide.* Cash breakeven usually requires a higher level of sales. Thus although an accounting profit is realized at the higher sales level, the firm simply breaks even on an aggregate cash flow basis.

ILLUSTRATION 6.2

Since insufficient data is available from W. T. Grant's financial statements to illustrate breakeven, assume the firm's cost and cash flow structure is as follows:

Cash operating fixed costs	$821,180
Depreciation and amortization	69,500
Interest on debt	69,750
Principal repayment on debt	30,000
Dividend to common shareholders	80,000
Variable cost/sales ratio	0.65
Effective tax rate	0.38

Table 6.7 summarizes the sales breakeven levels under two different assumptions about what should be included in fixed costs for traditional breakeven analysis and compares the results to cash breakeven. These

TABLE 6.7
Earnings versus Cash Breakeven

	Traditional breakeven		Cash breakeven
	Case 1	Case 2	
Sales	$2,544,800	$2,744,086	$2,930,723
Variable costs	1,654,120	1,783,656	1,904,970
Gross margin	$ 890,680	$ 960,430	$1,025,753
Fixed costs	890,680	960,430	960,430
Profit before tax	$ 0	$ 0	$ 65,323
Taxes	0	0	24,823
Net income	$ 0	$ 0	$ 40,500
Plus depreciation			69,500
Equals cash flow from operations			$ 110,000
Minus principal repayment			30,000
Minus dividends			80,000
Equals cash flow			$ 0

Note: In case 1 fixed costs include cash operating costs plus depreciation and amortization of $69,500. In case 2 fixed costs include case 1's fixed costs plus interest on debt.

breakeven levels have been calculated by starting at the bottom of the columns and working backward to determine sales. The traditional breakeven calculation, as discussed in Chapter 4, could have been used to find solutions for cases 1 and 2.

Cash breakeven indicates that sales must be about 6.8 percent higher than case 2 traditional earnings breakeven. Implicit in the cash breakeven calculation is the assumption of no change in accounts receivable, accounts payable, or inventory balances from the beginning of the period to the end of the period. Additionally, no expenditures for noncurrent assets have been made. If such expenditures were made for either net working capital items or fixed assets, they would be incorporated into the cash breakeven column of Table 6.7 in a manner similar to that used for principal and dividends. For instance, if net working capital investment increased $350,000, breakeven sales would need to be $4,543,626, a 55 percent increase over the $2,930,723 level (verify this result yourself, using the format of Table 6.7).

The company may not be able to meet this required cash breakeven sales level without adding additional capacity. For example, assume that another facility, costing $150,000, is required, as is the $350,000 increase in net working capital. At current costs and prices the additional space will allow the firm to sell $5 million worth of products. To acquire this space,

TABLE 6.8
Cash Breakeven with a New Facility and Additional Net Working Capital

Sales		$4,842,303
Variable costs		3,147,497
Gross margin		$1,694,806
Fixed costs:		
Before	$960,430	
Additional	27,500	
		987,930
Profit before taxes		$ 706,876
Taxes		268,613
Net income		$ 438,263
Plus depreciation:		
Old	$69,500	
New	15,000	
		84,500
Minus net working capital		350,000
Minus principal:		
Old	$30,000	
New	37,763	
		67,763
Minus dividends		80,000
Minus fixed assets		150,000
Plus long-term financing		125,000
Cash flow		$ 0

Note: Depreciation is included in fixed costs. The additional fixed costs consist of new interest payments and additional depreciation.

management will have to put $25,000 cash down and finance the balance of $125,000 at 10 percent with annual payments amortized over 3 years. The facility will be depreciated straight-line over 10 years.

Table 6.8 shows the new cash breakeven sales level to be $4,842,303. Additional sales of $1,911,580 are required to support the new facility and new net working capital investment.   □

Cash Breakeven Formula

It should be apparent from Table 6.8 that the cash breakeven sales level (*CBSL*) is based on the sources and uses concept and is similar to the statement of cash flows calculations. Indeed, the cash flow figure in Table 6.8 is saying that there is no change in the cash balance.

Rather than going through the detailed proforma income statement approach each time, one can determine the CBSL by applying the following equation:[11]

$$\text{CBSL} = \frac{\begin{array}{l}(\text{total fixed expenses})(1 - \text{tax rate}) \\ - \text{ depreciation expense} \\ + \text{ incremental use of balance sheet resources} \\ - \text{ incremental source of balance sheet resources}\end{array}}{(\text{contribution margin }\%)(1 - \text{tax rate})} \qquad (6.6)$$

ILLUSTRATION 6.3

To illustrate the formula, we use the data from Table 6.8:

$$\text{CBSL} = \frac{\$987,930(1 - 0.38) - \$84,500 + \$647,763 - \$125,000}{(1 - 0.65)(1 - 0.38)}$$

$$= \$4,842,303$$

The incremental use of balance-sheet resources of $647,763 consists of additional investment in working capital ($350,000), principal payments ($67,763), dividend payments ($80,000), and purchase of fixed assets ($150,000). The long-term financing arrangement of $125,000 represents the sole source of new resources on the balance sheet. □

The CBSL expression provides a simple technique for calculating the impact of additional investment, a desired profit or cash flow level, or a change in taxes and margin on cash breakeven sales levels. For instance, if management desires a cash flow of $10,000, this amount can be added to the numerator of the equation. Alternatively, simply dividing $10,000 by $(1 - 0.65)(1 - 0.38)$, indicates that sales must increase $46,083 beyond the current breakeven sales level of $4,842,303 to support the targeted cash flow level.

Cash Breakeven, ROE, and Cash Conversion Cycle

Changes in the cash breakeven level arising from net working capital accounts are directly correlated with cash conversion cycle. Since return on investment and cash conversion cycle are inversely related, the cash breakeven level and ROE must also be inversely related. Thus better manage-

---

[11]Total fixed costs in Eq. (6.6) include depreciation expense. When these fixed costs are multiplied by the tax rate, the depreciation expense provides a *tax shield*.

ment of cash and its flow results in improved shareholder wealth maximization.

Keep in mind, however, that useful though the cash breakeven point formula may be, it is not intended to replace cash budgeting (discussed in Chapter 8). *Cash breakeven analysis indicates the aggregate cash inflows and outflows and not their timing.* Timing is more critical than aggregate inflows and outflows. Only a cash budget can assess the timing risk.

Inflation-Adjusted Financial Analysis

According to economic theory, profit is the amount of money that may be withdrawn from a company and still leave its real capital untouched. Profit as calculated by conventional accounting procedures is more or less in line with this definition *if the quality of earnings are good and the purchasing power of money is stable.*

As Table 6.9 shows, approximately 84 percent of an American dollar's *purchasing power has been eroded by inflation* since World War II. Whenever there are various lengths between acquisition of inputs and realization of outputs, the time lag between acquisition and realization can cause these transactions to be measured by monetary units of different purchasing power, thereby raising reported accounting profit above its economic counterpart.

In most companies there are six major parties that lay claim to a share of the profit (and cash flow):

1. Managers through compensation.
2. Labor through wages and benefits.
3. Suppliers through payment for goods and services.
4. Government through income taxes.
5. Debtholders through amortization and interest.
6. Shareholders through dividends and capital gains.

During a period of inflation the upward bias of reported profit produced by conventional accounting often causes an unjustified withdrawal of resources from the company by the various claimants. For instance, dividends may be declared beyond the real earnings of the company. Income tax may withdraw some of the profit that is in fact only equity maintenance. Managers and labor may demand, and often receive, higher compensation based on illusory profit figures, which may in the long run endanger the company.

For a company to survive in the long run, its sales must at least equal the renewal value (costs) of the inputs used in generating the sales. Therefore only the income that is in excess of replacement requirements is **real profit**. According to this reasoning, in a period of inflation the historical

TABLE 6.9
Inflation in the United States (Based on the Consumer Price Index)

Year	Consumer price index (1967 = 100)	Rate of inflation	Purchasing power of a 1945 dollar
1945	53.9	2.6%	$1.00
1946	58.5	8.6	0.92
1947	66.9	14.2	0.81
1948	72.1	7.8	0.75
1949	71.4	−1.0	0.76
1950	72.1	1.0	0.75
1951	77.8	7.9	0.69
1952	79.5	2.2	0.68
1953	80.1	0.8	0.67
1954	80.5	0.5	0.67
1955	80.2	−0.3	0.67
1956	81.4	1.5	0.66
1957	84.3	3.6	0.64
1958	86.6	2.7	0.62
1959	87.3	0.8	0.62
1960	88.7	1.6	0.61
1961	89.6	1.0	0.60
1962	90.6	1.1	0.59
1963	91.7	1.2	0.59
1964	92.9	1.3	0.58
1965	94.5	1.7	0.57
1966	97.2	2.9	0.55
1967	100.0	2.9	0.54
1968	104.2	4.2	0.52
1969	109.8	5.4	0.49
1970	116.3	5.9	0.46
1971	121.3	3.7	0.44
1972	125.3	3.3	0.43
1973	133.1	6.2	0.41
1974	147.4	10.7	0.36
1975	161.2	9.4	0.33
1976	170.5	5.7	0.32
1977	181.5	6.4	0.30
1978	195.4	7.7	0.28
1979	217.4	11.3	0.26
1980	246.8	13.5	0.22
1981	272.4	10.3	0.20
1982	289.1	6.1	0.19
1983	298.4	3.2	0.19
1984	311.1	4.3	0.18
1985	322.2	3.6	0.17
1986	328.4	1.9	0.17
1987	340.4	3.7	0.16
1988	353.9	4.0	0.16

Source: U.S. Department of Labor, Bureau of Labor Statistics.

costs of asset inputs should be continually adjusted to replacement values. If this adjustment is made, current sales are matched with real current costs, and the bias of conventional profit calculation is greatly reduced.

Appraising the actual replacement cost of a company's existing assets is cumbersome and difficult; indeed, often it is not feasible in practice. A close estimate of replacement cost, which is feasible, can be obtained by using specific price indexes for asset revaluation. Revaluation by a general price level provides poorer estimates because of the divergence of individual price changes from the general one.

Replacement cost represents the cost, in current dollars, of replacing the productive capacity of an existing asset. It does not represent its sale value. Replacement is justified only if the economic value (the present value of future cash flows) of an asset exceeds its replacement cost. Thus replacement cost should be less than economic value to maintain long-run viability of the firm.

Financial versus Physical Assets and Capital

Usually, a company holds monetary (that is, financial) assets and liabilities in addition to nonmonetary (physical or real) assets and liabilities. The inflationary effect on most monetary assets and liabilities differs from that on nonmonetary assets and liabilities. Whereas the value of most nonmonetary assets and liabilities is, more or less, linked to price level, the value of most monetary assets and liabilities is usually not linked.

An asset or liability is said to be **monetary** if it is denominated in units of currency, and **nonmonetary** if it is not. Cash, marketable securities, and accounts receivable are monetary assets because when the assets mature, the company will receive a specified amount of currency. Inventories, plant and equipment, and land are nonmonetary assets whose ultimate value in units of currency depends, at least in part, on the future inflation rate. Most liabilities are monetary, while net worth (equity) is nonmonetary.

Since monetary assets are not linked to price level, during inflation they do not endow the company with potential gains, as is the case with nonmonetary assets. Thus the larger the share of monetary assets in the balance sheet, the fewer potential gains accrue to the company during a period of inflation.

ILLUSTRATION 6.4

Assume that a company has the following balance sheet at the beginning of the period:

Beginning Balance Sheet

Cash	$100	Equity	$300
Inventory	200		

If inflation level doubles during the year, and no transactions take place, then to be as well-off economically, the firm should have the following balance sheet at the end of the year:

Balance Sheet Required to Maintain a Constant Economic Position

Cash	$200	Equity	$300
Inventory	400	Purchasing power gains:	
		Cash	100
		Inventory	200

However, at the end of the period only $100 of cash will exist, and a purchasing power loss from holding a monetary asset will be experienced. Nonmonetary assets (e.g., inventory) do not represent a fixed claim; they retain their purchasing power. Thus the balance sheet adjusted for purchasing power will be as follows:

Balance Sheet Adjusted for Purchasing Power

Cash	$100	Equity	$300
Inventory	400	Purchasing power gain:	
		Inventory	200

□

Use of Inflation-Adjusted Financial Data

The rationale behind working capital ratios is that such current assets as marketable securities, accounts receivable, and inventory can be readily converted to cash in the event of an emergency. In an inflationary environment the historical cost conventions for valuing noncash current assets may not reflect the ability of the firm to raise cash by selling or pledging its current assets. For example, the LIFO method of inventory valuation leaves older, less inflated costs on the balance sheet, and so the book value LIFO inventory may be much lower than the amount of cash the firm could raise through sale.

Current value accounting provides that current assets and liability accounts be adjusted to reflect contemporary values so that they bear a closer relationship to cash-out values. Thus current value working capital ratios communicate more information about the short-run solvency of the firm.

Current value asset values also provide valuable information about the liquidity value of long-term assets. Although the degree of liquidity of long-term assets typically is less than that of working capital assets, a firm with a cushion of fixed assets is better able to quickly arrange sales, loans, or even leaseback arrangements to meet immediate cash needs.

Calculation of current cost can be complex. Since the purpose is to convey to you an appreciation of the need for understanding the impact of inflation on financial performance, simplifying assumptions have been used in the following discussion without impairing the overall conclusions that can be drawn from the analysis.

Inflation information can be used in conjunction with historical cost information to assess financial performance. Illustrative historic and *assumed* current cost income statements and balance sheets for W. T. Grant are summarized in Tables 6.10 and 6.11, respectively. Inflation rates shown in Table 6.9 were used to derive the current cost figures. The FASB did not require price-adjusted data to be reported until 1979 — thus the need to arbitrarily assume price-level effects for W. T. Grant. Appendix D of this chapter summarizes the rudiments of current cost accounting.

TABLE 6.10
W. T. Grant Company Comparative Income Statements for the Period Ended
January 31, 1974
($000)

	Historical cost	Current cost
Sales	$1,849,802	$1,849,802
Cost of sales	$1,163,998	$1,300,000
Depreciation	13,579	17,282
Selling and administrative	518,279	518,279
Leasing expense	105,367	105,367
Total costs	$1,801,223	$1,940,928
Net profit from operations	$ 48,579	$ (91,126)
Other income	7,033	7,033
Earnings before interest and taxes	$ 55,612	$ (84,093)
Interest expense	51,047	51,047
Earnings before taxes	$ 4,565	$ (135,140)
Taxes	787	787
Earnings before unconsolidated subsidiaries	$ 3,778	$ (135,927)
Equity in net earnings of unconsolidated subsidiaries	4,651	4,651
Net earnings	$ 8,429	
Current cost loss		$ (131,927)
Dividends	21,122	21,122
Retained earnings	$ (12,693)	$ (152,398)

TABLE 6.11
W. T. Grant Company Comparative Balance Sheets as of January 31, 1974
($000)

	Historical cost	Current cost
Assets		
Monetary assets:		
Cash and marketable securities	$ 45,951	$ 45,951
Receivables	598,799	598,799
Investment in debentures of unconsolidated subsidiaries	11,651	11,651
Unamortized debt expenses	1,362	1,362
Total monetary assets	$ 657,763	$ 657,763
Nonmonetary assets:		
Inventories	$ 450,637	$ 500,000
Property and equipment	100,984	128,525
Prepaid expenses	7,299	8,116
Stock of W.T. Grant and others	3,700	4,114
Investments in unconsolidated subsidiaries	32,600	36,248
Total nonmonetary assets	$ 595,220	$ 677,003
Total assets	$1,252,983	$1,334,766
Liabilities and equity		
Monetary liabilities:		
Current liabilities	$ 557,007	$ 557,007
Long-term debt	220,336	220,336
Indeterminate liabilities	151,902	151,902
Total liabilities	$ 929,245	$ 929,245
Monetary preferred stock	$ 7,465	$ 7,465
Nonmonetary equity:		
Shareholders' equity	$ 316,273	$ 398,056
Total liabilities and equity	$1,252,983	$1,334,766

ROE Analysis

Since ROE is considered a proxy for measuring wealth-maximizing performance, we may use it in measuring the impact inflation has on financial
results:

$$\text{ROE} = \text{ROS} \times \text{asset turnover} \times \text{leverage}$$

$$\text{ROE}_{\text{historical}} = 0.004 \times 1.476 \times 3.962 = 0.026 \tag{6.7}$$

$$\text{ROE}_{\text{current}} = \langle 0.071 \rangle \times 1.386 \times 3.353 = \langle 0.330 \rangle$$

These results dramatically illustrate the significant impact of inflation. The
use of *historical cost ignores the notion of economic asset value,* which is the pres-

ent value of future receipts generated by assets. The result is that the ROE based on historical costs is inflated. The current cost approach attempts to correct this problem by approximating current replacement costs (of the same age and same operating capacity). The following analysis of the ROE components provides insight into the problem.

Return on Sales

Calculation of profitability of sales (ROS) for W. T. Grant is very revealing and indicates serious problems with operations. The accounting (historical) ROS is 0.4 percent, whereas it is −7.1 percent for inflation-adjusted costs. Lower current cost net income is expected because costs increase as a result of higher costs of replacing inventories, property, and plant and equipment. Furthermore, W. T. Grant does not value its inventories on a LIFO basis and is thus more seriously affected than if it did, because LIFO acts as a partial surrogate for current cost. Also, firms with substantial physical assets or older physical assets are more affected by inflation than firms with few assets or new assets. Although W. T. Grant's physical assets are relatively new, they account for about 48 percent of total assets. Thus expenses like depreciation are increased under current cost accounting in order to reflect the cost of replacing the assets.

Another factor contributing to the variation in ROS is the effective income tax rate. This rate is almost always increased by inflation because income taxes are of a monetary nature not affected by inflation. Because income taxes are based on historical costs rather than current costs, the provision for taxes leverages the effect of increased costs on net income. In effect, inflation represents a tax on capital. For W. T. Grant the effective tax rate based on historical cost is 17.2 percent, whereas it is in excess of 100 percent under the current cost approach. W. T. Grant must pay taxes even though it has an inflation-adjusted operating loss.

Investment Turnover

W. T. Grant and other firms with low margins usually try to adopt a strategy of effective asset management to turn their investments over more frequently. Even so, inflation leaves its mark, particularly when physical assets comprise a significant proportion of total assets. The relatively long life of most plant assets means that there is a high probability for their replacement costs to depart substantially from original costs.

For W. T. Grant we estimate that fixed assets are understated from their replacement cost by about 27 percent (based on estimating the average age of fixed assets by dividing the accumulated depreciation by depreciation expense and then using the consumer price index in Table 6.9 to adjust them for price level). Since W. T. Grant does not use LIFO inventory accounting, historical inventories closely approximate replacement cost. However, as discussed previously, this practice leads to profits being misstated. Thus management is in a bind when it comes to deciding which technique to use for valuing inventories. With inflation a non-LIFO technique is better for approximating inventory value in the balance sheet, and LIFO is better for showing current cost in the income statement and the ROS calculation. Since consistency is required, whichever technique is used in presenting the balance sheet must also be used in the income statement.

The amount of net assets in the turnover ratio is increased for any unrealized holding gains. These unrealized gains occur on physical assets, such as inventories, property, and plant and equipment, because inflation increases the replacement cost of such assets. While such gains may be "realizable," they are not realized under present generally accepted accounting principles and do not apply to historical costs.

Leverage

An often-heard saying is that it is good to have fixed-rate debt during inflation because the debt is repaid in cheaper dollars in the future. This statement, however, assumes that creditors do not anticipate inflation and thus consistently lose money on their loans. The truth is that creditors attempt to anticipate what inflation will be by incorporating an inflation expectation into the interest rate they charge for the loans or by issuing variable-rate debt. Debtors only gain if creditors underanticipate the rate of inflation. Of course, the opposite is also true, and in such cases the creditors will gain even more than anticipated.

Leverage is measured in the ROE equation as total assets to total equity. The ratio measures the extent to which assets are financed and unrealized holding gains are leveraged by monetary liabilities. A high ratio signifies substantial debt or other monetary liabilities. Calculations based on current costs are always lower than those based on historical costs because holding gains are included in shareholders' equity when current costs are used. Inflation provides an incentive to increase the use of debt to the extent feasible without impairing liquidity in order to maximize the benefits to shareholders from holding physical assets.

Growth

An earlier section demonstrated that growth is positively associated with ROE and earnings retention. Since ROE based on historical accounting exceeds current cost ROE, inflation causes real growth to decline. Inflation also results in an implicit increase in dividend payout, which compounds the problem.

Since dividends represent a monetary flow, the retention ratio may be positive under the historical cost approach and negative under the current cost technique (note that W. T. Grant incurred negative retention under historical accounting techniques in 1974). The negative ratio thus causes negative growth in the current cost analysis. Effectively, the dividends represent liquidating dividends, although they would not be reflected as such under historical cost analysis or accounting techniques. Thus management has a critical role to play in monitoring inflation-adjusted performance and in explaining the problem to the various claimants of the organization.

In summary, current cost statements may give investors and managers an early warning of impending trouble and considerable lead time to take actions to preserve the company's financial integrity. An analyst investigates a large body of information when evaluating a company and projecting earnings, dividends, and cash flows. A substantial part, but not all, of this information is contained in the historical cost financial statements. Through the use of inflation-adjusted statements, the analyst is better able to look for insights that explain both change and change in the rate of change. The adverse cumulative effect of inflation may appear as a need for additional debt, a pressure on dividends to meet cash requirements, a dilution of the common shareholders' interest, or an inability to grow in real terms. Low-inflation-adjusted returns on capital may be a precursor of financial problems.

Summary

This chapter is an extension of traditional financial analysis discussed in Chapter 4. Imperfect indicators of a firm's liquidity have been discussed. They include a return-on-equity model, which is also used to determine debt levels and calculate the rate of sustainable growth. The firm's cash conversion cycle and cash breakeven were examined. Finally, the recasting of historical accounting statements to adjust for the impact of inflation was discussed.

Much interaction exists between these measures. Minimizing the cash conversion cycle and the cash breakeven point should lead to improved management of return on equity, sustainable growth, debt, and, of course, liquidity.

Ideally, analysis incorporates inflation's effects. Ignoring inflation can have a serious impact on both present and future performance. The use of historical accounting principles leads to gross overstatement of ROE during inflationary periods. If management fails to consider the impact of inflation on financial results, policy may be set that is inconsistent with sustainable growth and shareholder wealth maximization.

Key Concepts

Asset turnover
Cash breakeven
Cash conversion cycle
Cash inadequacy
Common-size statements
Debt capacity
Financial leverage
Life cycle cash needs
Maximization of ROE

Monetary versus nonmonetary assets/
  liabilities
Operating cycle
Profitability
Real profit
Significance of inflation
Sustainable growth
Yield curve

Appendix A

Relationship Between Residual Income and Return on Equity

Chapter 1 defined management's objective to be maximization of residual income (RI). This chapter uses return on equity (ROE) as the appropriate objective to maximize. The purpose of this appendix is to show the relationship between RI and ROE.

Residual income is defined as

$$RI = F(1 - \tau) - kI_o, \tag{A.1}$$

where F is net operating cash flow before tax, τ is the tax rate, k is the weighted average cost of capital, and I_o is investment.

This equation can be rewritten as

$$RI = NI_c + k_dD(1 - \tau) - kI_o. \tag{A.2}$$

where NI_c is after-tax net cash income and k_dD is the interest payment.

If both sides of Eq. (A.2) are divided by equity (E), and k is defined as the weighted average costs for debt (after taxes) and equity, the following equation results:

$$\frac{RI}{E} = \frac{NI_c}{E} + \frac{k_d(1 - \tau)D)}{E} - \left[\frac{k_d(1 - \tau)D}{I} + \frac{k_eE}{I} \right) \frac{I_o}{E}, \tag{A.3}$$

where k_e is the cost of equity. Recognizing that NI_c/E is ROE (in terms of cash flows) and simplifying the equation results in

$$\frac{RI}{E} = ROE - k_e \tag{A.4}$$

or

$$RI = NI_e - k_eE, \tag{A.5}$$

which can also be derived directly from Eq. (A.2) by substituting the debt and equity component cost of capitals for the weighted average cost of capital k.

Thus maximizing the residual income-to-equity ratio is equivalent to maximizing the difference between ROE and cost of equity, when ROE is defined in terms of cash flows and not accrual accounting profits.

Appendix B

Calculation of an ROE-Maximizing Capital Structure

Return-on-equity (ROE) models have received much attention as being useful for understanding management's stewardship of the firm. Modigliani and Miller's seminal article on corporate valuation in 1958, and books by Lerner and Carleton in 1966 and Fruhan in 1979 rely heavily on the concept of ROE to explain appropriate wealth-maximizing decisions by management.[12]

Return on equity is normally defined as

$$\text{ROE} = \frac{\text{profit after taxes}}{\text{equity}} = \frac{(rA - iD)(1 - \tau)}{E}, \tag{B.1}$$

where

r = EBIT/assets,

A = assets,

i = interest rate for debt,

D = debt (both short-term and long-term),

τ = corporate tax rate,

E = equity.

Since $A = D + E$, the equation can be rewritten as

$$\text{ROE} = \frac{[r(E + D) - iD](1 - \tau)}{E} = \left[r + (r - i)\frac{D}{E}\right](1 - \tau). \tag{B.2}$$

In the absence of taxes (i.e., $\tau = 0$), Eq. (B.2) is equivalent to Modigliani and Miller's (MM) proposition II. Inherent in MM's model are the implicit assumptions that the market values for the firm's debt and equity equal their book values and that the cost of debt is constant. Thus since both debt and equity sell at book values, the total cost of capital and the valuation placed upon the firm will not be affected by changes in the capital

---

[12]F. Modigliani and M. Miller, "The Cost of Capital, Corporate Finance, and the Theory of Investment," *American Economic Review* (June 1958): 261–97; E. M. Lerner and W. T. Carleton, *A Theory of Financial Analysis* (New York: Harcourt, Brace and World, 1966); W. E. Fruhan, Jr., *Financial Strategy: Studies on the Creation, Transfer, and Destruction of Shareholder Value* (Homewood, Ill.: Irwin, 1979).

structure. However, to get this result, MM assumed that the cost of equity k_e is a rising function of the debt-to-equity ratio D/E: $k_e = r + f(D/E)$. MM then proposed the following specification to describe the way the rate of discount changes as a function of the debt/equity ratio: $f(D/E) = (r - i)$ D/E, where, you recall, the cost of debt i is constant. Substituting this expression into the equation for k_e results in MM's proposition II. Note, however, that there is no inherent reason for choosing the precise functional form $f(D/E) = (r - i)D/E$ as a behavioral postulate. We could just as well assume that $f(D/E) > (r - i)D/E$, in which case the price would be less than the book value, or that $f(D/E) < (r - i)D/E$, in which case the price would be higher than its book value. Since Eq. (B.2) was derived as a pure accounting tautology, it follows that MM's proposition II by itself has no behavioral implications.

Relaxation of the unrealistic assumption that the cost of debt is constant as more debt is taken on allows a capital structure to be derived for maximizing return on equity. The proof follows.

The partial differentiation of Eq. (B.2) with respect to the leverage ratio is

$$\frac{\partial \text{ROE}}{\partial (D/E)} = \left\{ \frac{\partial r}{\partial (D/E)} + (r - i)\frac{\partial (D/E)}{\partial (D/E)} \right.$$
$$\left. + \left(\frac{D}{E}\right)\left[\frac{\partial r}{\partial (D/E)} - \frac{\partial i}{\partial (D/E)}\right] \right\}(1 - \tau). \tag{B.3}$$

Setting this equation equal to zero and solving in terms of D/E, in order to find the capital structure that maximizes return on equity, results in

$$\frac{D}{E} = \frac{(r - i) + \partial r/\partial (D/E)}{\partial i/\partial (D/E) - \partial r/\partial (D/E)}, \tag{B.4}$$

where $\partial r/\partial (D/E)$ and $\partial i/\partial (D/E)$ represent the change in r and i for a change in the debt/equity ratio, respectively.

To simplify the discussion, assume that the before-tax operating return on assets (r) does not change as the capital structure is changed; that is, $\partial r/\partial (D/E) = 0$. This assumption is reasonable whenever management realigns the capital structure without affecting the composition of the assets or their earning power. Hence ROE is maximized at the point where

$$\frac{D}{E} = \frac{r - i}{\partial i/\partial (D/E)}. \tag{B.5}$$

For example, if the interest schedule confronting management is approximated by the equation $i = a + b(D/E)^2$, then $\partial i/\partial (D/E)$, the change in the interest rate as the debt/equity ratio changes, is $2b(D/E)$. Substituting i and $\partial i/\partial (D/E)$ into Eq. (B.5) and solving for D/E leads to

$$\frac{D}{E} = \left(\frac{r - a}{3b}\right)^{1/2} \tag{B.6}$$

The solution to Eq. (B.6) represents the debt/equity capital structure that maximizes the ROE of the firm (assuming the interest schedule is appropriate).

ILLUSTRATION B.1

Assume that management has approached a number of lenders and asked them the following questions: If the debt/equity ratio is 0.25, how much would debt cost me? If it is 0.50, how much would debt cost me? And so on. If the interest schedule from this line of questioning is found to be $i = 0.10 + 0.117(D/E)^2$, then the optimal capital structure for maximizing ROE, when $r = 0.487$ and the tax rate is 50 percent, occurs when the debt/equity ratio is

$$\frac{D}{E} = \left(\frac{0.487 - 0.10}{3(0.117)} \right)^{1/2} = 1.05. \tag{B.7}$$

At this level the interest cost before taxes is

$$i = 0.10 + 0.117(1.05)^2 = 0.229, \tag{B.8}$$

and after-tax ROE is

$$\text{ROE} = (1 - 0.5)[0.487 + (0.487 - 0.229)(1.05)] = 0.379. \tag{B.9}$$

Deviations from the optimum result in lower ROE, as shown in Fig. B.1 and in the following illustration. Return on assets occurs where the curve intersects the ROE axis.   □

FIGURE B.1
ROE-Maximizing Leverage

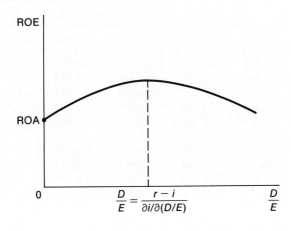

The return-on-equity maximization technique is contrasted with the EPS–EBIT analysis discussed in Chapter 4. Although EPS–EBIT analysis is frequently suggested as being appropriate for determining debt capacity, it is flawed as a wealth-maximizing criterion *whenever premiums paid for share repurchase result in a new equilibrium share price* (which is usually the case).

ILLUSTRATION B.2

Assume that the *pro forma* statement with all equity financing is EBIT = $9,905,000; assets = $20,340,000; tax rate = 50 percent; shares outstanding = 2,217,325; present stock price = $12 per share; and EPS = $2.23.

Assume that a minimum of $7 million debt can be issued; flotation costs are too expensive for anything less than this amount. If management replaces some equity with debt (which has no effect on assets or operating earnings), premiums payable for stock repurchases are as follows:

Up to $8 million   20% premium
$8.1 to $10 million   24% premium
Above $10.1 million   30% premium

From the interest rate schedule of Eq. (B.8) EPS is maximized when $8 million of debt is used, as shown in Table B.1. Note that all proposed debt levels result in an EPS as good as or higher than the firm's projection for an all-equity capital structure of $2.23.

The capital structure for ROE maximization is $10,418,000 debt and $9,922,000 equity (*D/E* = 1.05), with 1,549,504 shares outstanding. The EPS at the debt/equity ratio for ROE maximization is 7.6 percent lower than the EPS maximization debt level of $8 million.   □

TABLE B.1
Maximization of EPS ($000)

	Proposed debt levels					
	$7,000	$8,000	$9,000	$10,000	$10,418	$11,000
EBIT	$9,905	$9,905	$9,905	$9,905	$9,905	$9,905
Interest	926	1,193	1,563	2,094	2,386	2,885
Earnings	$8,979	$8,712	$8,342	$7,811	$7,519	$7,020
Taxes	4,490	4,356	4,171	3,906	3,760	3,510
Net income	$4,489	$4,356	$4,171	$3,905	$3,759	$3,510
Shares	1,731,214	1,661,769	1,612,486	1,545,282	1,549,504	1,512,197
EPS	$2.59	**$2.62**	$2.59	$2.53	$2.42	$2.32
D/E	0.525	0.648	0.794	0.967	1.050	1.123
ROE	33.7%	35.3%	36.8%	37.8%	**37.9%**	37.6%

TABLE B.1 (*Cont.*)

Interest Calculations

Debt	Interest schedule		Rate		Expense
$ 7,000	$i = 0.10 + 0.117(7000/13,340)^2$	=	0.132	→	$ 926
8,000	$i = 0.10 + 0.117(8000/12,340)^2$	=	0.149	→	1193
9,000	$i = 0.10 + 0.117(9000/11,340)^2$	=	0.174	→	1563
10,000	$i = 0.10 + 0.117(10,000/10,340)^2$	=	0.209	→	2094
10,418	$i = 0.10 + 0.117(10,418/9922)^2$	=	0.229	→	2386
11,000	$i = 0.10 + 0.117(11,000/9340)^2$	=	0.262	→	2885

Price-per-share calculations

Debt	Current price		1 + premium		New price		Shares retired
$7,000	$12	×	1.20	=	$14.40	→	486,111
8,000	12	×	1.20	=	14.40	→	555,555
9,000	12	×	1.24	=	14.88	→	604,839
10,000	12	×	1.24	=	14.88	→	672,043
10,418	12	×	1.30	=	15.60	→	667,821
11,000	12	×	1.30	=	15.60	→	705,128

Appendix C

Derivation of the Sustainable Growth Model

A key assumption of the sustainable growth model is that new equity is not raised to support growth. Additional equity is obtained from retained earnings, which are defined as

$$\text{Retained earnings} = \text{profits} - \text{dividends}$$
$$= (\text{return on sales}) \times \text{sales} - \text{dividends} \quad \text{(C.1)}$$
$$= R(S + \Delta S) \times (1 - p)$$

where R is return on sales, $S + \Delta S$ is last period's sales plus the increase in sales this period, and $1 - p$ is the retention ratio.

Because management wants to hold a targeted debt/equity ratio equal to D/E, each dollar of retained earnings allows debt to be increased in the proportion D/E. Thus,

$$\text{New debt} = \text{retained earnings} \times \text{targeted leverage}$$
$$= R(S + \Delta S) \times (1 - p) \times \frac{D}{E}. \quad \text{(C.2)}$$

The new debt and equity are then used to support growth in assets, which is measured as $\Delta S \times T$, where T is the asset/sales ratio.

Since the uses of funds must equal the sources of funds,

$$\Delta S \times T = R(S + \Delta S) \times (1 - p) \quad \text{(C.3)}$$
$$+ R(S + \Delta S) \times (1 - p) \times \frac{D}{E}.$$

Solving this equation algebraically results in the sustainable growth model, Eq. (6.3) in the text.

The alternative sustainable growth model (Eq. 6.4) is derived from this model by substituting A/S for T (since T is defined as A/S) and A/E for $(1 + D/E)$ (since $A = D + E$) and then multiplying both the numerator and the denominator by S (where $A = $ assets, $S = $ sales, $E = $ equity). Eliminating common terms and recognizing that $S \times R/E$ is ROE results in Eq. (6.4).

This formulation allows the dimension of capital structure (as embodied in ROE) to be explicitly recognized in growth analysis. Growth can be shown to be maximized, with respect to the capital structure, when

$$\frac{\partial(g_s)}{\partial(D/E)} = -\text{ROE}\frac{\partial p}{\partial(D/E)} + (1 - p)\frac{\partial(\text{ROE})}{\partial(D/E)} = 0. \quad \text{(C.4)}$$

If the retention rate $(1 - p)$ is fixed, then $\partial p/\partial(D/E) = 0$, and the growth-maximizing capital structure occurs when $\partial(\text{ROE})/\partial(D/E) = 0$. This point is the same point where ROE is maximized with respect to leverage, as shown earlier in Eq. (B.4). *Thus for a constant dividend payout policy, a management that concentrates its efforts on maximizing sustainable growth will also be meeting the primary objective of ROE maximization, that is, shareholder wealth maximization.*

Appendix D
Fundamentals of Current Cost Accounting

Our analysis of price-level effects differs from that of the accountants, as detailed for them in *FASB 33, Financial Reporting and Changing Prices* (superseded by FASB 89, which eliminates the calculation). We ignore adjusting the income statement for any holding gains. We do so intentionally to show the impact of inflation on the firm's production operations. Holding gains arise from holding assets, which increase in value with inflation. The objective of most businesses is to produce, sell, and profit from products that satisfy consumer demand. Most firms do not hoard assets to profit from holding gains. The accountant's inclusion of holding gains in the current cost income statement, in our opinion, detracts from the intent of isolating the influence of inflation on operations and management's ability to cope with it.

The following discussion provides a brief summary of the mechanics of current cost accounting. Deeper analysis can be found in an intermediate financial accounting book.

Adjustments to the Balance Sheet

Assets and liabilities are monetary if they are to be paid by currency; otherwise, they are physical. The company either receives or pays a specific amount of currency for monetary assets and liabilities, respectively. Thus these assets and liabilities are not restated for price changes. However, for physical assets current cost is the cost of replacing the asset by one of the same age and operating capacity. Current cost is usually approximated by using a specific price index to the book value of the asset.

Most liabilities are monetary, whereas equity is considered physical. Shareholders' equity is computed as the difference between adjusted assets and liabilities (that is, it is a plug figure).

Adjustments to the Income Statement

Sales are reported at current price levels when sold and therefore receive no adjustment. Cost of sales requires the following adjustment, since materials and labor were purchased in prior periods:

Beginning inventory (at historical cost)

+ purchases (at historical cost)

− ending inventory (at historical cost)

+ realized holding gain

= cost of sales (at current cost).

Realized holding gains (losses) are the difference between the current cost and the historical cost at the time of sale.

Selling and administrative expenses must be reflected at current cost. Unless these expenses are very late in being recorded and paid, current cost and historical cost will be the same.

Depreciation expense is adjusted to current cost as follows:

First cost of depreciable assets (historical cost)

− accumulated depreciation (historical cost)

+ first cost of depreciable assets (current cost)

= total

÷ 2

= average current cost balance

÷ useful life in years of the assets

= current cost depreciation expense.

Income taxes are reported at historical cost, which equals current cost.

Questions

1. Define the three major components of return on equity (ROE). What is the purpose of defining ROE in this manner?

2. How do common-size statements help an analyst understand a firm's financial condition?

3. Name some of the hidden problems in favorable return-on-sales and turnover ratios.

4. The leverage ratio in the ROE model, defined as total assets/equity, is also called the equity multiplier. It indicates the relation the debt of the firm has as a source of financing for the firm's assets. Discuss how this multiplier affects the firm's return on assets.

5. What does sustainable growth mean? How can managers manage sustainable growth? Does it affect liquidity?

6. Define the cash conversion cycle. Is it beneficial for managing liquidity? Explain.

7. How does cash breakeven analysis differ from traditional breakeven analysis? How is it useful for liquidity management?

8. What is the relationship among return on equity, sustainable growth, debt capacity, the cash conversion cycle, and the cash breakeven point?

9. How does an understanding of inflation accounting help one to manage liquidity? How does inflation accounting help satisfy the objective of maximizing shareholders' wealth?

Problems

1. Using the ROE model of Eq. (6.1) and the following data, calculate the return on assets and return on equity in both situations. Discuss your findings.

	No leverage	*Leverage*
Profit before interest and tax	$ 250	$ 250
Tax	40%	40%
Sales	1,000	1,000
Assets	1,500	1,500
Debt (8%)	0	750
Equity	1,500	750

The financial data in Table 6.12 are to be used in Problems 2–7. Make whatever assumptions you feel are necessary to answer the problems.

2. Calculate a common-size income statement and balance sheet. Comment on any significant changes.

3. Calculate return on equity for each year, using Eq. (6.1). Discuss apparent reasons for any change.

4. Calculate the sustainable growth rate for this year, using Eqs. (6.3) and (6.4). What is the actual growth rate? Discuss what management needs to do to ensure sustainable growth.

5. Calculate the cash conversion cycle for both years. Compare your results with calculated current ratios and quick ratios.

6. Calculate both the traditional operating breakeven sales level and the cash breakeven sales level for this year. Discuss the significance of your results.

7. Discuss how inflation affects your answers to Problems 2–6. What inflation information would you like to have to do a better analysis of the financial statements?

Problems 8–12 use the financial data for Homeland Variety Corporation given in Tables 4.5 and 4.6 of Chapter 4.

8. Develop common-size balance sheets and income statements for the years 1988 through 1990.

9. Estimate the sustainable growth rate for 1991, and discuss your answer. This problem requires you to do some projections for the year 1991.

10. Find the cash conversion cycle for the years 1988 through 1990, and discuss the results.

11. Find cash breakeven for the years 1989 and 1990, and discuss the results. Assume that no principal payments are made on the negotiated debt. How would your answers change if principal payments were made?

12. Evaluate the results of Homeland Variety, and comment on any differences from the analysis of Chapter 4.

TABLE 6.12
Financial Data

	This year	*Last year*
Balance Sheet		
Assets:		
Cash and short-term investments	$ 112,851	$ 140,690
Accounts receivable (net)	66,720	56,575
Inventory	20,848	17,798
Other current assets	33,521	31,667
Total current assets	$ 233,940	$ 246,730

TABLE 6.12 (*Cont.*)

	This year	Last year
Fixed assets (includes capitalized leases)	2,706,696	2,331,870
Less accumulated depreciation	479,548	386,933
Net fixed assets	$2,227,148	$1,944,937
Investment in other assets	182,281	162,339
Total assets	$2,643,369	$2,354,006
Liabilities:		
Accounts payable	$ 123,356	$ 161,641
Accrued liabilities	50,216	41,201
Accrued taxes	57,054	27,222
Current portion of long-term debt	38,756	44,243
Total current liabilities	$ 269,382	$ 274,307
Long-term debt	885,714	875,809
Capitalized lease obligations	84,076	90,314
Security deposits by franchises	59,651	54,633
Deferred income taxes	140,423	106,777
Total debt	$1,169,864	$1,401,840
Equity:		
Common stock issued and outstanding	4,515	4,515
Additional paid-in capital	93,508	93,508
Retained earnings	1,106,100	854,143
Total equity	$1,204,123	$ 952,166
Total liabilities and equity	$2,643,369	$2,954,006
Income statement:		
Sales	$2,215,463	$1,937,935
Cost of sales:		
Food and paper	660,869	602,647
Payroll	384,133	333,818
Rent	21,758	18,628
Rent (franchises)	27,791	23,725
Total	$1,094,551	$ 978,818
Gross margin	$1,120,912	$ 959,117
Expenses:		
General, selling and administrative	230,702	214,501
Depreciation and amortization	335,884	327,516
Earnings before interest and taxes	$ 554,326	$ 417,100
Interest charges	90,847	72,592
Profit before taxes	$ 463,479	$ 334,508
Income taxes	181,700	155,900
Profit after taxes	$ 281,779	$ 188,608
Earnings per share	$6.99	$4.68
Number of shares outstanding	40,300	40,300
Dividends per share	$.74	$.51
Dividends	$29,822	$20,553

PART III

Cash and
Risk Management

CHAPTER 7 □
Overview of Cash Management

Almost every business transaction involves cash, either at the time of the transaction or shortly after. Thus cash must be available to cover all purchases, and cash should result from every sale. Having cash available to cover business costs and utilizing it effectively after it is received is of vital importance for fulfilling the objective of maximizing shareholders' wealth.

The goal of cash management is to have enough cash when it is needed but to have as little excess cash as possible. Cash in itself is not a productive asset, because it earns nothing unless it is invested. A good treasurer minimizes the amount of cash on hand but is able to respond quickly to changing supply-and-demand relationships so that needs are satisfied.

The purpose of this chapter is to provide an overview of the basic principles of cash management.[1] The motives for holding cash and various near-cash instruments is deferred to the next chapter where they can be discussed with several techniques for minimizing cash balances. This chapter is devoted to understanding the true cash balance, discussing various methods to affect the speed of cash flows, examining important aspects of relationships with banks, and finally, surveying some international aspects of cash management.

Know the Cash Balance

Unless it is effectively controlled, cash has a tendency to accumulate or be deployed into numerous pools. For instance, payments are received at branch offices, bank accounts are established to support outlying plants,

---

[1]An excellent book on this subject is by M. C. Driscoll, *Cash Management: Corporate Strategies for Profit* (New York: John Wiley and Sons, 1983).

warehouses, or offices, and compensating balances are kept in these bank accounts to pay for bank services.

Many managers fail to recognize the potential of their cash system. Often substantial resources lie dormant for at least three reasons:

1. Accounting procedures misstate the cash balances.
2. Management has little understanding of the cash process.
3. Corporate policy hinders imaginative cash management.

Problem with Accounting Procedures

Generally, the amount of funds available to a company in its bank account is different from the cash balances indicated in the company's ledger. This difference is the cumulative result of a series of delays in payment of checks written by the company and the collection of checks received by the company. The difference is referred to as **float**. Checks written by the company result in **disbursement** (*positive*) **float**, which is an excess of bank net collected balances over corporate book balances. Conversely, checks received by the company and deposited in the banking system, but not yet shown by the bank, result in **deposit** (*negative*) **float** — an excess of book balances over bank net collected balances.

ILLUSTRATION 7.1

The following entries show disbursement and deposit floats.

Balance per bank statement, July 31	$42,165.10	
Balance per ledger, July 31	31,468.27	
Difference	$10,696.83	
Reconciliation:		
Outstanding checks	$15,830.47	(1)
Less: Deposit not recorded by		
bank	⟨4,700.00⟩	(2)
Customer check — NSF	⟨400.00⟩	
Bank charges	⟨33.64⟩	
Difference	$10,696.83	

Notes:
1. Disbursement (positive) float.
2. Deposit (negative) float.   □

Types of Float

Figure 7.1 outlines three types of floats found in the payment process. **Mail float** is the time the check is in the postal system. **Processing float** is the

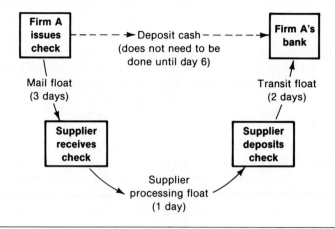

FIGURE 7.1
Deposit and Disbursement Floats

amount of time the company receiving the check takes to process it and deposit it in the bank. **Transit float** represents the amount of time it takes the check to clear the banking system and be charged against the company issuing the check. Obviously, a firm wants to maximize the positive float associated with disbursements to its suppliers and minimize the negative float associated with payments from its customers.

Another term for transit float is *Fed float.* The Federal Reserve Bank has established standard times for granting credit for checks deposited with it. These times are based upon the time required to present these checks to the banks on which they are drawn. Some checks are considered one-day items, and others are considered two-day items. Actual times in excess of these standard times are the responsibility of the Federal Reserve Bank. It bears the loss of the use of these funds for any extra time required to clear checks.

Understanding the Check Process

A basic need for the proper understanding of cash management is an understanding of how cash flows through commercial channels and, in particular, through the banking system. Many corporate decision makers have little or no knowledge of how checks are processed. A better understanding of the check-clearing process can aid in more effective use of company cash.

The **check-clearing process** involves several steps. Once a check is deposited into an account, the transaction information on the check is encoded. Since most checks are printed with codes for the bank of issue, the customer's account number, and routing information, it is the dollar amount that is added at this point, in magnetic ink. Machines that read the information sort the checks according to the bank of issue. The combination of encoding and sorting checks is known as processing.

The next step is for the check to be cleared. If it clears, settlement of accounts of the banks involved takes place. Settlement means the crediting and the debiting of funds to and from banks' accounts. After clearing, the check returns to the issuing bank, which debits the customer's accounts. Figure 7.2 summarizes the process.

A check may be sent to a payee in essentially two different ways. It can be mailed (or personally handed) to the payee, or it can be sent to a lockbox (discussed shortly). When checks are sent directly to the payee, the payee credits the payer's account, endorses the check, and deposits it in the bank. When checks are sent to a **lockbox**, the bank endorses and deposits the check and sends the payment-identifying data to the payee to be used in crediting the payer's account.

An advantage of using a lockbox is that it allows checks to be deposited sooner. They are processed by the lockbox bank during the night, or early in the day, so that on the same day the bank can charge them to the payer's account (if drawn on the bank where deposited) or send them to the local clearinghouse, to a correspondent bank, or to the Federal Reserve Bank or the Federal Reserve Regional Check Processing Center (RCPC) (if they are not drawn on the bank where deposited). A RCPC is a facility established in a commercially important city where there is no Federal Reserve Bank or branch. These facilities provide around-the-clock processing for checks and often allow institutions in the areas surrounding major cities the chance to receive same-day credit for their check deposits if certain deadlines are met.

A check does not follow a prescribed route in the collection process. Several alternatives exist at each step, and a check can take a number of different routes. A bank might handle the whole task itself. It processes the checks in-house and sends them directly to the issuing banks for clearing. Banks that follow this approach are usually large banks and use courier services to send checks directly to other banks for collection. A bank that does not handle the task itself might use several agents. A local service bureau encodes the checks, a correspondent bank sorts the checks, and a Federal Reserve facility clears the checks. A major reason for using these agents is to clear checks with distant banks. For the clearing of checks with local banks a local clearinghouse may exist that holds daily exchanges of checks among its members.

If a check is drawn on a bank outside the area of the local clearinghouse, the depositor bank has three options for collecting the funds. First, it can send the check directly to the bank on which drawn. This process is used normally when the sending bank has a correspondent relationship with the receiving bank and when it has a large number of checks to pre-

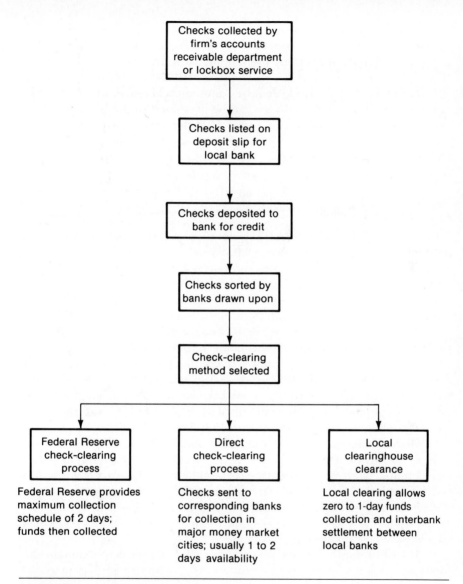

FIGURE 7.2
Check-Clearing Process

sent to it. The sending bank often uses a courier for this purpose if it has a large dollar volume of checks to present.

Second, the bank can send the check directly to the correspondent. The correspondent, in turn, presents the check to the bank on which it is drawn, either directly or through the local clearinghouse.

Third, the bank sends the check through the Federal Reserve system for clearing. This method usually involves two Federal Reserve banks or processing centers, one serving the sending bank and the other serving the receiving bank.

Most out-of-town checks require a minimum of one day from the time that they are deposited until they can be presented to the bank on which drawn. Some eastern banks, by using a courier plane, have been able to present checks to midwestern or western banks on the same day that they are received by the eastern bank. This technique greatly reduces the transit float.

Corporate Policy

An integral consideration regarding the type of cash management system used by the firm is the idea that a corporation's cash position depends upon all its asset and liability management policies. Cash is the result of all decisions involving investments in noncash assets, borrowing, the payment of dividends, and so on. Thus policies with respect to the minimum and maximum cash balances to maintain must be formulated.

The next chapter will discuss the minimum and maximum balances, using mathematical models. At this point we merely state that *the more control management exercises to maintain minimum balances, the more vulnerable the company is to random fluctuations in receipts and unexpected cash needs that were not forecast accurately.* Obviously, excess balances are nonearning assets and diminish profitability. Management must ascertain a cash management policy that contributes to maximization of shareholders' wealth.

Most managers set a minimum cash balance and do not want the balance to be less than this minimum except in periods of emergency. The idea is that regardless of how large cash outlays may be, except for emergencies, cash in excess of the established minimum should be available to meet any outlays. Such an attitude encourages the treasurer to maintain excess balances or to have excess standby lines of credit with banks, which require sizable compensating balances.

A second reason for keeping excess cash balances is to maintain the company's credit standing with creditors. As a matter of course, management takes advantage of all opportunities to buy goods and supplies on credit, but suppliers do not, as a matter of course, sell on credit to every company that asks for it. Suppliers sell on credit on the basis of an analysis of the prospective buyer's credit position. They evaluate the buyer to determine whether or not it has, or will have, the capacity to pay within the allowed credit period.

Maintaining good relations with banks from which it borrows is a third reason why management establishes minimum cash balances. Bankers argue that their lending capacity comes chiefly from deposits left with them by customers rather than from capital supplied by stockholders. Firms that wish to borrow should, therefore, contribute to this lending capacity by making it a practice to leave substantial balances with them.

Managing Cash Flows

Ever since the initiation of credit, management has sought ways to accelerate collection of outstanding accounts receivable, while at the same time it has searched for ways to slow the outflow of cash to satisfy trade payables without incurring penalties. Because checks are written on banks and deposited with banks, the speed at which checks are cleared is partially dependent on the banking system. The past several years have seen bankers join with management in actively pursuing ways to improve cash management practices — to accelerate cash inflows and delay cash outflows.

Accelerating Cash Inflows

Techniques available for accelerating cash flows include concentration banking, zero-balance accounts, lockbox services, preauthorized checks, preauthorized debits, depository transfer checks, wire transfers, and automated clearinghouse debits. Each of these is discussed in this section.

Concentration Banking

The primary goal of a **concentration banking** system is to channel all incoming cash into a cash pool for investment or borrowing offset so that no funds ever remain idle overnight. Such a system helps companies improve the timeliness and soundness of investment or borrowing decisions. The ability to achieve this goal is affected by the number of bank accounts and their locations and the bank services available. Figure 7.3 illustrates a cash concentration system.

There are three major types of balance control systems:

1. Automatic concentration
2. Discretionary concentration
3. Remote control

Automatic concentration can be achieved in one of three ways:

- *One operating account.* The cash control merits of this straightforward system are clear. However, a single operating account is probably unrealistic for any sizable company.
- *Automatic-transfer systems.* Account balances are transferred under standing instructions on set dates, on a periodic basis (e.g., each

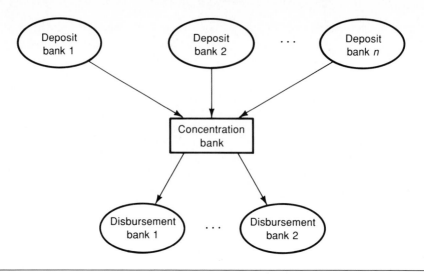

FIGURE 7.3
Cash Concentration System

Wednesday), on reaching a balance threshold (e.g., $12,000), or on some combination (e.g., each Wednesday, unless balances do not exceed $12,000). Automatic systems are a particularly effective means of managing specific operational accounts or of controlling cash balances where receivables and payables management is decentralized. Although float loss can occur, day-to-day policing is relieved.

□ *Cash concentration/pooling systems.* All balances held with one bank, irrespective of the branch, are consolidated for purposes of interest calculation. Pooling is particularly suited to situations where divisions or manufacturing and sales locations are spread throughout a country with a branch-banking network.

Discretionary concentration can be performed two ways:

□ *Depository transfer checks.* These checks are drawn on remote-control accounts and deposited to the main operating account. They are best used in conjunction with cash forecasts to concentrate cash in anticipation of funds inflows.

□ *Bank transfer.* Balances may be concentrated by instructing banks to transfer funds by telex, telephone, or other transfer mechanisms to the main bank operating account.

Remote control embraces all situations where funds are managed in one or more locations through unrelated operating accounts. The range is from single-location/several-account situations to autonomous accounts managed by division or manufacturing/sales personnel. A system of remote accounts supported by overdraft lines is common where large manufacturing or sales divisions are involved.

Zero-Balance Accounts

A product frequently used with an automatic concentration system is the **zero-balance account** (ZBA). ZBAs involve a formal interrelationship among deposit accounts in one institution, where the firm has a master or consolidation account and an unlimited number of subsidiary accounts. The ZBAs are special disbursement accounts having a zero dollar balance on which checks are written. As checks are drawn against the account, the amount to be funded is accumulated and the company is notified of the total amount needed to bring the account back to a zero balance. Funding can be done internally from a central control account or externally by transferring funds from other banks by wire, depository transfer checks, or other mechanisms.

ZBAs offer the following benefits:

□ Centralized cash control but decentralized disbursements

□ Elimination of petty cash accounts or balances at outlaying banks, thus freeing funds

□ Extension of disbursement float, thereby increasing the available cash pool

From a bank's perspective ZBAs require close attention. At some banks there is a one-day delay in funds collection. This delay occurs because the automated posting systems used by banks post credits to accounts first and then record the daily charges. With a ZBA the transfer of funds to the account is often for yesterday's overdraft. A negative balance is registered until funds are deposited. However, current daily charges are incurred, causing an overdraft for payment the next day. Many banks require an equivalent day's charges be on balance in the account to reduce the overdrawn status of the account.

The best use of a ZBA for most companies is in conjunction with an automated investment program where funds are transferred automatically to cover presentments, with the balance of the funding account invested each night. An extension of this service is the use of a money fund account with any number of money market funds available; high interest is earned, and checks or drafts are issued against the account. This technique eliminates the need for accurate daily forecasting since any excess funds continue to earn the money market rate.

Lockbox Services

A **lockbox** is a post office box to which the company's (payee's) bank has access. The purpose of the lockbox is to intercept corporate receivables so as to reduce the amount of mail float. The number and the location of lockboxes are very important since these factors affect the mailing time required for mail-in payments to reach the post office. Computer algorithms, using operations research techniques, are frequently employed to determine optimal lockbox locations that minimize mail float and the total cost of the system.

Several times a day the bank collects the lockbox receipts from the post office. The bank opens the receipts and deposits checks directly to the company's account. Details of the transactions are recorded either manually on a sheet of paper or in a machine-usable form such as a magnetic computer tape. Whatever form it takes, the accounts receivable department receives the customer name, the account number, and the amount paid, which it uses to update the accounts receivable ledger.

There are several advantages to a lockbox system. The processing float involved in physically handling receivables and depositing checks for collection is reduced. Collection time is reduced because checks are received at the post office, which reduces mail float time. The availability of funds is often increased by as much as one to four days over in-house remittance processing. This increase provides a significant infusion of liquid resources to the firm. Receivable-processing costs are often reduced. Reduced costs occur because banks that specialize in high-volume lockbox processing can provide the service for lower per-item cost than the firm. The company further benefits because its receivable data can be captured in machine-readable form by the bank and made available to update corporate accounts receivable records faster than that of the company using conventional in-house methods. A lockbox system is outlined in Fig. 7.4

ILLUSTRATION 7.2

Federal Equitable Company currently uses a centralized collection system. Customers make all payments to the central location. On average, customer mail float is 4 days. Processing float is generally 1.5 days. Average daily collections are $500,000.

The bank has recommended a lockbox system, which is expected to reduce the mail float by 2.5 days and processing float by 1 day.

The reduction in cash balances that can be realized using the lockbox is

3.5 days $\times$ $500,000 = $1,750,000.

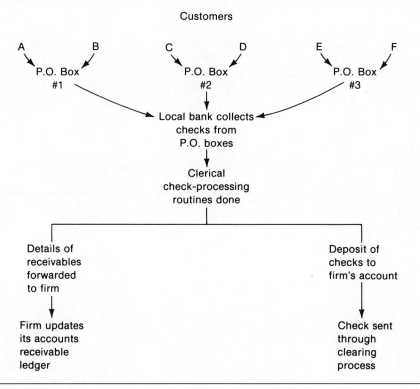

FIGURE 7.4
Lockbox System

The opportunity cost of the present system, assuming a rate of 9 percent, is

$$9\% \times \$1,750,000 = \$157,500.$$

If the annual cost of the lockbox system is \$90,000, then management can realize an incremental saving (i.e., residual income), which contributes to shareholder wealth maximization, of

$$\$157,500 - \$90,000 = \$67,500. \qquad \square$$

Preauthorized Checks

A **preauthorized check** (PAC) is a signatureless deposit check used for accelerating the collection of fixed payments. The customer signs an agreement with the corporation allowing the company — or, more usually, the company's bank — to write checks against the customer's account at speci-

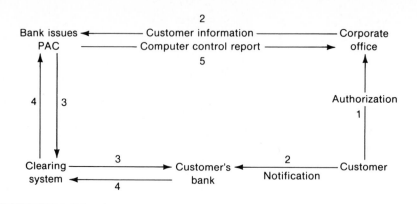

FIGURE 7.5
Preauthorized Check System

fied intervals for specified amounts. The company sends to its bank a file of customers and dates when PACs are to be produced. The bank maintains the file and updates it on instructions from the firm. The bank informs the firm, by means of a computer tape, of the deposit and the availability of funds. This process lowers the uncertainty in income flows and reduces mail float. Figure 7.5 illustrates the flow of a typical preauthorized check system.

Advantages to the cash management function from using PACs are as follows:

□ Increased cash flow predictability

□ Elimination of billing costs

□ Elimination of lockbox costs

□ Reduction of mail and processing floats

□ Reduction of corporate collection expenses

The disadvantages of PACs are the types of business transactions applicable to their use. Generally, PACs are only used with fixed-dollar repetitive types of payment (mortgage payments, insurance premiums, installment purchases). Another disadvantage, if it can be so classified, is the reluctance of customers to accept the arrangement.

Preauthorized Debits

A system very similar to PACs is the **preauthorized debit** (PAD). PADs are checkless or paperless transactions that require the customer's preauthorization to her or his bank to honor the selling firm's request. By the use of

PADs a customer's account is automatically charged for funds due on an agreed-upon date. Funds are electronically wired from the customer's bank to the firm's bank. The system accelerates the flow of cash and eliminates paperwork. Accounting entries to payer's and payee's accounts are made directly.

Although PADs are commonly used by insurance, finance, and utility companies, there is significant consumer resistance to this cash acceleration method. The accelerated payment and clearing process significantly reduces the disbursement float of the firm's customers. PADs eliminate in-transit mail time, late payments, and physical check processing.

Depository Transfer Checks

An inexpensive method of moving funds from one location to another is through the use of **depository transfer checks** (DTCs). A DTC is like a PAC in that it is a signatureless check. It does not require any corporate signature in order to move funds between two accounts for the same firm. DTCs are issued by the concentration bank against one of the firm's local collection banks on the basis of deposit information sent from the collection bank to the concentration bank, usually over a data-processing network. The concentration bank receives the deposit data and issues a check the same day for collection. Once the DTCs are presented at the local deposit banks, the checks deposited by the local collection office become collected funds. The bank then sends the information concerning the collected funds and their availability to the firm. Figure 7.6 illustrates the flow and the use of DTCs in a typical application.

The automated DTC system described here is the most commonly used system. Some firms, however, prefer to internally generate DTCs. This approach requires the cash manager to call daily to determine the amount of checks deposited. DTCs are then generated by the treasurer. The chief disadvantage of this approach is increased clerical costs for check production.

Wire Transfers

Wire transfers are alternatives to depository transfer checks. A criterion for the use of wire transfers is that all funds in excess of a base amount be automatically transferred from a local bank to a concentration bank. Alternatively, transfer may be initiated by the treasurer, who requests movement of funds from one bank to another. The bank where the funds presently reside sends a wire transfer of funds to the bank where management wants the funds to be.

There are two major wire services: the Federal Reserve Wire System (FEDWIRE), which is operated by the Federal Reserve Bank system, and

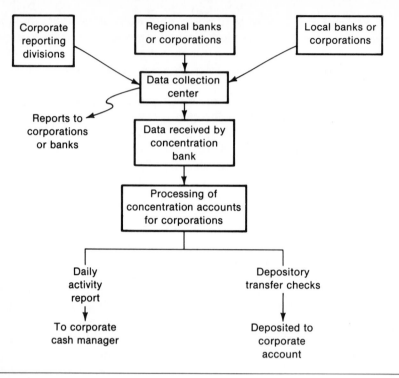

FIGURE 7.6
Depository Transfer Check System

the Bank Wire System (BANKWIRE), which is operated by a cooperative of bank members. Wire transfers are more costly than other transfer instruments, such as DTCs. However, same-day availability of funds is usually enough justification to incur the added expense.

Realistically, in determining whether DTCs are better to use than wire transfers, management needs to perform a marginal cost/benefit analysis. Daily depository amounts may be too small to justify DTCs. Transferring funds two or more times a week may be all that is necessary and may make the cost of a wire transfer feasible. The treasurer can calculate the cash balance that makes her or him indifferent between a DTC and a wire transfer by using the following equation:

$$\text{Indifference cash balance} = \frac{(\text{wire cost}) - (\text{DTC cost})}{(\text{daily opportunity cost of funds}) \times (\text{DTC float})} \tag{7.1}$$

If the cash balance to be transferred is in excess of the indifference amount, a wire transfer is used. Conversely, if the amount is less than the indifference amount, a DTC is used.

ILLUSTRATION 7.3

The bank charges $10 per wire transfer and $2 per DTC. If a DTC is used, it will be at least two days before the funds are available to the firm since the DTC has to be presented to the field office's local bank. The treasurer can invest funds overnight at an annual rate of 10 percent (net of transaction costs). The field office has $22,000 to be transferred. The treasurer must decide whether to use a wire or a DTC. The calculation is

Indifference cash balance

$$= \frac{\text{(wire cost)} - \text{(DTC cost)}}{\text{(daily opportunity cost of cash)} \times \text{(DTC float)}}$$

$$= \frac{\$10 - \$2}{(0.10/360) \times 2} = \$14,400.$$

A wire transfer should be used since the amount to be transferred exceeds the indifference balance.   □

There have been innovations in the use of wire transfers. Most notable is the ability of the treasurer to initiate a wire transfer from a computer terminal that interfaces either with the bank's computer-controlled wire system or with the data base of a third party that is used by the bank. Often this service is linked with other cash management services, such as programs that forecast a company's cash flows, and produces wire transfers that are less costly and that provide hard-copy verification of funds transferred.

Automated Clearinghouse Debit Transactions

Another method of transferring funds to and from another bank is through the use of automated clearinghouse (ACH) debit transactions. ACH debits can replicate wire transfers but are considerably cheaper, ranging from $0.10 to $0.50 per debit depending on the bank used.

An ACH debit is a transfer effected on a next-business-day basis (except when holidays are observed by the depository bank). For example, an ACH debit is created today against each one of a company's outlying accounts for the amount deposited today. Today's deposits will become available in the concentration account tomorrow, or one business day later.

Drafts

A *commercial draft* (also called a *bill of exchange*) gets a commitment from a buyer before goods are shipped. The seller has its bank draw a **draft** ordering payment by the customer and sends the draft and the shipping documents to the customer's bank. If payment is requested immediately, the draft is called a *sight draft;* otherwise it is referred to as a *time draft.* If the customer agrees, either funds are paid to the seller to cover the sight draft, or, if the draft is a time draft, the funds are segregated in the buyer's account and the shipping documents are given to the buyer.

If the customer's credit is questionable, the seller may ask the buyer to have its bank accept a time draft. In this situation, where the bank guarantees the buyer's obligation, the draft becomes known as a *banker's acceptance.* Banker's acceptances are frequently used in overseas trade since the credit standing of the bank is often better than the credit standing of the customer.

Another type of draft used in export trade is the *irrevocable letter of credit.* It provides the exporter (seller) with greater certainty of payment. The process is as follows. The buyer's bank sends the seller's bank a letter stating that it has established a credit payable to the seller at a bank in the United States. The seller then draws a draft on the customer's foreign bank but presents it to the bank in the United States together with the letter of credit and the shipping documents. The American bank arranges for the draft to be accepted or paid and forwards the documents to the customer's bank.

Delaying Outflows

The basic techniques used to manage cash outflows are staggered funding, controlled disbursements, ACH credits, and drafts. The first two techniques help the treasurer manage the *disbursement float* in an effort to decelerate cash outflows. This objective is accomplished by tracking disbursements through central bank accounts and not through the company's ledger. At 10 percent annual interest, an extra day's float on $1 million throughout the year is worth $100,000.[2]

Staggered Funding

Staggered funding is based on an analysis of historical clearing patterns. If clearing patterns of a firm's checks are reasonably predictable, then disbursement accounts can be funded on a percentage basis each business day. For example, if several checks have been mailed to suppliers today, the treasurer knows that on average she needs to transfer the following proportions of the total amount of checks written: 35 percent in two days, 50

---

[2]*Fortune* (April 18, 1983, p. 75) reported that Foremost-McKesson earned $5.5 million on float alone.

percent in three days, and the remaining 15 percent in four days. Typical applications of this technique are for dividend, interest, and payroll checks.

Obviously, there will be times when checks are presented in excess of the amount transferred to the account. So long as the treasurer has agreement from the bank that the bank will honor the checks with the payment of uncollected funds, then staggered funding is not a form of *check kiting*.[3]

Remote Disbursement

A technique for improving disbursement float is a process known as *remote disbursement*. In this practice the treasurer draws checks on several banks around the country. For any particular disbursement the treasurer chooses the bank that is the most removed from the seller in terms of float time.[4] Usually, the remote bank is located at some distance from the seller in a town where there is no Federal Reserve Bank or check-clearing center. Although the stated maximum Federal Reserve clearing time is two days, in reality it often takes longer for the physical check to be presented against the issuing bank.

The *Monetary Control Act of 1980* explicitly discourages remote disbursement. The act mandated that the Federal Reserve charge for Fed float at the federal funds rate and pass these charges on to the banking industry, which was expected to subsequently charge the remote-disbursing payer.

Controlled Disbursement

A technique that has gained widespread utilization now that remote disbursing has fallen out of favor is *controlled disbursement*. The concept of controlled disbursement is to provide early morning clearance information about the specific dollar amount clearing a zero-balance account (ZBA) of the firm. This information enables the treasurer to settle up the ZBA in one of several ways on a same-day basis. For example, the treasurer may use a wire transfer, may draw from a concentration account at a more central office of the same bank, or may invoke a standby line of credit. Any of these actions eliminates unnecessary balances in disbursement accounts.

The line between controlled and remote disbursement is so fine as to be obscure. Controlled disbursement still lets treasurers exploit the huge

---

[3]Kiting is defined as negotiable paper representing a fictitious transaction, as a bad check, used temporarily to sustain credit or raise money.

[4]L. J. Gitman, D. K. Forrester, and J. R. Forrester, Jr., "Maximizing Cash Disbursement Float," *Financial Management* (Summer 1976): 15–24, discuss a linear programming approach for maximizing disbursement float.

dollar potential in check-clearing float. It also enables treasurers to avoid idle checking account balances.

Controlled disbursement services are offered by a number of large banks through wholly owned subsidiaries or through branches that are located in less accessible areas such that check clearing is somewhat delayed. The key to effective controlled disbursement services is the bank's ability to provide a separate transit-routing number and to domicile all corporate accounts within that subsidiary or branch. It is desirable that this subsidiary or branch receive only one cash letter from the Federal Reserve daily, early in the morning, so that it can compute the dollar amount of clearances early each day and notify the corporate treasurer of the dollar amount required to cover disbursements. More frequent notifications make it difficult for the treasurer to know how much excess funds exist that can be invested.

A big city bank receives two or three check deliveries from the nearest Federal Reserve processing center. It also receives checks from the local clearinghouse, as well as *direct sends* — checks that arrive by courier from distant banks throughout the day and are debited to the customers' accounts that day. Thus big city banks cannot make the crucial early morning call to the treasurer. Illustration 7.4 provides an example of one company's approach to maximizing controlled disbursement float.

ILLUSTRATION 7.4

Levi Strauss, the San Francisco jeans manufacturer, uses a Troy printer and four controlled disbursement accounts at banks around the country. A Troy printer is a computer-controlled machine that turns out checks bearing the names of various banks. The printer automatically produces a check drawn on the bank that is most remote from the payee's postal ZIP code.   □

Payable-Through-Drafts

Payment by drafts provides improved disbursement control and improves the company's disbursement float. *Drafts,* as discussed earlier, are payable by the firm, not its bank. The drafts clear back to the bank they are issued on, which in turn presents them to the firm issuing them for review and approval before any payments are completed.

Automated Clearinghouse (ACH) Credits

ACH credits are frequently used for direct payroll deposits. Obviously, the employee's bank must be a member of an ACH network. Although the company gives up the disbursement float generated by paper-based pay-checks, it does reduce internal processing costs, and generates employee goodwill in many cases.

Role of Banks

As is apparent from the previous discussion, banks play an important role in moving funds. Banks make their profit by obtaining deposits of money borrowed from customers and relending these same funds at higher rates. Nonfinancial firms, however, in their pursuit of efficient cash management, desire to minimize idle cash and costs of services provided by banks. The apparent conflict between the firm and the bank is the heart of the relationship between firm and bank. Banks are essential to firms and must be treated as an important part of the firm's existence. So firms must provide sufficient deposit business if they expect the bank to help them. A firm can do so without putting too great a strain on its cash resources. That goal can be accomplished by concentrating as much banking activity as possible at one principal bank. What is a minimum working balance for a firm is usually a large and desirable account for a bank.

Working cash balances are significant in and of themselves. Often overlooked in the firm–bank relationship are such seemingly minor accounts as those set up for dividend payments, payrolls, branch petty cash, and other special purposes. It is a matter of average deposit balances. For example, all paychecks issued on the fifteenth of the month are not cashed that day. Meanwhile, the bank has the use of the funds in the payroll account.

Bank Evaluation

Traditionally, treasurers have evaluated banks when specific needs arose without systematically considering the bank's overall capabilities. This approach usually results in the company using an unnecessarily large group of banks.

Management's fundamental objective should be to develop bank relationships that provide the right mix of quality operational and financial services at a fair price. With respect to operational services the company's type of business, maturity, and size, and the frequency and the character of its cash flows are key factors. Low-volume, high-value cash flow firms have different operational needs than do high-volume, low-value cash flow businesses.

A basic rule to use for determining the number of operating banks is "the fewer the better." The use of a large number of operating banks is often rationalized on the basis of the reasoning that it provides competition among the banks, ensures credit availability during tight-money periods, provides specialized operational services, or satisfies some other business relationship. The use of too many banks, however, is counterproductive. Marginally profitable accounts seldom are granted favorable terms by the bank. Although availability to credit is important, strong relationships with fewer banks often can yield greater credit availability at better terms.

An important consideration in evaluating an existing bank or selecting a new one is the state of the bank's technology. If the company wants to use a bank for wire transfer purposes, does the bank system require initiation of each such transfer through an account officer? Or is there an on-line system available that the treasurer can access via a personal computer in his office? Does the bank have the technology that will enable it to allow the treasurer to access account balance information through a treasury workstation?

Is the bank a member of the National Automated Clearinghouse Association, which would allow it to transfer funds less expensively via the ACH network? If so, does the bank maintain only consumer-oriented ACH software, or does it also have software packages that facilitate corporation-to-corporation payments? Also, does the bank give the firm adequate control over periodic disbursements, particularly large-dollar items? The control that any bank can offer is affected by the number of Federal Reserve cash letters a bank receives during the day. The time at which the Fed presents the cash letters is another important factor. The best control is afforded by a bank that can report early in the day the value of all items to be presented against the company's account for that day.

Willingness

The most important service of most banks is the provision of credit. Without needed credit the firm may not be able to survive a period of economic hardship, take advantage of shareholder wealth-increasing investments, or have financial flexibility to conduct its affairs.

Here are some important considerations about credit:

□ Price of the credit relative to the price at other banks

□ Length of time it takes to receive approval for credit

□ Duration of the credit arrangement (the longer the better)

Senior management of the firm must foster the firm–bank relationship. If top management of the company and the bank have a good business relationship (and perhaps personal relationships), then difficult or rush situations may be resolved to the firm's benefit.

Ability

Management must determine whether a candidate bank fulfills the company's financial needs. This step requires answers to the following questions: What funding needs will the company have? What form will these funding needs take? What is the legal lending limit of the bank? If the company's needs exceed the legal limit of the bank, can the bank put together a syndicate of banks in order to meet the company's needs?

Management can segregate different types of funding into day-to-day needs, medium-term financing, and long-term requirements. It is not unusual to find different types of banks specializing in different kinds of financing.

Cost-Effective Operating Services

It is important for the company to have its banks provide high-quality competitively priced operating services for items such as deposits, lockboxes, paid checks, and account maintenance. Periodically, the treasurer requires access to particular expertise or operational capability from banks. The first is typically represented by domestic collections and disbursements, tax settlements, and balance-reporting systems. The second includes such elements as foreign exchange and export collections that can be segregated from main current account transactions.

Most banks want to provide a range of products and services to their customers and are less interested in relationships that involve only a single service. They prefer to be compensated in the form of balances rather than fees, although a growing number of banks are indifferent to the form of compensation if a relationship meets profitability targets. Balance compensation for credit lines has all but vanished from the large corporate banking market. The prime rate, historically the bellwether cost of borrowing for banks' most creditworthy customers, has been replaced by the London Interbank Offered Rate (LIBOR), daily Fed funds rate, and other more competitive price measures.

International Cash Management

Domestic cash management practices simply cannot be transferred to the international environment. The political, social, and economic environments are outside the control of cash managers but must be figured into policies, procedures, organizations, and so on. For instance, collecting cash, controlling balances, disbursing cash, and investing surplus funds are the primary activities of any treasury department. However, while a domestic treasury department operates within a self-contained banking system governed by one set of rules and procedures (well, almost), international treasury has to contend with a variety of banking systems each with its own distinct and often arbitrary conventions.

Different Banking Environments

A common problem experienced by international cash managers concerns a foreign country's banking practice of **value dating**. Value dating is akin to assigning float in the United States. Value dates assigned by foreign banks dictate when a transaction is completed for purposes of interest or funds availability, and are used by foreign banks as compensation for services. It is common for value dating to affect both ends of a payment transaction; for example, a bank executing a payment instruction on Tuesday may back-value the debit to the customer's account to Monday. The bank receiving the payment may then collect the funds and have use of those funds for a day or two before granting availability to the customer. This problem can be minimized either if one bank with a large global network of offices and an efficient international communications system is used, or if more than one bank is used, these banks are part of the Society for Worldwide Interbank Financial Telecommunications (SWIFT) network and it is used to facilitate transfer of funds at relatively low cost.

Bank Fees

Per-item handling charges vary from bank to bank and often are determined by the type of instrument used, destination of the payment, and amount of the payment. If a percentage of face value fee is imposed, companies making high-value transfers will find themselves footing relatively high transaction charges.

Each time a foreign exchange transaction is carried out, the company faces bank fees. Commissions usually are levied either at a flat rate or on a percentage basis. Bundling transactions reduces commissions. Specialized costs such as *netting*, discussed below, may be applicable.

Foreign Exchange Exposure[5]

In a world of fluctuating exchange rates, risk arises any time conversion takes place from one currency to another. Essentially, companies operating internationally face the following types of exchange risks:

---

[5]Hedging concepts discussed in Chapters 9 and 10 can be used to minimize this exposure.

□ *Transaction risk.* This occurs when the company receives funds or makes payments in a currency other than its own.

□ *Translation risk.* This is associated with translating foreign subsidiary balance sheets into the currency of the parent company.

□ *Economic risk.* This arises when companies expose themselves to exchange rate fluctuations by a future commitment to buy or sell at a fixed foreign currency price.

Foreign exchange exposure is encountered in each phase of the cash cycle. As a result, there are a variety of techniques that should be considered when faced with regular foreign exchange transactions:

□ Cover transactions on the *forward market.*[6]

□ Invoice in U.S. dollars, or buyer's currency if it is likely to appreciate, or in a strong third currency.

□ Offset expected receipts in one currency by making purchases in the same currency.

□ For intracompany flows, speed receipts that are likely to depreciate and delay payments likely to appreciate.

□ Obtain insurance against currency risks.

□ Establish multicurrency lines of credit.

International Funds Transfer

The combination of foreign exchange regulations in different countries, value dating, international communications, and national settlement systems can make international payments a harrowing experience. A key consideration is the currency of payment. U.S. dollars simplify matters, but this is a subject unto itself and will not be covered in this book. The following discussion simply pertains to moving funds to a foreign bank.

The cash manager must decide how fast settlement is to be made. If time is not of the essence, the simplest method is to mail a check drawn on the firm's local U.S. dollar account. Settlement can take from a few days to a few weeks. The next level of settlement is to use a *bank draft.* This is simply a check issued by a bank drawn on itself, a foreign branch, or a correspondent bank. Once again, settlement may take several days or even weeks since the draft must find its way to the bank of origin.

---

[6]A *forward exchange contract* is a binding contract between a firm and an international bank, in which the firm agrees to purchase a fixed amount of the needed foreign currency in exchange for dollars at an agreed exchange rate in, say, 120 days.

If time is more important, a *mail transfer* can be used. After the treasurer provides the firm's bank with the proper instructions, the bank then mails instructions to a correspondent bank to debit its account and credit the beneficiary's account with the payment. A speedier method is to telex a transfer.

If U.S. dollars are not the acceptable settlement currency, the process requires an additional step: purchase of foreign currency.

Netting

Netting is one of the most popular techniques used by larger companies with many *cross-border, intracompany cash flows*. Netting operates between entities within an organization and may be bilateral or multilateral, depending on the number of intersubsidiary payments. Clearly, some subsidiaries will be net payers and some net receivers of funds. Netting systems minimize the volume of dollars involved in intracompany payments between parent and subsidiaries and among subsidiaries, thereby freeing more cash for investments and other purposes.

In essence, netting involves the establishment of an extra step in the payment process. Although subsidiaries continue to invoice each other as usual, they do not affect settlement. On a prearranged date, they report the value of these transactions to a central department (or bank), which has responsibility for making settlement. The department converts all payables to a common currency, net all intersubsidiary flows and effect settlement, which results in each subsidiary making or receiving only one payment.

Figure 7.7 illustrates netting. The primary benefits of such a system are

□ reduced number of international payments, thus minimizing the group's foreign exchange commission, transaction exposure, and bank charges; and

□ improved central treasury control of local subsidiaries' cash positions.

One disadvantage is that netting is regulated in many countries and usually requires government approval before a system can begin operation. In fact, certain countries do not allow netting. A netting center must be in a country that is relatively free of exchange controls and where there is an active foreign exchange market.

Reinvoicing Center

A commonly used technique is to establish a separate legal entity to facilitate central control of cash and foreign exchange exposure. In common

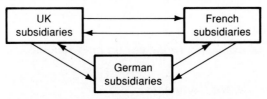

Before netting, all companies settle with each other, resulting in six separate foreign exchange transactions.

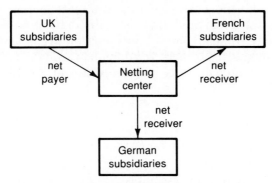

The netting center reduces the number of transactions from six to three.

FIGURE 7.7
Multinational Netting

with netting centers, a *reinvoicing center* represents an intermediary step in the flow of intracompany cash with the added benefit of favorable tax treatment. Instead of one subsidiary paying another in local currency, the transaction is routed via the reinvoicing center located in a favorable tax and exchange control location. The reinvoicing center, in effect, purchases goods from one subsidiary and then sells (reinvoices) them to another subsidiary. Although title to the goods passes to the reinvoicing center, actual possession does not. The selling subsidiary invoices the reinvoicing center in the selling subsidiary's currency; the reinvoicing center then bills the purchasing subsidiary in the purchasing subsidiary's local currency. This process eliminates the need for subsidiaries to conduct foreign exchange dealings from intracompany flows. All such dealings are controlled centrally, leading to the following benefits:

☐ The mechanism for grouping foreign exchange transactions ensures competitive rates, reduced commissions, and enhanced exposure management

□ Information concerning the company's cross-border transactions is centralized

□ There is favorable tax treatment on international transactions

Offshore Finance Company

An **offshore finance company** may operate as a separate legal entity or be established in conjunction with a reinvoicing center. These entities are established by multinational companies to centralize foreign transactions liquidity management and are located to optimize the group's tax position.

The finance company raises funds in its own right and then lends to other cash-short group members. In addition to acting as a source of liquidity, the finance company acts as an investment vehicle for cash-rich subsidiaries.

The benefits accruing from this type of structure generally include the following:

□ Financing at interest rates lower than subsidiaries could negotiate from their local sources

□ Access to the eurocapital markets

□ Pooling of excess cash for more favorable investment rates locally

□ In addition to fulfilling a pure financing role, and performing an exchange exposure management function (by providing intracompany currency loans), it assists subsidiaries in matching currency assets and liabilities, thus enhancing control of translation exposure.

Summary

This chapter provides an overview of cash management topics pertaining to understanding the cash balance, accelerating and delaying cash flows, evaluating the firm's relationship with its banks, and understanding some international cash management approaches. Knowing the cash balance requires an understanding of the differences between the bank balance and the ledger balance. Mail, processing, and transit floats, among other things, can cause these balances to differ. If management understands the check-clearing process, it can implement cash systems to make cash management more productive.

Several techniques were discussed for accelerating or decelerating cash flows. These techniques have received varying degrees of acceptance by customers, with the result that the most efficient form of cash management cannot always be routinely used by management. A second-best alternative must often be used.

An important aspect of cash management is the selection of banks and the relationship between the corporation and its banking system. Banks play an important intermediary role in the cash management system, and management should treat the banks as important partners. Failure to do so results in a less efficient cash management function of the company. But management cannot select just any banks. Banks used in the corporate cash management system must meet the needs of the company at a reasonable cost and provide the services and expertise needed by management.

Each year finds more firms expanding into international markets. This presents new liquidity problems to managers. They must have some understanding of international banking, decide how to move funds from one country to another, and manage foreign exchange risk. This chapter has provided but a glimpse at these problems.

Key Concepts

Automatic concentration
Check-clearing process
Concentration banking
Deposit float
Depository transfer check
Disbursement float
Discretionary concentration
Draft
Foreign exchange exposure
Lockbox

Mail float
Netting
Offshore finance company
Preauthorized check/debit
Processing float
Transit (fed) float
Value dating
Wire transfer
Zero-balance account

Questions

1. "Management can maintain too little as well as too much in its cash balances." Is this statement true? Explain.

2. What are the reasons that excess cash lies dormant?

3. What is the difference between a company's cash ledger balance and the bank's net collected balance?

4. Define and contrast mail float, processing float, and transit float.

5. Briefly describe some ways to accelerate cash inflows.

6. What is the difference between automatic concentration and discretionary concentration?

7. What are the advantages of concentration banking?

8. When one firm collects its outstanding accounts faster, another firm loses cash more rapidly. This situation is clearly a zero-sum game for the system as a whole. If there is no gain to business as a whole, why do firms try to streamline their collection system?

9. In the process of check clearing a bank has three options. The checks can be sent directly to the bank on which they were drawn, they can be sent directly to the correspondent bank, or they can be cleared through the Federal Reserve System. Give a brief description of each method.

10. Explain the meaning and operation of zero-balance accounts.

11. Compare and contrast the advantages of the lockbox system and the preauthorized check method.

12. Identify the meaning, the operation, and the differences between wire transfers and automatic clearinghouse (ACH) debit transactions.

13. Discuss the nature of staggered funding to a firm. Include in your answer a discussion of the risks involved in using this technique.

14. Discuss the role of banks in the collection procedures as they influence the acts of firm's managers.

15. Discuss the several types of risks that occur in international exchange transactions.

16. Cross-border cash flows are facilitated by a technique of netting transactions. Explain.

Problems

1. Prepare a bank reconciliation statement from the following data.

☐ The bank balance is $200,000.

☐ The bank has charged a service fee of $20 for the month, and it has not been recorded by the company.

☐ The company received but did not deposit $3200.

☐ The company maintains a compensating balance of $1500 with the bank.

☐ The company shows outstanding checks for its payables of $17,775.

2. The Chart Company deposits all receipts and makes all payments by check. The following information is available from the cash records.

April 30 Bank Reconciliation

Balance per bank	$11,020
Add: Deposits in transit	2,400
Deduct: Outstanding checks	(3,000)
Balance per books	$10,420

Month of May Results

	Per bank	Per books
Balance May 31	$14,000	$15,000
May deposits	6,400	9,180
May checks	5,000	4,200
May note collected (not in deposits)	2,000	
May bank service charge	20	
May NSF check of a customer returned — recorded by bank as a charge	400	

(a) Calculate the amount of the May 31 deposits in transit and outstanding checks.

(b) Given the information above, what is the May 31 adjusted cash balance? Label all work.

3. ABC, Inc., has $100,000 in the bank and issues $10,000 in checks on December 10. On the same day $20,000 in checks were written to the firm by different companies. How much cash is in ABC's bank account on December 15 under the following conditions?

(a) Disbursements clear in 9 days and incoming checks in 6 days.

(b) Disbursements clear in 6 days and incoming checks in 3 days.

(c) Disbursements clear in 4 days and incoming checks in 8 days.

4. Bruce, Inc., operates through 30 offices covering a 10-state region. Local managers have been mailing checks, totaling an average of $250,000 daily, to the home office in Lafayette. An average of 3 days elapse while checks are in the mail, ½ day while they are being processed in the home office, and 2 days while they are being collected through the banking system. Someone has recommended that each manager instruct the local bank to wire transfer receipts to the home office bank at 2:30 P.M. each day.

(a) How much money is presently tied up in float?

(b) What is the net amount of actual funds freed if each local bank requires a minimum compensating balance of $1500 be maintained at all times?

(c) For wire transfers costing $7 each, calculate the annual cost of this system, assuming 250 transfers per local bank per year. The annual cost of funds is 12 percent per annum before tax.

(d) Should the company use the wire transfer system?

(e) What other forms of cash acceleration should management look at?

5. Hurd Associates bills its customers and collects all accounts receivable at its home office, located in Buffalo, New York. Credit sales to customers in the Southwest region of the country are $48 million per year. Average mail, processing, deposit, and collection float is seven days. Valley Bank of Arizona has suggested a lockbox system be used. Valley Bank would collect the checks from the lockboxes and electronically transfer the collections daily to Hurd's main bank in Buffalo. It would also transmit records of collections to Hurd's computers on a daily basis. Valley requires a minimum compensating balance of $36,000 and charges a fee of $3600 per month for this service. Hurd's treasurer estimates that clerical and recordkeeping costs at the Buffalo office would be reduced by $1500 per month. Total float time would be reduced to three days.

(a) How much funds will be freed by the lockbox system? Use a 360-day year.

(b) How much is the actual annual dollar cost of the lockbox system?

(c) What is the net annual percentage cost of the funds freed?

(d) If the opportunity cost of funds for Hurd is 10 percent before taxes, should the system be adopted? Explain.

6. ValueDisc Corporation, headquartered in San Francisco, has annual credit sales of $840 million. It has eight regional sales offices. All billings and collections are handled by head office staff. Management is considering a concentration banking system under which collections are made by the regional offices and deposited in their local banks. Funds would then be transmitted to the concentration bank in San Francisco via wire transfers. The average elapsed time between customers' mailing checks and funds becoming available to the concentration bank would be reduced by one day. Compensating balances in the regional banks would be increased by $1,200,000. Annual service charges and regional office expenses would be increased $200,000 greater than the amount of reduction in the San Francisco headquarters.

(a) How much net cash is freed if the concentration banking system is adopted?

(b) What is the net annual cost of the actual funds freed? Ignore the opportunity cost at this point.

(c) If the opportunity cost of funds is 10 percent before tax, should the concentration banking system be adopted?

7.   The Wilt Company has an inventory turnover of 5 times and a receivables turnover of 11 times. All sales are on credit. It purchases inventory in equal amounts daily and issues checks to vendors 30 days after invoice dates. It experiences an average disbursement float of 9 days. Its clearing float on checks received from customers averages 4 days. Assume a 360-day year to answer the following questions, and adjust your answers to incorporate float.

   (a) What is the elapsed time of the operating cycle? How many days is the cash conversion cycle?

   (b) If daily payments for inventory are $100,000 and daily sales are $130,000, what are the total funds tied up in net working capital at any time according to the company's ledger? How is the ledger balance affected by receivable and disbursement float?

8.   The firm writes checks for $600,000 each day and charges them against its cash balance the same day (day 1). It takes the firm's bank, on average, three days (until day 4) to clear the checks. Any deposits made by the firm are credited to the firm's account by the bank on the same day.

   (a) Determine the firm's cash balance, per its ledger account and its bank account, if on day 1 the firm deposits $400,000.

   (b) If the firm continues to write $600,000 in checks daily, how much must it deposit, and when, in order to maintain a constant bank balance?

   (c) Assume that the bank borrowing rate is 12 percent. Determine whether the firm can profit by using float.

9.   Each business day Ashmore Corporation issues checks for $400,000 and deducts them from its cash ledger balance. Its bank clears the checks, on the average, the sixth business day after issue. Ashmore's $8 million bank line of credit requires a 10 percent compensating balance. This amount is in excess of any balance needed for precautionary purposes.

   (a) If the collected balance (available funds) is $800,000, how much must Ashmore deposit on days 1 through 6 to maintain this balance? Assume that collection patterns are stable and average two days of the checks included in Ashmore's deposits.

   (b) How much outgoing float does Ashmore have at all times?

   (c) What amount should Ashmore show on its books if the bank is to show a balance of $800,000?

10.   Westmount Mill wishes to determine whether or not it should establish a lockbox system with the local bank. The cost, net of any home office cost savings, would be $22,000 per year. The bank would require a $40,000 minimum balance be maintained. Collection float time would be reduced by four days. The firm's opportunity cost of funds is 12 percent before taxes. What is the breakeven credit sales level (where residual income equals zero)? Assume a 360-day year.

11. The Kitchener Company expects daily credit sales to average $50,000, with a standard deviation of $9500. A local bank has offered the company a lockbox service to accelerate cash receipts to the company. The bank requires a minimum balance of $45,000 be maintained and charges a service fee of $15,000 per year. The service would speed collection of credit sales by four days. Assume a 360-day year.

    (a) If the company's opportunity cost of capital is 12 percent, what is the breakeven credit sales level?

    (b) What is the probability of daily sales being below the breakeven sales level?

12. The following data indicates the intracompany sales for the current month.

	Detroit	Denver	London, U.K.	Calgary, Can.
Sales by:				
Detroit		2,500	4,750	3,200
Denver	3,950		2,900	4,000
London	5,000	1,900		4,000
Calgary	9,500	2,200	4,700	

Sales to:

Interpretation of the table is as follows. During the period Detroit sold $2,500 to Denver, $4,750 to London, and $3,200 to Calgary. All transactions are recorded in the currency of the selling branch.

    Exchange rates: £1 UK = $2.85 U.S.

                        $1 US = $1.20 Can.

                        £1 UK = $3.42 Can.

The firm uses a netting service provided by the ComericA Bank of Detroit. All monthly net balances are transferred to the Detroit office. Determine the amount of the total intracompany sales and the amount of the monthly settlement in U.S. currency.

CHAPTER 8 □
Minimizing Cash Balances

The most important of all the liquidity responsibilities of the financial manager is the managing of cash, both flows and balances. When a company is plagued with poor cash management, it often ignores its own carelessness with the explanation that it is in a dynamic industry where one cannot be sure of changes from one day to the next, a sink-or-swim market, and so on. In recent years increasing attention has been devoted to cash management to determine the appropriate level of safety and anticipation stocks of liquid assets and marketable securities. Management attention has focused on the proper level of liquidity with a view to reducing the risk of technical insolvency to an acceptable level. The higher the level of liquidity, the lower this risk.[1]

Any attempt to maintain a minimum cash balance that is consistent with maximization of shareholders' wealth requires input about liquidity needs and an understanding that cash has an economic value (an opportunity cost) apart from its being critical to the operations of the business. This value is the cost of possessing it, the cost of not lending it out for someone else to use, or the saving from not having to borrow it. In effect, cash is a commodity, an inventory. The cost of cash varies from day to day, and it varies significantly over months or years.

This chapter begins by discussing the motives for holding cash and then examines a number of cash management models that attempt to in-

---

[1] Theoretically, management should select the level of liquidity at which the expected cost of maintaining the optimal amount of liquidity exceeds the expected cost of bankruptcy by a margin large enough to satisfy the firm's shareholders.

corporate some of these motives. This discussion is followed by an examination of both monthly and daily cash budgets. The chapter concludes with
a discussion of liquidity indices.

Motives for Holding Cash

A broad definition of cash consists of currency and demand deposits and
near-money substitutes such as highly liquid securities. Management has
three basic motives for holding cash: (1) the transactions motive, (2) the
precautionary motive, (3) the speculative motive.

The **transactions motive** views cash strictly as a medium of exchange
to finance normal transactions, such as payments for supplies and wages.
The desired level of transactions balances depends to a great extent on the
size of the firm and the timing of cash inflows and outflows. Large firms
tend to make more transactions. If cash inflows and outflows are highly
synchronized, cash balances can be smaller.

The **precautionary motive** focuses on the ability of cash to provide
purchasing power in case of unexpected contingencies or unpredictable
opportunities. The precautionary balances act as a buffer against the increasing uncertainty of a changing industry, economy, and world. These
emergency balances are frequently provided through the use of a portfolio
of money market securities. Key attributes of this approach are high security or safety, high liquidity, and the immediate transferability from security to cash.

The **speculative motive** arises in connection with management's desire to have cash available to take advantage of profitable opportunities that
may arise unexpectedly. Management must have expectations of achieving
higher returns on such balances than are likely to be available in its normal
lines of business. Most firms do not hold cash balances for speculative
purposes.

Estimating the Level of Transaction Balances

The cash manager's goal should be to provide reasonable estimates of future cash positions that satisfy growth forecasts. Historically, the most common methods used to forecast aggregated transactional cash balances are
the ratio projection method, the adjusted-earnings method, and Baumol's
economic order quantity model.

Ratio Projection Method

The **ratio projection method** to estimating cash needs is couched in the
idea that management should keep a certain percentage of sales in its cash
account. The industry average is often suggested as the standard. This

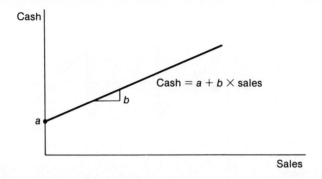

FIGURE 8.1
Ratio Approach to Forecasting the Cash Balance

technique assumes a fixed-regression slope (see Fig. 8.1) between cash and sales, which is most likely an inappropriate assumption because it fails to consider any economies of scale that can be realized.

Adjusted-Earnings Method

The **adjusted-earnings method** is nothing more than the *cash breakeven sales level* technique discussed in Chapter 6. It depends on the projected income statement and balance sheet. Naturally, the accuracy of the projected cash balance depends on the accuracy of the proforma profit and balance sheet projections.

Baumol Model

Early research by Baumol[2] on the demand for money used an *economic order quantity (EOQ)* model similar to that used in inventory management (which is discussed in Chapter 16). The idea is that cash is simply another commodity. Thus the **Baumol model** incorporates both the cost of holding idle cash balances and the cost of ordering (securing) cash. It can be used to find an optimal (average) cash balance.

The model incorporates the following features:

- A known demand for D dollars of cash for the period, which is used at a constant rate

[2]W. J. Baumol, "The Transactions Demand for Cash: An Inventory Theoretical Approach," *Quarterly Journal of Economics* (November 1952): 545–56.

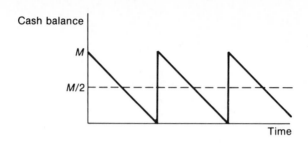

FIGURE 8.2
Baumol Cash Model

□ The requirement that all demands for payment from the cash balance be filled immediately

□ A lump cost of c dollars to transfer from assets into cash

□ An opportunity cost of $v/\$1$, which is equal to the interest forgone on bonds for the period

The last two items can be explained further as follows. If it is necessary to add to or subtract from the inventory of cash by making a transfer to or from a portfolio of securities, there is an order cost involved, partly in the form of internal clerical and decision-making costs and partly in the form of brokerage fees, wire transfer costs, and the like. In the other direction, if the cash manager tries to cut down these in-and-out costs by holding large cash balances, there is a substantial holding cost in the form of the interest lost on the funds tied up in the balance. The decision rule requires minimizing total costs with respect to the cash balance M. By the use of calculus, the optimal cash balance M is found to occur whenever

$$M = \left(\frac{2cD}{v}\right)^{1/2}, \tag{8.1}$$

the familiar square-root equation of the EOQ inventory model. The operating rule that leads to Eq. (8.1) generates a cash balance that takes the sawtooth pattern of Fig. 8.2. The average amount of cash is $M/2$.

ILLUSTRATION 8.1

The cash balance is steadily and uniformly drawn down over time. The cost of each transaction to secure cash is $50. Management anticipates $1,537,000 in cash outlays during the next six months. The company's annual opportunity cost of funds from investing in marketable securities is 8 percent, or 3.92 percent for six months $[(1.08)^{1/2} - 1 = 0.0392]$. All cash demands are met by selling marketable securities.

The optimal cash replenishment level is

$$M = \left(\frac{2 \times \$50 \times \$1,537,000}{0.0392}\right)^{1/2} = \$62,617.$$

Average cash balances are one-half of M, or \$31,309.   □

The next illustration highlights the fact that the optimal cash replenishment level, M, is not linearly related to the demand for dollars, D.

ILLUSTRATION 8.2

Cash outlays are anticipated to increase 10 percent over the \$1,537,000 amount used in Illustration 8.1. Ordering costs and opportunity costs are not expected to change. The optimal cash replenishment level is

$$M = \left(\frac{2 \times \$50 \times \$1,690,700}{0.0392}\right)^{1/2} = \$65,674.$$

or about 4.9 percent[3] greater than the level of Illustration 8.1   □

The Baumol model is oversimplified because it ignores uncertainty and assumes the treasurer makes cash disbursements at a uniform rate. However, the model is useful for proforma analysis since it does recognize opportunity costs, a feature missing in the *ratio projection model* and the *adjusted-earnings model*.

Miller–Orr Model

When cash flows are subject to much uncertainty, the **Miller–Orr model**[4] is more appropriate for estimating transactional balances. This model incorporates the following conditions:

□ The cash manager operates in a two-asset environment: One asset is the firm's cash balance, and the other is a separately managed port-

---

[3] An alternative calculation for the percentage change is $(1 + change)^{1/2} - 1$; for example, $(1 + 0.10)^{1/2} - 1 = 0.049$.

[4] M. H. Miller and D. Orr, "A Model for the Demand for Money by Firms," *Quarterly Journal of Economics* (July 1968): 413–35.

folio of liquid assets whose marginal and average yield is v percent per day.

□ Transfers between the two asset accounts can take place at any time at a marginal cost of c dollars per transfer. This cost is independent of the size of the transfer, the direction of the transfer, or the time since the previous transfer.

□ Transfers are regarded as taking place instantaneously.

□ Cash flows are completely stochastic (i.e., random).

□ The treasurer allows the cash balance to wander freely until it reaches either its lower bound, zero, or its upper bound, h, at which times a portfolio transfer is undertaken to restore the balance to a level of R. The policy implies that when the upper bound is hit, there is a lump-sum transfer from cash of $h - R$; and when the lower bound is triggered, a transfer of R is made to cash.

Management's objective is to minimize total costs associated with cash. By the use of stochastic calculus, the optimal return point (R) and average cash balance (ACB) in dollars are

$$R = \left(\frac{3c\sigma^2}{4v}\right)^{1/3},\tag{8.2}$$

$$\text{ACB} = \frac{4R}{3},\tag{8.3}$$

respectively, where σ^2 is the daily variance of changes in the cash balance. The upper bound is $h = 3R$, and the lower bound is a zero balance.

The optimal return point R is below the midpoint of the range over

FIGURE 8.3
Miller–Orr Model

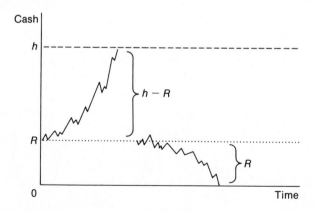

which the cash balance is allowed to wander. Thus there are more sales of portfolio assets than purchases. Figure 8.3 depicts the model.

The vertical orientation of the model can be changed without affecting the relationship between R and h. If management desires to keep a minimum balance, the lower limit becomes the minimum balance so desired. The Appendix to this chapter discusses an ad hoc technique for determining a minimum balance (for use with the Miller–Orr model or any other model or plan requiring a minimum balance).

ILLUSTRATION 8.3

Management uses the Miller–Orr model to monitor and control cash balances. It has estimated the transaction costs to be $75 per transaction, the annual opportunity cost of funds to be 11 percent, and the variance of daily cash flows to be $27,000. It is interested in determining the upper limit (h), the optimal return point (R), and the average cash balance. The minimum cash balance is zero. Assume a 360-day year. The calculations are as follows:

$$R = \left(\frac{3 \times 75 \times 27{,}000}{4 \times 0.11/360} \right)^{1/3} = \$1706,$$

$$h = 3 \times \$1706 = \$5118,$$

$$\text{Average balance} = \frac{4R}{3} = \$2275. \qquad \Box$$

Estimating the Level of Precautionary Balances

The level of precautionary balances is the difference between management's desired degree of liquidity and the level of transactional balances determined above. Part, or all, of this difference may be satisfied by line of credit or revolving credit agreements arranged with one or more banks. *Credit lines* are informal agreements and can be withdrawn by the bank at any time. A *revolving credit agreement* represents a legal commitment to lend up to a specified amount during a specified period. In return for this legal commitment, the firm must pay a commitment fee, typically between 0.25 and 0.5 percent, on the difference between the permitted maximum and the amount actually borrowed.

If lines of credit and/or revolving credit agreements do not provide satisfactory precautionary balances, the treasurer will use resources to invest in highly liquid marketable securities to attain the desired level.

A variety of investment alternatives serve as near-money substitutes. Table 8.1 summarizes the characteristics of principal near-money instruments.

TABLE 8.1
Near-Money Substitutes

Treasuries

Treasury bills
  Issued by U.S. Treasury with maturities of 91 days, 182 days, and 1 year. Yield earned
  by buying at a discount.
Treasury bonds and notes
  Issued by U.S. Treasury. Classified as a bond if maturity exceeds 10 years when issued;
  otherwise, classified as a note. Both bonds and notes issued in coupon-bearing form.

Agencies

Federal Farm Credit Bank (FFCB)
  Issues 3-, 6-, and until recently, 9-month coupon-bearing securities, discount notes with
  maturity of 5 to 270 days. The issues are of high quality but not explicitly guaranteed by
  the federal government.
Federal Home Loan Bank (FHLB)
  Issues both discount notes with maturities from 30 to 360 days and coupon-bearing
  issues. The issues are of high quality but are not explicitly guaranteed by the federal
  government.
Federal National Mortgage Association (FNMA or Fannie Mae)
  Issues discount notes with maturities of 30 to 360 days, and longer maturity capital
  debentures and coupon-bearing debt. Also issues pass-through securities backed by
  conventional (non-government-backed) mortgages.
Government National Mortgage Association (GNMA or Ginnie Mae)
  Issues mortgage pass-through securities which have the full faith and guarantee of the
  U.S. government for timely payment of both principal and interest on packages of
  mortgages issued by approved financial institutions. The mortgages are usually for 25 to
  30 years.
Federal Home Loan Mortgage Corporation (FHLMC or Freddie Mac)
  Issues guaranteed mortgage certificates and mortgage participation certificates based
  on conventional mortgages.
Collateralized Mortgage Obligation (CMO)
  Several variations of CMO exist. Example: $100 million worth of GNMAs, all having the
  same maturity and coupon rate, are divided into four blocks of $25 million each, labeled
  A, B, C, and Z. The trustee applies the monthly payments from groups B, C, and Z to
  group A, which causes A's principal to be returned much faster. Once all the principal has
  been paid off on group A, principal payments are then directed to group B. The effect is
  to shorten the average life of group A to 3 or 4 years, group B to about 7 years, group C
  to about 9 years, and lengthen group Z to about 20 years.

Money Markets

Eurodeposits
  The deposits are fixed, nonnegotiable, and usually pay interest at maturity. Maturities
  usually range from 1 day to 1 year.
Certificates of Deposit (CD)
  Issued by banks and thrifts for fixed periods from 2 weeks to a year. Earn a specific rate
  of interest, usually payable at maturity.
Commercial Paper
  Corporate IOUs usually sold on a discount basis, with maturities ranging from 1 to 270
  days. The paper is only as good as the reputation of the corporation issuing it.
Banker's Acceptances (BAs)
  Negotiable time drafts with maturities usually 1 to 6 months. They are high-quality
  instruments traded on a discount basis.
Repurchase Agreements (Repos)
  Issued by dealers in government securities, with maturities usually ranging from
  overnight to about 3 months. Repurchase price set higher than selling price.

Cash Budget

The techniques discussed to this point attempt to provide an estimate of cash needs by finding relationships (linear or otherwise) between cash and other factors, such as sales. These methods do not attempt to identify the various cash inflows and outflows. The **cash budget** is the primary technique used to capture these various flows. It attempts to identify the cash flows for periods short enough to permit the assurance that embarrassing intraperiod shortages will not be encountered.

In the short run a business can operate with an accounting loss. It cannot operate without cash for long. Table 8.2 shows a sampling of transactions to indicate why the results of operations forecasted in an income statement may be far different from the projected net change in cash balances expected to result from the cash transactions of the same period. This is followed by an illustration of a cash budget.

ILLUSTRATION 8.4

Management estimates total sales for the period January through July, based on actual sales for the immediate past quarter, to be as provided in Table 8.3.

The following assumptions are made:

1. All prices and costs remain constant.
2. Sales are 75 percent for credit and 25 percent for cash.
3. Sixty percent of credit sales are collected one month after the sale, 30 percent in the second month, and 10 percent in the third month. Bad-debt losses are insignificant.

TABLE 8.2
Effect of Transactions on Cash Budgets and Income Statements

	Income statement	Cash budget
Collection of receivables of past periods	Excluded	Included
Collection of current sales to customers	Included	Included
Current sales, payments in subsequent periods	Included	Excluded
Payment of current expenses	Included	Included
Depreciation charges	Included	Excluded
Purchase of new fixed assets for cash	Excluded	Included
Prepayment of expenses chargeable to later periods	Excluded	Included
Borrowing from banks	Excluded	Included
Repayment of bank loans	Excluded	Included
Payment of cash dividends to investors	Excluded	Included

TABLE 8.3
Sales: Past and Expected

Historical		Forecast			
October	$300,000	January	$150,000	April	$300,000
November	350,000	February	200,000	May	250,000
December	400,000	March	200,000	June	200,000
				July	300,000

4. The company operates with a 20 percent gross margin and purchases and pays for each month's anticipated sales in the preceding month.

5. Wages and salaries are as follows:

   January $30,000
   February $40,000
   March $50,000
   April $50,000
   May $40,000
   June $35,000

6. Rent is $2000 a month.

7. Interest on $500,000 of 16 percent bonds is due on the calendar quarter.

8. A tax prepayment of $50,000 is due in April.

9. A capital addition of $30,000 is planned in June.

10. The company has a cash balance of $100,000 at December 31, which is the minimum desired level.

11. Excess funds are invested in money market instruments and earn interest at 8 percent per annum in the month the excess occurs.

TABLE 8.4
Analysis of Sales ($00)

	Past			Future					
	Oct.	Nov.	Dec.	Jan.	Feb.	Mar.	Apr.	May	June
Cash	750	875	1000	375	500	500	750	625	500
Credit	2250	2625	3000	1125	1500	1500	2250	1875	1500
Total	3000	3500	4000	1500	2000	2000	3000	2500	2000

TABLE 8.5
Expected Cash Receipts ($00)

	Jan.	Feb.	Mar.	Apr.	May	June
Cash sales	375.0	500.0	500.0	750.0	625.0	500.0
Collections:						
60% prior month	1800.0	675.0	900.0	900.0	1350.0	1125.0
30% 2 months prior	787.5	900.0	337.5	450.0	450.0	675.0
10% 3 months prior	225.0	262.5	300.0	112.5	150.0	150.0
Total collections	3187.5	2337.5	2037.5	2212.5	2575.0	2450.0

12. Funds can be borrowed against a line of credit on a monthly basis at 16 percent per annum. Repayments are assumed to be made at the end of the following month if excess cash or marketable securities exist. Interest is payable on the end of the month in which the borrowing is incurred and is not accrued.

Given this information, a cash budget for the next six months is prepared. The total sales of the company are divided into cash and credit components according to assumption 2. Table 8.4 shows the results.

Since there is a lag in collections, according to assumption 3, the expected cash receipts are as set forth in Table 8.5.

Assumption 4 indicates that purchases are made in the month prior to sale and are paid in full in that month. Other cash outlays are calculated according to assumptions 5 through 9. Table 8.6 summarizes the payment patterns.

The monthly change in the firm's cash position, before any additional borrowing, is found by comparing the total cash receipts with the cash disbursements. Table 8.7 shows the expected change.

Any additional short-term borrowings or repayments depend on the

TABLE 8.6
Expected Cash Outlays ($00)

	Jan.	Feb.	Mar.	Apr.	May	June
Purchases (80% of sales)	1600	1600	2400	2000	1600	2400
Wages and salaries	300	400	500	500	400	350
Rent	20	20	20	20	20	20
Interest			200			200
Taxes payable				500		
New assets						300
Total	1920	2020	3120	3020	2020	3270

TABLE 8.7
Expected Change in Cash Before Additional Borrowing ($00)

	Jan.	Feb.	Mar.	Apr.	May	June
Cash receipts	3187.5	2337.5	2037.5	2212.5	2575.0	2450.0
Cash outlays	1920.0	2020.0	3120.0	3020.0	2020.0	3270.0
Surplus (shortage)	1267.5	317.5	(1082.5)	(807.5)	555.0	(820.0)

beginning cash position and the net change for the month. Borrowings and repayments happen according to assumptions 10 through 12 and are summarized in Table 8.8. □

Although Illustration 8.4 shows borrowing from a line of credit, management could possibly postpone payment to some of its suppliers and, in effect, rely more heavily on trade credit. Another option is to try and im-

TABLE 8.8
Expected Borrowings and Repayments ($00)

	Jan.	Feb.	Mar.	Apr.	May	June
Beginning balance	1000.0	1000.0	1000.0	1000.0	1000.0	1000.0
Gain (loss)	1267.5	317.5	(1082.5)	(807.5)	555.0	(820.0)
Total	2267.5	1317.5	(82.5)	192.5	1555.0	180.0
Borrowings*						
(repayments)				286.2	(286.2)	560.8
Interest†				(3.8)	(3.8)	(7.5)
(Investment)						
liquidation	(1267.5)	(317.5)	1082.5	525.1	(265.0)	266.7
Ending						
balance	1000.0	1000.0	1000.0	1000.0	1000.0	1000.0
Investment in securities						
Beginning balance	0	1276.0	1604.1	525.1	0	266.7
Additions						
(deletions)	1267.5	317.5	(1082.5)	(525.1)	265.0	(266.7)
Cumulative						
investments	1267.5	1593.5	521.6	0	265.0	0
Interest income	8.5	10.6	3.5	0	1.7	0
Ending						
balance	1276.0	1604.1	525.1	0	266.7	0

*Short-term loan required = (loss − short-term investment)/(1 − 0.16/12).
†Interest expense = (0.16/12) × (short-term loan).

prove the cash position by accelerating the flow of payments from its debtors.[5]

While the cash budget shows which factors give rise to changes in the firm's cash position, it does not take into account changes in other balance-sheet items and overall profitability. For example, is inventory being accumulated too rapidly? Is the ratio of sales to outstanding receivables being maintained at a reasonable level? What is the impact on profits? To answer questions such as these, one can look at how ROE changes as a result of changing cash budget scenarios in order to ascertain the effect on shareholders' wealth.

Daily Management of Cash Balances

Cash forecasts inevitably focus on period-end positions (e.g., end of month). However, management must not hesitate to change the focal point of the projection when another date has more meaning, such as weekly or daily cash forecasts. More important than the period-end balance is the range of cash positions during the period. Two models that can be used by the cash manager to manage daily cash balances are the *Miller–Orr model*, discussed earlier, and the *Stone model*.

Miller–Orr Revisited

The Miller–Orr model is appropriate for forecasting transactional balances under uncertainty. It is also very useful for monitoring daily cash balances since its control limits trigger buy and sell transactions for cash.

In a study[6] of Union Tank Car Company's daily cash management practices, the Miller–Orr model was superior to the ad hoc procedures utilized by the company's assistant treasurer. The model resulted in fewer transactions while allowing the firm to keep a lower average cash balance. This translates into increased wealth for shareholders.

Stone Model

In practice, cash managers attempt to consider not only their present cash position but also their cash position over the next few days. They attempt to minimize unnecessary transactions.

---

[5]One way of minimizing the risk associated with cash budgeting is to prepare several budgets, using different "optimistic" and "pessimistic" estimates for sales, collections, and payments.

[6]M. H. Miller and D. Orr, "An Application of Control-Limit Models to the Management of Corporate Cash Balances," in *Financial Research and Management Decisions*, edited by A. A. Robichek (John Wiley and Sons, 1967), pp. 133–51.

The Miller–Orr model automatically and immediately returns the cash balance to the target level R whenever a control limit is pierced. If cash forecasts, however crude, are available, such a system is generally not optimal. For example, consider a firm with an R of \$4 million and control limits of \$12 and \$0 million. If current balances are \$15 million, an automatic-return model such as Miller–Orr requires the purchase of \$11 million in marketable securities to restore the balance to \$4 million. If additional inflows of \$1 million and \$2 million are expected over the next two days, the cash manager might want to purchase \$14 million so that the balance would be back on target in two days rather than immediately. In another situation, if expected outflows of \$1 million and \$3 million are expected over the next two days, then the cash manager might prefer to make no purchase (depending on the overnight money rate), since the cash balance will automatically restore itself below the upper limit over the next two days.

The **Stone model** operationalizes such an approach. It uses two sets of control limits and does not depend on stochastic calculus to set the limits, as does the Miller–Orr model. Figure 8.4 depicts the structure. The target level of cash balances is denoted by TB. The outside set of control limits, denoted by U and L, are the upper and lower control limits for initiating consideration of a transaction. The inside limits are defined by $U - \alpha$ and $L + \alpha$. These inside limits determine whether a transaction will actually be made.

FIGURE 8.4
Stone Model

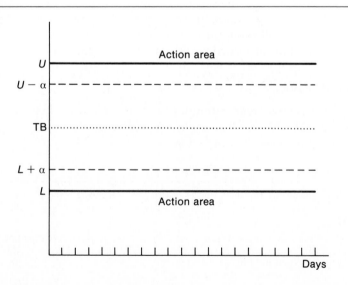

The cash manager takes no action unless the actual current cash balance is outside the outer control limits (i.e., in the action areas). When either U or L is exceeded, then the cash forecast for the next N days (which can be arbitrarily chosen) is used to determine whether a market security transaction should be made. A transaction is made only if the expected cash balance in N days exceeds the inner control limits, $U - \alpha$ or $L + \alpha$. If a transaction is made, the amount is such that expected balances in N days will be at the target level of cash balances, TB. This procedure is illustrated later.

Both the number of days used in the forecast and the values of the control limits are parameters that the cash manager assigns. Typical values of N are between 3 and 12 days. The limits can be assigned arbitrarily or calculated by using classical statistical techniques, $X \pm Z\sigma$; that is, the upper and lower limits are Z standard deviations from the mean. The value for Z indicates the probability of the measures being within the limits. A table for the area under the normal curve is included at the end of the book.

The Miller–Orr model could be used to determine the limits. Thus L could be assigned the value of 0, and U could be assigned the value of h. *The important point is that the values of the control limits and the length of the forecast period should not be treated as fixed parameters.* The target level of cash balances can be an adjusted target to reflect past history. If balances are either too low or too high for some part of the period, the cash manager can adjust the limits to bring the cash balance into line so that the average balance is as expected for the month.

Daily Cash Forecasting

Daily cash forecasts are needed to implement the Stone model. Unless cash flows are constant from day to day, dividing the monthly forecast by the number of days in the month to obtain daily forecasts is grossly inaccurate. A technique developed by Stone and Wood[7] can be used in which daily cash forecasts are separated into major items (which are easily identifiable) and many minor receipts and disbursements (which are not readily identifiable). Taxes, dividends, and debt repayments are examples of the first case. Payments for materials, office supplies, and telephone expenses are examples of the second case. The focus of daily cash forecasting is the forecasting of nonmajor items, with the major items subsequently added to this forecast to get a total daily budget.

With the use of bank statements, all major items can be identified and deleted from the analysis to derive the nonmajor flows. This deletion is

---

[7]B. K. Stone and R. A. Wood, "Daily Cash Forecasting: A Simple Method for Implementing the Distribution Approach," *Financial Management* (Fall 1977): 40–50.

necessary to minimize statistical bias of the results. The nonmajor flows can be identified for day of the month and day of the week. This identification allows the calculation of the proportion of the monthly cash flow that occurs on work day j as well as the calculation of the proportion of total flows occurring on weekday i.

The *day-of-the-week effect* attempts to recognize that many payers have payment patterns that are affected by the *day of the month*. For instance, many companies pay about the 25th of the month to bring their accounts to current status by the end of the month. The day-of-the-week effect also has a powerful impact on cash flows. For instance, many companies experience their greatest collection volume on Mondays, with a sharp drop-off on Tuesdays, and varying patterns over the remaining three days. The primary cause of this pattern is that, generally, checks mailed on Thursday and Friday are received on Monday.

Once having recognized the influence of the day-of-the-month and day-of-the-week effects, the cash manager can set up a simple model. For example, assume that Table 8.9 summarizes both day-of-the-month and day-of-the-week proportions for the month of March for the past three years, as well as the average values for this period. Furthermore, assume that the major items have been purged from the data.

Since the jth day of the month is not always the same day of the week, one must adjust the day-of-the-month proportion (a_j in Table 8.9) for any day-of-the-week proportion (d_i). A day-of-the-week effect may arise for the following reasons: Management may schedule payments to out-of-state vendors on a Thursday; payments to other vendors occur on Wednesday; payroll is paid on Friday; and collections are normally larger on Monday than any other day.

The day-of-the-week adjustment is accomplished by calculating a factor d_i^*. It is calculated as follows, where $\bar{d}$ represents the average of the d_i's:

	d_i	$d_i - \bar{d}$		d_i^*
M	0.264	0.264 − 0.200	=	0.064
T	0.203	0.203 − 0.200	=	0.003
W	0.153	0.153 − 0.200	=	−0.047
T	0.083	0.083 − 0.200	=	−0.117
F	0.297	0.297 − 0.200	=	0.097
	1.000		=	0

This information, coupled with that in Table 8.9, allows a monthly cash budget for nonmajor items to be distributed over the days of the month.

TABLE 8.9
Cash Flow Distributions*

	Last year	First prior year	Second prior year	Average (a_j)
Day of the month				
1	0.045	0.040	0.042	0.042
2	0.050	0.052	0.048	0.050
3	0.060	0.055	0.058	0.058
4	0.065	0.060	0.067	0.064
5	0.070	0.075	0.069	0.071
6	0.070	0.080	0.072	0.074
7	0.065	0.064	0.066	0.065
8	0.060	0.058	0.062	0.060
9	0.055	0.060	0.058	0.058
10	0.050	0.050	0.048	0.049
11	0.050	0.048	0.052	0.050
12	0.045	0.049	0.046	0.047
13	0.040	0.035	0.039	0.038
14	0.030	0.033	0.041	0.035
15	0.030	0.034	0.033	0.032
16	0.025	0.020	0.024	0.023
17	0.030	0.027	0.025	0.027
18	0.035	0.040	0.033	0.036
19	0.040	0.041	0.037	0.039
20	0.040	0.045	0.039	0.042
21	0.045	0.034	0.041	0.040
	1.000	1.000	1.000	1.000
Day of the week				(d_i)
M	0.250	0.280	0.260	0.264
T	0.200	0.220	0.190	0.203
W	0.150	0.140	0.170	0.153
T	0.100	0.080	0.070	0.083
F	0.300	0.280	0.310	0.297
	1.000	1.000	1.000	1.000

*Ideally, many more years of data should be used to compute the averages.

ILLUSTRATION 8.5

Assume that next March's monthly net cash budget for the minor items is $75,000, and the first workday of the month is a Friday. Table 8.10 summarizes the daily budget for these minor items. The total $a_j + d_i$* sums to more than 1.0 since an extra day, Friday, appears in the month. The normalized column restates the proportions so that they sum to 1.0. The daily budget column is simply each day's normalized factor times $75,000.

TABLE 8.10
Allocation of Monthly Budget by Day

Day	a_j	d_i^*	$a_j + d_i^*$	Normalized	Daily budget	Cumulative
1	0.042	0.097	0.139	0.1266	$ 9,493	$ 9,493
2	0.050	0.064	0.114	0.1033	7,751	17,244
3	0.058	0.003	0.061	0.0555	4,166	21,410
4	0.064	− 0.047	0.017	0.0159	1,193	22,603
5	0.071	− 0.117	− 0.046	− 0.0416	− 3,121	19,482
6	0.074	0.097	0.171	0.1554	11,655	31,137
7	0.065	0.064	0.129	0.1170	8,776	39,913
8	0.060	0.003	0.063	0.0577	4,325	44,238
9	0.058	− 0.047	0.011	0.0101	760	44,998
10	0.049	− 0.117	− 0.068	− 0.0615	− 4,611	40,387
11	0.050	0.097	0.147	0.1335	10,016	50,403
12	0.047	0.064	0.111	0.1007	7,555	57,958
13	0.038	0.003	0.041	0.0376	2,823	60,781
14	0.035	− 0.047	− 0.012	− 0.0108	− 810	59,971
15	0.032	− 0.117	− 0.085	− 0.0770	− 5,773	54,198
16	0.023	0.097	0.120	0.1090	8,172	62,370
17	0.027	0.064	0.091	0.0827	6,203	68,573
18	0.036	0.003	0.039	0.0360	2,697	71,270
19	0.039	− 0.047	− 0.008	− 0.0068	− 513	70,757
20	0.042	− 0.117	− 0.075	− 0.0680	− 5,102	65,655
21	0.040	0.097	0.137	0.1246	9,345	75,000
	1.000		1.097	1.0000	$75,000	

Note: Normalized calculation for day 1: 0.139/1.097 = 0.1266, where the numerator is the adjusted day-of-the-month factor and the denominator is the column total.

The major cash flow items need to be added to these daily projections. This information can then be used with Stone's control limit cash management model if the budget amount is still appropriate as of the time management must make a cash decision. If it is not, a new forecast must be made.   □

ILLUSTRATION 8.6

Assume that $10,000 and $30,000 are the lower (*L*) and upper (*U*) control limits, respectively. The inner control limits are arbitrarily set at ±$3000 of the outer control limits. Management has a target balance of $20,000, which is the balance on the first workday of March. Table 8.11 details the cash flows and management action based on a four-day moving forecast. This illustration assumes no major flow items for purposes of simplification.

TABLE 8.11
Cash Management Activities for a Four-Day Moving Forecast

Day	Beginning cash balance	Actual cash flow	Adjusted cash balance	Marketable securities	Ending cash balance	Next four-day forecast
1	$20,000	$ 8,430	$28,430		$28,430	
2	28,430	6,000	34,430	⟨$28,323⟩	6,107	13,893*
3	6,107	3,905	10,012		10,012	
4	10,012	1,214	11,226		11,226	
5	11,226	−5,000	6,226		6,226	25,516
6	6,226	7,281	13,507		13,507	
7	13,507	6,430	19,937		19,937	
8	19,937	8,700	28,637		28,637	
9	28,637	2,000	30,637	⟨26,420⟩	4,217	15,783
10	4,217	−7,308	−3,091		−3,091	19,584
11	−3,091	8,570	5,479	10,727	16,205	3,795
12	16,205	7,500	23,705		23,705	
13	23,705	3,111	26,816		26,816	
14	26,816	0	26,816		26,816	
15	26,816	−4,310	22,506		22,506	
16	22,506	8,325	30,831	⟨14,117⟩	16,714	3,286
17	16,714	6,415	23,129		23,129	
18	23,129	2,100	25,229		25,229	
19	25,229	−1,204	24,025		24,025	
20	24,025	−6,111	17,914		17,914	
21	17,914	9,512	27,426		27,426	
		$65,560		⟨$58,134⟩		

Average daily ending: cash balance = $17,890
marketable securities = $2,768

Note: A ⟨⟩ represents investment in marketable securities. No ⟨⟩ means a sale of marketable securities.
*This forecast is from Table 8.10, the daily cash budget column, for days 3 through 6.

The decision to buy or sell securities is based on the following decision rule: Whenever an outer limit is pierced, the forecasted cash flows for the next four days are summed to see whether the cash balance will be within the inner control limits by day 4. If it is, no action is taken. If it is not, then cash is transferred to marketable securities if the upper limit is violated, while marketable securities are sold and cash transferred to the cash account if the lower limit is violated. In Table 8.11 there were four transactions actually made, whereas the limits were violated six times. Thus in three cases the forecasted cash balances during the next four days were expected to bring the system back into control. The transactions for days 2, 9, 11, and 16 are shown in Table 8.12.

Table 8.13 summarizes the situation if a no-forecast policy exists. Marketable securities are bought once the upper limit is violated. They are sold

TABLE 8.12
Marketable Security Transactions

Day	Adjusted cash balance	Four-day forecast	Expected cash balance in four days	Target balance	Marketable securities	
2	$34,430	$13,893	$48,323	$20,000	$28,323	Buy
9	30,637	15,783	46,420	20,000	26,420	Buy
11	5,479	3,795	9,273	20,000	10,727	Sell
16	30,831	3,286	34,117	20,000	14,117	Buy

Note: No transaction is undertaken for day 5 even though the adjusted cash balance plus the next four-day forecast exceeds the outer upper control limit. In this example it is management's decision to avoid transactions when the situation goes from violating one limit to violating the opposite limit within the forecast period. Such a policy may not be the most efficient. Computer simulation of this possibility would help determine whether another decision rule would be more profitable.

TABLE 8.13
Cash Management Activities for a No-Forecast Policy

Day	Beginning cash balance	Actual cash flow	Adjusted cash balance	Marketable securities	Ending cash balance
1	$20,000	$ 8,430	$28,430		$28,430
2	28,430	6,000	34,430	($14,430)	20,000
3	20,000	3,905	23,905		23,905
4	23,905	1,214	25,119		25,119
5	25,119	−5,000	20,119		20,119
6	20,119	7,281	27,400		27,400
7	27,400	6,430	33,830	⟨13,830⟩	20,000
8	20,000	8,700	28,700		28,700
9	28,700	2,000	30,700	⟨10,700⟩	20,000
10	20,000	−7,308	12,692		12,692
11	12,692	8,570	21,262		21,262
12	21,262	7,500	28,762		28,762
13	28,762	3,111	31,873	⟨11,873⟩	20,000
14	20,000	0	20,000		20,000
15	20,000	−4,310	15,690		15,690
16	15,690	8,325	24,015		24,015
17	24,015	6,415	30,430	⟨10,430⟩	20,000
18	20,000	2,100	22,100		22,100
19	22,100	−1,204	20,896		20,896
20	20,896	−6,111	14,785		14,785
21	14,785	9,512	24,297		24,297
		$65,560		($61,263)	

Average daily ending: cash balance = $21,818
marketable securities = $2,917

Note: A ⟨⟩ represents investment in marketable securities.

whenever the lower limit is violated. The amount bought or sold restores the cash balance to its target level of $20,000.

A comparison of the next four-day forecast with the no-forecast model reveals two things: The no-forecast policy has a higher investment in marketable securities at the end of the period (which will not happen in all situations), and it has a higher average balance invested in cash for the period (which is likely to be the case in all situations).

The residual income model can be used to evaluate each approach. Table 8.14 summarizes the analysis and indicates that the forecast approach is clearly superior. The results are misstated somewhat since weekend effects are not included in the calculation of income earned from marketable security investments.

Different examples would produce similar results. The ability to forecast a few days' cash flows with a reasonable degree of accuracy generally results in lower investment in cash and a higher residual income amount.   □

TABLE 8.14
Residual Income Analysis of Forecasting Versus Not Forecasting

Investment		Days invested		Daily rate		Interest earned
Four-day forecast						
$28,323	×	7	×	0.1/360	=	$ 55.07
54,743	×	2	×	0.1/360	=	30.41
44,016	×	5	×	0.1/360	=	61.13
58,134	×	5	×	0.1/360	=	80.74
						$227.35
No forecast						
$14,430	×	5	×	0.1/360	=	$ 20.04
28,260	×	2	×	0.1/360	=	15.70
38,960	×	4	×	0.1/360	=	43.29
50,833	×	4	×	0.1/360	=	56.48
61,263	×	4	×	0.1/360	=	68.07
						$203.58

Residual income = cash flow − k(average cash + marketable securities investment)

$$RI_{fcst} = \$227.35 - 21 \times \frac{0.1}{360}(\$20,658) = \$106.85$$

$$RI_{no\ fcst} = \$203.58 - 21 \times \frac{0.1}{360}(\$24,735) = 59.29$$

Advantage to forecasting $47.56

Note: The average investment amounts are stated in Tables 8.11 and 8.13.

The results of Illustration 8.6 take on added importance as the size of the cash budget increases. For instance, if the amounts were in millions of dollars rather than thousands, the advantage to forecasting would be $47,560 for this *one month*, or $570,720 when annualized. Thus management could invest a considerable amount of resources (assuming it is done productively) in the cash management area, which would result in increased profits, cash flow, and shareholder wealth.

Liquidity Indices

Management frequently wants information presented in a summary form rather than in a detailed form. Chapter 4 indicated that there is disagreement about what constitutes a good summary indicator of liquidity. The liquidity indices discussed next are superior to those measures discussed in Chapter 4 since much of the data used in their calculation is taken directly from the cash budget.

Liquidity Flow Index (LFI)

The cash budget's ratio of operating cash flows to the required rate of cash outflow for a particular period is termed the **liquidity flow index (LFI)**.[8] The operating cash inflows are defined as the total amount of cash available per unit of time to meet required outflows without temporarily drawing on a line of credit or long-term funds or prejudicing future operating efficiency. The required rate of outflow is defined as the amount of obligations falling due for payment per unit of time.

Mathematically, the index is defined as

$$\text{LFI} = \frac{\begin{array}{c}\text{opening} \quad \text{expected} \quad \text{expected} \\ \text{cash} \quad + \quad \text{cash} \quad - \quad \text{closing} \\ \text{balances} \quad \text{receipts} \quad \text{cash balances}\end{array}}{\text{expected cash payments}} \tag{8.4}$$

$$= 1 + \frac{\text{lending} - \text{borrowing}}{\text{expected cash payments}}. \tag{8.4a}$$

The numerator in Eq. (8.4) represents cash inflows from the cash budget; the denominator is the cash budget's outflows. In the restated Eq. (8.4a), *lending* refers to excess funds that can be invested in marketable securities; *borrowing* means that excess funds accumulated from prior periods are liquidated and/or funds are borrowed externally.

---

[8]This measure was developed by K. W. Lemeke, "The Evaluation of Liquidity: An Analytical Study," *Journal of Accounting Research* (Spring 1970): 47–77.

ILLUSTRATION 8.7

The cash budget discussed in Illustration 8.4 is used to calculate the index (refer to Table 8.8). Table 8.15 summarizes the results.

Whenever the cumulative index drops below 1.0, this is indicative of having to borrow externally. Near cash balances have been liquidated to support the cash shortfall but are insufficient to cover it entirely. The index reveals that external borrowings take place in the months of April and June. The noncumulative index reveals cash outflows exceeding minimum required cash inflows in the months of March, April, and June (as indicated by values less than 1.0).

A comparison of cumulative and noncumulative indices indicates the near-cash balances (precautionary balances) are expected to be sufficient to support cash requirements in March (noncumulative index is less than 1.0, but the cumulative index is greater than 1.0) but not in April (when the cumulative index is less than 1.0). □

Over a period of time (say, 12 months), the LFI should tend to a numerical value of 1.0. An index much in excess of 1.0 suggests inefficient or ultraconservative cash management. An index much below 1.0 indicates cash deficiency problems. Minor variations in the ratio, either above or below the 1.0 level, can be due to seasonal influences, and while they can-

TABLE 8.15
Calculation of the Liquidity Flow Index ($00)

	January	February	March	April	May	June
Cumulative index						
Lend	1276.0	1604.1	525.1		266.7	
Borrow				286.2		560.8
Expected payments	1920.0	2020.0	3120.0	3023.8	2310.0	3277.5
Index	1.67	1.79	1.17	0.91	1.12	0.83
Noncumulative index						
Lend	1276.0	328.1			266.7	
Borrow			1079.0	807.5		820.0
Expected payments	1920.0	2020.0	3120.0	3023.8	2310.0	3277.5
Index	1.67	1.16	0.65	0.73	1.12	0.75

Notes:

1. *Lend* includes interest earned on invested principal. *Expected payments* include operating cash outlays, interest, and principal payments.

2. Data for the calculations come from Tables 8.6 and 8.8. For example, May's expected payments consist of $2020 operating cash outlays + $286.2 principal repayment + $3.8 interest payment.

not be ignored, generally they require only minor attention, as is apparently the situation in Illustration 8.7.

Although the ratio can be calculated by using data of varying period lengths, if the time is too long (quarterly or annual periods), two limitations are evident. First, much of the data would be outdated by the time of reporting and may be of little use for projecting cash flows. Second, longer periods smooth out intrayear fluctuations. Thus cash flow problems may not be discovered soon enough.

Relative Liquidity Index (RLI)

The **relative liquidity index**[9] measures the extent to which deviations in net cash flows, during some time period, are covered by cash on hand, unused lines of credit, and cash generated by operations. The index is a component of a complex mathematical process that gives the likelihood that the firm will become temporarily insolvent. This mathematical process provides the index with a strong theoretical base, which is lacking with most liquidity ratios. The index is defined as follows:

$$\text{RLI} = \frac{\begin{array}{c}\text{initial liquid}\\ \text{reserve}\end{array} + \begin{array}{c}\text{total anticipated net cash flow}\\ \text{during the analysis horizon}\end{array}}{\begin{array}{c}\text{uncertainty about net cash flow during the analysis}\\ \text{horizon as measured by the standard deviation}\end{array}} \qquad (8.5)$$

$$= \frac{L_o + \mu\sigma}{\sigma\sqrt{T}} \qquad (8.5\text{a})$$

where T is the length of the analysis horizon in months.

The index is the ratio of cash flow resources to potential cash flow requirements. Low values of the RLI correspond to increased probabilities of technical insolvency. Table 8.16 illustrates the calculation of RLI by using the cash budget data of Illustration 8.4.

The probability of insolvency can be readily computed by treating the index as the number of standard deviations that cash balances are from zero, as shown in Fig. 8.5. According to a table of areas under the normal curve (see the Appendix at the end of the book), 1.916 standard deviations indicates about a 3 percent chance of insolvency. Low initial reserves, low net cash flows, and high variability in the net cash flows attribute to a low RLI. If each of these factors is working against the firm at the same time, insolvency may be the result.

For computing the ratio, the analyst may obtain a value of initial re-

---

[9]This measure was developed by G. W. Emery and K. O. Cogger in an article titled "The Measurement of Liquidity," *Journal of Accounting Research* (Autumn 1982): 290–303.

TABLE 8.16
Calculation of the Relative Liquidity Index ($00)

Initial liquid reserve

Cash and securities (Table 8.8)	$1000.0
Line of credit (assumed)	4000.0
Total (L_o)	$5000.0

Net operating cash flows (Table 8.7)

January	$1267.5
February	317.5
March	⟨1082.5⟩
April	⟨807.5⟩
May	555.0
June	⟨820.0⟩
Total (μT)	⟨$570.0⟩
Standard deviation (σ)	$ 944.2

$$\text{RLI} = \frac{5000 - 570}{944.2 \sqrt{6}} = 1.916$$

serves fairly easily by using internal financial reports. The initial liquid reserve is the sum of opening cash and marketable security balances plus the company's short-term borrowing capacity. The net cash flows during the planning period should be adjusted to control for the effect of any large, regularly recurring items. If there are cash inflows (outflows) that are matched with uses for (sources of) resources, then they should be excluded from the data used to estimate net cash flow and variability of net cash flow. Failure to do so injects a systematic bias into the calculation of the index.

FIGURE 8.5
Probability of Cash Inadequacy

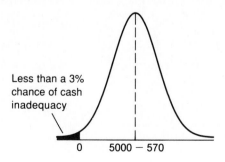

Less than a 3% chance of cash inadequacy

0   5000 − 570

Summary

Cash balances are held for transactional and precautionary purposes, and sometimes for speculative reasons. This chapter suggests several models for determining transaction balances. At one extreme is the simplistic ratio approach, which fails to consider either economies of scale or uncertainties in managing cash. At the other extreme is the Miller–Orr control-limit model, which allows cash flows to be uncertain and does consider ordering and holding costs. Between these two extremes are the adjusted-earnings model, Baumol's EOQ model, and Stone's control-limit models.

Efficient cash management requires managers to maintain minimal cash balances, since idle cash balances are nonearning (or minimal earning) assets. Monthly cash budgets are frequently used in an effort to determine the minimum balances. Monthly forecasts fail to indicate intramonth cash needs and surpluses, with the result that management may find itself unexpectedly short of cash or with large balances. In an effort to minimize this problem, a method for allocating monthly cash budgets to daily budgets was discussed. Stone and Wood's look-ahead model was incorporated into this approach in an effort to minimize costs associated with the holding and ordering of cash.

Liquidity indices, which attempt to capture the firm's liquidity position, were also discussed. The liquidity flow index is calculated from cash budget data and provides management with summary statistics of the cash budget. The relative liquidity index is another measure examined. It incorporates available lines of credit and revolving credit agreements, and factors the uncertainty of cash flows into the index.

Key Concepts

Adjusted-earnings method
Baumol model
Cash budget
Liquidity flow index
Miller–Orr model
Precautionary motive

Ratio projection method
Relative liquidity index
Speculative motive
Stone model
Transactions motive

Appendix

Ad Hoc Procedure for Determining a Minimum Cash Balance

A simple procedure that the treasurer can use to determine what the bank considers to be the minimum cash balance is to reduce the average bank balance, say 5 percent, every other month. When the balance becomes too low, a bank officer will call to find out what the problem is. At that point a working cash level is attained that if not maintained will cause problems with the bank.

This crude procedure can be improved upon with a little understanding of how banks assess required balances. Using cost accounting procedures, banks analyze their accounts to determine the profit or loss on each account. Unfortunately, the general principle they follow is to contact only customers whose accounts run at a loss for them. The basic procedure most banks follow in analyzing profitability is to determine what funds left on deposit are available for investment, assign an assumed rate of earnings to calculate gross revenues from the available funds, and then subtract the costs of all transactions associated with the account.

The bank starts with the average level of funds on deposit in the company's account and then reduces the level by an amount equal to the required reserves the bank must keep at the Federal Reserve Bank. Note that the balance on the company's ledger is not used. This fact is elementary but is often overlooked. The treasurer must analyze the cash account the way a banker does, not the way an accountant does. Because of the various types of float (mentioned in Chapter 7), the bank balance most likely does not equal the company's ledger balance.

An earnings rate is next applied by the bank to the usable funds to determine the gross revenue from the account. This arbitrary earnings figure supposedly gives the gross revenue available to the bank from the customer's account. Wide disagreement exists among banks about the proper rate for computing earnings. The effect of using too low a rate is that the bank will require customers to keep larger deposit balances than necessary. Finally, by subtracting the actual costs of the checks written and deposited, the bank derives either a positive or a negative earnings figure for each account.

The corporate treasurer can use this procedure to estimate necessary minimum balances. Estimates are required since the bank is generally unwilling to disclose certain information about its required-earnings rate.

ILLUSTRATION A.1

The bank is required to keep 20 percent of the company's deposit on reserve (R) with the Federal Reserve Bank. The cash manager forecasts the bank's earning rate (ER) to be 5 percent and its profit margin (M) to be 1 percent. Costs (C) incurred by the bank to maintain the company's account and various requests are estimated to be $5000. From these estimates the cash manager determines that the average deposit (AD) should be $156,250. This amount is calculated by using the following breakeven formula:

$$\text{AD} = \frac{C/(1 - R)}{\text{ER} - M} = \frac{\$5000/(1 - 0.2)}{0.05 - 0.01} = \$156{,}250. \tag{A.1}$$

The sensitivity of the estimated average required deposits to changes in any of the variables in the breakeven equation can be readily examined by substituting new values into the equation. For example, if the reserve requirement declines to 15 percent, the average required deposit is about $147,060, or approximately 6 percent lower.   □

Questions

1. Discuss the motives for a firm to hold cash balances.

2. What is a major deficiency of the ratio approach in estimating the required cash balance?

3. What are the key factors that should be incorporated into a model for determining minimum and maximum cash balances?

4. Are the concepts of inventory theory applicable when cash inflows and cash outflows are variable but completely predictable? Explain.

5. How would you judge whether or not a given corporation is maintaining excessive cash balances?

6. What do h and R refer to in the Miller–Orr model?

7. A cash budget cannot tell one what specific course of action to follow to alter the firm's cash flows. What considerations are involved in this direction?

8. What is the difference between a cash budget and a projected income statement or a projected balance sheet?

9. If cash flows are random, of what significance is a cash budget?

10. What is the major problem with monthly cash forecasts? How can this problem be overcome?

11. Of what significance are daily and monthly cash reports in cash budget control?

12. Contrast the actions management takes when either the upper or the lower control limits are pierced in the Miller–Orr model and in the Stone look-ahead model.

13. Define the LFI and RLI models, and explain why they are better measures of liquidity than the current and quick ratios.

Problems

1. The Artie Corporation expects $2 million in cash outlays during the next year. The outlays are expected to occur uniformly during the year. Management's opportunity cost of funds is 10 percent from investments in marketable securities. The cost of each transaction to secure cash is $90, which includes both direct and indirect costs. All cash demands are met by selling marketable securities.

    (a) Determine the optimal size of a transfer of funds from marketable securities to cash.

(b) What is the average cash balance?

(c) How many transfers to cash from marketable securities are needed during the year?

(d) What is the total cost associated with the firm's cash requirements?

(e) How are the answers to (a) and (b) affected if transaction costs are $50 per transaction? $125 per transaction?

2.   At the start of a 90-day planning period, the cash manager estimates cash needs of $27,000. The market rate of interest on government securities is 10 percent per annum, and the brokerage commission is a constant $50 per buying-and-selling transaction.

(a) Determine the economic order quantity of cash, using the Baumol model.

(b) What is the average cash balance?

(c) If the brokerage cost doubles, how much does the economic order quantity increase?

3.   Determine the maximum cash balance, the average cash balance, and the optimal return point, using the Miller–Orr model for each of the following situations:

	Variance of daily cash flows	*Transaction cost*	*Annual interest rate*
(a)	$ 5,000	$90	12%
(b)	5,000	90	15
(c)	5,000	45	15
(d)	50,000	45	15
(e)	50,000	45	10
(f)	30,000	55	10

4.   To help management with the preparation of the cash budget and a *pro forma* income statement for the year, you are asked to prepare a table of the following transactions, showing their individual and net effects upon income, cash receipts, and cash disbursements. Total the amounts in each category.

(a)   Cash sales for the year: $1,200,000.

(b)   Credit sales for the year: $18,000,000.

(c)   Collections from this year's credit sales: $16,800,000.

(d)   Collections from accounts outstanding at the beginning of the year: $1,800,000.

(e)   Returns and allowances: $200,000.

(f)   Refunds to customers on account of foregoing returns and allowances: $15,000.

(g)   Purchases of raw materials on account: $8,700,000.

(h)   Payments to suppliers on foregoing purchases: $7,800,000.

(i)   Payments to suppliers for goods bought last year: $650,000.

(j)   Total wage and salary charges for the year: $4,300,000.

(k)   Total payroll disbursements: $4,175,000.

(l) Purchase of equipment for cash: $875,000.

(m) Purchase of equipment, payment to be made next year: $250,000.

(n) Sale of surplus equipment for cash; book value is $120,000, and tax rate is 40 percent: $65,000.

(o) Depreciation charges: $450,000.

(p) Cash dividend declared, to be paid next year: $310,000.

(q) Bank loan obtained this year, to be repaid next year: $200,000.

5. Prepare a cash budget for Barney Associates for the months of June, July, and August. Discuss your results. The necessary data follow.

Forecasted sales	June	$2000
	July	3000
	August	2500
Historical sales	March	$1500
	April	2250
	May	1500

Sales are 75 percent for credit and 25 percent for cash. Credit sales are paid 70 percent in the current month, 15 percent the following month, and 15 percent the month following that. Wages and salaries are 10 percent of sales. Rent is $200 a month. A tax payment of $150 is due in August. Purchases are 80 percent of sales and are paid one month following the month of sale.

6. The cash manager of Xtra Company gathered the following data related to the company's cash position for the next six months.

Cash balance, January 1	$ 5,000
Estimated monthly payroll	40,000
Payroll accrued at the end of the year as well as at the end of each month	4,000
Interest payable in June	500
Taxes payable in March	10,000

Other data are given Table 8.17. Credit sales are collected 50 percent in the month sales are made, 45 percent in the month following, and 5 percent in the second month. Accounts payable represent unpaid purchases. Prepare a monthly cash budget for the period January through June.

TABLE 8.17
Financial Data

	Cash sales	Credit purchases	Accounts payable	Credit sales
November				$60,000
December			$18,000	70,000
January	$15,000	$12,000	14,000	65,000
February	14,000	16,500	30,000	80,000
March	12,000	14,000	25,000	72,000
April	16,000	18,000	30,000	60,000
May	14,500	25,000	24,000	75,000
June	18,000	12,500	30,000	68,000

7. The C&W Manufacturing Company had sales of $90,000 last month. It expects sales of $80,000 next month. Sales levels should increase 10 percent per month for the next five months. Cash sales normally are 30 percent of total sales, with the remainder collected in the following month. Other cash income is approximately 5 percent of monthly sales. Payroll costs are constant at $30,000 per month. Rent and utilities are constant at $3500 and $3000, respectively. Operating expenses have a fixed component of $6000 per month and a variable portion that is 2 percent of monthly sales. Cost of sales is approximately 45 percent of sales and is paid in the month of purchase. The firm has $8000 in its bank account and $15,000 in a money market fund. Prepare a monthly cash budget for the next six months.

8. The Siggle Company must pay off a $2000 loan on July 31. Its January 1 cash balance is zero. From the following information, will there be enough funds to repay the loan?

□ Raw materials are purchased at 50 percent of their final sales price. These purchases are made two months in advance of sales. The company pays its suppliers one month after it receives the goods.

□ Ten percent of sales are for cash, with 60 percent of sales collected the following month and another 25 percent collected the month after that. The remaining 5 percent are uncollected.

□ Estimated collections are $1140 in January and $350 in February for its November and December sales. Projected sales for the first nine months of the year are as follows:

Jan.	$600	Apr.	$1600	July	$1500
Feb.	800	May	2000	Aug.	1000
Mar.	900	June	1800	Sept.	900

□ Other monthly cash expenditures are $200. Taxes of $150 are paid each quarter, beginning in March.

9. Beta Food Services is trying to forecast its cash position as of its fiscal year end. Its opening balance was $50,000. Sales last year were $1 million, evenly spread over the 12 months. Sales were expected to grow at an annual rate of 4 percent. All sales are for credit, with collection 50 percent in the month of sale and 50 percent in the following month. Purchases are paid for with cash, and products are marked up 100 percent for sale. Selling prices and purchase costs are expected to be the same as last year. Expenses are $30,000 per month. Funds may be borrowed from the bank at an annual rate of 15 percent, up to a maximum of $250,000. What is the cash balance at the end of the new year under the (a) ratio approach and (b) cash budget approach?

10. Given average day-of-the-week proportions of

$$M = 0.246, \quad T = 0.198, \quad W = 0.152, \quad Th = 0.117, \quad F = 0.287,$$

calculate day-of-the-week adjustment factors.

11. Given the historical information shown in Table 8.18, determine the allocation of the month's $80,000 budget by day. Assume that day 1 is a Monday.

TABLE 8.18
Historical Proportions

	Day-of-month proportions							Day-of-week proportions	
1	0.040	9	0.060	17	0.029			M	0.244
2	0.052	10	0.047	18	0.034			T	0.196
3	0.056	11	0.052	19	0.041			W	0.090
4	0.066	12	0.045	20	0.040			T	0.271
5	0.069	13	0.040	21	0.044			F	0.199
6	0.072	14	0.033		1.000				1.000
7	0.067	15	0.034						
8	0.058	16	0.021						

12. Use the Stone model and the data that follow. What should XYZ Company's strategy be with regard to marketable securities if a four-day forecast is used?

Target balance = $10,000,
Upper outer limit = $20,000,
Upper inner limit = $15,000,
Lower outer limit = $0,
Lower inner limit = $5000.

Forecasted cash flow:

Day	2	3	4	5	6
Amount	$1000	$6000	−$10,000	500	−$5000

The adjusted balance for day 1 is $25,000.

13. A company uses the Stone model for managing cash. The target balance is $15,000, with upper and lower control limits of $25,000 and $5000, respectively. Inner control limits are ±$2000 of the outer limits. On Friday, August 1, the company's cash balance was $12,000. Actual cash flows during August occurred as listed in Table 8.19. The firm's daily cash budget is as shown in Table 8.10 (in the chapter).

TABLE 8.19
Cash Flow

Day	Cash flow	Day	Cash flow	Day	Cash flow
1	$4500	8	$ 3,020	15	$4900
2	2400	9	945	16	4150
3	4210	10	−1,900	17	5970
4	2090	11	11,640	18	9900
5	−2300	12	6,750	19	620
6	9900	13	−9,000	20	1370
7	6980	14	−7,790	21	8250

(a) Set up a table showing the beginning, adjusted, and ending daily cash balances for August. Indicate any investment activity in marketable securities. Do not assume any look-ahead forecast.

(b) Redo part (a) assuming a three-day look-ahead forecast.

(c) Using a 12 percent cost of money, calculate the residual income for parts (a) and (b). Which method is preferred?

14. Management has determined the extreme lower and upper control limits of the Stone cash management model to be $7,000 and $28,000, respectively. The inner lower and upper limits are $10,000 and $25,000, respectively. The target balance is $17,500. Using the daily budget data shown in Table 8.10 and a three-day moving forecast, reconstruct Tables 8.11, 8.12, 8.13, and 8.14. Use the actual cash flows shown in Table 8.11. The opening cash balance is $20,000.

15. The data shown in Table 8.20 have been revealed from an audit of the Sun Devil Company's current year budget and next year forecast. For each period, calculate the liquidity flow index, and compare it with the current ratio. Which measure provides a better indicator of liquidity? Discuss.

16. Assume that the Sun Devil Company (Problem 15) had an expected standard deviation of net cash flows of $12 and $72 in the budget and the forecast, respectively.

(a) Calculate the relative liquidity index for each period, and comment on the results.

(b) Determine the necessary line of credit to make the forecast index equal to the budget index. Discuss the impact the credit line would have on the firm.

TABLE 8.20
Sun Devil Company Data

	Budget	*Forecast*
Cash payments to creditors:		
Purchases	$720	$2820
Cash expenses	170	680
Taxes and dividends	10	40
Cash receipts:		
Cash sales	480	1920
Collection of receivables	450	1800
Cash balances:		
Opening	10	20
Closing	20	40
Current assets	50	120
Current liabilities	20	80

CHAPTER 9 □
Duration Analysis and Hedging with Futures

Most executives have identified the corporation mission for their firms. It may be explicitly articulated in a statement of objectives and supporting strategies or loosely defined in the collective minds of top management. Whichever the case, the mission normally states the firm's desire to meet the needs of a specific market with various goods or services, priced reasonably so as to compensate its investors adequately and to ensure the continued existence of the firm. Seldom does the mission statement expressly define the mission as speculation or gambling in high-risk situations. Very few corporate charters mention the firm's anticipated involvement in speculative or gaming activities.

Nearly all managers, however, implicitly speculate with their assets and liabilities.[1] For example, speculation occurs whenever cash is held for temporary investment or borrowed on a floating-rate basis. The speculation is implicit since management speculates about the higher yield of cash holdings or the lower cost of cash borrowings. Considerable market fluctuations in interest rates (and thus prices) increase the uncertainty involved in cash management.

During the decade of the 1970s and into the 1980s, corporate life was significantly affected by changing interest rates and prices. For instance, in the 1974–76 period the prime rate ranged from a low of 6 percent to a high of 12 percent. It reached just about 16 percent in 1979 and was at 21 percent by December 1980. It then changed 29 times during 1981. Change

---

[1]Chapter 8 mentioned that management might hold excess cash balances for speculative purposes. The use of the word "speculate" in this sentence refers to management's risk management practices.

was less frequent in 1982 and 1983, but when it happened, it was generally to lower the rate. In ensuing years, the prime rate reached a low of 7.5 percent before advancing steadily to 10 percent as of October 1990.

The purpose of this chapter is to provide an overview of how the treasurer can use duration analysis and futures to protect liquidity and shareholders' wealth. Although the fundamentals of hedging are fairly straightforward, much expertise is required in managing hedging. This chapter and the next merely touch on hedging concepts.

Rate-Sensitive Assets and Liabilities

Corporate borrowings have continued to grow in recent years as the result of increased working capital requirements of most firms. Companies have had to borrow because of reduced operating margins and their inability to generate sufficient cash flow from operations. When funding needs arise, the response is to borrow funds from prearranged lines of credit. When needs diminish, lines are paid back to minimize interest expense. In this respect the treasurer merely reacts to production requirements.

Net interest expense as a percentage of sales and as a percentage of earnings before interest and taxes has continued to grow in recent years for many firms. The reason interest cost has become so significant lies not only in the rate itself but also in the volume of credit.[2] This situation has resulted in many firms having a **duration gap.** This means that there is no *cash matching* between the firm's interest-sensitive assets and its interest-sensitive liabilities as interest rates change; that is, the interest-sensitive assets are not **immunized** — interest-rate risk exists.

ILLUSTRATION 9.1

For simplicity, assume the planning horizon for the firm is one year and that a flat interest yield curve exists. Management expects to collect $1000 of receivables at the end of the year. It is able to earn a 10 percent annual return on investments (that is, the opportunity cost of capital is 10 percent) and to borrow at an annualized rate of 8 percent for 90 days. The present value of receivables is $904.94 (i.e., $1000e^{-0.10}$, where $e^{-0.10}$ represents the continuous discounting factor). This amount is financed with debt.

In three months $923.12 (= $904.84e^{0.08(0.25)}$, where $e^{0.08(0.25)}$ represents the continuous compounding factor) will be paid and a new loan

---

[2]Much debt has been raised through the use of *junk bonds*, which are bonds classified as speculative grade, with ratings below BBB (Standard and Poor's) or below Baa (Moody's).

taken out for the amount of the principal and interest payment. The loan will continue to be rolled over every 90 days. With borrowing rates remaining constant at 8 percent, management will roll over the loan at days 180 and 270 into new loans of $941.77 and $960.79, respectively. At the end of the year, the rolled-over loan will have an outstanding balance of $980.20.

The cash flows of this transaction are as shown in Table 9.1. The balance sheet is exposed to interest rate risk (change in interest rates causing change in value) because the 10 percent earning rate of the receivables is fixed, whereas borrowings must be refunded every 90 days. The asset's longer *duration* implies that a given change in interest rates will change the present value of the receivable more than it will affect the present value of the liability. This change, of course, will change the value of the firm's equity.

Suppose that immediately after the firm obtains the September loan, the yield curve shifts upward 200 basis points (2 percentage points). The increase raises the anticipated refunding costs and the opportunity cost of funds to the firm. The new loan at day 90, of $923.12, will now have an interest cost of 10 percent when it is refinanced. Thus $946.49 ($= \$923.12e^{0.10(0.25)}$) is the amount that will be refunded at day 180. As a result, the amount the firm expects to pay at year end increases to $995.02. Net cash flow falls to $4.98, and its present value is $4.42. Table 9.2 summarizes the impact of increased interest rates.   □

TABLE 9.1
Cash Flow Analysis: Stable Interest Rates

	Day				
	0	90	180	270	360
Investment	(904.84)				
Borrow	904.84	923.12	941.77	960.79	
Refund/pay debt		(923.12)	(941.77)	(960.79)	(980.20)
Collection					1000.00
Net flow	0	0	0	0	19.80
Equity	17.92 ←		Present value		
			$19.80e^{-0.10}$		

Present-value balance sheet (using 10%)

Receivables (1)	$904.84	Debt (2)	$886.92
		Equity	17.92

Notes:
1. $\$1000e^{-0.10} = \$904.84$.
2. $\$980.20e^{-0.10} = \$886.92$.

TABLE 9.2
Cash Flow Analysis: Increasing Interest Rates

	Day				
	0	90	180	270	360
Investment	⟨904.84⟩				
Borrow	904.84	923.12	946.49	970.45	
Refund/pay debt		⟨923.12⟩	⟨946.49⟩	⟨970.45⟩	⟨995.02⟩
Collection					1000.00
Net flow	0	0	0	0	4.98
Equity	4.42 ←		Present value ———————		⌐
			$4.98e^{-0.12}$		

Present-value balance sheet just before debt repayments on day 360 (using 12%)

Receivables (1)	$886.92	Debt (2)	$882.50
		Equity	4.42

Notes:
1. $\$1000e^{-0.12} = \$886.92$.
2. $\$995.02e^{-0.12} = \$882.50$.

As the illustration shows, if the firm is in interest rate disequilibrium, its management is speculating that rates or prices will always move in the firm's favor. A company that has a surplus of short-term investments assumes that rates will continually increase so that their yields continue to increase as time goes on. But when the firm is a net borrower of funds, its management hopes that interest rates will decline and that its cost of borrowing will be lower in the future. In either case, as a net seller or a net borrower of cash, management is clearly speculating about the future yield or the future cost of the quantity of cash it has placed.

Duration Analysis[3]

In its simplest form, **duration** is defined as follows:

$$\text{Duration} = \frac{\text{PV}(C_1)}{V} \times 1 + \frac{\text{PV}(C_2)}{V} \times 2 + \cdots + \frac{\text{PV}(C_n)}{V} \times n, \qquad (9.1)$$

where $\text{PV}(C_t)$ is the present value of the cash flow in period t, V is the sum of all the $\text{PV}(C_t)$s, and $1, 2, \ldots, n$ represent time periods. For securities that make a single payment at maturity, duration is equal to maturity. For securities that

---

[3]This section relies heavily on the article by G. G. Kaufman, "Measuring and Managing Interest Rate Risk: A Primer," *Economic Perspectives* (Federal Reserve Bank of Chicago, January-February 1984): 16–29.

make intermediate payments, duration is shorter than term to maturity, and is a weighted average as given in Eq. (9.1). Duration effectively calculates the number of periods for a zero-coupon security to be equivalent (in a present-value sense) to a multiperiod paying security.

In Table 9.1, the receivable has a duration of one year, whereas the loan has a duration of 0.25 year (their maturity dates since both are single-payment securities). The duration measure for equity is a function of asset duration and debt duration:

$$\text{Equity duration} = \left[\text{asset duration} - \frac{\text{debt}}{\text{asset}} \times \text{debt duration}\right], \qquad (9.2)$$

where the debt/asset ratio is measured in market terms. Thus, equity duration in Table 9.1 is $1 - (886.92/904.84) \times 0.25 = 0.755$ year. This figure is referred to as the **duration gap.**[4]

The estimated impact of interest rate changes on the change in the equity-to-asset ratio is

$$\frac{\Delta \text{ Equity}}{\text{Assets}} = -[\text{equity duration}] \times \Delta k, \qquad (9.3)$$

where Δk is the change in interest rate. Substitution into Eq. (9.3) indicates that equity decreases about 1.5 percent of total assets: $-0.755 \times 0.02 = -0.0151$, or -1.51 percent. This is approximately the percentage decline found by comparing the change in equity in Tables 9.1 and 9.2 to the original asset amount in Table 9.1: $(\$17.92 - \$4.42)/\$904.84 = 0.0149$, or 1.49 percent.

When the duration gap is zero, the balance sheet is insensitive to changes in interest rates; the balance sheet is said to be *immunized*. To immunize equity in Table 9.1, the treasurer needs to restructure the balance sheet so that equity duration equals zero. The treasurer can reduce the duration gap (equity duration) to zero either by shortening the duration of the receivable to 0.245 year, or by lengthening the duration of the debt to 1.02 years.[5] Of course, some combination of asset duration and debt duration between these two extreme points also exists. The treasurer can immunize the balance sheet by using the futures market,[6] which is discussed next.

---

[4]The duration gap can be defined differently. See Kaufman, ibid., p. 20.

[5]This number is the result of substituting the debt/asset ratio (886.92/904.84) and debt duration (0.25) into Eq. (9.3), setting the equation equal to zero, and solving for asset duration. A similar calculation results in the new debt duration figure.

[6]The duration gap can also be changed by adjusting the asset mix in the cash market. For instance, the treasurer could reduce the gap by judicious use of asset-based financing, which is the topic of Chapter 11.

TABLE 9.3
Futures Traded on U.S. Exchanges

Financial Futures

Treasury bonds	Treasury notes
5-Year Treasury notes	2-Year Treasury notes
30-Day interest rate	Treasury bills
Municipal bond index	S&P 500 index†
NYSE composite index*	Major market index
Value Line index	CRB index‡
Mortgage backed	Eurodollar
Sterling	Long gilt
Japanese yen	Deutsche Mark
Canadian dollar	British pound
Swiss franc	Dollar–Deutsche Mark difference
Dollar–yen difference	Dollar–sterling difference

Commodity Futures

Corn	Oats
Soybeans	Soybean meal
Soybean oil	Wheat
Barley	Flaxseed
Canola	Rye
Cattle-feeder	Cattle–live
Hogs–live	Pork bellies
Cocoa	Coffee
Sugar	Cotton
Orange juice	Copper
Gold	Silver
Platinum	Palladium
Crude oil	Heating oil
Gasoline	Gas oil
Lumber	Aluminum
Propane	Rice
Sorghum	

*NYSE = New York Stock Exchange.
†S&P = Standard and Poor's.
‡CRB = Commodity Research Bureau.

Background on Futures

Until late 1975 there was no effective and inexpensive way for treasurers to reduce the risk associated with changing interest rates.[7] However, in October 1975 the Chicago Board of Trade introduced the first futures market in interest rates in Government National Mortgage Association (GNMAs)

---

[7]Futures contracts have existed for foreign currencies and various commodities for several decades.

TABLE 9.4
Survey of Use of Financial Futures

Industry	Total respondents	Have used	Have considered	Have no interest
Mining	13	1	10	2
Construction	6	0	4	2
Manufacturing	225	2	150	73
Transportation and communication	28	1	19	8
Wholesale trade	12	0	6	6
Retail trade	10	0	5	5
Financial services	80	11	56	13
Other services	20	0	6	14
Total	394	15	256	123
Percentages		3.8%	64.9%	31.3%

Source: J. Miller et al. (Arthur Anderson & Co.), *Interest Rate Futures: The Corporate Decision* (Financial Executives Research Foundation, New York, 1982). Used by permission.

pass-through certificates, and in January 1976 the International Monetary Market of Chicago Mercantile Exchange provided a market for futures trading in three-month treasury bills. Today, several interest rate futures contracts are actively traded on three exchanges in the United States, with additional contracts traded in London and Singapore. Table 9.3 lists both financial and commodity futures traded on U.S. exchanges.

The use of futures to reduce risk is done through a process called **hedging.**[8] Hedging enables treasurers to shift risks to persons willing to assume those risks (speculators). Many treasurers do not use the futures market (see Table 9.4) because of the risky image created by speculators who buy and sell contracts at the most volatile ends of the marketplace.

Fundamentals of Hedging with Futures

Futures have an image that is difficult to sell to top management. Hedging entails winning most of the time and losing sometimes. Many managers view hedging as an instance where money is ventured and lost. They have difficulty understanding that unhedged investments stand to suffer greater losses during market swings than do hedged investments.

Contrary to its risky image, hedging allows the participant to mitigate most or all risks of ownership by balancing a cash position against a roughly

[8]In perfect markets, hedging transactions have zero net present values. In reality, the firm has to pay small transaction costs and may not be as well informed as professional traders.

equivalent opposite stance in a futures market. Taking a position in the cash market means trading in actual hard commodities or financial instruments. In contrast, the futures market allows traders to control large blocks of these items with a small amount of cash and without purchasing the actual commodities or financial instruments. It often happens that winning in the futures market means losing in the cash market and vice versa.

To develop any hedging strategy, a corporate treasurer must be familiar with both the cash and futures markets. These markets are sophisticated and volatile and should be monitored constantly. It is not the purpose of this section to describe all the characteristics or nuances of either of these markets. Rather, the purpose here is to provide you with a basic understanding of concepts, terminology, and mechanics of hedging.

The basic concept behind hedging is to trade assets (or liabilities) and futures contracts that parallel an equivalent position in a cash or hard goods market. That is, you sell (buy) a futures contract if you intend to sell (buy) securities in the cash market in the future. The stance taken in futures trading is 180 degrees opposite the cash position. A hedge is undertaken with the objective of controlling or eliminating risk; there is little expectation of making an overall profit in the hedge transaction. The expectation is that any futures gains or losses offset price fluctuations in the cash market.

Cash Market

There are two kinds of **cash markets,** the spot market and the forward market. In the **spot market** transactions are made for current sales at current prices. Delivery is to occur within normal commercial periods, that is, the amount of time it would take to deliver the instrument or commodity. The forward cash market, called the **forward market,** is a direct placement market where the purchase and sale of instruments or commodities is for future delivery. Prices are determined at the time of contract.

The attributes of the cash markets are the following: A legal contract is made between two parties; physical delivery is expected and must be performed; price is negotiated between buyer and seller and is specified in the contract. In this sense there is no standard cash contract. Moreover, cash market contracts are not generally regulated by government agencies. Most important, they are not cancelable unless mutually agreed upon. Payment is not standardized and depends on the trade terms that exist between the parties.

Futures Market

The economic functions of futures markets are to provide a competitive market price mechanism, a hedging mechanism for price risk, and a means to improve market efficiency. Prices of futures contracts for the various commodities and financial instruments provide a current consensus of knowledgeable opinions of a large number of buyers and sellers. The futures markets help eliminate market imperfections and contribute to more efficient economic activity.

Futures contracts, simply stated, are a promise between two persons to exchange a commodity at a specified time and place in the future for a stated price. As a commitment between a buyer and a seller, a futures contract specifies precisely the commodity being traded and the terms of delivery. The clearinghouse of the commodity exchange, made up of exchange members, guarantees contract performance by both parties. Individual traders cease to deal with each other and instead become obligated to the clearinghouse, which becomes the guarantor of performance of all futures traded on a particular exchange. At the close of every trading day the clearinghouse matches buy-and-sell contracts for the day and informs every exchange member of its net settlement status.

Table 9.5 illustrates information for Treasury bond futures as of June 18, 1990.

Mechanics of Interest Rate Futures

Interest rate futures are based on long- and short-term financial debt instruments with prices that vary inversely to their interest rates. For example, treasury bills are sold on a discount basis and then redeemed at maturity at face value. The difference between the face value and the dis-

TABLE 9.5
Treasury Bond Futures

FUTURES

TREASURY BONDS (CBT) – $100,000; pts. 32nds of 100%

	Open	High	Low	Settle	Chg	Yield Settle	Chg	Open Interest
June	94-10	94-12	93-26	93-29	– 13	8.646	+ .045	26,491
Sept	94-01	94-06	93-16	93-20	– 13	8.677	+ .045	229,274
Dec	93-23	93-26	93-08	93-11	– 13	8.708	+ .045	19,844
Mr91	93-09	93-09	93-02	93-03	– 13	8.737	+ .046	7,075
June	92-28	93-00	92-28	92-28	– 12	8.761	+ .042	3,068
Sept	92-24	92-27	92-22	92-22	– 11	8.782	+ .038	591
Dec	92-19	92-19	92-16	92-16	– 10	8.804	+ .036	172
Mr92	92-13	92-13	92-10	92-10	– 10	8.825	+ .035	260

Est vol 160,000; vol Fri 448 155; op int 287,360, –6,478

Explanation:

As of the close on Monday, June 18, 1990, the June contract closed (settled) at 93 29/32, down 13/32 from the previous day. This resulted in the yield increasing 0.045 points to close at 8.646 percent. The June contract opened the day at 94 10/32, reached a high of 94 12/32 and a low of 93 26/32. There are 26,491 contracts still open as of the previous Friday.

Estimated volume of all Treasury bond contracts traded on Monday was 160,000, down from Friday's volume of 448,155.

Contracts with longer maturities show higher yields.

counted selling price equals the amount of interest earned. Similarly, the price of a futures contract is inversely related to the interest rate of the underlying debt instrument.

Participants in futures markets can take one of two positions in the market: a long position or a short position. A buyer of a futures contract takes a *long position* in the market. A *long hedge* is the purchase of futures contracts as temporary substitutes for a purchase of an actual instrument in the future. The most common reason to place a long hedge is the desire to lock in a high yield on a future investment, coupled with a fear that yields will fall before an actual investment is made. By using a long hedge, the treasurer can attempt to ensure that an attractive return will be earned on funds that will be investable at a later time but that presently are not available. The long position is offset at the time the cash commodity is purchased.

To profit from a long position, the treasurer must sell the contract at a higher price than the purchase price. For an interest rate futures contract, a long position profits from a decline in interest rates. A lower interest rate means a higher contract price, since interest rates (or yields) are inversely related. An increase in interest rates produces a loss in a long position.

A seller of a futures contract takes a *short position* in the market. That is, the seller sells a contract that is a promise to deliver, on a specified date, a financial asset even though he or she may not currently own that asset. The *short hedge* is used by management as a temporary substitute for the sale of the actual asset in the cash market at a later date. It is used to protect the price at which the manager wishes to eventually sell the asset. The short position is offset at the time the asset is sold.

To profit from a short position, the treasurer must purchase the contract at a lower price than the selling price. In financial instruments a short position profits from an increase in interest rates, because the contract price then declines, allowing the contract to be bought at a profit. Conversely, a decline in interest rates produces a loss in a short position.

The process of hedging is temporary. The futures contract is typically made with the intent to offset the futures position prior to the expiration of the contract. The sale (purchase) of futures contracts can be offset by the purchase (sale) of an equal number of identical futures contracts at a later date — as long as it is done before the contract matures. *Offset* is the most frequently used method of settling a futures market position. Offset is extremely important from a risk management viewpoint. Though some cash market participants use futures contracts as delivery vehicles, only a small percentage of futures transactions result in delivery.

By turning over the risk to the market, management forgoes some profit potential. One case where hedging reduces profit potential is when a cash market increases, resulting in a lower-valued futures market. If, on the other hand, management accurately predicts a decline in the cash market, it does not have to accept a diminished return or reduced value in that market. *By purchasing a futures contract that exhibits a high amount of correlation with the cash market asset, the manager can minimize much of the risk of loss of value.*

Managers wishing to hedge in futures should make sure that the hedging vehicle they choose has sufficient trading volume. A healthy futures offering should have a minimum of 5000 open-interest contracts. Open interest is the number of contracts not yet balanced by trade or closing. At least 2000 contracts for the particular commodity being traded each day gives a strong indication that the futures market is liquid. A liquid market offers assurance to the manager that purchases and sales can be done freely. Liquidity is important because it enables traders to minimize losses if the market declines.

Receivables Example Revisited

Illustration 9.1 involving accounts receivable showed the effect that mismatched maturity of assets and liabilities can have on the firm's equity. Futures contracts can be used to hedge the interest rate risk caused by the mismatch.

Confusion exists about the appropriate hedging objective of management and how the hedge should be constructed. One strategy is to protect the present value of the equity of the firm from interest rate fluctuations. Another strategy is to minimize discrepancies in cash flows over time. From the standpoint of wealth maximization, protecting wealth (that is, protecting the present value of the equity) is more meaningful. As the following illustration shows, meeting the second objective of reducing cash flow mismatches to zero does not minimize the exposure of shareholders' wealth to interest rate changes.

ILLUSTRATION 9.2

Suppose that on September 15 management undertakes the receivable transaction and its associated financing as shown earlier in Table 9.1. Uncertainty prevails about what will happen to future interest rates. To protect its equity of $19.80 (nondiscounted amount), management sells a treasury bill futures contract yielding 10 percent. Since the loan is renewable every 90 days at the then-prevailing interest rate, contracts are sold now for maturity in 90 days, 180 days, and 270 days (December, March, and June, respectively). Since the interest yield curve is flat, these contracts are sold for $975.31, $951.23, and $927.74, respectively (using the continuous discounting model).

TABLE 9.6
Futures-Protected Balance Sheet (Not Discounted)

Cash (1)	$ 28.14	Debt (3)	$995.02
Receivables (2)	1000.00		
		Equity:	
		Futures (4)	$ 28.14
		Receivables (5)	4.98
			$ 33.12

Note: (1) and (4) are the profit on the future contracts; (2), (3) and (5) are taken from the top part of Table 9.2.

Shortly after management sells these contracts, interest rates increase 200 basis points. It now costs the firm 10 percent to finance operations; futures contracts are priced to yield 12 percent. In terms of refinancing the maturing 90-day debt, the costs are as shown earlier in Table 9.2. As that analysis indicates, equity shrinks from $19.80 to $4.98 because of the higher refunding costs.

However, since management has sold futures contracts short, it is cheaper to buy contracts to close the open positions. If the yield curve stays flat at the 12 percent level, the higher interest rates translate into futures prices of $970.45, $941.76, and $913.93, for the December, March, and June contracts, respectively (using continuous discounting at 12 percent). Thus the $28.14 difference between the selling prices and the buying prices represents profit earned on the futures contracts. The balance sheet, just before collection of the receivables and payment of the outstanding debt but after the closing of all open futures positions, is as shown in Table 9.6.

Management has been able not only to protect its equity by using future contracts but actually to add to it. The higher borrowing costs have been more than offset. Table 9.6 can be made directly comparable to Table 9.1 by discounting cash flows at 12 percent, as will be shown later in Table 9.7.   □

We stated earlier that some disagreement exists about whether the hedging strategy should attempt to minimize discrepancies between cash flows over time or to minimize the loss of equity. Quite clearly from Table 9.7 (as shown by the cash flow line), minimizing discrepancies in the cash flows can lead to significant loss of equity. To contribute to the strategy that maximizes shareholders' wealth, one must attempt to maintain (or add to) equity value during periods of uncertainty about interest rates. This objective is accomplished by allowing net cash receipts to vary.

The present value of the firm's balance sheet just before collection of the receivable and payment of the debt is given in Table 9.8.

TABLE 9.7
Total Cash Flow with a Hedged Position

	Day				
	0	90	180	270	360
Investment	(904.84)				
Borrow	904.84	923.12	946.49	970.45	
Refund/pay debt		(923.12)	(946.49)	(970.45)	(995.02)
Collection					1000.00
Cash flow	0	0	0	0	4.98
Futures:					
Sell December (1)		975.31			
Sell March (1)			951.23		
Sell June (1)				927.74	
Buy December (2)		(970.45)			
Buy March (3)			(941.76)		
Buy June (4)	(913.73)				
Net flows	0	4.86	9.47	13.81	4.98

$$4.72 \leftarrow e^{-0.12(0.25)}$$
$$8.92 \leftarrow e^{-0.12(0.50)}$$
$$12.62 \leftarrow e^{-0.12(0.75)}$$
$$4.42 \leftarrow e^{-0.12(1)}$$

| Present-value equity | 30.68 | | | | |

Notes:
1. Transaction date is September 15, 19X1.
2. Transaction date is December 14, 19X1.
3. Transaction date is March 14, 19X2.
4. Transaction date is June 14, 19X2.

The variability of these cash flows should not be a serious problem for liquidity management since the hedged position should only be maintained when interest rates are increasing. If interest rates are falling, refinancing costs will be less, with the result that equity will increase. If

TABLE 9.8
Present-Value Balance Sheet (Discounted at 12 Percent)

Cash	$ 26.26	Debt		$882.50
Receivables	886.92			
		Equity:		
			Futures	$ 26.26
			Receivables	4.42
				$ 30.68

management enters a hedge, and interest rates subsequently decline, the appropriate strategy is to close the position as soon as possible and take the small loss. Maintaining the hedge throughout the period will not cause the equity to decline from the prehedged balance. It will simply not allow lower refinancing costs to contribute to shareholders' wealth.

Basis Risk

While futures provide opportunities to reduce risk exposure, they have pitfalls as well. Their use can actually increase risk under certain circumstances and can result in lower income. In an extreme case the use of futures can jeopardize solvency. Generally, hedging in the futures market replaces the risk of price fluctuation in the cash market with the risk of a change in the relationship between the cash price and the futures price of an instrument. This relationship is called the **basis.** Basis is both stable and predictable because of the tendency of the cash and futures prices of commodities or financial instruments to move together.

Three market forces operate to ensure similar price movements in the cash and futures markets:

□ Changes in economic and financial market conditions influence cash and futures prices simultaneously.

□ The possible delivery of the cash instrument forces cash and futures prices to converge as the delivery date approaches.

□ Arbitrage between the cash and futures markets helps remove distortions in the basis.

Arbitrage is the simultaneous purchase of one commodity against the sale of the same commodity in order to profit from distortions from usual price relationships. For example, if carrying costs and expectations are thought to be at a certain level and the actual cash/futures price is at another level, there is a distortion; the futures price is either too low or too high relative to the cash price. Thus it benefits the market participant to buy futures and sell in the cash market, or vice versa. As a result, the futures price remains relatively close to the asset's cash price; movements in the cash market are reflected by similar movements in the futures market.

The basis can be positive or negative, depending on whether the futures price is under or over the cash price:

$$\text{Basis} = \text{cash price} - \text{futures price.} \tag{9.4}$$

The greater (wider) the basis (that is, the more positive), the greater is its strength; the smaller (narrower) the basis (more negative), the weaker it is. Basis strength or weakness reflects the relative yields on the underlying instrument vis-à-vis the financing cost.

Futures prices for commodities are normally higher than cash prices, reflecting the financing costs or short-term interest rates relative to the yield on the cash commodity. However, *the normal configuration for long-term interest rate futures is for the futures price to lie below the cash price,* reflecting a positively sloped yield curve. This behavior is shown in Fig. 9.1. Note that in Fig. 9.1 if the *Y*-axis was yield, the top curve would be the futures market and the bottom curve would be the cash market.

Though cash and futures prices do not always fluctuate equally, their movements in response to changing market conditions are generally in the same direction. It is this common directional movement that makes the basis more predictable and, therefore, less risky at a given time than the movement of either the cash prices or the futures prices. At the contract's maturity date, the basis must be zero.

Through basis management the manager can seek to profit from changes in the basis given her or his expectations, cash position, and willingness and ability to absorb risk. Vital for hedging in any commodity is consideration of the direction of the market.

Table 9.9 summarizes the accounts receivable example illustrated in Tables 9.1, 9.2, and 9.6 with the basis calculated for both the opening and the closing transactions. Since the basis has strengthened (become less negative), a small net economic gain has resulted — the realized gain exceeds the opportunity loss. Whenever a gain or a loss occurs from the hedge, the hedge ratio is not perfect. Calculation of the hedge ratio will be shown shortly.

A change in equity, relative to anticipations, can occur because the basis may not be the same at the time a futures position is offset as it was

FIGURE 9.1
Behavior of the Basis for Financial Contracts

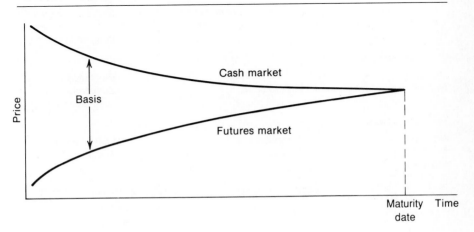

TABLE 9.9
Hedging the Equity of the Firm

Date	Cash market	Futures market
September 15, 1985	Management wants to protect the unrealized equity of $19.80	Sells December, March, and June treasury bill futures for $2854.28 (short)
	Basis = −$2834.48	
September 14, 1986	Receivable is collected; actual equity is $4.98	By this date the open futures contracts have been closed; they were bought for $2826.14 (long)
	Basis = −$2821.16	
	Opportunity loss $14.82	Realized gain $28.14

when the position first was taken, as is the case in Table 9.9. Only if a hedge is perfect (this means the basis does not change), is the opportunity loss in the cash market offset exactly by the gain in the futures market. Usually, a gain or loss in the cash market is not offset exactly. *Depending on the size and the direction of the change in basis, profit rises or falls.*

Certain relationships exist between the basis and profitability. They are summarized in Table 9.10. When the dollar basis weakens (narrows), a

TABLE 9.10
Hedging Strategies and Outcomes

	Expectations for interest rates (prices)	
	Increase (decrease)	*Decrease (increase)*
Hedging strategy	Short hedge	Long hedge
(a) Dollar basis		
Narrows	Loss realized	Profit made
No change	Zero profit	Zero profit
Widens	Profit made	Loss realized
(b) Percent basis		
Narrows	Profit made	Loss realized
No change	Zero profit	Zero profit
Widens	Loss realized	Profit made

Note: If the basis narrows, it becomes more negative or less positive; if it widens, it becomes more positive or less negative.

short hedge results in a net loss and a long hedge results in a net gain. When the dollar basis strengthens (widens), the short hedge results in a net gain and the long hedge results in a net loss. If the basis remains unchanged from the initial futures transaction (putting on the hedge) to the offsetting transaction (lifting the hedge), there is no net gain or loss on either a long or a short hedge other than the costs of the commission and of providing the margin deposit.

The hedge's gain or loss can be calculated using the following equation, where the subscripts *long* and *short* refer to transactions in the futures market:

$$\text{Profit} = \$\text{basis}_{long} - \$\text{basis}_{short}. \tag{9.5}$$

For example, Table 9.9 indicates the *long basis* is $-\$2821.16$ and the *short basis* is $-\$2834.48$. Substituting these amounts into Eq. (9.5) results in an overall economic profit of $13.32.

Although the discussion of the basis has been in terms of dollar amounts, the basis is frequently measured by yield spreads. Table 9.10 (b) also shows results when the basis is calculated by using interest rates. Not surprisingly, the results are exactly opposite to dollar-denominated basis results, since increasing interest rates mean declining prices and vice versa.

A necessary requirement for any successful hedge is to monitor the hedge. Once a futures position is undertaken, it has to be watched in much the same way that investment managers monitor cash investments. Of primary concern are movements in the basis and changes in expectations for future interest rates. In short, *the manager must manage basis risk.* While unnecessary placing and lifting of futures positions can amount to *speculation*, placing a hedge and forgetting it in the face of fundamental changes in the basis can amount to imprudent hedging.

For the profit-maximizing firm hedging contains a paradox. If management decides to hedge only part of its overall interest rate risk, it should not be surprised to find its hedging program reporting losses. The reason is that by hedging only part of the risk, management accepts some cash market risk and effectively endorses an interest rate forecast. If this forecast for the cash market is correct, net interest margin will be positive. But by definition, profits in the cash market position mean losses in the futures market. Thus losses in the futures market when only part of the risk is hedged probably mean that the business plan embodied in the cash position was the correct one.

Appendix A of this chapter contains several other examples of hedging and basis calculations. Since an understanding of this material may be difficult, you may wish to spend time working through the examples in this appendix.

Establishing the Hedge

Once the interest rate risk is assessed and the hedge vehicle selected, the proper amount for the hedge transaction must be determined. This process has four steps:

1. Determine the dollar amount to be hedged.
2. Determine the face value of the futures contract.
3. Determine the maturity of the asset or liability in question.
4. Determine the correlation between cash and futures prices.

If all securities fluctuate by equal yield and dollar amounts (i.e., are perfectly correlated), one could always use a hedge ratio of one unit of the hedge vehicle security per one unit of the target security, or a 1:1 ratio. Obviously, securities fluctuate by different dollar amounts even if there are identical yield changes, so the interest rate sensitivity of the hedge vehicle must be compared with the dollar impact of the risk. However, if the risk is associated with yield changes on a security or market that exhibits different yield moves than does the hedging vehicle, this difference must also be taken into account.

A number of techniques are used to calculate the hedge ratio. The following discussion describes the computation used extensively by Salomon Brothers, Inc. Other methods are shown in Appendix B of this chapter. Through the use of a regression model and elasticity measures, Salomon's approach considers both the dollar impact of the risk and the different yield movements for the cash and futures market securities. Three steps are involved in calculating the hedge ratio:

1. Determine the yield volatility of the asset to be hedged relative to that of the futures contract. The slope coefficient β in the regression,

$$\text{Spot} = a + \beta \times \text{futures} + e. \tag{9.6}$$

is used to measure the yield volatility. The spot (cash market) and futures variables are measured as percentage price changes. For instance, if an 11-basis-point change in the security to be hedged is associated with a 10-basis-point change in the futures security, the relative yield volatility, β, is 11/10, or 1.1.

2. Determine the percentage dollar price change (the elasticity) of both the cash market security and the futures market security for a 1-basis-point change in yield.

3. Calculate the *hedge ratio* by using the following equation:

$$\text{Hedge ratio} = \beta \times \frac{\text{elasticity of the corporate bond}}{\text{elasticity of the treasury bond}}. \tag{9.7}$$

ILLUSTRATION 9.3

Assume that a corporation's treasurer holds an XYZ Corporation 11 percent bond due September 1, 2002, currently valued at a price of 85 (for a yield of 13.139 percent). The treasurer determines that a 1-basis-point change will cause the price of the bond to change by 6.1 percent. She also expects that the yield will fluctuate 1.1 times as much as the treasury bond she will use in the hedge. This result has been estimated by using regression analysis on past data. The 14 percent treasury bond of February 15, 2002, has a price value per basis point of 7.9 percent (at its price of 112).

The hedge ratio is

$$\frac{0.061}{0.079} \times 1.1 = 0.85 \text{ futures.}$$

The logic behind the calculation of the hedge ratio is straightforward. If treasury yields move by 1 basis point, the XYZ bond is expected to change by 1.1 basis points. Since each basis point move causes a change of 6.1 percent for the XYZ bond, 1.1 basis points would cause a change of 6.71 percent. Now to counteract the risk of one security being likely to move 6.71 percent per 1-basis-point change in treasuries with another that will move 7.9 percent, management needs 0.0671/0.079, or 0.85, of the treasury (the futures security) per XYZ bond held.   □

A number of books discuss both portfolio and price-sensitivity approaches to calculating hedge ratios. Unfortunately, it is almost impossible to determine a perfect hedge with the known hedge ratios. Thus to some extent, every hedge remains a speculation of the basis.

Summary

The volatile interest rate and price environment of the 1980s led many financial executives to obtain a better understanding of interest rate risk and price volatility and of ways to manage it so as to protect or improve corporate liquidity. Through the use of duration analysis, management can determine the relationship between rate-sensitive assets and rate-sensitive liabilities and undertake hedging strategies to minimize the effect of interest rate risk on liquidity and shareholders' wealth.

A financial disaster can occur, though, from a hedging strategy if management does not understand the nature of the hedging function. Hedging is meant to protect corporate liquidity, not to generate profits for the sake of earning more income. In order to successfully hedge, it is necessary to establish the proper hedge ratio and carefully monitor the basis.

Key Concepts

Basis

Cash market

Duration

Duration gap

Forward market

Futures market

Hedge ratio

Hedge profit or loss

Immunization

Rate-sensitive assets/liabilities

Spot market

Appendix A

Further Illustrations of Futures Hedging

This appendix illustrates four additional uses of futures for hedging purposes.

Case 1

A corporation's treasurer undertakes a futures market hedge expecting to lock in a level of earnings from a particular investment strategy. Table A.1 summarizes the transactions. Table A.2 indicates the change in the profitability of the hedge resulting from changes in the basis.

Managers need not be completely in the dark about how a change in the basis will affect the firm's earnings. As the delivery date of a futures contract approaches, the price of that contract and the cash market price of the underlying securities should move toward equality. Thus the basis should be approximately zero by the last trading day of a futures contract, and this characteristic can be used to get some idea of how the basis might change.

If the basis for a June delivery contract is -0.20 on April 1, for example, a reasonably good guess is that from April 1 to the last trading day

TABLE A.1
Lock in a Level of Earnings (Long Hedge)

Date	Cash market	Futures market
April 1	Proceeds of $1 million from maturing investment expected June 1. Treasurer wishes to lock in current yield of 13%. Cost of $1 million in 3-month T-bills at 13% is $967,500. The discount is $32,500: $1 million × 0.13 × 90/360	Purchases $1 million, June, 3-month T-bills for $967,000. Yield is 13.20%, and the discount is $33,000: $1 million × 0.132 × 90/360
	Basis = −0.20%, or $500	
June 1	Buys $1 million of 3-month T-bills for $968,625. Yield is 12.55%, and the discount is $31,375: $1 million × 0.1255 × 90/360	Sells $1 million, June, 3-month T-bills for $968,125. Yield is 12.75%, and the discount is $31,875: $1 million × 0.1275 × 90/360
	Basis = −0.20%, or $500	
	Opportunity loss $1125	Real gain $1125

TABLE A.2
Basis Risk and Profitability

	Cash market	Futures market	Basis	Profit
April 1				
Amount	$967,500	$967,000	$500	
Yield	13.00%	13.20%	−0.20%	
June 1				
Rates fall, dollar (percent) basis unchanged (unchanged)				
Amount	$968,750	$968,250	$500	
Yield	12.50%	12.70%	−0.20%	
Gain ⟨loss⟩	⟨$1,250⟩	$1,250		$0
Rates fall, dollar (percent) basis decreases (increases)				
Amount	$968,750	$968,875	−$125	
Yield	12.50%	12.45%	+0.05%	
Gain ⟨loss⟩	⟨$1,250⟩	$1,875		$625
Rates fall, dollar (percent) basis increases (decreases)				
Amount	$968,750	$967,625	$1125	
Yield	12.50%	12.95%	−0.45%	
Gain ⟨loss⟩	⟨$1,250⟩	$625		⟨$625⟩
Rates rise, dollar (percent) basis unchanged (unchanged)				
Amount	$966,250	$965,750	$500	
Yield	13.50%	13.70%	−0.20%	
Gain ⟨loss⟩	$1,250	⟨$1,250⟩		$0
Rates rise, dollar (percent) basis decreases (increases)				
Amount	$966,250	$966,375	−$125	
Yield	13.50%	13.45%	+0.05%	
Gain ⟨loss⟩	$1,250	⟨$625⟩		$625
Rates rise, dollar (percent) basis increases (decreases)				
Amount	$966,250	$965,125	$1125	
Yield	13.50%	13.95%	−0.45%	
Gain ⟨loss⟩	$1,250	⟨$1,875⟩		⟨$625⟩

around the third week in June, the change in the basis would be +0.20. An increase in the basis would add to the earnings from a long hedge and reduce those from a short hedge.

Case 2

As shown in Table A.3, the treasurer plans to borrow funds for 60 days one month hence. Since economists expect interest rates to rise, the treasurer locks in April 30 borrowing costs on April 1 by selling seven certifi-

TABLE A.3
Borrowing for Seasonal Needs

Date	Cash market	Futures market
April 1	Determine need to issue $10 million in 60-day commercial paper. Current 60-day rate is 12.6%. Projected interest expense is $210,000: $10 million × 0.126 × 60/360	Sells 7* June CD futures contracts at 86.80. Yield is 13.2%, and the discount is $231,000: $7 million × 0.132 × 90/360
	Basis = −0.6%, or $3,021,000	
April 30	Issues $10 million in 60-day commercial paper at prevailing rate of 13.5%. Actual interest expense is $225,000: $10 million × 0.135 × 60/360	Buys 7 June CD futures contracts at 85.80. Yield is 14.2%, and the discount is $248,500: $7 million × 0.142 × 90/360
	Basis = −0.7%, or $3,023,500	
	Opportunity loss $15,000	Realized gain $17,500

*The face value of a CD futures contract is $1 million, so it would be logical to assume that 10 CD futures would be used to hedge $10 million in commercial paper. However, in this case 60-day paper is being hedged with 90-day CD futures. Therefore the hedge is "weighted" by reducing the number of CD futures contracts used by approximately one-third.

cate of deposit (CD) futures contracts. If interest rates increase, prices of futures will decline and the profit from the futures position will help offset the higher rate paid when the commercial paper is issued. Should rates unexpectedly decline and futures prices rise, the futures position loss is offset by the decreased cost of issuing the commercial paper.

Without the hedge the treasurer would have incurred an increased interest expense of $15,000. The futures transaction not only offset this opportunity loss but also generated a net gain of $2500 per contract. This gain allowed the treasurer to achieve an effective borrowing rate of 12.45 percent on the 60-day paper, 15 basis points less than the April 1 rate:

$$\frac{\$210,000 - \$2500}{60/360 \times \$10,000,000} = 0.1245.$$

Case 3

Table A.4 shows that on June 1 the treasurer expects a seasonal inflow of $10 million one month hence. To protect the present yield of 16.5 percent on CDs, he buys ten September CD futures contracts. After 30 days, when the cash is received and invested, the hedge is offset by selling the ten contracts back into the futures market. The 1.25 percent decline in interest rates over the 30-day period in the cash market created an opportunity loss for the company of $31,250. The hedge, however, offset the loss with a

TABLE A.4
Investing Excess Seasonal Needs

Date	Cash market	Futures market
June 1	Anticipates $10 million cash inflow in 30 days. Current 90-day CD rate is 16.5%. Projected return is $412,500: $10 million × 0.165 × 90/360	Buys 10 September CD futures contracts at 83.75. Yield is 16.25%, and the discount is $406,250: $10 million × 0.1625 × 90/360
	Basis = +0.25%, or −$6250	
July 1	Receives $10 million and invests in 90-day CDs at a rate of 15.25%. Actual return is $381,250; $10 million × 0.1525 × 90/360	Sells 10 September CD futures contracts at 85.05. Yield is 14.95%, and the discount is $373,750: $10 million × 0.1495 × 90/360
	Basis = +0.30%, or −$7500	
	Opportunity loss $31,250	Realized gain $32,500

$32,500 gain. When the net gain of $1250 on the hedge is added to the income stream for the next 90 days, the treasurer achieves an effective yield on his CD investment of 16.55 percent — an improvement of 5 basis points over the rate prevailing on June 1:

$$\frac{\$412,500 + (\$32,500 - \$31,250)}{90/360 \times \$10,000,000} = 0.1655.$$

Case 4

This last example hedges foreign exchange risk. In foreign exchange the basis primarily reflects the interest rate differential among countries and expectations.

The procedure is summarized in Table A.5. On June 1 the importer contracts to buy 100,000 German widgets to be delivered on December 1 at a price of DM500,000. What will be the exchange rate when she takes delivery? She can lock in the cost of those Deutsche Marks now by purchasing futures contracts for delivery of DM500,000 in that month. On June 1 the Deutsche Mark is selling from $0.37 on the spot (cash) market and $0.3726 for future delivery in the month of December. The importer hedges her exchange risk in the futures market.

When purchasing the December contracts in Deutsche Marks, the importer knows that the price quoted is for delivery on December 15 (the third Wednesday of the month). The importer will be lifting her hedge on December 1, when she will offset her futures contracts and purchase spot Deutsche Marks to pay for the widgets. Since futures and spot prices

TABLE A.5
Hedging Foreign Exchange Risk

Date	Cash market	Futures market
June 1	Bid for widgets contract on the estimated price of December 1 spot DM at $0.3724/DM	Buy 4 DM futures contracts (500,000 DM) for December delivery at $0.3726/DM
	Basis = −0.0002	
December 1	Buy spot DM to pay for widgets at $0.3741/DM	Sell 4 DM futures contracts for December at $0.3746/DM
	Basis = −0.0005	
	Opportunity loss $0.0017/DM	Realized gain $0.0020/DM

roughly coincide only on the last trading day, the importer would expect the basis to have narrowed from the June 1 basis but not to have disappeared.

The importer can interpolate between the cash price for Deutsche Marks on June 1 and the futures price for delivery on December 15. The number she derives from this interpolation is her estimated basis for December 1, six months from now. The arithmetic is as follows: December 1 is 12/13 of the way between June 1 and December 15. The basis of June 1 is $0.0026. By December 1 that basis should have progressed 12/13 of the way from 26 points to zero, or down to 2 points. In other words, on December 1 the same futures contracts should be above cash by $0.0002. Since the futures price is known, the importer can compute the cash estimate for that day to be $0.3724. This figure is used by the importer when she makes her bid for the widgets.

The actual cash price on December 1 for Deutsche Marks ($0.3741) is quite a bit higher than the estimate of $0.3724. The December 1 basis is $0.0003 higher than anticipated. This results in a small profit on the entire hedge transaction. The small profit on this hedge could just as easily have been a small loss if the importer had overestimated the basis.

This forward-pricing example utilizes basis estimation as an alternative for actual spot price forecasting. Because of the relationship between the cash and futures prices, basis estimation is much more reliable than cash price forecasting.

The preceding example may be applied to a variety of actual situations. The following are just a few categories in which futures hedging can be used:

☐ Companies building plants abroad
☐ Companies financing subsidiaries abroad

□ Manufacturers importing raw materials and exporting finished goods

□ Exporters taking payment in foreign currencies

□ Companies abroad financing operations in Eurocurrencies

□ Firms involved in the purchase or sale of foreign securities

The possibilities are limitless. Virtually everyone who deals in or with foreign countries has a need for this hedge mechanism to avoid major loss due to fluctuations in exchange rates.

Appendix B

Mathematical Determination of the Hedge Ratio

An objective of hedging is to minimize the risk of unanticipated changes in the value of cash market positions over some period of time t. In the context of differential calculus the hedging model can be written as

$$X_c \frac{dP^c}{dt} = -\left(P^h \frac{dX_h}{dt} + X_h \frac{dP^h}{dt} \right). \tag{B.1}$$

where X_c and X_h are the number of units in the cash and hedge positions, respectively, and P^c and P^h are the cash and hedge market prices per unit, respectively. The model shows that the change in the value of the cash position is opposite to the change in the value of the hedge position.

A *static hedge* exists when the size of the hedge position X_h is constant over the hedge period. In this case the hedge condition is

$$X_c \frac{dP^c}{dt} = -X_h \frac{dP^h}{dt}. \tag{B.2}$$

This relationship implies that the optimal (static) hedge ratio is

$$\frac{X_c}{X_h} = -\frac{dP^h}{dP^c}. \tag{B.3}$$

A regression model is frequently used to determine this hedge ratio.

There are a number of potential problems involved in hedging. The most important are the differences associated with risk and the term to maturity of the assets. To find a hedge asset that has the same risk as the cash market asset to be hedged is often difficult. And even if a hedge asset is found that has comparable risk, finding one that has the same time to maturity as the cash market asset may be difficult. While no sure methods exist to remedy these problems, the following approaches are suggested as being useful.

Nonmatching Maturities

If the term to maturity for the cash asset is less than the term to maturity for the hedge asset, then the hedge ratio (HR) can be written as

$$HR = -\frac{COV(c, h)}{\sigma_c^2} = -\frac{r\sigma_h}{\sigma_c}, \tag{B.4}$$

where $\text{COV}(c, h)$ is the covariance between the cash and hedged assets, σ_c and σ_h are the standard deviations for the cash and hedge assets, respectively, and r is the correlation between the cash and hedge assets.

Duration

Duration D is a measure of the maturity horizon of an asset. It may be written as an elasticity measure:

$$D = \frac{dP/P}{dR/R},$$ (B.5)

where the numerator is the rate of change in price and the denominator is the rate of change in return. With the use of Eq. (B.3) the hedge ratio can be written in terms of duration as

$$\text{HR} = -\left(\frac{P^h}{P^c}\right)\left(\frac{D^h}{D^c}\right)\left(\frac{R^c dR^h}{R^h dR^c}\right).$$ (B.6)

This formulation indicates the contribution of price effects, relative changes in the elasticity of discount rates in the cash and hedge markets, and the ratio of the cash and hedge market durations.

Questions

1. Define the terms *hedging* and *speculating*. How do they differ from each other?

2. What does *rate-sensitive equilibrium* mean? What causes a duration gap to occur? How can it be resolved?

3. Define *duration* mathematically. What is the concept underlying this measure?

4. What is a futures contract? What is the cash (spot) market? What is the difference between the cash forward market and the futures market?

5. What is the difference between a long hedge and a short hedge? What is meant by the term *selling hedge*? How is it different from a buying hedge?

6. Hedging strategy should attempt to minimize discrepancies between cash flows over time and to minimize the loss of equity. Discuss.

7. Define *basis*. What happens to the basis as the futures contract approaches maturity? Why does this happen?

8. How can profit or loss on the hedge be determined from basis calculations?

9. What is the purpose of the hedge ratio? How is it defined?

10. Discuss why it is possible to make a profit on a hedge when interest rates or prices move contrary to expectations.

Problems

1. The accounts receivable for Micro Valuation, Inc., show $1000 outstanding for Fremont Corporation. The payment is due two years from now. The account for F. T. Griggs, Inc., shows a balance of $1500, payable in installments of $500 in each of the next three years. What are the durations for each of these accounts if the firm's opportunity cost of funds is 10 percent?

2. The market value of a firm's assets are $2 million. These assets are financed with 40 percent debt and 60 percent equity. The assets have an expected duration of three years, whereas debt duration is four years. Does a duration gap exist? Explain. How much is the equity duration?

3. Rossco Corporation has an equity duration of six years, an asset duration of 10 years, and a debt duration of four years. What is the debt/asset ratio? If interest rates are forecasted to change 75 basis points, how will the equity-to-asset ratio be affected?

4.   Rework Tables 9.2, 9.5, 9.6, and 9.7 under the assumption that interest rates fall 200 basis points immediately after the firm receives the September loan. Discuss your results in terms of the appropriate hedging strategy to follow.

5.   XYZ Company wants to ensure a minimum price that it can sell its product for three months from now. The basis differential between the cash and the futures markets is − $0.15.

(a) What does management expect is going to happen to selling prices, and how can it hedge its position?

(b) What will happen in the cash and futures markets if the basis declines to − $0.10? What happens if the basis becomes − $0.20?

6.   The treasurer has a portfolio of high-grade corporate bonds with a face value of $5 million (an average price of 73–15 per bond), an average coupon of 8 percent, an average maturity of 20 years, and a current market value of $3,674,000 on January 2. She wants to protect the value of the portfolio from a possible increase in interest rates. There is no corporate bond futures market in which to hedge this risk, so she sells 50 June treasury bond futures at 81–20 in the treasury bond futures market. By March 15 interest rates have risen, and the treasurer decides to sell the corporate bonds. She sells them for 64–13 per bond. The futures are trading at 69–20. Compute the gains/losses in the cash and futures markets. Discuss your results in terms of a change in the basis. (*Note:* The bonds are priced in 32nds.)

7.   On March 15 the treasurer of Apex Corporation was worried about the price the company would have to pay to buy gold for use in the company's fabrication process. The present inventory of gold would be depleted in two months. Recent reports have suggested that gold will increase from its present level of $310 an ounce, as quoted in the spot market. On the basis of this news, the treasurer called a broker to hedge the company's position. He is told that two-month gold is selling for $330 an ounce. Assume that in early May gold is purchased for production. Also, assume that brokerage commissions are zero. What are the gains or losses in the cash market and in the futures market if gold has the following prices?

(a) $320 an ounce in the spot (cash) market and $322 in the futures market.

(b) $350 in the cash market and $355 in the futures market.

8.   Quick Kamera uses silver in its film-manufacturing process. In early April it will have to purchase more silver to replenish supplies.

(a) If prices are expected to increase during the next couple of months, what strategy should Quick use to protect against higher prices?

(b) If the cash price of silver in February is $5 per ounce and the present futures price is $5.25 per ounce, what is the basis?

(c) Two months later, on April 1, these silver futures contracts are trading at $6 per ounce and the cash price is $5.50 per ounce. What is the new basis? Has the basis strengthened or weakened?

(d) Assume that Quick hedged silver prices on February 1 and offset its position on April 1. Did Quick earn a profit on its hedging activities? Discuss the results.

9. Determine the appropriate hedge ratio to provide a perfect hedge in this scenario: A corporate treasurer holds a 12 percent corporate bond that is expected to move 4.9 percent in price for every 1-basis-point change. If a 14 percent treasury bond were used to hedge the current position, expectations are that the yield on the corporate bond would move 1.3 times as much as the yield on the treasury bond. The treasury bond has a price movement of 5.9 percent per 1 basis point.

10. The portfolio manager of Hurt Company holds a Smith Corporation 10 percent bond due October 1, 2010. The yield on the bond is 14.12 percent. Some calculations indicate that a 1-basis-point change causes the Smith Corporation bond to change by 7.3 percent. The portfolio manager wants to hedge the position by using treasury bonds. She expects the yield of the Smith bond to fluctuate 1.33 times as much as the treasury bond. The 15 percent treasury bond of November 1, 2010, has a price per basis point of 10.7 percent. To hedge her position, how many treasury bonds per Smith Corporation bond does she have to buy?

11. Rogo Company has an overseas plant in Japan that makes pogos. On June 1 Rogo bids for a part used in the manufacture of pogos. On that day the yen is valued at 0.35 American dollars in the spot market. October futures contracts are valued at 0.37 yen to the dollar. If on October 1 the yen is valued at 0.40 American dollars and the futures contract can be sold for 0.45, what is the gain or loss?

CHAPTER 10 ☐

Hedging with Options, Options on Futures, and Interest Rate Swaps

This chapter extends the examination of hedging corporate assets and liabilities through a discussion of options, options on futures, and interest rate swaps. Exchange-traded options on common stock were introduced by the Chicago Board of Options Exchange (CBOE) in 1973. In the past few years options on futures have been introduced. **Options** are contracts that give the holder the right, but not the obligation, to buy or sell a specific quantity of an underlying asset at a given price on or before a specified delivery date. Table 10.1 lists various options and options on futures traded on exchanges in the United States.

The other topic discussed in this chapter is interest rate swaps. These swaps were introduced in the early 1980s and quickly became an important tool for liquidity management. An **interest rate swap** is an agreement between two parties in which the parties agree to swap a series of interest payments or cash flows without affecting the underlying debt involved. Appendix A of this chapter provides a glimpse at other products used to manage interest rate risks.

Options versus Futures

Options and options on futures share the characteristics of futures in that they have limited life and derive their value from an underlying instrument such as bonds, stocks, or currencies. In contrast to futures, an option contract provides the option holder the right but not the obligation to require the seller (the option writer) to perform under the contract, and the seller is obligated to do so only if the buyer exercises this right. The converse, however, is not true. The seller of an option cannot require the buyer to exercise.

TABLE 10.1
Options and Futures Options Traded on U.S. Exchanges

Options

U.S. Treasury bond	5-Year U.S. Treasury note
Short-term interest rates	Long-term interest rates
S&P 100 index	S&P 500 index
Major market index	International market index
Oil index	Institutional index
NYSE index	Financial news composite index
Gold/silver index	Value Line index
Utilities index	Eurodollar
Long gilt	Mortgage backed
Treasury bills	

Futures Options

Treasury bonds	Treasury notes
Municipal bond index	NYSE composite index
S&P 500 stock index	Japanese yen
Deutsche Mark	Canadian dollar
British pound	Swiss franc
Australian dollar	
Corn	Soybeans
Soybean meal	Soybean oil
Wheat	Cotton
Coffee	Sugar
Cocoa	Crude oil
Heating oil	Gasoline
Cattle-feeder	Cattle–live
Hogs–live	Pork bellies
Gold	Silver
Copper	Lumber

Source: Data from the *Wall Street Journal*.

An important feature of an option contract is the limited liability of the purchaser. The potential loss to an option purchaser is limited to the *premium* the treasurer pays to the seller at the time of the purchase of the option. The potential gain, theoretically, is limited only by the extent of the price movement of the underlying instrument. In contrast, the holder of a futures contract remains liable for *margin calls* as long as the futures contract remains open (see Appendix B of this chapter). Losses on short future positions essentially are unlimited; losses on long futures positions are limited to the price of the contract.

The major advantage of options over futures is that when prices are extremely volatile, options can reduce the demands on cash flow. For example, if the treasurer buys a futures contract and it declines, she has to pay more margin, which, of course, is paid in cash. On the other hand, if she has purchased a call option, the treasurer has no further obligation beyond the initial premium paid. Thus, the limited risk of options provides staying power, or the ability to maintain a market position that has initially moved against the option buyer in the hope that it will eventually become profitable.

Fundamentals of Options

The price of an option depends on expectations of future economic conditions as they affect the value of the underlying security. To make options as versatile an investment vehicle as possible, the options exchange conducts simultaneous trading in options with a number of different exercise prices and a number of different expiration months. Exercise prices exist both below and above the current underlying asset price, and as the underlying asset price increases or decreases, the exchange may introduce additional options with higher or lower exercise prices.

Table 10.2 contains examples of price quotations for exchange-traded options. Each option is identified by the delivery month of the underlying security, by its strike (exercise) price, and by whether it is a **call** or a **put**. For example, under the column headed *Futures Options,* an option to purchase a September S&P 500 stock index futures contract at an strike price of 370, with a premium of 7.75, is shown. This option is referred to as a "September 370 call." The value of this call is $500 times the premium, or $500 × 7.75.

Since options differ in their exercise price, in the underlying contract, and in whether they are calls or puts, it follows that the premium also differs. While the premium reduces the potential for financial gain, the option provides protection from an unfavorable market swing. Options covering long periods of time tend to have greater premium prices. Premiums are determined daily on exchange floors and are the only component of the options agreement that fluctuates during the life of the option. The owner of the option can check the profit or loss of the option contract by comparing it with the initial purchase. If because of market movement, the option contract becomes more desirable and worth more, the treasurer may decide to sell the contract back to the market for a profit.

Option premiums are related directly to an option's intrinsic value and its time value. The **intrinsic value** is the greater of zero or the difference between the price of the contract's underlying asset and the **strike** (i.e., **exercise**) **price** — the amount at which the option's call holder may buy, or its put holder may sell, the underlying security.

The **time value of an option** is the difference between the option price and its intrinsic value. This time premium represents the amount that the option purchaser is willing to pay for the chance that the option will

TABLE 10.2
Example Price Quotes for Options and Options on Futures

Tuesday, June 19, 1990

OPTIONS

Chicago Board

S&P 100 INDEX

Strike Price	Calls–Last Jul	Aug	Sep	Puts–Last Jul	Aug	Sep
295	....	....	....	1/4	....	....
300	....	....	....	3/8	7/8	....
305	....	....	....	7/16	1 1/8	....
310	....	....	....	1/2	1 7/16	2 7/8
315	28	....	....	3/4	1 3/4	3 1/8
320	24	....	27 1/2	1	2 3/8	4
325	20 1/4	....	....	1 3/8	3 1/8	5 1/8
330	15 3/4	18 1/2	22	1 7/8	4	5 7/8
335	11 3/4	15	....	2 13/16	5 1/8	7
340	8 1/4	11 1/4	14 1/2	4 3/8	6 7/8	9
345	5 1/4	8 1/4	10 1/2	6 1/2	8 7/8	....
350	3 1/8	5 3/4	8 1/2	9 5/8	12	14
355	1 11/16	3 3/4	6 3/8	13 3/8	16 1/4	17 1/4
360	13/16	2 3/8	4 1/4	18 1/4	....	....
365	7/16	1 5/16	2 7/8	25 1/2	....	....

Total call volume 77,811 Total call open int. 239,529
Total put volume 89,576 Total put open int. 261,686
The index: High 342.41; Low 339.63; Close 341.86, +1.26

S&P 500 INDEX

Strike Price	Calls–Last Jul	Aug	Sep	Puts–Last Jul	Aug	Sep
310	....	....	....	....	....	1 1/16
315	....	....	....	....	....	1 3/8
320	....	....	....	....	....	2
325	....	....	40	1/2	....	2 3/4
330	....	....	....	....	....	3
335	....	....	....	7/8	2 1/4	3 3/4
340	....	....	....	1 1/4	3	4 1/4
345	....	....	....	2	3 3/4	5 1/2
350	....	14 5/8	19 1/2	2 1/2	5 1/4	6 5/8
355	....	....	15 1/8	3 7/8	....	8 7/8
360	9 1/2	....	11 3/4	5 1/2	8 5/8	9 1/2
365	6	....	8 7/8	8	....	11 3/4
370	3 5/8	4 3/8	6 7/8	12 1/8	....	14
375	2	....	5 3/4	15 3/4	....	....
380	1	1 3/8	4	21 1/2	....	....
385	7/16	....	2 3/8	....	....	24 1/2
390	1/4	....	....	....	....	....

Total call volume 8,456 Total call open int. 256,462
Total put volume 31,367 Total put open int. 345,082
The index: High 358.90; Low 356.18; Close 358.47, +1.59

FUTURES OPTIONS

T-BONDS (CBT) $100,000; points and 64ths of 100%

Strike Price	Calls–Last Sep-c	Dec-c	Mar-c	Puts–Last Sep-p	Dec-p	Mar-p
90	3-55	4-10	4-28	0-23	0-62	1-32
92	2-17	2-50	....	0-50	1-37	2-12
94	1-08	1-48	2-14	1-38	2-32	....
96	0-30	1-02	1-28	2-58	3-44	....
98	0-10	0-35	0-60	4-36	....	....
100	0-05	0-18	0-38	6-29	....	....

Est. vol. 60,000, Mon vol. 30,964 calls, 30,313 puts
Open interest Mon 288,317 calls, 314,547 puts

S&P 500 STOCK INDEX (CME) $500 times premium

Strike Price	Calls–Settle Jly-c	Aug-c	Sp-c	Puts–Settle Jly-p	Aug-p	Sep-p
355	11.60	....	16.35	3.05	5.30	7.95
360	8.05	....	13.15	4.50	6.95	9.65
365	5.20	7.65	10.30	6.55	9.05	11.65
370	3.05	5.35	7.75	9.40	11.60	14.00
375	1.65	3.50	5.70	12.95	....	16.85
380	0.85	2.15	4.05	17.10	....	20.10

Est. vol. 3,223; Mon vol. 1,650 calls; 2,437 puts
Open interest Mon; 17,557 calls; 32,479 puts

GOLD (CMX) 100 troy ounces; dollars per troy ounce

Strike Price	Calls–Last Aug-c	Sep-c	Oct-c	Puts–Last Aug-p	Sep-p	Oct-p
330	22.50	27.10	27.70	0.70	1.30	2.40
340	13.60	18.70	20.00	1.80	2.80	4.50
350	6.40	11.70	13.80	4.60	5.50	7.60
360	2.40	6.50	8.70	10.60	10.20	12.50
370	0.90	3.40	5.20	18.90	17.00	19.00
380	0.50	1.70	3.00	28.70	25.20	26.50

Est. vol. 3,500, Mon vol. 2,893 calls, 2,043 puts
Open interest Mon 63,592 calls, 25,367 puts

Explanation for the S&P 500 index option:
As of June 19, 1990, there were 256,462 call options outstanding and 345,082 put options outstanding for contracts expiring in July, August, and September. On June 19, trading occurred in 8,456 call contracts and 31,367 put contracts, and the S&P 500 index traded as high as 358.90, as low as 356.18, and closed the day at 358.47, up 1.59 from the previous day.

With the index closing at 358.47, a call option with a strike price below this amount is **in the money**. A put option with a strike price above 358.47 is in the money.

Source: Reprinted by permission of the *Wall Street Journal*, © Dow Jones and Company, Inc., 1990. All Rights Reserved Worldwide.

become profitable prior to the expiration date. This explains why an **out-of-the-money-option** (for which the underlying asset price is less than the exercise price) still will be traded at a positive premium. That is, some buyers are willing to take the chance that some event will change the underlying asset's price enough to make this option a profitable one. Similarly, premiums may be greater than intrinsic value because buyers are willing to pay for the chance that further changes in the underlying asset price may make a profitable option even more profitable before it expires.

Figure 10.1 summarizes the value of options. In Fig. 10.1(a), for example, if the strike price is 315 when the September S&P 500 stock index futures are trading at 324.65 and the call option premium is 16.25 (which equates to a value of $8125 = $16.25 × 500), the option's intrinsic value is 9.65 (= 324.65 − 315.00), and its time value premium is 6.60 (= 16.25 − 9.65), that is, the difference between the premium value and

FIGURE 10.1
Value of Options or Futures

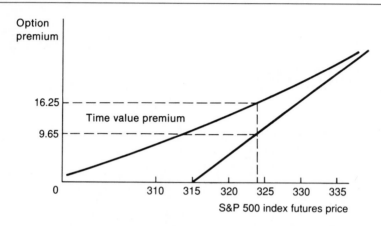

(a) September call option

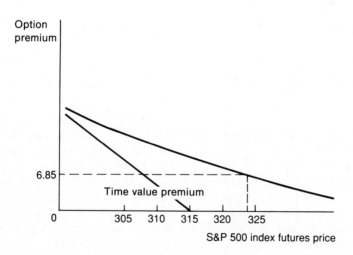

(b) September put option

the intrinsic value. Similarly, in Fig. 10.1(b) if the strike price is 315 when the September futures are trading at 324.65 and the put option premium is 6.85, the option's intrinsic value is zero, since the option is *out-of-the-money*, and its time value premium is 6.85.

An option's expiration date is the key factor in determining its time value. As the length of time until expiration decreases, there is less time for the underlying asset price — and, therefore, the option's profitability — to change markedly. Conversely, an option of long duration has more time value because the profitability of an unexpected event changing its profitability is greater.

Hedging with Options

Options can be used like futures to hedge the risk of an underlying asset. The treasurer must determine which option contract is appropriate and once a hedge is in place, continually manage the *basis of the hedge*. Profit and loss of the option hedge is computed the same way the futures hedge was calculated, that is profit = $\$\text{basis}_{\text{long}} - \$\text{basis}_{\text{short}}$, where *long* and *short* refer to transactions in the options market and have special meaning. *Long* means to buy calls to open a hedge (or sell puts to close a hedge), whereas *short* means to buy puts to open a hedge (or sell calls to close a hedge). When placing a hedge with options, the purchase of calls indicates the underlying asset is expected to appreciate in value. Puts would be purchased if the underlying asset was expected to depreciate in value.

If the firm is short in the cash market, it hedges by going long in the options market (that is, it buys calls). If it is long in the cash market, it needs to go short in the options market (it buys puts). A hedging strategy using options has the treasurer buying either calls or puts when the hedge is initially placed — not selling these instruments. Option contracts have simply replaced futures contracts in the hedge.

ILLUSTRATION 10.1

A firm does not have sufficient supplies of silver to satisfy production requirements for the next fiscal year and management expects the price of silver to continue to increase. If silver prices do in fact increase, future silver purchases will be more expensive, resulting in higher manufacturing costs. If management is not able to pass the higher costs on to consumers, cash flows and profits will decline. However, by following strategies similar to those used with management of futures contracts price risk can be minimized.

Since the firm is short in the cash market (it does not have enough silver to meet its production needs), the treasurer should buy silver call option contracts. The purchase of call options will position the firm long in the options market. If silver prices increase, the call options will appreciate in value and help offset the increased production costs the firm will incur when it buys silver in the cash (spot) market.   □

Hedge Ratio

It is necessary to determine how many option contracts to purchase to hedge the cash market position. The **hedge ratio** is the change in the price of an option for a $1 increase in the price of the underlying security. For example, if a $1 change in the cash market instrument is associated with a $0.60 change in the option price, the hedge ratio is 1/0.6 = 1.67 dollars of options per dollar of cash market security. It is necessary for the hedge ratio to be continually monitored and adjusted.

Hedging with Options on Futures

Options on futures can be used to hedge open futures contracts. The option position will be 180 degrees opposite the futures position. If the treasurer is *short futures*, then call options on futures are purchased (long options) to provide a hedge. If a *long futures* position exists, then put options on futures are purchased (short options) to provide a hedge. And since futures are used to hedge the cash market, the various positions would be as follows: long cash market, short futures market, and long options on futures market, and just the opposite if initially short in the cash market.

ILLUSTRATION 10.2[1]

Call options on futures might be bought by the treasurer to ensure an investment yield. For example, it is now May 15 and the treasurer expects to have about $600,000 available for investment on August 1. The September futures price for the S&P 500 index is 324.65 but the index is expected to be about 340 by August. The risk of losing this potential appreciation of 4.7 percent [that is (340/324.65) × 100] in the market can be reduced by either buying S&P 500 futures contracts or buying call options on S&P 500 futures contracts. If the stock market increases, the lost appreciation of having to wait to invest $600,000 in August should be roughly offset by the

---

[1]The illustrations in this section use the S&P 500 stock index. The use of futures and futures options on commodities, such as gold or sugar, could have been used to show how management can alleviate upward price pressures on cost of materials used in production.

TABLE 10.3
Hedging with Futures

Date	Cash market	Futures market
May 15	$600,000 is expected to be available August 1. Stock market is forecasted to appreciate and treasurer wants to realize some of the appreciation now.	Treasurer takes a long position by buying four S&P 500 index contracts for $649,300.
	Basis = −$49,300	
Aug. 1	The stock market gained. A $600,000 investment on May 15 would be worth $632,343.	Treasurer offsets the hedge by selling four S&P 500 contracts for $684,300.
	Basis = −$51,957	
	Opportunity loss $32,343	Real gain $35,000

profit realized on the sale of either the futures contracts or the options contracts.

On May 15, the treasurer places a long hedge by buying four futures contracts on the S&P 500 index. This amounts to a futures position[2] of $649,300 (index × contract multiplier × number of contracts = 324.65 × 500 × 4). The basis is −$49,300, which is the difference between the cash value of $600,000 and the futures position of $649,300.

On August 1, when $600,000 is available for investment, the S&P 500 index is 342.15, or 5.4 percent higher than it was on May 15. Thus, 5.4 percent, or $32,343, appreciation has been forgone in the cash market because of the treasurer's inability to invest on May 15. The August 1 basis is −$51,957 (= $600,000 + $32,343 − [342.15 × 500 × 4]). The overall profit from the hedge is $basis_{long} − $basis_{short} = −$49,300 − (−$51,957) = $2657. The real futures profit of [342.15 − 324.65] × 500 × 4 = $35,000 offsets the cash market opportunity loss of $32,343, leaving an overall economic profit of $2657. Table 10.3 summarizes the hedge.

Instead of using futures, the treasurer could have used *options on futures*. On May 15, a long position would be taken in options by buying four September 325 calls at a premium of 10.30 each, for a total cost of $20,600 (= 10.30 × 500 × 4). The basis is −$579,400, which is the difference between the cash market amount of $600,000 and the options investment of $20,600. This transaction provides an option on S&P 500 index futures with a value of $650,000 (= 325 × 500 × 4).

---

[2]If three futures contracts were purchased, the futures position would be $486,975. Since the futures contracts cannot be purchased in fractional units, the treasurer must decide if the hedge will be more than or less than the cash market position.

On August 1, the S&P 500 stock index is 342.15 and the September call futures options are selling at a premium of 25. The value of the calls is $50,000 (= 25 × 500 × 4). The basis is $582,343, which is the potential value of the $600,000 if it had been invested on May 15 ($600,000 × 342.15/324.65 = $632,343) less the value of the call options of $50,000. Investing in call options has resulted in a real option profit of $29,400 [= (25 − 10.30) × 500 × 4]. The opportunity loss in the cash market is $32,343. The overall loss on the hedge is $2943 (= $32,343 − $29,400), as opposed to the unhedged economic loss of $32,343 in the cash market. Alternatively, the total economic loss is calculated as $basis$_{long}$ − $basis$_{short}$ = $579,400 − $582,343 = −$2943, where *long* and *short* refer to transactions in the options market. Long represents the purchase of call options. Short represents the sale of the call options initially purchased. Table 10.4 summarizes this hedge.   □

Illustration 10.1 shows how futures or options on futures can be used to reduce opportunity losses. If the S&P 500 stock index had gone down, the long futures hedge would have been unprofitable, as would have the options on futures hedge. As explained earlier, the use of options on futures is less risky than the futures themselves because only the options premium can be lost, whereas the futures can result in market-to-market requirements (see Appendix B to this chapter). These circumstances seem to suggest that futures should never be used whenever options on futures exist. However, as Illustration 10.3 shows, a profitable hedging strategy may be to use both futures and options on futures. Such a strategy provides downside protection but allows the upside potential to run.

TABLE 10.4
Hedging with Options on Futures

Date	Cash market	Options market
May 15	$600,000 is expected to be available August 1. The stock market is forecasted to appreciate and treasurer wants to realize some of the appreciation now.	Treasurer takes a long position by buying four S&P Sept. 325 calls for $20,600.
	Basis = $579,400	
Aug. 1	The stock market gained. A $600,000 investment on May 15 would be worth $632,343.	Treasurer offsets the hedge by selling the four Sept. 325 calls for $50,000.
	Basis = −$582,343	
	Opportunity loss $32,343	Real gain $29,400

A joint futures and options on futures hedging strategy requires the futures position to be 180 degrees opposite the cash market position, with the options on futures position to be the same as the cash market position. For example, a *short position in the cash market requires a long position in the futures market and a short (buy puts) position in the options on futures market.*

From a conceptual standpoint, the expectation of hedging with futures is to make a profit on the futures to offset the expected opportunity loss in the cash market. However, if events turn out differently than expected, the cash market can have an **opportunity gain** and the futures investment can have a **realized loss**. If in addition to hedging the cash position with futures, the futures in turn are hedged with options on futures, management can reduce any real losses on the futures by real gains on the options. If the futures contracts are profitable, all that is lost on the options on futures is the premium (i.e., the cost of insurance).

ILLUSTRATION 10.3

Assume the same information as given in Illustration 10.2 for events on May 15; that is, the treasurer is short $600,000 to take advantage of an expected increase in the stock market. However, on May 15 she buys four September S&P 500 index futures contracts at 324.65 (in other words, she takes a long position in futures), which have a value of $649,300, and establishes a basis of − $49,300.

Although she expects the S&P 500 index to increase, she buys four September 325 futures put options on the S&P 500 index to provide some insurance against the futures contracts if expectations are not fulfilled with respect to the direction of the market. The options are bought at a premium of 10.25 each, for a total cost of $20,500 (= 10.25 × 500 × 4). These options can be exercised against futures contracts with a market value of $650,000 (= 325 × 500 × 4). Thus, the net value of the options on futures is $650,000 less the $20,500 premium, or $629,500. It is this amount that is used to calculate the basis between futures and options on futures. The *basis, defined as futures market minus options on futures market,* is $649,300 − $629,500 = $19,800.

Assume as of June 10 that the stock market has suffered a relapse — contrary to expectations of May 15. The S&P 500 index has fallen to 310.05, the futures contracts are selling for 312.25, and the put options premium is 23.75. This means that if the $600,000 had been invested on May 15, it would have depreciated to $573,017 (= $600,000 × 310.05/ 324.65) as of June 10 — an opportunity loss of $26,983. The futures have a value of $624.500 (= 312.25 × 500 × 4) — a real loss of $24,800 if the futures hedge is offset. The futures options premium is $47,500 (= 23.75 × 500 × 4) — a profit of $27,000 if the hedge is offset. The June 10 bases are

$$\text{Cash market} - \text{futures market} = \$573,017 - \$624,500$$
$$= -\$51,483,$$
$$\text{Futures market} - \text{options market} = \$624,500 - \$602,500$$
$$= -\$22,000,$$

where the option market value represents the June 10 value of the futures controlled by options less the option premium ($650,000 − $47,500). Table 10.5 summarizes the hedge.

The overall economic profit position on June 10, assuming the total hedge is offset, is

$$\text{\$basis}_{\text{long}} - \text{\$basis}_{\text{short}}$$

Cash vs. futures:	$-\$49,300 - (-\$51,483) =$	$2183
Futures vs. options:	$\$22,000 - (\$19,800) =$	$\underline{2200}$
Economic profit		$\underline{\underline{\$4383}}$

TABLE 10.5
Hedging with Futures and Options on Futures

Date	Cash market	Futures market	Options market
May 15	$600,000 expected to be available August 1. Stock market expected to appreciate.	Take a long position by buying four September S&P 500 index future contracts with a value of $649,300.	Take a short position by buying four September 325 put options for $20,500. Net value of futures controlled is $629,500.
	Basis = −$49,300		Basis = $19,800
June 10	Stock market has fallen. A $600,000 investment on May 15 would be worth $573,017.	Futures have lost value and are now worth $624,500.	Put options have appreciated to $47,500. Net value of futures controlled is $602,500.
	Basis = −$51,483		Basis = $22,000
	Opportunity gain $26,983	Real loss $24,800	Real gain $27,000

Note:
Net value of futures controlled is the contract value of the futures less the option premium:
  May 15 $325 × 500 × 4 − $20,500 = $629,500
  June 10 $325 × 500 × 4 − $47,500 = $602,500

The *cash versus futures* profit of $2183 is based on the *opportunity savings* of $26,983 by not investing the $600,000 in the cash market on May 15 and the *real loss* in the futures market of $24,800. The *futures versus options* profit is the difference between the profit on options ($27,000) and the loss on futures ($24,800).

If the market is expected to continue its decline, the treasurer should lift the futures hedge but keep the options hedge in place. Thus there will be no further losses on the futures, so long as prices keep declining, and the put options on futures will continue to appreciate in value. This hedge continues to provide downside protection. However, if prices advance, the put options could lose all their value. □

Interest Rate Swaps

One of the more creative approaches available to the treasurer to reduce interest rate risk is the interest rate swap.[3] The **interest rate swap** transfers the repricing interval of two firms' assets or liabilities. This enables firms to choose from a wider variety of asset and liability markets without having to incur additional interest rate risk — that is, risk that arises because of changes in market interest rates. For example, one firm has long-term assets that yield a fixed rate of return; but it also has liabilities with interest payments that fluctuate with market rates of interest (floating-rate liabilities). This firm loses when interest rates rise unexpectedly, because the interest cost of its liabilities rises, but the revenue from its fixed-rate assets remains the same.[4] Conversely, this firm gains from an unexpected drop in interest rates. This sensitivity of a firm's net earnings and cash flows to interest rate fluctuations is the firm's exposure to interest rate risk. The other firm involved in the swap faces the opposite situation: Its assets yield a return that fluctuates with market rates, but the interest payments on its liabilities are fixed for a longer period of time. A rise in interest rates benefits this firm, because its revenues rise faster than its cost of borrowing; but a drop in market rates reduces its net earnings.

Basics of Swaps

When firms such as these have opposite interest rate exposures, they can come together — usually through an intermediary — and, in effect, ex-

---

[3]The basic concepts discussed here also apply to a currency swap, which is an arrangement between two firms to exchange principal and interest payments in two different currencies at prearranged exchange rates. Currency swaps are frequently used to alleviate foreign exchange currency risk.

[4]You should recognize this problem as being similar to the accounts receivable illustration discussed in Chapter 9.

change some of their interest payments. The firm with floating-rate debt essentially takes over some of the interest payments of the firm with fixed-rate debt, and in return the firm with the fixed-rate debt takes over some of the interest payments of the firm with floating-rate debt. In effect, one firm converts the interest payments on its liabilities from a floating-rate to a fixed-rate basis, and the other converts its liabilities from fixed to floating rate.

Parties to a swap agree to make interest payments to each other. They do not actually swap liabilities, nor do they lend money to each other. Each firm remains responsible for paying the interest and principal on its own liabilities. Therefore, *swaps do not appear on a firm's balance sheet;* instead they are used to alter the exposure to interest rate risk implied by the balance sheet.

The amount of interest paid is based on some agreed principal amount, which is called the **notional principal** because it never actually changes hands. Moreover, the two parties do not exchange the full amounts of the interest payments. Rather, at each payment a single amount is transferred to cover the net difference in the promised interest payments.

ILLUSTRATION 10.4

In May 1989 an intermediary arranged a $100 million, seven-year interest rate swap between Financial Services Corporation (FSC) and Basic Manufacturing Inc. (BMI). FSC has most of its dollar-denominated assets yielding a floating rate of return based on London Interbank Offered Rate (LIBOR). BMI's large asset investment basically generates a fixed return.

In the swap, BMI agrees to pay FSC a fixed rate of 11 percent per year on $100 million, every six months. This payment covers the interest FSC has to pay on a $100 million bond it recently issued in the capital markets. BMI also agrees to pay FSC the 2 percent underwriting spread FSC incurred issuing the bonds. In exchange, FSC agrees to make floating-rate payments to BMI at 35 basis points (0.35 percent) below LIBOR. The intermediary receives a broker's fee of $500,000.

Twice a year, the intermediary (for a fee) calculates FSC's floating-rate payments by taking the average level of LIBOR for that month, deducting 35 basis points, dividing by 2 (since it is for half a year), and multiplying by $100 million. If this amount is larger than BMI's fixed-rate payment, FSC pays BMI the difference. Otherwise, BMI pays FSC the difference. Table 10.6 sets forth the calculations.

The swap allows FSC and BMI to reduce their exposures to interest rate risk. FSC can now match its floating-rate assets priced according to

TABLE 10.6
Interest Rate Swap Payments ($000)

Date	LIBOR	Floating-rate payment	Fixed-rate payment	Net payment from FSC to BMI	Net payment from BMI to FSC
May 1989	8.98%				
Nov. 1989	8.43	$4040	$5500		$1460
May 1990	11.54	5595	5500	$95	
Nov. 1990	9.92	4785	5500		715
May 1991	8.44	4045	5500		1455

Note: Payments are calculated as follows, using May 1991 as an example:

$$[0.0844 - 0.0035] \times \$100{,}000/2 = \$4045$$
$$0.11 \times \$100{,}000/2 = \$5500$$

LIBOR with an interest payment based on LIBOR, while the fixed-rate interest payments on its bond issue are covered by BMI. At the same time, BMI can hedge part of its fixed-rate earning assets with the fixed-rate payment it makes to FSC.   □

Why Not Just Use Futures or Options?

As discussed in the last chapter and earlier in this chapter, companies can hedge their risk with the use of exchange-traded futures and/or options. However, one disadvantage of exchange-traded futures and options is that they are standardized contracts that exist only with certain specific delivery dates and deliverable types of instruments. In particular, futures are available only for delivery dates at three-month intervals out to about two and one-half years. This makes it impossible to hedge beyond this period. Interest rate swaps, in contrast, are private contracts with virtually every aspect of the agreement open to negotiation. Thus, a swap can be tailor-made to fulfill one firm's particular needs, assuming another firm can be found to fit the other end of the contract. This flexibility allows firms to set up long-term arrangements, thereby filling the gap left by futures and options. Most swaps have a final maturity of three to ten years.

Why Not Refinance?

A firm that has only floating-rate liabilities but now desires fixed-rate debt could buy back some of its floating-rate debt and issue fixed-rate debt. However, swaps may be less costly than refinancing for several reasons. One is that firms with lower credit ratings may have to pay relatively higher interest rates in the fixed-rate market than in the floating-rate market and a subsequent swap transaction. Another reason is that swaps circumvent transactions costs associated with refinancing (costs of legal fees, advertising, and regulatory restrictions) because swaps do not involve new borrowing. Additionally, swaps can usually be arranged in a few days whereas refinancing can take several weeks.

In summary, the existence of interest rate swaps makes it possible for firms to borrow in the markets in which they have a comparative advantage rather than refinance in markets in which they do not. These firms can then swap interest payments with firms that have a comparative advantage in another market to achieve the interest payment characteristics they desire.

Risk of Swaps

Among the more important risks associated with interest rate swaps are interest rate risk and default risk. Interest rate risk arises because changes in market interest rates cause a change in a swap's value. Default risk occurs because either party may default on a swap contract. Both participants in a swap are subject to each type of risk.

Interest rate risk. As market interest rates change, interest rate swaps generate gains or losses that are equal to the change in the replacement cost of the swap. These gains or losses allow swaps to serve as a hedge that a company can use to reduce its risk or to serve as a speculative tool that increases the company's total risk. A swap represents a hedge if gains or losses generated by the swap offset changes in the market values of a company's assets, liabilities, and off-balance-sheet activities such as trading in interest rate futures and options. However, a swap is speculative to the extent that the firm deliberately increases its risk position to profit from predicted changes in interest rates.

Default risk. Participants in interest rate swaps are subject to the risk that the other party will default and thus be unable to continue the agreement. Although the other party has no principal at risk, it would again be stuck with an interest risk exposure. It could negotiate a new swap arrangement with another firm, but the terms of that agreement would depend on current market interest rates, which may be more or less advantageous to the firm. Default risk can be reduced by requiring collateral, standby letters of credit, or a third-party guarantee — all of which are costly.

Other risks. The lack of standardization of swap contracts can make it more difficult to find another party and to negotiate a mutually agreeable contract. It also costs more to close out a swap contract (at least 25 basis points) if the need arises, than a futures contract position (2 to 5 basis points), which can be closed out readily.

Summary

This chapter has extended the discussion of hedging by examining options, options on futures, and interest rate swaps. The primary advantage options have over futures is limited liability. The only downside risk with an option is loss of the premium. Futures, on the other hand, have to mark to market. The combination of futures and options on futures allows management to change the return distribution to its favor. Options on futures minimize downside profit risk but allow management to realize any upside profit potential.

Interest rate swaps have become popular hedging instruments because frequently they are better suited than other hedging techniques. Swaps are freely negotiated agreements between private parties and, thus, can be tailor-made. But this customization also makes swaps more expensive than futures and options.

Key Concepts

Call option
Default risk
Exercise price
Hedge ratio
In-the-money-option
Interest rate risk
Interest rate swaps
Intrinsic value
Long position
Notational principal

Opportunity gain or loss
Options
Options market
Option on futures
Out-of-the-money option
Put option
Realized gain or loss
Short position
Strike price
Time value of option

Appendix A

Overview of Some Other Hedging Instruments

There are several products available to hedge risks that have not been discussed in either Chapters 9 or 10. This appendix provides an overview of some of these products. Readers wanting a discussion in more depth should refer to any recently published book on interest rate risk management.

Caps. A buyer of a *cap* buys the right to be paid the interest rate differential between the strike price and the then current rate at certain times during the life of the cap. It is like a series of purchased put options. The purchase price is usually an initial fee, although it may be amortized over the life of the cap.

For example, the treasurer buys from the bank a five-year 11 percent cap on three-month LIBOR on a notional principal of $100 million. The initial payment may be about $2.5 million. In return, every three months if the three-month LIBOR rate is above 11 percent, say it is at 12 percent, the bank pays the treasurer the difference for that interest rate period: $100,000,000 \times (0.12 - 0.11) \times 90/360 = \$250,000$. This type of calculation is repeated every three months during the term of the cap.

Caps are frequently used when the treasurer is concerned about borrowing on a floating rate but finds the fixed rate of a swap too expensive.

Floor. This is similar to a cap, except it is triggered by rates falling below the negotiated rate. Payments and mechanics are identical to swaps.

Collar. A *collar* is the use of both a cap and a floor. The treasurer buys a cap, and pays the premium associated with it, but at the same time sells a floor at a lower (or sometimes same) strike price than the cap and receives a premium.

Participating Interest Rate Agreement (PIRA). With a PIRA, the treasurer buys a cap on a notional amount and sells back a floor *at the same strike level* but on some smaller fraction of the notional principal. The primary purpose of the PIRA is to reduce the initial premium paid on the cap.

Corridor. The treasurer buys a cap at one level, say five years at 11 percent, and in the same transaction sells a five-year cap at a higher strike, say 13 percent. At rates between 11 and 13 percent the treasurer is protected, but if rates go above 13 percent, he becomes unprotected. Corridors are simply another way of reducing the initial premium of the purchased cap.

Swaptions. A "swaption" is an option to enter into an interest rate swap. The treasurer pays a premium at the time of purchasing the swaption. The option provides the right but not the obligation to enter into a swap at a pre-agreed level.

Interest Rate Guarantees (IRG). The simplest type of interest rate option, an IRG is an option to buy or sell a forward rate agreement. This is effectively identical to a cap with only one interest period.

Forward Rate Agreements (FRA). A FRA is contract between two parties (a buyer and a seller) for a stated sum of principal at a stated price of interest for a stated period.

Appendix B

Mark to Market for Futures Contracts

The operation of the futures market is best illustrated by an example. Assume a trader wishes to buy one treasury bill futures contract that calls for the delivery of $1 million face value of treasury bills upon the maturity of the futures contract. The trader's broker may require an initial margin of $1500. The $1500 is deposited and the purchase is consummated. Assume the price moves against the trader so that he suffers paper losses of $600. The value of the margin account will now be $900, which is below the maintenance margin of $1000. This maintenance margin is the minimum value of the margin account that the trader can have without having to post more margin. The broker then requires the trader to make another margin deposit to restore the margin account to the original level of $1500.

This process of monitoring the market proceeds through the technique of daily settlement, or *marking to the market*. It consists principally of realizing the gains or losses sustained on a futures position each day. When the losses bring the value of the margin account below the maintenance margin level, it triggers a margin call. But when one gains on the futures contract, one can withdraw funds in excess of the $1500 initial margin amount.

Questions

1. Differentiate between an option contract and a futures contract.

2. Why are options safer hedge vehicles than futures?

3. Explain the difference between put and call options. What are the main factors determining put and call premiums? What do the terms *intrinsic value* and *time value* mean?

4. Who are the parties to the sale of a put and call option, and what function is performed by each party?

5. Explain how options can be used as hedging instruments.

6. Describe how to hedge a short position in the cash market using (a) options or (b) options on futures. If management exercises the option, what happens in each situation?

7. Describe how to hedge a long position in the spot market using both futures and options. What is the advantage in using both futures and options?

8. How is the basis used to calculate the profit or loss for the option hedge on the futures contract?

9. What is meant by an interest rate swap?

10. Discuss how firms manage and settle interest rate swaps.

11. Discuss the risks involved in interest rate swaps.

Problems

1. A call option for a treasury bond has a strike price of 65–00, and its premium is 4–00. The treasury bond futures are trading at 68–00.

   (a) What is the intrinsic value of this option?

   (b) What is the option's time value premium?

2. A call option to purchase a treasury bond futures contract has a strike price of 62–00. Given the accompanying information, calculate each option's intrinsic value and time value in dollars.

	March	June	September
Futures price	62–05	62–14	62–23
Options premium	1–38	2–61	3–42

3.   Verbex Company is expecting $200,000 worth of investments to mature in three months. Management would like to reinvest the money in some risk-free government bonds currently selling at 88 and yielding 11.9 percent. It feels that interest rates will decline before the money is available for investment.

(a) What futures strategy can it follow?

(b) What options strategy can it follow?

(c) Can management use a strategy that combines both futures and options? Explain.

4.   Two months ago, a firm's treasurer placed a hedge by buying futures and then hedging the futures in the option-on-futures market. The June 1 cash-futures basis was −$600, while the basis between the futures and the option-on-futures was −$75. Moments ago, the treasurer calculated the basis between the cash and the futures markets to be −$550 and the basis between the futures and option on futures to be −$45. How much is the economic profit on this hedge if it is to be closed in the next few minutes (assuming the bases do not change)?

5.   Ten August 350 futures call options on the S&P 500 index were purchased for a premium of $20 each. What is the value of the futures contracts that these options can be exercised against?

6.   Rework Illustration 10.3 using the following information for June 10. The S&P index has risen to 330, the futures contracts are selling for 332, and the put options premium is 2. Calculate the overall economic profit or loss on June 10, assuming the hedge is offset at this time.

7.   Rework Table 10.6 in Illustration 10.4 under the assumption FSC agrees to make payments to BMI at 45 basis points below LIBOR. All other information remains the same.

8.   Assume in Problem 7 that BMI agrees to pay FSC a fixed rate of 10 percent per year on $100 million every six months. How much are the net payments to each of the participants over the period covered in Table 10.6?

CHAPTER 11 □
Asset-Based Financing

In recent years relatively rapid business growth, general inflation, broader economic uncertainties, and unique financing situations have frequently resulted in inadequate liquidity levels. As a result, fewer firms have been able to raise required cash and working capital through short-term unsecured loans. To facilitate the borrowing needs of these companies, an alternative source of financing is proving highly beneficial. Referred to as **asset-based financing**, this alternative has gained increasing popularity and credibility in recent years. Asset-based financing uses such assets as accounts receivables, inventories, plant and equipment, and real estate as collateral for loans.

The subject of asset-based financial services is a total balance sheet concern and, therefore, is of importance to both businesses and creditors alike. The purpose of this chapter is to examine some of the reasons for the importance of asset-based financing and its recent growth, examine characteristics of borrowers, and discuss the various forms of collateral used to improve the firm's liquidity.

Conditions Conducive to Asset-Based Financing

The asset-based financial services industry has matured rapidly in recent years. Historically, the industry was characterized as "lenders of last resort," mainly because of a lack of public understanding and negative attitudes often associated with secured financing. As the number of businesses unable to satisfy borrowers' requirements increased, the need for asset-based financial services also increased; and the industry inevitably gained credibility.

Asset-based financing is selected by the borrower for a variety of reasons. Some of these reasons include marginal creditworthiness, above-average growth, business seasonality, industry cyclicality, turnaround financing for a troubled firm, acquisition financing, and monetization of illiquid assets. Each of these reasons is examined in the next section. Asset-based financing can also be for reasons to adjust the duration gap caused by the sensitivity of assets and liabilities to interest rate changes. This was discussed in Chapter 9.

Marginal Creditworthiness

During the 1970s corporate debt increased faster than either the book value or the market value of equity. The capitalization ratios of many corporations became so low that lenders feared liquidity of borrowers would be impaired by major capital expenditures unless all layers of capitalization were expanded. High interest rates on debt and low market values of equity made conventional methods of raising capital less attractive.

Thus if a borrower's credit risk is suspect and the firm is characterized by high leverage, poor earnings trends, or weak financial ratios, management may rely on secured financing to provide cash or working capital. In this situation the lender prefers the asset-based loan to an unsecured loan. However, both borrower and lender should determine why the poor financial situation exists before relying on asset-based financing.

Business Growth

Firms experiencing above-average growth may require external funds to provide an appropriate level of net working capital to finance the cash conversion cycle — the difference between the period of conversion of inventories and accounts receivable into cash, and the length of time creditors are willing to wait for payment. Cash or borrowing capacity must be available to sustain the sales growth rate. Asset-based financing can be used to supply the needed additional net working capital and at the same time allow a company to reserve its debt capacity, which leaves bank lines open for future needs.

Business Seasonality

A firm may need to carry higher receivables or inventories owing to the seasonality of its business. Management may borrow from external sources if not enough cash is generated internally to carry temporarily higher levels of receivables or inventories. This situation is particularly well-suited for asset-based financing because such borrowing can be tied directly to asset account balances in an effort to maintain an appropriate ratio of loans to asset value and an appropriate level of net working capital. In effect, as the inventory levels increase, so does the borrowing capacity. Thus the borrower gains access to a revolving line of credit based on the liquid value of the collateralized assets.

Industry Cyclicality

Highly cyclical businesses such as steel and automobile manufacture require large amounts of permanent net working capital. If internal cash generation is insufficient to maintain a minimum level of net working capital, meet capital expenditures, service debt, pay reasonable dividends, or maintain some borrowing level throughout the economic cycle, asset-based financing may be used to avoid periodic cash shortfalls.

Even though profitability may decrease during an economic recession for a cyclical firm, an asset-based lender may still be willing to provide the firm with needed funds. The lender will do so because the collateral gives the lender additional protection against risk (if the collateral is properly valued and monitored).

Financial Turnarounds

Sometimes, financially troubled firms seek new cash to alleviate creditor pressure or avoid bankruptcy. Loans collateralized by receivables can provide funds that may not otherwise be available to these firms since the loan is self-liquidating. As cash is received on outstanding receivables, it is applied to the loan in full or in some proportion.

Acquisition Financing

Asset-based financing has become popular in leveraged buyouts. In its simplest terms a leveraged buyout (LBO) is the purchase of a company or the subsidiary of a company by an investor group, largely with borrowed funds. In a typical deal an investment banker or other deal maker assembles a group of investors, almost always including the management of the organization to be bought and usually one or more financial institutions. These investors acquire the stock or assets of the company by contributing a relatively small amount of equity and arranging a relatively large amount of debt financing. The investment banker packaging the buyout purchases an interest in the equity along with the management on the assumption that the leveraging will net the investors as much as $25 for every dollar risked.

The amount of debt financing is based on that company's existing assets. Thus the borrower is able to raise significantly greater amounts of funds than would otherwise have been possible.

These highly levered transactions entail collateral monitoring and detailed negotiations. Because equipment and inventory are often undervalued on the balance sheets of many midsized privately held companies, asset-based lenders have been able to apply higher lending ratios in delivering required funds. The *lending formulas used are often based on the company's assets rather than on cash flow predictions, as in conventional borrowing.*

Asset-based lending packages for these leveraged buyouts may combine a nonamortizing loan with one tied to a repayment schedule. The term loan is based on a quick liquidation value of the acquired company's fixed assets. The nonamortized portion of the financing is provided through a revolving loan against receivables and inventories. The lending formulas typically advance a percentage against the liquid value of eligible receivables, inventory, and the liquidation value of fixed assets.

Acquisitions by purchase of corporate shares are also handled by the asset-based financing industry, although not as frequently as purchase of assets. Acquisition of shares would be indicated if the acquiring firm were interested in utilizing the target company's tax loss. Other possibilities might be that the target corporation has an advantageous lease franchise or other contract.

In summary, *the main advantage to the borrower of an asset-based loan is that the firm can maximize leverage and maintain an appropriate level of liquidity.* An asset-based loan gives management the ability to borrow additional funds beyond moneys obtained from more conventional financing. Indeed, many times management cannot take advantage of market opportunities because of the unavailability of conventional unsecured bank financing.

Asset-based financing also gives the firm the opportunity to grow and become more profitable by taking advantage of the leveraging power provided by the collateralized assets. Since an asset-based loan does not require an annual cleanup, this type of financing is very helpful to companies experiencing rapid growth. Moreover, because the company borrows only what it needs at the time needed, borrowings can be kept at a minimum, and the cost of borrowed funds can be reduced.

An unfavorable feature of asset-based financing is that it increases the cost of unsecured debt. That is, asset-based transactions are invariably levered beyond the limits of normal unsecured bank loans. Hence unsecured lenders are exposed to more risk; there are fewer assets available to repay the loan should a liquidity crisis occur.

Evaluation of Borrowers

The evaluation of borrowers is perhaps the most important part of the asset-based financing decision to lenders. This evaluation determines whether or not the lending institution makes an appropriate return on equity. The factors that receive primary consideration in the credit evaluation are cash flow and analysis of collateral.

Cash Flow Analysis

The preliminary evaluation of an asset-based borrower differs from that of a conventional unsecured borrower. In the conventional approach to lending, the lender's protection is primarily in the cash flow of the entity that is being financed. Loans are tied to the expected cash flow of the borrowing firm or of the entity guaranteeing the loan. In this situation the lender must have a history of stable cash flow, and the loan represents a conservative multiple of that proven cash flow.

In asset-based lending the lender has a different orientation. Although cash flow analysis is used to determine whether the firm generates sufficient cash flow from operations, protection is based primarily on the assets and secondarily on the cash flow of the borrowing firm. Therefore, rather than tie the loan amounts to the cash flow, the leverage, or the amortization ability of the borrower, the asset-based lender should tie the loan to the forced liquidation value of the borrowing firm's assets offered as collateral.[1] This is not to say that credit analysis is ignored. The lender must remember that collateral is not a substitute for performing a thorough credit analysis of the borrower. Lenders do not often make money in liquidations, and the presence of collateral does not make a difference in whether or not there will be a liquidation. Collateral only assures a lender that if liquidation does occur, the lender will have the right to negotiate for the proceeds of the borrower's collateral.

Analysis of Collateral

Collateral of superior quality can partially offset poor credit quality. However, collateral analysis should be separated from credit analysis. *Collateral analysis should address the worst case.* In the event that liquidation is necessary, the lender should be able to obtain maximum recovery. Collateral only assures a lender the right to negotiate for the proceeds of liquidation.

Two factors that influence acceptable collateral are the life of the collateral and the suitability and liquidity of the collateral.

1. *Life of the collateral.* Lenders of secured short-term funds prefer collateral that has a life closely related to the term of the loan. In this way lenders are assured that the collateral is sufficiently liquid to satisfy the loan in the event of a default. For short-term loans, collaterals are a firm's short-term (current) assets — accounts receivable, inventories, and marketable securities.

2. *Suitability and liquidity of the collateral.* Although virtually any asset may be pledged to ensure payment, not all assets are equally desirable.

---

[1]An obvious example where this was not done is in the savings and loan industry.

The suitability of various assets is determined largely by the borrower's line of business. Elements for consideration when one is analyzing the suitability of collateral include standardization of grading, durability, marketability, and stability of demand. The lender of short-term secured funds is more apt than not to find only liquid current assets acceptable as collateral. The *liquidability of an asset refers to the asset's ability to be converted into cash.* The quality of the ability is measured in terms of speed of conversion and value of exchange. Accounts receivable or inventories having an average age of 180 days are questionable candidates as security for a 90-day note.

Almost any of the firm's assets can be used as collateral, as discussed in the next section. The lender determines the desirable percentage advance to make against certain collateral. This percentage advance is normally between 30 and 90 percent of the book value of the collateral. It varies according to both the type of collateral and the type of security interest being taken. It is low if the collateral is not very liquid and high if the collateral is highly liquid. Several kinds of collateral can be employed. The following sections examine several forms.

Marketable Securities

Marketable securities make excellent collateral because of their highly liquid status. Despite this positive attribute, marketable securities do not play a dominant role as loan collateral. When businesses operate in tight credit environments, large security portfolios are uncommon.

Accounts Receivable

Some businesses find it advantageous to borrow money through the pledging (assignment) of accounts receivable or the selling of them. With the pledging of accounts receivable as security for a loan, a business usually applies to either a commercial credit company or a bank.

The selling of accounts receivable has been traditionally associated with **factoring**. Until recently, most financial managers prescribed factoring as a last resort to satisfy their credit needs. Today factoring is a highly recommended way of raising resources. It has gained increased popularity in industries as diverse as apparel, automotive parts, consumer electronics, furniture, paint, textiles, and watch manufacturing.

A new technique has recently emerged for selling receivables. It is called **asset securitization**. Securitization helps firms improve their credit quality by allowing them to liquify assets and lower leverage. The removal of assets from the company's balance sheet may enable the firm to obtain off-balance-sheet financing.

Pledging Accounts Receivable

Financing through **pledging of accounts receivable** is typically a continuing arrangement rather than a one-time transaction. If a financial agreement exists between the borrower and the lender covering a year, or perhaps covering an unspecified time period, the agreement would normally provide for the assignment of accounts receivable on a selective basis. Effectively, a pure line of credit is established that increases as sales increase.

The lender scrutinizes the borrower's billing and collections procedures carefully and evaluates the acceptable collateral on a liquidation basis rather than on a "going-concern" basis. The lender agrees to advance funds up to a specified percentage of the accounts pledged.[2] This percentage incorporates an amount for any sales returns and allowances. The borrower draws against this amount only as funds are needed and is charged interest on the net daily amount outstanding each day and not the full amount available. The interest rate ranges between 2 and 5 percent over the prime rate, although it is negotiable.

Accounts receivable may be financed on a notification or nonnotification basis. Under a **notification plan** the receivables are pledged and payment is made directly to the lender, but the borrower remains responsible for the payment. The lender receives power of attorney to endorse notes and checks in the assignor's name.

Under the more satisfactory and more commonly used **nonnotification arrangement**, the borrower collects as agent for the lender. This allows the financing arrangement to remain confidential. Uncollectible accounts are the responsibility of the borrower.

The advantages to a company borrowing through the pledging of accounts receivable are several:

☐ Receivables financing is sometimes effectively used to offset delays in receivables collection time and to finance an increase in receivables.

☐ An increased investment in receivables presents an opportunity to increase leverage and thereby improve the firm's return-on-equity.

☐ Income tax deductibility of interest paid on new receivables loans significantly subsidizes the cost of carrying additional receivables, especially during times of high interest rates.

---

[2]An evaluation of payment proportions or balance fractions is the logical place to start when one is evaluating accounts receivable collateral and setting an advance rate. Frequently, the lender uses aging schedules and historical turnover ratios, which can lead to questionable conclusions (see Chapter 14).

□ An increase in receivables financed by external sources produces a swift conversion of receivables to cash (it decreases the cash conversion cycle) and creates reinvestment opportunities or the ability to deploy funds on a timely basis to other areas of the business where the return may be higher.

The chief disadvantages of pledging receivables are also several:

□ The lender probably will be willing to lend only some portion of the face value.

□ The extra burdens of complying with the lender's requirements fall upon the bookkeeping department, which is less likely than the credit department to be under direct control of the treasurer.

□ The lender may insist that all accounts be pledged, even though the amount to be borrowed is much less in amount and the loan is not continuous.

□ The lender may insist on notification to customers and require them to make payments on account directly to the lender.

Factoring Accounts Receivable

Although similar in nature to pledging, **factoring of accounts receivables**[3] differs from a pledging arrangement in that it is not a form of secured financing and the factor assumes all credit risks. A factoring arrangement is accomplished through a written contract established between the factor and the client. In this arrangement a factor buys a client's accounts receivable for cash on an open account. The factor guarantees or purchases the firm's receivables as they arise, either with or without recourse concerning credit losses. This guarantee is subject to the condition that the firm must obtain the factor's approval before shipping any goods, and the merchandise must be received and accepted by the customers without dispute. This straightforward credit and collection service is referred to as *maturity factoring (factor nonborrowing)*. *Old-line factoring (factor borrowing)* pertains to firms that wish to have funds advanced on uncollected receivables. Such advances are *unsecured* financing.

The benefits of factoring are the following:

□ The rate of cash flow and the flexibility afforded are greatly increased. To companies exposed to the cyclical hazards of seasonal

---

[3]Most readers participate in a form of factoring, without realizing it, each time they use a credit card. The cardholder is the customer, the merchant is the client, the credit card issuer is the factor who does the credit checking, bookkeeping, and risk taking. The merchant is charged a commission for the factor's services.

sales, factoring can facilitate the smoothing out of cash flows by drawing advances against expected sales for needed material purchases.

- The greater availability of working capital to fund production and sales leads to higher utilization of fixed assets and greater profits.

- Cost savings can result in the purchase of stock and new materials, because with the improved liquidity from factoring a client can obtain discounts from suppliers for prompt payment on bulk purchases.

- Budgeting becomes easier with an assured cash flow geared to sales and not dependent on debtor payments.

- Unlike other forms of financing, factoring imposes no requirement to set aside funds for loan repayment, since the factoring debt is repaid by the client's customers.

- The rapidity of cash flows aids the firm in avoiding the dilution of ownership equity by enabling it to acquire additional net working capital without seeking new investors.

- The predictability of future cash flows is enhanced through the elimination of uncertainty and risk by fixing the percentage of credit sales receipts that will be absorbed by credit and collection expenses (including bad-debt losses). This percentage will be the commission on credit sales the firm agrees to pay the factor.

- The services of a factor eliminate the salaries and wages for credit and collection personnel. Also, office costs such as invoice mailing, long-distance telephone calls, and telex costs are reduced. These cost savings make the actual costs of factoring lower than explicitly stated.

- Factoring also gives management time to concentrate efforts on other business concerns such as production and marketing.

- Factors help define and organize customer profiles while providing useful business information to allow a business to take on certain credit risks that would have otherwise been unacceptable. Risk reduction is clearly advantageous to firms considering a potential buyer whose credit loss could jeopardize the financial security of the business.

Factoring is not for everyone, though, and there are disadvantages to be considered:

- When invoices are numerous and relatively small in dollar amount, the administrative costs involved may render this method of financing inconvenient and expensive. A prospective client must decide whether the benefits outweigh the costs.

□ A nonborrowing client must compare the factoring charge with the cost savings of not maintaining a credit and collection department.

□ Qualitative elements must be considered, such as the quality of service, one's ability to work with the account executives, and the ability to turn over receivables.

□ In some circumstances the firm will have reached its maximum credit extension with the bank, so the main consideration will be the cost to owners in terms of dilution of majority ownership or the cost of venture capital.

□ For a long time accounts receivable financing was frowned on by most trade creditors; it was regarded as a confession of a firm's unsound financial position. It is still regarded as such by some people, although many sound firms engage in either receivables pledging or factoring. Still, the traditional attitude causes some trade creditors to refuse to grant credit to a firm involved in this method of financing on the ground that this practice removes one of the firm's most liquid assets.

ILLUSTRATION 11.1

Management is considering an offer by a local bank to (old-line) factor the company's receivables. Management expects to need an average monthly balance of $150,000 for the months of July through October, with a peak cash need of $200,000 during this period. The terms of the factor agreement are:

□ The bank will hold 20 percent of the face value of the receivables in reserve.

□ A 1.5 percent commission will be assessed each month on the basis of the face value of the receivables.

□ The annual interest charge on borrowed funds will be 12 percent, calculated on a discounted basis.

□ Factoring will be on a nonrecourse and notification basis.

The company's credit terms are net 30 days. Customers remit their payments an average of 30 days after sale. Bad-debt expense is generally 0.75 percent of sales. Monthly clerical and credit-checking costs during the period of the loan average about $2125 each month. Management forecasts monthly sales of $350,000 during the period the loan is needed.

The maximum amount of loan available to the company is calculated as follows:

Accounts receivable balance	
(outstanding one month)	$350,000.00
Less:	
Reserve ($350,000 × 20%)	⟨70,000.00⟩
Commission ($350,000 × 1.5%)	⟨5,250.00⟩
Maximum loan amount	$274,750.00
Interest ($274,750 × 12%/12)	2,747.50
Cash proceeds realized from loan	$272,002.50

If the receivables are (old-line) factored and an average loan balance of $150,000 exists, the effective annual cost of the factoring arrangement is 16.16 percent, as is shown next. The net cash proceeds are as follows:

Commission ($350,000 × 1.5%)	$ 5,250
Interest ($150,000 × 12%/12)	1,500
Gross cost	$ 6,750
Less savings:	
Bad debts ($350,000 × 0.75%)	⟨2,625⟩
Clerical and credit checking	⟨2,125⟩
Net monthly cost	$ 2,000
Average loan balance	$150,000
Interest ($150,000 × 12%/12)	1,500
Cash proceeds	$148,500

The effective annual cost is $= \dfrac{\$2,000}{\$148,500} \times 12 = 0.1616.$ □

Remember that many companies using factors are doing so for their credit, collection, and bookkeeping services. Companies that are factor borrowing are generally healthy enterprises that have found liquidity tight because of a high investment in current assets. On this same point, we stress that not every company requiring factoring will receive it. Potential clients must meet a number of criteria, including good management, favorable product acceptability, a desired financing package, and, for a new company, imminent profit forecasts supported by orders on hand.

Securitization

Issuers of credit are following the lead of mortgage lenders and adopting asset securitization as a new means of raising funds and disbursing risk. The new asset-backed debt securities (ABS) are patterned after mortgage-related securities and provide many of the same benefits. However, non-mortgage-backed finance has taken longer to evolve because of the lack of any governmental payment guarantee as well as various legal and accounting uncertainties.

Figure 11.1 shows the basic structure of an ABS. In general, ABSs are *pass-through certificates* issued by a *grantor trust,* who is also the registrant for purposes of filing under the Securities Act of 1933. Certificates are sold to investors through an underwritten public offering or private placement. The certificates represent fractional undivided interests in one or more pools of financial assets. The selling company transfers assets with or without recourse to the grantor trust, which is deemed to be formed and owned by the investors, in exchange for the proceeds from the issuance of the certificates. Thus, except for any recourse provision, the assets are sold outright and the selling company has no obligation with respect to the re-payment of the certificates.

The asset cash flows are remitted to the trustee, who pays scheduled interest and principal payments to the investors on the same business day of every month at the pass-through or coupon rate of interest. Typically, any prepayments on the assets are also paid by the trustee to investors on these payment dates. The aggregate cash flow from the assets is always equal to or greater than the required payments on the ABS. The differ-

FIGURE 11.1
Basic Structure of an Asset-Backed Security

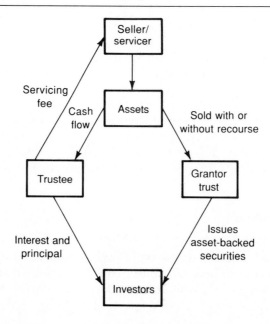

ence, if any, is usually paid to the selling company as compensation for its role as servicer. A portion may also be used for credit enhancement, including paying a letter of credit fee and/or funding a reserve account.

ABSs rely on structure and collateral to achieve their creditworthiness and therefore their marketability. An ABS is made "bulletproof" (i.e., bankruptcy proof) so that it is effectively insulated from any misfortunes of the selling company. This is done by legal contracts stipulating that the pooled assets collateralizing the ABS would not be consolidated into the estate of the bankrupt company.

ABS structures can accommodate receivables with fixed amortization schedules or revolving credits, either fixed or floating rates, either simple or effective interest methods, and different levels of quality. In general, the securitized assets have the following characteristics:

- Predictable cash flows
- Consistently low delinquency and default experience
- Total amortization of principal at maturity
- Average life of more than one year
- Many demographically and geographically diverse obligors
- Underlying collateral with high liquidation value and utility to the obligors.

There are several reasons why a company might decide to sell financial assets through an ABS structure:

- *Facilitate rapid asset growth and increase economies of scale.* ABSs enable companies to increase financing activity without inflating their balance sheets. In addition, greater economies of scale can be achieved in loan underwriting and servicing.
- *Decrease barriers to entry.* Securitization makes it easier for entities to originate consumer loans.
- *Liquify assets.* Securitization makes receivables more marketable and permits asset redeployment.
- *Manage earnings.* Receivable sales can be timed so that gains or losses can be recognized in the quarters or years desired, from both tax and financial reporting perspectives.
- *Improve asset/liability matching.* The interest rate, maturity, and duration risks associated with financing a specific pool of assets are completely removed when the assets are sold. For foreign currency denominated assets, any currency risk is also eliminated.
- *Achieve sale treatment for financial reporting purposes.* Sold assets are off-balance-sheet, except for any estimated liability associated with a recourse provision.

□ *Improve financial measurements.* Unlike asset financing, sold assets require little or no underpinning of equity. The reduction of assets and liabilities on the balance sheet, combined with the retention of servicing income, improves a variety of financial measurements such as returns on equity and assets, and coverage and capitalization ratios.

□ *Increase borrowing capacity.* A company can often leverage financial assets more through an asset-based security structure than through on-balance-sheet debt financing.

To date, the primary private sector ABSs have been securitized by automobile and credit card receivables. Securities have also been supported by the cash flows of computer leases, truck leases, land and property leases, commercial mortgages and commercial loan receivables.

Inventory

Inventory management considerations are not unlike those associated with receivables. Often pressure on net working capital results from the need to carry higher inventories in anticipation of larger sales volume, seasonal stock buildups, or cyclical production patterns. Seasonally patterned inventories accumulate, peak, then fall rapidly as sales grow. Without the ability to invest larger dollars in inventory, the firm may lose out on sales or market share. Therefore, as with investment in accounts receivable, the firm is faced with deciding on how to finance the greater investment in inventories.

A large volume of credit is secured by business inventories. Inventory is a useful form of collateral because it is physical — it can be seen and counted. Businesses that use inventory loans generally are typified by one or more of the following characteristics:

□ Their manufacturing and/or distribution pattern is such that there is an extended period between receipt of raw materials and the sale of finished goods.

□ Inventory is a major current asset.

□ Alternative sources of finance are inadequate for current needs.

□ Major increases in inventory occur sporadically in the normal course of business owing to special purchase opportunities or variances in deliveries, production, or sales.

□ The business is highly seasonal, requiring large purchases or accumulation of finished goods that do not result in sales until a specific time of year.

□ The company anticipates rapid growth in sales that requires an even larger anticipatory buildup of inventory.

Physical possession of the inventory is specified as part of the collateral arrangement. In some cases the borrower retains the pledged inventory and pays the lender when that inventory is sold or used. This procedure typically is used for consumer durables, such as appliances and automobiles, where the presence of a serial number on each inventory item is an easy way to keep track of the collateral. It is not as easy to keep track of parts, materials, and nondurable goods, and the pledged inventory may be entrusted to a third party for safeguarding.

If pledged inventory is kept off the premises of the borrowing firm, it is held in a *public warehouse* by a bonded company that provides warehousing services as part of collateral arrangements. If, instead, the inventory is kept on the premises of the borrower but under the control of a bonded warehouse operator, the arrangement is referred to as a *field warehouse.*

The lender decides the worth (on the basis of cost or market value) of particular items of inventory and then agrees to advance some prescribed percentage of the value as a loan to the firm. The lender will set the advance rate at less than 100 percent and usually less than the advance rate for receivables. Otherwise, full-cost recovery would not be realized should liquidation become necessary. The inventory valuation method used by the borrower can affect the amount of borrowings. The first-in, first-out (FIFO) method of inventory (discussed fully in Chapter 15) reflects the maximum inventory valuation during a period of increasing prices, thus permitting maximum borrowings. Consistency and accuracy in whatever method of inventory valuation is adopted is paramount.

The nature of a particular inventory and its relative stage in the production process affects its estimated value as collateral. Perishability is one property that may cause the inventory to be unacceptable collateral. Specialized items may not be acceptable if the market for them is small. Another characteristic to be considered is the physical size of the inventory. Very large items may not be desirable because of the expense associated with their transportation and storage.

All types of inventories may be offered as collateral, but typically only raw materials and finished goods are considered acceptable. Raw material can often be resold in the market for close to market value. Important considerations regarding finished goods are the spread between manufacturer's cost and the wholesale price, and the marketability of the product. The wider the spread and the stronger the demand for the goods, the higher the advance rate is. Work-in-process inventory is seldom used as collateral. The partially completed goods will not realize a return near either market value or cost in a liquidation. Therefore advance rates are low, if they are made at all.

Types of Collateral

There are three types of collateral in inventory financing: floating inventory liens, trust receipt inventory liens, and warehouse receipt loans. **Floating inventory liens** represent a general claim on a group of inventory. When a firm has a stable level of inventory that consists of a diversified group of merchandise, and no single item has an excessively high dollar value, the lender will generally advance less than 50 percent of the book value of the average inventory, and the interest charge is usually 3 to 5 percent above the prime rate.

A **trust receipt inventory loan** is a loan made against specific collateral, which can be identified (e.g., serial number), and the borrower physically holds the inventories (collateral) as the lender's trustee. These loans against inventory are available not only from the captive finance subsidiaries of manufacturers but also from commercial banks and commercial finance companies. Loans against collateral are relatively expensive. The legal and control pitfalls of this form of loan security are well recognized. This technique is usually limited to use as a supplemental protection on loans to firms that generally qualify for unsecured credit.

Warehouse receipt loans allow the lender to maintain control over the collateral, which is placed in either a bonded terminal or a field warehouse chosen by the lender. The borrower cannot sell any of the collateral without the lender's written permission. Warehouse receipt loans provide the lender with the best position with respect to collateral — the lender has direct control over its disposition. This type of loan involves greater clerical costs than the floating lien; this increased cost is carried by the borrower. The interest rate is 3 to 5 percent above the prime rate plus a 1 to 3 percent warehouse fee.

Advantages and Disadvantages

Major benefits of inventory financing are twofold. First, cash can be freed up earlier in the inventory-sale-receivable-cash cycle (that is, the cash conversion cycle is reduced). As raw materials are acquired, the firm may use increased borrowing power, assuming the lender will lend on a secured basis tied to the value of inventories. Cash freed from inventory via secured borrowing can be reinvested or used to satisfy other liabilities such as salaries, taxes, or other maturing debts.

Second, by resorting to asset-based financing, the firm effectively mortgages out its assets. By doing so, the firm earns the tax benefit of interest expense deductibility. This feature lowers the firm's effective carrying rate. In short, the firm alters the cost of capital by leveraging more assets at the secured borrowing rate. At the same time, it improves the velocity of cash flows.

The major disadvantages of inventory loans can be briefly summarized as follows:

☐ Financing costs are typically 3 to 5 percent above the prime rate.

☐ Not all forms of inventory are equally acceptable.

☐ Inventory may be physically removed from the borrower's premises and placed in a bonded warehouse, which may cause production or sales disruptions.

☐ A lower proportion of financing is given for inventories.

ILLUSTRATION 11.2

A bank is willing to lend $150,000 on a two-year note to a customer. Interest would be charged at 20 percent annually and require the loan to be secured by a warehouse receipt. The costs to the customer to maintain a field warehouse arrangement would be $2400 annually. The loan would enable the customer to pay for purchases within the discount period.

The *monthly* cost of the warehouse receipt loan is as follows:

Field warehouse arrangement	$ 200
Interest ($150,000 × 20%/12)	2500
Monthly cost	$2700

The effective interest rate is $2700/$150,000 = 1.8 percent monthly, or 21.6 percent annually.   ☐

Fixed Assets

Management is becoming increasingly aware of the underutilized value of its real property interests and the implied opportunities this value represents with regard to the basic business. A company does not need to own the buildings it uses in order to conduct a profitable business. It does need cash to conduct its business. Thus the question becomes, "How can a company's real assets be utilized to raise cash in the most cost-efficient manner, cash that will be use to support the company's primary business operations?"

There are a number of alternatives that management can use singularly or in combination to address this question. The objective is to make more effective use of assets in order to meet liquidity needs. The alternatives to be discussed in the following subsections are as follows:

1. Disposing of excess properties
2. Pledging plant and equipment
3. Mortgaging real estate
4. Using sale and leaseback agreements
5. Arranging a tax exchange
6. Selling an ownership interest

Sale of Excess Property

Management must identify those real assets that are integral to the company's operations and those assets that are, or will be in the near future, excess. The excess assets could be sold, leased, offered for joint-venture development, or exchanged for other properties. Net present-value analysis that incorporates abandonment value is the ideal technique to use to identify properties for potential sale.

Pledging Plant and Equipment

Plant and equipment can be used in asset-based financing by pledging the asset as collateral. The liquidating appraisal value should be used for secured loans made against plant and equipment. A fair market value appraisal, a replacement value appraisal, and an insurance value appraisal are inadequate since they do not tell the lender what the collateral will bring in a distress sale. Background information on the plant and equipment (including their past use) is necessary. If the plant and equipment are highly specialized, their relative liquidity is reduced.

The plant and equipment user assumes the risks and benefits of ownership and operates under a lien until the debt is repaid. The advantage of a loan secured by plant and equipment is that the income generated by the equipment helps offset the cost of its financing. In addition, the cost of acquiring equipment is fixed, providing stability during a time of volatile interest rates.

Mortgages on Real Estate

Mortgages on real estate may be taken as security for a loan, but they are used infrequently and usually as a last resort. Transactions involved in securing loans on real estate are usually heavily detailed in tax and title searches, valuation procedures, and execution of instruments. Should the borrower fail in repayment, the carrying cost of the real estate can quickly dissipate the value of the initial arrangement.

Sale-and-Leaseback Agreement

In a **sale-leaseback agreement** the owner of the asset sells the asset to a second party. The second party then leases the asset to the seller. Sale-leaseback agreements often arise because historical accrual accounting is unable to reflect the impacts of inflation. Any long-term assets that have appreciated in value are understated on the balance sheet. This understatement, in turn, can affect the firm's ability to raise needed capital.

Through a sale-leaseback the selling firm realizes a large, positive initial cash flow and retains the benefits of using the asset. The firm should be able to obtain funds at a reasonable rate because the sale-leaseback is, in effect, the ultimate in a secured loan; the lender obtains title to the collateral at the inception of the loan. In addition to raising needed funds, a sale-leaseback can result in a better-looking financial statement if it can be structured as an operating lease. Under this arrangement the firm will show no additional debt on its books even though it has an obligation to make periodic payments. If the asset sold had a book value lower than the selling price, the total reported assets will be increased by the amount of gain on the sale. The result is that the firm's debt/equity ratio decreases, net assets increase, and the current and quick ratios increase (due to cash received).

Even if the lease is capitalized and debt is recorded, when book value of the asset is less than the selling price, a gain is recognized under certain conditions. If the gain is recognized, ratios are affected in the same manner as with an operating lease, except that the debt/equity ratio may increase or decrease depending on the ratio prior to the sale-leaseback (assets will increase, but so will debt).

ILLUSTRATION 11.3

The sale of assets for $55 million, which have a book value of $47 million, results in a gain reported in the income statement of $8 million and an increase in liquid assets. The old, undervalued assets are replaced on the balance sheet with the higher amount of cash (or notes) received for the assets. Earnings may increase because the reduction of interest expense on corporate borrowings, and annual depreciation on the disposed asset may exceed the newly created operating lease expense. However, annual cash flow from operations may not improve by this decision. For cash flow to improve, the following condition must hold:

New operating lease expense

$$< \text{(interest savings)} + \text{(depreciation)}\left(\frac{\tau}{1 - \tau}\right),$$

where τ is the marginal corporate tax rate. Thus the cash flow benefit of the sale-leaseback usually comes from the large infusion of cash at the time of the transaction. Subsequent periods' cash flows are usually negative.   □

Although sale-leasebacks are normally associated with capital equipment, creative financial managers can use this method to raise cash by utilizing other assets. For instance, IU International sold macadamia nut orchards to investors but retained a 99-year right to manage the orchards and market the nuts. This technique allowed the company to **monetize** $10 million of assets being carried on the books at ridiculously low values. It was more profitable for the firm to utilize the assets than to own them.

Tax Arrangement Exchange

In an exchange of similar assets, the firm trades one nonmonetary asset used in a trade or business, or for investment, for another that performs the same function. The earning process is considered to be uninterrupted by the exchange of assets. When the exchange is viewed from this perspective, it is logical to transfer the book value of the old asset to the new asset. This is exactly how the Internal Revenue Service views the process.

The tax advantage of *like-kind* **tax arrangement exchange** of assets arises for two reasons. First, the taxpayer defers the payment of tax until the second asset (the asset acquired) is sold. Second, the taxpayer continues to take the same depreciation deductions as were taken on the first asset (the asset exchanged).[4] Gains on exchanges of similar assets are not recognized unless cash (commonly called *boot*) is received. In such cases, the old asset is considered to be partially sold and partially exchanged.

No loss can be recognized in a tax-free exchange, even if cash is paid by the party suffering the loss. A loss occurs when the asset exchanged has a book value greater than either its own fair market value or the fair market value of the asset received.

ILLUSTRATION 11.4

Assume that the company finds that its corporate offices are inadequate. The building has a market value of $35 million, a book value of $3 million, and initially cost $10 million. The marginal tax rate is 28 percent, as is the

---

[4]The Tax Reform Act of 1986 resulted in lower depreciation deductions for assets placed in service after passage of the Act. Tax-free exchanges result in continued use of the higher depreciation of the surrendered asset, if it was purchased before 1986.

capital gains rate. A new office complex would cost $20 million to construct. Sale of the old property would result in $8.96 million taxes: 28 percent × ($10 million − $3 million) + 28 percent × ($35 million − $10 million). Therefore the firm would net $26.04 million ($35 million − $8.96 million) from the sale but would pay $20 million for the new facilities.

Suppose this property could be exchanged for $18 million cash plus property valued at $15 million. The $2 million difference between the market price ($35 million) of the building to be given up and the total value of the exchange ($15 million + $18 million) is considered equity to the purchaser for buying the inadequate property. The company will be taxed only on the $18 million cash portion of the sales price. Therefore only $4.2 million in taxes will be paid: 28 percent × ($10 million − $3 million) + 28 percent × ($18 million − $10 million). The company will net $13.8 million in cash from this transaction, as opposed to netting only $6.04 million from the sale and new purchase.   ☐

The advantages of this transaction are obvious. The company has more liquidity, higher profits from the gain on the sale, and newer facilities that fit into its operating plan.

Sale of an Ownership Interest

Rather than sell an asset outright, a firm may choose to sell an ownership interest in an asset. Ownership interests can take many forms, including an equity participation by a lender, a loan-and-option agreement, a convertible mortgage, and a right to future income streams from an asset.

Lenders looking for an inflation hedge may find **equity participation** in projects involving appreciating assets to be an attractive alternative to conventional loans. The lender puts up a portion of the cost of the asset from its own funds and lends the borrower the remaining funds at a lower-than-normal rate. The borrower gives up some of the advantages of total ownership but gains liquidity benefits from not having to commit 100 percent of the required funds and obtains funds at below-normal rates.

A **loan-and-option agreement** gives lenders the option to purchase an asset (or a portion thereof) that the lender has been financing. The option is usually not exercisable until several years after the loan is made. In return for this option the lender supplies funds at a below-market rate.

ILLUSTRATION 11.5

General Motors obtained needed liquidity by obtaining a loan on its former New York headquarters building. The Aa bond rating for General Motors at the time was 15 percent, while the loan rate was 10 percent. The lender had the option of buying the building in 10 years for $500 million — the principal amount of the loan. If the option was not exercised, General Motors was required to repay the loan. General Motors was effectively paid $25 million a year for the option (the 5 percent rate difference times the $500 million principal). □

A **convertible mortgage** allows the lender to convert a mortgage debt into an equity interest.

ILLUSTRATION 11.6

Cadillac-Fairview secured a $37.7 million mortgage at well below market rates, thus lessening interest expense and alleviating liquidity needs. In return for the rate concession the lender obtained the right, after ten years, to convert the mortgage to a 50 percent ownership interest. Otherwise, Cadillac-Fairview has a 30-year mortgage at below-market rates. Unlike General Motors in its loan-and-option agreement, Cadillac-Fairview faces no balloon payment of principal if the option is not exercised. □

Selling the rights to future income derived from an asset allows a firm to obtain cash immediately for assets that are not currently productive.

ILLUSTRATION 11.7

Tucson Electric Power Company and Public Service of New Mexico put a portion of their coal reserves into a grantor trust. Shares in the trust were sold for $60 million. The investors were treated for federal income tax purposes as if they owned the assets of the trust directly. The investors obtained the rights to a 23-year stream of royalty income from the mining of the coal. The royalties were indexed to inflation, 3 percent above the GNP deflator. The utilities estimated that they would have had to pay 6 percent above the GNP deflator for conventional floating rate financing. If coal reserves are greater than expected, the investors will earn a higher-than-minimum return. If the reserves are depleted before 23 years pass, the investors get their money sooner. The utilities have given up future, uncertain income for current, low-rate money, which helps corporate liquidity. □

An interesting development in the sale of an ownership interest was Echo Bay Mines creation of securities.

ILLUSTRATION 11.8

In 1981 Echo issued some securities, which had returns dependent on the future value of gold. The company offered units consisting of one preferred stock share and four *warrants*[5] to purchase gold at a fixed price for a period of three years beginning in 1986. The company was able to take advantage of its proven gold reserves to obtain immediate cash flow.   □

Pensions

Chapter 5 discussed unfunded pension obligations as an off-balance-sheet item. The present discussion examines pensions as an asset-based financing source. Many companies have vast amounts of available capital in surplus **defined-benefit pension funds** that they can recapture.[6] These surpluses have arisen as a result of the following conditions:

1. *Minimum-funding standards.* The Pension Benefit Guaranty Corporation (PBGC) prescribes how to compute payments per employee per year. These formulas result in overfunding for a young worker and underfunding as he or she ages. The funding is expected to come out even when the employee retires. A company with a new pension plan or a young work force is likely to be overfunded.

2. *Stock market.* Pension fund assets are invested about 40 percent in stocks. When a bull market occurs, increased equity values boost the value of pension fund assets.

3. *Recession.* Economic downturns result in layoffs of employees and elimination of jobs. The same pension fund assets therefore cover fewer workers.

4. *High interest rates.* Many companies have purchased high-yielding annuities to cover their pension promises. The higher the stated yield, the lower the purchase price is for a bundle of pension benefits. Also, the more the annuity rate exceeds the assumed earnings rate of the pension fund, the greater is the paper surplus created.

Table 11.1 lists the 25 most overfunded pension plans as of 1988.

---

[5]A **warrant** is a long-term call option issued by a company.

[6]W. Alderson and A. Chen, "Excess Asset Reversions and Shareholder Wealth," *Journal of Finance* (March 1986): 225–41, show that the market reacts positively to the announcement of pension plan terminations. They conclude that the positive market reaction implies a redistribution of wealth from the participants to stockholders.

TABLE 11.1
Overfunded Defined Benefit Pension Plans as of 1988

Company	Plan assets in excess of projected benefit obligations	Surplus as % of equity
Large excesses		
Ameritech	$ 3,571.4	45.5
AT&T	10,305.0	89.9
Bell Atlantic	1,472.0	16.0
Du Pont	4,561.0	29.3
Eastman Kodak	1,446.0	21.3
Exxon	1,223.0	3.9
Ford*	2,148.9	10.0
General Electric	6,029.0	32.6
General Motors*	3,820.4	10.7
GM Hughes	1,244.7	16.5
GTE	3,293.0	34.7
IBM	4,132.0	10.5
Lockheed	1,443.0	58.3
McDonnell Douglas	1,765.0	55.4
NYNEX	2,272.0	24.1
Pacific Telesis	1,739.0	21.4
Prudential	1,345.0	35.7
Rockwell International*	1,265.0	34.2
Southwestern Bell	2,258.4	26.6
US West	2,310.0	29.7
Other well-known companies		
Boeing	392.0	7.3
Inland Steel	255.0	16.3
International Paper	654.0	14.4
Martin Marietta	653.8	54.5
Monsanto	529.0	13.9
Teledyne	634.6	29.6

*The company also had an underfunded plan. It is not included in the above numbers.
Source: Companies' 1988 annual reports.

Plan Termination as a Source of Capital

A major reason for terminating overfunded defined-benefit pension plans is to provide an immediate source of cash.[7] An alternative to terminating a

---

[7]A study of A. E. S. Hamdallah and W. Ruland, "The Decision to Terminate Overfunded Pension Plans," *Journal of Accounting and Public Policy,* 5 (1986): 77–91, indicates that the type of management compensation plan is correlated with the decision to terminate overfunded plans. Managers are more willing to terminate a plan when they share directly in the benefits of plan termination (if compensation is tied to reported profits and terminating the plan will increase profits).

plan is simply to reduce future funding. Obviously, the former approach provides a faster source of funds.

Even though pension funds are managed separately from other corporate assets and for the benefit of employees, *a company that terminates a defined-benefit plan can take back any assets left over after accrued benefits are paid.* The excess of the old plan assets on termination and reversion over the amount needed for either employee "cash-out" or contribution to a new plan is recognized as a fully taxable gain on plan termination if the replacement plan is not closely linked to the terminated plan. If the new plan is linked to the old plan, the gain is amortized over time as a reduction in future pension expense.[8]

The basic procedure for plan termination is simple. The company must notify the PBGC of its intention to terminate the plan at least 10 days in advance of the proposed termination date. If the PBGC finds that the plan is overfunded, it issues a notice of sufficiency within 90 days of the original notification, and the termination proceeds as scheduled.

There is, however, more than one way to terminate a defined-benefit plan:

1. Terminate and replace with a **defined-contribution plan**. This method is the most common and is indisputably legal. The company simply ends its plan and pays off all the accumulated benefits of both retirees and active workers, nonvested as well as vested, usually with annuities or a lump sum. Starting from scratch, it then creates a defined-contribution plan for the active employees.

2. Terminate and replace with a new defined-benefit plan. The new plan that is set up is usually a slight improvement on the original. The legal issue is whether or not a real termination has occurred. If it has not, the excess funds in the plan should not go to the corporation but, rather, to the employees.

3. Spin off the retired workers. The old plan is divided into two parts: one for active and one for retired workers. The first group continues with its defined-benefit plan. After allocating enough assets to cover those benefits, the company places the remaining assets into the retirees' plan. That plan is then terminated, with the company buying annuities for the participants and the company taking whatever surplus cash is left over. The Employee Retirement Income Security Act (commonly called ERISA) has attacked this plan as not being a true termination.

---

[8]Generally, an employer who receives surplus assets from a terminated defined-benefit plan is subject to both income taxes and excise taxes on the amount it receives. The excise tax is 10 percent and is nondeductible for income tax purposes.

Many critics of these practices exist. Corporate managers offer the logical explanation that they are still offering retirement benefits at the same time that they are strengthening the company that issues the employees' paychecks.

Indirect Sources of Capital

Many companies view pension assets as a source of capital in a more indirect way. They hold on to the cash they would normally contribute to their retirement plans — thus avoiding the need to tap the capital markets as heavily — and, instead, send along their own corporate bonds (as does LTV Corporation), common and preferred stock (as do Eastman Kodak, Reynolds Metals, American Airlines), real estate (Exxon Corporation), and even gas well royalty interest (Diamond Shamrock). Other companies have been raising capital through the sale and leaseback of corporate property with their own pension funds as the buyer (United Technologies, Burroughs Corporation).

Summary

Asset-based financing has expanded rapidly in recent years. Inflation has been a significant reason for this growth. Many businesses have doubled their sales because of inflation alone. Thus firms have become more leveraged, making it more difficult for them to finance growth and operations with conventional unsecured loans.

Asset-based financing is playing an extremely important role in the management of net working capital. In general, the advantages for the borrower of asset-based financing include improved liquidity and working capital and the ability to increase leverage when additional borrowing would not otherwise be available.

From the lender's perspective, the lender must evaluate risk/reward trade-offs on asset-based loans by using two types of criteria — one for evaluating the prospective borrower's general creditworthiness and one for evaluating the quality of collateral used to support the loan. After the lender has thoroughly evaluated the collateral, a written document should be prepared setting forth the price and terms of the loan. All terms should be thoroughly documented to protect both parties and prevent misunderstandings. Once the loan is made, the lender should monitor the collateral to determine whether any problems are developing.

The assets involved in asset-based loans can be of any type and can be either pledged as collateral or sold outright. The only criterion that can be advanced for any asset to be included is that it is presently owned and unpledged by the borrower and the lender considers it to have sufficient value to collateralize the loan. The assets discussed in this chapter include marketable securities, accounts receivable, inventory, fixed assets, and pensions. The discussion of accounts receivable examined pledging, factoring, and securitization arrangements. The discussion of fixed assets examined sale of excess assets, pledging agreements, mortgages, sale-leaseback arrangements, tax exchanges, and sale of an ownership interest. Terminating overfunded defined-benefit pension plans was also examined as a means of obtaining liquidity.

Key Concepts

Asset-based financing
Asset securitization
Collateral analysis
Convertible mortgage
Equity participation
Factoring of accounts receivable
Floating inventory lien
Defined-benefit pension plan
Defined-contribution pension plan
Loan-and-option agreement

Monetize assets
Notification versus nonnotification
  basis
Pension surplus
Pledging of accounts receivable
Sale-leaseback agreement
Selling the rights to future income
Tax arrangement exchange
Trust receipt inventory loan
Warehouse receipt loan

Questions

1. Name the conditions conducive to asset-based financing. Briefly discuss each condition.

2. What are the factors influencing acceptable collateral?

3. Which of the following would be most suitable as collateral for a 90-day note from the company's lender? Discuss.

   (a) Units of electric switches premounted on circuit boards

   (b) Accounts receivable due within 30 days

   (c) Share of stock of IBM

   (d) Stock options on American Can stock to buy at $45 per share; the current price is $48.25, and the expiration date is in six months

   (e) Vacant land adjacent to the plant

   (f) Government marketable securities

   (g) Ninety-day commercial paper from Xerox

   (h) Life insurance on the company's president paid for by the company

4. How might the use of assets as specific loan collateral influence existing and future nonsecured loan arrangements?

5. How does pledging of accounts receivable differ from factoring of accounts receivable? Discuss the advantages and disadvantages of each.

6. Discuss the concept and the operations behind asset-backed debt securities (ABS).

7. What are the characteristics of firms that use inventory as loan collateral?

8. Distinguish between floating inventory liens, trust receipt inventory liens, and warehouse receipt loans.

9. What are the advantages and disadvantages of inventory loans?

10. Discuss the factors that will influence the percentage of face value that will be loaned against (a) accounts receivable and (b) inventories.

11. How does a sale-leaseback transaction impact on the demand and supply of liquidity of the selling firm?

12. What is a loan and option transaction?

13. What is a tax arrangement exchange?

14. What factors lead to firms using the employees' pension fund as an asset-based financing vehicle?

Problems

1. The XYZ Corporation wishes to decrease its cash conversion cycle by pledging its accounts receivable. After the firm is analyzed by ABC Credit Company, an agreement is reached. XYZ can pledge its short-term receivables to ABC, who will lend to XYZ at 1/20 of 1 percent against net daily debt and a service fee of 1/100 of 1 percent against net daily pledge. ABC reduces the short-term receivables by a 5 percent dilution factor and an additional 10 percent margin-of-error factor. Management can earn 8 percent per annum on surplus funds. The marginal tax rate for the company is 40 percent.

(a) What is ABC's advance rate to XYZ Corporation?

(b) How much must XYZ pledge if it needs $50,000 for 30 days?

(c) What is the cost of pledging for 30 days?

(d) If ABC advances $50,000 to XYZ and then collects receivables to pay off the loan, as indicated in the accompanying schedule, how much will XYZ owe in interest and service costs at the end of 30 days? Assume collections are at the end of the day.

Day	4	7	14	18	21	25	29
Collect ($000)	$9	$5	$10	$8	$12	$9	$6

(e) Suppose the XYZ Corporation has the choice of repaying ABC by following either (c) or (d). Discuss which method it should choose. Use the residual income model discussed in earlier chapters (e.g., Chapter 1) to make the decision. The marginal tax rate is 40 percent.

2. The Diamond D Company needs an additional $325,000 to satisfy the payment of seasonal purchases. It will need this financing for one month. Management is negotiating with its local bank to factor the company's accounts receivable. The bank's interest rate is 12.5 percent annually, and in addition, the bank charges a commission of 1.25 percent on the loan amount. The bank will accept 90 percent of the new credit sales.

(a) How much will the company have to factor?

(b) What will be the total new accounts receivable level?

(c) What will be the total cost of this method of financing?

3. The Diamond D Company (Problem 2) could pledge its account receivable to achieve the required $325,000 cash demand. The bank's policy is to charge interest at prime plus 2 (which is currently 13.75 percent) on average daily receivables pledged.

(a) Determine the dollar interest cost of pledging.

(b) Determine the effective annual percentage cost.

(c) Determine the amount of receivables pledged if the advance rate is 85 percent.

4. Management wishes to increase its liquidity balance by negotiating a 90-day inventory loan with a local bank. Relations between the company and the bank are good and expected to continue so in the future. The company's inventory, as stated on its ledger, is as follows:

Raw materials	$ 375,268.00
Work in process	3,450,847.82
Finished goods	785,490.90
	$4,611,606.72

The bank charges interest at 1.75 percent per month, based on acceptable inventory pledged.

(a) What is the maximum loan amount the bank will be willing to allow if raw materials and finished goods are discounted between 5 percent and 10 percent and work in process is discounted between 20 percent and 50 percent? (Do the calculations for the extreme values.)

(b) What is the range of the dollar interest cost?

Discuss the impact of a change in assumptions about the amount and cost of the loan.

5. The Joy Company has determined that it could field-warehouse $3 million of its inventory for 90 days under a trustee arrangement with the ABC Finance Company. Interest charges would be 1.5 percent per month (30 days). Warehouse setup costs would be $6250 annually, plus 1/6 of the warehouse manager's annual salary of $30,000. Determine the total cost and the effective interest rate of the arrangement.

6. Hunt Corporation faces a need for seasonal working capital over the next 90 days. The required funds will average $250,000 over the period. However, the peak requirement is estimated at $300,000. The alternatives available to management are as follows:

(a) The corporation will obtain an inventory loan under a field warehousing arrangement. The initial setup cost of the loan is $1000 and warehousing charges of 1 percent of the goods warehoused. Credit will be extended up to 75 percent of the value of inventory at a cost of 15 percent.

(b) Management will use factoring of accounts receivable at a cost of 0.75 percent of all accounts factored plus 12 percent on the amount of any cash advances against the receivables. Cash advances will be limited to 60 percent of accounts factored.

(c) Second National Bank will make the necessary loan for 90 days at an annual interest rate of 13 percent, secured by a pledge of the company's inventory. The bank requires a minimum compensating balance of 10 percent, and a 1 percent prepayment penalty will apply.

Evaluate the dollar cost of meeting the firm's seasonal needs under each of the alternatives.

7. Five years ago the Thames Company purchased land and a building for $250,000 and $3,500,000, respectively. This purchase was financed by a long-term loan at a 10 percent interest rate. The loan was to be amortized over the estimated 30-year life of the building. The building was to be depreciated on a straight-line basis. The company has reached the maximum limit of its debt/equity ratio. Since inflation is expected to continue its 5-year annual rate of 7.5 percent, it was not considered prudent by the Thames management to sell additional equity. To secure additional financing, management is considering a sale-leaseback of the land and building. It is expected that the sale can be made at the inflation-adjusted value of the assets less any accumulated depreciation. Management desires to have the maximum operating lease start immediately (refer to Chapter 5 for a discussion of leases). The company's before-tax cost of debt is 10 percent. Presently, the firm has current assets of $2.9 million, current liabilities of $1.525 million, net fixed assets of $10 million, long-term debt of $8 million, and equity of $3.375 million. The firm's marginal tax rate is 30 percent. The capital gain rate is 30 percent.

(a) If the sale-leaseback is arranged, what changes would occur in the current balance sheet?

(b) Determine the changes to the current and debt-equity ratios before and after the sale-leaseback.

(c) Determine the after-tax operating cash flows with and without the sale-leaseback.

8.   The Mountain Apple Company (MAC) owns a cold-storage facility. The building was recently constructed at a cost of $6,000,000 and has an estimated life of 12 years. The total cost amount is being financed and amortized as an annuity due over 10 years at 12 percent. Management is negotiating a sale-leaseback agreement for the facilities. The sale value would be $5,676,724, and the lease would be for 10 years. Annual lease payments would be $882,254.26 and be paid at the beginning of each year. The capital gains tax rate is 30 percent, and the marginal corporate tax rate is 30 percent. MAC plans to invest the sale proceeds in a 10 percent (before-tax) low-risk investment. The cost of debt funds is 12 percent before taxes.

(a) Determine whether the lease qualifies as an operating lease.

(b) Compare the after-tax profits and cash flows of the sale-leaseback arrangement versus owning the facility. Use straight-line depreciation if the lease is capitalized. What should MAC do?

9.   The Charles Company has assets of $250,000, debt of $175,000, and equity of $75,000. Management needs the use of $150,000 of assets next year. This expansion can be financed by a term loan at 12 percent for 5 years or by a lease agreement at the same terms. Management has assurance that the lease qualifies as an operating lease. Determine the firm's financial leverage at the end of next year under each of these possible financing arrangements.

10.   Caves and Company has warehouse facilities located in the North End industrial park area. Land costs were higher in this area than in the city's old industrial core area. Caves' production facilities were in the old core area. Caves wished to move the warehouse closer to the production facilities. The estimated

cost of this move was $28 million. Bauer Bros. owned a general purpose building immediately adjacent to Caves' production facilities. For some years Caves has been negotiating with Bauer for the Bauer old core facilities.

Bauer proposed that they exchange warehouse (general purpose) facilities. Caves' North End facilities cost $22 million with a current book value of $15 million. Because of the desirability of this location the current market value is estimated to be $45 million. Caves would exchange its North End facilities for $25 million plus the Bauer old core facilities. Current market value of these facilities is $15 million. Income tax rate is 30 percent and capital gain rate is 30 percent.

Should Caves and Company accept this exchange?

PART IV

Trade Credit and Inventory Management

CHAPTER 12 □
Credit Selection Models

The credit sale relationship between customer and supplier is a trust based on mutual need. The customer selects the supplier on the basis of its reputation as a source of a quality good at an acceptable price. The supplier accepts the order and extends the credit necessary to facilitate the sale if it believes the customer will honor the contract by paying the invoice according to the terms agreed. Usually, this procedure is completed without complication. Both parties agree to a contract and are expected to live up to its terms. While much is written about poor suppliers and late-paying customers, it is sometimes forgotten that the bulk of all transactions flow through the system in the normal way. If they did not, business transactions would not take place and the entire commercial system would grind to a halt.

The system works because both parties to every transaction do the necessary pretransaction investigation and are prepared to contract. The quality of the seller's product is evaluated by the buyer according to criteria that the buyer deems important. This information can usually be gathered through discussions with other buyers and trade associations. In the same way, credit managers gather information about customers.

Credit managers use different techniques for evaluating credit applicants. At one extreme is the approach used by W. T. Grant Company, as reported by a former financial executive of the company, to *Business Week* magazine (July 19, 1976): "We gave credit to every deadbeat who breathed. The stores were told to push credit and had certain quotas to fill." This chapter describes more reasoned approaches that provide better control over credit risks. The discussion starts with an examination of various sources of credit information. The "five C's of credit" are then discussed and a simple scoring model developed. This is followed by discussion of more complex credit evaluation models.

Sources of Credit Information

The modern credit manager does very little credit checking personally. Instead, the manager generally relies on one or more of the following sources: credit reporting agencies, industry interchange reports, banks, references, and customers.

Credit Reporting Agencies

A prime source of information for the average credit manager is the credit agency. There are many agencies operating all over the country. The services they offer are varied but are usually limited to reference books, ratings, recommendations, and reports.

Dun & Bradstreet, the best known and largest agency, provides all these services and more, while others offer perhaps only one or two. Where recommendations only are offered, you have, in effect, a credit checking agency, for the agency concentrates its best efforts upon furnishing enough information within a specific recommendation so that the credit manager's task is reduced to a minimum. Generally, this information pertains to the customer's antecedents, type of operation, financial resources and current condition, buying and paying habits.

When the credit manager uses a reference book supplied by the agency, he or she finds the credit rating of the potential customer and then makes a decision based upon that rating. The rating system used by Dun & Bradstreet ("D&B") is a combination of numbers and letters signifying financial strength, as shown in Table 12.1.

D&B's system is used as follows. Suppose the credit manager receives a $3000 order for a new account and finds the account listed in the D&B reference book as BB1. A BB1 account shows an estimated financial strength of $200,000 to $300,000 and could easily absorb an order for $3000 or higher.

Suppose the new account was rated BB3. In this case, the account is not a high-rated account, but one that is fair and may also be slow in its payments. With this type of rating, a $3000 order might not be approved without additional investigation or a review of the entire credit report. Now faced with a marginal account, the credit manager must use other sources of information in order to make an informed decision.

The same process is applied to any order, regardless of the dollar amount. Whether the credit manager relies upon an agency that offers recommendations only, or consults a rating book, checking credit on most orders should give little difficulty.

TABLE 12.1
Dun & Bradstreet Key to Ratings

<table>
<tr><td colspan="4">Estimated financial strength</td><td colspan="4">Composite credit appraisal</td></tr>
<tr><td></td><td></td><td></td><td></td><td>HIGH</td><td>GOOD</td><td>FAIR</td><td>LIMITED</td></tr>
<tr><td>5A</td><td>$50,000,000</td><td>and over</td><td></td><td>1</td><td>2</td><td>3</td><td>4</td></tr>
<tr><td>4A</td><td>$10,000,000 to</td><td>49,999,999</td><td></td><td>1</td><td>2</td><td>3</td><td>4</td></tr>
<tr><td>3A</td><td>1,000,000 to</td><td>9,999,999</td><td></td><td>1</td><td>2</td><td>3</td><td>4</td></tr>
<tr><td>2A</td><td>750,000 to</td><td>999,999</td><td></td><td>1</td><td>2</td><td>3</td><td>4</td></tr>
<tr><td>1A</td><td>500,000 to</td><td>749,999</td><td></td><td>1</td><td>2</td><td>3</td><td>4</td></tr>
<tr><td>BA</td><td>300,000 to</td><td>499,999</td><td></td><td>1</td><td>2</td><td>3</td><td>4</td></tr>
<tr><td>BB</td><td>200,000 to</td><td>299,999</td><td></td><td>1</td><td>2</td><td>3</td><td>4</td></tr>
<tr><td>CB</td><td>125,000 to</td><td>199,999</td><td></td><td>1</td><td>2</td><td>3</td><td>4</td></tr>
<tr><td>CC</td><td>75,000 to</td><td>124,999</td><td></td><td>1</td><td>2</td><td>3</td><td>4</td></tr>
<tr><td>DC</td><td>50,000 to</td><td>74,999</td><td></td><td>1</td><td>2</td><td>3</td><td>4</td></tr>
<tr><td>DD</td><td>35,000 to</td><td>49,999</td><td></td><td>1</td><td>2</td><td>3</td><td>4</td></tr>
<tr><td>EE</td><td>20,000 to</td><td>34,999</td><td></td><td>1</td><td>2</td><td>3</td><td>4</td></tr>
<tr><td>FF</td><td>10,000 to</td><td>19,999</td><td></td><td>1</td><td>2</td><td>3</td><td>4</td></tr>
<tr><td>GG</td><td>5,000 to</td><td>9,999</td><td></td><td>1</td><td>2</td><td>3</td><td>4</td></tr>
<tr><td>HH</td><td>Up to</td><td>4,999</td><td></td><td>1</td><td>2</td><td>3</td><td>4</td></tr>
</table>

GENERAL CLASSIFICATION

ESTIMATED FINANCIAL STRENGTH			COMPOSITE CREDIT APPRAISAL		
			GOOD	FAIR	LIMITED
1R	$125,000	and over	2	3	4
2R	$50,000 to	$124,999	2	3	4

EXPLANATION
When the designation "**1R**" or "**2R**" appears, followed by a 2, 3 or 4, it is an indication that the Estimated Financial Strength, while not definitely classified, is presumed to be in the range of the ($) figures in the corresponding bracket, and while the Composite Credit Appraisal cannot be judged precisely, it is believed to fall in the general category indicated.

ABSENCE OF RATING (--) THE
BLANK SYMBOL
A blank symbol--should not be interpreted as indicating that credit should be denied. It simply means that the information available to Dun & Bradstreet does not permit us to classify the company within our rating key and that further inquiry should be made before reaching a credit decision.

KEY TO THE D&B PAYDEX
(PAYMENT INDEX)

PAYDEX	PAYMENT
100	ANTICIPATE
90	DISCOUNT
80	PROMPT
70	SLOW TO 15 days
50	SLOW TO 30 days
40	SLOW TO 60 days
30	SLOW TO 90 days
20	SLOW TO 120 days
UN-0	UNAVAILABLE

EMPLOYEE RANGE DESIGNATIONS IN
REPORTS ON NAMES NOT LISTED IN
THE REFERENCE BOOK

Certain businesses do not lend themselves to a Dun & Bradstreet rating and are not listed in the Reference Book. Information on these names, however, continues to be stored and updated in the D&B Business Information File. Reports are available on such businesses and instead of a rating they carry and Employee Range Designation(ER) which is indicative of size in terms of number of employees. No other significance should be attached.

KEY TO EMPLOYEE
RANGE DESIGNATIONS

ER1	1000 or more	Employees
ER2	500-999	Employees
ER3	100-499	Employees
ER4	50-99	Employees
ER5	20-49	Employees
ER6	10-19	Employees
ER7	5-9	Employees
ER8	1-4	Employees
ERN		Not Available

Industry Interchange Reports

Industry reports cover either a variety of industries or just a single industry. They indicate the experience credit managers from all sections of the country have had with the customer.

Many local groups offer a limited interchange of credit information. They are generally councils or bureaus organized within a specific geographical area, and possibly within a given industry. But there is a national organization called the National Association of Credit Management (NACM), which has about 72 reference bureaus in both major and minor markets all over the country. These local bureaus cooperate with one another in compiling credit information so that it is possible for any participating member of the Association to obtain credit information on a customer for other members.

A credit interchange report provides the following information: how long sold, date of last sale, highest recent credit, amount owing, amount past due, when due, terms of sale, paying record. The report also provides comments other credit managers have made, such as, "takes unearned discount," "makes unauthorized returns," "skips invoices," "placed for collection."

Other Sources of Information

Banks play a vital role for the credit manager. With the customer's permission, the customer's bank can be approached as a credit source either directly or through the credit manager's bank.

References supplied by a credit applicant can be misleading. Credit seekers will obviously supply a *selected* list of references — suppliers who have been paid on time, possibly only because their merchandise was desperately needed, or simply to establish a presumptive history of prompt payments.

The customer provides current financial statements, where its banking activity is done, and a list of references.

Five C's of Credit

A popular way of categorizing credit information received is by the **five C's of credit**: character, capacity, capital, collateral, and conditions.

- □ *Character.* Those moral qualities and actions of a credit applicant which impel the applicant to pay.
- □ *Capacity.* The ability to pay when a debt is due.
- □ *Capital.* The financial strength of a risk as measured by the equity or net worth of the applicant.
- □ *Collateral.* Those possessions or equities from which payment might be expected should character and capacity fail.
- □ *Conditions.* The current and expected general economic situations as they might affect the applicant.

Embodied in the five C's is a judgment of risk, based on the following factors:

- The probability that the customer will pay on time
- Whether or not the customer is living within the credit line
- The customer's overall financial condition

Ad Hoc Scoring Model

The importance of the five C's is that they cause the credit manager to consider the overall financial and operational circumstances of both the credit-granting firm and of the applicant seeking credit. It is not unusual for the credit manager to design an ad hoc **scoring model** to encompass the five C's. Table 12.2 provides an example.

TABLE 12.2
Credit Application Summary

Assign points in the range of 0 to 15. The higher the points assigned, the more favorable is your evaluation.

				Points
Character				
Average past payment		On time Up to 30 days late Up to 60 days late		_____
Capacity				
Profit margin	0%–5%	6%–12%	13%–20%	_____
Quick ratio	<1.0	1–2	>2.0	_____
Cash flow	Low	Average	High	_____
Capital				
Current ratio	<2.0	2–3	>3.0	_____
Debt to equity	<1.0	1–2	>2.0	_____
Interest earned	$<2\times$	$2\times-3\times$	$>3\times$	_____
Collateral				
Net worth	Low	Average	High	_____
Percent assets free	Low	Average	High	_____
Market value of net worth	Low	Average	High	_____
Conditions				
Recession		Average	Prosperity	_____
			Total points	_____

In each of the items in Table 12.2, a high degree of subjective judg-ment is required. As an example, the credit manager must decide whether or not a quick ratio of 1:1 differs substantially from a ratio of 1.1:1. Many of the items are divided among low, average, and high. Who, or what, dis-tinguishes among these categories? If, in the example of a scoring model illustrated in the table, point values can range from a low of 0 to a high of 15, then the total score can range from 0 to 165 points. The next problem becomes, What constitutes an acceptable score for credit extension?

Evaluation

This system creates almost as many problems as it attempts to solve. Why did the managers include only 11 items? How did they decide on the var-ious steps in each category? Where do they get their information? Does an applicant have to receive a minimum value in each group to be acceptable? Does a forecast of recession change any of the values in the other items, and conversely, does a forecast of prosperity outweigh a negative value of another item? The answers to these questions are critical to the success of the firm and deserve substantial debate before resolution.

Each firm has its own criteria in the establishment of this system. The credit manager decides which of the items are relatively more important variables and to what degree. Each variable is assigned a threshold value for acceptable performance, and the applicant's credentials are measured against this list. The applicant's total points are determined and then com-pared with a predetermined, overall, minimum acceptable value. If the credit manager prepares the system carefully and has properly evaluated the data supplied by the applicant, then the decision should have a reason-able expectation of success.

Window Dressing

While a good system is critical, its results are influenced by the data input. The following example is offered to call attention to problems that might arise in interpreting the data supplied by the applicant. Assume that a point method is used that relies strictly on the current ratio of the applicant. Also, assume that the minimum acceptable ratio is 6:1. The balance sheets in Table 12.3 indicate that applicant A is denied credit whereas applicant B receives it.

The two balance sheets shown in Table 12.3 could be of the same applicant at virtually the same time. In this case the difference for B is that this applicant knew of the firm's standards and simply adjusted the figures in balance sheet A to produce the desired ratio. This operation is referred

TABLE 12.3
Analysis of Credit Applicants

Applicant A's balance sheet			
Cash	$100	Payables	$200
Receivables	960	Equity	860
Current ratio: 5.3			
Applicant B's balance sheet			
Cash	$ 72	Payables	$172
Receivables	960	Equity	860
Current ratio: 6			

to as "**window dressing**," since $28 is taken from the cash account and is used to reduce payables to produce a current ratio of 6:1. Is there any real change between A and B? This operation reduced cash and payables an equal amount, and net working capital has not changed. Liquidity, however, may be lower. Although payables are lower, the balance sheet fails to indicate off-balance-sheet liabilities and all future known liabilities that will be paid after this date. Also, the reduction in cash could possibly threaten any minimum cash position requirements imposed by creditors.

There are other ways the applicant could produce the desired result, but the danger of bias due to poor design is inherent in any *ad hoc* system of evaluation the credit manager might establish. In addition, the credit manager must investigate and carefully consider the information offered by potential customers.

Credit managers who use simple point scoring systems usually recognize the limitations inherent in them. They believe, and rightly so, that these systems are better than nothing at all. They allow organization of the applicant's information within the parameters of what management believes to be important. The following sections discuss more complex models for capturing information.

Simple Probability Model

The acceptance or rejection of a specific credit request must be made by the credit manager with care and with reason. While the past payment record of the applicant may be the single most important item, the credit manager must question the future financial viability of the applicant. This task is made easier if the applicant is considered from the perspective of expected cash flow contributions to the supplier's firm. A decision rule can be established that indicates that the firm should extend credit or should carry an existing customer as long as the probability of the customer paying is equal to or greater than some predetermined level.

For example, let us assume that

probability of collection = P,

probability of noncollection = $1 - P$,

sales = S,

and costs are as follows:

variable production costs = vS,

finance charge per month = fS,

collection charge per month on overdue accounts = c,

where v and f are decimal proportions. **Breakeven** for this problem implies that the expected profit of a successful sale equals the expected cost of an uncollectible sale:

$$P(S - vS - fS - c) = (1 - P)(vS + fS + c).$$

$$\underbrace{}_{\text{Expected profit}} \qquad \underbrace{}_{\text{Expected cost}}$$

(12.1)

Solving in terms of P yields

$$P = \frac{vS + fS + c}{S}.$$

(12.2)

The breakeven probability (P) is the total cost-to-sales ratio (which is less than or equal to 1). This relationship may be used to solve for the probability of collection for any number of months into the future.

ILLUSTRATION 12.1

Assume that $S = \$22.71$, $v = 0.7$, $f = 0.01$ per month, and $c = \$2$ per month for each month that the bill is overdue. Terms are net one month. The breakeven probabilities of sales collections, using Eq. (12.2), are as follows:

$$\text{By the due date} = \frac{0.7 \times \$22.71 + 0.00 \times \$22.71 + \$0}{\$22.71} = 0.700;$$

$$\text{One month late} = \frac{0.7 \times \$22.71 + 0.01 \times \$22.71 + \$2}{\$22.71} = 0.798;$$

$$\text{Two months late} = \frac{0.7 \times \$22.71 + 0.02 \times \$22.71 + \$4}{\$22.71} = 0.896.$$

The breakeven point changes over time because of the impact of the assessed collection charge and the time value of money. Other cost variables could be included and the flows discounted to better reflect the costs of credit. The point of this analysis is to indicate that the firm needs a higher assurance of payment the longer the account is expected to be outstanding. In other words, the necessary breakeven probability is higher for slower payers than it is for prompt payers.   □

A more theoretically correct model excludes the finance term, fs, and discounts the relevant cash flows as follows:[1]

$$P\left[\frac{S - c(n - 1)}{(1 + k)^n} - vS\right] = (1 - P)\left[\frac{c(n - 1)}{(1 + k)^n} + vS\right], \qquad (12.3)$$

where k is a monthly opportunity cost of capital rate and n is the month being analyzed. Solving in terms of P yields

$$P = \frac{c}{s}(n - 1) + v(1 + k)^n. \qquad (12.4)$$

If $k = 0.01$ per month, the breakeven probabilities of sales collections become

$$\text{By the due date} = \frac{\$0}{\$22.71} \times (1 - 1) + 0.7 \times (1.01)^1 = 0.707;$$

$$\text{One month late} = \frac{\$2}{\$22.71} \times (2 - 1) + 0.7 \times (1.01)^2 = 0.802;$$

$$\text{Two months late} = \frac{\$2}{\$22.71} \times (3 - 1) + 0.7 \times (1.01)^3 = 0.897.$$

Management should be able to assign probabilities that accounts will either pay or become bad debts. Credit information collected both externally (obtained from Dun & Bradstreet, for example) and internally can help in this task.[2] This information is used in conjunction with the breakeven data just developed to determine how long uncollected accounts should remain on the books before they are deemed uncollectible. Figure 12.1 depicts an example.

The decreasing curve in Fig. 12.1 depicts the probability of accounts being paid when they are current, when they are one month past due, and when they are two months past due. The increasing curve indicates the

---

[1] We use the probabilities shown in Illustration 12.1 later in this chapter when we discuss sequential decision systems. It simplifies the discussion without seriously distorting the results.

[2] Appendix 1 (at the end of the book) discusses a sophisticated mathematical approach that could possibly be used to calculate these probabilities.

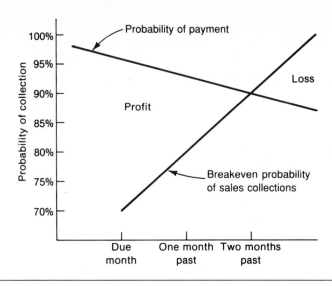

FIGURE 12.1
Breakeven Analysis of Accounts Receivable

probability of collecting sales that is necessary for the firm to break even. *Wherever the probability of payment curve exceeds the sales collection breakeven probability curve, a profitable sale is expected to result.* Conversely, wherever the probability of payment curve is less than the breakeven probability of sales collection curve, a loss is expected from the sale. The example indicates that if management intends to offer credit to customers with payment profiles captured by the probability-of-payment curve, then it should not extend credit to any customers who are expected to take longer than three months to pay (that is, customers whose accounts are two months past due).

Linear Discriminant Model

Linear discriminant models have been used in credit selection decisions for several years. These models attempt to discriminate among customers on the basis of a profile of several variables. The linear discriminant function is expressed as a score based on the linear relationship between variables.

This score indicates an indifference point between success and failure of customers relative to some objective relationship of similar customers. The basis of the score is usually past financial data and, consequently, is biased by this procedure. The basic strength of linear discriminant models is that they do relate, in an objective fashion, several variables that the credit manager deems important to the evaluation of customers.

The Model

Assume that the credit manager feels that the current ratio (R) and the debt-to-equity ratio (L) of the applicant are important for assessing credit risk — they are not contaminated by window dressing. A multiple linear discriminant model would then be specified as follows:

$$Z = b_0(R) + b_1(L), \tag{12.5}$$

where Z is the *score* and the b_i's are the *coefficients* of the ratios.

The mathematics of this method is outlined in Appendix A of this chapter. In summary, the theory of discriminant analysis implies that if the credit manager can compare the past financial data of customers with the individual success or failure of these customers in honoring their credit contracts over time, then like applicants in the future can be expected to behave in a similar fashion. This assumption is not unreasonable, since its basis is empirical. In the past, credit managers simply extended credit to customers to determine which ones would prove to be good payers and which would not. However, discriminant models provide a less risky way of deciding who is credit worthy. They can be sensitive to changing economic conditions. A prudent procedure is for the credit manager to reevaluate the model periodically to determine if it should be updated with the passage of time.

The criterion of success is the absence of financial difficulty in paying the outstanding receivable. If the Z score is to discriminate between good and bad applicants, then the score should be significantly different for each type of customer. Thus the credit manager should be able to determine an *indifference* or *cutoff point* between the different risk categories such that new applicants can be evaluated by using the discriminant model.

A new applicant's score can be calculated by multiplying the current ratio by b_0 and the leverage ratio by b_1. If the applicant's score is in the rejection region, this result is viewed as strong evidence for not extending credit. Credit will be extended if, in the opinion of the credit manager, this applicant has other significant attributes such as never having been delinquent or always paying, albeit late. The point is that this system offers a better approach to credit evaluation than does the simple five C's point system. It still does not, however, replace the intelligence and experience of a well-trained credit manager or analyst; it supplements her or his knowledge.

ILLUSTRATION 12.2

Assume that in the past year the majority of the firm's customers fulfilled their credit contracts, yet a few were delinquent. The credit manager re-

TABLE 12.4
Classification of Credit Customers

Customers	Current ratio	Leverage ratio	Z score
Successful			
1	3.0	0.6	1.08
2	3.3	0.2	1.92
3	3.9	0.3	2.17
4	4.0	0.4	2.07
5	2.9	0.5	1.17
6	2.7	0.3	1.35
7	3.0	0.2	1.72
8	3.1	0.6	1.14
9	4.2	0.7	1.73
10	4.6	0.1	2.96
Delinquent			
11	1.0	1.0	−0.92
12	0.9	0.9	−0.83
13	1.1	1.2	−1.17
14	0.8	1.3	−1.53
	$Z = 0.6782(R) - 1.5969(L)$		

Note: See Appendix A for the calculations.

quests that all credit applicants submit audited financial statements. In this way the credit manager has the current ratio and the leverage ratio of each customer prior to the extension of credit. At a later period management conducts an analysis of credit customers to determine the result of extending credit. The customers are divided into successful or delinquent groups, depending upon the outcome of the credit extension. The ratios and Z scores of each customer are shown in Table 12.4.

The Z scores range from a low of -1.53 (for customer 14) to a high of 2.96 (for customer 10), with no scores between -0.82 and 1.07. Any credit applicant with a score of 1.08 (the lowest successful score) or greater is offered credit, whereas any applicant with a score of -0.83 (the highest delinquent score) or less is denied credit. Any applicant whose score falls between -0.82 and 1.07 is investigated further before credit is granted or denied.   □

Concerns

This system seems to offer the credit manager a relatively simple method for evaluating credit applicants. As with any statistical technique, though, there are a number of potential problems. For example, are the ratios employed in the model the best ratios, or are they even usable as an indication of future success of credit customers? Throughout this text many warnings have been given about the possibility of firms' using creative accounting methods. It is folly to suggest that customers, as a general rule, establish accounting procedures to defraud. However, manipulation of accounting data is done frequently in order to allow the firm to gain some advantage. Thus the credit manager has no guarantee that the ratios selected are the best indicators of creditworthiness.

The Z scores in Table 12.4 were designed to give clear signals of successful and delinquent customers. Generally, there is an overlap of the groups. In this case the credit manager must decide what is desirable, what is not desirable, and where the "maybe" range is. Also, if two variables are good, possibly three or more are even better. The question of how many variables to include can only be determined through analysis and testing of the model. In reality, how many variables end up in the final model is a subjective decision.

Sequential Decision System

Collection of information is costly and time consuming. It is to the firm's benefit to expedite the decision process as much as possible. In this context the standard rule of marginal analysis is applied: Continue the process until marginal cost equals marginal revenue. The essence of the rule is that some applicants are better than others and therefore need less evaluation. Although concerned with all credit accounts, the credit manager should be more concerned with the marginal accounts and leave the clear-cut applications to be handled in a routine fashion. This technique is the very nature of the **sequential decision approach**.[3]

This system is based on several principles. First, information gathering is costly and time consuming. Second, some information is virtually impossible to gather, while other information is useless. Third, past experience with the applicant is meaningful and may be used as a predictor of the future.

The intention in using this system is to facilitate the granting of credit. In this regard there are three possible outcomes for each application: grant the credit, refuse the credit, or postpone the decision. Each of these decisions has its own associated cost.

---

[3]A more comprehensive exposition of the approach is given in an article by Dileep Mehta, "The Formulation of Credit Policy Models," *Management Science* (October 1968): B30–B50.

If the credit is granted, then the firm may experience the costs of nonpayment. These costs include the following:

□ The variable costs of the goods sold

□ The opportunity cost of the investment in the accounts receivable

□ The average collection cost

If the credit is not granted, the cost includes the opportunity cost of the lost contribution margin. If the decision is postponed in order to investigate the applicant further, then the incremental cost is the cost of further investigation. These incremental costs must be included in the costs of the subsequent rejection or approval decision.

ILLUSTRATION 12.3

Assume that the credit manager has recently completed an analysis of outstanding accounts. The relevant information is summarized in Table 12.5.

If these customers, or customers of similar risk characteristics, request credit, the opportunity cost of granting credit becomes the cost of nonpay-

TABLE 12.5
Accounts Receivable Payment and Cost Data

Average sales per customer	$22.71
Variable costs incurred	15.90
Contribution margin	$ 6.81

Other costs:
Finance charge $0.01 × sales × months overdue
Collection charge $2/month on overdue accounts

Credit terms   Net 30 days

	Accounts currently		
	Current	One month overdue	Two months overdue
Probability of accounts staying or becoming:			
current	0.664	0.335	0.311
1 month overdue	0.248	0.491	0.199
2 months overdue	0.088	0.174	0.490
Probability of:			
Paying	0.979	0.947	0.884
Defaulting	0.021	0.053	0.116

ment of the debt, or in other words, the cost the firm incurs by making a wrong decision. In the same sense, if the firm refuses to grant credit, the opportunity cost is the margin forgone when the correct decision was to allow credit, that is, the cost incurred by making a wrong decision. Using the data of Table 12.5 and testing according to the current status of accounts (current, one month overdue, two months overdue), we can determine the **opportunity costs of credit**. These calculations are shown in Appendix B, Part 1, of this chapter. Figure 12.2 summarizes the results. Conceptually, the calculations are made by equating the incremental costs incurred in extending credit to nonpaying customers to the incremental profits lost by not extending credit to customers who would pay.

An analysis of Fig. 12.2 indicates the following points:

☐ For accounts presently classified as current, the opportunity cost of refusing to extend credit for new orders is greater than the opportunity cost of granting credit whenever more than 0.136 of a full order is placed.

☐ For accounts presently one month overdue the opportunity cost of refusing credit for new orders is greater than the opportunity cost of granting credit whenever more than 0.310 of a full order is placed.

☐ For accounts presently two months overdue the opportunity cost of refusing credit for new orders is greater than the opportunity cost of granting credit whenever more than 0.603 of an order is placed.

FIGURE 12.2
Indifference Curve for Granting or Refusing Credit, Based on Current Age of Account

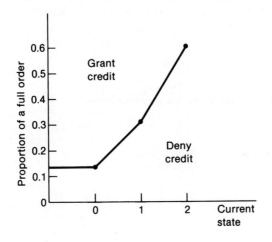

The conclusion is that the credit manager should not arbitrarily grant new credit to any account. The granting of credit (and profitability) depends on the size of the potential new order. It may not be in the firm's best interest to immediately refuse credit for quantities less than the indifference values. Additional information might prove the orders to be worthwhile.   □

Additional information may be supplied by a **point evaluation system**. This system is expensive and time-consuming, but it can be useful. Assume that customers presently one month overdue in payment can be divided into three subgroups having the characteristics shown in Table 12.6. The collection period information has been upgraded by investigation.

The opportunity costs of granting or refusing credit to accounts one month overdue are determined by combining the payments and cost data in Table 12.5 with that of Table 12.6. The calculations are shown in Appendix B, Part 2, of this chapter. Figure 12.3 summarizes the new decision rules.

The original data for accounts one month overdue indicated that for orders of less than 0.310 unit credit should be refused. As Figure 12.3 shows, further investigation by the credit manager indicates that credit should be extended if the applicant is classified as having a good credit rating and orders at least 0.076 of a full order; otherwise, credit should be refused. If the applicant has an average credit rating, then credit should be extended if at least 0.334 order is placed. Credit should not be extended to customers whose credit rating is bad unless they order at least 1.23 units. Similar analyses can be conducted on customers denied credit whose accounts are two months overdue.

The information derived from the point evaluation system is useful in structuring a cost function for the linear discriminant model examined earlier. From the information of Table 12.4 the credit manager believes that customers who default on credit usually have a Z score of -0.83 or

TABLE 12.6
Subgrouping Data for Accounts One Month Overdue

Rating	Probability of payment	Probability of bad debts	Probability of collection in period			Per-period marginal collection costs
			0	1	2	
Good	0.99	0.01	0.40	0.55	0.05	$0.75
Average	0.96	0.04	0.35	0.35	0.30	2.00
Poor	0.89	0.11	0.25	0.10	0.65	3.50

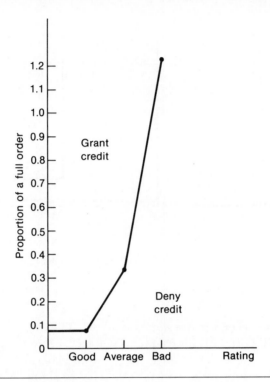

FIGURE 12.3
Indifference Curve for Granting or Refusing Credit to Accounts One Month Overdue, Using the Point Evaluation System

less, and customers who usually pay their outstanding credit have a score of 1.08 or more. Experience may indicate that these two groups have the characteristics shown in Table 12.7.

The data of Table 12.7 can be combined with the opportunity costs of granting and refusing credit to determine a new opportunity cost sched-

TABLE 12.7
Summary of Credit Information

Z score	Probability of payment	Probability of bad debt	Probability of collection in period			Marginal collection costs
			0	1	2	
≤ -0.83	0.10	0.90	0.20	0.10	0.70	$3.50
≥ 1.08	0.95	0.05	0.30	0.60	0.10	0.75

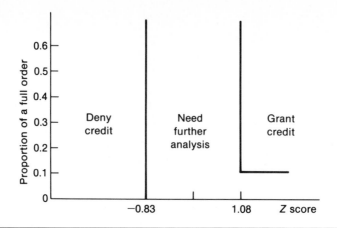

FIGURE 12.4
Indifference Curve for Granting or Refusing Credit, Using the Linear Discriminant Model

ule for credit by using the discriminant model. The calculations are shown in Appendix B, Part 3 of this chapter. Figure 12.4 summarizes the results.

From the figure the credit manager would conclude that applicants with a linear discriminant Z score of -0.83 or less should always be denied credit. If the score is 1.08 or more, credit should be granted if at least 0.109 order is placed. For orders less than 0.109, the cost of granting credit exceeds the cost of refusing credit. Applicants in this situation, and applicants whose scores fall between -0.83 and 1.08, need to be evaluated in a different way. The best method is to conduct a thorough credit analysis of the applicant.

With the use of additional investigation the credit manager has better information for making the credit decision. A reasonable conclusion is that this approach results in improved probability of collection of accounts and better overall profitability of the company. This conclusion is reasonable since the analyses are based on equating marginal benefits to marginal costs.

Summary

This chapter examined a number of techniques for determining who should receive credit. The use of credit reference organizations, such as Dun & Bradstreet, was discussed. Information from such firms was then analyzed in terms of the five C's of credit and a simple model derived. Such a model has two basic problems: The categorization of applicants into high, low, average, and so on, is subjective; and credit evaluation costs are generally ignored.

The remaining models discussed in this chapter are based on statistical probability concepts and incorporate opportunity cost functions. In a theoretical sense, these models should be useful guides to help credit managers contribute to the shareholder wealth objective of the firm.

Key Concepts

Breakeven

Five C's of credit

Linear discriminant model

Opportunity cost of credit

Point evaluation

Scoring models

Sequential decision making

Window dressing

Appendix A
Fundamentals of Discriminant Analysis

Discriminant analysis begins with the wish to statistically categorize two or more groups of cases, such as good and bad credit risks or solvent and insolvent companies. To distinguish between the groups, the analyst selects a collection of discriminating variables that measure characteristics on which the groups are expected to differ. The mathematical objective of discriminant analysis is to weigh and linearly combine the discriminating variables in some fashion so that the groups are forced to be as statistically distinct as possible. In other words, the analyst wants to be able to discriminate between the groups in the sense of being able to tell them apart.

Discriminant analysis attempts to form one or more linear combinations of the discriminating variables. These discriminant functions are of the form

$$Z_i = b_{i1}X_1 + \cdots + b_{ip}X_p,$$

where Z_i is the score on the discriminant function i, the b's are weighting coefficients, and the X's are the standardized values of the p discriminating variables used in the analysis. The maximum number of functions that can be derived is equal to one less than either the number of groups or the number of discriminating variables, whichever is less. The functions are formed in such a way as to maximize the separation of the groups.

An example based on two groups and two variables follows. The variables used to discriminate are simply called B and L. Group 1 has 10 observations, and group 2 has 4 observations. Table A.1 shows the calculation of the discriminant function.

The b_i coefficients can be interpreted much as they are in regression analysis. They serve to identify the variables that contribute most to differentiating the function.

The discriminant function for this two-variable model is

$$Z = 0.6782R - 1.5969L.$$

This model can be used to classify observations. Assuming that variables R and L provide satisfactory discrimination for cases with known group membership, a set of classification functions can be derived that will permit the classification of new cases with unknown memberships.

TABLE A.1
Two-Variable Discriminant Function

Observation	R	L	$(R - \bar{R})$	$(R - \bar{R})^2$	$(L - \bar{L})$	$(L - \bar{L})^2$	$(R - \bar{R})(L - \bar{L})$
Group 1							
1	3.0	0.6	-0.47	0.2209	0.21	0.0441	-0.0987
2	3.3	0.2	-0.17	0.0289	-0.19	0.0361	0.0323
3	3.9	0.3	0.43	0.1849	-0.09	0.0081	-0.0387
4	4.0	0.4	0.53	0.2809	0.01	0.0001	0.0053
5	2.9	0.5	-0.57	0.3249	0.11	0.0121	-0.0627
6	2.7	0.3	-0.77	0.5929	-0.09	0.0081	0.0693
7	3.0	0.2	-0.47	0.2209	-0.19	0.0361	0.0893
8	3.1	0.6	-0.37	0.1369	0.21	0.0441	-0.0777
9	4.2	0.7	0.73	0.5329	0.31	0.0961	0.2263
10	4.6	0.1	1.13	1.2769	-0.29	0.0841	-0.0290
Sum	34.7	3.9		3.8010		0.3690	0.0674
Average	3.47	0.39					
	(a)	(b)		(c)		(d)	(e)
Group 2							
1	1.0	1.0	0.05	0.0025	-0.10	0.0100	-0.0050
2	0.9	0.9	-0.05	0.0025	-0.20	0.0400	0.0100
3	1.1	1.2	0.15	0.0225	0.10	0.0100	0.0150
4	0.8	1.3	-0.15	0.0225	0.20	0.0400	-0.0300
Sum	3.8	4.4		0.0500		0.1000	-0.0100
Average	0.95	1.1					
	(f)	(g)		(h)		(i)	(j)

$$b_1 = \frac{(a - f)(d + i) - (b - g)(e + i)}{(c + h)(d + i) - (e + i)^2} = 0.6782$$

$$b_2 = \frac{(b - g)(c + h) - (a - f)(e + i)}{(c + h)(d + i) - (e + i)^2} = -1.5969$$

Appendix B

Calculation of Indifference Values

The calculations shown in the three parts of this appendix are more detailed than necessary. The details have been provided for the convenience of those readers who have difficulty understanding the relevant costs. The calculations are simply identification of incremental costs and benefits incurred by either granting or refusing credit. The following discussion uses the state 0 results to explain the input to the equations.[1]

The number 0.021 represents the probability of a customer who is granted credit who will not pay. The number 15.90 is the dollar sales margin associated with a sale before any financing or collection costs are incurred. Thus if a sale is uncollectible, this amount will be lost. The next series of decimal numbers — 0.664, 0.248, and 0.088 — are the probabilities that an account, presently in state 0, will end in state 0, state 1, and state 2, respectively. These numbers, shown in Table 12.5, are actually calculated from Table A1.6 in Appendix 1 at the end of the book, as follows: $2.17/3.27 = 0.664$, $0.81/3.27 = 0.248$, and $0.29/3.27 = 0.088$. The numbers within the brackets are as follows, reading from left to right: (the finance charge of 1 percent) × (state i) × (the sale value per unit × units sold — which is an unknown called X) + (collection charge) × (state i), where $i = 0, 1, 2$. The unknown X represents the number of orders, with $X = 1$ being a full order for $22.71.

Part 1: Opportunity Cost of Granting or Refusing Credit, Based on the Current State (See Table 12.5)

The current state is 0; credit is granted. The opportunity cost is

$$
\begin{aligned}
(0.021)\{15.90X & \\
+\ 0.664[0.01(0)(22.71X) &+ 2(0)] \\
+\ 0.248[0.01(1)(22.71X) &+ 2(1)] \\
+\ 0.088[0.01(2)(22.71X) &+ 2(2)]\} \\
=\ 0.336X + 0.018. &
\end{aligned}
$$

---

[1]State 0 refers to accounts classified as current. States 1 and 2 refer to accounts one month and two months overdue, respectively.

The current state is 0; credit is refused. The opportunity cost is

$$(0.979)\{6.81X$$
$$-\ 0.664[0.01(0)(22.71X)\ +\ 2(0)]$$
$$-\ 0.248[0.01(1)(22.71X)\ +\ 2(1)]$$
$$-\ 0.088[0.01(2)(22.71X)\ +\ 2(2)]\}$$
$$=\ 6.573X\ -\ 0.830.$$

Also,

indifference value for $X = 0.136$.

The current state is 1; credit is granted. The opportunity cost is

$$(0.053)\{15.90X$$
$$+\ 0.335[0.01(0)(22.71X)\ +\ 2(0)]$$
$$+\ 0.491[0.01(1)(22.71X)\ +\ 2(1)]$$
$$+\ 0.174[0.01(2)(22.71X)\ +\ 2(2)]\}$$
$$=\ 0.853X\ +\ 0.089.$$

The current state is 1; credit is refused. The opportunity cost is

$$(0.947)\{6.81X$$
$$-\ 0.335[0.01(0)(22.71X)\ +\ 2(0)]$$
$$-\ 0.491[0.01(1)(22.71X)\ +\ 2(1)]$$
$$-\ 0.174[0.01(2)(22.71X)\ +\ 2(2)]\}$$
$$=\ 6.269X\ -\ 1.589.$$

Also,

indifference value for $X = 0.310$.

The current state is 2; credit is granted. The opportunity cost is

$$(0.116)\{15.90X$$
$$+\ 0.311[0.01(0)(22.71X)\ +\ 2(0)]$$
$$+\ 0.199[0.01(1)(22.71X)\ +\ 2(1)]$$
$$+\ 0.490[0.01(2)(22.71X)\ +\ 2(2)]\}$$
$$=\ 1.875X\ +\ 0.274.$$

The current state is 2; credit is refused. The opportunity cost is

$$(0.884)\{6.81X$$
$$-\ 0.311[0.01(0)(22.71X)\ +\ 2(0)]$$
$$-\ 0.199[0.01(1)(22.71X)\ +\ 2(1)]$$
$$-\ 0.490[0.01(2)(22.71X)\ +\ 2(2)]\}$$
$$=\ 5.783X\ -\ 2.084.$$

Also,

indifference value for $X = 0.603$.

Part 2: Opportunity Costs of Credit to State 1, Using the Point Evaluation System (See Table 12.6)

The credit rating is good; credit is granted. The opportunity cost is

$$0.01\{15.90X$$
$$+ 0.40[0.01(0)(22.71X) + 0.75(0)]$$
$$+ 0.55[0.01(1)(22.71X) + 0.75(1)]$$
$$+ 0.05[0.01(2)(22.71X) + 0.75(2)]\}$$
$$= 0.160X + 0.005.$$

The credit rating is good; credit is refused. The opportunity cost is

$$0.99\{6.81X$$
$$- 0.40[0.01(0)(22.71X) + 0.75(0)]$$
$$- 0.55[0.01(1)(22.71X) + 0.75(1)]$$
$$- 0.05[0.01(2)(22.71X) + 0.75(2)]\}$$
$$= 6.596X - 0.483.$$

Also,

indifference value for $X = 0.076$.

The credit rating is average; credit is granted. The opportunity cost is

$$0.04\{15.90X$$
$$+ 0.35[0.01(0)(22.71X) + 2(0)]$$
$$+ 0.35[0.01(1)(22.71X) + 2(1)]$$
$$+ 0.30[0.01(2)(22.71X) + 2(2)]\}$$
$$= 0.645X + 0.076.$$

The credit rating is average; credit is refused. The opportunity cost is

$$0.96\{6.81X$$
$$- 0.35[0.01(0)(22.71X) + 2(0)]$$
$$- 0.35[0.01(1)(22.71X) + 2(1)]$$
$$- 0.30[0.01(2)(22.71X) + 2(2)]\}$$
$$= 6.330X - 1.824.$$

Also,

indifference value for $X = 0.334$.

The credit rating is poor; credit is granted. The opportunity cost is

$$0.11\{15.90X$$
$$+ 0.25[0.01(0)(22.71X) + 2(0)]$$
$$+ 0.10[0.01(1)(22.71X) + 2(1)]$$
$$+ 0.65[0.01(2)(22.71X) + 2(2)]\}$$
$$= 1.784X + 0.539.$$

The credit rating is poor; credit is refused. The opportunity cost is

$$0.89\{6.81X$$
$$- 0.25[0.01(0)(22.71X) + 2(0)]$$
$$- 0.10[0.01(1)(22.71X) + 2(1)]$$
$$- 0.65[0.01(2)(22.71X) + 2(2)]\}$$
$$= 5.778X - 4.361.$$

Also,

indifference value for $X = 1.227$.

Part 3: Opportunity Costs of Granting or Refusing Credit, Based on the Linear Discriminant Model (See Table 12.7)

The Z score is less than or equal to -0.83; credit is granted. The opportunity cost is

$$0.9\{15.90X$$
$$+ 0.20[0.01(0)(22.71X) + 3.5(0)]$$
$$+ 0.10[0.01(1)(22.71X) + 3.5(1)]$$
$$+ 0.70[0.01(2)(22.71X) + 3.5(2)]\}$$
$$= 14.617X + 4.725.$$

The Z score is less than or equal to -0.83; credit is refused. The opportunity cost is

$$0.1\{6.81X$$
$$- 0.20[0.01(0)(22.71X) + 3.5(0)]$$
$$- 0.10[0.01(1)(22.71X) + 3.5(1)]$$
$$- 0.70[0.01(2)(22.71X) + 3.5(2)]\}$$
$$= 0.647X - 5.25.$$

Also,

indifference value for $X = -0.376$.

The Z score is greater than or equal to 1.08; credit is granted. The opportunity cost is

$$0.05\{15.90X$$
$$+ 0.30[0.01(0)(22.71X) + 0.75(0)]$$
$$+ 0.60[0.01(1)(22.71X) + 0.75(1)]$$
$$+ 0.10[0.01(2)(22.71X) + 0.75(2)]\}$$
$$= 0.804X + 0.030.$$

The Z score is greater than or equal to 1.08; credit is refused. The opportunity cost is

$$0.95\{6.81X$$
$$- 0.30[0.01(0)(22.71X) + 0.75(0)]$$
$$- 0.60[0.01(1)(22.71X) + 0.75(1)]$$
$$- 0.10[0.01(2)(22.71X) + 0.75(2)]\}$$
$$= 6.297X - 0.570.$$

Also,

indifference value for $X = 0.109$.

Questions

1. Indicate the sources of credit information. Which are the most expensive? Which provide the best information?

2. Credit managers generally give more weight to character than to any of the other five C's. Explain.

3. What is the advantage of an *ad hoc* point-scoring model? What are the disadvantages?

4. What is meant by the term *window dressing*? Explain whether or not you think it an honorable practice.

5. Extending credit to any customer rests on the ability of the seller to determine the probability that the customer will pay. Evaluate this statement.

6. Discuss the advantages and disadvantages of using a linear discriminant analysis model for evaluating credit risk.

7. Describe an approach for handling numerous small accounts when making credit decisions. Will your system differ for large accounts?

8. When management chooses credit customers, what should its attitude be toward bad-debt losses?

Problems

1. The Wellington Fabricating Company has a large number of customers. Credit losses are about normal for the industry, yet customer turnover seems relatively high. No formal, consistent credit analysis is performed on credit applicants. Management wants this practice changed and has given you the responsibility of developing a point system. The information shown in Table 12.8 has been gathered from the credit files.

TABLE 12.8
Credit Application Survey Information on Customers' Characteristics

Customer	1	2	3	4	5	6	7	8	9	10
Past 10 payments										
On time	4	5	10	4	7	6	9	4	0	2
30 days late	4	2	0	5	3	0	0	5	8	2
60 days late	2	3	0	1	0	4	1	1	2	6

382   Chapter 12 □ Credit Selection Models

TABLE 12.8 (Cont.)

Customer	1	2	3	4	5	6	7	8	9	10
Profit margin										
5% or less				X	X	X				
6% to 12%	X	X					X	X	X	
13% or more			X							X
Quick ratio										
<2	X			X	X					X
2 to 3		X				X	X	X		
>3			X						X	
Inventory turnover										
<4	X			X	X	X		X		
4 to 7		X					X			
>7			X						X	X
Debt/equity										
<1	X			X				X	X	
1 to 2		X	X			X	X			
>2					X					X
Times interest earned										
<2			X	X					X	X
2 to 3		X					X	X		
>3	X				X	X				
Net worth										
Low										
Average	X	X	X	X	X	X	X	X	X	X
High										
Percent free assets										
Low		X		X		X				
Average	X		X				X	X	X	X
High					X					

(a) If you assign 15 points to each classification, what will be your good, average, and bad customer scores?

(b) Discuss the relative value of each piece of information to the total.

(c) Should each type of information be weighted the same? If not, how would a different weighting system influence the results?

(d) Discuss what other information might be included.

(e) How might the credit manager apply this information to new customers?

2. Quigley Containers experiences the following financial conditions: The average sale (S) value is $85, with variable production costs of $0.65S$. Monthly finance and collection charges on overdue accounts are $0.015S$ and $2.50, respectively. Terms of sale are net 30 days.

   (a) Determine the breakeven probability of sales collection by (i) the due month, (ii) one month late, (iii) two months late.

   (b) Determine how the following situations influence the breakeven probability of sales collection. Evaluate each change independently: (i) Variable cost of sale increases to $0.7S$; (ii) average sales value doubles; (iii) finance charge doubles; (iv) collection charge doubles.

   (c) Discuss the cause of the results found in (b) as compared to those in (a).

3. Credit terms are net 30 days. Average sales value is $150, and variable cost is 70 percent of sales ($0.7S$).

   (a) Determine the maximum carrying charges (the financial and collection charges) the firm could accept in order simply to break even.

   (b) If the finance and collection charges per month are $0.05S$ and $7 per account, respectively, and management expects the probability of collection of credit sales to average 90 percent, how many months can credit accounts be outstanding and still allow a profit?

   (c) How many months should the company carry these credit accounts?

4. Analysis of credit policy decisions of the Albright Company found the following relationships between the probability of payment (P) and the probability of bad debts (B) and the current status of accounts.

	P	B
Current	0.90	0.10
1 month overdue	0.75	0.25
2 months overdue	0.65	0.35

Average sales values range between a low of $30 and a high of $285, with an expected value of $85. Incremental variable costs are 65 percent of sales. Monthly finance and collection charges on overdue accounts are 1.5 percent and $2.50, respectively, of sales. Prepare a graph similar to Fig. 12.1 and discuss the interpretation of the results.

5. The 13–5 Company has been in business since the turn of the century and is now recognized as the leader in its markets. Over these many years the 13–5 Company's credit policy has been the model used by the competition. Because of the company's dominance in the markets, management has been able to be relatively selective in who it extends credit to. Recently, the company experienced a substantial increase in delinquent accounts. In an attempt to correct this problem, the credit manager decided to develop a linear discriminant model to evaluate potential credit customers. After sampling past records of customers, the credit manager decided to develop a model that used cash flow as a percentage of sales (C) and inventory turnover (T) as the discriminating variables. Table 12.9 identifies successful and delinquent customers based on these two ratios.

TABLE 12.9
Customer Analysis

Customer	Successful		Customer	Delinquent	
	C	T		C	T
1	0.27	15.4	1	0.10	2.7
2	0.19	9.6	2	0.12	5.1
3	0.34	12.9	3	0.30	4.0
4	0.42	10.4	4	0.06	3.7
5	0.20	21.2			
6	0.36	14.7			
7	0.14	8.4			

(a) Determine the linear discriminant function from the data.

(b) Apply the function in (a) to the customer, and evaluate the results.

(c) Discuss the application of this procedure in this situation.

6.   Kinderspiel A. G. (KAG) of West Germany is just starting to sell in North America. The firm has successfully used a discriminant analysis model in West Germany to analyze credit risks. The model is

$$Z = 1.6X - 0.5Y,$$

where X is the cash conversion cycle as a percentage of business days per month and Y is the total debt-to-equity ratio.

(a) Given the following information for North American customers, how should KAG rank the prospective clients?

Customer	1	2	3	4	5	6
X	0.6	0.4	0.8	0.2	0.5	0.3
Y	1.4	0.8	2.0	1.6	1.0	1.0

(b) Table 12.10 shows the credit experience KAG has in West Germany. Determine the ranking of customers in part (a), and discuss your results.

TABLE 12.10
Customer Analysis

Customer	Successful		Customer	Delinquent	
	X	Y		X	Y
1	0.6	1.2	9	0.3	2.0
2	0.9	0.8	10	0.9	1.7
3	1.0	1.1	11	0.3	0.9
4	0.4	0.6	12	0.7	1.8
5	0.7	0.0	13	0.8	2.8
6	1.1	0.4			
7	0.9	1.4			
8	0.6	2.5			

7.   Assume that sales revenue could be $50, $90, or $145. Variable costs are 65 percent of the sales level, and the finance charge is 5 percent of sales per month overdue. A collection charge of $5 per month is incurred on overdue accounts. Collection experience analysis indicates that current accounts are collected 65 percent of the time, accounts one month old are collected 50 percent of the time, and accounts two months old are collected 35 percent of the time.

(a) How long should an account be carried for each scenario? Usual terms of sale are net 30 days.

(b) Management has the opportunity to purchase a superior credit investigation system. Experience with this system indicates that the probability of collecting current accounts is 92 percent, the probability of collecting accounts one month old is 75 percent, and the probability of collecting accounts two months old is 65 percent. How much should management pay for the system?

(c) Discuss the cause of the results found in (b) as compared to those in (a).

8.   Change the probabilities in paying and defaulting in Table 12.5 to those shown in the following table:

Accounts Receivable

	Current	One month overdue	Two months overdue
Paying	0.95	0.90	0.80
Defaulting	0.05	0.10	0.20

Leave all other information as it is, and determine the opportunity cost of granting or refusing credit based on the current status of an account receivable. Refer to Appendix B of this chapter for an example. Discuss your conclusion.

CHAPTER 13 □
Analysis of Credit Policy

Extending credit to customers often involves a trade-off between holding inventory or holding accounts receivable.[1] The credit decision should be taken only after the credit manager has considered completely all aspects of granting credit and the way this decision integrates with other decisions and policies of the firm. The decision involves factors such as how much should be invested in credit, what the credit terms should be, who the recipients of credit should be, how the receivables should be monitored, and how the collection process should be structured. These factors must be evaluated in conjunction with other corporate policies. If scarce funds are used for credit extension, then fewer investable funds are available for both long-term purposes such as investment in plant and equipment and short-term investments such as inventory. Of course, most firms help finance the extension of credit by using trade credit (accounts payable) themselves. As a major component of the cash conversion cycle, trade credit is a significant tool for management to use in maximizing the use of its resources.

The goal of credit decisions is to maximize shareholder wealth. Unfortunately, all too often the decision to extend credit is a passive one. Many firms sell on credit because other firms in the industry do so. Too little consideration is given to the effect of credit extension on the firm's revenue and cost structures. For instance, W. T. Grant Company until 1975 allowed customers 36 months to pay, with a minimum payment of $1 per month.

---

[1]Theoretical discussions are found in two articles by G. W. Emery: "A Pure Financial Explanation for Trade Credit," *Journal of Financial and Quantitative Analysis* (September 1984): 271–85, and "An Optimal Financial Response to Variable Demand," *Journal of Financial and Quantitative Analysis* (June 1987): 209–25.

Given the serious cash flow problems the firm had, this policy was not in the best interests of either investors or creditors — particularly in light of the fact that receivables were sold for about 15 percent of their face value when W. T. Grant liquidated.

The purpose of this chapter is to analyze the establishment of credit policies that contribute to shareholder wealth. First, some theoretical underpinnings are discussed. Next, the effect of changing credit terms on assets, liabilities, and cash flows is examined. Finally, a steady-state model for evaluating credit terms is discussed. A graphical solution is shown in Appendix A of this chapter.

Theoretical Foundations

Credit is extended in response to either direct or indirect customer demand for the firm's products or services. This principle implies that sales might not occur without the extension of credit. While that may be true, management cannot afford the luxury of such a narrow view of its affairs. Instead of starting with the question, "Do customers receive the credit requested?" a firm should establish a policy involving all credit decisions.

The decision to extend credit and the decision about the terms offered can be viewed as similar to a change in the price of the product or service. Price is the result of a great number of market forces, some of which are controllable but most of which are not. Under the assumption that the firm operates within the classic definition of imperfect competition in both the product and the factor markets, then management has some influence over product demand. Although the firm's products or services may be similar to those offered by competitors, sufficient diversity of product or service can be created by the firm through customer relations, pre- and postservices, and pricing policies.

The establishment of a market price implies that a quantity of goods is offered and taken in a market exchange setting. This statement does not suggest that all possible demanders are satisfied or that the supply cannot be changed. Rather, it means that a given amount of product is offered and the same amount is purchased at the market price. From the firm's view, does the transaction price allow for a profit? Can profit be enhanced by charging some other price?[2]

Answers to these questions require analysis of marginal revenue and marginal cost relationships. Marginal analysis should also be chosen by

---

[2]In some cases (gasoline, for example) there exists a cash price and a credit price. The customer is given the option of deciding which to accept. However, the Robinson–Patman Act prohibits the seller from charging different classes of customers different credit prices unless the different prices can be justified by volume considerations. This idea is inconsistent with the risk-return concept underlying finance theory.

management to establish terms of credit. Failure to do so results in lower shareholder wealth. Since most firms differ with respect to their production capabilities, their access to the capital markets, the types of customers they serve, and so forth, their credit terms should also differ in the pursuit of the goal of maximizing shareholders' wealth.

Credit and Collection Variables

Investing in accounts receivable requires consideration of several interrelated aspects: investment costs, losses from bad debts, the impact of credit terms on sales, and the related cash flows, for instance, for inventory purchases. The important decision variables can be divided into two groups. The first group contains three **credit policy variables**: cash discounts, discount period, and credit period. The second group consists of three **collection policy variables** that are associated with late payments and bad debts: the seller's collection expense as a percentage of overdue accounts, the penalty rate charged on overdue accounts, and the time when accounts are sold to a collection agency.

The credit policy variables directly affect total credit sales and the proportion of early payments and indirectly affect the proportion of overdue payments. Generally, as the discount is increased, more customers take advantage of the discount. Conversely, as the credit period is lengthened, fewer customers take the discount since the implicit cost is reduced.

Value of Cash Discounts

Cash discounts offer substantial financial advantage to buyers. The traditional belief was that should a firm not take the discount, then it was on the first step of bankruptcy. A more realistic view is that these funds are no different from other funds employed in the firm, except for their cost.

The buyer's major decision is whether or not to take the discount or whether to delay payment beyond the due date, which is called "stretching payables." If payables are not to be stretched, the economically correct decision for the buyer is to pay the invoice on the last date of the discount or the last day to the credit period. If the buying firm can earn interest from its demand deposits at the bank or can invest the resources in a money market account, it should never pay before the last day of the discount period or before the final credit period day. The credit community has traditionally used the postmark on the envelope in which the check is received to determine the date of payment receipt.

An understanding of the full value of the cash discount is important. Consider credit terms of "2/10, n/30" where n is read as "net." That is, a 2 percent cash discount can be taken if the invoice is paid within 10 days; otherwise, the invoice is due in full in 30 days. The approximate cost of a missed discount under these terms is 36 percent per annum: 2 percent $\times$ 360/20 = 36 percent, where 360 represents the number of days in the year and the number 20 is the difference between the credit period (30 days) and the discount period (10 days). This type of calculation can be seriously misleading for three reasons:

1. The length of the payment acceleration assumed (payment is in 10 days instead of 30 days; therefore payment is accelerated 20 days).
2. The implicit assumption that the transaction will not be repeated.
3. The worth of the discount once taken.

The calculation should reflect the actual acceleration period. Rarely do companies not accepting discounts pay on the due date (usually the 30th day). Also, the benefit should be compounded to approximate the ongoing value of the discount to the buyer. Whenever sales are continuous, the **annualized implicit cost** (AIC) of a cash discount may be measured by the formula

$$\text{AIC} = \left(\frac{1}{1-y}\right)^{360/\alpha} - 1, \tag{13.1}$$

where α is the number of days of actual acceleration and y is the discount rate offered (stated as a decimal number). When a transaction is unlikely to be repeated, a simple interest equivalent is more appropriate:

$$\text{AIC} = \left(\frac{y}{1-y}\right)\left(\frac{360}{\alpha}\right). \tag{13.2}$$

ILLUSTRATION 13.1

Assume that invoices displaying 2/10, n/30 credit terms are normally paid 40 days from the invoice date. The traditional approach assigns a cost of 36 percent, as shown previously. Actually, the benefit of discount settlement, or the AIC, after 10 days (i.e., $\alpha = 40 - 10 = 30$) is equivalent to about 27.4 percent on a continuous basis,

$$\text{AIC} = \left(\frac{1}{1-0.02}\right)^{360/30} - 1 = 0.274,$$

or 24.5 percent on a single-event basis,

$$\text{AIC} = \left(\frac{0.02}{1-0.02}\right)\left(\frac{360}{30}\right) = 0.245.$$

If the invoices were normally paid 30 days from the invoice date, the single-event AIC would be 36.7 percent, whereas the continuous-event AIC would be 43.8 percent (prove these figures for yourself). $\square$

Failure to take the discount is equivalent to borrowing the amount of the payable for 20 days at an annual implicit cost (AIC) of 27.4 percent on a compound interest basis and 24.5 percent on a single-event basis. Alternatively, taking the discount is comparable to not taking a loan for 20 days at the costs shown.

Figure 13.1 graphically depicts annual implicit costs for discount rates of 1, 2, and 3 percent and for payment accelerations up to 60 days. Generally, as either the discount rate or the discount period is increased, more customers should take advantage of them, since forgoing the cash discount increases the implicit cost. Conversely, as the credit period is lengthened, fewer customers will take the discount, since the implicit cost is reduced.

If the discount amount, discount period, or credit period is increased, sales should improve. The firm gains sales from competitors and from new customers to the market since increasing these credit variables effectively lowers the market price. The increased discount amount results in the buyer remitting a smaller amount. Lengthening the discount period and the credit period means that the present value of the amount due is now less.

Delayed Payment

Payments delayed beyond the credit period should signal to the credit manager that one or more of the following reasons may be the cause:

FIGURE 13.1
Cost of Discounts: Compound Interest Case

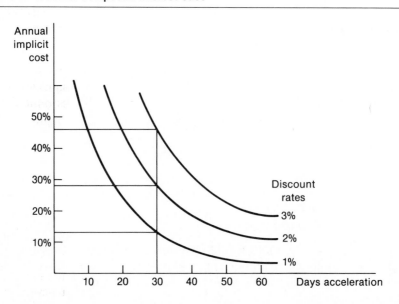

☐ Payment has been simply overlooked.

☐ The debtor is having financial problems.

☐ The discount is not an attractive enough incentive to induce early payment.

The first two possibilities are properly part of the credit review and granting function of the credit department (discussed in Chapter 12). However, if the discount is not enticing enough, the credit manager should attempt to understand why this is the case. As part of this analysis, it is useful to analyze why customers **stretch payables**.

The critical questions the debtor must ask when paying invoices are these:

☐ Should payables be stretched?

☐ If payables are stretched, for how long should they be?

The factors to consider are the loss of credit standing and reputation against the value of using the stretched funds. These considerations require quantification of loss of credit standing and reputation, which is obviously a difficult task. Stretching for a short period of time is less damaging to the firm than stretching for a long period. The cost of stretching is also affected by the firm the payable is owed to. Factors such as the seller's size and relative financial strength, goodwill between the two companies, and alternative sources of supply influence the credit and reputation loss function.

ILLUSTRATION 13.2

The AIC associated with stretching can be calculated by using Eqs. (13.1) and (13.2). Assume that payment terms are 1/10, n/60, but management normally pays 80 days from the invoice date. The AIC is

$$\text{AIC} = \left(\frac{1}{1 - 0.01}\right)^{360/70} - 1 = 0.0531$$

on a compound interest basis. It is

$$\text{AIC} = \left(\frac{0.01}{1 - 0.01}\right)\left(\frac{360}{70}\right) = 0.0520$$

on a single-event basis.

The interpretation of these results is that the *effective annualized borrowing cost* resulting from not taking the discount and stretching payables 20 days beyond the credit period is a little over 5.2 percent. If this cost is less than any alternative forms of borrowing that might be available to the firm, management should consider stretching payables.   ☐

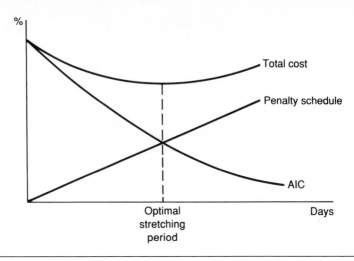

FIGURE 13.2
Optimal Stretching Period

If the use of a linear penalty schedule is appropriate for incorporating the credit and reputation costs incurred by the debtor from stretching, then the credit manager can infer that the payment period equals the optimal stretching period.[3] Figure 13.2 depicts this situation. The credit manager can then use this information to support a need to change credit terms. For instance, by increasing the discount 0.5 percentage points, so that terms are now 2.5/10, n/30, the AIC increases from 15.7 percent to 20 percent on a compound basis, and from 14.7 percent to 18.5 percent on a single-event basis. In Fig. 13.2, the new AIC curve will shift upward and to the right, as will the total cost curve. The credit manager may feel that the intersection of the new AIC curve with the penalty schedule exceeds debtors' borrowing rates, say, on lines of credit, providing incentive for them to take advantage of the discount and pay earlier. The extension of this type of analysis in a marginal revenue, marginal cost context is formalized later in this chapter.

Asset, Liability, and Cash Flow Considerations

Changes in credit policy, and specifically in the credit terms, can significantly affect asset and liability balances and cash flows. New credit terms can stimulate sales growth, which in turn causes production to increase to

---

[3]The underlying concept is similar to economic order quantity analysis where the optimal amount of inventory to order is where ordering costs equal holding costs — or in the present case, where AIC equals penalty costs.

meet the higher sales demand. Higher production results in increased inventory requirements, financing, and so on.

In an effort to indicate the dynamics of the problem, assume that the firm is in a relatively stable operating position. The market sets the price of the product, and the firm produces a given quantity for sale at that price. The internal structure of purchasing and using materials and labor in production, creating inventory, and selling takes place on a repetitive basis. The lead times necessary for delivery of raw materials, the manufacturing cycle, and the sales pattern are known. This information allows management to establish an asset-liability structure, establish sources and uses of funds, project profits, and predict the cash cycle of the firm.

No Credit Extended

In the previous market setting the cash flow pattern of a firm that does not extend credit follows a predictable and stable pattern. This pattern means that the firm's liquidity risk is greatly reduced, as indicated in the following illustration.

ILLUSTRATION 13.3

Assume that the firm operates in the type of environment outlined in the preceding paragraph. Relevant data are as follows: market demand per month is 100 units; market price per unit is $10; fixed labor cost per month is $150; variable cost per unit is $5; the corporate tax rate is 34 percent; and credit available for financing inventory is $500. All sales are made for cash. These data result in profit of $231 for month 1, as shown in Table 13.1.

Assuming that the opening balance sheet for month 1 consists only of

---

TABLE 13.1
Income Statement for the First Month (No Credit Extended)

Sales		$1000
Costs:		
Variable	$500	
Fixed	150	
Total		650
Profit before taxes		$ 350
Taxes		119
Profit after taxes		$ 231

TABLE 13.2
Balance Sheet

(a) As of the start of the first month of no credit

Cash	$ 0	Accounts payable	$500
Receivables	0	Accrued wages	0
Inventories	500	Taxes payable	0
		Retained earnings	0
Total	$ 500	Total	$500

(b) As of the end of the first month of no credit

Cash	$1000	Accounts payable	$ 500
Receivables	0	Accrued wages	150
Inventories	0	Taxes payable	119
		Retained earnings	231
Total	$1000	Total	$1000

inventory and accounts payable (see Table 13.2a), then the closing financial position is represented by Table 13.2(b).

Immediately following the end of month 1 the firm makes payments for accrued wages, outstanding accounts payable,[4] taxes, and dividends, in this order. It then purchases, on credit, new materials to satisfy month 2's sales demand. The new financial position beginning month 2 is the same as that shown in Table 13.2(a). Since market and production conditions in month 2 are similar to those in month 1, month 2's ending financial position is as shown in Table 13.2(b). This process continues month after month, with the result that cash flows follow the predictable pattern shown in Figure 13.3.

This highly simplified system ignores replacement of fixed assets. They could be included, but they are not necessary to show the effects of credit. Thus the firm achieves a stable and repetitive situation.

It is the nature of this situation that is important. Net working capital reaches a high of $231 (see Table 13.2b) and a low of $0 (see Table 13.2a), and inventory turnover is every 30 days. Cash inflows occur evenly throughout the month, and all cash outflows take place on the last moment of the month. Corporate financing is arranged through suppliers of materials. If these traditional forms of liquidity analysis are used by the firm and its creditors, the conclusion is that although some degree of liquidity risk exists, it is within acceptable limits.   □

---

[4] For simplicity, we assume accounts payable terms are net 30 days.

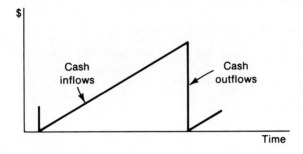

FIGURE 13.3
Cash Flow Patterns: No Credit Offered

Whenever cash flow stability is lacking, creditors and stockholders experience different degrees of risk exposure. They may react to such a situation to the detriment of management. Hence management must satisfy these special-interest groups.

Credit Extended

How might these special-interest groups and the firm be affected by changing credit terms? As the following illustration indicates, the firm enters a **transition period** that takes it from its current steady state to a new steady state. Liquidity management can be subjected to much stress during this transition period.

ILLUSTRATION 13.4

Assume that management decides to change from a policy of cash on delivery (COD) to one in which the terms are 2/10, n/30. Management forecasts that these credit terms will encourage new customers to purchase 50 units per month. It is expected that the cash discount will be taken by all the original customers but by none of the new customers. In addition, a credit and collection department will need to be established. It is estimated that costs of this department will have both variable and fixed components: 15 percent of incremental sales plus $5 fixed costs per month. As a support for the new credit policy additional inventory must be purchased and financing arranged before the time of sale.

Table 13.3 indicates the start of the new credit policy. Inventory and accounts payable have increased by $250 to support the new credit terms.

During the month, production and sales occur in the usual fashion, except that the scale of each has increased. The consolidated income state-

TABLE 13.3
Balance Sheet as of the Start of the First Month of Credit

Cash	$ 0	Accounts payable	$750
Receivables	0	Accrued wages	0
Inventory	750	Taxes payable	0
		Retained earnings	0
Total	$750	Total	$750

ment, shown in Table 13.4, indicates that the new credit terms result in profit increasing $103.36 to a level of $334.36. Assuming that sales occur at a constant rate, Table 13.5 shows daily receivable balances and collections.

The end of the first period's and the beginning of the next period's financial positions when credit is extended are reflected by Tables 13.6(a) and 13.6(b), respectively. As a result of selling on credit, cash flow during the first month of the credit transition period is less than before. The initiation of credit results in total cash flow of $653.20 ($32.66 per day times 20 days), as opposed to $1000 in the period before the change. The difference is a result of no cash inflow during the first 10 days of the discount period and amounts deducted for discounts. Increased inventory requirements result in higher accounts payable (under the assumption that the needed financing is available through material suppliers). In addition, sizable accounts receivable are now outstanding.

After the settlement process shown in Table 13.6(b), and including new credit purchases of materials for the second month, the firm is unable to pay suppliers in full for prior purchases. Only $423.20 (that is, $653.20

TABLE 13.4
Income Statement First Month That Credit Is Offered

	Without credit	With credit	Change
Sales	$1000.00	$1500.00	$500.00
Less cash discounts	0	13.40	13.40
Net sales	$1000.00	$1486.60	$486.60
Costs:			
Variable	$ 500.00	$ 825.00	$325.00
Fixed	150.00	155.00	5.00
Total	$ 650.00	$ 980.00	$330.00
Profit before taxes	$ 350.00	$ 506.60	$156.60
Taxes	119.00	172.24	53.24
Profit after taxes	$ 231.00	$ 334.36	$103.36

TABLE 13.5
Daily Sales, Receivable Balance, and Cash Inflow

Day	Sales per day		Receivable balance	Cash inflow
	Original	New		
1	$33.33	$16.67	$ 50.00	$ 0
2	33.33	16.67	100.00	0
3	33.33	16.67	150.00	0
4	33.33	16.67	200.00	0
5	33.33	16.67	250.00	0
6	33.33	16.67	300.00	0
7	33.33	16.67	350.00	0
8	33.33	16.67	400.00	0
9	33.33	16.67	450.00	0
10	33.33	16.67	500.00	0
11	33.33	16.67	516.67	32.66*
12	33.33	16.67	533.34	32.66
13	33.33	16.67	550.01	32.66
14	33.33	16.67	566.68	32.66
15	33.33	16.67	583.35	32.66
16	33.33	16.67	600.02	32.66
17	33.33	16.67	616.69	32.66
18	33.33	16.67	633.36	32.66
19	33.33	16.67	650.03	32.66
20	33.33	16.67	666.70	32.66
21	33.33	16.67	683.37	32.66
22	33.33	16.67	700.04	32.66
23	33.33	16.67	716.71	32.66
24	33.33	16.67	733.38	32.66
25	33.33	16.67	750.05	32.66
26	33.33	16.67	766.72	32.66
27	33.33	16.67	783.39	32.66
28	33.33	16.67	800.06	32.66
29	33.33	16.67	816.73	32.66
30	33.33	16.67	833.40	32.66
1	33.33	16.67	833.40	49.33†
2	33.33	16.67	833.40	49.33

*Collection of day 1 sales from customers who take the discount; that is,

$33.33 − $0.67 discount = $32.66.

†Collection of day 1 sales from customers who do not take the discount plus collection of day 21 sales from customers who take the discount; that is,

$16.67 + ($33.33 − $0.67) = $49.33.

cash − $230.00 wages) is available to pay supplier debt of $750, since employees are paid first. Therefore accounts payable increase to $1076.80 to start the second period. It is one thing for suppliers to expand their sales and resultant receivables, but it is an entirely different matter for them to be asked to carry additional obligations to finance buyers. Suppliers, how-

TABLE 13.6
Financial Position When Credit Is Offered (1)

(a) Balance sheet as of the end of the first month of credit

Cash	$ 653.20	Accounts payable	$ 750.00
Receivables	833.40	Accrued wages	230.00
Inventories	0	Taxes payable	172.24
		Retained earnings	334.36
Total	$1486.60	Total	$1486.60

(b) Balance sheet as of the start of the second month of credit

Cash	$ 0	Accounts payable	$1076.80
Receivables	833.40	Accrued wages	0
Inventories	750.00	Taxes payable	172.24
		Retained earnings	334.36
Total	$1583.40	Total	$1583.40

ever, are not the only group financing the new credit policy. The lack of sufficient cash flow results in taxes payable remaining outstanding and stockholders receiving no dividends. Therefore both the government and the shareholders are also financing the new credit policy.

Table 13.7 represents the start of the new static phase. Daily collections of $49.33 (see Table 13.5) result in a cash buildup of $1479.90 at the end of the second month. Outstanding receivables are constant at the prior period's level of $833.40. Higher retained earnings reflect the current period's profit after taxes of $329.94. Profit decreases $4.42 from the pre-

TABLE 13.7
Financial Position When Credit Is Offered (2)

(a) Balance sheet as of the end of the second month of credit

Cash	$1479.90	Accounts payable	$1076.80
Receivables	833.40	Accrued wages	230.00
Inventories	0	Taxes payable	342.21
		Retained earnings	664.29
Total	$2313.30	Total	$2313.30

(b) Balance sheet as of the start of the third month of credit

Cash	$ 0	Accounts payable	$ 750.00
Receivables	833.40	Accrued wages	0
Inventories	750.00	Taxes payable	169.10
		Retained earnings	664.30
Total	$1583.40	Total	$1583.40

TABLE 13.8
Financial Position When Credit Is Offered (3)

(a) Balance sheet as of the end of the third month of credit

Cash	$1479.90	Accounts payable	$ 750.00
Receivables	833.40	Accrued wages	230.00
Inventories	0	Taxes payable	339.06
		Retained earnings	994.24
Total	$2313.30	Total	$2313.30

(b) Balance sheet as of the start of the fourth month of credit

Cash	$ 0	Accounts payable	$ 750.00
Receivables	833.40	Accrued wages	0
Inventories	750.00	Taxes payable	0
		Retained earnings	833.40
Total	$1583.40	Total	$1583.40

vious period's level since cash discounts are now taken for the full 30-day period as opposed to 20 days when credit was initiated.

In the settlement for month 2 (see Table 13.7b) wages are paid and accounts payable are restored to a current status. The tax obligation, however, is about the same as the previous settlement period's balance, and shareholders still do not receive dividends.

Table 13.8 represents the financial positions at the end of month 3 and the start of month 4, respectively. From an analysis of Table 13.8(b) we see that all liabilities are current, and residual cash flows of $70.44 have been paid as dividends to shareholders. This result is evident from the decrease in the retained-earnings balance.

A fourth month of sales, collections, and payments are necessary to bring the system to full stability. Table 13.9 reflects the closing position for month 4 and the opening position for month 5 now that credit influences have worked their way through the system. Cash flows are regular and predictable, suppliers are paid on a regular basis for the amount of current purchases, and stockholders receive regular dividends of $329.94, which are in excess of the precredit policy period.   □

Important Considerations

The previous illustrations highlight three important considerations. First, credit decisions have a significant influence on cash flows. An unstable transition period may follow the initiation of new credit terms because of insufficient funds. Management must know how the credit policy will be financed. Management needs to project all inflows and outflows since failure to do so can lead to unhappy creditors and shareholders.

TABLE 13.9
Financial Position When Credit Is Offered (4)

(a) Balance sheet as of the end of the fourth month of credit

Cash	$1479.90	Accounts payable	$ 750.00
Receivables	833.40	Accrued wages	230.00
Inventories	0	Taxes payable	169.96
		Retained earnings	1163.34
Total	$2313.30	Total	$2313.30

(b) Balance sheet as of the start of the fifth month of credit

Cash	$ 0	Accounts payable	$ 750.00
Receivables	833.40	Accrued wages	0
Inventories	750.00	Taxes payable	0
		Retained earnings	833.40
Total	$1583.40	Total	$1583.40

Second, suppliers are often required to expand their investment in the firm making a credit change. From the buyer's perspective the higher accounts payable amount is permanent and considered costless, unless, of course, discounts are not taken. However, from the supplier's point of view the commitment is only for a short period of time. Therefore how stable is this "permanent" incremental investment? Should the firm attempt to replace short-term capital with more permanent and stable long-term funds? If the answer is yes, then the new long-term capital has a cost to the firm, either a real cost in the case of debt or an opportunity cost in the case of equity. The firm should look upon this added cost as a form of insurance payment to reduce liquidity risk.

Finally, the posture of the stockholders must be considered. In Illustration 13.4 shareholders lost two dividends and received a smaller than usual one in another period. It was not until a new *steady state* was reached that dividends were greater than before and as stable. However, what if the steady state takes a long time to reach or is never reached? Has management now contributed to stockholder dissatisfaction, with the result that a successful takeover can occur? Also, is the present value of the new dividend stream greater than that of the original stream? If not, the value of stockholders' wealth is diminished.

ILLUSTRATION 13.5

Under the no-credit policy shareholders receive $210 in dividends each period. The new credit policy results in no dividends in periods 1 and 2, $160.84 in period 3, and $329.94 in period 4 and thereafter.

If the new credit policy is expected to stay constant for the foreseeable future, and shareholders can earn 1 percent per period on their investments for comparable risk, it takes about 7.1 periods before the new policy contributes more to shareholder wealth than does the old policy. This is determined by solving for n, the number of periods, in the following present value equation:

No credit   Credit

$210(PVIFA 1\%, n)$ = $160.84(PVIF 1\%, 3)$
$$+ \ 329.94[(PVIFA \ 1\%, n)$$
$$- \ (PVIFA \ 1\%, 3)].$$

Rearranging and solving for the annuity factor (PVIFA 1%, n) results in an answer of 6.7887. This value is approximately equivalent to the annuity discount factor for 1 percent, 7.1 periods.   □

Steady-State Time Value Approach

The balance-sheet approach illustrated in the preceding section is a laborious technique for analyzing proposed credit decisions. A generalized net-present-value (NPV) formulation of a credit model in a noninflationary environment[5] is

$$NPV = \sum_{t=0}^{M} \frac{-I_t + F_t(1 - \tau)}{(1 + k)^t} \geqslant 0, \tag{13.3}$$

where

I_t = incremental investment in time period t as a result of credit decision,

F_t = marginal net cash flow occurring at time period t,

τ = marginal corporate tax rate,

k = appropriate risk-adjusted discount rate,

M = number of periods policy is expected to remain in effect.

The decision rule is to accept the credit policy if NPV is greater than or equal to zero. If two mutually exclusive credit policies are compared, the decision is to accept the policy with the higher NPV, assuming it is positive. Since positive NPVs accrue to shareholders, the result is improved shareholder wealth.

Under the often-invoked assumptions that investments are only made

---

[5]Appendix B of this chapter shows an inflation-adjusted credit model.

at $t = 0$ and that cash flows are constant and exist in perpetuity, Eq. (13.3) becomes

$$\text{NPV} = -I_0 + \frac{F(1 - \tau)}{k} \geq 0, \tag{13.4}$$

where I_0 is the incremental investment at the start of the new credit policy.

Multiplying both sides of Eq. (13.4) by k results in the residual income model:

$$\text{RI} = k(\text{NPV}) = F(1 - \tau) - kI_0. \tag{13.5}$$

Both academicians and practitioners view this model as a useful decision model. The expression $F(1 - \tau)$ is after-tax cash flow; the expression kI_0 represents an adjustment for the opportunity cost of funds invested. The decision rule is to undertake the new credit policy whenever RI is greater than or equal to zero. When this is the case, marginal revenue is greater than or equal to marginal cost.

The RI model provides results that are *equivalent to the balance-sheet approach discussed earlier as long as a steady state prevails.* If a new credit policy results in investment and financial changes that require time for establishing a new steady state, then the balance-sheet approach and the residual income approach are not equivalent.

In an effort to make the discussion that follows easier to understand, the RI model is restated as

$$\text{RI} = [S_n(1 - V) - w - f](1 - \tau) - kI_0 \geq 0, \tag{13.6}$$

where the new variables are

S_n = new incremental gross sales,
V = incremental variable-cost ratio,
w = incremental amount of cash discounts taken,
f = any incremental fixed costs and bad debt incurred.

Explanation of I_0: Changing Credit Terms

It is important to understand how to interpret incremental investment I_0 under **changing credit terms**. Easing credit by lengthening the credit period should stimulate sales. Receivable balances, in turn, should increase because present customers will now take longer to pay and new customers will be attracted by more attractive credit terms. Inventory investments will likely increase because of the changing credit policy's stimulus on sales. Increases in spontaneous liabilities, such as accounts payable and accrued wages, will offset some of the asset investments. In this case the incremental investment is

I_0 = (increased investment in receivables associated with
  original sales, stated at cost plus profit — in other words,
                 selling price) (a)

 + (investment in receivables associated with new sales,
                stated at cost) (b)

 + (increased investment in inventories, stated at cost) (c)

 − (increased spontaneous non-interest-bearing liabilities), (d)

or

$$I_0 = \text{DSO}_o\left(\frac{S_o}{360}\right) + V(\text{DSO}_n)\left(\frac{S_n}{360}\right) + H - L.$$

    (a)   (b)   (c) (d)

(13.7)

Here DSO represents incremental days sales outstanding in receivables; S and V are incremental dollar sales and percent variable costs, respectively; the subscripts o and n refer to old and new customers, respectively; H represents incremental inventory investment; and L represents incremental spontaneous liabilities arising as a result of the credit decision.

The *increased investment in accounts receivable for original sales* [expression (a) of Eq. 13.7] *includes the full dollar amount of those receivables,* that is, both inventory cost and profit.[6] However, *the investment in receivables from new sales* [expression (b) of Eq. 13.7] *excludes all profit margin.* The difference is that only variable costs are invested in new receivables, whereas there is an opportunity cost associated with the existing outstanding receivables. If management does not change the credit period, then the receivables that are stated at cost plus profit (the selling price) will be collected at the normal average collection period. If the **average collection period** for the old accounts changes as a result of changing credit terms, then the profit embedded in the receivable balance will not be collected at the normal time and, therefore, will not be available for reinvestment. Thus an opportunity cost is associated with the profit amount since management implicitly has reinvested it in the outstanding accounts by extending the payment period.

---

[6]We assume that old customers are affected by the changing credit terms. If they are not, DSO will not change and there will be no incremental investment for old accounts.

ILLUSTRATION 13.6

Implementation of the RI model is illustrated by using the following data: current annual sales (S_o) are \$12,000, variable costs are \$6000, and fixed costs are \$1800. Presently, all sales are made for cash. Assume that management is considering the introduction of credit sales with terms of 2/10, n/30. These terms are expected to increase sales (S_n) by \$6000 per year; variable costs by \$3900 [resulting in the incremental variable-cost ratio (V) becoming 65 percent — that is, incremental variable costs divided by incremental sales: \$3900/\$6000]; fixed costs (f) by \$60; and inventory (H) by \$250. Spontaneous liabilities (L) of accounts payable and accrued wages increase \$250 and \$80, respectively.

   Ninety percent of the old customers are forecasted to take the discount and pay on the 10th day (DSO_o) that their receivables are outstanding. The remaining old customers and all the new customers are not expected to take the discount. They are expected to pay on the 35th day (DSO_n). Discounts taken (w) will be \$216. The opportunity cost of funds (k) is 10 percent after taxes, and the corporate tax rate (τ) is 34 percent. No bad debts are expected.

   Incremental investment is

$$I_0 = DSO_o\left(\frac{S_o}{360}\right) + V(DSO_n)\left(\frac{S_n}{360}\right) + H - L$$

$$= \left[\left(0.90 \times 10 \times \frac{\$12,000}{360}\right) + \left(0.10 \times 35 \times \frac{\$12,000}{360}\right)\right]$$

$$+ \left(0.65 \times 35 \times \frac{\$6000}{360}\right) + \$250 - \$330$$

$$= \$795.83 + \$250 - \$330 = \$715.83.$$

Residual income is

$$RI = [S_n(1 - V) - w - f](1 - \tau) - kI_0$$

$$= [\$6000(1 - 0.65) - \$216 - \$60](1 - 0.34) - 0.1(\$715.83)$$

$$= \$1203.84 - \$71.58 = \$1132.26.$$

Since RI is positive, the new credit policy should be implemented.   □

Explanation of I_0: Changing Credit Standards

Whenever the credit decision relates to **loosening credit standards**, the incremental investment is redefined to exclude the first expression on the right-hand side of Eq. (13.9); that is, expression (a) of the equation equals zero:

$$I_0 = V(\text{DSO}_n)\left(\frac{S_n}{360}\right) + H - L. \tag{13.8}$$

The revised specification indicates the incremental investment in receivables and inventories, stated at cost, that arises from new customers being granted credit. *A loosening of credit standards has no effect on present credit customers since they already qualify* under the old credit standards.

ILLUSTRATION 13.7

Subsequent to implementation of the credit policy in Illustration 13.5, management decides to loosen credit standards. This policy is expected to attract an additional $5000 in sales ($S_n$) from new customers. The variable-cost ratio (V) is expected to remain at 65 percent, inventory investment (H) will increase $225, and spontaneous liabilities (L) will increase $200. The new accounts are not expected to pay until 45 days after the sale. The opportunity cost of capital for this type of risky customer is 15 percent after taxes. Present accounts should not be affected by this change.

Incremental investment is

$$
\begin{aligned}
I_0 &= V(\text{DSO}_n)\left(\frac{S_n}{360}\right) + H - L \\
&= 0.65(45)\left(\frac{\$5000}{360}\right) + \$225 - \$200 \\
&= \$406.25 + \$225 - \$200 = \$431.25.
\end{aligned}
$$

Residual income is

$$
\begin{aligned}
\text{RI} &= [S_n(1 - V) - w - f](1 - \tau) - kI_0 \\
&= [\$5000(1 - 0.65) - 0 - 0](1 - 0.34) - 0.15(\$431.25) \\
&= \$1155 - \$64.69 = \$1090.31.
\end{aligned}
$$

Since RI is positive, management should loosen credit standards. $\square$

Whenever credit standards are tightened, some present customers will be affected. In this situation Eq. (13.8) is still appropriate.

ILLUSTRATION 13.8

Management is considering tightening the credit standards, with the expectation of losing $3000 in sales ($S_n$). Inventories ($H$) should decline $1000, and accounts payable (L) should decrease $500. The variable-cost ratio (V) is expected to remain at 65 percent. Average days sales outstanding (DSO_n) for these accounts is 50 days. The tax rate is 34 percent, and the opportunity cost of funds is 15 percent.

The incremental investment freed is

$$I_0 = V(DSO_n)\left(\frac{S_n}{360}\right) + H - L$$

$$= 0.65(50)\left(\frac{-\$3000}{360}\right) + (-\$1000) - (-\$500) = -\$770.83,$$

whereas the residual income generated by this decision is

$$RI = [S_n(1 - V) - w - f](1 - \tau) - kI_0$$

$$= [-\$3000(1 - 0.65) - 0 - 0](1 - 0.34) - 0.15(-\$770.83)$$

$$= \$-577.38.$$

Since residual income is negative, management should not institute the proposed change in credit standards. □

Reconciliation of the RI Model and the Balance-Sheet Approach

The RI model requires steady-state conditions. The following example reconciles the simplistic *steady-state RI model* results to the *changing balance-sheet approach*. The balance sheet data have been annualized and used in the RI model that follows.

In summary, the data are as follows:
Precredit period:

Current annual sales (S_0) = $12,000

Variable costs = $6000,

Fixed costs = $1800.

Upon initiation of credit:

Incremental sales (S_n) = $6000,

Variable costs = $3900,

Fixed costs (f) = $60,

Inventory (H) = $250,

Spontaneous liabilities (L) = $330,

Discounts taken (w) = $240.

Old customers take the discount and pay on day 10; new customers do not take the discount and pay on day 30.

Opportunity cost of funds = 10%,

Tax rate = 34%.

On the basis of this data incremental investment is

$$I_0 = (\text{DSO}_o)\left(\frac{S_o}{360}\right) + V(\text{DSO}_n)\left(\frac{S_n}{360}\right) + H - L$$

$$= 10\left(\frac{\$12,000}{360}\right) + \left(\frac{\$3900}{\$6000}\right)(30)\left(\frac{\$6000}{360}\right) + \$250 - \$330$$

$$= \underline{\$658.33} + \$250 - \$330$$

Receivable
investment

$$= \$578.33.$$

Residual income is

$$\text{RI} = [S_n(1 - V) - w - f](1 - \tau) - kI_0$$

$$= [\$6000(1 - 0.65) - \$240 - \$60](1 - 0.34) - 0.1(\$578.33)$$

$$= \underline{\$1188} - \underline{\$57.83}$$

Profit   Cost of capital

$$= \$1130.17.$$

A quick check of the two approaches reveals that incremental profits are equal — or nearly so; $1188 for the RI model (see the previous results) versus $1187.28 for the balance-sheet illustration [see Table 13.1 and the discussion following Table 13.8: ($329.94 − $231) × 12]. Incremental investments in inventories, accounts payable, and accrued wages are the same for both approaches. An investment difference of about $175 exists in accounts receivable between the two models (RI model: $658.33 — see the previous I_0 calculation; balance-sheet model: $833.40 — see Table 13.9).

The investment difference is the profit margin included in receivables in the balance-sheet approach. For example, outstanding receivables are calculated as

$$\text{DSO}_o \times \frac{\text{old sales}}{360} + \text{DSO}_n \times \frac{\text{new sales}}{360} \tag{13.9}$$

$$= 10 \times \frac{\$12,000}{360} + 30 \times \frac{\$6000}{360} = \$833.$$

This result agrees with the balance-sheet model in Table 13.9, with the exception of a small rounding difference. If the profit embedded in the new receivables is excluded, for the reasons discussed earlier, the investment in receivables is $658, the amount used in the calculation of I_0:

$$10 \times \frac{\$12,000}{360} + 0.65 \times 30 \times \frac{\$6000}{360} = \$658,$$

where 0.65 is the variable-cost factor to exclude profit in the new receivables.

Given the assumptions that have been made, it is apparent that *once a steady state is reached, the simple RI model is appropriate for analyzing receivables.* However, if the steady state takes a long time to reach, or if it is never reached, the usefulness of the RI model is uncertain. During the transition from one steady state to another, the cash demands may be too great for the firm to remain solvent. Careful planning is as much a prerequisite in establishing credit policy as it is in other types of investments.

Summary

Credit terms are often used by management to stimulate sales or meet competition without much regard for how they influence other facets of the business. Since management's objective should be to maximize long-term wealth of shareholders, analysis must be conducted in this frame of reference. The models presented in this chapter adhere to the wealth maximization concept.

A balance-sheet approach was presented first. This technique is laborious to use and overstates the economic investment in receivables. It does, however, pinpoint potential cash flow problems that management faces before a steady state is attained.

The residual income (discounting) model was discussed next. This model is prevalent in most finance book discussions of receivables. Major shortcomings of the model, as normally stated, are the assumptions of a steady state and no inflation. Appendix B of this chapter extends the residual income model to incorporate inflation. The only remaining weakness of the residual income model is the necessity of assuming a steady state. This problem can be overcome, however, by using a discrete net-present-value model that allows conditions (assumptions) to change from period to period.

The appendices of this chapter are essential for readers desiring insight into more complex credit models. The application of computers to credit problems allows management to use more sophisticated models to determine simultaneously the optimal discount amount, discount period, and credit period. Needless to say, these optimums are unique to each firm. If sales, cost, and payment functions are reasonably well specified by management, then there is little reason to match credit terms with competition. Terms considered optimal for one company are very likely not optimal for another firm.

Key Concepts

Annualized implicit cost
Average collection period
Change in credit standards
Change in credit terms
Collection policy variables

Credit policy variables
Steady state
Stretching payables
Transition period

Appendix A

A Graphical Solution for Optimal Credit Terms

A graphical solution for determining optimal credit terms is provided in Fig. A.1. Expected sales, shown in Fig. A.1(a), are a positive function of credit terms. Lengthening the credit period and increasing the cash discount lead to greater sales, since customers view these credit changes as implicit price reductions. The firm loses sales as restrictive credit terms force some customers to buy from competitors. Failure to offer credit terms results in only cash sales (and lower profits).

The level of accounts receivable in Fig. A.1(b) bears the expected close relationship with sales. Easier credit terms lead to higher sales and higher receivable balances.

Figure A.1(c) shows expected profit on sales (exclusive of any revenues and costs directly associated with credit) as a function of sales. This function reaches a maximum at the point that marginal revenue from sales equals marginal cost of sales. The intercept of the curve with the expected-sales axis indicates breakeven sales for the firm.

Figure A.1(d) is used to determine optimal credit policy. The profit-on-sales curve is shown in relation to expected level of accounts receivable and is derived geometrically from the three functions given in Figs. A.1(a), A.1(b), and A.1(c). The dotted lines trace three points in the construction of the curve.

For example, credit policy 1 results in expected sales of A in Fig. A.1(a), expected receivables of B in Fig. A.1(b), and expected profit (before credit revenues and costs) of C in Fig. A.1(c). This policy translates into point D in Fig. A.1(d). The cost of carrying accounts receivable is an increasing function of accounts receivable. Its position and shape indicate both fixed and variable carrying costs. The revenue curve represents interest charged on overdue accounts. It is an increasing function of accounts receivable balances since large accounts receivable balances are likely to have more overdue accounts, which are assessed interest charges. The total profit curve is derived by adding credit charge income to the profit on sales and subtracting the cost of carrying receivables.

The highest point on the total profit curve occurs where total marginal revenue from both product sales and credit charges equals the marginal cost of product sales and carrying receivables. This point determines the profit-maximizing level of receivables in Fig. A.1(b), the profit-maximizing level of sales in Fig. A.1(a), and the optimal credit terms (that is, the optimal set of credit and collection policies).

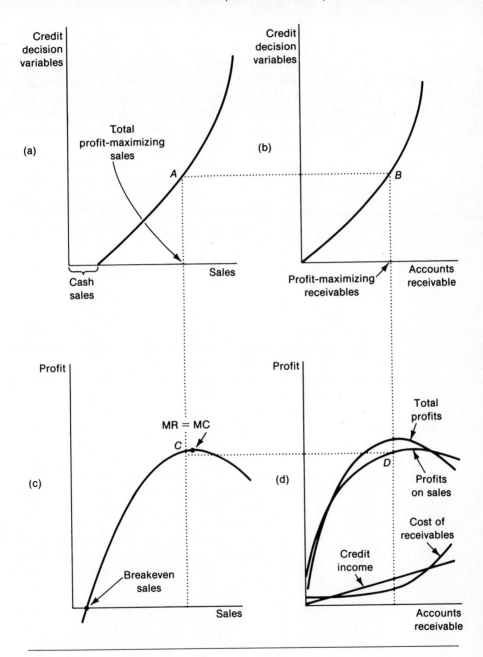

FIGURE A.1
Graphical Solution for Optimal Credit Terms

The multifaceted nature of optimal receivable balances is evident from this graphical representation. A changing sales function, cost function, cost of capital function, or receivable investment function affects optimal credit terms and receivable investment. Managers must be cognizant of the interrelationships that exist, since it is evident that *full* marginal analysis is required in order to choose the path most likely to enhance shareholders' wealth. Appendix C of this chapter describes a mathematical approach for implementing this graphical solution.

Appendix B

Inflation-Adjusted Credit Model

When discussing the RI (NPV) model, we stated that the conversion of the finite NPV model to a perpetuity NPV model assumed a noninflationary environment. Under inflationary conditions the expected cash flows must be adjusted for inflation-induced increases in product, factor, and financial prices.[1] Failure of management to raise product prices to offset increased costs results in reduced cash flow (assuming no possibility of making up the deficiency in increased volume).

The incorporation of inflation adjustments for both cash inflows and cash outflows result in the following NPV model:

$$
\begin{aligned}
\text{NPV} = -I_0 &\left[1 + \sum_{T=1}^{M} \frac{(1 + d)^T - (1 + d)^{T-1}}{(1 + r)(1 + i)^T} \right] \\
&+ \sum_{T=1}^{M} \frac{F(1 + u)^T(1 - \tau)}{[(1 + r)(1 + i)]^T} \geq 0,
\end{aligned}
\tag{B.1}
$$

where

d = rate of increase in net investment per period because of inflation,

u = increase in net cash inflows per period because of inflation,

r = real rate of return required on investment,

i = financial market's perception of inflation.

The expression $I_0[(1 + d)^T - (1 + d)^{T-1}]$ represents the increase in net investment that is required in period T because of inflation.

For example, the following time line shows the incremental inflation investment required at times 0, 1, and 2:

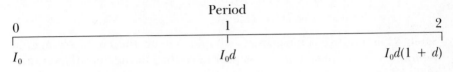

	Period	
0	1	2
I_0	$I_0 d$	$I_0 d(1 + d)$

---

[1] This appendix is based on the article by J. A. Halloran and H. P. Lanser, "The Credit Policy Decision in an Inflationary Environment," *Financial Management* (Winter 1981): 31–38.

In Eq. (B.1) the expression $F(1 + u)^T$ reflects the fact that the net cash inflows are growing over time at a constant rate of inflation of u percent per period. The discount factor $(1 + r)(1 + i)$ can be restated as $(1 + k)$, where k is the required rate of return in nominal terms and is usually stated as $k = r + i$. The cross-product term ri is often ignored since it is generally insignificant and r and i are estimates. Rate k is strictly greater than both d and u since it is a market-determined rate that incorporates any inflation premiums.

If cash flows are assumed to exist in perpetuity, then Eq. (B.1) can be simplified to

$$\text{NPV} = -I_0\left(\frac{k}{k - d}\right) + \frac{F(1 + u)(1 - \tau)}{(k - u)} \geq 0. \tag{B.2}$$

The most general form of the model is derived from Eq. (B.2) by analyzing it where NPV = 0:

$$F(1 - \tau)(1 + u)(k - d) - k(k - u)I_0 = 0. \tag{B.3}$$

If no inflation exists in the factor, product, or financial markets, then $u = d = i = 0$, with the result that $k = r$. The model then reduces to the simple RI model shown as Eq. (13.5).

ILLUSTRATION B.1

Assume the same facts as in the reconciliation of the residual income model and the balance-sheet approach. However, inflation is now expected to cause investment to increase at the rate (d) of 5 percent per period, cash inflows are expected to increase (u) 6 percent per period, the real rate of interest (k) is 10 percent, and the nominal rate (i) is 12 percent.

Residual income is

$$\begin{aligned}
\text{RI} &= [\$6000(1 - 0.65) - \$240 - \$60] \\
&\quad (1 - 0.34)(1 + 0.06)(0.12 - 0.05) \\
&\quad -0.12(0.12 - 0.06)(\$578.33) \\
&= \$88.15 - \$4.16 = \$83.99
\end{aligned}$$

Since RI is positive, management should initiate the credit change, although it is now considerably less profitable than in the no-inflation situation. Different assumptions about inflation obviously lead to different residual income expectations.   □

Appendix C
Comprehensive Credit Model

A comprehensive credit value maximization model[1] can be constructed that incorporates most of the concepts discussed in the chapter. Since customers have no incentive for making early payments within the discount or credit periods, it is assumed that all payments are made at the end of these time intervals. A realistic picture of payments is depicted in Table C.1. Some proportion q of total credit sales (S), less the cash discount of y percent, is paid at the end of the discount period i, another proportion $(1 - x)$ $(1 - q)$ is paid at the end of the credit period j, and the balance is either paid $[x(1 - q)(1 - b)]$ to the firm or sold $[xb(1 - q)]$ to a collection agency at time m, with z percent of the account amount remitted to the firm. Accounts not paid by the credit period are assessed an interest charge of r percent of the face value of the overdue account.

TABLE C.1
Payment Sequence

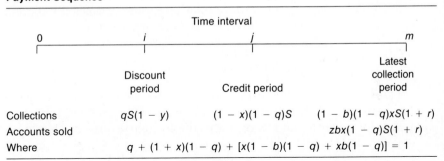

	Time interval		
0	i	j	m
	Discount period	Credit period	Latest collection period
Collections	$qS(1 - y)$	$(1 - x)(1 - q)S$	$(1 - b)(1 - q)xS(1 + r)$
Accounts sold			$zbx(1 - q)S(1 + r)$
Where	$q + (1 + x)(1 - q) + [x(1 - b)(1 - q) + xb(1 - q)] = 1$		

The present value of these cash flows can now be calculated. For payments received at the end of the discount period, the present value, discounted at a risk-adjusted rate k, is

$$\frac{(1 - y)qS}{(1 + k)^i}. \tag{C.1}$$

[1]This appendix is based on the following articles: Ned C. Hill and Kenneth D. Riener, "Determining the Cash Discount in the Firm's Credit Policy." *Financial Management* (Spring 1979): 68–73; Zvi Lieber and Yair E. Orgler, "An Integrated Model for Accounts Receivable Management," *Management Science* (October 1975): 202–11.

Credit balances paid at the end of the credit period have a present value of

$$\frac{(1 - x)(1 - q)S}{(1 + k)^j}.$$ (C.2)

If the proportion of early payments (q) increases, the proportion of overdue accounts (x) may increase. A possible reason is as follows: The proportion of early payments will increase because of the higher implicit cost associated with not taking the discount. Thus some customers who originally planned to pay at time j will now pay at time i and receive the cash discount. Since customers with financial difficulties will be the last ones to pay, a higher proportion of overdue balances will exist among customers who do not take the discount. There will be no change in overdue balances only if the change in early payments does not affect the average risk profile of customers who do not take the discount.

Balances that are not paid within the credit period, $x(1 - q)S$, are classified as overdue and are subject to collection efforts by the seller up to time m, that is, within the period $m - j$. For simplicity, assume that any successful collection efforts result in payments being made at time m for the face amount of the invoice plus an interest charge of r percent of invoice value. Unsuccessful efforts result in the overdue balances being sold to a collection agency for z percent of their face value and penalty charge. The NPV of the collections and sale of accounts at time m is

$$\frac{x(1 - q)(1 + r)(1 - b + bz)S}{(1 + k)^m}.$$ (C.3)

There are two cash outflow streams associated with the revenue streams. The first stream is for normal variable cost incurred in production and sales (for materials and labor, for example). These costs can be represented as

$$\frac{vS}{(1 + k)^n},$$ (C.4)

where v is the fraction of sales (S) that represents variable costs paid at time n. Time n is not necessarily equal to times $i, j,$ or m since the firm's payment schedule can differ from its receipts schedule.

The second category of costs is for collection expenses incurred (for simplicity, assumed to be at time m) in the attempt to collect overdue accounts:

$$\frac{cx(1 - q)S}{(1 + k)^m},$$ (C.5)

where c represents the percentage these costs are of overdue collections.

Profit (P) from accounts receivable is determined by summing all the elements of the model indicated by Eqs. (C.1) through (C.5):

$$P = \frac{(1 - y)qS}{(1 + k)^i} + \frac{(1 - x)(1 - q)S}{(1 + k)^j}$$
$$+ \frac{x(1 - q)(1 + r)(1 - b + bz)S}{(1 + k)^m} - \frac{vS}{(1 + k)^n} - \frac{cx(1 - q)S}{(1 + k)^m}. \qquad \text{(C.6)}$$

Optimal credit and collection policies can be derived through the use of calculus. The partial derivatives of P with respect to each decision variable — y, i, j, c, r, m — must be taken. This manipulation results in six equations and six unknowns, which are then solved simultaneously. *A straightforward solution is not possible without specifying credit sales (S) and customer payment (q) functions*, since these both depend on the credit terms y, i, and j, that is, y percent in i days, net in j days. Computer methods need to be used to solve this problem quickly.

The model can be simplified to make it easier to use for decision-making purposes by combining all receipts realized after the discount period, that is, by combining the second, third, and fifth terms of Eq. (C.6). The result is

$$P = \frac{(1 - y)qS}{(1 + k)^i} + \frac{g(1 - q)S}{(1 + k)^j} - \frac{vS}{(1 + k)^n}, \qquad \text{(C.7)}$$

where

$$g = (1 - x) + x\{[1 - b(1 - z)](1 + r) - c\}(1 + k)^{j-m}.$$

The second expression in Eq. (C.7) approximates the present value of the net amount collected after time i. Because of bad debts and collection expenditures, g is less than 1. Overall, Eq. (C.7) states that profit from accounts receivable is equal to the present value of payments at time i (the first expression), plus later collections (the second expression), less variable costs (the third expression).

In the situation where management knows values for i, j, and n, the discount rate y is the only remaining decision variable in Eq. (C.7). And since the discount w affects sales (S), customer payments patterns (q), and bad debts and collection expenditures (impounded in g), the simplified model incorporates all important factors associated with the credit decision.

The optimal value of the cash discount is found by equating the derivative of P with respect to y to zero. Since q and S are influenced by w, and g is influenced by q, the derivative is

$$[(1 - y)q'S + (1 - y)qS' - qS](1 + k)^{-i}$$
$$+ [g'q'(1 - q)S + g(1 - q)S' - gq'S](1 + k)^{-j} \qquad \text{(C.8)}$$
$$- vS'(1 + k)^{-n} = 0,$$

where primes denote partial derivatives with respect to the discount rate y. The optimal discount can be calculated when the sales and the payment functions and all parameters are specified.

In the case where the cash discount has no effect on sales ($S' = 0$) and bad debts exist but are constant ($g < 1$ and $g' = 0$), then Eq. (C.8) reduces to

$$y = 1 - g(1 + k)^{i-j} - \frac{q}{q'}. \tag{C.9}$$

Given a further assumption that no bad debts exist ($g = 1$), then Eq. (C.9) becomes

$$y = 1 - (1 + k)^{i-j} - \frac{q}{q'}. \tag{C.10}$$

In either case the cash discount depends on the seller's time value of money and the ratio of customer payment proportions to the change in the proportions as the discount is increased (q/q'). Terms q and q' represent the proportion of earlier payment and change in that proportion, respectively. They are positive values with an increase in the discount rate. If money has no time value, $k = 0$. Thus in Eq. (C.9) the discount depends on whether $1 > g + q/q'$. In Eq. (C.10) no discount should be offered since the right-hand side would be negative; the seller has no incentive to want to receive early payment. Therefore in the absence of time value of money, the risk of not being paid (that is, $g < 1$) is sufficient incentive to offer a discount to induce payment.

In the situation where the cash discount affects sales ($S' > 0$), and bad debts exist and are constant ($g < 1$ and $g' = 0$), the optimal discount is given by

$$y = 1 - g(1 + k)^{i-j} - [qS(1 + k)^{-i} \tag{C.11}$$
$$- gS'(1 + k)^{-j} + vS'(1 + k)^{-n}](q'S + qS')(1 + k)^{-i}.$$

A solution for this situation requires specification of the credit sales (S) and customer payment (q) functions. If the discount has not effect on sales ($S' = 0$), Eq. (C.11) reduces to Eq. (C.9). Furthermore, if bad debts are zero ($g = 1$), the equation reduces to Eq. (C.10).

Assume the sales and payments functions are specified as

$$S = -ey^2 + (e + d)y + L, \tag{C.12}$$

$$q = \frac{(J + D)y^u}{(J + Dy^u)}. \tag{C.13}$$

The sales function is quadratic and indicates L dollars of sales are realized when the discount y is zero. The early payment function is S-shaped and is equal to zero whenever no discount is offered. It rises slowly for low values of y and sharply at high values of y. The partial derivatives of these functions, with respect to w, are

$$S' = -2ey + (e + d), \tag{C.14}$$

$$q' = \frac{u(J + D)y^{u-1}}{(J + Dy^u)} - \frac{(J + D)uDy^{2u-1}}{(J + Dy^u)^2}. \tag{C.15}$$

ILLUSTRATION C.1

The optimal cash discount can be found by solving for y in Eq. (C.11), where S, q, S', and q' are specified by Eqs. (C.12) through (C.15), respectively. Assume that empirical values of the parameters in these equations are defined as $e = 275$, $d = 47.95$, $L = 255$, $J = 0.01$, $D = 50$, and $u = 4$. Assuming that the seller's cost of funds before taxes is 12 percent per annum, that $j = 2$ months and that $i = 1$ month, then the discount factor from j to i is about 0.99 [that is, $(1 + 0.12/12)^{-1}$].

Let the average loss from bad debts, $1 - g$, be 1 percent of credit sales, and let the variable cost v be equal to 69 percent of sales. Assume that these costs are paid at period $n = i$. Thus the discount factor is 0.99. The optimal discount is found by substituting these functions and parameters into Eq. (C.11) and solving for y. The result is a discount of approximately 2 percent. □

Questions

1. It is often said that a firm's credit policy is a passive policy. Discuss.

2. Accounts payable are said to be spontaneous financing. Explain. Your answer should include a discussion of the cash conversion cycle.

3. "The firm that misses a trade discount has taken the first step to ruin." Discuss.

4. The stretching of trade accounts payable is another example of indifference analysis. Discuss the conflicting forces of such an analysis.

5. What probable effects would the following changes have on the level of the company's accounts receivable?

(a) The company changes credit terms from 4/15, n/25 to 2/10, n/30.

(b) Interest rates increase.

(c) Production costs associated with the firm's product decrease.

(d) The economy worsens and slips into a mild recession.

6. Suppose that Williams Company and the local bank are considering extending credit to the same customer. Why might the Williams Company and the bank arrive at different decisions?

7. Explain why the credit decision and the inventory decision should be analyzed jointly.

8. What is the difference between a change in credit terms and a change in credit standards?

9. How would you decide whether or not to loosen credit standards? Describe the decision analysis.

10. What is the relationship between residual income and marginal cost/marginal revenue in a situation where additional credit is extended?

11. What is the impact of inflation on investment in accounts receivable?

Problems

1. Calculate the annual implicit cost of interest for terms of purchase of 3/15, n/45 and 4/10, n/30 when payments are made on days 45 and 30, respectively. Calculate for (a) nonrepeated sales and (b) continuous sales.

2. The 16–1 Company has been offered a change in trade credit terms by its supplier. The present terms are 2/10, n/45. Proposed terms are 1.5/20, n/36 or

2.5/cash, n/54. Determine and discuss the probable reaction of management to these proposed terms. The company usually forgoes the discount and pays on day 50. Use the compound interest equation to calculate the annualized implicit cost. Assume 360 days in the year.

3.   The AXE Company estimates that its opportunity cost of funds is 18 percent annually. Creditor terms offered the AXE Company are 3/15, n/30. Should management take the discounts offered if the company usually pays on day **(a)** 20, **(b)** 30, **(c)** 60, **(d)** 80, or **(e)** 90? Discuss the implications of your answer. Use the continuous case.

4.   The Berry Company purchases materials from a number of suppliers. Purchase discounts range between 1 percent and 4 percent (in 1 percent increments), with the discount period either 10 or 15 days. The net period is always 30 days. Management wishes to develop a cost profile of stretching trade payables. Prepare a profile that allows the acceleration period to vary between 20 and 90 days, in 10-day increments. Use the continuous-compounding formula, and assume 360 days in the year.

5.   A firm purchases $80,000 of goods monthly on credit terms of 2/10, n/50. Assume 360 days in the year.

   (a) Calculate the annual implicit cost of credit in percentage and dollar terms if the firm usually pays on the net date.

   (b) Calculate the annual implicit cost of credit in percentage and dollar terms if the firm usually pays 40 days after the invoice date.

   (c) Discuss the implications of these two payment arrangements.

6.   Oasis Company is considering changing its credit standards in order to attract more customers. These customers will generate an estimated $450,000 additional sales. The collection period for these new accounts is expected to be about 55 days. Present accounts are outstanding an average of 35 days. Variable costs are about 60 percent of sales. If the credit terms are changed, administrative costs are expected to increase $7000 annually. Management estimates the required return (before taxes) to be 20 percent. Using a 360-day year, decide whether the credit standards should be relaxed.

7.   The Hazel Company purchases $750,600 of goods annually at a constant monthly rate. Its suppliers offer terms of 2/10, n/50. Management has investigated the relationship between credit rating and time of payment of credit purchases and found it to be

$$0.02P + 0.0001 \text{ (number of days after discount date)} \left(\frac{P}{30}\right)^2,$$

where P is the average monthly purchases. Construct a graph similar to Fig. 13.2, and discuss your findings. Assume 360 days in the year.

8.   Grignomics Corporation is evaluating whether to change its credit terms from net 15. The sales manager estimates that 75 percent of the company's $400,000 annual sales, which are all sold on credit, will take advantage of any discount. The company presently finances its accounts receivable at an after-tax interest cost of 14 percent. Its marginal tax rate is 35 percent and variable costs are 60 percent of sales. Assuming that management can expect the annual sales, default costs, and inventory increases shown in Table 13.10 with each set of alternative credit terms, which credit term alternative is the most profitable? It is expected that 75 percent of new sales will be discounted. Assume 360 days in the year.

TABLE 13.10
Credit Term Alternatives

	Default costs	Credit terms	Additional inventory	Sales
(a)	$6000	2/10, n/45	$50,000	$600,000
(b)	4000	2/10, n/30	25,000	500,000
(c)	5000	net 30	40,000	525,000

9. From the information in Problem 8, calculate the average investment in accounts receivable, the number of days accounts receivable are outstanding, and the turnover ratio for each alternative.

10. Calculate the breakeven sales level where variable costs are 75 percent of incremental sales and incremental fixed costs are $13,500. The incremental sales will be 80 percent for credit and will be collected, on average, 60 days after sale. The opportunity cost of capital is 25 percent.

11. Determine how sensitive the breakeven sales level in Problem 10 is under the following conditions.

(a) The collection period increases to 66 days.

(b) The new administrative costs increase to $14,850.

(c) The variable-cost ratio increases to 82.5 percent of new sales.

12. Jakobstettel, Inc., is considering the extension of credit terms in expectation that sales will increase. Management believes that sales will increase 100 units if the current terms of 1/10, n/15 are changed to 3/10, n/20. Presently, 75 percent of customers take the discount. With new terms all old customers are expected to take the discount, but only 50 percent of new customers are expected to do so. Customers who do not take the discount are expected to pay by the net period. No bad debts are expected. Presently, 300 units are sold per month at a price of $15 per unit. Variable costs are $7.50 per unit, and total fixed costs are $1200. The new credit terms are expected to increase monthly sales by 100 units. The per-unit variable cost for these 100 units will be $8. Incremental fixed costs will be $325. The marginal tax rate is 42 percent. (Assume 30 days in a month, and round your answer to two decimal places.)

(a) Determine the expected change in monthly profit under the new credit terms.

(b) Calculate the daily accounts receivable balances and cash flows under the new credit policy. Use Table 13.5 as a model. Assume that the old terms started on day 1 (no outstanding sales prior to day 1) and the new terms become effective on day 16. All customers are expected to abide by the sale terms as on the day of their purchase.

13.   The Forwell Company wishes to evaluate a change in credit terms by calculating residual income. The current and proposed business conditions are as follows:

Current	Terms of sale	Cash
	Sales	$54,000
	Variable costs	$27,000
	Fixed costs	$ 1,200
Proposed	Terms of sale	2/10, n/30
	Incremental sales	$18,000
	Incremental variable costs	$ 9,600
	Incremental fixed costs	$250
	Incremental inventory	$900

When the new terms are implemented, 90 percent of the old customers are expected to discount and pay on the 10th day. Only 30 percent of the new customers are expected to discount. Management does not expect any bad debts. Sales to nondiscounters are expected to be paid on the 40th day after the sale. The after-tax opportunity cost of funds is 12 percent. The income tax rate is 42 percent. Should management implement the new credit terms?

14.   Management of Forwell Company (Problem 13) is concerned with the downside risk of the proposed change in credit terms.

(a) Calculate the minimum change in sales necessary for the company to break even at zero residual income.

(b) If the expected level of new sales is $7500 with a standard deviation of $2740, what is the probability of the company having negative residual income?

15.   The Sybil Company is proposing to change its credit standards in the hope that annual sales will increase from $11,000,000 to $14,000,000. Annual bad debts are expected to increase from $800,000 to $1,200,000 if the credit policy is implemented. The average collection ratio is currently 90 days sales outstanding. The ratio most likely will increase to 120 days outstanding if the policy change is made. An extra $20,000 investment in inventories will be necessary to support the higher sales. The company's variable-cost ratio is 60 percent. The after-tax opportunity cost of capital is 15 percent and the marginal tax rate is 28 percent. Assume a 360-day year to decide if management should change its credit policy. (*Hint:* You need to calculate the days sales outstanding for the new sales.)

16.   Harris, Inc., currently has average receivables of $100,000. Its sales terms are net 20 days; but accounts average 30 days outstanding from the point of sale. No account has ever defaulted on payment. The company's variable-cost ratio is 80 percent of sales. It has an after-tax required return of 12 percent on investment in receivables, and a tax rate of 34 percent.

Evaluate the following proposed change in credit policy: Adopt more lenient credit standards, which are expected to double sales and increase average receivables to $200,000; bad debt losses increase to 2 percent of incremental sales; average days sales outstanding for all accounts increase to 40 days. Assume a 360-day year.

CHAPTER 14 □
Monitoring Trade Credit

The financial significance of credit transactions is evidenced by statistics reporting that 20 to 25 percent of the typical manufacturer's total assets is trade receivables, while trade payables represent approximately 10 to 15 percent of total firm financing. Along with the dramatic growth in credit has come a need to monitor credit balances more effectively. Monitoring includes an evaluation of the quantity and the quality of outstanding credit amounts (both owed and owing) as well as the planning and execution of policies should deviations from norm occur.

Most companies exercise far greater control over disbursements than over collections. The extent of control is the key difference between these two elements in the cash cycle. In collections, management's goal is to prompt cash payments by others. The seller is responsible for timely and accurate invoice dispatch and subsequent enforcement of credit terms. By contrast, the purchaser's concerns are control of and response to credit terms and payment requests. In most circumstances companies possess flexibility in both purchase negotiations and subsequent timing and method of payment.

An account receivable to one firm is an account payable to another firm, of course. Because of this duality, the techniques available to monitor accounts receivable can be extended very naturally to monitor the firm's accounts payable. This chapter emphasizes the monitoring of accounts receivable.

Traditionally, credit and disbursement managers use turnover ratios (or their complement, days sales outstanding) and aging schedules to analyze outstanding credit balances. This chapter reviews these approaches and shows their shortcomings. Techniques that offer better insight into credit management are examined next. This is followed by a discussion of evaluation of deviations and ways to correct deviations.

Traditional Analysis

The monitoring of accounts receivable can be complex. Most credit managers attempt to ascertain the overall status of receivables by analyzing the aggregate balance outstanding. Many factors influence this balance, with the result that a number of the factors may offset each other. Nevertheless, credit managers continue to employ aggregate models because of the ease of calculating performance indices. The traditional models used are days sales outstanding and aging schedules.

Days Sales Outstanding

When managers monitor total accounts receivable, the most prevalent method they use is the **days sales outstanding** (DSO) procedure.[1] This method attempts to express accounts receivable as a number of equivalent days of credit sales:

$$\text{DSO} = \frac{\text{accounts receivable}}{\text{sales/(number of days in the period)}}. \tag{14.1}$$

For example, on an annual basis, if daily credit sales equal \$10 and accounts receivable equal \$30, then it is expected that current credit sales will not be collected for three days [= \$30/(\$3600/360)].

However, this conclusion may not be sensible. The numerator and the denominator are both historical numbers, whereas the interpretation of the ratio is a projection. It is often argued that the DSO is not intended to be used in this fashion but, rather, as a measure to compare one period with another. The measure is used only to report a general trend between periods so that management has an index of comparison. If the intention of the analyst is to study the collection of a specific day's sales, then some other analytical method must be used.

A change in any of the conditions that govern the accounts receivable balance makes the interpretation of the DSO index difficult. If the DSO index does not change, but the firm adds new credit customers or prices change, then the meaning of the DSO index is obscure. The DSO measure

---

[1] Aging of accounts payable follows a comparable procedure.

TABLE 14.1
Sales, Collections and Accounts Receivable ($000)

Month	Sales	Collection in period T of sales made in periods:				Receivables outstanding at period T consisting of sales made in periods:			
		T	T − 1	T − 2	Total	T	T − 1	T − 2	Total
11	100	20				80			
12	100	20	40			80	40		
1	100	20	40	40	100	80	40	0	120
2	125	25	40	40	105	100	40	0	140
3	150	30	50	40	120	120	50	0	170
4	175	35	60	50	145	140	60	0	200
5	200	40	70	60	170	160	70	0	230
6	175	35	80	70	185	140	80	0	220
7	150	30	70	80	180	120	70	0	190
8	125	25	60	70	155	100	60	0	160
9	100	20	50	60	130	80	50	0	130
10	100	20	40	50	110	80	40	0	120
11	100	20	40	40	100	80	40	0	120
12	100	20	40	40	100	80	40	0	120

simply will not answer questions concerning the impact on cash flow and the firm's investment in receivables from credit sales.[2]

ILLUSTRATION 14.1

Table 14.1 can be used to illustrate some of the problems with the DSO index. Keep in mind that credit sales are the result of two forces:

1. The general economic climate and how it applies to the firm's products.
2. The general efficiency of the selling firm's sales, production, and shipping functions, and its credit-granting policy.

A change in one or more of these forces affects current and future sales (both cash and credit sales). In the same way, the accounts receivable balance is affected by the credit payment pattern of all customers.

---

[2]Much of the material in this and the next section is attributed to Wilber G. Lewellen and Robert W. Johnson, "Better Way to Monitor Accounts Receivable," *Harvard Business Review* (May-June 1972): 101–9; and Bernell K. Stone, "The Payments-Pattern Approach to the Forecasting and Control of Accounts Receivable," *Financial Management* (Autumn 1976): 65–82.

The data of Table 14.1 indicate that the sales have a large seasonal effect, with the high sales period occurring in the fifth month. The *collection pattern is the same for each month;* that is, collections of the month are composed of 20 percent current sales, 40 percent from last month's sales, and 40 percent from sales of two months ago. Accounts receivable, thus, are composed of 80 percent of current sales and 40 percent of last month's sales. No bad debts exist. Total collections increase from $100 in month 1 to a maximum of $185 in month 6, and then they fall back to $100 in month 11. Accounts receivable increase from $120 in month 1 to a maximum of $230 in month 5. They decrease to $120 in month 10.

Various DSO calculations for these sales are listed in Table 14.2. The reason for showing different DSO calculations is that credit managers use different historical sales periods for the calculation. It is possible to reflect the DSO calculation in a favorable light simply by choosing a different historical sales period.

The interpretation of these DSO calculations is difficult. On the basis of sales per day for the past 30 days (column 2), the DSOs (column 3) for months 2 through 5 are less than the DSO for the first month. This result

TABLE 14.2
Days Sales Outstanding

Month	For the last 30 days Sales per day	DSO	For the last 60 days Sales per day	DSO	For the last 90 days Sales per day	DSO
1	3.33[1]	36.0[2]	3.33	36.0	3.33	36.0
2	4.17	33.6	3.75[3]	37.3[4]	3.61	38.8
3	5.00	34.0	4.58	37.1	4.17[5]	40.8[6]
4	5.83	34.3	5.42	36.9	5.00	40.0
5	6.67	34.5	6.25	36.8	5.83	39.5
6	5.83	37.7	6.25	35.2	6.11	36.0
7	5.00	38.0	5.42	35.1	5.83	32.6
8	4.17	38.4	4.58	34.9	5.00	32.0
9	3.33	39.0	3.75	34.7	4.17	31.2
10	3.33	36.0	3.33	36.0	3.33	33.2
11	3.33	36.0	3.33	36.0	3.33	36.0
12	3.33	36.0	3.33	36.0	3.33	36.0

Notes:
1. $100/30 = $3.33
2. $120/$3.33 = 36.0
3. ($100 + $125)/60 = $3.75
4. $140/$3.75 = 37.3
5. ($100 + $125 + $150)/90 = $4.17
6. $170/$4.17 = 40.8

occurs because sales are increasing during this period. As sales decrease in months 6 through 9, the DSO begins to increase and reaches a maximum in month 9, when the sales level returns to its preseasonal level.

On the basis of sales per day for the past 60 days (column 4), DSO (column 5) jumps from the preseasonal level of month 1 to a maximum in month 2 but then declines each month during months 3 through 9, when sales are either increasing or decreasing. The DSO index of 36.0 is the same for months 1, 10, 11, and 12 for calculations based on both 30 and 60 days sales. This result occurs because sales are level at $100 per month for these months.

On the basis of sales per day for the past 90 days (column 6), the DSO (column 7) reaches a maximum in month 3, which is greater than the high under either of the previous two cases. The low for both the 60-day and the 90-day methods occurs in the same month in which the high occurs for the 30-day method. The 90-day DSO index increases similarly to the sales increase for months 2 through 5 but falls below the preseasonal level as sales start to decrease to the preseasonal level in months 7 through 10.   □

Which of the indices in Illustration 14.1 is correct? Actually, none of them are. A DSO index confounds sales effects and collection efficiency and allows the credit manager to select a sales base that reflects the so-called collection effort in the best possible light. *The basic difficulty of the DSO index is that it is sensitive to both changing sales patterns and changing collection patterns.* These patterns can cause the DSO index to signal the need for corrective action when none is needed or to overlook the need for action when it is needed. This difficulty is evident in Illustration 14.1. Note, again, an assumption of this illustration: Customers' payment patterns are identical, and they pay for 20 percent of their purchases in the current month, 40 percent in the next month, and 40 percent in the month after that. Thus *it is possible for customer payment patterns to be constant even though the DSO index is not.*

Aging Accounts Receivable

The **aging of accounts receivable** is another of the traditional methods used to analyze these balances. The **aging schedule** attempts to show the proportions of the current outstanding balance that originates from sales of the previous periods. It is believed that if these proportions change, then something of significance has happened to accounts receivable.

Illustration 14.1 assumed that the payment patterns associated with each month's sales were constant. This assumption was made to show the fallacy of DSO calculations. Constant payment patterns are unreasonable to expect in practice. Assume that the *new* monthly payment patterns are represented by the data in Table 14.3. Here the credit manager recognizes bad debts once an account is more than three months old.

The cumulative payment patterns of Table 14.3 allow end-of-month accounts receivable balances to be calculated. These results are shown in Table 14.4. The origination of these balances is identified with the month in which the sale occurred. Sales for months $T - 3$, $T - 2$, and $T - 1$ are assumed to be $100 each. The payment patterns for these months are the same as those for months 10, 11, and 12, respectively. All amounts are rounded to the nearest dollar.

The conventional way to age the outstanding accounts receivable balances is to classify the various amounts making up the outstanding balance at the end of month T as a percentage of the total outstanding balance. Generally, it is desirable to have the largest and fastest growing percentage originating from the most recent sales. The rationale is that as an account ages, the probability of collection decreases. Table 14.5 summarizes the aging of accounts shown in Table 14.4.

From Table 14.5 we see that the monthly age of receivables for the past 12 months has been predominantly current, ranging from a low of 55 percent in month 8 to a high of 65.2 percent in month 5. It is important to note that the interpretation of these aging schedules differs considerably from the interpretation of the cumulative payments patterns in Table 14.3. The problem is that the aging schedules are wrong. They are wrong be-

TABLE 14.3
Payment Patterns

Period	Sales ($000)	Cumulative payment pattern of period T's sales in period:				Accounts delayed
		T	T + 1	T + 2	T + 3	
1	$100	20.0%	60.0%	90.0%	99.0%	1.0%
2	115	19.7	61.3	89.7	98.4	1.6
3	122	19.8	58.7	91.6	99.4	0.6
4	140	20.1	59.2	87.5	98.6	1.4
5	158	18.5	58.0	90.3	98.5	1.5
6	175	19.2	59.5	91.4	99.1	0.9
7	164	20.2	60.1	90.7	99.3	0.7
8	125	20.1	60.2	89.4	99.4	0.6
9	119	19.7	60.1	88.6	99.6	0.4
10	104	19.5	60.7	91.2	98.7	1.3
11	102	20.2	59.4	90.4	99.1	0.9
12	100	20.6	59.2	90.1	98.9	1.1
Mean		19.8	59.7	90.1	99.0	1.0

TABLE 14.4
Accounts Receivable Balance ($000)

Month	Sales	At end of month: 1	2	3	4	5	6	7	8	9	10	11	12
T − 3	100	1											
T − 2	100	10	1										
T − 1	100	41	10	1									
1	100	80	40	10	1								
2	115		92	45	12	2							
3	122			98	50	10	1						
4	140				112	57	18	2					
5	158					129	66	15	2				
6	175						141	71	15	2			
7	164							131	65	15	1		
8	125								100	50	13	1	
9	119									96	47	14	0
10	104										84	41	9
11	102											81	41
12	100												79
Total		132	143	154	175	198	226	219	182	163	145	137	129

Note: Total sales in month 1 were $100, with $20 of this amount collected in month 1. By the end of month 2, $60 of the $100 sales has been collected. After three months, $90 has been collected. $1 remains outstanding after 4 months.

TABLE 14.5
Traditional Accounts Receivable Aging Schedule

Month	Distribution by months 1	2	3	4	5	6	7	8	9	10	11	12
T − 3	0.008											
T − 2	0.076	0.007										
T − 1	0.305	0.070	0.006									
1	0.611	0.280	0.065	0.006								
2		0.643	0.293	0.069	0.010							
3			0.636	0.285	0.050	0.004						
4				0.640	0.288	0.080	0.009					
5					0.652	0.292	0.069	0.011				
6						0.624	0.324	0.082	0.012			
7							0.598	0.357	0.092	0.007		
8								0.550	0.307	0.090	0.007	
9									0.589	0.324	0.102	0.000
10										0.579	0.300	0.070
11											0.591	0.318
12												0.612

Note: These entries represent Table 14.4's column amounts expressed as a proportion of their respective column total.

cause the *aging percentages are directly affected by the sales trend, which can cause significant distortion in the aging.* This characteristic is examined in more detail later in this chapter.

Use of Balance Proportions[3]

Rather than review accounts receivable data in conventional ways, a credit manager should review the payment patterns of customers relative to how they pay for each sale. That is, the credit manager should analyze the proportion of the sale of month T that is still outstanding in months T, $T + 1$, $\ldots$, $T + n$. Table 14.6 summarizes this approach using **balance proportions** (rounded to two decimal places).

Interpretation of Balance Proportions

The interpretation of Table 14.6 is clear and simple. For instance, the row for month 5 indicates that 82 percent of month 5's sales are outstanding at

TABLE 14.6
Accounts Receivable Outstanding as a Proportion of Original Sales

Month	Sales ($000)	Proportion by month 1	2	3	4	5	6	7	8	9	10	11	12
$T - 3$	100	0.01											
$T - 2$	100	0.10	0.01										
$T - 1$	100	0.41	0.10	0.01									
1	100	0.80	0.40	0.10	0.01								
2	115		0.80	0.39	0.10	0.02							
3	122			0.80	0.41	0.08	0.01						
4	140				0.80	0.41	0.12	0.01					
5	158					0.82	0.42	0.10	0.01				
6	175						0.81	0.40	0.09	0.01			
7	164							0.80	0.40	0.09	0.01		
8	125								0.80	0.40	0.11	0.01	
9	119									0.80	0.40	0.11	0.00
10	104										0.80	0.39	0.09
11	102											0.80	0.41
12	100												0.79

Note: These balance proportions can be derived from either Table 14.3 or 14.4.

---

[3]Balance proportions for accounts payable relate the outstanding invoice to the purchase that originated the liability. Mechanically, the procedure is the same as calculating balance proportions for accounts receivable.

the end of month 5, 42 percent of month 5's sales are still outstanding at the end of the next month, 10 percent of month 5's sales are still outstanding two months after the initial sale, and 1 percent of month 5's sales are still outstanding three months after the initial sale. The accounts receivable balance for month 5 (see the column for month 5) consists of 82 percent of month 5's sales, 41 percent of month 4's sales, 8 percent of month 3's sales, and 2 percent of month 2's sales. This column's set of numbers provides a distinctly different view of balances than that provided by the aging schedule. Overall, the use of balance fractions allows the credit manager to readily see whether any shifts are taking place in customer payment patterns, since the analysis is related directly to the sale initiating the account receivable. The conventional methods shown in Table 14.4 and 14.5 do not allow such interpretation.

Criticism of DSO and the Aging Schedule

Considerable controversy exists as to whether the DSO and aging procedures are acceptable methods for monitoring accounts receivable. While these methods are still widely used, their results may be misleading and are capable of frequent error. The difficulty with using DSO and aging schedules is that an upward trend in sales produces an impression of improved customer payment behavior when, in fact, behavior may be just the opposite or have changed very little. A comparison of month 5 of the aging schedule (Table 14.5) with month 5 of the balance fraction schedule (Table 14.6) highlights this fact. The aging schedule indicates that receivables are more current than normal, as shown by the 65.2 percent current month outstanding figure. The other "current" months range from a low of 55 percent in month 8 to a high of 64 percent in month 4. The balance fractions, however, indicate the true state of the receivables. A smaller proportion of current month's sales have been paid in month 5 than in any of the other months, contrary to implicit conclusions of the traditional aging method.

The criticism of DSO and aging schedules centers on the sensitivity of the calculations to the sales pattern and the sales averaging period selected (for example, see Table 14.2). If sales are falling, both monitoring techniques give the appearance of receivables being less current than they really are. This is the case even though total sales may be the same for both the upward and downward trend patterns. It is only when the sales pattern is flat that misleading signals are not emitted by DSO and aging schedules. Most analysts recognize the influence of sales pattern and attribute it to a seasonal factor. They attempt to eliminate, or at least minimize its effect, by comparing calculated DSO ratios and aging schedules against comparable historical periods. This approach is not satisfactory, though, since history seldom repeats itself exactly. Also, it may be hard to find data with which relevant comparisons can be made, especially when one is comparing companies of different sizes and types.

Variance Analysis Model

Another technique that can be used to overcome the problems associated with traditional techniques of DSO and aging schedules is to use a *weighted-DSO scheme*. This technique allows the DSO calculation to be independent of both the sales averaging period and the sales pattern. Also, it provides a comparison with a standard (such as budget or last year's results) and gives information that an aging schedule attempts to provide.

Relevant information for discussing the variance analysis model is summarized in Table 14.7. The actual receivables and sales data are taken from Table 14.4; the budget data for receivables and sales is new. Notice-

TABLE 14.7
Sales and Receivables Information ($000)

Sales and receivables

Month	Receivables Actual	Receivables Budget	Receivables Difference	Sales Actual	Sales Budget	Days*
January	$ 1	$ 0	$ 1	$100	$120	30
February	12	12	0	115	120	30
March	50	36	14	122	120	30
April	112	54	58	140	120	30
Total	$175	$102	$73	$477	$480	120

Days sales outstanding

$$\text{Actual} \quad 120 \times \frac{\$175}{\$477} = 44.0 \text{ days}$$

$$\text{Budget} \quad 120 \times \frac{\$102}{\$480} = 25.5 \text{ days}$$

Aging schedule

Month	Actual	Budget
January	0.6%	0%
February	6.9	11.8
March	28.5	35.3
April	64.0	52.9
Total	100.0%	100.0%

*30 days is used for ease of later computations.

TABLE 14.8
Variance Analysis of Accounts Receivable Balances ($000)

Month	Actual sales per day × actual DSO	Actual sales per day × budget DSO	Sales per day restated in budget proportions × budget DSO	Budget sales per day × budget DSO
January	$ 1	$ 0	$ 0	$ 0
February	12	11.50	11.93	12
March	50	36.58	35.78	36
April	112	63.00	53.66	54
	$175	$111.08	$101.37	$102

| | Collection experience variance $63.92; unfavorable | Sales pattern mix variance $9.71; unfavorable | Sales quantity variance $0.63; favorable |

Sales pattern variance
$9.08; unfavorable

able in this table is that actual receivables exceed the budget even though total sales are only marginally lower than the budget. The conventional DSO measure indicates that actual receivables are outstanding longer than expected. However, the traditional aging schedule reveals a higher proportion of receivables to be current than expected. These traditional measures are in conflict with each other.

Table 14.8 allocates the $73,000 receivable balance variance shown in Table 14.7. The variance is unfavorable since the actual receivable investment exceeds the budget. Stated differently, more resources have been invested in accounts receivable than budgeted. The credit manager's responsibility is to understand the factors contributing to this variance. A first level of analysis can partition the variance into two components:[4]

1. A collection experience variance
2. A sales pattern variance

---

[4]An article by J. A. Gentry and J. De La Garza ["Monitoring Accounts Receivable: Revisited," *Financial Management* (Winter 1985): 28–38] recommends that a joint variance be calculated so as to make the collection effect and sales pattern variances "pure." An article by G. W. Gallinger and A. J. Ifflander ["Monitoring Accounts Receivable Using Variance Analysis," *Financial Management* (Winter 1986): 69–76] discusses some reasons for not calculating the joint variance.

If greater understanding of the sales pattern variance is sought, a second level of analysis partitions this variance into two parts:

1. A sales pattern mix variance
2. A sales quantity variance

The calculation of these variances is shown in the Appendix to this chapter. Discussion of each variance is given in the sections that follow.

Collection Experience Variance

The **collection experience variance** (CEV) is a direct measure of collection efficiency. This variance is free of any influence of changing sales pattern, which hampers the traditional measures of DSO and aging schedules. This freedom exists because *a new budget for receivables is derived on the basis of the sales level actually achieved. This new budget recognizes that outstanding receivables should increase or decrease directly with changes in sales.*

Analysis of the CEV indicates that actual receivables are $63,920 higher than expected on the basis of the new budget's expected collection efficiency. The most pronounced problem is with the latest month's collections. Days sales outstanding for April are about 78 percent higher than the new budget indicates they should be. This figure translates into excess receivables of $49,000, or approximately 77 percent of the total CEV variance. The variance for March's outstanding receivables is the other major component of the variance; it represents 21 percent of the total CEV variance.

The credit manager needs to ascertain the following:

☐ Has collection efficiency really deteroriated?

☐ Are customers experiencing cash flow problems?

☐ Have credit terms changed from those used in the budget?

The third question is relatively easy to answer, since the credit manager is one of the decision-makers establishing credit terms. The first two points require more analysis. For the first point the manager should consider questions such as the following: How effective is the company's lockbox collection system? Is transit float being minimized? How long is processing float? Are there an inordinate number of invoices in dispute? For the second point analysis of payment patterns of individual accounts and follow-up conversations with customers, where deemed necessary, can provide insight into customer cash flow problems.

Sales Pattern Variance

The **sales pattern variance** (SPV) is the other major component of the receivables variance. This variance indicates the effect that changing sales pattern has on receivable balances. One might argue that credit managers cannot be held accountable for the sales pattern variance. Although this is generally true, circumstances can exist that negate this claim. For example, one of the credit manager's duties is to determine whether credit should be extended to customers. A too lenient credit-granting policy, as a result of inadequate analysis of credit applications, results in higher sales and in higher receivable balances that are outstanding longer. In this case the credit manager is responsible for at least a portion of the sales pattern variance. The credit manager should be aware of her or his responsibilities here, since a company officer may raise questions about the trend of accounts receivable and about management's effectiveness with regard to investment in productive assets. Selling goods to poor credit risks is generally not a good use of scarce investment dollars.

Regardless of who is responsible for the sales pattern variance, an understanding of this variance is important in analyzing resource allocations. However, the sales pattern variance can be difficult to interpret. For example, in Table 14.7 the fact that total actual sales are practically equal to total budgeted sales may lead management to conclude that sales are not the cause of any receivable variance, when in fact they contribute $9080 to the higher receivable level (see Table 14.8). This result occurs because sales in April are $20,000 higher than budgeted.

The real significance of any sales pattern on receivables can be discovered by separating the sales pattern variance into a sales pattern mix variance and a sales quantity variance.

Sales Pattern Mix Variance

Although total sales are practically as budgeted, the proportion of each month's sales to total sales differs from the budget proportions. These different proportions give rise to the **sales pattern mix variance**.

Analysis of this variance provides insights that an aging schedule attempts to reveal. The mix variance indicates that $430 (i.e., $11,500 − $11,930) less receivables are outstanding for February than expected, $800 (i.e., $36,580 − $35,780) more receivables are outstanding for March than expected, and $9340 (i.e., $63,000 − $53,660) more receivables are outstanding for April than expected. The aging schedule in Table 14.7, however, provides contrary information when it is interpreted in the usual manner. It shows a much larger proportion of receivables to be current versus the budget (64 percent versus 52.9 percent) and smaller proportions to be one and two months old versus the budget. The interpretation is that accounts receivable are more current than budgeted. It is the higher April sales that are causing this conclusion to be drawn. Thus a simple aging schedule is unable to effectively identify aging (sales mix) problems.

Sales Quantity Variance

The remaining component of the sales pattern variance is the **sales quantity variance**. This variance represents the true volume influence of sales on receivables and is not influenced by collection efficiency or change in sales pattern.

Since total sales are marginally lower than budget, sales volume has a minimal effect on receivable balances. The $3000 lower sales result in receivables being lower by $630. This is the true effect of sales volume on receivables.

Overall Analysis

An overall analysis of Table 14.8 indicates that the total receivable variance of $73,000, as of April, is largely attributable to the collection experience variance, which may indicate serious collection problems. The imbalance in sales, as compared with budget, contributes a lesser amount to the total variance, but it is by no means insignificant. If sales continue to deviate from budget, and if collection effort continues to lag, cash flows may be significantly reduced. As a result of such reduced liquidity, management may have to delay both required and discretionary investments or revise plans if the cash flow problem cannot be corrected.

Neither the DSO calculations nor aging schedules provide the same insights. For instance, conventional DSO calculations in Table 14.7 indicate that actual performance (44 days) has deteriorated from budget expectations (25.5 days) but fails to provide a reason why. The aging schedule leads to similar misleading conclusions (as discussed earlier).

Although our discussion and illustration have pertained to an analysis of total outstanding receivables, the proposed variance techniques can effectively be used to analyze receivables at the customer level. Such analysis simply requires budget figures for individual accounts, which can be compared with actual receivable balances. Analysis at this level will provide credit managers with information about the effectiveness of credit-granting procedures, about the impact of changing credit policies (different payment terms, for example) on individual accounts, about the influence of changing credit standards (loosening credit, for example) on receivable balances, and about customer purchase patterns and volumes that may be overlooked by management in its effort to keep abreast of various other facets of the business.

Changes in Payment Habits

A sale facilitated by credit is worthwhile to the firm only if the receivable is eventually collected. The credit manager's functions include the evaluation and the extension of credit to specific customers and the enforcement of the contract. As discussed in Chapter 12, certain information is available to the credit manager concerning each customer before credit is actually extended. Once credit is extended, the manager should be concerned if the customer deviates substantially from her or his expected **payment pattern** norm.

As an example, if an old and well-known company fails to take a discount when it has regularly done so in the past, this behavior may be a signal that the customer is experiencing financial difficulty. The cost of lost discounts is usually high enough to be of major concern.

Change in the customer's payment habits may be the result of any of the following three conditions:

1. internal change in the customer's firm,
2. a change in the mix of purchases by the customer,
3. some exogenous change in economic conditions.

In all three cases the credit-extending firm experiences a decrease in its cash inflows and an increase in the probability of default by the customer.

Internal Change

An internal change may be caused by one of the following problems:

□ The payment procedure of the customer errs or fails through some administrative error.

□ The customer experiences cash flow problems.

□ The opportunity cost of discounts lost is less than the opportunity cost of funds invested in the customer's firm.

If the problem is the result of an administrative error, then the corrective action can be made quickly, with the result that the customer returns to her or his earlier payment pattern. If the change is a result of cash flow problems, then the possibility of potential insolvency exists. If the opportunity cost of lost discounts is irrelevant to the customer, then the seller's discount policy is apparently meaningless (at least to this customer). It does not facilitate rapid payment of credit sales, since the decrease in the cost of goods is less than the earning power of funds held to the net credit period in the customer's firm.

Each of these conditions stems from a fundamentally different set of circumstances. The credit manager must have some information concerning these conditions so that he or she can properly monitor the account and make appropriate recommendations to senior management.

Change in Product Mix

A change in the product mix the customer purchases may cause her or his payments to change. As an example, for highly seasonal and high-style products there is a long production and marketing lead time. The high-style product is usually produced and sold long in advance of the consumer market period. Terms of credit for this product may be as long as six to nine months. These terms are frequently referred to as *seasonal-dating terms*. If the firm produces this type of product as well as products having the more usual shorter lead time, with sales to the same customer, then the collection pattern of this customer reflects the type of products purchased.

The usual practice in industrial credit is that all bills are paid by invoice. Thus the credit manager must be informed not only of the amount of credit outstanding but also of the type of product for which credit has not been paid in order to keep collection difficulties to a minimum.

Economic Conditions

Economic conditions have an important influence on the actions of creditors. Economic slowdowns cause creditors to decrease their purchases, to delay their payments, and possibly to deteriorate in terms of credit quality. The overall result is that cash flows and subsequent profits of the credit-granting firms are adversely affected.

Later Payments

The situations just described, while of concern to the credit manager, differ considerably if the customer is in default. The term **default** has both a legal meaning and an operating meaning. Legally, default means that the customer has not paid the invoice by the end of the credit period. In an extremely loose operating context, default means that a customer has not paid by her or his usual payment time. Delayed payment can give cause for concern, of course; but unless the customer goes beyond the credit period, the credit manager certainly has no recourse against the customer.

It is not unusual for large firms to miss the discount date of payment yet still take the discount when payment is made. Also, some large firms do not pay by the net credit period. They are financially sound and not considered to be bad debts, even though they are technically in default. There are two possible reasons for this behavior:

1. A cycle payment procedure is used that ignores the seller's discount date.
2. The firm buys on its own terms and not on the terms of the seller.

Both reasons can be summarized by the statement that the large firm simply uses its competitive powers to its own advantage. This situation presents the credit manager with a problem. The manager must decide whether to grant this account special consideration or to enforce the contract and probably lose future sales. This decision is not an easy one, since the profit margin on these accounts is generally assured relative to smaller and less financially strong firms. Usually, management concedes to the larger firm.

However, the majority of sales are made to relatively small firms. These firms have common conditions in that individually they buy only a small percentage of the seller's output and they have relatively limited financial resources. Collectively, these small firms constitute a large proportion of the seller's total sales and take up the majority of the administrative time of the credit department. Owing to the size and the financial similarities of small customers, the credit manager knows that adverse economic conditions will probably affect most of the small firms in a similar fashion. As the country's gross national product decreases or interest rates increase, the credit manager expects that sales to and collections from these firms will decrease. Thus the credit manager must monitor these accounts daily and be aware of changing environmental conditions.

The corrective action for the smaller firm's account differs from that of the large firm. The credit manager might attempt to determine the cause of any payment behavior change by direct contact with the customer or by making inquiries to other credit managers who sell to the same customer. If the best information is that the customer is experiencing cash flow problems, then the credit manager might request additional information regarding the ability of the buyer to pay, should an additional order be placed. A warning flag may be put on the account so that the customer will be notified promptly when the account is overdue, which may minimize any possible loss to the seller. If the situation deteriorates further, then immediate action to collect is warranted.

Default versus Bad Debt

The question of what to do with an account in default is not easily answered. All accounts that are overdue are not bad debts. Most firms with overdue accounts pay, given some additional time. The dividing line between default accounts and bad debts is one that gives credit managers much concern.

When is an account a **bad debt**? Some situations lend themselves to a simple definition: The probability of collection is low, and the probability of future sales or the willingness of the seller to engage in further credit sales to this customer is also low. In this case there is every reason to label this account a bad debt and to attempt full collection by whatever means possible.

The usual situation is that a particular invoice is significantly overdue, yet the customer continues to purchase and pay for additional goods. Is this account a bad debt? Most likely it is not. Although the default invoice can be classified as a bad debt, to do so risks the loss of a customer who apparently has a good payment record in all but this one invoice.

A better practice is to substitute an interim condition to create a credit spectrum: good account — disputed account — bad-debt account. Before payment of an invoice is made, all aspects of the invoice (product quality and quantity, price, sales taxes, and contract conditions) must be correct.

Usually, goods are shipped with transportation documents and a bill of lading, and the invoice is mailed separately. The bill of lading is used by the buyer's receiver to justify the goods being received. The invoice is received by the accounting office and sent to purchasing for approval. This approval amounts to justifying both the physical character of the goods, by matching the invoice with the bill of lading, and the costs, by matching the invoice with the purchase order. A dispute occurs when there is a discrepancy between the documentation and the merchandise received. Generally, these disputes are resolved with relative ease, and the invoice does not linger outstanding as a bad debt.

If disputes are not solved fairly and amicably, they could cost the seller far more through the loss of future sales than through a significant number of bad-debt customers. It is not surprising, then, that many firms have a policy of accepting any returns without question and of satisfying any dispute to the customer's satisfaction.

Corrective action to collect overdue accounts must recognize two possibilities:

1. There exists some chance (however small) that the account can be saved to become a continuing good account.

2. There exists a concern that not only will the firm fail to realize any margin on the sales but the entire sale value will not be collected; that is, cost of sale *plus* profit margin is lost.

Summary

This chapter has focused on techniques for evaluating outstanding credit balances. The traditional measures of days sales outstanding and aging schedules have serious shortcomings. They are influenced by changing sales patterns (or purchase patterns in the cash of payables) and fail to correctly identify changing collection (or disbursement) patterns. Balance fractions, payment proportions, and variance analysis offer superior evaluation techniques. Each method associates the outstanding credit amount with its source. These methods overcome the aggregation problems inherent in number of days sales (or purchases) outstanding as well as in aging schedules.

The variance model allows superior analysis since it forces reconciliation of differences between budget expectations and actual performance. This reconciliation provides the credit manager with better information for evaluating outstanding credit.

The chapter also examined explanations for changing payment behavior. Changes in payment habits can occur because of internal changes within the customer's business, changes in amounts owed because of changes in the product mix purchased, and changes in the economic environment. What constitutes a default payment was examined and found to be largely a subjective decision by management.

Key Concepts

Aging of accounts receivable
Aging schedule
Bad debt
Balance proportions
Collection experience variance
Days sales outstanding

Default
Payment patterns
Sales pattern mix variance
Sales pattern variance
Sales quantity variance

Appendix

Mechanics of Variance Analysis

The calculation of accounts receivable variances requires information pertaining to *each month* that is represented in the accounts receivable balance. As shown by the headings in Table 14.8, the information needed includes actual and budget sales per day for each month, actual and budget days sales outstanding for each month's sales, and actual sales per day for each month, restated as a proportion of each month's budget sales per day to the total budget sales per day for the entire period.[1] The following computations outline the steps for calculating the variances, using the data presented in the chapter. These data are repeated in Table A.1.

Collection Experience Variance

The collection experience variance is calculated as

$$\sum_i \{(\text{actual sales per day})_i \times [(\text{actual DSO})_i - (\text{budget DSO})_i]\},$$

where $i = 1, 2, 3, 4$, which correspond to January (J), February (F), March (M), and April (A), respectively.

The actual variance is as follows:

$$
\left.
\begin{array}{lll}
\text{J:} & \$3.333(0.30 - 0) = & \$\ 1.00 \\
\text{F:} & \$3.833(3.13 - 3.00) = & 0.50 \\
\text{M:} & \$4.067(12.30 - 9.00) = & 13.42 \\
\text{A:} & \$4.667(24.00 - 13.50) = & \underline{49.00}
\end{array}
\right\}
\begin{array}{l}
\text{column (a)} \times \\
\quad [\text{column (d)} - \text{column (e)}]
\end{array}
$$

$$\underline{\underline{\$63.92}}$$

---

[1] When calculating variances for accounts payable, replace these items with "actual" and "budget purchases per day" for each month, "actual" and "budget days purchases outstanding" for each month's purchases, and "actual purchases per day for each month, restated as a proportion of each month's budget purchases per day to the total budget purchases per day for the entire period."

The variance names change to payment experience variance, purchase pattern variance, purchase mix variance, and purchase quantity variance.

TABLE A.1
Data for Variance Calculations

Sales per day by month

Month	Actual (a)	Budget (b)	Budget proportion (c)
January	$100/30 = $ 3.333	$120/30 = $ 4.00	0.25
February	115/30 = 3.833	120/30 = 4.00	0.25
March	122/30 = 4.067	120/30 = 4.00	0.25
April	140/30 = 4.667	120/30 = 4.00	0.25
	$15.900	$16.00	1.00

Days sales outstanding by month

Month	Actual (d)	Budget (e)
January	30 × $1/$100 = 0.30	30 × $0/$120 = 0
February	30 × $12/$115 = 3.13	30 × $12/$120 = 3.00
March	30 × $50/$122 = 12.30	30 × $36/$120 = 9.00
April	30 × $112/$140 = 24.00	30 × $54/$120 = 13.50

Restatement of actual sales per day in budget proportions
(f)

January	$15.90 × 0.25 = $ 3.975
February	15.90 × 0.25 = 3.975
March	15.90 × 0.25 = 3.975
April	15.90 × 0.25 = 3.975
	$15.900

Sales Pattern Variance

The sales pattern variance is calculated as

$$\sum_i \{(\text{budget DSO})_i \times [(\text{actual sales per day})_i - (\text{budget sales per day})_i]\}.$$

The actual calculation is as follows:

$$
\begin{aligned}
\text{J:} &\quad 0(\$3.333 - \$4.000) = \$\ \ 0 \\
\text{F:} &\quad 3.00(\$3.833 - \$4.000) = -0.50 \\
\text{M:} &\quad 9.00(\$4.067 - \$4.000) = 0.58 \\
\text{A:} &\quad 13.50(\$4.667 - \$4.000) = 9.00 \\
\end{aligned}
$$

column (e) ×
[column (a) − column (b)]

$$\$9.08$$

Sales Quantity Variance

The sales quantity variance is calculated as

$$\sum_i \{(\text{budget DSO})_i \times [(\text{actual sales per day in budget proportions})_i - (\text{budget sales per day})_i)]\}.$$

The actual variance is as follows:

$$
\left.
\begin{array}{llr}
\text{J:} & 0(\$3.975 - \$4.000) = \$ & 0 \\
\text{F:} & 3.0(\$3.975 - \$4.000) = & -0.07 \\
\text{M:} & 9.0(\$3.975 - \$4.000) = & -0.22 \\
\text{A:} & 13.5(\$3.975 - \$4.000) = & \underline{-0.34}
\end{array}
\right\}
\begin{array}{l}
\text{column (e)} \times \\
\quad [\text{column (f)} - \text{column (b)}]
\end{array}
$$

$$\$-0.63$$

Sales Pattern Mix Variance

The mix variance is the difference between the sales pattern variance and the sales quantity variance:

$$\sum_i [(\text{sales pattern variance})_i - (\text{sales quantity variance})_i].$$

The actual calculation is as follows:

$$
\left.
\begin{array}{llr}
\text{J:} & \$0 - \$0 = \$ & 0 \\
\text{F:} & \$-0.50 + \$0.07 = & -0.43 \\
\text{M:} & \$0.58 + \$0.22 = & 0.80 \\
\text{A:} & \$9.00 + \$0.34 = & \underline{9.34}
\end{array}
\right\}
\begin{array}{l}
\text{Alternatively:} \\
\text{column (e)} \times \\
\quad [\text{column (a)} - \text{column (f)}]
\end{array}
$$

$$\$9.71$$

Questions

1. Discuss the necessity for improved monitoring of trade credit.

2. The use of days purchases outstanding as a control measure for accounts payable contains a basic flaw. Discuss.

3. The average collection period for ABC Company is 46 days, whereas the XYZ Company collects its accounts in 35 days. As the financial manager of ABC, react to this observation.

4. In an evaluation of how well a company's receivables are managed, what advantage does the aging schedule have over the days sales outstanding and accounts receivable turnover ratios?

5. What is meant by *payment proportions* and *balance fractions*? How are they calculated? What advantage does each have?

6. How is the collection experience variance calculated? What does it measure?

7. What is the usefulness of the sales pattern mix variance? How is it calculated?

8. Which technique is best for evaluating accounts receivable? Why?

9. What are some causes of changing customer payment patterns? Discuss.

Problems

1. Alpha, Inc., had the following sales over the past 20 months:

Month	−1	0	1	2	3	4	5	6	7	8
Sales	100	100	100	120	140	225	400	500	450	380
Month	9	10	11	12	13	14	15	16	17	18
Sales	350	200	180	120	120	142	168	270	480	580

Collections for each month are composed of 25 percent of current sales, 40 percent of last month's sales, and 35 percent of sales made two months ago. Assume each month has 30 days.

(a) Calculate the monthly cash flow from collections and the monthly accounts receivable balances for months 1 through 18.

(b) Calculate the days sales outstanding for months 1 through 18 based on sales of the last 30 days and of the last 90 days.

(c) Discuss the days sales outstanding patterns in part (b) in relation to the sales pattern.

2. The Karlin Corporation wishes to analyze its accounts payable record for the year ending December. Management decides to evaluate payables by calculating days payables outstanding, using 30, 60, and 90 days purchases. Complete this analysis by using the data in Table 14.9.

TABLE 14.9
Purchase Data

Month	Purchases	Payables
Last year		
November	$4250	$2750
December	5170	4010
This year		
January	3200	3000
February	1800	1000
March	1250	1000
April	1450	1300
May	2700	2240
June	3240	2587
July	4950	3094
August	6500	5700
September	7100	6250
October	8400	6570
November	8950	7040
December	9400	7190

3. During the year the Karlin Corporation (Problem 2) had the accounts payable aging schedule shown in Table 14.10.

(a) Discuss the firm's payment behavior, using the aging schedule.

(b) Determine the dollar amount of purchases discounted. Assume all purchases allow a discount.

TABLE 14.10
Accounts Payable Aging Schedule

Month	30 days	%	60 days	%	90 days	%	Total
Jan.	$1956	0.652	$ 912	0.304	$132	0.044	$3000
Feb.	586	0.586	364	0.364	50	0.050	1000
Mar.	429	0.429	503	0.503	68	0.068	1000
Apr.	781	0.601	490	0.377	29	0.022	1300
May	1577	0.704	634	0.283	29	0.013	2240
June	1485	0.574	999	0.386	103	0.040	2587
July	2033	0.657	987	0.319	74	0.024	3094
Aug.	3944	0.692	1693	0.297	63	0.011	5700
Sept.	3463	0.554	2575	0.412	212	0.034	6250
Oct.	3705	0.564	2792	0.425	73	0.011	6570
Nov.	4231	0.601	2703	0.384	106	0.015	7040
Dec.	3983	0.554	3063	0.426	144	0.020	7190

4. Home Bakery Company has sales and cumulative payment patterns for receivables as shown in Table 14.11. Assume payments for months -1, -2, and -3 are the same as for months 12, 11, and 10, respectively.

(a) Calculate the end-of-month accounts receivable balances (round to zero decimal places).

(b) Calculate the traditional accounts receivable aging schedule and the balance proportions of accounts receivable outstanding (to three decimals — for example, 0.001 instead of 0.1 percent).

(c) Discuss the results of the two methods used in part (b).

TABLE 14.11
Sales and Payment Patterns

	Sales	Cumulative payment pattern				
Period	($000)	T	T + 1	T + 2	T + 3	Later
−3	185					
−2	210					
−1	225					
1	250	20.0%	45.6%	84.8%	98.0%	2.0%
2	350	18.6	46.9	86.9	98.9	1.1
3	375	21.1	44.8	85.9	98.4	1.6
4	400	19.8	44.8	84.8	98.0	2.0
5	380	22.4	46.1	86.1	99.2	0.8
6	600	21.5	45.8	85.2	98.8	1.2
7	550	22.0	44.9	84.7	99.3	0.7
8	425	22.1	44.9	85.6	98.8	1.2
9	375	21.6	44.5	85.3	98.4	1.6
10	250	22.0	45.2	84.8	98.9	1.1
11	190	20.5	46.8	87.1	99.0	0.8
12	200	21.0	44.8	84.4	98.2	1.8

5. Suppose sales of the Home Bakery Company in Problem 4 increase by 20 percent next year. How may accounts receivable balances change? Consider real and inflationary increases, as well as a change in credit quality of customers.

6. Management of Edmonds Emporium wishes to investigate how much of the trade payables are being discounted. The firm buys on credit terms of 2/10, n/30. The data given in Table 14.12 relate purchases to accounts payable balances.

(a) Determine the traditional aging of accounts payable.

(b) Determine the percentage of each month's purchases that are discounted.

TABLE 14.12
Monthly Purchases and Outstanding Accounts Payable ($000)

Month	1	2	3	4	5	6	7	8	9	10	11	12
−2	400											
−1	1500	100										
1	3000	600	50									
2		3250	780	130								
3			3713	1185	395							
4				5200	900	100						
5					5800	1200	240					
6						4320	1080	270				
7							4080	800	80			
8								3975	825	0		
9									2450	700	100	
10										2160	540	135
11											2000	360
12												2346
Sum	4900	3950	4543	6515	7175	5620	5400	5045	3355	2860	2640	2841
Purchases	5800	6500	7900	10,000	12,000	9000	8000	7500	5000	4500	4000	4600

7. Approximately 20 percent of sales are paid in cash, with the remaining 80 percent sold to established credit customers on a 30-day charge account. Historically, 70 percent of the charge accounts are paid in the month following sale, with the remaining 30 percent being paid the second month following sale. Bad-debt losses are insignificant. Accounts receivable at the end of April amounted to $4200. Credit sales for the year were as follows:

January	$2000	May	$10,000	September	$21,000
February	2000	June	9,000	October	15,000
March	4000	July	8,000	November	13,000
April	3000	August	14,000	December	18,000

Starting with April, calculate the following:

(a) End-of-month accounts receivable balances for each month

(b) End-of-month aging schedule for each month

(c) Days sales outstanding for each month, using 30-, 60-, and 90-day intervals. Assume 30 days in each month

Compare your results, and draw conclusions about why differences exist among them. Which approach is best for analyzing accounts receivable balances?

8. Iffinger Corporation's budget for credit sales and accounts receivable is as follows:

Month	Sales	Receivables
July	$ 5,000	$ 7,000
August	11,000	14,000
September	22,000	19,000

The September receivable balance consists of $15,000 from September sales, $3,000 from August sales, and $1,000 from July sales. Using the actual credit sales and receivables balances for these months as determined in Problem 7, calculate the collection experience variance, the sales pattern variance, the sales pattern mix variance, and the sales quantity variance. Assume each month has 30 days. What conclusions do you draw from the analysis to present to senior management?

9. The Hartley Corporation uses a budget control system. Actual and budgeted data for the last three months is given in Table 14.13. Use this data to perform a three-way variance analysis. Assume each month has 30 days.

TABLE 14.13
Actual and Budget Data

	Payables		Purchases	
Month	*Actual*	*Budget*	*Actual*	*Budget*
October	$ 6,570	$ 6,200	$ 8,400	$ 8,500
November	7,040	6,800	8,950	8,750
December	7,190	7,000	9,400	9,000
Total	$20,800	$20,000	$26,750	$26,250

10. Table 14.14 shows the sales and receivable balances as of the end of September for the Maloof Manufacturing Company. Management wishes to know the contribution of the collection experience and sales pattern variances to the total variance. Assume that each month has 30 days.

TABLE 14.14
Sales and Receivables

	Receivables		Sales	
Month	*Actual*	*Budget*	*Actual*	*Budget*
June	$ 10	$ 15	$110	$100
July	25	35	95	100
August	90	106	121	110
September	107	110	130	120
Total	$232	$266	$456	$430

11. Actual purchases for the months of May through July were substantially larger than budgeted. Management wants a three-way analysis of variance performed to explain what has happened. Payables and purchases are summarized in Table 14.15. Discuss your results.

TABLE 14.15
Payables and Purchases

| Month | Payables | | Purchases | | Days |
	Actual	Budget	Actual	Budget	
May	$ 270	$ 116	$ 7,000	$ 3,500	31
June	1420	612	6,250	3,600	30
July	3185	1372	5,000	3,400	31
	$4875	$2100	$18,250	$10,500	

Inventory Accounting and Cash Flow Effects

The financial executive is charged with safeguarding company assets and ensuring that they are properly managed. This responsibility applies equally well to inventories. The changing and renewable nature of inventory demands constant attention. The accounting for inventories is an important part of this attention since one must determine the proper assignment of costs to periods.

From an accounting perspective the total cost of goods available for sale or use during a period must be allocated between the current period's use (cost of items sold or used) and the amounts carried forward to future periods (the end-of-period inventory). This allocation affects cash flow through the amount of profits reported and the taxes paid on these profits.

Inventory valuation problems arise because there are two unknown quantities in the basic inventory equation:

$$\text{Ending inventory} = \text{beginning inventory} \qquad (15.1)$$
$$+ \text{ purchases} - \text{withdrawals.}$$

The values of beginning inventory and purchases are known, but unknown are the values of withdrawals or ending inventory. The question is whether to value the ending inventory by using the most recent costs, the oldest costs, the average cost, or some other alternative. Of course, the question could have been put in terms of valuing the withdrawals, because once the value of one is determined, the inventory equation automatically values the other. The relation between the two unknowns in the inventory equation is such that the higher the value given to one of them, the lower must be the value given to the other.

There are no historical cost-based accounting methods for valuing inventories and, inversely, withdrawals *that allow the accountant to show current values on both the income statement and the balance sheet.* If current, higher costs are to be shown on the income statement, then older, lower costs must be shown on the balance sheet, and vice versa. The accountant can present current values in one place but not in both. Of course, combinations of current and out-of-date information can be shown in both places. It is this problem that leads to cash flow considerations when one is selecting an inventory accounting technique.

Therefore, if the financial manager is to have significant input in inventory decisions, the manager must have a basic understanding of inventory accounting and its effect on cash flows. This understanding, in turn, requires knowledge of inventoriable costs, valuation bases, and flow assumptions. Each of these topics is examined in this chapter.

As a means of emphasizing the importance of this material, one needs only to read published reports about W. T. Grant. For instance, buyers relied on vendors to keep them posted on inventory needs; significant delays existed between the time the goods were received and accounting entries were made; and inventory was understated about $70 million when the firm declared bankruptcy. In summary, no controls existed, which meant that management was never sure of inventory's effect on liquidity.

Inventoriable Costs

What costs are to be included in inventories? Of course, costs not included in inventory become an expense of the period. Thus *the true cash flow consideration arises at the time of the transaction* in the factor (material and labor) markets. **Inventoriable costs** are simply costs deferred until the eventual time of sale as far as recognition of income is concerned. But income is not cash flow, and depending on tax implications, these costs can affect cash flow.

Definition of Inventoriable Costs

In order to understand cost as it relates to inventories, one must define inventoriable costs, that is, those costs that are said to attach to the inventory and are considered to be part of the inventory valuation. Charges directly connected with bringing goods to the marketplace in a salable condition are proper inventoriable costs. Such charges include materials costs and associated freight charges on goods purchased, labor, and indirect (overhead) production costs incurred in processing the goods up to the time of sale. Indirect costs allocable to inventories include expenses of storage and handling, and all general and administrative expenses related to the production function (for purchasing, quality control, warehousing, and so forth).

Ideally, to increase cash flow, management should attempt to expense as much cost associated with inventory as possible. Since material, labor, and overhead cash outflows are incurred in the production of the product, regardless of the accounting procedures adopted, the ability to expense as much cost as possible leads to lower taxes and improved cash flows.[1]

Variable versus Absorption Costing

Two concepts are involved in costing inventory. These concepts are variable (direct) costing and absorption (full) costing. For external reporting purposes and in determining taxable income, absorption costing must be used. Either method can be used for internal reporting purposes.

In a **direct (variable) costing system** all costs must be classified as either variable or fixed. Only those costs that vary directly with the volume of production are charged to products and subsequently appear either in the balance sheet as inventory or in the income statement as cost of goods sold. Fixed costs are considered period costs; that is, they are charged as expenses to the current period.

Under **absorption costing** all manufacturing costs, variable and fixed, direct and indirect, incurred in the factory or in the production process attach to the product and are included in the cost of inventory. The firm that uses absorption costing has higher inventory amounts and lower cumulative expense totals. The firm that uses variable costing has lower inventory amounts and higher cumulative expense totals. *From a cash flow perspective variable costing results in a closer matching of costs and cash outflows.* Variable costing accounts for costs in a manner that parallels a firm's cost behavior and, presumably, provides management with better information for its decisions. This result is shown in Table 15.1, which also shows the impact of inventory costing on ratio analysis.

Absorption costing creates a false impression of economic flows and distorts liquidity and costs incurred. Both the current ratio and net working capital are higher under absorption costing, whereas total costs are lower. The $30,000 lower cost of absorption accounting results because this amount has been deferred to the balance sheet as part of ending inventory. The reality of the situation is that the differences exist solely because of accounting methodology — not because of cash flow management.

Implicit in the discussion of the example of Table 15.1 is that variable

---

[1]The Tax Reform Act of 1986 resulted in more costs being inventoried for tax purposes. For example, depreciation taken for tax purposes which is in excess of that reported in financial statements must be included in inventory. Any differences between inventory for financial reporting purposes and tax purposes result in changes to the deferred tax account.

TABLE 15.1
Variable Versus Absorption Costing

Assumptions

1. No beginning inventory; ending inventory is 25,000 units.
2. Total production costs of $200,000 are split between variable and fixed costs as $80,000 and $120,000, respectively; 100,000 units produced.
3. All production costs are paid before the end of the year.
4. Current assets, excluding inventory, are $100,000. Current liabilities (excluding production expenditures) are $75,000.

Data	Absorption	Variable
Beginning inventory	$ 0	$ 0
Plus production costs	200,000	80,000
Minus ending inventory	50,000	20,000
Equals cost of sales	$150,000	$ 60,000
Plus period costs	0	120,000
Equals total costs	$150,000 ⌐	$180,000 ⌐
Cash outflow	$200,000	$200,000
Minus total costs "incurred"	150,000 ←	180,000 ←
Equals ending inventory	$ 50,000	$ 20,000
Current ratio	2.0	1.6
Net working capital	$ 75,000	$ 45,000

costing corresponds to the typical cost-volume-profit (that is, operating breakeven) analysis. The correspondence between variable costing and breakeven analysis is a result of variable costing income being a function only of sales volume. Absorption costing, on the other hand, is a function of both sales and production volume. In order to illustrate this point, suppose that, in comparison to last year's sales, this year's sales are up. However, this year's net income is lower than last year's, and management is puzzled as to why. Analysis reveals that this year's production is considerably below this year's sales. The result, of course, is a decline in the inventory. Under absorption costing the effect of this is to release against this year's revenue an amount of fixed cost that is greater than the amount incurred during this year. This is due to the fixed costs of preceding periods, which have been included in the beginning inventory, being released when the inventory was reduced.

The relationship between production units and sales quantities leads to the following conclusions:

☐ If production exceeds sales, then variable costing income is less than absorption costing income.

☐ If production is less than sales, then variable costing income exceeds absorption costing income.

□ If production equals sales, then variable costing income equals absorption costing income.

It should be stated that differences between variable and absorption costing income are strictly timing differences. That is, in the long run, the total net income will be the same under either method, assuming that income taxes and other expenses remain constant over time.

Bases of Inventory Valuation

The valuation method used to price inventories affects periodic income, cash flow, and any ratios that reflect inventories. Currently, there are at least four bases of valuation in use:

□ Original cost

□ Lower of cost or market

□ Standard cost

□ Selling price

Original Cost

Conceptually, the simplest of all inventory policies is the specific-invoice method, which requires that the cost of each item sold or inventoried be known. With this **original-cost** technique the gains on items sold are simply the difference between their selling prices and their costs, and the value of inventory is the sum of items in stock. There is a complete correspondence between the flow of goods and the reported flow of costs. The inventory amount shown in the balance sheet, however, is usually out of date, depending on how prices have changed.

Lower of Cost or Market

The **lower-of-cost-or-market (LCM) valuation basis** (original cost or replacement cost, whichever is lower) is not always feasible in practice, particularly in a manufacturing firm. However, it is the generally accepted accounting rule when no other procedures have been adopted.

Use of the LCM basis involves the determination of both cost and market information for each item in the inventory. A problem immediately arises in defining *market*. Basically, three different types of market valuation must be determined: replacement cost, net realizable value, and net realizable value less a normal markup. The use of the LCM rule requires the accountant to follow the decision process shown in Fig. 15.1.

Realization value is, of course, a paraphrase of "what you can get for it." Replacement cost, on the other hand, is something quite different, and,

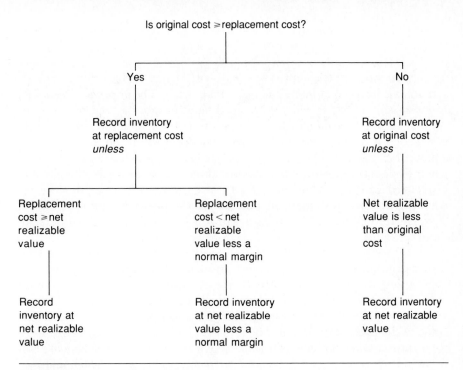

FIGURE 15.1
Lower-of-Cost-or-Market Decision Rule

indeed, one may question why it needs to be considered at all in the determination of market. To this question accountants have two answers, conservatism and expediency. The extreme of conservatism is to consider market as the lower of realization value or replacement cost. Even when there is no conscious effort at such conservatism, to determine replacement cost and to demonstrate that it is below realization value is often easier than to determine an exact or even an approximate realization value.

The difficulty in determining realization value is that additional costs must be incurred to realize on any item in the inventories. And such costs must be deducted from the selling price of the item to determine the true net amount that can be realized from its sale.

The difficulty of gathering the necessary market information for each of the hundreds or thousands of items in an inventory — to say nothing of the difficulty of calculating the cost of work in process and finished goods on the basis of present material prices, present labor costs, and present prices for each of the other costs of production operations — certainly leads to the conclusion that the method has limited application. Its use is frequently restricted to the case where valuable raw materials and other items have had significant price declines.

As mentioned earlier, the lower-of-cost-or-market basis for inventory valuation is justified as being a conservative policy. The approach, however, is questionable and, as will be discussed later, cannot be used with the inventory flow assumption of last-in, first-out (LIFO). The effect of the rule is to take a loss when the market price has declined but not to take a gain when it has risen. Such losses are "paper losses," which are only realized when the items are sold. That an unrealized loss is recognized while any unrealized gain is not does not conform entirely with logic. But the accounting profession defends its position on the principle of conservatism, characterized by fearing to overstate profits but not fearing to understate them.

For any one unit of goods there is only one income or loss figure, the difference between the original cost and the selling price. The valuation rule merely determines how this figure of income or loss is to be spread over the accounting periods, with total disregard for how the cash flows were incurred. When the lower-of-cost-or-market price is used, the net income of the present period may be lower than if the original cost basis were used, but the net income of the period when the unit is sold will then be higher. *It is the timing of reported profit that affects tax liabilities and cash flows.*

Standard Costs

One of the most convenient methods of assigning costs to an inventory is to use predetermined **standard costs** for the items in it. A standard cost reflects what an item should cost to produce under assumed conditions for prices, technology, and operational efficiency. It is generally based on studies of past cost data and planned production methods. This method is probably more widely used than any other in valuing the labor and overhead elements of inventories. It is particularly convenient where goods pass through a number of processes or are manufactured on mass production lines.

There is always a danger that when standard costs are used to value inventories, they may not reflect current conditions unless they are revised frequently. Of course, if the revisions are too frequent, inventories are effectively priced at current replacement costs, which may violate the accountant's conservatism principle of lower of cost or market. The use of standard costs, however, can greatly aid management in quickly evaluating various inventory investment, profit, and cash flow scenarios.

Selling Price

Selling price is occasionally used in inventory valuation. This approach indicates the value of the goods to the firm. Agricultural products and by-products of manufacturing operations, on hand at the close of an accounting period, are often valued at selling price less costs of marketing, so *the income is recognized in the period of production rather than in the period of sale. The tax liability, however, is not incurred until the product is actually sold. Cash flow is realized at the time of a cash sale or whenever the receivable is collected.*

The influence of the accounting valuation methods on financial analysis should be obvious. Ratios that use cost of sales and/or inventory balances (current ratio, inventory turnover ratio, all profitability ratios, and the calculation of net working capital and cash flow) will be directly affected. It is critical that the analyst make adjustments for significant inventory valuation differences (if possible) when comparing one firm with another or a firm's present performance against its historical performance. Failure to do so makes financial comparisons less meaningful.

Flow Assumptions

If individual units can be identified, ascertaining original cost does not present a special problem. The cost can be marked on the unit or on its container, or the item can be traced back to its purchase invoice or cost record. The accounting profession and the IRS have long recognized that even small businesses find it difficult to keep track of the cost of each specific item in inventory. In most cases new items are mixed with old on shelves, in bins, or in other ways, and physical identification is impossible or impractical. If more than one purchase of the same item at differing prices is made, then some assumption must be made about the flow of costs in order to estimate the original cost applicable to the inventory.

Therefore several inventory accounting procedures have been developed that break the direct link between flow of goods and flow of costs. The discussion that follows concentrates on two such methods — first-in, first-out (FIFO) and last-in, first-out (LIFO) — because of their importance and because they generally represent the extremes in the range of choices faced by management. Of several other inventory accounting methods, two relatively common ones are the average cost method and the retail cost method. A complete discussion of the mechanics of the various techniques can be found in most intermediate accounting textbooks. Keep in mind that these different flow assumptions can affect financial analysis as do different inventory valuation methods.

First In, First Out (FIFO)

Under the **FIFO inventory method** the cost of goods sold is computed as if these items were the oldest in inventory. As this is probably a reasonable flow-of-goods assumption, the resulting costs (and, therefore, profits) that are reported in the firm's income statement are probably similar to those that would result from using the specific-invoice method. The remaining inventory, which is entered in the balance sheet, is valued at the cost of the most recently acquired or produced items and therefore approximates market value or replacement cost of the inventoried stock.

Last In, First Out (LIFO)

The logic of the **LIFO method** is the opposite of that of the FIFO method. With this technique the cost of goods sold is taken as the cost of the items most recently produced or added to inventory. This cost approximates the expense of replacing the item in inventory, whereas FIFO values the sold good at close to its original cost. Generally, LIFO cannot be physically justified since it assumes current operations and sales are carried on with the use of items purchased most recently. No attempt is made to link the actual flow of goods and flow of costs: Nobody would seriously recommend a policy of shipping the most recently produced goods and holding the oldest output in stock. The advocates of LIFO explain that it does not matter which of any identifiable goods are taken out of stock first, since *it is the flow of costs and not the flow of goods that is to be considered*. It is also important to note that under LIFO, inventory is composed of layers. When more units are produced (or purchased) than sold, the increase in inventory results in a new layer of inventory. Layers are eliminated when sales exceed production (or purchases).

Since LIFO charges the most recently produced or inventoried items against goods sold, the stocks carried forward and reflected on the balance sheet are treated as if they were the earliest acquired or produced. In times of inflation this practice can seriously understate the value of inventory relative to current or replacement value on the balance sheet of firms that have produced or acquired at least as many items as they sold for several years. This drawback is partially overcome since most LIFO firms report the cumulative balance sheet difference between LIFO and FIFO. Also, since the tax liability is reduced under LIFO (during a period of increasing prices), *more cash is available*. And in an economic sense the firm is better able to replace inventory under LIFO than under FIFO.

Comparison of Methods

In an environment of permanently stable prices, LIFO and FIFO policies yield identical income statements and balance sheets. However, in a world with relative and absolute price changes, the two methods yield significantly different results.

Prior to the early 1970s inflation was reasonably low. So most firms used FIFO inventory accounting. However, as inflation grew to double-digit levels during the 1970s and into the 1980s, many firms switched to LIFO. The rationale for switching is straightforward. Under FIFO the inventory amount in the balance sheet reflects costs relatively close to current costs, because the latest purchases dominate the inventory valuation. In the income statement, however, the cost of goods sold reflects older purchase prices, because FIFO assumes earlier purchases are sold first. During inflationary periods FIFO leads to the highest reported net income of the two methods, and it leads to the smallest net income when prices are falling. When FIFO is used, both perpetual- and periodic-inventory methods provide the same cost-of-goods-sold figure and the same ending inventory amount.

LIFO provides opposite results. LIFO results in balance sheet figures that may be far removed from present costs and a cost-of-goods-sold amount that is close to current costs. The cost-of-goods-sold figure under LIFO is the largest of the two methods when prices are rising and the smallest when prices are falling. LIFO ordinarily results in the least fluctuation in reported income, because selling prices tend to change as current prices of inventory items change.

ILLUSTRATION 15.1

The difference between LIFO and FIFO can be shown further by examining the income statement and inventory balance sheets of a very simple hypothetical firm. This company may be viewed as acquiring and selling the same product. At any time the acquisition and selling prices are the same, so the only type of profit possible for this firm is that due to the appreciation of inventoried goods, that is, inventory profits. Table 15.2 lists the activities, income, and inventory valuation for this firm for 14 periods.

In period 0 the firm simply acquires a stock of 10 items. Periods 1 through 4 are characterized by a steady increase in price and by sales that just match acquisitions. Thus ending inventory remains constant at 10 units. Although selling price equals the latest purchase price, FIFO accounting reports profits of $54 during the first four periods; LIFO profits are zero. The value of inventory under FIFO accounting approximates market value, whereas LIFO accounting, relative to FIFO, greatly understates it.

Both sales and inventories grow in periods 5 through 7. This growth changes the situation very little with FIFO, since profits are still reported as the increase in value of each period's initial stock of inventories. There are no LIFO profits as long as acquisitions at least match sales.

TABLE 15.2
FIFO Versus LIFO Inventory Accounting

Period	Price ($)	Units Purchased	Units Sold	Revenues ($)	Unit inventory Initial	Unit inventory Final	Cost of sales ($) FIFO	Cost of sales ($) LIFO	Value of ending inventory ($) FIFO	Value of ending inventory ($) LIFO	Profits ($) FIFO	Profits ($) LIFO
0	8	10	0	0	0	10	0	0	80	80	0	0
1	8	7	7	56	10	10	56	56	80	80	0	0
2	10	7	7	70	10	10	56	70	94	80	14	0
3	12	7	7	84	10	10	64	84	114	80	20	0
4	14	7	7	98	10	10	78	98	134	80	20	0
5	16	8	7	112	10	11	92	112	170	96	20	0
6	18	9	8	144	11	12	122	144	210	114	22	0
7	20	10	9	180	12	13	156	180	254	134	24	0
8	20	10	10	200	13	13	194	200	260	134	6	0
9	18	10	10	180	13	13	200	180	240	134	⟨20⟩	0
10	16	10	10	160	13	13	186	160	214	134	⟨26⟩	0
11	16	8	10	160	13	11	166	166	176	96	⟨6⟩	⟨6⟩
12	16	6	10	160	11	7	160	136	112	56	0	24
13	16	0	7	112	7	0	112	56	0	0	0	56
All periods		109	109	1716			1642	1642			74	74

Notes:

Acquisition prices = selling prices in each period.

Cost of sales: FIFO 3 units × $10 + 4 units × $12 = $78
LIFO 7 units × $14 = $98

Value of ending inventory: FIFO 3 units × $12 + 7 units × $14 = $134
LIFO 10 units × $8 = $80

Prices stabilize in period 8 and decline in periods 9 and 10. Sales just match acquisitions, so inventories remain stable at 13 units. While LIFO profits remain zero, FIFO accounting results in a loss (and, hence, tax savings or credit) for these periods.

Prices are stable in periods 11 through 13, but the firm gradually liquidates inventories. The FIFO method now reports zero profits, while the LIFO method reports large profits as inventoried items (some still valued at the acquisition cost of period 0) are sold.

As the last row of the table shows, the firm has a cumulative pretax profit of $74 under either system (because all inventory is sold), but the time patterns of income differ. Under the FIFO system income is reported as the value of inventory increase, but under LIFO it is recorded only when the inventory is liquidated. The source of the $74 LIFO profit is clear when one tabulates net acquisitions as 10 units at $8 (period 0), 1 unit at $16 (period 5), 1 unit at $18 (period 6), and 1 unit at $20 (period 7), for a total cost of $134. These 13 units were sold in periods 11 through 13 at $16 apiece for a total revenue of $208.   □

There is some logic behind both sets of numbers. Table 15.3 attempts to capture it. For instance, in periods 1 through 4 the firm has generated no cash inflow since each item is replaced as it is sold (see Table 15.2). This fact is reported under LIFO (the cumulative cash flow has stayed constant at −$80, indicating no additional cash inflow or outflow since period 0). But the stock on hand has appreciated in nominal value, as reflected by cumulative FIFO profit of $32.40.

LIFO does not record any profit or loss until periods 11 through 13, because unit purchases have either exceeded or equaled unit sales for periods 1 through 10. Thus, *any inventory profits stay hidden in the balance sheet.* However, when unit sales exceed unit purchases, these inventory profits emerge. They emerge because lower cost inventory layers are released from the balance sheet.

In the absence of the corporate income tax cash flows for FIFO and LIFO are the same in our example. This result can be easily verified by calculating the cash flow for any period in Table 15.2 as net income plus or minus the change in inventory. An increase in inventory is subtracted from income and vice versa. For example, in period 7,

FIFO cash flow = ($24 income before taxes)
                 − ($44 increase in inventories) = −$20,

LIFO cash flow = ($0 income before taxes)
                 − ($20 increase in inventories) = −$20.

However, in the presence of taxes cash flows vary by period and by method. For example, in period 7 FIFO has an after-tax cash flow of

TABLE 15.3
Cash Flow Analysis

	FIFO			LIFO		
	After-tax profits		Cumulative net cash	After-tax profits		Cumulative net cash
Period	Current	Cumulative	flow	Current	Cumulative	flow
0	0	0	⟨80.0⟩	0	0	⟨80.0⟩
1	0	0	⟨80.0⟩	0	0	⟨80.0⟩
2	8.4	8.4	⟨85.6⟩	0	0	⟨80.0⟩
3	12.0	20.4	⟨93.6⟩	0	0	⟨80.0⟩
4	12.0	32.4	⟨101.6⟩	0	0	⟨80.0⟩
5	12.0	44.4	⟨125.6⟩	0	0	⟨96.0⟩
6	13.2	57.6	⟨152.4⟩	0	0	⟨114.0⟩
7	14.4	72.0	⟨182.0⟩	0	0	⟨134.0⟩
8	3.6	75.6	⟨184.4⟩	0	0	⟨134.0⟩
9	⟨12.0⟩	63.6	⟨176.4⟩	0	0	⟨134.0⟩
10	⟨15.6⟩	48.0	⟨166.0⟩	0	0	⟨134.0⟩
11	⟨3.6⟩	44.4	⟨131.6⟩	⟨3.6⟩	⟨3.6⟩	⟨99.6⟩
12	0	44.4	⟨67.6⟩	14.4	10.8	⟨45.2⟩
13	0	44.4	44.4	33.6	44.4	44.4
Total	44.4			44.4		

Notes: (1) Tax rate = 40%. (2) Total numbers of units sold are the same for both methods. (3) All inventory is sold. (4) Total cumulative cash flow is the same for both methods because of items 2 and 3.

−$29.60 (i.e., ⟨$182.0⟩ − ⟨152.4⟩, as shown under the column for cumulative net cash flow for periods 7 and 6, respectively). But LIFO has an after-tax cash flow of −$20 (i.e., ⟨$134.0⟩ − ⟨114.0⟩). The $9.60 difference in favor of LIFO is the tax paid on the FIFO profits ($24 × 0.40 = $9.60); see Table 15.2.

Advantages of LIFO

As long as purchased units exceed or equal sales units, LIFO results in lower tax liability, higher quality of earnings if management is not manipulating income, and higher cash flow during periods of rising prices. *LIFO is consistent with an economic perspective that includes only realized gains,* whereas *FIFO reflects accounting profits and losses as they accrue.*

It is the economic perspective and not the accounting viewpoint that is important to shareholder wealth maximization. In terms of financial analysis Tables 15.2 and 15.3 implicitly indicate how profitability ratios, the inventory turnover ratio, and the current ratio are influenced by the inventory flow assumption. However, these ratios should be of secondary importance. *Cash flow is the most significant factor in the management of firm liquidity, and it should be emphasized in any analysis.*

There is no doubt that during inflationary times LIFO results in a higher after-tax cash flow to shareholders. The economic income of a firm before taxes may not be easily identifiable, but it is certainly not affected by management's arbitrary decision to use FIFO versus LIFO. On a pretax basis the selection of LIFO or FIFO simply affects the level of reported profits — it can have no impact on pretax economic income. Yet since the government bases taxes due to it on reported taxable income, actual taxes are lower under LIFO. Thus after-tax economic profit and cash flows are higher under LIFO. Besides reducing (but not eliminating) taxes on inventory profits, LIFO has the additional advantage of stating reported income closer to real economic income than does FIFO. Economic profits are best estimated by using replacement costs of inventory, and LIFO is a closer estimate of such replacement costs than FIFO.

Recognizing the difference as that between realizations and accruals should make it clear that the tax savings arising from choosing LIFO in an inflationary period may actually amount to the deferral of taxes. Should prices drop to their original level or should the firm liquidate its inventory, LIFO inventory profit and taxes would exceed those under FIFO. The gains would be completely eliminated or "repaid," although no interest would have been charged on the "loan."

For maximum tax benefits the optimal time to adopt LIFO may be when inventories are relatively low. With proper management the difference between tax savings and tax deferral may be virtually eliminated; the postponement may be made sufficiently long to permit virtual escape of taxes under the realization (LIFO) system. Furthermore, even if taxes avoided in one year must be made up in a subsequent year, financial managers are generally pleased with the deferment. Cash saved from current tax payments can be used temporarily for expanded operations, and expanded operations may be expected to increase the corporation's capacity to pay taxes in future years. For a variety of reasons managers are inclined to think that improvements in future years will be less burdensome than they would be at the moment. And there is always the hope that tax rates in the future will be lower than they are at present.

Another reason for the choice of inventory valuation methods that result in the lowest possible profit figures is the avoidance of pressures on corporate directors to raise the rate of cash dividends to be paid to the stockholders. In ordinary circumstances the higher a company's profits, the greater are the stockholders' expectations for generous dividends. If the directors prefer to use available cash for expansion rather than for increases in cash dividend rates, they will hold down, by whatever means possible, the amount of profits to be reported — which means choosing carefully among inventory valuation methods. Lower reported earnings might be attractive, as well, to regulated firms or to firms that face negotiations with powerful labor unions.

Disadvantages of LIFO

Lowering reported earnings may, however, impose difficulties on the corporation and its management. Often a firm is constrained in its dividend and borrowing policies by the terms of its existing bonds and bank credit. These constraints often depend on such figures as reported net income and the firm's ratio of liabilities to either assets or net worth, both of which will be lower under LIFO in an inflationary economy. Furthermore, most profit-sharing and executive bonus plans are tied directly to reported earnings. Altering these programs to compensate for the switch from FIFO to LIFO may be difficult.

Further reasons for not switching to LIFO can be extracted from the examples given in Tables 15.2 and 15.3. The first is the expectation of falling prices, which may be important in a few industries (for example, semiconductors). The second reason is that companies whose inventories are frequently liquidated — perhaps involuntarily — owing to strikes, bad weather, or particularly volatile demand or supply conditions experience little benefit from LIFO because of the frequent realization of the gains on the value of their inventories. In other words, falling prices and the need to sell inventory carried at a relatively low cost result in higher profit and tax obligations.

Inventories may also be liquidated voluntarily. Such practice allows income manipulation under LIFO. The liquidation can be easily accomplished by changing purchasing policy at the end of the year. This causes lower cost layers to be released to costs of goods sold with the result that reported profits increase. This is not possible under FIFO accounting.

When the LIFO flow assumption is elected for tax returns, the Securities and Exchange Commission requires that it also be used for reports to stockholders. Furthermore, all firms must request permission from the Internal Revenue Service to use the LIFO flow assumption. Once a firm has chosen to adopt the LIFO flow assumption, it must request permission to change back to FIFO and may incur a tax liability if it does so. In recent years many firms that earlier adopted LIFO so that income taxes would be lower (at the cost of reporting lower net income in the financial statements) have switched back to FIFO so that reported earnings per share will be higher (at the cost of paying larger current income taxes).

The emphasis on earnings per share is a questionable practice. A corporation using LIFO may indicate, by footnote in the annual financial statements, the effect on earnings if FIFO were used in the year of change. Also, there is some question about whether the reduction in earnings as a result of switching to LIFO affects the price of the corporation's stock. The sophisticated investor realizes that in a period of rising prices inflated inventory values artificially inflate profits. As the investing public becomes more sophisticated, the emphasis will increasingly be on the quality of profits rather than on the quantity. Accordingly, LIFO should continue to be the more popular inventory valuation method.

When a company changes from LIFO to FIFO it is obligated to pay taxes on its LIFO reserves.[2] This obligation may be spread over a period of 20 years. If the company switches back to LIFO, then the obligation must be paid immediately.

The Internal Revenue Service requires that if LCM valuation basis is used, it may not be coupled with a LIFO flow assumption. Consider the effect of allowing both LIFO and LCM techniques. When prices are rising, the LIFO flow assumption results in a lower closing inventory amount and lower reported income than does FIFO. When prices are falling, the lower-of-cost-or-market basis with LIFO leads to a closing inventory amount equal to that of FIFO coupled with a lower-of-cost-or-market basis. The Internal Revenue Service is unwilling to allow a flow assumption that results in lower taxable income when prices are rising and no higher taxable income when prices are falling. LIFO coupled with a lower-of-cost-or-market basis, were it allowed, would result in a guarantee of no worse position (falling prices) and the hope of a better position (rising prices), as compared with FIFO plus a lower-of-cost-or-market basis.

If a firm has been using FIFO and LCM, and wishes to adopt LIFO, it must restore its inventory to original cost. The restoration of the inventory "write downs" causes the company's tax liability to increase, and thereby unfavorably affects cash flow.

Summary

This chapter discussed inventory accounting and the effect of taxes on financial ratio analysis and cash flows. Inventory measurements affect both the cost-of-goods-sold expense on the income statement for the period and the amount shown for the asset inventory on the balance sheet at the end of the period. The sum of the two must be equal to the beginning inventory plus the cost of purchases.

The allocation between expense and asset depends on three factors: (1) the types of manufacturing costs included in inventory, (2) the valuation basis used, and (3) the flow assumption. The first factor involves a choice

---

[2]Many companies use LIFO for tax and external reporting purposes but maintain a different system (often FIFO) for internal reporting purposes. The difference between LIFO and the internal system is referred to as the *LIFO reserve.*

between absorption costing and variable costing. The second factor involves a choice between the cost basis and the lower-of-cost-or-market basis. The third factor involves a choice among FIFO, LIFO, or some other flow assumption (such as average cost). The allocation decision directly affects the firm's cash flow via the tax calculation and the analysis of various ratios that incorporate cost of sales and/or inventory balances.

The tax code is the common element running through these three factors. Without taxes the argument of which inventory accounting alternatives to use becomes moot. *If there were no taxes, the different inventory techniques would have no effect on cash flow.* A number of different financial ratios would still be affected by the different accounting alternatives. However, as discussed elsewhere in this book, it is the analyst's responsibility to interpret ratios with caution. This chapter has identified the reasons for exercising caution in analysis of inventory.

Key Concepts

Absorption costing

Direct (variable) costing

FIFO

Inventoriable costs

LIFO

Lower-of-cost-or-market basis

Original-cost basis

Periodic inventory

Perpetual inventory

Selling price

Standard costs

Appendix A

Inventory Methods: Periodic versus Perpetual

There are two types of inventory procedures used to arrive at the quantity and the amount of an inventory: the periodic-inventory method and the perpetual-inventory method. The perpetual method offers more advantages for planning and controlling the investment in inventories and in periodically calculating cash flow from operations.

Periodic Inventories

The **periodic-inventory procedure** consists of making a physical count of all articles in stock at least once a year at the end of the accounting period. At all other times during the year there is no complete information available on the amount of the inventory of goods or the cost of goods sold. The main benefit of this inventory system is its simplicity.

It is seldom possible to prepare operating (and cash flow) statements more frequently than once a year when the inventory figures are obtained only from periodic counts. An assumption of the periodic approach is that all goods not accounted for by the physical count of inventory have been sold or used. Any shrinkages or losses from such causes as theft, evaporation, and waste are hidden in the cost of goods sold or the cost of materials used.

The periodic-inventory method determines the ending inventory figure of units by physical count multiplied by cost per unit and uses the inventory equation to determine the withdrawals. A problem arises when a change in the replacement price has taken place since certain items were acquired. Accordingly, the question arises whether the units will be priced at the cost price or at the current market price. The answer to this question is discussed in more detail later, but it is based on the generally accepted rule that the items in inventory be priced at cost or at market, whichever is lower.

Perpetual Inventories

Under the **perpetual- (or continuous) inventory method** the system of records is designed so that the cost of merchandise sold or the cost of material used is recorded at the time these assets are sold or consumed. The perpetual method determines the withdrawals by physical observation (for example, using material withdrawal requisitions) and uses the inventory equation to determine (what should be in) the ending inventory. This method allows operating (and cash flow) statements to be prepared without a physical count and allows for greater analysis of inventory investment and its impact on liquidity.

When a perpetual-inventory system is used, there is a constant record of goods in stock. Nevertheless, the book inventory must periodically be verified by a physical count because goods become lost, are stolen, or deteriorate. The dollar amount of any missing goods is treated as a loss, contrary to what is done in the periodic method. Analysis of the loss account should thus result in more efficient operations and better control. All items should be counted at least once a year, and certain items may be checked more frequently, either because of their high value or because of a high probability or errors in recording their withdrawals.

A FIFO/LIFO Aside

FIFO yields the same cost of goods sold and ending inventory in either the periodic or perpetual systems. During periods of rising prices, LIFO yields different results for ending inventory and cost of goods sold using a periodic system than when using a perpetual system. The difference occurs because LIFO in a periodic system assumes sale of the most recent purchases in the total accounting period, whereas LIFO in a perpetual system assumes sale of the most recent purchases as of the time of each sale.

Appendix B
Inventory Accounting Errors

If inventory items are incorrectly (maybe, purposefully) included or excluded for inventory purposes, there will be errors in the financial statements and analysis. To illustrate, suppose that certain goods that the firm owns are either not recorded as a purchase or not counted in ending inventory. To disregard such purchases results in an understatement of inventories and accounts payable in the balance sheet and an understatement of purchases and ending inventories in the income statement. The net income for the period is not affected by the omission of such purchases, since purchases and ending inventories are both understated by the same amount, with the error offsetting itself in cost of goods sold. Total working capital is unchanged, but the current ratio, assuming it is greater than 1 before the omission, is higher because of the omission of equal amounts from current assets and current liabilities. (The use of the current ratio in this example is done for expediency.)

To illustrate the effect of errors, assume the following balances are reported at the end of the period:

Current assets	$120,000	Cost of sales	$100,000
Current liabilities	$40,000	Ending inventory	$25,000
Current ratio	3:1	Inventory turnover	4.0

If $40,000 for goods in transit should have been included in ending inventory, then the following balances would be presented:

Current assets	$160,000	Cost of sales	$100,000
Current liabilities	$80,000	Ending inventory	$65,000
Current ratio	2:1	Inventory turnover	1.5

The correct current ratio is 2:1 instead of 3:1, and the turnover ratio should be 1.5 times instead of 4 times. In other words, the missing inventory should be reported in purchases, ending inventory, and accounts payable.

What would happen if the beginning inventory and the goods purchased are recorded correctly, but some items on hand are not included in ending inventory? In this situation ending inventory, net income, current ratio, and net working capital are all understated, and inventory turnover is overstated. Net income is understated because cost of goods sold is larger than it should be; the current ratio and the net working capital are understated because a portion of ending inventory is omitted; the inventory turnover ratio is overstated because cost of goods sold are overstated while ending inventory is understated.

To illustrate the effect on operating funds flow, assume that the ending inventory is understated and that all other items are correctly stated. The effect of this error will be to decrease net income and funds from operations in the current period and to increase net income and funds from operations in the following period. The error will be offset in the next period, because the beginning inventory will be understated and net income and funds flow will be overstated. In other words, both net income and funds flow are misstated, but the total for the two periods is correct.

If a purchase is not recorded but is included in ending inventory, the reverse result occurs. Net income, the current ratio, and net working capital are all overstated, and inventory turnover is understated. The effect on net income and funds flow will be offset in the subsequent period (assuming purchases are recorded in the next period), but both periods' financial statements will be misstated.

These illustrations indicate that an accurate computation of purchases and inventory is needed to ensure that proper income, assets and liabilities, and funds flow figures are presented for analysis.

Questions

1. What is the distinction between an inventoriable cost and a period cost? How does absorption costing differ from variable costing? What is the significance of each of these approaches for cash flow management?

2. "Original cost for inventory valuation is reasonable from the standpoint of the income statement but misleading for balance sheet purposes." Comment.

3. Two retailers have identical stock of goods on hand, but their inventory balances, as stated in their respective balance sheets, differ. Explain.

4. What is the basic conceptual difference between a standard cost system and an historical cost system? Which system is more appropriate for helping one to manage cash flows?

5. Why would a financial manager select an inventory valuation method that would result in lower reported profits? Does not this choice directly clash with the oft-stated doctrine that corporations seek always to maximize their profit? Explain.

6. In a period of falling prices, is it better for a firm to value its inventory by FIFO or by LIFO? Why?

7. Ignoring income taxes, what effect does a change from FIFO to LIFO have on net earnings, working capital, and cash flow during a period of rising prices? During a period of falling prices?

8. Why is it claimed that the LIFO valuation method gives a "truer" picture of operating results than do other methods of inventory valuation?

9. Chapter 6 discussed the importance of the cash conversion cycle in planning liquidity needs. The cash conversion cycle was defined as the number of days of inventory outstanding plus days sales outstanding in receivables less trade credit days outstanding. How does the choice of an inventory valuation method affect the cash conversion cycle?

10. Distinguish between a periodic-inventory method and a perpetual-inventory method. Which one is more appropriate for providing information about inventory cash flows? (*Note:* This question requires you to be familiar with the material in Appendix A of this chapter.)

Problems

1.   At the start of the year Anchor Company had $3000 invested in inventory, which represented 1500 units. During the year management purchased the following quantities:

June 15	1700 units @ $2.50
August 15	2190 units @ $2.75
November 15	1400 units @ $3.10
February 15	2100 units @ $3.45

Inventory on hand at the end of the year was 2700 units. Freight-in costs averaged $0.50 per unit. The purchasing department's direct and allocated overhead costs for the year were $10,450 and $3200, respectively. Selling price averaged $7.50 per unit, and the corporate income tax rate was 30 percent. As of February 28, current assets were $125,000, and current liabilities were $92,500.

(a) Determine the value of ending inventory, first by using variable costing and then by using absorption costing.

(b) Determine the difference in after-tax profit for the year between the two methods in part (a).

(c) For each method, determine the cash flow for the year and the net working capital at the end of the year. Assume all sales and purchases are on a cash basis.

2.   Calculate the inventory of Department K at the original cost, the present market cost, and the lower of cost or market from the data in Table 15.4. Apply the method on an item-by-item basis. How does this accounting procedure affect cash flow? Does it affect either the current ratio or the inventory turnover ratio? Explain.

TABLE 15.4
Data for Department K

Item	Quantity	Original unit cost	Present unit cost
P	50	$15	$14
Q	70	18	20
R	20	25	25
S	100	27	28

3.   For the data in Table 15.5, compute the gross margin on sales for each year (a) under the cost basis and (b) under the lower-of-cost-or-market basis in valuing inventories. Assume that the beginning inventory is zero. Discuss whether the lower-of-cost-or-market basis is conservative in terms of cash flows, inventory turnover, and the current ratio. (*Hint:* If inventory is written down to lower of cost or market, the journal entry is a debit to a loss account and a credit to inventory.)

TABLE 15.5
Sales and Inventory Data

	Year 1	Year 2	Year 3
Sales	$300,000	$330,000	$450,000
Purchases	280,000	260,000	350,000
Inventory:			
At cost	80,000	95,000	95,000
At market	75,000	80,000	100,000

4. The Stelz Corporation started business three years ago on January 1. It purchased inventory costing $100,000 in the first year, $125,000 in the second year, and $135,000 in the third year. Information about Stelz's inventory, as it would appear on the balance sheet under different valuation methods and flow assumptions, is shown in Table 15.6.

(a) Did prices go up or down in the first year?

(b) Did prices go up or down in the third year?

(c) Which inventory basis would show the highest income in the first year? The second year? All three years combined?

(d) For the third year, how much higher or lower would income be on the FIFO cost basis than it would be on the lower-of-cost-or-market basis?

(e) Why can't LIFO be used with a lower-of-cost-or-market basis?

TABLE 15.6
Data for Stelz Corporation

Year	LIFO	FIFO	Lower of (FIFO) cost or market
1	$40,800	$40,000	$37,000
2	36,400	36,000	34,000
3	41,200	44,000	44,000

5. Determine the proper unit inventory price in the following cases applying the lower of cost or market rule.

	A	B	C	D	E
Cost	$9.00	$9.00	$9.00	$9.00	$9.00
Net realizable value	6.90	9.15	8.40	10.20	8.70
Net realizable value less normal profit	6.30	8.55	7.80	9.60	8.10
Market replacement cost	6.30	9.30	8.55	9.45	7.80

6. The Ajax Manufacturing Company uses a standard cost system for internal control of inventory. The opening inventory was 750 units, valued at a standard cost of $3 per unit. The following entry was made to record this inventory:

Debit	Raw materials	$2250	
Debit	Price variance	375	
Credit	Cash		$2625

During the next year, three inventory purchases were made:

- **(a)** 300 units at $4.00 per unit
- **(b)** 400 units at $4.25 per unit
- **(c)** 500 units at $2.75 per unit

Determine the cost of goods available for sale after each of the new purchases, using the standard cost system. Discuss how a standard cost system influences cash flows and profits.

7. The firm produces a product that is sold through a government marketing board that values inventory at selling price. Using the data in Table 15.7, determine the profit after taxes and cash flow for years 1 and 2. The tax rate is 40 percent. Discuss your answers, and compare them with the more usual cost basis of inventory valuation.

TABLE 15.7
Sales and Cost Data

	Year 1	Year 2
Sales	$ 0	$12,000
Beginning inventory:		
Cost	0	9,000
Selling price		12,000
Purchases at cost	9,000	0
Ending inventory:		
Cost	9,000	0
Selling price	12,000	0
Operating expenses	1,000	1,000

8. In comparing and contrasting FIFO with LIFO inventory procedures, the following listing is used. Complete the tabulation with an answer *Yes* or *No* as demonstrated by the first item.

	FIFO	LIFO
(a) Usually matches the actual flow of goods	*yes*	*no*
(b) Emphasizes the balance sheet in that more recent costs are contained in the inventory account.	_____	_____
(c) Possibility of liquidating the base may be a significant negative aspect.	_____	_____
(d) May be theoretically less valid if prices lag behind costs (if there is not an immediate response in selling price to an increase in replacement costs).	_____	_____
(e) Has an adverse effect on assets, working capital and shareholders' equity, in a period of rising prices.	_____	_____
(f) Is acceptable to the IRS.	_____	_____
(g) Perpetual-inventory results may be different from periodic-inventory results.	_____	_____

	FIFO	LIFO
(h) Income figure is more "real" in that it does not contain "paper profits."	_____	_____
(i) Income figure more accurately reflects cash available for dividends, investments, etc.	_____	_____
(j) In periods of rising prices, the method may have an adverse effect on profit sharing plans, retirement plans, etc., from the point of view of participants in such plans.	_____	_____
(k) Somewhat opens the door for profit manipulation and may cause poor purchase decisions.	_____	_____
(l) Improve cash flow in periods of rising prices.	_____	_____
(m) Will probably not be adopted if prices are expected to decline.	_____	_____
(n) Defers tax payments in times of rising prices.	_____	_____
(o) Emphasizes the income statement in that it matches the more recent costs with revenue.	_____	_____
(p) Gives lower profits when prices rise.	_____	_____
(q) Will probably be adopted if inventory quantities are at unusually high levels.	_____	_____
(r) A change to this method must be justified (to the auditors) other than solely on the basis of tax effect.	_____	_____
(s) Tends to smooth income in periods of fluctuating prices.	_____	_____
(t) Switching to this method could cause problems with loan covenants.	_____	_____
(u) Is a current value, rather than a historical cost, valuation method.	_____	_____
(v) Quick inventory turnover may have a somewhat mitigating effect on some of the method's claimed disadvantages.	_____	_____
(w) If used for tax purposes, it must be used for financial reporting purposes.	_____	_____

9. Packard Corporation was formed on December 1 of last year. The following information is available from inventory records for Product HEW:

	Units	Unit cost
January 1 (beginning inventory)	800	$ 9.00
Purchases:		
January 5	1500	10.00
January 25	1200	10.50
February 16	600	11.00
March 26	900	11.50

A physical inventory on March 31 shows 1600 units on hand.

Prepare schedules to compute the ending inventory at March 31, for both FIFO and LIFO.

10. The Manhatton Publishing Company had in its inventory on July 1 three units of item K, all purchased on the same date at a price of $60 per unit. Information relative to item K is given in Table 15.8. Compute the cost of goods sold and the ending inventory in accordance with the following valuation methods: specific identification of units sold, FIFO, LIFO. Assume that a perpetual-record approach is followed for both quantities and dollar amounts. What effect does each method have on profits, on balance-sheet investment, and on cash flow?

TABLE 15.8
Data for Item K

Date	Explanation	Units	Unit cost	Tag number
July 1	Inventory	3	$60	k–515,516,517
3	Purchase	2	65	k–518,519
12	Sale	3		k–515,518,519
19	Purchase	2	70	k–520,521
25	Sale	1		k–516

11. The management of Fluke, Inc., wishes to have a better understanding of the differences that occur to (i) ending inventory, (ii) cost of sales, and (iii) profit before tax when goods are valued by using FIFO and LIFO. Use Table 15.9 to prepare a table showing the ending inventory values under each approach. Assume that there is no beginning inventory.

TABLE 15.9
Data for Fluke, Inc.

Period	Purchase price per unit	Units Purchased	Units Sold	Selling price per unit
1	$10	40	30	$15
2	11	44	28	14
3	9	35	55	15
4	8	36	35	14
5	10	40	30	13
6	12	35	35	14

12. The inventory records of a company show the following picture for the last fiscal year:

On hand, at start of year	500 units @ $5.00 = $ 2,500
Purchases during the year:	
February 1	500 units @ $6.00 = 3,000
May 1	1000 units @ $6.50 = 6,500
August 1	3000 units @ $6.50 = 19,500
November 1	2000 units @ $7.00 = 14,000
On hand, at end of year	800 units

A periodic-inventory record approach is kept in amounts as well as quantities. Calculate the cost of sales under both FIFO and LIFO. What is the value of ending inventory under each method? Which method results in larger cash flows, assuming the tax rate is 40 percent? How are the current ratios and inventory turnover ratios affected by each method?

Appendix B Problems

1. The income statement of the Furniture Centre for the year ended December 31 is as follows:

Sales		$244,700
Cost of sales:		
Opening inventory	$ 40,900	
Purchases	156,000	
Total	$197,000	
Ending inventory	35,900	
		161,200
Gross margin		$ 83,500
Operating expenses		74,800
Profit before taxes		$ 8,700

After this statement was prepared, the following errors were discovered:

☐ Opening inventory was overstated by $3400.

☐ A $4200 invoice has not been recorded, although the goods have been received and counted in ending inventory.

☐ A $3000 invoice, terms FOB shipping point, was recorded in December, but since the goods have not arrived, they are not included in the ending inventory's physical count.

Revise the income statement for these errors and omissions. How will liquidity be affected? What is the impact on net working capital? If the corrections are not made, will current year net income be overstated or understated? How is cash flow affected?

2. On December 31 of last year inventory amounting to $750 was received and included in the December 31 inventory. The invoice was not received until

January 4 of this year, at which time the acquisition was recorded. Indicate the effect (overstatement, understatement, none) on each of the following amounts:

	Last year	This year
Inventory, December 31		
Cost of sales		
Net income		
Accounts payable		
Retained earnings		
Net working capital		
Cash flow		

Assume that the error was not discovered by the firm when the invoice was received.

CHAPTER 16 □
Inventory Investment: How Much?

Inventories represent an investment and must, therefore, compete with other investments for the firm's limited funds. As a consequence, total investment in inventories must be related to some optimal investment level that contributes to the overall wealth objective of shareholders. The optimal level can be determined (at least theoretically) through the use of sophisticated operations research models. To expect financial managers to have an in depth knowledge of these techniques is unrealistic. However, they should be able to ask probing questions, since the proper management of inventory has a significant influence on profitability. Excessively large inventories, on the one hand, penalize profits through costs that are higher than necessary. On the other hand, keeping inventories too low handicaps sales, thus lowering potential profits.

For most firms the investment in inventories is a very significant dollar amount and percentage of assets.[1] The 1986 Statistics of Income issued by the U.S. Department of the Treasury reports that in the aggregate manufacturing U.S. corporations have about 11 percent of their resources invested in inventory. Firms in the wholesaling and retailing sectors have in excess of 28 percent of total assets invested in inventory.

The purpose of this chapter is to provide financial managers with a fundamental understanding of inventory management.

---

[1]It is important to keep in mind the discussion of Chapter 15. Firms that use LIFO have artificially low inventory book values. During the 1970s companies increasingly switched to LIFO accounting.

Need for Inventories

If production and delivery of goods are instantaneous, there is no need for inventories except as a hedge against price changes.[2] However, uncertainties exist between the production and delivery phases. Traditional types of inventory include the following:

- *Lot-size inventory.* Making or buying lots larger than immediately needed results in purchase and production economies.
- *Safety-stock inventory.* Acts as a buffer against uncertain demand and lead times.
- *Work-in-process inventory.* Reduces work stoppages that result from variability in scheduled flow or processing problems.
- *Anticipation inventory.* Stabilizes production against seasonal variation.
- *Pipeline inventory.* Fills the process and/or transportation pipeline.
- *Hedge inventory.* Purchased in advance of anticipated price increases, suppliers' strikes, and so on.

In many respects inventories are more sensitive to general business fluctuations than are other assets. Large and costly swings in inventory have exacerbated just about every recorded business cycle. In periods of prosperity, when sales are high, merchandise can be disposed of readily, and quantities on hand may not appear excessive. But when even a slight downward trend in the business cycle occurs, many lines of merchandise begin to move slowly, stock piles up, and obsolescence becomes a real possibility. Because of the heavy costs of carrying surplus inventory, an intense effort must be made by management to liquidate surpluses. Prices will fall until either consumption increases or production falls off sufficiently.

These problems are compounded by the fact that there are several conflicting views about the appropriate inventory investment:[3]

- The *marketing manager* has a natural desire to have plenty of finished goods inventory on hand so that no customer is ever turned away or forced to wait because of lack of stock.
- The *production manager* likes to have large quantities of both raw materials and work-in-process inventories available to ensure continuous production runs. This allows spreading costs for setup, changeover, spoilage, and learning over longer production runs.

---

[2]Management can use futures or options to hedge against expected price changes.

[3]These conflicting views are essentially the same views expressed in Chapter 2 with respect to Fig. 2.1.

□ The *purchasing agent* often prefers to buy in large quantities in order to take advantage of quantity discounts and lower freight costs. Sometimes, the purchasing agent tries to outguess changing market prices and either postpone or accelerate purchases accordingly.

□ The *finance manager's* responsibility is to pry loose as much inventory investment as is feasible in order to rechannel it into more profitable opportunities.

Because of these conflicting functional objectives, inventory policy must be carefully drawn so as to benefit the business as a whole.

Inventory Overinvestment

It is unrealistic for a company to carry the amount of stock that would virtually guarantee no stockouts. Inventory investment increases at an increasing rate as the customer service standard approaches 100 percent. A typical cost relationship is illustrated in Fig. 16.1. For example, in order to be able to fill 85 percent of the total received orders from existing stock, the company has to carry an inventory valued at $400,000. To raise the customer service standard by 5 percentage points, to 90 percent, the inventory investment must be increased by $100,000. To raise the customer ser-

FIGURE 16.1
Trade-off Between Inventory Investment and Level of Customer Service

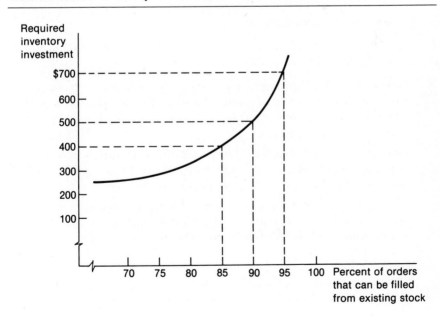

vice standard another 5 percentage points, to 95 percent, inventory investment must be increased by $200,000.

This acceleration of investment does not mean, however, that increases in customer service are never warranted. Obviously, increases in service spell increases in patronage and sales. But how much do sales, profits, and cash flow increase with product availability? This is the crucial question. The graph does not indicate whether sales, profits, and cash flow will increase enough to justify the higher investment in inventories. This issue requires careful analysis of expected demand and acceptable stockout rates.

The evils that result from overinvestment in inventories are obvious:

□ *Liquidity problems.* The erring management is likely to find itself short of cash for other purposes. Management is likely to find it necessary to increase borrowings, thereby adding to the risk of insolvency.

□ *Misuse of facilities.* Facilities that could be better used for other purposes may have to be used for storage, or indeed, additional facilities may have to be bought, erected, or rented.

□ *Inventory losses.* Losses through shrinkage, spoilage, theft, and obsolescence may increase substantially.

□ *Competitiveness problems.* Management may find itself with a high-cost inventory at a time when its competitors are carrying on their operations with goods purchased more recently at lower prices.

Inventory Underinvestment

A management that is unduly niggardly in its inventory investment policy also faces problems. Here are just a few:

□ *Loss of customers.* Customers may go elsewhere because they cannot find a sufficient variety of goods of a given line to make reasonable selection, or because they experience unreasonable delays in the delivery of goods ordered.

□ *Unnecessary costs of operations.* Shortages of raw materials may bring temporary shutdowns, with many kinds of overhead expenses continuing to accumulate during the periods of idleness.

□ *Being at the mercy of rising prices.* Lack of foresight in the accumulation of inventories, at a time of plentiful supplies and relatively low prices, may result in substantial increases in costs of goods sold.[4]

---

[4]This problem can be minimized by hedging, as discussed in Chapters 9 and 10.

Methods for Managing Inventory and Production

The problem of how much inventory to carry is a serious one for management. The dominant inventory models used to address how much to invest in inventory go by the abbreviations EOQ/ROP, MRP, and JIT. Each of these models will be discussed in terms of its relationship with the following profit function:

$$\text{Profits} = \text{revenue} - [\text{production costs}] - [\text{inventory costs}] \qquad (16.1)$$
$$- [\text{costs of customer dissatisfaction}].$$

Economic Order Quantity/Reorder Point Model (EOQ/ROP)

The EOQ/ROP model minimizes Eq. (16.1)'s production costs and inventory costs. These costs vary with quantity ordered as shown in Fig. 16.2. Other assumptions of the model[5] include

□ Demand annually or per period is known with certainty and is at a constant (linear) rate.

□ Purchase and preparation (setup) costs are fixed, and no discounts are offered for volume purchases.

□ Lead time is known with certainty and equals zero.

□ Stockouts are not permissible.

□ Replenishment is instantaneous.

Under these assumptions, the optimal order quantity is provided by Eq. (16.2):

$$\text{EOQ} = \left(\frac{2 \times \text{demand for inventory} \times \text{cost per order}}{\text{total holding cost per unit of item per period}} \right)^{1/2} \qquad (16.2)$$
$$= \left(\frac{2DC_o}{C_h} \right)^{1/2}$$

Reorder points are arbitrarily set to provide sufficient stock to cover demand over the reorder lead time.

---

[5]Appendix A of this chapter reconciles the EOQ model to the RI model. Appendices B and C show that many of the EOQ assumptions can be relaxed and still derive EOQs. Some weaknesses of the model, from a financial perspective, are discussed by F. Lindman, R. Gagne, and G. W. Gallinger, "Firm Value and Optimal Inventory Investment," in *Readings on Short-term Financial Management*, 3rd ed. K. V. Smith and G. W. Gallinger, editors (St. Paul, MN: West Publishing Co., 1988): 500–503, and Y. H. Kim, G. C. Philippatos, and K. H. Chung, "Evaluating Investment in Inventory Policy: A Net Present Value Framework," *The Engineering Economist* (Winter 1986): 119–36.

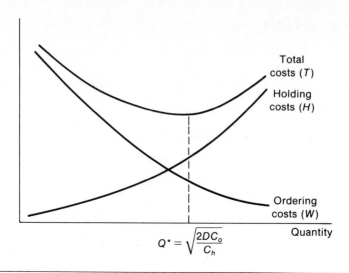

$$Q^* = \sqrt{\frac{2DC_o}{C_h}}$$

FIGURE 16.2
Inventory Costs in the EOQ Model

ILLUSTRATION 16.1

Assume annual demand for an item is 600,000 units, ordering cost per order is $100, and carrying cost per unit is $0.25. The EOQ ($Q^*$) is

$$Q^* = \left(\frac{2 \times 100 \times 600,000}{0.25}\right)^{1/2} = 21,909.$$

This value results in an average number of units of 10,955 being carried in inventory. The total number of orders placed for the year is 27 ($=D/Q^*$).   □

The unrealistic assumptions of the EOQ model can be relaxed to allow more practical applications of the model. Appendix A of this chapter examines some of these situations. The conceptual nature of the model remains intact, however. Thus the basic EOQ model is still useful to financial managers for evaluating inventory levels and asking intelligent questions of production and purchasing personnel.

Materials Requirement Planning Model (MRP)

The **materials requirement planning (MRP) inventory system**[6] is a computer simulation for each product of its bill of material structure, inventory status, and process of manufacture. When a master schedule of end items to be produced and due dates are put into the computer, the model first accesses the structured bill of material, lead times, and on-hand and on-order inventory balances. It then *explodes* the bill of material to obtain component-parts requirements, nets gross requirements against available inventory balances, offsets net requirements over lead times, and generates a time-phased set of components and materials requirements.

The projected components requirements are in turn exploded through their manufacturing routings to provide a time-phased projection of the loads on the various manufacturing departments that would result from the given time schedule. These loads are compared with the capacities of each department to determine the feasibility of meeting the master schedule. If bottlenecks occur, the master schedule is revised to solve the problem. When this is done purchase orders are placed and shop operations are scheduled.

Just-in-Time (JIT)[7]

The system of **just-in-time (JIT) inventory** is also known as *Kanban*[8] (because of the cards used), *zero inventory,* or *stockless production.* In JIT, authorization for a part to be made at any work station is generated by a requirement for the part at the next work station in the production line. As parts are consumed in final assembly, cards associated with these parts are posted to indicate the need for, and to authorize production of, replacement parts. The process is repeated at all upstream work stations, pulling parts through the production system as they are needed and eventually pulling raw materials and purchased parts from suppliers.

The objective of JIT is to assign the fewest possible number of parts to each authorization card. Work-in-process (WIP) inventory is reduced,

---

[6]The section draws on the work of O. Wright, *MRP II: Unlocking America's Productivity Potential* (Boston: CBI Publishing, 1982).

[7]The section relies on several articles published in *P&IM Review,* a journal devoted to production and inventory management.

[8]Kanban and JIT are not synonymous. Kanban is a pull production and inventory management system. JIT is a philosophy of viewing the production network from a systems perspective and involves continuously striving to improve process efficiency, reduce inventory, and improve quality. Although JIT normally uses a pull system to accomplish its goals, the JIT philosophy is recommended whether a MRP or Kanban method is used.

and the authorization of single parts that arrive "just in time" to be consumed results in "zero inventory" and "stockless production."

JIT imposes two major production problems. For each work station to make the variety of parts called for by downstream work stations in small quantities requires great flexibility and frequent machine setups. The other problem is that the final assembly schedule cannot be permitted to impose a changing load on the factory.

Reconciliation of the Methods

EOQ/ROP inventory management is reactive. New orders for parts to support future demand result from reorder points that are triggered when inventories are depleted by past demand. In contrast, MRP is proactive. Inventory management and production management are guided by forecasts of future demand.

MRP does not make EOQ obsolete; it simply uses new techniques for answering what to order, when to order, and what priorities to assign. MRP still uses EOQ concepts to determine how much to order (lot size). The only refinement that MRP makes to the classical EOQ method of setting lot sizes is that the MRP model seeks to minimize the total inventory costs of Eq. (16.1) using demand as projected from the demand forecast and the master schedule, rather than assuming a continuously repetitive and smooth usage pattern.

JIT proposes minimal (theoretically, zero) lot sizes. It treats *preparation costs* as variable costs (contrary to assumptions of EOQ and MRP, which treat them as fixed). As preparation costs are driven to zero, then EOQ and MRP are consistent with the zero inventory concept of JIT.[9] Under JIT, Fig. 16.2 takes on the profile of Fig. 16.3.

Safety stock serves to minimize the combined inventory and customer dissatisfaction costs of Eq. (16.1). The EOQ/ROP model optimizes safety stock levels by setting statistical reorder points that establish sufficient reserve material to protect against variability in demand and replenishment time to reach acceptable levels of customer dissatisfaction.

The MRP approach poses no new procedure for handling safety stocks. Although JIT advances the goal of zero inventory, it recognizes the need for safety stock to cover uncertainties in demand.

Work-in-process (WIP) inventory is intended to reduce the production cost component of Eq. (16.1) by reducing idle time, permitting combined setups, and so on. Used improperly, however, it increases all three of the cost components of Eq. (16.1). Production costs are increased because

---

[9]This is obvious from Eq. (16.2). When total ordering costs (preparation costs) become zero, the EOQ becomes zero.

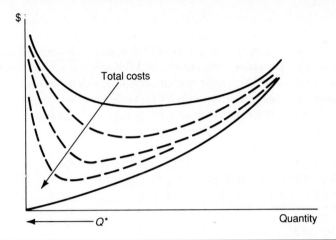

FIGURE 16.3
EOQ under a JIT System

excessive WIP clogs the production system, more space is taken up for equipment and storage, and handling costs rise. WIP inventory increases customer dissatisfaction in EOQ/ROP systems by increasing lead times, because the time parts spend waiting in WIP queues typically makes up about 75 percent of manufacturing lead time. Since WIP ties up resources, it also is an inventory cost.

The EOQ/ROP model, because it addresses only lot-size economies and not production efficiencies, does not directly address WIP inventory. In addition, because EOQ/ROP is a reactive system, it often calls for parts to be made that are not needed to support demand in the near future.

MRP does not propose any new techniques for determining optimal WIP inventory levels. It does, however, have the capability to drastically reduce WIP inventory abuses. The forward-looking capability of MRP anticipates future changes in needed capacity in time to minimize WIP bottlenecks.

The objective of JIT is to reduce WIP inventory to zero. Low WIP levels force processing problems to quickly emerge so that they can be eliminated. This results in a decrease in the inventory cost component of Eq. (16.1). Production costs and customer dissatisfaction costs are also reduced through increased quality and decreased lead times. Striving to achieve zero inventory results in continued improvement of the production process.

Anticipation inventory is "stored capacity." It attempts a joint reduction of the production costs and inventory costs in Eq. (16.1). The EOQ/ROP model does not address anticipation inventories. MRP increases the importance of the production planning process when anticipation levels are established. JIT, through its emphasis of production flexibility, attempts to eliminate the need for anticipation inventory.

Pipeline inventory consists of WIP inventory and materials-in-transit from suppliers, interplant shipments, and finished goods in transit to warehouses or customers. JIT attempts to minimize this inventory by reducing transit time. JIT accomplishes this by locating suppliers' facilities closer to customers, delivering directly to process points, and shipping smaller quantities of finished product at more frequent intervals. Close attention is paid to routes and schedules.

Although the goal of reducing pipeline inventory in the traditional view is to reduce capital investment, the major objective of JIT is to force process improvements in the total system.

Why JIT?

EOQ ignores even the simple relationships that exist among the parts that make up a finished product. MRP using the power of the computer takes a significant step toward integration by considering each component as part of the larger system of parts defined by the bill of material, and by anticipating the production capacity required to meet forecasted demand. But both EOQ and MRP take as given parameters, or constants, the time and cost associated with operations such as setups and quality control.

JIT, unlike the other two systems, explicitly seeks process efficiency improvements and uses inventory management as a tool for doing so. JIT attempts to minimize the sum of the cost components of Eq. (16.1) in its entire rather than only the inventory cost component. JIT takes a more long-term view by accepting short-run diseconomies, such as those that result from reducing inventories to below optimal EOQ levels, in order to force process inefficiencies to surface and thereby reduce total costs in the long run.[10]

Transitional Problems[11]

Few manufacturing organizations are very flexible, either in their operations or in the minds of their managers. In this environment, change comes

---

[10]By adopting a JIT system, Cincinnati Milacron's Electronic Systems Division was able to reduce inventories by more than 60 percent, manufacturing lead times from 12 weeks to 4 weeks, and manufacturing costs by 24 percent. This was accomplished in an 18-month period. And it is not only manufacturing companies using JIT principles. Harris Bank of Chicago has an agreement with a supplier for daily delivery of office products.

[11]R. C. Walleigh, "What's Your Excuse for Not Using JIT?" *Harvard Business Review* (March–April 1986): 38–54, discusses a number of impediments often encountered when implementing JIT.

slowly, if at all. Attempts to implement JIT may consume considerable resources.[12] People are the cornerstone of the foundation of JIT implementation. External suppliers must cooperate in terms of meeting quality standards and delivery times. Employees must adopt a state of mind[13] that encourages competitive excellence, continuous improvements, value-added activities, and 100 percent quality items. Parallel production systems may have to be run until JIT is successfully implemented.

In short, considerable problems may exist in changing to a JIT system. A period of transition will require additional resources with the result that greater resource constraints may arise until management is able to successfully implement a JIT system.

Target Inventory Balances

JIT, with its goal of zero inventory balances, is the ideal inventory system. However, zero balances are seldom reached and not all inventory items are treated in the same manner, regardless of which inventory control technique is used. The inventory classification method discussed next provides an approach for allocating effort to control inventory.

A–B–C Method

Many managers find it difficult to divide materials, parts, supplies, and finished goods into subclassifications for purpose of stock control. For example, Table 16.1 shows inventory items that are subclassified step by step by (1) itemizing total annual volume of each item needed and (2) grouping in decreasing order of annual costs. This technique is often called the **A–B–C method**. This approach allows for management by emphasis, where emphasis is placed on the few items that bring about the most results.

The final A–B–C classification in Table 16.1 demonstrates that only 7 percent of the items represent 82 percent of the total cost. The standard relationship normally cited in A–B–C analysis is that 20 percent of the items handled will contribute 80 percent of the annual sales dollars. However, the selection of A, B, and C items is mostly subjective. It should be dependent on whether different types of control are planned for each group and on what resources (such as control system, people, computer assistance) are available for controlling inventory activities.

---

[12]E. J. Hay, writing a guest editorial column for *P&IM Magazine* (July 1988): 22, states that it could take "10-or-more years" to fully successfully implement JIT throughout a large manufacturing entity.

[13]Success in inducing this state of mind relies on persuasive communication skills, discussion of which is beyond the scope of this book.

TABLE 16.1
A–B–C Inventory Classification

Step 1: Calculate total sales volume and costs

Item	Unit sales	%	Unit price	Costs	%
1	10,000	7.0	$10.00	$100,000	81.8
2	1,000	0.8	0.05	50	0.0
3	10,000	7.0	0.02	200	0.2
4	11,000	7.7	1.00	11,000	9.0
5	110,000	77.5	0.10	11,000	9.0
	142,000	100.0		$122,250	100.0

Step 2: Group items in descending order of total cost

Item	Classification
1	A
4	B
5	B
3	C
2	C

The A–B–C analysis allows priorities to be established for control of replenishment ordering, with top control on A and B items and little control over C items. Class A items should be under continuous review since they represent the high-cost items. Class B items are less costly, and thus on a unit basis contribute less to any dollar inventory buildup than do A items. A JIT system works well with both A and B items. On the other hand, EOQ and MRP systems are not appropriate for A items since they rely on periodic reviews based on point forecasts.

Class C items consist of nuts, bolts, washers, and other small hardware items. These items are not critical from a dollar investment viewpoint, so an arbitrary fixed-time supply (a six-month supply) order quantity could be used. A two-bin system is often established by management to control C items. When the first bin is depleted, an order is placed to replenish the inventory consumed. The C items result in less frequent ordering, higher safety stocks, and less paperwork.

Inventory Turnover Ratios

The computation of an **inventory turnover ratio** is frequently relied upon by management to get an idea of whether inventory investments are appropriate. This method was used by W. T. Grant. It was corporate policy to have a constant turnover ratio — inventories were to increase by the same percentage change that sales increased. This technique is, at best, a very rough method of testing for the reasonableness of inventory investment. Very serious errors can result if turnover figures are accorded greater weight than they deserve in arriving at judgments. Many complex circumstances bear upon policy formulation in the individual firm, and these factors can influence inventory investment. Thus turnover ratios cannot be used routinely or mechanically in judging inventory investment policies; they must be used in conjunction with an analysis of underlying economic and financial factors.

The inventory turnover for a given period of time can be computed by the solution of either of the following two formulas:

$$\text{Turnover} = \frac{\text{cost of goods sold}}{\text{average inventory}} \qquad (16.3)$$

or

$$\text{Turnover} = \frac{\text{sales}}{\text{average inventory}} \qquad (16.4)$$

Equation (16.3) is often advocated as being the correct formula. Some analysts, however, find the use of Eq. (16.4) more convenient; department stores, for example, customarily value their inventories at selling prices, using the so-called retail method for this purpose. As long as consistency is maintained, which equation is used is generally immaterial.

For greatest accuracy in the computation of inventory turnover, monthly inventories should ordinarily be used, especially if the size of inventories fluctuates substantially in the course of the year. Average inventory for a year, then, is the sum of the opening inventory and the inventory at the end of every month, this total to be divided by 13. Many firms operate on a fiscal year other than the calendar year, for the very reason that they want their yearly operations to conclude at a time when inventories are at or near their lowest level. This arrangement makes possible appreciable economies in the work of inventory taking and valuation. However, as Table 16.2 shows, for a firm in this position a turnover ratio computed on the basis of the average of opening and closing inventories would be much higher than one computed on the basis of an average of monthly inventories; accordingly, it would be quite misleading.

An inventory turnover ratio, standing by itself, generally means absolutely nothing. To state that the turnover of a particular firm is, say, 3.6 times indicates nothing about the wisdom of its inventory management policies. To give meaning to a turnover ratio, management often compares it with the firm's historical turnover ratio, with a budgeted value, or with those of other firms operating in the same area of business activity, that is, with the ratios of the firm's competitors. It is very difficult, however, to gain access to competitors' figures that would prove useful.

TABLE 16.2
Monthly Inventory Balance and Turnover Ratios

January 1 balance	$ 55,000	July	$160,000
January	70,000	August	175,000
February	85,000	September	190,000
March	100,000	October	145,000
April	115,000	November	100,000
May	130,000	December	55,000
June	145,000		

Assume cost of goods sold = $420,000

	Average inventory	Turnover
Based on monthly balances	$117,308	3.6
Based on opening and closing balances	55,000	7.6

Should a firm's turnover ratio be decreasing over time, some evidence of growing deficiencies in inventory management is brought out — not conclusive evidence, by any means, but likely sufficient to warrant a thorough analysis of the situation. Likewise, should a firm's turnover ratio be lower than those of competitors, an investigation of the causes of what appears to be a record of poor performance might be in order.

A comparison of turnover ratios can easily lead to unsound conclusions. Comparative ratios, standing alone, can never wisely be taken as proof that inventory management has been good or bad. When ratios are found to be out of line, praise or blame to the makers of policy must be withheld until the reasons for the out-of-line result have been sought and found.

Inventory ratios vary according to the methods of inventory valuation that are used (LIFO versus FIFO, for example), especially if the methods of valuation are changed. For example, a relatively low ratio may result from the heavy stocking of inventory in anticipation of price increases; should price increases actually come about, the managers would surely be deserving of praise rather than of blame. Or it may result from a stabilization of production, that is, the spreading out of productive operations over the year, as by a manufacturing firm whose sales are heavily concentrated in a few months.

On the other hand, a relatively high turnover ratio may not really be an indicator of favorable results and prospects. It may indicate a serious underinvestment in inventories. Surely there would be strong evidence of underinvestment should sales be falling off while the turnover figure is rising or should a firm's sales be expanding at a slower rate than those of other firms while its turnover ratio is rising. A loss of customers because of an inability to show them complete lines or to make prompt deliveries could hardly be regarded as a favorable development.

EOQ-Based Turnover Ratio

The question that arises from the previous discussion is what to compare the turnover ratio with. Ideally, management wants inventories to contribute to the wealth maximization objectives of the company. However, what ratio is consistent with this objective? The EOQ model can be tied to the turnover calculation to help answer this question. Of course, the answer depends on accepting the assumptions and usefulness of the EOQ model. The following illustration demonstrates this approach.

ILLUSTRATION 16.2

W.T. Grant's policy was to maintain a fixed relationship between inventory and sales. For the year ended January 31, 1974, sales of $1,644,747,000 were supported by year-end inventory of $399,533,000. Thus inventory was 24.3 percent of sales and turnover (based on sales) was 4.12 times. The following year, sales were $1,849,802,000 and inventory was on target at $450,637,000.

This approach is inconsistent with the EOQ wealth maximization approach. The percentage-of-sales technique overstates inventory balances relative to the EOQ model. The EOQ model shows inventory to be a function of sales demand, holding costs, and ordering costs. If the ratio of holding costs to ordering costs does not change, W. T. Grant's inventory ending January 1974 should be $423,707,000, or $26.9 million less than what it actually was.

This amount is calculated as follows: *Assume* that last year's inventory was optimal. Therefore with the EOQ formula (stated in thousands of dollars and not in units), the ordering cost-to-holding cost ratio, C_o/C_h, is as follows:

$$\$Q^* = \left(\frac{2DC_o}{C_h} \right)^{1/2},$$

$$\$399{,}533 = \left(\frac{2 \times \$1{,}644{,}747 \times C_o}{C_h} \right)^{1/2}. \tag{16.5}$$

Solving for the ordering cost-to-holding cost ratio gives

$$\frac{C_o}{C_h} = 48{,}526.$$

When this ratio is held constant, the January 1974 inventory balance should be

$$\$Q^* = (2 \times \$1{,}849{,}802 \times 48{,}526)^{1/2} = \$423{,}707.$$

An alternative method of calculating the forecast balance is as follows:

$$(\text{Last period's inventory}) \times (1 + \text{expected growth in sales})^{1/2}. \qquad (16.6)$$

For W.T. Grant the calculation is

$$\$399,533 \times \left(\frac{\$1,849,802}{\$1,644,747}\right)^{1/2} = \$423,707.$$

At the (assumed) efficient inventory level of $423,707,000, turnover increases from 4.12 times to about 4.37 times; the inventory-to-sales percentage decreases from 24.3 percent to about 22.9 percent. Thus *the traditional percent-of-sales method allows $26.9 million excess inventory.* If 1971 is used as the base period (sales = $1,254,131,000, inventory = $260,492,000), $134 million excess inventory exists as of January 31, 1974; that is,

$$\underbrace{\$450,637}_{\substack{1974 \\ \text{actual} \\ \text{inventory}}} - \$260,492 \times \left(\frac{\$1,849,802}{\$1,254,131}\right)^{.1/2}$$

Since management frequently thinks of inventory in terms of turnover (and percentages simply being the inverse of the turnover ratio), the targeted turnover ratio that incorporates the wealth-maximizing objective of the EOQ model is

$$
\begin{aligned}
\text{Turnover} &= \frac{\text{forecast sales}}{\text{EOQ forecast inventory}} \\
&= \left[\frac{(\text{forecast sales})(\text{last year's sales})}{(\text{last year's inventory})^2}\right]^{1/2}.
\end{aligned}
\qquad (16.7)
$$

Substituting numbers from this example into the revised turnover equation results in a turnover of 4.37 times:

$$\text{Turnover} = \left[\frac{\$1,849,802 \times \$1,644,747}{(\$399,533)^2}\right]^{1/2} = 4.37.$$

The targeted percentage of sales is the inverse of this figure, or 22.9 percent.

The inventory turnover amount of 4.37 can also be derived from the following equation:

$$
\begin{aligned}
[\text{Inventory turnover}]_{t+1} \\
= [\text{inventory turnover}]_t \times [1 + \text{growth in sales}]^{1/2}
\end{aligned}
\qquad (16.8)
$$

where t represents period t. For example,

$$[\text{Inventory turnover}]_{t+1} = 4.12 \times [1.1246]^{1/2} = 4.37. \qquad \square$$

The major advantage of the turnover ratio is its simplicity. Unfortunately, this is also its major disadvantage. *The inventory turnover ratio is not able to measure the efficiency of inventory management.* The mere relationship of cost of sales (or sales) to inventory fails to tell much of anything about efficiency. Adjusting it to incorporate EOQ concepts does lead to more efficient inventory balances. However, there is still no indication of how any change in price, product mix, or quantity affect efficiency. These factors are examined in the next chapter.

Summary

Many firms have a substantial proportion of their total assets invested in various kinds of inventories, and pressures to increase inventories are substantial. So effort must be made to keep inventories within reasonable limits. However, inventory management is usually not under the direct responsibility of the financial manager. He or she must rely on many non-financial specialists in an effort to determine the "proper" inventory investment level.

This chapter examined inventory costs and models that provide the financial manager with a conceptual basis for overseeing inventory investments. The traditional cost categories used in analyzing inventories are carrying (holding) costs and ordering (setup) costs. The trade-off between these two costs leads to a cost-minimization solution for the economic order quantity (EOQ) model. The model is consistent with shareholder wealth maximization as embodied in the residual income model (discussed in Chapter 1).

Another model, which has gained acceptance in Japan and is finding acceptance with some large companies in other parts of the world, is the just-in-time (JIT) technique. This technique is an improvement over the EOQ system in that if properly implemented, product quality improves, management attains a better understanding of the production process, and lower inventory investment results. Unfortunately, the characteristics that make the system so successful in Japan are not easily transferred to Western cultures.

The next topic discussed in the chapter was monitoring inventory balances. The A–B–C system of physical inventory control was discussed first. This system can be implemented with either an EOQ or JIT system. It is based on the premise that a small fraction of the items generate a large fraction of the total revenues of the business. These items require a different type of control than items that contribute little to the revenues of the business.

Financial techniques for monitoring inventories were discussed next. Traditional turnover ratios are fraught with problems. An EOQ turnover ratio provides more efficient inventory targets since it implicitly incorporates the inventory costs of holding and carrying, which are instrumental to a cost minimization strategy.

Even though the complexity of inventory management is enormous, proper inventory management is important to the short-run liquidity and the long-run profitability of the firm. Lack of control over inventories can be ruinous to a business.

Key Concepts

A–B–C– method
Anticipation inventory
Economic order quantity (EOQ)
    model
JIT

MRP
Pipeline inventory
Safety stock
Turnover ratio
Work-in-process inventory

Appendix A

EOQ as a Wealth-Maximization Model

The EOQ formula is based on a cost-minimization criterion that assumes separation among production, investment, and financing (a common assumption of finance theory). Under these conditions it is compatible with management's value-maximization objective, where value maximization is defined as maximizing residual income (RI).

In terms of inventory analysis, the RI model assesses the incremental contribution of inventory to profits less a deduction for the opportunity cost of funds invested in average inventory. Hence

$$\text{RI} = \text{revenue} - (\text{cost of goods sold}) - (\text{ordering costs})$$
$$- (\text{out of pocket holding costs}) - (\text{opportunity holding costs}),$$

or

$$\text{RI} = VD - PD - C_o \left(\frac{D}{Q} \right) - i_1 \left(\frac{PQ}{2} \right) - i_2 \left(\frac{PQ}{2} \right), \tag{A.1}$$

where

V = selling price per unit,
D = unit demand rate per period,
P = cost price per unit,
C_o = order cost per order,
Q = units of item per order,
i_1 = carrying cost, expressed as a percentage of P, exclusive of the opportunity cost of funds tied up in inventory,
i_2 = opportunity cost of funds tied up in inventory, as a percentage of P,
$(i_1 + i_2)P = C_h$ = total holding cost per unit of item over time period.

Taking the first derivative of Eq. (A.1) with respect to Q, setting the result equal to zero, and solving for Q leads to the RI-maximizing order quantity:

$$Q_{RI}^* = \left[\frac{2DC_o}{(i_1 + i_2)P} \right]^{1/2}. \tag{A.2}$$

This equation is identical to the traditional EOQ formula. The following discussion shows that maximizing accounting return on investment (ROI) or profit (π) does not lead to the same conclusion.

If management's objective is to maximize accounting ROI, Eq. (A.1) becomes

$$\text{ROI} = \frac{VD - PD - C_o(D/Q) - i_1 P(Q/2)}{P(Q/2)}, \tag{A.3}$$

where the numerator represents profits and the denominator is average inventory investment. Differentiating with respect to Q, setting the result equal to zero, and solving for Q results in

$$Q^*_{\text{ROI}} = \frac{2C_o}{V - P}. \tag{A.4}$$

This maximum is distinctly different from the EOQ (and RI) maximum.

Where management's objective is to maximize accounting profits, the numerator of Eq. (A.3) is differentiated with respect to Q, set equal to zero, and solved in terms of Q. The maximizing order quantity is

$$Q^*_{\pi} = \left(\frac{2DC_o}{i_1 P}\right)^{1/2}. \tag{A.5}$$

Although this result is similar to the EOQ (and RI) result, it differs in the denominator. The profit-maximizing approach results in higher inventory order quantities since the opportunity cost of funds (i_2) is ignored.

Appendix B

Extensions of the Classic EOQ Vendor Model

Nonzero Lead Times

One of the assumptions of the classic EOQ model is zero lead time. Consider the case where lead time is greater than zero. As before, assume that lead time is deterministic and stationary, as opposed to being stochastic.

Figure B.1 illustrates situations where the number of days of lead time is either less than the optimal cycle time ($t_L < t_C$) or greater than the optimal cycle time ($t_L > t_C$). Note the following:

- The optimal reorder quantity Q^* is unaffected by the magnitude of the lead time, which means that the EOQ model is still relevant.
- The optimal reorder point R^* must be determined such that replenishment arrives exactly at the beginning of a new cycle.
- Time t_C equals the economic order quantity divided by the use per day: $Q^* \times 360/D$.

First, consider the case when $t_L < t_C$. Demand during the lead time is $t_L \times D/360$, which is less than Q^* because $Q^* = t_C \times D/360$ and $t_L < t_C$. Thus one simply places an order when inventory level drops to $R^* = t_L \times D/360$, thereby guaranteeing that replenishment arrives exactly at the end of the current cycle.

Next, consider the case where $t_L > t_C$. Lead time demand is still $t_L \times D/360$; however, this demand is now greater than Q^*. In this case it is not possible to reorder at an inventory level that will exactly absorb lead time demand.

Therefore lead time demand must be satisfied both by the amount of inventory on hand when an order is launched (i.e., by R^*) and by replenishments (from previous orders) that arrive during the lead time under consideration. Thus

$$R^* = \left(t_L \times \frac{D}{360} \right) - \left[\frac{t_L}{t_C} \right] Q^*, \tag{B.1}$$

where $[t_L/t_C]$ represents the integer part of the quotient t_L/t_C, that is, the number of complete cycles during a lead time. Note that $[t_L/t_C] = 0$ when $t_L < t_C$, in which case Eq. (B.1) is simply the result for Fig. B.1(a).

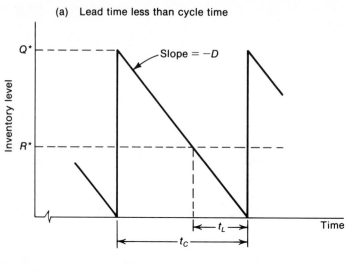

(a)   Lead time less than cycle time

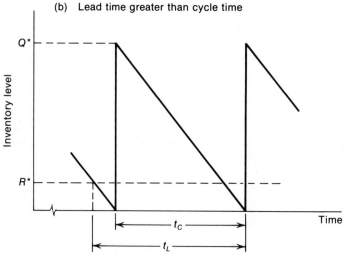

(b)   Lead time greater than cycle time

FIGURE B.1
Reorder Points for Lead Times Greater Than Zero

ILLUSTRATION B.1

If the inventory cycle t_C is 18 days and the lead time is 7.2 days, then from Eq. (B.1) the economic order quantity Q^* of 250 items, with an annual demand D of 5000 units, should be placed whenever inventory drops to

$$R^* = 7.2 \times \frac{5000}{360} - \left[\frac{7.2}{18}\right]250$$

$$= 100 - 0 = 100 \text{ items.}$$

If the lead time is 28.8 days, then

$$R^* = 28.8 \times \frac{5000}{360} - \left[\frac{28.8}{18}\right]250$$

$$= 400 - [1]250 = 150 \text{ items.} \qquad \square$$

Shortages Allowed

This extension to the model allows shortages to be back-ordered. As before, all demands must be met ultimately; hence at the moment of replenishment all back orders are satisfied prior to meeting new demands. These back orders, however, incur a shortage cost. When back orders are allowed, the assumption of unaffected demand requires that all demand be met. If purchases are delayed, however, part of each incoming order is immediately allocated to back-order demand. Consequently, fewer orders may be made, resulting in lower ordering costs; and average inventory levels may be lower, resulting in reduced carrying costs. This trade-off between ordering and carrying costs, on the one hand, and back-ordering costs, on the other hand, can be exploited, as shown next.

Figure B.2 portrays the inventory behavior for this model. New variables are defined as follows:

S = maximum number of units short,

C_s = shortage cost per unit per time period,

t_1 = time within a cycle during which inventory is held,

t_2 = time within a cycle during which a shortage exists.

Appendix C shows the derivation of the EOQ back-order model. The optimal order quantity is

$$Q^* = \left(\frac{2DC_o}{C_h} \times \frac{C_h + C_s}{C_s}\right)^{1/2}, \tag{B.2}$$

and the maximum shortage quantity is

$$S^* = \left[\frac{2DC_o/C_h}{(C_hC_s + C_s^2)}\right]^{1/2}. \tag{B.3}$$

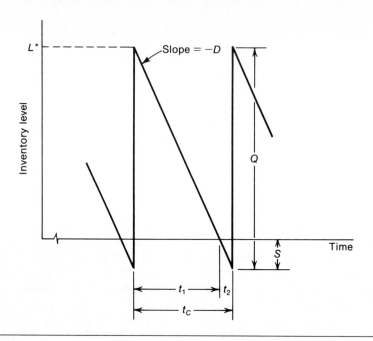

FIGURE B.2
EOQ Behavior with Back Orders

ILLUSTRATION B.2

Assume annual demand for an item is 600,000 units, ordering cost per order is $100, carrying cost per unit per year is $0.25, and back-ordering cost per unit is $2. Ignoring back-ordering possibilities for the moment, the EOQ is calculated, using Eq. (16.2), as

$$Q^* = \left(2 \times 100 \times \frac{600{,}000}{0.25}\right)^{1/2} = 21{,}909 \text{ units.}$$

This EOQ results in an average number of units of 10,955 being carried in inventory. The total number of orders placed for the year is 27 $(= D/Q^*)$.

Compare these results with the case where back ordering is allowed. From Eq. (B.2) the optimal order quantity is

$$Q^* = \left[\left(2 \times 100 \times \frac{600{,}000}{0.25}\right)\left(\frac{0.25 + 2}{2}\right)\right]^{1/2} = 23{,}238 \text{ units.}$$

From Eq. (B.3) the maximum shortage quantity is

$$S^* = \left(\frac{2 \times 100 \times 600,000 \times 0.25}{(0.25 \times 2 + 2^2)}\right)^{1/2} = 2582 \text{ units.}$$

The average inventory on hand is $[Q^* - S^*]/2 = 10,328$ units, and the total number of orders placed during the year is $D/Q^* = 26$. This example shows that being able to back-order product can result in lower inventory investment. □

Quantity Discounts Offered

Frequently, suppliers offer discounts if buyers purchase in large quantities. The motivation for doing so is straightforward. In vendor models the supplier moves more inventory forward in the distribution channel and lowers carrying costs if buyers purchase in larger quantities. By purchasing a large lot size, the buyer is trading off lowered purchasing and ordering costs (fewer orders) with higher carrying costs.

If a company is offered a single quantity discount, then one approach is to compare the total cost for the best inventory policy without the discount with the total cost if the discount is accepted. Total annual cost (T_d) is defined as the sum of annual ordering cost, annual carrying cost, annual shortage cost, and annual purchasing cost, or

$$T_d = T_s + D \times P \qquad\qquad\qquad (B.4)$$

for the back-order model, and

$$T_d = T + D \times P \qquad\qquad\qquad (B.5)$$

for the no-shortage model. Cost T_s is defined by Eq. (C.6) in Appendix C of this chapter, T is defined as the sum of annual holding costs and ordering costs, D is annual demand, P is purchase cost per unit of item, and $D \times P$ represents the annual purchasing cost.

Often suppliers offer a progression of discrete discounts to buyers, each discount corresponding to a larger minimum purchase quantity. To simplify presentation, assume no shortages, and assume ordering costs and carrying costs per unit per period are constant. Since these costs are not functions of price, the purchase price is not a factor in the determination of Q^*. It follows, therefore, that decreases in the purchase price of items do nothing but lower the vertical orientation of the total cost function. In other words, total inventory cost for any order quantity Q is less when the unit purchase cost is lower.

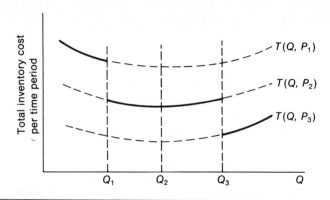

FIGURE B.3
Total Inventory Costs When Two Price Breaks Are Present

Assume in Fig. B.3 that a supplier will sell at price P_1, unless the buyer agrees to purchase in quantities of Q_1 or more units, in which case P_2 is the selling price. Similarly, if the buyer agrees to buy in quantities of Q_2 or more units, the lower price P_3 applies. If the objective is to minimize the total inventory cost per time period, then this objective is achieved when the order size is Q_2 units and the price is P_3. This action results in a total cost of D. The buyer will not purchase any more than Q_2 units since total cost will increase. Note that Q^*, the economic order quantity, is not permissible at price P_3 since $Q^* < Q_2$.

The result in this example cannot be generalized; that is, the lowest inventory cost will not always be associated with the policy of purchasing the minimum allowable quantity at the lowest price offered. In general, the minimum cost solution is found by first computing Q^*. (Remember that Q^* is independent of purchase price, provided that ordering cost and unit carrying cost remain the same.) Next, compute the total inventory cost for Q^* and the appropriate unit purchasing price for that order size, $T_d(Q^*, P^*)$. The only way in which total cost might be lower is if the buyer purchases the minimum quantity corresponding to a unit purchase price that is lower than P^*. Total costs under these lower-price alternatives must be compared with $T_d(Q^*, P^*)$ to determine the best policy.

ILLUSTRATION B.3

Consider a steel casing that has an annual demand of 2000 units. The cost per order is $90, and the annual inventory carrying rate is $1 per unit. The vendor of this part offers a quantity discount schedule as follows:

0 to 500 units	$18 per unit
501 to 700 units	16 per unit
701 to 1000 units	14 per unit
1001 and more units	13 per unit

There are three price breaks, occurring at quantities of 500, 700, and 1000 units, respectively. The EOQ (ignoring unit purchase price) is 600 units — this is left for you to verify.

The total cost incurred at the EOQ level is $32,600:

$$\text{Holding costs} = \frac{600}{2} \times \$1 = \$ \quad 300.00$$

$$\text{Ordering costs} = \frac{2000}{600} \times \$90 = \quad 300.00$$

$$\text{Purchase costs} = 2000 \times \$16 = \underline{\quad 32,000.00}$$

$$\text{total cost} \quad \underline{\$32,600.00}$$

Next, compute total cost at the $14-per-unit price level, and compare it with the EOQ level total cost:

$$\text{Holding costs} = \frac{701}{2} \times \$1 = \$ \quad 350.50$$

$$\text{Ordering costs} = \frac{2000}{701} \times \$90 = \quad 256.78$$

$$\text{Purchase costs} = 2000 \times \$14 = \underline{\quad 28,000.00}$$

$$\text{total cost} \quad \underline{\$28,607.28}$$

Since total cost declines if 701 units are purchased, this purchase volume dominates the EOQ level. We must see whether costs can be lowered further; we do so by checking the next price break level:

$$\text{Holding costs} = \frac{1001}{2} \times \$1 = \$ \quad 500.50$$

$$\text{Ordering costs} = \frac{2000}{1001} \times \$90 = \quad 179.82$$

$$\text{Purchase costs} = 2000 \times \$13 = \underline{\quad 26,000.00}$$

$$\text{total cost} \quad \underline{\$26,680.32}$$

Buying 1001 units results in the lowest total cost. This is the amount that should be purchased.   □

Appendix C

Derivation of the EOQ Back-Order Model

In the back-order model the decision variables are Q, the order quantity, and S, the maximum shortage. The order cost component is the same as in the classical EOQ model:

$$W_s = \left(\frac{D}{Q}\right) C_o. \tag{C.1}$$

Carrying cost per cycle is determined as in the classic model. It can be stated as

$$(Q - S)^2 \frac{C_h}{2D}. \tag{C.2}$$

When carrying cost is annualized (by multiplying by the number of cycles per period, D/Q), total annual carrying cost (H_s) becomes

$$H_s = (Q - S)^2 \frac{C_h}{2Q}. \tag{C.3}$$

The final component is the shortage cost, which is determined in a manner similar to that used for carrying cost. Shortage cost per cycle is given by (average number of units short) × (time short per cycle) × (shortage cost per unit per time period). It is stated as

$$\frac{S^2 C_s}{2D}. \tag{C.4}$$

Multiplying by the number of cycles, D/Q, gives the annual shortage cost C_s:

$$C_s = \frac{S^2 C_s}{2Q}. \tag{C.5}$$

Combining the three cost components, we can express the total variable cost T_s for this model as

$$T_s = C_o \left(\frac{D}{Q}\right) + (Q - S)^2 \frac{C_h}{2Q} + \frac{S^2 C_s}{2Q}. \tag{C.6}$$

Taking partial derivatives of Eq. (C.6), with respect to Q and S, and solving for the stationary point gives the optimal order and shortage quantities, Eqs. (B.2) and (B.3) of Appendix B of this chapter, respectively.

Questions

1. What is the primary function of inventory?

2. How is proper inventory management linked to the short-run liquidity of the firm? How is it linked to the long-run profitability of the firm?

3. What are the evils of carrying inventories that are excessive in relation to current sales?

4. Describe the disadvantage of underinvestment in inventories.

5. How do various inventory carrying or ordering costs affect decisions concerning the size of inventory to be carried?

6. What costs are associated with procurement of materials and with carrying inventories?

7. Discuss some of the problems of determining the variables that enter into the determination of the EOQ.

8. In a graph of cost-quantity inventory relationships, why is the total cost curve high at both low and high quantities and lower between them?

9. What are some limitations of the economic order quantity approach to the analysis of inventory problems?

10. The materials requirement planning model attempts to integrate the flow-through of inventory. Evaluate this statement and indicate the basic assumptions necessary to make this system an efficient operating procedure.

11. Discuss the JIT approach to inventory management.

12. What is the purpose of safety stock? Will the size of the safety stock be influenced by the firm's attitude toward risk? Why? How will a JIT system affect safety stock?

13. What is the A–B–C method?

14. What is the significance of inventory turnover ratios in testing the soundness of inventory investment policies?

15. In calculation of the turnover ratio, when might the use of an average of beginning and ending inventories lead to an inaccurate result?

16. Does the choice of an inventory valuation method affect the turnover ratio? Explain, using examples.

Problems

1.   The Brutus Manufacturing Company carries a wide assortment of items for its customers. One item is particularly popular. Wishing to keep its inventory under control, management selects this item to initiate its new problem of ordering only the optimal economic order quantity each time. From the following information, help them solve the problem.

Annual demand	160,000 units
Price per unit	$2.00
Carrying costs	$0.10 per unit, or 5% of value
Cost per order	$5.00

Fill in the missing amounts:

Number of orders	1	10	20	40	80	100
Size of order						
Average inventory						
Carrying costs						
Order costs						
Total costs						

Determine the optimal EOQ by inspection and by the use of the formula in Eq. (16.2).

2.   Vanessa's Bridal Shop stocks rolls of flowered ribbon. The annual demand reaches 2000 for these rolls. Each roll costs $10, and the order cost is $40 per order. Carrying costs are 10 percent of purchase price. The Bridal Shop is currently ordering on an optimal basis. The wholesaler, in an effort to shift some of its inventory to the Bridal Shop, points to the high ordering cost of $40 and suggests that orders be placed only once a year. As an inducement, the wholesaler offers Vanessa a 3 percent discount if the annual ordering policy is adopted. Evaluate this offer, and make a reasonable recommendation to accept or reject it. Show your calculations. If you reject the offer, what reasonable counteroffer might you make? (See Appendix B.)

3.   Using the following data, determine and discuss the sensitivity of EOQ, total inventory policy costs, and average investment to changes in cost and usage. Carrying cost is 5 percent of purchase price.

	Annual demand	Ordering costs	Price per unit
(a)	100,000	$5.00	$10.00
(b)	150,000	5.00	10.00
(c)	100,000	5.00	15.00
(d)	100,000	7.50	10.00

4.   The Cormick Industries Group had the following inventory balances during the year:

January 1	$25,000	July	$ 90,000
January	45,000	August	75,000
February	25,000	September	25,000
March	15,000	October	101,000
April	80,000	November	60,000
May	60,000	December	35,000
June	45,000		

Cost of goods sold = $360,000

Determine average inventory and inventory turnover based on beginning and closing balances, and compare the answer with a calculation based on a 13-point average. Explain the differences.

5.   Last year's sales of $15,000 were supported by an average inventory of $5000. The forecast for the coming year estimates sales of $25,000. Using the EOQ dollar approach, calculate the following:

(a) The implied ratio of ordering cost to holding cost

(b) The EOQ dollar amount

(c) The average inventory investment

6.   Last year's sales were $800,000 and the average inventory balance was $200,000. This year's sales are expected to be $1,000,000.

(a) What should be the average inventory balance, using the dollar-EOQ model?

(b) What should it be using the percent-of-sales approach?

(c) What should it be using a JIT approach?

(d) Which method is best? Discuss.

7.   Lyons Manufacturing Company followed an EOQ inventory policy. Over the years it found that the relation of ordering costs to holding costs was about 150/1. Sales last year were $19,500,000. The average sales growth over the last few years was 5.5 percent.

(a) If a dollar-EOQ model was followed, what should have been the year-end inventory level for last year?

(b) Determine the expected inventory value for next year-end using the dollar EOQ model.

8.   GHI Company forecasts sales for the period to be $200,000. Last period's sales were $150,000, and the beginning inventory balance was $25,000.

(a) What is the targeted turnover ratio if the beginning inventory balance for this period is $35,000?

(b) What is the targeted percentage of sales? Use the EOQ turnover equation to work this problem.

Appendix B Problems

1.   A company purchases a part that is a component of one of the assemblies it manufactures. This component is used at a uniform rate throughout the year, and the supplier delivers the entire lot at one time. The manufacturer finds it necessary to take the following factors into consideration when ascertaining the economic lot size:

consumption rate per year = 25,000 units,
cost of placing and receiving an order = $10,
cost of carrying 1 unit of inventory for 1 year = 20% of price,

price per unit =
$1 for lot sizes of 1 to 1999 units,
$0.50 for lot sizes of 2000 to 4999 units,
$0.30 for lot sizes of 5000 or more units.

(a) What is the economic order size at each of these prices?

(b) In what order quantity should the manufacturer purchase the part? What annual cost will this order quantity generate?

2.   Compute the reorder points, given the following information:

	(a)	(b)	(c)
Lead time	15 days	25 days	25 days
Cycle time	25 days	15 days	25 days
EOQ	694 units	417 units	694 units
Annual demand	10,000 units	10,000 units	10,000 units

Assume 360 days in the year.

3.   Stevenson Corporation sells a single product that has an annual demand of 75,000 units. As best can be determined, carrying costs per unit of this product amount to $0.01, and ordering costs are $60. Back-ordering cost per unit is estimated at $10 per unit. Price per unit is $100.

(a) What is the EOQ in units and in dollars?

(b) What is the maximum shortage quantity in units and dollars?

(c) How many orders are placed per year if optimal inventories are maintained?

(d) What is the average investment in inventory in dollars?

CHAPTER 17 □
Monitoring Inventory Balances

The predominant aim of inventory management is to keep inventory investments in line with targets (or budgets) so that resources are allocated efficiently and profit targets are realized. The previous chapter discussed the use of turnover ratios for measuring performance. This technique has serious deficiencies, for it is not able to answer the following questions: How do actual reported inventories compare with budgeted inventories? What factors have caused variations? Who or what is responsible for favorable or unfavorable variances? Is the product mix appropriate? The factors upon which answers to these questions may be based will be considered in this chapter through analysis of sales and cost of sales in the income statement, and of inventory levels in the balance sheet.

The importance of monitoring inventories is vividly indicated in the following excerpts about W. T. Grant, which were published in *Business Week* magazine (July 19, 1976):

> Grant was unable to keep track of its inventory. The company was reluctant to reduce inventories by taking markdowns because that reduced gross selling margins. . . . Headquarters did not know what was going on in the field. . . . It was easy for managers to manipulate their inventory. They would order goods and delay passing the invoice to [headquarters for payment]. This increased their ordering budget and understated the cost of sales.

> Further complicating the inventory problem was Grant's lack of a sales classification system to indicate what specific items were selling.

> Procedures were so lax that I am not sure how any reasonable estimate of inventory, accounts receivable or profit could be obtained.

The specific means of testing the reasonableness of inventory invest-ment in this chapter is the computation of inventory variances. *Variance analysis models* offer a significant improvement over turnover ratios in eval-uating inventory performance. Since the primary function of inventory is to decouple sales and production, it is beneficial to conduct the evaluation in terms of analysis of the components of gross profit — sales and cost of sales — and then translate this analysis into analysis of cash flow from operations.

The discussion begins with an examination of the traditional inven-tory turnover ratio, and its deficiencies. The discussion then proceeds through various levels of variance analysis, from one-way analysis to three-way analysis. These analyses take as given whatever accrual accounting pol-icy the firm's management follows with respect to inventories. For simplic-ity, analysis of these variances focuses on changes in gross profit. A subsequent section incorporates cash flows directly into the variance anal-ysis model. The final section reveals the superiority of variance techniques over turnover ratios.

Inventory Turnover Ratios

An inventory turnover ratio is used in one form or another in virtually every firm that has inventory. One advantage of the ratio is that it is easy to calculate. However, as will be shown later, this is also its chief disadvan-tage. Assume the data given in Table 17.1 (which are used throughout the chapter) correctly states inventory and cost of sales results for the year. Turnover ratios for *actual* and *budget* performance are easily determined by dividing cost of sales by average inventory. Since actual turnover of 1.06 times is less than budgeted performance of 1.31 times, there appears to be an inventory problem. However, the reasons for this problem are not read-ily apparent.

TABLE 17.1
Inventory Turnover Ratios

	Actual	*Budget*
Cost of sales:		
Beginning inventory	$337,000	$194,250
+ Purchases	159,750	117,500
	$496,750	$311,750
− Ending Inventory	208,750	111,750
Total	$288,000	$200,000
Average inventory	$272,875	$153,000
Turnover ratio	1.06	1.31

One-Way Variance Analysis

Comparative dollar analysis of inventory levels in the balance sheet and of cost-of-goods-sold amounts in the income statement are often used as a means of inventory analysis to augment turnover ratio analysis. The procedure is simple and sometimes provides satisfactory results. However, it can often be more misleading than informative. Percentages have significance only when the base remains stable and provides truly comparative data. Very often, a change in the base obscures facts that should be brought to light. The data given in Table 17.2 illustrates the point.

The cost percentages appear to be entirely unfavorable. A 20 percent increase in volume required a 44 percent increase in cost, and unit cost increased 20 percent. The analyst cannot conclude that all costs increased. Because some of the costs are fixed, the increase in volume could cause a decrease in fixed unit costs. Therefore the analyst must determine what part of the change in unit cost is attributable to volume and what part, if any, is the result of cost reduction. If the variable and fixed inventory costs are identified, the analyst may find that some costs have increased, as shown in Table 17.3.

According to the data in the table, a favorable **volume variance** has partially offset an increase in per-unit variable costs. This conclusion is apparent from looking at the $0.58-per-unit decrease in fixed costs.

A more reliable comparative analysis of inventories is gained by examining gross profit variances, which are shown in Table 17.4. Since gross profit equals the difference between sales and cost of sales, this **one-way analysis of variance** results in a fuller understanding of how inventories affect profits.

A cursory glance at the figures in Table 17.4 indicates deteriorating performance relative to budget. It appears that sales volume is up marginally, while costs are up significantly. If the increase in sales revenue is caused by higher selling prices, this result is less desirable than an increase arising from greater volume of sales. The market forces that have allowed an increase in selling price can react to drive the price down, resulting in excess inventories. Similarly (although not apparent in the data), cost de-

TABLE 17.2
Analysis of Cost of Sales

	Actual	Budget	Change Amount	%
Cost of goods sold	$288,000	$200,000	$88,000	44
Units	24,000	20,000	4,000	20
Cost per unit	$12.00	$10.00	$2.00	20

TABLE 17.3
Analysis of Fixed and Variable Cost of Sales

	Actual		Budget	
	Total	Per unit	Total	Per unit
Cost of sales:				
Variable	$158,000	$ 6.58	$ 80,000	$ 4.00
Fixed	130,000	5.42	120,000	6.00
Total	$288,000	$12.00	$200,000	$10.00

creases that result from increased sales volume are not as desirable as those achieved through more efficient use of labor, materials, and equipment. The former type of decrease may be temporary, and the latter type is more likely to be permanent.

Cost-of-sales analysis indicates that opening inventory has released $142,750 additional cost, relative to budget, from the balance sheet to the income statement. Since ending inventory exceeds budget by $97,000, this amount of additional cost has been *deferred* to the balance sheet, to be released next period. A large and unfavorable purchase variance represents the remaining variance in cost of sales. Do these cost-of-sales variances lead to the conclusion that the manager of inventory deserves criticism? This comparative analysis is unable to provide the answer.

The change in gross profit is the result of change in sales revenue and change in cost of sales. If a single product is sold, each of these sources is affected by two factors: price and volume. When, as usual, more than one product is sold, gross profit is also influenced by the product mix (discussed later in this chapter) because all products do not normally bear the same profit margins.

TABLE 17.4
One-Way Variance Analysis of Gross Profit

	Actual		Budget		Variance	
	Amount	%	Amount	%	Amount	%
Sales	$403,200	100.0	$400,000	100.0	$ 3,200	0.8
Cost of sales:						
Beginning inventory	$337,000	83.6	$194,250	48.5	$142,750	73.5
Purchases	159,750	39.6	117,500	29.4	42,250	36.0
Ending inventory	⟨208,750⟩	51.8	⟨111,750⟩	27.9	⟨97,000⟩	86.8
Total	$288,000	71.4	$200,000	50.0	$88,000	44.0
Gross profit	$115,200	28.6	$200,000	50.0	⟨$84,800⟩	⟨42.4⟩

Usually, the net change in gross profit results from an interplay of several factors, some causing increases and some causing decreases. An increase in selling price may be accompanied by an increase in volume, thereby causing a substantial increase in sales revenue. However, consistent with the downward-sloping demand curve facing most firms, an increase in selling price is often accompanied by a decrease in volume, with the result that sales revenue and gross profits may increase only a small amount or perhaps even decline. Knowledge of the elasticity of the demand curve is important for understanding the price-volume relationship.

Responsibility for gross profit changes varies. For example, whereas a sales manager may not be able to claim credit for sales revenue generated by price increases, he or she is more likely to be responsible for increases generated by volume. A production manager cannot be held responsible for cost increases and higher inventory caused by a drop in production due to lack of sales, but he or she can be charged with increases traceable to inefficiencies in production or excessive spending. Ideally, answers need to address how these variances affect operating cash flows. For simplicity, much of the discussion that follows in this chapter focuses on analysis of changes in gross profit. *Cash flows will be directly incorporated into the analysis in a later section.*

Two-Way Variance Analysis

The analysis of changes in gross profit can be better understood by examining changes in sales revenues and cost of sales such that the various influencing factors are isolated separately. As indicated earlier, three factors can affect sales and cost of sales: *price, volume,* and *mix.* For the present the complexities of mix are deferred, and it is assumed here that a single product is manufactured and sold.

If price and volume factors are to be separated,[1] two basic principles must be adhered to:

1. The volume factor must be held constant when one is determining the effect of a price change.

2. The price factor must be held constant when one is determining the effect of a change in volume.

---

[1]Some people argue that price and volume factors are contaminated by a joint variance and that is necessary to separately identify the joint effect. Although all cost accountants recognize the existence of the joint variance, most accountants disregard it because assigning responsibility for it and interpreting it are difficult. As will become clear shortly, variances are generally labeled as favorable or unfavorable. Whenever a joint variance is calculated, it is possible to have favorable pure price and pure volume variances and an unfavorable joint variance. Under such circumstances it is difficult to have much enthusiasm for the joint variance.

Application and explanation of these principles is given in the following illustration, which uses the information in Table 17.4.

ILLUSTRATION 17.1

(a) Analysis of Change in Sales Revenues

Assume that budgeted sales for a given year were 20,000 units at a $20 selling price, or a total of $400,000. Actual sales for the year of $403,200 were obtained by selling 24,000 units at price of $16.80 each. Under a horizontal form of analysis sales revenue variances can be calculated as shown in Table 17.5.

Two-way variance analysis provides obvious benefits over the one-way model. Interpretation is as follows, going from right to left in Table 17.5. Column (c) represents the budget, or 20,000 units to be sold at $20 each. Column (b) represents a *flexible* sales budget. It shows what sales dollars should be given actual sales volume and no change in the budgeted price. When compared with column (c), the $80,000 favorable variance is a result of selling 4000 more units than budgeted. Column (a) is total actual sales. The variance between columns (a) and (b) represents the effect of changing prices, relative to budget. Total sales variance, relative to budget, is the difference between columns (a) and (c). The favorable total sales variance is a result of lower selling prices stimulating sales volume. Has this pricing strategy resulted in more profits? Analysis of cost of sales provides some insight.

(b) Analysis of Change in Cost of Sales

The same principles of analysis used in relation to change in sales revenue are also applicable to analysis of change in cost of sales. Here, assume that

TABLE 17.5
Two-Way Variance Analysis of Revenues

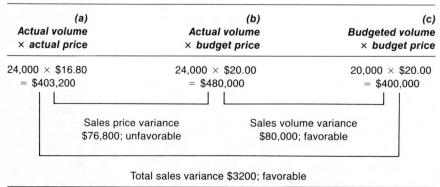

(a) **Actual volume × actual price**	(b) **Actual volume × budget price**	(c) **Budgeted volume × budget price**
24,000 × $16.80 = $403,200	24,000 × $20.00 = $480,000	20,000 × $20.00 = $400,000

Sales price variance $76,800; unfavorable   Sales volume variance $80,000; favorable

Total sales variance $3200; favorable

the budgeted cost of sales is 20,000 units at a unit cost of $10, or a total of $200,000. The actual cost of sales for 24,000 units sold is $288,000, or $12.00 per unit. Analysis of the $88,000 difference between actual and budget requires examination of purchases (or production) and the change between opening and closing inventory balances. Assume that quantities and unit costs for opening and closing inventories are as shown in Table 17.6.

TABLE 17.6
Two-Way Variance Analysis of Cost of Sales

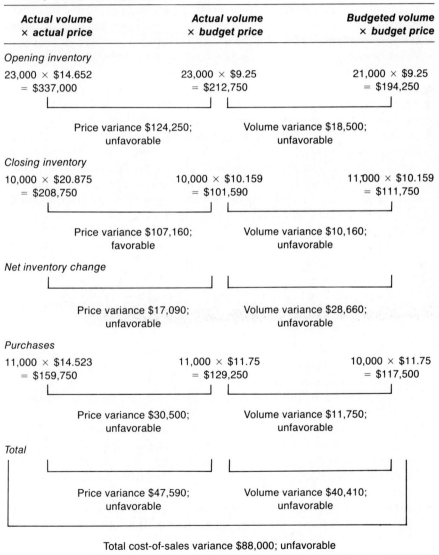

Actual volume × actual price	Actual volume × budget price	Budgeted volume × budget price
Opening inventory		
23,000 × $14.652 = $337,000	23,000 × $9.25 = $212,750	21,000 × $9.25 = $194,250
	Price variance $124,250; unfavorable	Volume variance $18,500; unfavorable
Closing inventory		
10,000 × $20.875 = $208,750	10,000 × $10.159 = $101,590	11,000 × $10.159 = $111,750
	Price variance $107,160; favorable	Volume variance $10,160; unfavorable
Net inventory change		
	Price variance $17,090; unfavorable	Volume variance $28,660; unfavorable
Purchases		
11,000 × $14.523 = $159,750	11,000 × $11.75 = $129,250	10,000 × $11.75 = $117,500
	Price variance $30,500; unfavorable	Volume variance $11,750; unfavorable
Total		
	Price variance $47,590; unfavorable	Volume variance $40,410; unfavorable

Total cost-of-sales variance $88,000; unfavorable

The analysis reveals that the cost-of-sales variance is relatively complex and requires careful interpretation. The change in inventory level contributes a net unfavorable variance of $45,750 — consisting of a net balance of $17,090 nonbudgeted price increases and $28,660 nonbudgeted volume changes released from the balance sheet (thus increasing the cost of sales). Purchases (or production) for the period were $42,250 more than budgeted, resulting in an additional cost-of-sales increase. Higher prices contribute $30,500 to the total purchase variance; the balance is due to a volume effect. The total unfavorable variance of $88,000 consists of $47,590 in price increases and $40,410 in volume changes.

Care must be exercised in interpreting opening and closing inventory variances. For example, with the price variance, whenever actual inventory exceeds (actual volume) × (budgeted price), an unfavorable variance results for opening inventory and a favorable variance results for closing inventory. The reason is as follows: The *opening inventory represents costs deferred to the balance sheet in the previous period* under the generally accepted accounting principles of accrual accounting. All these costs are released to the income statement in the present period. *Thus the higher prices incurred in the earlier period are now realized (in terms of profit determination — not cash flow) in the present period.*

The reverse situation occurs with closing inventories. The higher prices (relative to budget) embedded in ending inventory are not realized in the current period for calculating profits — but they can have a significant influence on cash flows if some or all of the purchases are paid for in the current period. Instead, these higher prices are deferred to the balance sheet and will be released to operations next period. Hence the favorable price variance for ending inventory will become an unfavorable price variance for opening inventory next period. Similar analysis applies to the volume variance.

(c) Analysis of Change in Gross Profit

When the sales analysis in Table 17.5 is combined with the cost analysis in Table 17.6, the influence of inventories and purchases on gross profit can be explained, as shown in Table 17.7.

A comparison of this summary with the one-way variance analysis of Table 17.4 reveals the two-way variance model to be more informative. The gross profit deficit from budget of $84,800 is caused by lower selling prices and higher (net) inventory and purchase prices. Higher-than-expected sales and purchase (production) volume offsets some of the unfavorable price effects. The change in inventory investment from its opening to closing balance has contributed about 52 percent [that is, ($142,750 − $97,000)/$88,000] of the total unfavorable cost of sales variance. This result simply means that more costs were released from the balance sheet's opening inventory than were deferred to it through ending inventory.

TABLE 17.7
Summary of the Two-Way Variance Analysis

	Price	Volume	Total
Sales	$ 76,800 U	$80,000 F	$ 3,200 F
Cost of sales:			
Opening inventories	$124,250 U	$18,500 U	$142,750 U
Purchases	30,500 U	11,750 U	42,250 U
Closing inventories	107,160 F	10,160 U	97,000 F
Total	$ 47,590 U	$40,410 U	$ 88,000 U
Gross profit	$124,390 U	$39,590 F	$ 84,800 U

Note: F represents favorable variance; U represents unfavorable variance.

The overall results could be due to management lowering selling prices in an attempt to obtain larger market share, to protect current market position, or to liquidate some inventories because of expected business slowdown. Whatever the underlying reason, the two-way analysis of variance allows managers to evaluate the impact of inventory and pricing decisions on performance (and cash flow, once the payment patterns for accounts receivable and accounts payable are known) better than they can with the one-way model.   □

Three-Way Variance Analysis

Most firms purchase (or produce) and sell more than one finished product and budget some given normal or standard combination of each to be sold. Because all products do not have the same profit margins, gross profit varies with a change in the proportion of each item produced and/or sold, that is, with the mix. One must then determine the influence of change in mix on the gross profit — and subsequently on cash flows.

If selling prices and costs remain constant, a shift in volume from less profitable to more profitable products increases the average gross profit per unit on all units sold and thereby improves profit. Conversely, shifts from more profitable to less profitable products lower the average gross profit per unit and cause profits to drop. Therefore the mix element must be brought into the analysis.

Building on the illustration in Table 17.7, assume that actual and budget product line information for revenues and costs is as given in Table 17.8. Also, assume that a periodic FIFO inventory procedure is used. It is noted from the budget that the average gross profit is $10 per unit and, as a percentage, is 50 percent of sales. As long as the unit sales of products X and Y remain in the ratio 1:1 (10,000:10,000), the average gross profit per unit (and as a percentage of sales) will remain the same. In this case, none

TABLE 17.8
Product Line Information

	Product X		Product Y		Total	
	Price	Amount	Price	Amount	Price	Amount
Actual						
Sales	$6.00	$90,000	$34.80	$313,200	$16.80	$403,200
Cost of sales	5.10	76,500	23.50	211,500	12.00	288,000
Gross profit	$0.90	$13,500	$11.30	$101,700	$ 4.80	$115,200
%	15.00		32.47		28.57	
Units		15,000		9000		24,000
Budget						
Sales	$8.00	$80,000	$32.00	$320,000	$20.00	$400,000
Cost of sales	5.50	55,000	14.50	145,000	10.00	200,000
Gross profit	$2.50	$25,000	$17.50	$175,000	$10.00	$200,000
%	31.25		54.69		50.00	
Units		10,000		10,000		20,000

Cost-of-sales data

	Product X			
	Actual		Budget	
	Units	Price	Units	Price
Opening inventory	11,000	$5.00	12,000	$5.50
Plus purchases	6,000	5.375	5,000	6.75
Minus closing inventory	2,000	5.375	7,000	6.393
Equals cost of sales	15,000	$5.10	10,000	$5.50

	Product Y			
	Actual		Budget	
	Units	Price	Units	Price
Opening inventory	12,000	$23.50	9,000	$14.25
Plus purchases	5,000	25.50	5,000	16.75
Minus closing inventory	8,000	24.75	4,000	16.75
Equals cost of sales	9,000	$23.50	10,000	$14.50

of the change in gross profit is caused by a **mix variance**. It is attributable entirely to a **quantity variance**. In Table 17.8, since the actual average gross profit of $4.80 is not equal to budgeted gross profit, a mix variance exists. Appendix B of this chapter summarizes the mix and quantity variance calculations.

TABLE 17.9
Three-Way Variance Analysis of Sales

Actual volume × actual price	Actual volume × budget price	Actual volume in budget % × budget price	Budget volume × budget price
Product X			
15,000 × $6 = $90,000	15,000 × $8 = $120,000	24,000 × 0.5 × $8 = $96,000	10,000 × $8 = $80,000
Price variance $30,000 U	Mix variance $24,000 F	Quantity variance $16,000 F	
Product Y			
9000 × $34.80 = $313,200	9000 × $32 = $288,000	24,000 × 0.5 × $32 = $384,000	10,000 × $32 = $320,000
Price variance $25,200 F	Mix variance $96,000 U	Quantity variance $64,000 F	
Total			
$403,200	$408,000	$480,000	$400,000
Price variance $4,800 U	Mix variance $72,000 U	Quantity variance $80,000 F	

Total sales variance $3200 F

Note: F represents favorable variance; U represents unfavorable variance.

Table 17.9 details the calculation of the sales price, mix, and quantity variances for products X and Y. **Three-way analysis** of these variances provides valuable insight into the influence of sales on cost of sales and inventory — and thus on the change in *operating cash flows*.

These variances (relative to budget) reveal that the 25 percent price reduction in product X stimulated its sales volume by 50 percent. A 9 percent price increase for product Y reduced its volume by 10 percent. The result of these pricing decisions was a shift in sales mix from product Y to product X, resulting in a net $72,000 unfavorable mix variance. The favorable quantity variance of $80,000 is the result of selling 4000 units more than budgeted times the weighted average budgeted price of $20 per unit.

The influence of the sales effort on cost of sales requires analysis of opening and closing inventory positions and purchases. These items are shown in Table 17.10; the analysis uses a three-way analysis of variance.

TABLE 17.10
Three-Way Variance Analysis of Cost of Sales

Actual volume × actual price	Actual volume × budget price	Actual volume in budget % × budget price	Budget volume × budget price

Opening Inventory

Product X

| 11,000 × $5 = $55,000 | 11,000 × $5.50 = $60,500 | 23,000 × $12/21$ × $5.50 = $72,285 | 12,000 × $5.50 = $66,000 |

| | Price variance $5500 F | Mix variance $11,785 F | Quantity variance $6285 U |

Product Y

| 12,000 × $23.50 = $282,000 | 12,000 × $14.25 = $171,000 | 23,000 × $9/21$ × $14.25 = $140,465 | 9000 × $14.25 = $128,250 |

| | Price variance $111,000 U | Mix variance $30,535 U | Quantity variance $12,215 U |

Total

| | Price variance $105,500 U | Mix variance $18,750 U | Quantity variance $18,500 U |

Total opening inventory $142,750 U

Closing inventory

Product X

| 2000 × $5.375 = $10,750 | 2000 × $6.393 = $12,785 | 10,000 × $7/11$ × $6.393 = $40,680 | 7000 × $6.393 = $44,750 |

| | Price variance $2035 U | Mix variance $27,895 U | Quantity variance $4070 U |

Product Y

| 8000 × $24.75 = $198,000 | 8000 × $16.75 = $134,000 | 10,000 × $4/11$ × $16.75 = $60,910 | 4000 × $16.75 = $67,000 |

| | Price variance $64,000 F | Mix variance $73,090 F | Quantity variance $6090 U |

Total

| | Price variance $61,965 F | Mix variance $45,195 F | Quantity variance $10,160 U |

Total closing inventory $97,000 F

TABLE 17.10 (Cont.)

Actual volume × actual price	Actual volume × budget price	Actual volume in budget % × budget price	Budget volume × budget price
Purchases			
Product X			
6000 × $5.375 = $32,250	6000 × $6.75 = $40,500	11,000 × 5/10 × $6.75 = $37,125	5000 × $6.75 = $33,750

Price variance $8250 F   Mix variance $3375 U   Quantity variance $8375 U

Product Y			
5000 × $25.50 = $127,500	5000 × $16.75 = $83,750	11,000 × 5/10 × $16.75 = $92,125	5000 × $16.75 = $83,750

Price variance $43,750 U   Mix variance $8375 F   Quantity variance $8375 U

Total

Price variance $35,500 U   Mix variance $5000 F   Quantity variance $11,750 U

Total purchases $42,250 U

Summary

Product	Price variance	Mix variance	Quantity variance
X	$11,715 F	$19,485 U	$13,730 U
Y	90,750 U	50,930 F	26,680 U
Total	$79,035 U	$31,445 F	$40,410 U

Total cost of sales variance: $88,000 U

Note: F is favorable variance; U is unfavorable variance.

The analysis indicates that the $88,000 unfavorable cost-of-sales variance is largely caused by unit price variations from budget. The release of the prior period's price increases from the balance sheet to the income statement, through the opening inventory, contributes $105,500 additional cost in this period's cost of sales. On the other hand, higher ending inventories have deferred some of this period's higher purchase costs to the balance sheet. These costs will be released to the income statement next period, since this period's closing inventories become opening inventories next period.

Similar reasoning applies to the mix and quantity variances. Not only are total opening inventories larger than budget, but the actual proportion of each product to its budgeted proportion is out of line with the budget. The more expensive product Y represents about 52 percent of opening units, whereas it was budgeted to represent only 43 percent. Thus a disproportionate amount of cost is released to the income statement through the opening inventory than was expected. This cost is represented by the unfavorable mix variance for opening inventories. And since opening inventories are larger than budgeted, in terms of total units, an unfavorable quantity variance exists.

Similar analyses of purchases and closing inventories lead to the overall conclusion that although both products have contributed to the unfavorable cost of sales variance, product Y has contributed about three times as much as has product X. The most significant problem area concerns the acquisition cost of product Y. If it can be brought into line, gross profit should quickly improve. Of almost equal importance is the physical quantity of inventory for product Y. The sales strategy (either explicitly or implicitly) appears to be to move the sales emphasis from product Y to product X. The closing inventory is heavily weighted in favor of product Y. Close attention needs to be paid to this product. A cutback in purchases is required to bring product Y back into line.

The overall impact of inventory management on gross profit can be determined by netting the sales variances against the component-cost-of-sales variances, as shown in Table 17.11. A comparison of this three-way product-line analysis with the two-way aggregate analysis summarized in Table 17.7 reveals significant differences in the variances. Although the total variance is the same, the allocation of variances differs. This difference is caused by the manner in which actual volume × budget price vari-

TABLE 17.11
Three-Way Variance Analysis of Gross Profit by Product Line

	Price	Mix	Quantity	Total
Sales	$ 4,800 U	$72,000 U	$80,000 F	$ 3,200 F
Opening inventory	$105,500 U	$18,750 U	$18,500 U	$142,750 U
Purchases	35,500 U	5,000 F	11,750 U	42,250 U
Closing inventory	61,965 F	45,195 F	10,160 U	97,000 F
Total	$ 79,035 U	$31,445 F	$40,410 U	$ 88,000 U
Gross margin	$ 83,835 U	$40,555 U	$39,590 F	$ 84,800 U

Note: F is favorable variance; U is unfavorable variance.

ances are calculated in each case. The three-way model ensures correct allocations since it uses disaggregated data (product-line data). The two-way analysis is not concerned with the influence of product mix on inventory investment, sales, or profits, with the result that it combines price and mix variances. This result is undesirable from an analysis-and-control perspective since different people are responsible for each of these variances.

The interpretation of results in Table 17.11 is that total beginning inventories exceed their budget levels by $142,750. Since beginning inventories are released to cost of sales at the start of the period, cost of sales is increased by this amount over budget. In the case of total closing inventories, the amount is greater than budget by $97,000. Thus, $97,000 more cost, relative to budget, is deferred to the balance sheet. This manipulation has a short-term favorable impact since all this cost will be released to the income statement at the start of the next period. The unfavorable purchase variance of $42,250 arises primarily from the fact that more of product X was purchased than budgeted and the purchase price of product Y increased in excess of 52 percent of the budget price (see Table 17.10).

Table 17.11 highlights unfavorable performance relative to budget. The problem is attributable mainly to nonbudgeted cost increases, since total mix and quantity variances largely offset each other. Management has been unable to offset these cost increases with selling price increases.

Incorporating Cash Flows

The significance of variance analysis is that it directly focuses attention on problem areas. The previous examples have concentrated analysis on gross profit variances by analyzing sales and cost of sales. The analysis indicates that one must analyze opening and closing inventories and purchases to understand the impact of inventory management on profits. Ending inventories are shown to simply represent *deferred expenses* (in an accrual accounting framework). This feature should come as no surprise, since it has been discussed in previous chapters. *Cash outflows are incurred for inventory investment when accounts payable are paid, and until the inventory is sold and collections of accounts receivable are made, there is no cash inflow.* Management, therefore, needs to finance this excess investment by managing the cash conversion cycle, as discussed in Chapter 6. This financing is accomplished by stretching accounts payable, using existing lines of credit, or negotiating a new loan.

The gross profit variance analysis can be converted to a cash flow analysis simply by identifying changes in accounts receivable and accounts payable balances, relative to budget. As discussed in Chapter 6, cash flow from operations is defined as (net income) + (depreciation) ± (changes in accounts receivable, accounts payable, inventories, prepaids, and accruals).

TABLE 17.12
Cash Flow Analysis of Gross Margin

(a) Receivables and payables data (assumed)

	Actual	Budget
Opening receivables	$44,800	$50,000
Closing receivables	60,600	55,000
Opening payables	34,500	35,000
Closing payables	42,800	45,000

(b) Variance analysis

	Change in		Variance
	Actual	Budget	
Accounts receivable	$ 15,800 U	$ 5,000 U	$10,800 U
Accounts payable	8,300 F	10,000 F	1,700 U
Inventory change (Table 17.10)*	128,250 F	82,500 F	45,750 F
			$33,250 F
Gross margin (Table 17.11)			84,800 U
Gross margin cash flow variance			$51,550 U

Note: U is unfavorable variance; F is favorable variance.
*[Opening inventory variances + closing inventory variances] × (−1)

Table 17.12 converts Table 17.11 from an accrual accounting gross income variance analysis to a cash flow analysis of gross margin variance.

Given the assumptions for changes in accounts receivable and accounts payable, analysis of *cash flow gross margin* indicates that problems are less severe than revealed by the accrual accounting analysis. The variances arising from receivable and payable balances should be analyzed by using the variance models discussed in Chapter 14. This analysis will allow management to understand how its various net working capital decisions and actions have affected resource allocations, profitability, and liquidity.

Importance of Variance Analysis Relative to Turnover Ratios

Analysis of the **inventory turnover ratio** by using a variance analysis framework reveals the weakness of the turnover ratio. The three-way variance analysis example illustrated in Table 17.11 shows an $88,000 unfavorable variance between actual and budgeted cost of sales, and ending inventories are $97,000 higher than the budget. Average inventories (using opening and closing balances) are $119,875 higher than budgeted.

Computation of *average* inventory turnover, shown in Table 17.13, is based on the cost-of-sales data from Table 17.10. Total turnover shows a

TABLE 17.13
Variance Analysis of Turnover Ratios

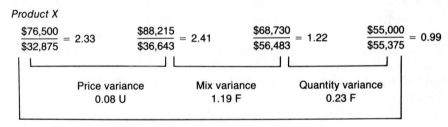

Actual turnover	Actual turnover restated in budget prices	Actual quantities in budgeted % × budget prices	Budget turnover
Total			
$\dfrac{\$288,000}{\$272,875} = 1.06$	$\dfrac{\$208,965}{\$189,143} = 1.10$	$\dfrac{\$240,411}{\$157,170} = 1.53$	$\dfrac{\$200,000}{\$153,000} = 1.31$

Price variance   Mix variance   Quantity variance
0.04 U   0.43 U   0.22 F

Total variance 0.25 U

Product X			
$\dfrac{\$76,500}{\$32,875} = 2.33$	$\dfrac{\$88,215}{\$36,643} = 2.41$	$\dfrac{\$68,730}{\$56,483} = 1.22$	$\dfrac{\$55,000}{\$55,375} = 0.99$

Price variance   Mix variance   Quantity variance
0.08 U   1.19 F   0.23 F

Total variance 1.34 F

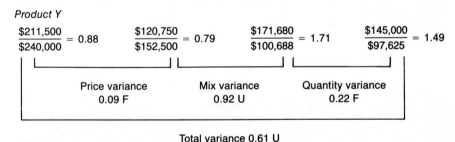

Product Y			
$\dfrac{\$211,500}{\$240,000} = 0.88$	$\dfrac{\$120,750}{\$152,500} = 0.79$	$\dfrac{\$171,680}{\$100,688} = 1.71$	$\dfrac{\$145,000}{\$97,625} = 1.49$

Price variance   Mix variance   Quantity variance
0.09 F   0.92 U   0.22 F

Total variance 0.61 U

Note: Numerators are cost of sales; denominators are average inventory. For instance, Product Y's "Actual turnover restated in budget prices" of 0.79 = ($171,000 + $83,750 − $134,000 = $120,750) ÷ ([$171,000 + $134,000]/2 = $152,500). Also, F is favorable variance; U is unfavorable variance.

decrease from the budgeted level of 1.31 times to an actual figure of 1.06 times — indicating poor performance. This result translates into excess average inventory of $53,028, assuming that the budget turnover figure is appropriate. This figure is calculated as follows: (actual average inventory) − (what actual average inventory should be so that turnover is 1.31), or ($272,875 − $288,000/1.31). The causes of the declining turnover ratio can be pinpointed by casting the turnover ratio into a three-way variance analysis format. The numerators in these calculations represent cost of sales; the denominators represent average inventory amounts.

Interpretation of Table 17.13 is as follows: Increased sales quantities favorably influenced inventory turnover, both in total and at the product level. However, the sales shift from the more expensive product Y to the less expensive product X has caused actual turnover performance to fall considerably short of budget expectations for product Y and in total (see the mix variances). Price changes have resulted in a decrease in the turnover ratio in total and for product X. The turnover ratio indicates favorable price performance is associated with product Y. (Previous analysis indicates otherwise, which makes the turnover ratio a suspect technique.)

The relationship between these turnover calculations and the cost-of-sales dollar variances summarized in Table 17.11 is shown in Table 17.14. In terms of overall analysis the data summarized in Table 17.14 shows that although the price variance is the most significant variance in dollar terms, it has a minimal effect on total inventory turnover. At the product-line level, price (cost) increases have contributed to improved turnover performance for product Y (see Table 17.13), and price (cost) decreases have caused deteriorating turnover performance for product X (see Table 17.13).

These relationships are perverse. At the aggregate level an unfavorable turnover variance accompanies an unfavorable price variance, as one would expect. As mentioned earlier, the mix variance is the primary factor influencing the turnover ratio, contributing negatively to product Y and total inventories and favorably to product X. The shift in sales mix from

TABLE 17.14
Joint Variance–Turnover Analysis of Inventories

	Total		Product X		Product Y	
	$	T/O*	$	T/O*	$	T/O*
Budgeted cost of sales	$200,000	1.31	$55,000	0.99	$145,000	1.49
Price variance	79,035 U	0.04 U	11,715 F	0.08 U	90,750 U	0.09 F
Mix variance	31,445 F	0.43 U	19,484 U	1.19 F	50,930 F	0.92 U
Quantity variance	40,410 U	0.22 F	13,731 U	0.23 F	26,680 U	0.22 F
Actual cost of sales	$288,000	1.06	$76,500	2.33	$211,500	0.88

Note: F is favorable variance; U is unfavorable variance. Add unfavorable variances and subtract favorable variances.

*T/O means turnover.

the expensive product Y to the cheaper product X has resulted in significantly increased investment in product Y and lower investment in product X relative to budget. Unfortunately, increased sales quantities were not sufficient to overcome the unfavorable product mix influence on the turnover calculation.

An important benefit of this comparison should be apparent. Although turnover ratios are easy to compute, they provide relatively little useful information, other than at a gross level for planning aggregate inventory, as discussed in the previous chapter. For example, price variance is the most significant factor contributing to the difference between budgeted cost of sales and actual sales in Table 17.14. However, price variance plays an insignificant role in explaining the turnover variance. An unfavorable contribution of 0.04 to the turnover ratio is insignificant and does not warrant management's attention. The $79,035 unfavorable price variance, representing 90 percent of the difference between actual and budgeted cost of sales, most certainly requires management's attention.

Two other bothersome observations of the turnover ratio, as shown in Table 17.14, are that (1) unfavorable dollar variances are generally aligned with favorable turnover variances and vice versa (the only exception is the total price variance), and (2) the reconciliation of change in the turnover ratio (identifying the impact of price, mix, and quantity on the ratio) fails to identify the most significant dollar variance. The problems identified with the turnover ratio should be sufficient to cause management serious concerns about its use.

Summary

This chapter extends the analysis of inventory begun in the previous chapter. The extension analyzes variances to budget, starting with turnover ratios calculations and then introduces variance analysis models.

One-way variance analysis offers little information for management to use. It compares actual performance with budget without being able to provide much direction about the cause of differences.

Two-way variance analysis separates the total variance into price and volume components. This analysis allows management to begin to assess the impact of changing product and factor market environments, relative to budget, on performance. A problem with this model is that a changing product mix is not identified. In fact, it is hidden in the so-called price variance.

Three-way variance analysis overcomes this problem. This model identifies the true price, mix, and quantity variances and allows management to assign responsibility where it belongs.

The chapter concludes with a discussion of the inadequacy of the much-used inventory turnover ratio. Turnover ratios fail to adequately pinpoint problem areas, as is shown by a comparison of the dollar variance model with an inventory turnover variance model. Variance analysis of dollar amounts shows the areas where management needs to direct its attention.

Key Concepts

Inventory turnover ratio	Quantity variance
Mix variance	Three-way variance analysis
One-way variance analysis	Two-way variance analysis
Price variance	Volume variance

Appendix A

Analysis of Variance Using Prior Year's Data

In many cases analysis is made of a given year's sales or cost of sales with their counterparts in the prior year rather than with their budgeted amounts for the year in question. The analysis is essentially the same as the one conducted in this chapter. All that needs to be done is to substitute the prior year's volume and price for the budget data.

Sometimes, the required analysis is made slightly more complicated when the prior year's figures are used as the basis of comparison because one does not have information concerning unit prices or the number of units sold for either of the years in question. For example, assume that the sales data are as follows:

1st year	$400,000
2nd year	403,200
Change	3,200

The required analysis can still be made if either the percentage of change in the selling price or the percentage of change in the sales volume can be determined.

Assume, first, that during year 2 the selling price was 1.18 percent lower than in year 1. With this information the sales revenue of year 2 can be converted into year 1 selling prices as follows:

$$\frac{\text{Year 2 sales at year 2 prices}}{1 + \text{decimal change in price}} = \frac{\$403,200}{0.9882} = \$408,000.$$

This calculation eliminates the effect of the 1.18 percent decrease in selling price. It is now know that if the price had not decreased, sales revenue in year 2 would have been $408,000. With this figure one can determine the effect of the price change and the volume change, as shown in Table A.1.

TABLE A.1
Two-Way Variance Analysis

Year 2 sales × year 2 prices	Year 2 sales × year 1 prices	Year 1 sales × year 1 prices
$403,200	$408,000	$400,000

Price volume $4800; unfavorable   Volume variance $8000; favorable

Next, assume that the price decrease of 1.18 percent is unknown but that the volume of sales increased by 2 percent in year 2. The effect of any price change must be eliminated by converting the sales revenue of year 2 into year 1 selling prices. Since the volume in year 2 was 2 percent greater than in year 1, the sales revenue in year 2 would have been 2 percent higher than the sales revenue in year 1 if the price had not changed. The year 2 sales volume at year 1 selling price would have been $408,000, computed as follows:

(Year 1 sales at year 1 prices) × (1 + decimal change in volume)
= $400,000 × 1.02 = $408,000.

With year 2 sales converted to year 1 selling prices, the revenue changes from price and volume factors can be determined as before.

This model can also be used to assess the influences of inflation on the firm. By separating price effects from volume effects, management is able to determine whether any real growth has occurred.

Appendix B
Explanation of Mix and Quantity Variances

An explanation of the mix and quantity variances can best be described by using the sales data of Table 17.8. Assume that actual and budgeted quantities are as given in Table B.1.

A two-way variance analysis model calculates the volume variance as the sum of the differences between actual and budget units times the budget price for each product. For example, the total volume variance for this example is $8000. It is found as follows:

$$\$8(15,000 - 10,000) + \$32(9000 - 10,000) = \$8,000.$$

The separation of the volume variance into its mix and quantity components requires that the total actual number of units be allocated over the product lines in their budget proportions, as in Table B.2. The comparison of columns (1) and (2) by product line allows a mix variance to be calculated. A quantity variance results from analysis of columns (2) and (3) (either by product line or in total, it does not matter).

The original budget, column (3), forecasts 20,000 total units. Since 24,000 units were actually sold, column (2) effectively restates the budget in terms of actual units sold by maintaining the same proportional quantity of each product to the total quantity. Thus the quantity variance is as follows:

X	$ 8(12,000 − 10,000)
Y	32(12,000 − 10,000)
Total	$80,000 favorable

TABLE B.1
Sales Data

Product	Actual	%	Budget	%	Budgeted sales price
X	15,000	62.5	10,000	50	$ 8.00
Y	9,000	37.5	10,000	50	32.00
Total	24,000	100.0	20,000	100	$20.00

TABLE B.2
Actual and Budgeted Quantities

Product	(1) Actual units	(2) Actual total units in budgeted proportions	(3) Budget units
X	15,000	12,000	10,000
Y	9,000	12,000	10,000
Total	24,000	24,000	20,000

Another way to look at this variance is to multiply the 4000 difference in units sold versus budget by the weighted average selling price of $20, that is, 4000 [(0.5 × $8) + (0.5 × $32)] = $80,000.

The mix variance abstracts from any change in total units. It is concerned with the actual proportion of each product to total units, compared with actual total units allocated to each product in budget proportions. The different proportions between actual and budget represent the change in product mix:

X	$ 8(15,000 − 12,000)
Y	32(9,000 − 12,000)
Total	$72,000 unfavorable

Although this explanation has used but two products, three or more products can readily be incorporated. The logic used to compute the variances is the same.

Questions

1.   What does a one-way variance analysis show?

2.   How are price and volume variances calculated?

3.   What is meant by the term *mix*? How does it affect inventory analysis?

4.   Explain the difference between a quantity variance and a mix variance.

5.   What is meant by the expression "unfavorable price variance" for (a) sales, (b) closing inventory, and (c) purchases?

6.   Cost of sales has a price variance of $10,000 above the revised budget amount. Is this variance favorable or unfavorable? Why?

7.   When should the three-way variance analysis be employed in preference to the two-way analysis?

8.   What is the usefulness of a three-way variance analysis technique for analyzing inventory turnover?

Problems

1.   Given the budgeted and actual sales information in Table 17.15, calculate and discuss the gross profit variance, using a one-way variance analysis.

TABLE 17.15
Sales Data

	Budget		Actual	
Sales	$250,000	100%	$185,000	100%
Beginning inventory		32%		28%
Purchases		27%		32%
Ending inventory		40%		35%

2.   Assume that budgeted sales for the year were 10,000 units at a price of $10 per unit. Actual sales turned out to be 12,000 units at $8.50 per unit. Calculate the total sales variance, sale price variance, and sales volume variance.

3.   Perform a two-way variance analysis of cost of sales for the information given in Table 17.16. Management values inventory with LIFO.

TABLE 17.16
Cost of Sales

	Actual	Budget
Sales volume	20,000 units	18,000 units
Purchases	15,000 units	13,500 units
Closing inventory	14,000 units	15,000 units
Purchase price per unit	$11.50	$11.25
Opening inventory price per unit	$12.00	$11.00

4. The actual and budgeted ending inventory amounts for products X and Y are as follows:

Actual X	$22,000 and 18,000 units
Budgeted X	$20,000 and 16,000 units
Actual Y	$14,000 and 15,000 units
Budgeted Y	$15,000 and 16,000 units

Determine the price variance, mix variance, quantity variance, and total variance for the ending inventory.

5. The unit sales price for widgets was $10 actual and $12 budget; for gadgets it was $5 actual and $5 budget. Actual sales of widgets was 10,000 units, whereas 9500 units were budgeted. Gadgets had actual sales of 12,000 units, whereas they had a budget of 9500 units. Compute the price, mix quantity, and volume variances for widgets and gadgets.

6. The data in Table 17.17 has been taken from the company's records. Management uses FIFO inventory accounting procedures.

 (a) Calculate a two-way variance report, showing revenues, cost of sales, and gross margin.

 (b) Calculate a cash flow analysis of gross margin (see Table 17.12 for an example).

TABLE 17.17
Data from Company Records

	Budget	Actual
Sales	100 units	90 units
Price per unit	$10	$15
Beginning inventory	70 units	80 units
Price per unit	$8	$12
Ending inventory	60 units	75 units
Price per unit	$?	$?
Purchases	90 units	85 units
Price per unit	$7.50	$12.50
Accounts receivable:		
Beginning	$500	$550
Ending	$700	$600
Accounts payable:		
Beginning	$400	$500
Ending	$350	$510

7. Use the data below to explain the variance in the period's gross profit.

	Actual	Budget
Sales volume	$350,000	$300,000
Beginning inventory	107,500	105,000
Purchases	157,500	120,000
Ending inventory	140,000	150,000

8. The Wentworth Company had the following sales for the month of June.

	Actual	Budget
Sales units	25,000	30,000
Price per unit	$14.00	$10.00

Calculate the total sales, price, and volume variances. Discuss the results.

9. The Wentworth Company, Problem 8, had the following cost of sales for the month of June. Prepare a two-way variance analysis. Inventory is valued using LIFO.

	Actual		Budget	
	Units	Price/unit	Units	Price/unit
Sales	25,000		30,000	
Beginning inventory	21,500	$5.00	26,250	$4.00
Purchases	21,000	7.50	20,000	6.00
Ending inventory	17,500	5.00	16,250	4.00

10. Assume the Wentworth Company, Problems 8 and 9, values its inventory using FIFO. Calculate revenue, cost of sales, and gross margin variances.

11. Using the Wentworth Company's situation and data of Problem 10, calculate and discuss the price and volume variances of the actual and budget turnover ratios.

PART V □
Summary

CHAPTER 18 □
A Summary

Management of liquidity is usually viewed as a series of interesting and vital assets and/or liability groupings and analyses. Clear-cut objectives are usually missing. The reason for this shortcoming is that the linkages are fully understood neither by practitioners nor by theorists. Most studies of this problem have relied on some variation of a constrained mathematical model. Much work still needs to be done to derive a meaningful valuation model that explicitly incorporates liquidity objectives.

The purpose of this chapter is to briefly summarize the discussion of economic foundations, techniques of liquidity analysis, and management of various assets and liabilities that influence corporate liquidity. These three areas represent the essential ingredients in determining a cohesive strategy for managing liquidity that is consistent with creating value for shareholders.

Economic Foundations

The theory of finance states that the objective of the firm is to maximize shareholders' wealth. Such a statement assumes that risk can be quantified and (possibly) expressed as the effective rate to discount returns over time as in the residual income (net-present-value) model. The usual assumption employed with this model is that resources flow freely between firms so as to maximize returns for the entire economic system. In other words, the theory assumes perfect market conditions.

In the real world of the competitive firm the classical perfect-market assumptions do not prevail. Resources used by the firm are classified as fixed or variable, depending on the time frame. For instance, liquidity in the immediate time is fixed, whereas it is variable in the short-run or the long-run time dimension. It is the immediate and short-run dimensions that are important for liquidity. Management must recognize the existence of conditions that limit its ability to reach a desired wealth-maximizing state because of liquidity needs.

Both the desired state and the liquidity level are affected by the firm's imperfect input and output markets. Market participants have the ability to directly influence the pricing of outputs and/or inputs and thereby influence market demand and/or supply. Management must use whatever information is available to make decisions that attempt to enhance the firm's value. This objective requires managers to combine various factor inputs so that output is salable at a quantity and price that maximize economic profit — that is, to operate where marginal revenue equals marginal cost.

In an operational sense this maximizing output level must be prepared in a cost/benefit framework that explicitly incorporates the timing of cash flows. If management simply assumes that sufficient liquidity exists and is being properly managed, then the analysis most likely will be faulty, and actual results will not be as intended. Each expenditure, whether it be for factor inputs or capital requirements, represents an investment of funds and must be evaluated in terms of its contribution to satisfying the liquidity-constrained shareholder wealth maximization objective — or, in the economist's terms, maximization of economic profit.

Economic profit is defined as the difference between investment and expected future cash flows generated by that investment that is discounted at the opportunity cost of funds. As shown in Fig. 18.1, economic profit is the difference between the discounted terminal value I_n and the initial investment value I_o, where k is the appropriate opportunity cost of capital rate.

Obviously, for an economic profit to exist, the discounted terminal value of investment must exceed the initial investment. Whenever the reverse situation occurs (that is, an *economic loss* exists), it may simply be a matter of time before periodic *accounting profit* changes from profit to loss and eventual failure of the firm because of the lack of availability of liquid resources from the financial markets. The element of time is crucial to overall corporate objectives and managing the trade-off between liquidity

FIGURE 18.1
Investment and Profit Through Time

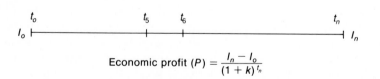

$$\text{Economic profit } (P) = \frac{I_n - I_o}{(1 + k)^{t_n}}$$

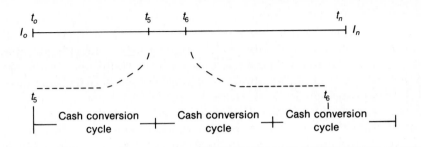

FIGURE 18.2
Cash Conversion Cycle versus Accounting Cycle

and profitability. Management simply cannot wait for the termination of the project to measure economic profit.

The time interval from t_5 to t_6 in Fig. 18.1 can be thought of as the usual annual accounting period. This period is chosen for estimating performance and satisfying reporting requirements both internally and externally. The time dimension has little relationship to the production-sales pattern (operating and cash conversion cycles) of the firm. The relationship between the cash conversion cycle and the annual accounting reporting period is stylized in Fig. 18.2.

Annual accounting profit can only estimate the resultant profit from approximately two and one-half cash conversion cycles, as shown in Fig. 18.2. Since accounting profit is determined by following generally accepted accounting principles, these profits do not fully account for all opportunity costs. If anything, these accounting profits overstate true economic profits, since adjustments are not made for either inflation or increase in value because of other market conditions.

Note that operations during any cycle are highly dependent on (1) the composition of the investments and (2) the time dimension. Some of these investments are variable and may be easily withdrawn from the process, while other investments are completely fixed or locked into the production-sales process and become available for alternative use only at the end of the process. The appropriate mixture of fixed and variable investments is determined by the technological rules of the production-sales process. If management finds it necessary to disrupt the process, operating efficiency can be severely damaged, with the result that the recovery values of many of the investments (such as receivables, inventories) may become but a small fraction of their original value. If management has time to change some of its constraining conditions, then liquidity is of lesser concern and profit is the more demanding objective. However, while profits can be viewed as an accumulation over time, liquidity must be viewed as some minimum amount of liquid resources at each moment in time.

The lack of liquidity supply, relative to liquidity demand, is the most common reason for disrupting the cycle. Each cycle involves a certain amount of time, and within this time parameter management invests most of its funds into fixed or quasi-fixed investments. Unfortunately, the obligations of the firm do not always match its revenue-deriving operations. The firm's suppliers demand payment according to the terms of the purchase contract. Should these demands exceed the existing supply at the current time, the firm runs the risk of insolvency and eventual bankruptcy.

If the demands at the present time can be temporarily satisfied, management has a number of options to resolve liquidity problems. Additional time provides management with flexibility to adjust the firm's financial position and scale of operations so as to reduce the risk of liquidity shortfall. In other words, within a confined operating structure there exist some variable inputs that, when combined in various proportions with fixed inputs, result in different levels of output and sustainable growth. Understanding the relationship between sale of this output and sustainable growth is crucial. Thus management must make every effort to understand both the endogenous factors (such as asset and employee capabilities, debt capacity) and the exogenous factors (such as product demand conditions) that affect wealth-maximizing decisions.

In the long run, where time is not a restriction, management can vary any of the factors involved in production and sales. In this way attention can be diverted from the liquidity objective to the economic profit objective.

Liquidity Analysis

The traditional historical accounting-based balance sheet and income statement are used to summarize the economic activity of the firm during the immediate and short-run time dimensions. Many ratios purporting to explain the economic activity are derived from these financial statements and are subsequently used to help management plan future direction. However, the balance-sheet and income-statement presentations of information are questionable with regard to their usefulness for understanding liquidity. It is not that the information is incorrect; rather, it is that the information presented in these financial statements is often inappropriate for analyzing many management problems.

The importance of managing cash and funds flow is apparent from Chapter 1's illustration "How to Go Broke" and by the frequent references throughout this book to management practices of W.T. Grant Company. The generation of accounting profits is not a guarantee of corporate solvency. Indeed, profits can generally be improved by adopting some alternative and generally accepted accounting principle. The quality of these earnings, however, is suspect. *Solvency and value depend on cash flow*, not some artificially created accounting profit figure that causes economic profits to lag further behind accounting profits.

Sustainability of the firm requires well thought-out strategic decisions pertaining to investments in both short-term and long-term assets, dividend policy, and the firm's capital structure. Often this objective means that conventional financing sources cannot be relied on. Inflation and increased economic instability may mean that some financing sources cannot be used — often at critical times when the firm needs them the most. As a result, managers must be more creative in their financing arrangements without causing perceptible changes in the risk of the firm. Hence they have used creative *asset-based financing* and *off-balance-sheet financing* as a means of raising needed capital funds. These financing alternatives cause assets that are important to the production-sales process to also become as important to the financing and liquidity needs of the company.

Management of Liquidity

Interactions between various assets and liability accounts are real and complex. Unfortunately, they are not very well understood from the perspective of their effects on the firm's value and on maximization of shareholders' wealth. Financial analysts use traditional ratios (such as current ratio and return on investment) calculated from the financial statements to reveal the complexities. The emphasis of the analysis is frequently on the firm's financial coverage in case of disaster. Under most conditions where disaster is imminent, such information is often useless because it is too late for management to use the information in an effort to avert bankruptcy.

In a world of certainty, management has no need for liquidity balances since all cash inflows and outflows are known. However, managerial decisions are usually made with imperfect information. Thus some level of liquid balances is required to reduce risk. A computer simulation study[1] indicates that an optimal liquidity level does exist and that this level contributes to increasing shareholder wealth. Thus in a practical operational sense management must try to find the optimal liquidity level.

What is needed is information that truly signals, with a sufficient lead time, whether the firm is likely to continue without serious disruptions. Consequently, emphasis must be placed on the firm's cash and funds flows, management's ability to manage inflation and sustain growth, and the creation of shareholder wealth.

The most critical asset in the liquidity portfolio is *cash*. Its function is to bridge the gap between cash receipts and cash disbursements. Thus forecasts must be made of expected requirements, and action points must be identified for investing surplus balances or securing additional funds to ensure uninterrupted operations. Understanding the float associated with

---

[1]A.K. Bhattacharya, "The Influence of Liquidity on Corporate Valuation," (Ph.D. dissertation, Arizona State University, 1984).

cash payments and receipts can increase the productivity of cash. This point is important, since cash per se is a nonearning asset and must be carefully monitored so that it does not accumulate unnecessarily in non-productive balances.

Various cash management models can be used to increase the pro-ductivity of cash. Regardless of the model chosen, though, improvement in cash management is likely to result, because the models, in one way or another, analyze the trade-off between holding costs (the opportunity costs associated with having too much cash on hand) and ordering costs (the transaction costs incurred to buy or sell cash). Theoretically, this result is consistent with the economist's profit-maximization argument.

The investment in *accounts receivable* depends on the credit and col-lection policy of the firm. Management uses credit terms as a pricing vari-able in the hope of influencing the demand curve so as to increase sales and profitability. However, profitability is of low quality if the sales are slow in being collected. The credit decision must be part of an integrative deci-sion based on marginal analysis that addresses changing sales, production, and inventory requirements, as well as spontaneous financing that may result.

Needless to say, if the credit decision results in too many resources being invested in accounts receivable, then less are available for allocation to other productive areas, such as expanding capacity or meeting liquidity needs. A number of credit evaluation models are available for the credit manager to use.

Monitoring of accounts receivable balances has come under increased scrutiny in recent years. The traditional techniques of receivables turnover, days sales outstanding, and aging schedules can provide incorrect conclu-sions about the status of receivable balances. If sales are not constant from one period to another, these techniques usually give incorrect indicators of the status of receivables. Techniques such as balance fractions, payment proportions, and variance analysis have emerged in recent years as supe-rior monitoring tools.

Inventory is the largest single asset in many firms. It is held in different forms to accomplish a number of objectives. As raw material, inventory provides for uninterrupted production; as work in process and finished goods, inventory recognizes the production constraint that the product cannot be produced instantaneously.

A critical question concerns the necessary level of inventory invest-ment. From the marketing manager's view no customer should be lost ow-ing to the firm's inability to fill an order. From the production manager's view inventory should facilitate production efficiency (allow production at the least costly level). From the accounting and financial view inventory represents a consumption of scarce resources and must be analyzed with marginal analysis. Clearly, compromises are made by the different factions within the firm, but if the scarce-resource allocation argument is ignored, the firm may be headed for serious financial difficulties.

It is the finance manager's job to convince other managers that investment in inventory must be consistent with the shareholder wealth objective. The economic order quantity (EOQ) model is a useful tool to help convey this message. Although EOQ is questionable as an operating tool — because of its restrictive assumptions and the existence of better models (such as just-in-time systems) — it does provide a useful conceptual approach for explaining the trade-offs involved in minimizing inventory investment while satisfying the shareholders' wealth-maximization objective.

Management of inventory from a financial perspective also requires analysis of price changes and knowledge of whether *cash flow* savings can result from using a particular valuation approach (for example, FIFO or LIFO inventory accounting). Depending on the direction of price changes, the valuation method, and the inventory balance, cash flow (economic profit) may be improved at the expense of accounting profit. Managers in other functional areas must be educated in the validity of this procedure. The discussion in Chapter 2, on the relationship between physical and monetary flows, is useful for explaining this process.

A critical role needs to be assumed by financial management in monitoring inventories. As many firms have discovered, too much inventory can result in significant disruptions within the company — employee layoffs, plant shutdowns, price competition, and so on — which may eventually result in liquidity problems too severe to overcome. The traditional techniques for monitoring inventories are the inventory turnover ratio or days sales in inventories. However, these techniques can provide faulty information. Analysis of variances between actual and budget inventory levels allows management to isolate problems and take corrective actions.

Management of *liabilities* plays an important role in the shareholders' wealth-maximization objective. As discussed earlier, that sufficient funds be available to meet obligations as they become due is critical. Failure to have sufficient funds can result in a wide range of responses from creditors. At one extreme, they may simply be annoyed that payment is not made on time. At the other extreme, they may bring court action that could result in the firm having to file bankruptcy, with eventual liquidation a possibility.

In recent years the importance of asset-based financing has emerged as a means of obtaining much needed funds. This form of financing is highly dependent on the form of collateral offered to secure the loan. In many cases asset-based financing allows more debt to be raised than does conventional unsecured financing, because the book values of the assets are carried at values much below market values. Thus management is able to monetize unrealized gains it is carrying on the balance sheet.

The wealth objective will also be affected by the cost of financing.

Trade accounts payable are frequently viewed as being a costless source of capital. However, if discounts offered by suppliers are not taken, the annualized cost of these missed discounts can be higher than most types of financing. As a result, the opportunity cost of funds is high, and economic profit is decreased.

The cost of other forms of financing is also important. The financial leverage of the firm affects not only value but also liquidity. In recent years management has realized the advantages associated with commodity/financial futures and options as a means of minimizing the financing costs and removing some of the uncertainty so as to improve the liquidity position of the firm.

In Conclusion

When management needs to better understand the firm's liquidity status, it must shed many of the traditional or preconceived notions about how to measure liquidity. Current and quick ratios, accounts receivable and inventory turnover ratios, as well as many other ratios, must be recognized as providing relatively little information. The fact that they have been used for decades and are easy to calculate should not allow them to take precedence over more insightful measures that are newer and usually more tedious to calculate. Cash breakeven analysis, inflation-adjusted ROE, cash and funds flow statements, cash budgeting, and variance analysis models, to name but a few of the techniques, provide management with a better understanding of the firm's financial status than the traditional measures.

Management of liquidity can be described as the daily operating decisions of financial personnel so as to keep the firm solvent while directing policy and operating actions toward maximizing shareholder wealth. This type of management requires an understanding of marginal analysis, since it is the basis for maximizing economic profits. In an operational sense the unifying models for achieving this objective are the maximization of residual income (RI) and return on equity (ROE). Under certain assumptions these models are compatible with net-present-value models. Management of ROE is better from a practical standpoint since it incorporates the profitability of sales and production, the utilization of assets, and the use of both debt and equity to finance the company. Also, maximization of ROE is consistent with maximizing sustainable growth. The importance of managing sustainable growth is underscored by its implicit definition: Sustainable growth means operating within the firm's limits so as to perpetuate growth at a level that avoids liquidity problems. If management does not understand the firm's liquidity, the reason it does not is that it has abdicated the responsibility — usually to the detriment of employees, customers, and investors.

Appendices

Appendix 1
Forecasting Accounts Receivable Flows

The objective of extending credit (see Chapter 11) or changing existing credit terms (see Chapter 12) is to influence sales demand in an effort to enhance profitability. Two questions are of much concern when addressing the issue of whether to change credit policy:

1. What are the appropriate values to choose for receivables paid by the discount date, paid subsequent to this date, or written off as bad debts?

2. How does the extension of credit to new customers affect the total value of receivables and the mix of credit risks already accepted?

This appendix discusses a technique called Markov chain analysis (MCA) that has been used to address both of these questions, although the focus here will be on the first issue.[1] MCA, in the context of receivables, is based on learned behavior about customers' payment patterns. An important concept in MCA is that of a **steady state**; that is, a balance (or equilibrium) is reached between the resource outflows and the resource inflows.

Analysis of Historical Patterns

Assume a firm is presently at a steady-state condition wherein its current sales are equal to the current cash receipts from prior credit sales plus the current period write-off of bad debts.[2] This state results in a stable level of investment in accounts receivable and in a reasonably stable age distribution of outstanding accounts.

---

[1] The first issue is discussed by R. M. Cyert, H. J. Davidson, and G. L. Thompson in "Estimation of the Allowance for Doubtful Accounts by Markov Chains," *Management Science* (April 1962): 287–303. The second issue is discussed by R. M. Cyert and G. L. Thompson in "Selecting a Portfolio of Credit Risks by Markov Chains," *Journal of Business* (January 1968): 39–46. A number of authors have subsequently used Markov chains to analyze receivables.

[2] There are two methods available for determining bad-debt deductions — the direct write-off method and the reserve method. Markov chain analysis uses the direct write-off method, in which a receivable is charged off only when it is clear that it cannot be collected. Most companies use the reserve method, which estimates bad debts using either of the following techniques: percentage of sales or aging schedules. The reserve method generally accelerates the timing of a bad-debt deduction.

Constant Credit Risk

Appendix Table A1.1 presents customer information taken from the company's accounts receivable ledger. The "Ending state" columns in the July and August statements identify each account in the following way:

P = account is paid in full,
B = account is written off as a bad debt,
0 = oldest invoice is a current charge,
1 = oldest invoice is one month beyond date of sale,
2 = oldest invoice is two months beyond date of sale.

The receivable balance for August is determined as follows:

End of July receivables balance	$348	(a)
Plus sales in August	159	(b)
Minus cash collections	142	(c)
Minus bad debts written off	17	(d)
End of August receivables balance	$348	(e)

The August report differs slightly from the July report, particularly in that it also reflects bad debts. The firm has a policy that if any invoice is more than two months past the point of sale, it is classified as a bad debt (as is customer 250 in the table). Those customers who purchase and pay in full but do not repurchase every month (like customer 100 in the table), normally would not be included in the report. Similarly, the bad-debt invoice normally does not appear on the account summary. Why these accounts are included here will become apparent later.

Aging of Accounts

The aging of accounts is shown in Table A1.2. An explanation of how this table is constructed is given next. Note that the format of Table A1.2 would be the same even if the ledger (Table A1.1) contained hundreds of entries.

The following explanation of the entries in Table A1.2 uses the state 0 transactions. Only four customer accounts had ending state 0 at the end of July, and these four accounts changed during the month of August as follows:

□ Customer 100 paid in full and did not purchase in August.

□ Customer 275 settled the July balance of $10 and purchased $23 more goods in August.

□ Customer 300 owed $45 at the end of July and only paid $5 of this debt in August. Thus the remaining balance aged from group 0 to group 1.

TABLE A1.1
Accounts Receivable Reports

July report

Customer number	Months outstanding 0	Months outstanding 1	Months outstanding 2	Receivable balance	Ending state
100	$ 13			$ 13	0
125	16		$15	31	2
150	8	$ 5		13	1
175	14	20	9	43	2
200	25	20		45	1
225		15	17	32	2
250			17	17	2
275	10			10	0
300	45			45	0
325		18		18	1
350		21		21	1
375			14	14	2
400	25			25	0
425		10	11	21	2
Total	$156	$109	$83	$348	

(a)

August report

Customer number	Cash collections	Bad debts	Months outstanding 0	Months outstanding 1	Months outstanding 2	Receivable balance	Ending state
100	$ 13						P
125	15		$ 10	$ 16		$ 26	1
150	5			8		8	1
175	9			14	$20	34	2
200			30	25	20	75	2
225	17				15	15	2
250		$17					B
275	10		23			23	0
300	5			40		40	1
325	18		17			17	0
350					21	21	2
375	14		6			6	0
400	25		35			35	0
425	11		38		10	48	2
Total	$142	$17	$159	$103	$86	$348	
	(c)	(d)	(b)	(f)	(g)	(e)	

TABLE A1.2
Aging of Accounts Between July and August

Initial state	Ending state					
	P	B	0	1	2	Total
0	$ 53		$ 58	$ 40		$151
1	23		47	33	$41	144
2	66	$17	54	30	45	212
	$142	$17	$159	$103	$86	$507
	(c)	(d)	(b)	(f)	(g)	

☐ Customer 400 paid the outstanding balance of $25 and purchased $35 worth of more goods.

The cash inflows from these customers amounted to $53, while new sales were $58. The August accounts receivable balance for this group was $98. There can be no bad debts from this group since they started the month as current charges (the initial state was 0) and management does not recognize a bad debt until an invoice is more than two months past due. The remaining rows of Table A1.2 are determined in the same fashion. Table A1.3 summarizes this discussion.

Tables A1.2 and A1.3 are value analyses showing the possible changes in economic activity of sales and credit outstanding between two periods. These dollar amounts can be converted to percentages based on the initial state (end of July) and the ending state (end of August) of all the firm's regular customers. This conversion is shown in Table A1.4.

The economic activity of customers whose accounts started out the month classified as current (initial state 0 accounts) is explained as follows: 35 percent of the total activity for the month represents payments, 38 per-

TABLE A1.3
Analysis of July's State 0 Accounts

Account number	July balance	August activity					August ending state
		P	B	0	1	2	
100	$13	$13					P
275	10	10		$23			0
300	45	5			$40		1
400	25	25		35			1
		$53	$0	$58	$40	$0	

TABLE A1.4
Economic Activity of Accounts

Initial state	Ending state					Total
	P	*B*	*0*	*1*	*2*	
0	0.35	0	0.38	0.27	0	1.00
1	0.16	0	0.33	0.23	0.28	1.00
2	0.31	0.08	0.26	0.14	0.21	1.00

cent represents invoices outstanding as current charges, and 27 percent represents invoices that are one month past due. No invoices are two months old. The remaining rows of Table A1.4 can be interpreted in a similar manner.

If this pattern is the usual activity pattern of customers' accounts, and if the firm attracts new customers with similar characteristics using the same credit standards, then we would expect that these new customers would, on average, show the same pattern as the old customers. Thus by analyzing these payment- and credit-outstanding probabilities, the credit manager is able to forecast various aspects of accounts receivable for increasing sales to current customers or extending credit to new customers of comparable risk.

Absorbing States

The payment (P) and bad debts (B) are referred to as *absorbing states*. If an invoice is paid or declared delinquent, it is removed from the accounts receivable ledger. Nothing further can happen to it in the next month. Therefore the invoice is absorbed.

Nonabsorbing States

States 0, 1, and 2 are *nonabsorbing states*, or *transitional states*. Accounts in these states can change their status during the month. The change, however, is limited by the passage of one month and the bad-debt policy of the firm. It is perfectly possible in the model's framework for a transitional (customer's) account to never become absorbed into either state P or state B. This result does not mean that the individual invoices are never paid or classified as uncollectible. It simply means that at least one invoice is not paid, which causes the account to be classified in one of the nonabsorbing states.

Transition Matrix

Adding the absorbing states P and B to Table A1.4 results in a square *transition matrix* that can be subdivided into different partitions, as shown in Table A1.5. The upper left matrix is a 2-by-2 identity matrix (*I*) composed of 1s and 0s to represent the absorbing states. The lower left 3-by-2 matrix (*R*) indicates the probability of moving from nonabsorbing states (0, 1, 2) to absorbing states (P, B). The upper right matrix is a 2-by-3 null (*O*) matrix. The lower 3-by-3 matrix (*Q*) yields the probability that a customer account in a given nonabsorbing state will end in a particular nonabsorbing state. In other words, it is neither paid in full nor declared delinquent. *The Q matrix represents a set of typical payment patterns and is used to find the joint probability of a large number of like experiences.* The sum of each row of the *Q* matrix is positive but less than 1.

Projections Based on Historical Payment Patterns

Of interest is the number of periods it takes nonabsorbing states 0, 1, and 2 to reach absorbing states P and B, that is, how long on average a receivable starting in any particular nonabsorbing state remains outstanding before it is paid or declared delinquent. A relatively simple way to calculate this relationship is to find the value of the inverse of the matrix $[I - Q]$, that is, $N^{-1} = [I - Q]^{-1}$, where *I* is a 3-by-3 identity matrix (it is not the previously defined 2-by-2 identity matrix).

Fundamental Matrix

The N^{-1} matrix is a *fundamental matrix* of the absorbing chain. The elements of N^{-1} indicate the average number of times that a receivable starting in a particular state will continue to be outstanding before it is either paid in full or declared delinquent. Table A1.6 shows the calculations.

TABLE A1.5
Transition Matrix

		P	B	0	1	2
	P	1	0	0	0	0
$T =$	B	0	1	0	0	0
	0	0.35	0	0.38	0.27	0
	1	0.16	0	0.33	0.23	0.28
	2	0.31	0.08	0.26	0.14	0.21

$$= \begin{bmatrix} I & O \\ R & Q \end{bmatrix}$$

TABLE A1.6
Calculation of Payment Patterns

From Table A1.5:

$$Q = \begin{bmatrix} 0.38 & 0.27 & 0 \\ 0.33 & 0.23 & 0.28 \\ 0.26 & 0.14 & 0.21 \end{bmatrix}$$

N^{-1}, the fundamental matrix:

$$N^{-1} = [I - Q]^{-1} = \left[\begin{pmatrix} 1 & 0 & 0 \\ 0 & 1 & 0 \\ 0 & 0 & 1 \end{pmatrix} - \begin{pmatrix} 0.38 & 0.27 & 0 \\ 0.33 & 0.23 & 0.28 \\ 0.26 & 0.14 & 0.21 \end{pmatrix} \right]^{-1} = \begin{array}{c} 0 \\ 1 \\ 2 \end{array} \begin{bmatrix} 2.17 & 0.81 & 0.29 \\ 1.27 & 1.86 & 0.66 \\ 0.94 & 0.60 & 1.48 \end{bmatrix}$$

The values in the N^{-1} matrix are interpreted as follows:

□ A customer account that is *current* at the start will, on the average, pass through the future states of being current, one month old, and two months old for 2.17 times, 0.81 time, and 0.29 time, respectively, before it is absorbed.

□ A customer account that is *one month old* at the start will, on the average, pass through the future states of being current, one month old, and two months old for 1.27 times, 1.86 times, and 0.66 time, respectively, before it is absorbed.

□ A customer account that is *two months old* at the start will, on the average, pass through the future states of being current, one month old, and two months old for 0.94 time, 0.60 time, and 1.48 times, respectively, before it is absorbed.

A more important interpretation of the N^{-1} matrix is that the sum of each row ($2.17 + 0.81 + 0.29 = 3.27$) indicates how many months in the future it takes a receivable balance, which is presently in a particular state, to be absorbed in state P (paid in full) or in state B (declared a bad debt). Thus the average number of months customer balances are outstanding is as shown in Table A1.7.

TABLE A1.7
Number of Months Outstanding

Current state	Months outstanding from current state	Months outstanding from point of sale*
0	3.27	3.27
1	3.79	4.79
2	3.02	5.02

*All sales occur in state 0.

Probability of Payment

What is the importance of this information? Since the N^{-1} matrix indicates the average number of times that a customer account will be in a particular state, and the R matrix shows the probability of passing from that state to one of the absorbing states, the credit manager can determine the probability that a receivable will either be paid in full or be declared a bad debt by multiplying the N^{-1} and R matrices. This calculation is shown in Table A1.8.

The probability that an outstanding receivable that is now current will ultimately be paid is 0.979, and the probability that it will become delinquent is 0.021. An outstanding receivable that is presently one month old has a probability of 0.947 of being collected and a probability of 0.053 of becoming a bad debt. A two-month-old balance, on the average, will be collected with a probability of 0.884 and be classified as uncollectible with a probability of 0.116.

TABLE A1.8
Probability of Payment

$$
N^{-1} \times R = \begin{bmatrix} 2.17 & 0.81 & 0.29 \\ 1.27 & 1.86 & 0.66 \\ 0.94 & 0.60 & 1.48 \end{bmatrix} \begin{bmatrix} 0.35 & 0 \\ 0.16 & 0 \\ 0.31 & 0.08 \end{bmatrix} = \begin{matrix} 0 \\ 1 \\ 2 \end{matrix} \begin{matrix} P & B \\ \begin{bmatrix} 0.979^* & 0.021 \\ 0.947 & 0.053 \\ 0.884 & 0.116 \end{bmatrix} \end{matrix}
$$

*(2.17 × 0.35) + (0.81 × 0.16) + (0.29 × 0.31) = 0.979.

ILLUSTRATION A1.1

The fundamental matrix N^{-1} is defined as

$$
N^{-1} = [I - Q]^{-1} = \left[\begin{pmatrix} 1 & 0 & 0 \\ 0 & 1 & 0 \\ 0 & 0 & 1 \end{pmatrix} - \begin{pmatrix} 0.38 & 0.27 & 0 \\ 0.33 & 0.23 & 0.28 \\ 0.26 & 0.14 & 0.21 \end{pmatrix} \right]^{-1}
$$

$$
= \begin{bmatrix} 0.62 & -0.27 & 0 \\ -0.33 & 0.77 & -0.28 \\ -0.26 & -0.14 & 0.79 \end{bmatrix}^{-1}.
$$

The first step in finding the inverse of N (that is, N^{-1}) is to recall that $N^{-1}N = I$. Substituting for N and I yields

$$N^{-1} \begin{bmatrix} 0.62 & -0.27 & 0 \\ -0.33 & 0.77 & -0.28 \\ -0.26 & -0.14 & 0.79 \end{bmatrix} = \begin{bmatrix} 1 & 0 & 0 \\ 0 & 1 & 0 \\ 0 & 0 & 1 \end{bmatrix}.$$

Let the elements of N^{-1} be designated by the letters a, b, c, and so on:

$$N^{-1} = \begin{bmatrix} a & b & c \\ d & e & f \\ g & h & i \end{bmatrix}.$$

Then recalling the procedure for multiplication of matrices, we can write the following:

$$\begin{bmatrix} (0.62a - 0.33b - 0.26c) & (-0.27a + 0.77b - 0.14c) & (0a - 0.28b + 0.79c) \\ (0.62d - 0.33e - 0.26f) & (-0.27d + 0.77e - 0.14f) & (0d - 0.28e + 0.79f) \\ (0.62g - 0.33h - 0.26i) & (-0.27g + 0.77h - 0.14i) & (0g - 0.28h + 0.79i) \end{bmatrix}.$$

Equating corresponding elements of $N^{-1}N$ and I gives the following equations:

$$\left. \begin{array}{r} 0.62a - 0.33b - 0.26c = 1 \\ -0.27a + 0.77b - 0.14c = 0 \\ 0a - 0.28b + 0.79c = 0 \end{array} \right\} \quad \text{which can be solved for } a, b, c$$

$$\left. \begin{array}{r} 0.62d - 0.33e - 0.26f = 0 \\ -0.27d + 0.77e - 0.14f = 1 \\ 0d - 0.28e + 0.79f = 0 \end{array} \right\} \quad \text{which can be solved for } d, e, f$$

$$\left. \begin{array}{r} 0.62g - 0.33h - 0.26i = 0 \\ -0.27g + 0.77h - 0.14i = 0 \\ 0g - 0.28h + 0.79i = 1 \end{array} \right\} \quad \text{which can be solved for } g, h, i$$

Solving these nine equations in sets of three for the elements of N^{-1} gives

$$N^{-1} = \begin{bmatrix} 2.17 & 0.81 & 0.29 \\ 1.27 & 1.86 & 0.66 \\ 0.94 & 0.60 & 1.48 \end{bmatrix}.$$

The solution for $N^{-1} \times R$ is straightforward if the rules of matrix multiplication are followed. The R matrix is shown in Table A1.8.

$$N^{-1} \times R = \begin{bmatrix} 2.17 \times 0.35 + 0.81 \times 0.16 + 0.29 \times 0.31 \\ 1.27 \times 0.35 + 1.86 \times 0.16 + 0.66 \times 0.31 \\ 0.94 \times 0.35 + 0.60 \times 0.16 + 1.48 \times 0.31 \end{bmatrix}$$

$$\begin{bmatrix} 2.17 \times 0 + 0.81 \times 0 + 0.29 \times 0.08 \\ 1.27 \times 0 + 1.86 \times 0 + 0.66 \times 0.08 \\ 0.94 \times 0 + 0.60 \times 0 + 1.48 \times 0.08 \end{bmatrix}$$

$$= \begin{bmatrix} 0.979 & 0.021 \\ 0.947 & 0.053 \\ 0.884 & 0.116 \end{bmatrix}.$$
□

Forecast of Receivable Balances

Suppose management plans to expand sales via a new advertising promotion with the result that more will be sold to old customers and at the same time more customers with the same creditworthiness will be enticed to purchase goods. In effect, new sales are a reflection of past sales. In August (see Table A1.1) the total sales (the sum of column 0) were $159 to seven customers, or $22.71 per customer. If sales are expanded in this fashion, what will be the distribution of receivables at some future date when this impulse in sales has reached a new *steady-state* condition?

Since there are, on average, $22.71 of new sales per customer each period, multiplying the row vector $[22.71, 0, 0]$ by the N^{-1} matrix gives the answer:

$$N^{-1}$$

$$[22.71 \quad 0 \quad 0] \begin{bmatrix} 2.17 & 0.81 & 0.29 \\ 1.27 & 1.86 & 0.66 \\ 0.94 & 0.60 & 1.48 \end{bmatrix} = [49.28 \quad 18.40 \quad 6.59].$$

Subsequently, there is an *outstanding receivable balance per customer* of $74.27 once a new steady state is attained:

$$\$49.28 + \$18.40 + \$6.59 = \$74.27.$$

This receivable balance is recorded at sales value. Illustration A1.2 provides further mathematical explanation about how this new steady state is reached.

The new steady state occurs when sales equal collections plus bad debts, and gross investment is defined as total accounts receivable outstanding at the steady state. The receivable balances, by the ending state, are multiplied by the R matrix to determine the monthly cash flow of collections and the monthly bad debts:

$$[49.28 \quad 18.40 \quad 6.59] \begin{bmatrix} 0.35 & 0 \\ 0.16 & 0 \\ 0.31 & 0.08 \end{bmatrix} \begin{matrix} P & B \end{matrix}$$

Expected value of collections (B) = $22.19
Expected value of bad debts (P) =   0.52
Total $22.71

(A rounding error of $0.05 exists; the answer for the matrix multiplication is $22.76.) The steady state has occurred since sales are equal to cash inflows plus bad debts.

ILLUSTRATION A1.2

This illustration shows the transition from one steady state to another. For the transition matrix of Table A1.5, each customer's average accounts receivable balance at the new steady state is $74.27, based on sales each period of $22.71 and a constant payment pattern. At the new static state funds flows are in equilibrium, and no new investment is required. However, prior to that time the firm faces a net liquidity outflow. To determine this outflow and its estimated timing, we may make further use of the original transition matrix.

The original transition matrix is an estimate of the probability of payment of incremental sales through time to the average customer. The steady state, or equilibrium, is calculated as the sum of the following payment series to infinity:

$$I + T + T^2 + \cdots + T^\infty,$$

where I represents the matrix for period 1's transition, T represents the matrix for period 2's transition, T^2 represents the matrix for period 3's transition, and so on. Table A1.9 summarizes the transitions for the first 5 periods *for row 0 of the transition matrix.* Only these entries are reported because the concern is with new sales that can only be generated at time 0.

Accounts receivable for each period may be determined by adding each of the transitional values (states 0, 1, 2) of each new sales row in a cumulative fashion (the last column of Table A1.9), and multiplying each row's cumulative sum by the sales of that period (assumed constant at $22.71). These manipulations are reflected in the data of Table A1.10.

TABLE A1.9
Row 0 of the Transition Matrices

Period	P	B	0	1	2	Total
$I \rightarrow 1$	0	0	1.0000	0	0	1.0000
$T \rightarrow 2$	0.3500	0	0.3800	0.2700	0	0.6500
$T^2 \rightarrow 3$	0.5262	0	0.2335	0.1647	0.0756	0.4738
$T^3 \rightarrow 4$	0.6577	0.0060	0.1627	0.1115	0.0620	0.3362
$T^4 \rightarrow 5$	0.7517	0.0110	0.1148	0.0783	0.0442	0.2373

Note: I is the identity matrix; T is the T matrix of Table A1.5; T^2 is found by multiplying $T \times T$; T^3 is found by multiplying $T^2 \times T$; and so on.

By period 5 accounts receivable have increased from \$22.71 to \$61.25. As the number of periods approach infinity, the receivable balance will approach \$74.27. This sum is calculated by realizing that

$$I + T + T^2 + \cdots + T^\infty = [I - T]^{-1}.$$

Solving this inverse matrix gives the desired new steady-state result.   ☐

Changing Credit Risk

To this point, the basic assumption has been that the new sales are to customers with the same creditworthiness as that of the regular customers. While this situation is possible, certain other cases should be discussed. A very common case is the expansion of sales by selling on credit to customers with a different (say lower) creditworthy condition. In this case management is lacking direct information about the payment patterns of these potential customers. Information on these new customers may be gathered

TABLE A1.10
Estimated Accounts Receivable Balance

Period	Sum of row values for states 0, 1, 2 — Sum	Sum of row values for states 0, 1, 2 — Cumulative		Sales		Ending accounts receivables
1	1.0000	1.0000	×	\$22.71	=	\$22.71
2	0.6500	1.6500	×	22.71	=	37.47
3	0.4738	2.1238	×	22.71	=	48.23
4	0.3362	2.4600	×	22.71	=	55.87
5	0.2373	2.6973	×	22.71	=	61.25
⋮	⋮	⋮	⋮	⋮	⋮	⋮
∞	—	3.2704	×	22.71	=	74.27

from a number of sources, such as competitors, Dun & Bradstreet, or Creditel. Whatever the source of the basic information on these new customers, the credit manager is still responsible for making a decision of whether or not to extend credit.

To illustrate the impact that low-creditworthy customers might have on the firm, the transition matrix of Table A1.5 has been arbitrarily adjusted to show a slow down in cash flow (column P), an increase in bad debts (column B), and an increase in receivables aging (columns 1 and 2). These changes are shown in Table A1.11.

With the same procedures as used before, comparative results of these different risk situations are shown in Table A1.12. The results of Table A1.12 indicate that significant changes may occur through the introduction of low-creditworthy customers.

You are cautioned to appreciate that the transition matrix used in Table A1.11 has no basis other than as an example to show that acceptance of less creditworthy customers, or a decrease in the firm's credit standards, can have a significant impact on receivable investment. In the illustration cash inflow decreases about 7.5 percent ($20,52/$22.19), while at the same time receivable investment increases 64 percent ($121.71/$74.27) and bad debts increase 321 percent ($2.19/$0.52). Many other illustrations can be chosen, but they will not change the basic conclusion that if a firm lowers its credit standards, then investment and bad debts will increase, while cash inflows will decrease. Whether the firm should make such a change depends on the profit margin and whether the firm has *sufficient liquidity* to finance this investment demand.

Timing of Liquidity Drain

If the firm changes one or more of its policies governing the allowance of credit, this change affects sales, cash inflows, and receivables. The impact does not happen instantaneously; often considerable time elapses before

TABLE A1.11
Revised Transition Matrix

	P	B	0	1	2
P	1	0	0	0	0
B	0	1	0	0	0
0	0.20	0	0.38	0.42	0
1	0.10	0	0.33	0.23	0.34
2	0.20	0.12	0.26	0.14	0.28

Note: The cell (0, P) has decreased from 0.35 to 0.20; the cell (2, B) has increased from 0.08 to 0.12; and cells (0, 1), (1, 2), and (2, 2) have changed from 0.27 to 0.42, 0.28 to 0.34, and 0.21 to 0.28, respectively.

TABLE A1.12
Comparative Results of Transition Matrices of Tables A1.5 and A1.11

Accounts receivable outstanding from point of sale

Initial state	Table A1.5	Table A1.11
0	3.27	5.37
1	4.79	6.55
2	5.02	6.41

Dollar value of receivables balance per customer based on monthly sales of $22.71

		Ending state			
	Initial state	0	1	2	Total
Table A.1.5	0	$49.28	$18.40	$ 6.59	$ 74.27
Table A.1.11	0	64.92	38.73	18.29	121.71

Cash flow and bad debts per customer per month

	Cash flow	Bad debts	Total
Table A.1.5	$22.19	$0.52	$22.71
Table A.1.11	20.52	2.19	22.71

Probability of collection and bad debts at a steady state

	Table A1.5		Table A1.11	
Initial state	P	B	P	B
0	0.979	0.021	0.903	0.097
1	0.947	0.053	0.857	0.143
2	0.884	0.116	0.771	0.229

the full impact of the policy change is known. (See Chapter 13, Table 13.5 for an illustration of the time involved between the initiation of the policy change and the establishment of the new steady state.) During the growth period the firm experiences an incremental liquidity demand to finance changes in inventory, production, and accounts receivable.

The timing and the amount of the liquidity drain for the earlier illustration of no change in credit risk are shown for five periods in Table A1.13. The net liquidity drain is the investment necessary to finance the growth in accounts receivable (similar to the "How to Go Broke" example in Chapter 1). Outflows for cost of sales are assumed to be 80 percent of sales. Accounts receivable per customer grow from $0 to $61.25. If this series is continued to infinity, accounts receivable will maximize at $74.27.

Liquidity Needs

The most significant conclusion that can be drawn from the data in Table A1.13 is that *the liquidity drain to finance receivables happens in the early periods,*

TABLE A1.13
Timing and Amount of Liquidity Drain

	Period				
	1	2	3	4	5
Beginning accounts receivable	$ 0	$22.71	$37.47	$48.23	$55.87
Plus sales	22.71	22.71	22.71	22.71	22.71
Minus ending accounts receivable	22.71	37.47	48.23	55.87	61.25
Cash inflow	$ 0	$ 7.95	$11.95	$15.07	$17.23
Minus cost of sales*	18.17	18.17	18.17	18.17	18.17
Liquidity drain	$18.17	$10.22	$ 6.22	$ 3.10	$ 0.94

*Paid in the current month.

whereas the cash inflow buildup occurs in later periods. For the firm to benefit from these incremental sales, management must ensure that sufficient liquidity exists to finance the expansion.

The rate of change of cash inflows is not linear and places a great burden on the firm's resources in the early periods. The result of the expansion is that while profits have increased, so have the costs and the level of investment. The necessary funds for expansion may come from existing liquidity resources. Usually, though, part of this expansion is provided from outside sources via an expansion in trade accounts payable. Sometimes, the expansion is financed through long-term sources. This action might be viewed as a mismatch of sources and uses of funds, particularly once the steady state is reached. Expansion can create an imbalance, since it does the firm little good to expand and at the same time to plant the seeds of its own destruction.

Summary

The appendix discussed Markov chain analysis as a technique for analyzing credit balances and for setting credit policy. The objectives of the technique are multifold: (1) to determine the average number of months before an account is settled in some manner, (2) to calculate the probabilities that the account will be paid or declared a bad debt, (3) to estimate the average number of times the account will be classified in some aging category before it is either paid or declared a bad debt, and (4) to forecast the liquidity drain caused by changing some aspect of credit policy.

An in depth understanding of Markov chain analysis depends on an understanding of matrix algebra. However, on a conceptual level the technique models the flow of receivable balances through an aging process. The dynamics of the flow process model the transition from one steady state to another.

Appendix 1 Questions

1. Discuss the meaning of the new steady-state accounts receivable balance, given a constant sales stimulus.

2. What type of information is shown in the transition matrix? What does the fundamental matrix reveal?

3. How are the probabilities of payment and bad debts determined?

Appendix 1 Problems

1. Company policy is to write off delinquent accounts if the accounts are of age three months. The transition probabilities are given next.

	P	B	0	1	2
P	1	0	0	0	0
B	0	1	0	0	0
0	0.5	0	0.4	0.1	0
1	0.4	0	0.3	0.2	0.1
2	0.3	0.2	0.1	0.1	0.3

It is expected that 100 new accounts will be created each month. The average dollar value of accounts in states 0, 1, and 2 is estimated to be $20, $30, and $40, respectively. Cash costs are 70 percent of sales.

(a) Compute the fundamental matrix N^{-1} and explain what it means.

(b) What is the expected number of months before an account, initially in a nonabsorbing state, is absorbed?

(c) Calculate the probability that an account that is initially in a nonabsorbing state will be written off.

(d) What is the expected number of accounts in each nonabsorbing state? What is the expected dollar value of receivables in each nonabsorbing state?

(e) What is the expected dollar value of monthly cash flow and accounts written off?

2. The Wright Company expects to increase monthly sales to its present customers by $150 monthly. From past experience the credit manager has determined that the transition matrix for these customers is as shown in Appendix Table A1.11. Variable production cash costs are estimated to be 72 percent of sales and are paid monthly as incurred. What will the firm's incremental investment in accounts receivable be after four months and at the new steady state?

Appendix 2
Corporate Bankruptcy, Reorganization, and Liquidation

The magnitude of corporate bankruptcy and reorganization in the United States has never been as great as it has been within the past 20 years. As proven by Penn Central in 1970, W. T. Grant in 1975, Wickes and Braniff in 1982 (and Braniff again in 1989), and Texaco in 1987, just to name a few, corporate failure is no longer limited to the small, undercapitalized firms. It is also affecting large industrial and financial corporations. In fact, between 1972 and 1979, from 29,500 to 35,200 firms a year petitioned the courts to liquidate or to reorganize under the protection of the nation's bankruptcy laws. Since 1979 bankruptcy levels have increased steadily and by 1983 had reached levels exceeding that of the 1922 depression. These facts exemplify the significance of liquidity management in the economy today.

The paragraphs that follow provide an overview of bankruptcy, reorganization, and liquidation. However, a procedure that is frequently pursued prior to forcing bankruptcy is examined first.

National Association of Credit Managers

Bankruptcy statistics indicate that only about one in eight businesses is successfully reorganized in bankruptcy court. The rest cease operations. The National Association of Credit Managers (NACM) and its nationwide affiliates have become an effective alternative to the bankruptcy courts, at least in the initial stages. The reason for NACM's emergence is that its constituency comprises tens of thousands of suppliers who have made independent decisions to extend credit to debtors on an unsecured basis. Those creditors are in desperate need of a unified voice in negotiations with the secured creditors — principally banks and asset-based lenders — who can so strongly influence the directions in which troubled borrowers are moving.

In severe cases where financially ailing firms cannot pay their debts when due, and they can no longer negotiate with unsecured general creditors on a one-on-one basis, they often call on NACM affiliates to hastily convene meetings so they can explain their problems. This is the functional equivalent of inviting creditors to attend the first meeting under a Chapter 11 proceeding. If solutions can be worked out, management avoids having to file for protection under Chapter 11.

Corporate Bankruptcy and the Courts

In the United States the procedure of bankruptcy is a sophisticated legal process of fair treatment to both creditors and debtors, used as a last resort in cases of corporate insolvencies. All bankruptcy cases are heard in federal court.

The Constitution gave Congress the right to enact federal laws governing both personal and corporate bankruptcy procedure. Not until 1898, however, did Congress enact a comprehensive bankruptcy act. The 1898 Nelson Act, although amended some 50 times in the twentieth century, stood for 80 years. The Chandler Act of 1938 was the only significant revision of the Nelson Act during those years. By the 1970s a major reform of the bankruptcy law was long overdue. That came with the Bankruptcy Reform Act of 1978. The new Bankruptcy Code became effective on October 1, 1979, after nine years in the making.

One big difference between the acts is the role of the bankruptcy judge. Under the old law the judge acted as both judge and administrator. Now these roles are separated. The new act also introduced a new federal bankruptcy court system, effective April 1, 1984, consisting of 95 judicial districts.

The Bankruptcy Code is made up of several odd-numbered chapters:

- □ *Chapter 1* defines several of the rules and procedures and describes who is a debtor.

- □ *Chapter 3* describes how a bankruptcy case is initiated for both voluntary and involuntary cases and defines the role of trustees in the proceedings.

- □ *Chapter 5* covers the duties and obligations of both creditors and debtors.

- □ *Chapter 7* applies to cases where liquidation of corporate assets (straight bankruptcy) is sought by the party that petitioned the proceedings.

- □ *Chapter 9* deals with debt adjustments of municipalities.

- □ *Chapter 11* is a synthesis of old Chapters VIII (railroad reorganizations), X (other corporate reorganizations), XI (arrangements), and XII (real estate arrangements). The new Chapter 11 deals with any corporate reorganization: The company continues to operate under the protection of the court while it attempts to work out a plan for paying its creditors.

For a firm with insolvency problems *Chapter 11 allows the firm protection from creditors while it attempts to reorganize and survive as a going concern.* Management must decide whether reorganization is the proper course to follow or whether the interests of the firm's owners might not be better served by merger with another company or by liquidation.

Reorganization is an attempt to keep a company in continued operations by correcting and modifying its present financial structure. This strategy should be pursued whenever the firm's future prospects are projected to be profitable. *Liquidation* should occur when the assets of a business are worth more when sold than when used in the continuing business. Liquidation involves the sale of a firm's assets and the application of the proceeds to the satisfaction of all creditors according to their relative priorities; the payment of any residual goes to the stockholders in the form of a (generally) nontaxable liquidating dividend.

Reorganization in Bankruptcy

Reorganizations may be voluntary or involuntary, judicial or nonjudicial. Voluntary reorganizations are those pursued by management on its own initiative, while involuntary reorganizations are imposed on the firm by creditors. Judicial reorganizations are those occurring through the courts, as in bankruptcy proceedings, while nonjudicial reorganizations involve a settlement with creditors outside the courtroom.

Voluntary Reorganizations

Voluntary reorganizations may occur as the firm takes it on itself to find alternatives to its financial difficulties. Such alternatives include the following:

- □ *Partial liquidation.* A partial sale of a firm's assets or divestiture of product segments to generate cash.
- □ *Dissolution.* A voluntary closing followed in the belief that more can be realized by a piecemeal sale of assets by the existing management than by the sale of the entire business as a unit.
- □ *Extension.* A voluntary agreement by one or more of the firm's creditors to delay the date of payment of their claims.
- □ *Composition.* The voluntary agreement of all the creditors to accept partial payment in full satisfaction of their debts.
- □ *Combination settlements.* A combination of extension and composition.
- □ *Sale and merger.* A sale of the business or a merger with a more financially secure firm before problems become too severe.
- □ *Refinance/readjustment.* A change in a firm's capital structure to bring debt and other fixed payment charges and terms into line.

Even if these voluntary methods are successful, the firm may still be without current funds to purchase inventory, meet payroll, finance receivables, and meet other liquidity needs.

When a company is insolvent and its creditors are demanding payment, management generally seeks protection in the bankruptcy courts under the protection of Chapter 11 of the Bankruptcy Code.

Tool for Restructuring Debt

A business in financial distress has a wide array of tools available for restructuring its debt under Chapter 11.

1. *The automatic stay.* The most powerful weapon available to a business that seeks the protection of the bankruptcy court under Chapter 11 is the automatic-stay provision. It provides that as long as the debtor is under protection of the bankruptcy court, a creditor cannot take any action to collect its debt without the permission of the bankruptcy court. The stay prevents creditors from commencing or continuing any litigation against the debtor, enforcing any judgment against the debtor, attempting to obtain possession of any property of the debtor, attempting to enforce any lien against the debtor, and attempting to collect any debts against the debtor, including the set off of any debt by any creditor. The automatic-stay provision gives breathing room to the debtor to allow management to propose a plan of reorganization.

2. *Utility turnoffs.* The code prevents a utility from discontinuing service to the debtor solely on the basis of bills that had accumulated prior to the filing of the Chapter 11 proceeding, provided that the debtor, within 20 days of filing, furnishes adequate assurance of payment for current bills.

3. *Strong-arm provisions.* The code allows a debtor in possession to set aside several kinds of prefiling actions such as preferential payments to creditors, the granting of liens or security interests, and transfers of property.

4. *Executory contracts.* A debtor in possession, subject to the court's approval, may assume or reject any executory contract or unexpired lease. An executory contract is one that has not yet been fully performed. Therefore the debtor (management) can pick and choose among contracts he will perform and reject those that are onerous. Included in this category have been labor union contracts. As can be seen from the controversy that erupted over the Continental Airlines Chapter 11 filing, a debtor in possession may, with court approval, reject a collective bargaining agreement with a labor union.

5. *Cessation of interest on unsecured debt.* Under the Bankruptcy Code interest will cease on unsecured debt as of the date of the filing.

6. *Orderly liquidation.* A debtor can use Chapter 11 to liquidate the business in an orderly manner so that one group of creditors is not preferred over another.

7. *The plan.* Under a plan of reorganization both secured and unsecured debt can be restructured in any way acceptable to the debtor and the requisite majority of creditors. For example, secured creditors might receive a lower interest rate on loans in return for more collateral; unsecured creditors might receive a percentage of their debt immediately or payments on a debt over time; or stockholders may consent that creditors be given a portion of their equity. The main point is that the plan can be tailored to the needs of the parties. Acceptance of a plan requires the vote of two-thirds of the creditors in amount in each class of creditors and more than one-half in number of allowed claims. If a class of creditors is not impaired, it has no vote.

8. *Impairment of classes of claims.* Section 1124 of the code defines an unimpaired claim as one that will not be extended, modified, or lessened in duration or amount. Once claimants are classified, each member of a particular class must be treated the same. In preparing a plan, a debtor has almost unlimited leeway in impairing claims of the creditors. For example, interest rates might be lowered on a class of claims, another class might take less than 100 cents on the dollar, and so forth.

9. *Cram down.* Although the code requires two-thirds in amount and more than one-half in number of each class of claims to accept the plan before confirmation, if one or more classes of claims have not accepted the plan, the court may confirm the plan over their objections, that is, the plan can be "crammed down their throats."

Procedure

A Chapter 11 case is commenced by filing a petition with the U.S. Bankruptcy Court. The petition contains schedules of all assets and liabilities. Liabilities are categorized generally into priority, secured, and unsecured creditors. Upon filing a Chapter 11 proceeding, management of the debtor firm continues to operate the business as a "debtor in possession" unless the judge orders otherwise. A trustee will be appointed only for cause or if the appointment is in the interest of creditors or equityholders of the business.

Management has 120 days from the filing of the petition to submit a plan of reorganization to the court and the creditors. If management does not file within this time, any party in interest may file a plan. The plan designates the correction of any managerial defects, reduction of fixed charges, reduction of floating debt, and provision of new capital. The plan includes an identification of problem areas and proposals for realistically revising a firm's financial condition in a manner that is both fair to the firm's creditors and shareholders and feasible from the firm's view toward continued operations.

Once a plan has been submitted to the court and the creditors, a hearing is held to confirm or reject the plan. If the plan is confirmed, it will go into effect and will be overseen by the bankruptcy court. If the plan is rejected, then the *debtor in possession* must come up with an alternative plan, or any interested party may submit a plan for approval.

The feasibility of the plan depends on the extent to which the trustee or receiver can utilize various financial expedients in efforts to minimize the initial cost and cash drain to the firm as it tries to improve its ability to continue operations on its own without additional outside support. If the problems cannot be corrected, or if a fair and feasible plan of reorganization does not exist, the matter proceeds to liquidation and dissolution of the corporation.

The troubled firm and its attorneys attempt to convince the creditors that it is in their best interests to keep the company alive for one or more of the following reasons:

- Creditors will receive little or no money if they ultimately force the troubled firm into liquidation.
- If they allow the firm to survive, they can continue doing business with the firm.
- The troubled firm will pay for new supplies, materials, or services on a COD basis while it is in Chapter 11.
- The plan will allow each creditor to end up with more money than it is likely to receive if it plunges the troubled firm into liquidation.

Reorganization Process

The reorganization process passes through three phases of financial correction:

1. Operating trusteeship or receivership.
2. Revaluation of assets and reallocations of claims.
3. Provision of essential new capital.

Trusteeship/Receivership

The trusteeship or receivership phase consists of actions designed to improve the company's short-run financial position and to correct any managerial defects that may exist. These actions may include the suspension of interest payments and dividends to improve cash flow, the sale of unnecessary assets, and other borrowing — all designed to provide temporary funds for continued operations while awaiting final reorganization.

Revaluation of Assets and Reallocation of Claims

The second phase, after the company has made its most immediate changes, is the revaluation of assets and reallocation of claims. At this stage the trustee determines the worth of a potential reorganization, scales down existing priorities as to principal and income preferences, extends maturities as much as possible, and substitute contingent interest for dividend preference. These approaches seek to assess the firm's continued ability to sustain operations and to reduce the impact that existing claims will have on the initial phase of reorganization operations.

The company focuses primarily on reducing fixed charges and deferring close maturities at this point. To reduce fixed charges, management may pursue the following actions:

☐ Exchange noncumulative preferred or common stock for debt issues.

☐ Exchange debt issues with a contingent interest payment for those with a fixed charge.

☐ Retire bonds by means of proceeds from a sale of nonessential assets only.

☐ Lower the interest rate on bonds issued in the reorganization.

To defer close maturities, the company may pursue these actions:

☐ Extend the maturity dates.

☐ Refund maturing obligations.

☐ Grant bondholders liberal conversion privileges.

☐ Eliminate the bond issues in reorganization entirely by exchanging them for equity securities.

Provision of New Capital

The final phase is the provision of essential new capital. It attempts to properly capitalize the firm so that management will be able to fund continued operations. This phase deals with the company's need to raise immediate cash for net working capital requirements and with its ability to facilitate sound future financing. To raise cash, the company may pursue the following courses of action:

☐ Sell new securities or warrants.

☐ Obtain term loans.

☐ Sell unneeded assets.

☐ Assess existing stockholders.

Pros and Cons of Chapter 11

The overwhelming advantage of a Chapter 11 proceeding is that the creditors of the business can be held off for a minimum of four months while a plan is proposed to satisfy their obligations. A reorganization plan can extend the maturity of the various obligations, reduce them to a certain extent, and provide for adjustment of interest rates.

There are serious disadvantages to filing a Chapter 11, though, such as adverse reaction by the public, stockholders, suppliers, employees, and customers. The bankruptcy court is not likely to tolerate, for an extended period, a business with a negative cash flow after filing, and operating capital must be available to avoid cash losses. There are serious time and legal cost constraints involved in filing, and if fraud or serious mismanagement is found, a trustee may be appointed to run the business.

Liquidation

If a reorganization cannot be effected, *liquidation* of the firm occurs. The trustee and the creditors' committee act to convert all assets into cash. Appraisers are appointed by the court to set a value on the property. The property cannot be sold at less than 75 percent of the value set by the appraisers unless the court consents.

The creditors receive distributions of the estate according to a list of *priority of claims* established by the law. The priorities for unsecured creditors are as follows:

1. The trustee's costs for administering the liquidation.
2. Unsecured claims in an involuntary case arising from the ordinary course of business after the bankruptcy proceedings began but prior to the appointment of a trustee.
3. Unsecured wages, salaries, or commissions of up to $2000 per employee earned within 90 days of the filing of the bankruptcy petition. Claims in excess of $2000 are treated as general unsecured claims.
4. Unsecured contributions of up to $2000 per employee for employee benefit plans for services rendered within 180 days prior to the petition for bankruptcy.
5. Unsecured claims of up to $900 for money deposited with the bankrupt company for services and property that were not delivered.

6. Taxes due within three years prior to the bankruptcy petition filing.

7. General creditors' claims.

After all these priorities have been satisfied, any remaining general unsecured creditors participate pro rata in any remaining realization proceeds. The final distribution to unsecured creditors is termed a dividend and is generally expressed in terms of the percentage of the total unsecured claims that will be paid.

A senior priority exists for creditors whose collateral is depleted and for whom the trustee cannot provide adequate protection. In such circumstances the secured creditor has a priority over selected other claims.

The preferred stockholders participate if there is anything left after the unsecured and secured creditors' claims are satisfied. The common shareholders represent the residual claimants. They get the remaining assets, if any still exist.

The liquidation process can take years to complete and is constantly in a state of change as the trustee attempts to value the assets, identify all claims, and liquidate the firm piecewise. The following illustration reveals some of the circumstances in W. T. Grant's liquidation. A hypothesized liquidation, which shows the allocation of the firm to the various claimants, is shown in Illustration A2.2.

ILLUSTRATION A2.1

As of January 29, 1976, while W. T. Grant was under the protection of Chapter 11 of the Bankruptcy Code, it was reported to have total assets of $512.1 million, including $45 million of inventories when valued at cost (which were subsequently discovered to be undervalued by $70 million). Its total liabilities were $1.11 billion, of which $200 million were established to be claims of landlords. Trade creditors were owed $110 million, which included $82 million in secured liens against inventories, $26 million of bank subordination, and $2 million for unsecured creditors. Secured-debenture holders were owed $24 million, and debtor-in-possession certificates amounted to $90 million. General creditors, administrative costs, and legal fees made up the difference.

Consultants hired during the bankruptcy period cautioned creditors that it would take six to eight years to determine whether W. T. Grant would survive. Because $320 million cash had been accumulated from closing stores and liquidating inventory, bankers on the Committee of Secured Creditors favored liquidation. Representatives of trade creditors on this committee were against liquidation since they were fully secured and were still doing business with W.T. Grant. However, the bankers eventually won out.

Liquidation resulted in claims of $15 million for severance pay to employees, which was not a priority item. The Internal Revenue Service claimed W. T. Grant owed $67 million, an amount later reduced to $29 million. Administrative fees were expected to be about $30 million. Legal fees were expected to have priority status and be in the millions of dollars. It was doubtful that unsecured creditors would receive anything.

Liquidation resulted in the accounts receivable being sold for about 15 percent of face value plus 5 percent of the first year's profit earned on them by the purchaser. Secured creditors were offered two alternatives: 90 percent payment in full satisfaction or a 75 percent payment with reservation of the right to sue for additional money. The controlling interest in Zeller's was sold for $32.7 million. It had been carried on the books for about $30 million.

In other developments Ernst & Whinney, the CPA firm, paid the W. T. Grant estate $2 million plus interest to settle a suit out of court. The suit stemmed from charges that Ernst & Whinney's auditing of W. T. Grant's accounts, inventory, and internal controls before its collapse in 1975 was inadequate. Morgan Guaranty paid $2.8 million to settle a class action suit by shareholders that accused the bank of concealing the retailer's financial condition and of selling substantial holding of W. T. Grant's stock on inside information.   □

ILLUSTRATION A2.2

As an illustration of the liquidation process, assume that the Lang Company had the balance sheet shown in Table A2.1 on the date if filed for a

TABLE A2.1
Lang Company
Balance Sheet As of March 31, 1989

Assets		Liabilities and equity	
Cash	$ 8,200	Bank note payable	$ 32,000
Notes receivable	24,000	Accounts payable	195,000
Accounts receivable	47,000	Accrued wages	13,500
Inventories:		Accrued interest:	
Finished goods	56,000	Bank notes	1,100
Work in process	24,000	Mortgage	8,500
Raw materials	39,000	Mortgage note	200,000
Prepaid expenses	1,200	Capital stock	250,000
Investment in Gale	26,500	Retained earnings	(141,200)
Land	42,000		
Buildings (net)	198,000		
Equipment	93,000		
Total assets	$558,900	Total liabilities	$558,900

voluntary bankruptcy petition. Additional information concerning estimated realizable values and other balance sheet relationships follow.

- The notes receivable are expected to be fully realized, and they have
  been pledged as collateral on a bank note in the principal amount of
  $20,000 plus accrued interest of $600.
- Accounts receivable have an estimated collectible value of $28,000.
- Finished-goods inventory can be sold at a markup of 20 percent
  over cost, with selling expenses estimated at 10 percent of selling
  price. Work in process has no value unless completed. The estimated cost to complete this work totals $12,000, of which $5000
  represents the costs of raw materials. The estimated selling price of
  the work-in-process inventory (after allowing for selling expenses) is
  $25,000. The remaining raw materials inventory has an estimated
  selling price of 70 percent of its cost.
- The recovery value of prepaid expense is $600.
- The Gale Company stock has a current market value of $30 per
  share and is pledged as collateral on a bank note payable in the
  principal amount of $12,000 plus accrued interest of $500.
- Land and buildings have appraised values of $60,000 and $120,000,
  respectively, and serve as collateral on the mortgage note payable.
- Much of the equipment is special-purpose equipment having an estimated disposal value of $28,000.

Tables A2.2 and A2.3 incorporate this information to show the position of creditors and the deficiency report, respectively. Several features
should be noted:

- Assets pledged with fully secured creditors have realizable values in
  excess of the secured debt in an amount of $20,900 (see Table A2.2:
  $3400 + $17,000), which becomes available for distribution to unsecured creditors.
- Assets pledged with partially secured creditors have a realizable
  value that is $28,500 less than the total related debt (see Table
  A2.2: $180,000 − $208,000). Thus mortgage holders have a
  $28,500 remaining debt that ranks as an unsecured one.
- Free assets are those that have not been pledged with specific liabilities and are available to satisfy general unsecured creditors. Note
  that the free assets include the excess of the realizable value of
  pledged assets over the related debts of fully secured creditors.
- In the deficiency account (see Table A2.3) the capital stock and retained earnings are included in the estimated gains column only to
  indicate the extent to which total potential deficiency is covered by
  stockholders' equity.

TABLE A2.2
Position of Creditors

	Book value			Realizable value
Assets pledged with fully secured creditors				
Notes receivable	$ 24,000		$ 24,000	
Bank note payable		$ 20,000		
Accrued interest		600	20,600	$ 3,400
Investment in Gale	26,500		$ 30,000	
Bank note payable		$ 12,000		
Accrued interest		500	12,500	17,500
Assets pledged with partially secured creditors				
Land	42,000	$ 60,000		
Buildings	198,000	120,000	$180,000	
Mortgage note payable		$200,000		
Accrued interest		8,500	208,500	
Free assets				
Cash	8,200			8,200
Accounts receivable	47,000			28,000
Prepaid expenses	1,200			600
Inventories:				
Finished	56,000			60,480
Work in process	24,000			18,000
Raw materials	39,000			23,800
Equipment	93,000			38,000
Total net realizable value				$197,980
Liabilities having priority:				
Accrued wages				13,500
Net free assets				$184,480
Estimated deficiency to				
unsecured creditors				39,020
Total	$558,900			$223,500
Liabilities having priority				
Accrued wages	$ 13,500		$ 13,500	
Fully secured creditors				
Notes payable	32,000		$ 32,000	
Accrued interest	1,100		1,100	
Partially secured creditors				
Mortgage note payable	200,000		$200,000	
Accrued interest	8,500		8,500	
Total			$208,500	
Land and buildings			180,000	$28,500

TABLE A2.2 (Cont.)

	Book value	Realizable value
Unsecured creditors		
Accounts payable	195,000	195,000
Stockholders' equity		
Capital stock	250,000	
Retained earnings	⟨141,200⟩	
Total	$558,900	$223,500

☐ The final settlement with the unsecured creditors can be computed by dividing the net free assets by the estimated deficiency to unsecured creditors (see Table A2.2):

$$\frac{\$184,480}{\$223,500} = 0.825.$$

Thus each unsecured creditor will receive approximately 82.5 percent of the amount due under the claim.

Conclusion

More probing analysis of corporate distress is required if the financial analyst is to enhance her or his understanding of bankruptcy, reorganization, and liquidation proceedings.

TABLE A2.3
Lang Company Deficiency Account March 31, 1989

Estimated losses		Estimated gains	
Accounts receivable	$19,000	Investment in Gale	$ 3,500
Inventory	16,720	Land	18,000
Prepaid expenses	600	Capital stock	250,000
Buildings	78,000	Retained earnings	⟨141,200⟩
Equipment	55,000	Deficiency to unsecured creditors	39,020
Total	$169,300	Total	$169,300

Appendix 2 Questions

1.   Distinguish between solvency in an accounting sense and in a legal sense.

2.   Distinguish between fully secured, partially secured, and unsecured creditors.

3.   Discuss some of the tools available under Chapter 11 of the Bankruptcy Code that the firm can use to restructure its debt.

4.   Distinguish between *reorganization* and *liquidation*.

5.   What is the reasoning behind the court's attempt to conserve the firm as an ongoing entity rather than liquidate it?

Appendix 2 Problems

1.   The following data are taken from the trustee's records:

Assets pledged with fully secured creditors (realizable value $100,000)	$125,000
Assets pledged with partially secured creditors (realizable value $45,000)	70,000
Free assets (realizable value $60,000)	90,000
Fully secured creditor claims	55,000
Partially secured creditor claims	65,000
Unsecured creditor claims with priority	15,000
General unsecured creditor claims	150,000

Determine the amount that will be paid to each class of creditor.

2.   Columbus Cabinets is facing bankruptcy proceedings. Its most current balance sheet is as follows:

Cash	$ 4,000	Accounts payable	$ 80,000
Receivables	35,000	Accrued wages	35,000
Inventories	40,000	Notes payable	45,000
Fixed assets	115,000	Common stock	75,000
		Retained earnings	⟨41,000⟩
Total	$194,000	Total	$194,000

Estimated realizable values of the assets are receivables, $15,000; inventories, $20,000; fixed assets, $70,000. Receivables and inventories are both pledged as collateral on the notes payable in the amounts of $20,000 and $25,000, respectively. Prepare a Position of Creditors Statement, and determine the estimated settlement per dollar for general unsecured creditors. Assume that accrued wages are a priority item.

Appendix 3

Normal Probability Distribution Table

Area of the Normal Distribution that Is Z Standard Deviations to the Left or Right of the Mean

Number of standard deviations from the mean (Z)	Area to the left or right	Number of standard deviations from the mean (Z)	Area to the left or right
0.00	0.5000	1.55	0.0606
0.05	0.4801	1.60	0.0548
0.10	0.4602	1.65	0.0495
0.15	0.4404	1.70	0.0446
0.20	0.4207	1.75	0.0401
0.25	0.4013	1.80	0.0359
0.30	0.3821	1.85	0.0322
0.35	0.3632	1.90	0.0287
0.40	0.3446	1.95	0.0256
0.45	0.3264	2.00	0.0228
0.50	0.3085	2.05	0.0202
0.55	0.2912	2.10	0.0179
0.60	0.2743	2.15	0.0158
0.65	0.2578	2.20	0.0139
0.70	0.2420	2.25	0.0122
0.75	0.2264	2.30	0.0107
0.80	0.2119	2.35	0.0094
0.85	0.1977	2.40	0.0082
0.90	0.1841	2.45	0.0071
0.95	0.1711	2.50	0.0062
1.00	0.1577	2.55	0.0054
1.05	0.1469	2.60	0.0047
1.10	0.1357	2.65	0.0040
1.15	0.1251	2.70	0.0035
1.20	0.1151	2.75	0.0030
1.25	0.1056	2.80	0.0026
1.30	0.0968	2.85	0.0022
1.35	0.0885	2.90	0.0019
1.40	0.0808	2.95	0.0016
1.45	0.0735	3.00	0.0013
1.50	0.0668		

Appendix 4

Time-Value Tables

TABLE A
Future Value of $1

n					Percent					
	2	4	6	8	10	12	14	16	18	20
1	1.0200	1.0400	1.0600	1.0800	1.1000	1.1200	1.1400	1.1600	1.1800	1.2000
2	1.0404	1.0816	1.1236	1.1664	1.2100	1.2544	1.2996	1.3456	1.3924	1.4400
3	1.0612	1.1249	1.1910	1.2597	1.3310	1.4049	1.4815	1.5609	1.6430	1.7280
4	1.0824	1.1699	1.2625	1.3605	1.4641	1.5735	1.6890	1.8106	1.9388	2.0736
5	1.1041	1.2167	1.3382	1.4693	1.6105	1.7623	1.9254	2.1003	2.2878	2.4883
6	1.1262	1.2653	1.4185	1.5869	1.7716	1.9738	2.1950	2.4364	2.6996	2.9860
7	1.1487	1.3159	1.5036	1.7138	1.9487	2.2107	2.5023	2.8262	3.1855	3.5832
8	1.1717	1.3686	1.5938	1.8509	2.1436	2.4760	2.8526	3.2784	3.7589	4.2998
9	1.1951	1.4233	1.6895	1.9990	2.3579	2.7731	3.2519	3.8030	4.4355	5.1598
10	1.2190	1.4802	1.7908	2.1589	2.5937	3.1058	3.7072	4.4114	5.2338	6.1917
11	1.2434	1.5395	1.8983	2.3316	2.8531	3.4785	4.2262	5.1173	6.1759	7.4301
12	1.2682	1.6010	2.0122	2.5182	3.1384	3.8960	4.8179	5.9360	7.2876	8.9161
13	1.2936	1.6651	2.1329	2.7196	3.4523	4.3635	5.4924	6.8858	8.5994	10.6993
14	1.3195	1.7317	2.2609	2.9372	3.7975	4.8871	6.2613	7.9875	10.1472	12.8392
15	1.3459	1.8009	2.3966	3.1722	4.1772	5.4736	7.1379	9.2655	11.9737	15.4070
16	1.3728	1.8730	2.5404	3.4259	4.5950	6.1304	8.1372	10.7480	14.1290	18.4884
17	1.4002	1.9479	2.6928	3.7000	5.0545	6.8660	9.2765	12.4677	16.6722	22.1861
18	1.4282	2.0258	2.8543	3.9960	5.5599	7.6900	10.5752	14.4625	19.6733	26.6233
19	1.4568	2.1068	3.0256	4.3157	6.1159	8.6128	12.0557	16.7765	23.2144	31.9480
20	1.4859	2.1911	3.2071	4.6610	6.7275	9.6463	13.7435	19.4608	27.3930	38.3376
21	1.5157	2.2788	3.3996	5.0338	7.4002	10.8038	15.6676	22.5745	32.3238	46.0051
22	1.5460	2.3699	3.6035	5.4365	8.1403	12.1003	17.8610	26.1864	38.1421	55.2061
23	1.5769	2.4647	3.8197	5.8715	8.9543	13.5523	20.3616	30.3762	45.0076	66.2474
24	1.6084	2.5633	4.0489	6.3412	9.8497	15.1786	23.2122	35.2364	53.1090	79.4968
25	1.6406	2.6658	4.2919	6.8485	10.8347	17.0001	26.4619	40.8742	62.6686	95.3962
26	1.6734	2.7725	4.5494	7.3964	11.9182	19.0401	30.1666	47.4141	73.9490	114.4755
27	1.7069	2.8834	4.8223	7.9881	13.1100	21.3249	34.3899	55.0004	87.2598	137.3706
28	1.7410	2.9987	5.1117	8.6271	14.4210	23.8839	39.2045	63.8004	102.9666	164.8447
29	1.7758	3.1187	5.4184	9.3173	15.8631	26.7499	44.6931	74.0085	121.5005	197.8136
30	1.8114	3.2434	5.7435	10.0627	17.4494	29.9599	50.9502	85.8499	143.3706	237.3763
40	2.2080	4.8010	10.2857	21.7245	45.2593	93.0510	188.8835	378.7212	750.3783	1469.7716
50	2.6916	7.1067	18.4202	46.9016	117.3909	289.0022	700.2330	1670.7038	3927.3569	9100.4382

TABLE B
Present Value of $1

					Percent					
n	2	4	6	8	10	12	14	16	18	20
1	0.9804	0.9615	0.9434	0.9259	0.9091	0.8929	0.8772	0.8621	0.8475	0.8333
2	0.9612	0.9246	0.8900	0.8573	0.8264	0.7972	0.7695	0.7432	0.7182	0.6944
3	0.9423	0.8890	0.8396	0.7938	0.7513	0.7118	0.6750	0.6407	0.6086	0.5787
4	0.9238	0.8548	0.7921	0.7350	0.6830	0.6355	0.5921	0.5523	0.5158	0.4823
5	0.9057	0.8219	0.7473	0.6806	0.6209	0.5674	0.5194	0.4761	0.4371	0.4019
6	0.8880	0.7903	0.7050	0.6302	0.5645	0.5066	0.4556	0.4104	0.3704	0.3349
7	0.8706	0.7599	0.6651	0.5835	0.5132	0.4523	0.3996	0.3538	0.3139	0.2791
8	0.8535	0.7307	0.6274	0.5403	0.4665	0.4039	0.3506	0.3050	0.2660	0.2326
9	0.8368	0.7026	0.5919	0.5002	0.4241	0.3606	0.3075	0.2630	0.2255	0.1938
10	0.8203	0.6756	0.5584	0.4632	0.3855	0.3220	0.2697	0.2267	0.1911	0.1615
11	0.8043	0.6496	0.5268	0.4289	0.3505	0.2875	0.2366	0.1954	0.1619	0.1346
12	0.7885	0.6246	0.4970	0.3971	0.3186	0.2567	0.2076	0.1685	0.1372	0.1122
13	0.7730	0.6006	0.4688	0.3677	0.2897	0.2292	0.1821	0.1452	0.1163	0.0935
14	0.7579	0.5775	0.4423	0.3405	0.2633	0.2046	0.1597	0.1252	0.0985	0.0779
15	0.7430	0.5553	0.4173	0.3152	0.2394	0.1827	0.1401	0.1079	0.0835	0.0649
16	0.7284	0.5339	0.3936	0.2919	0.2176	0.1631	0.1229	0.0930	0.0708	0.0541
17	0.7142	0.5134	0.3714	0.2703	0.1978	0.1456	0.1078	0.0802	0.0600	0.0451
18	0.7002	0.4936	0.3503	0.2502	0.1799	0.1300	0.0946	0.0691	0.0508	0.0376
19	0.6864	0.4746	0.3305	0.2317	0.1635	0.1161	0.0829	0.0596	0.0431	0.0313
20	0.6730	0.4564	0.3118	0.2145	0.1486	0.1037	0.0728	0.0514	0.0365	0.0261
21	0.6598	0.4388	0.2942	0.1987	0.1351	0.0926	0.0638	0.0443	0.0309	0.0217
22	0.6468	0.4220	0.2775	0.1839	0.1228	0.0826	0.0560	0.0382	0.0262	0.0181
23	0.6342	0.4057	0.2618	0.1703	0.1117	0.0738	0.0491	0.0329	0.0222	0.0151
24	0.6217	0.3901	0.2470	0.1577	0.1015	0.0659	0.0431	0.0284	0.0188	0.0126
25	0.6095	0.3751	0.2330	0.1460	0.0923	0.0588	0.0378	0.0245	0.0160	0.0105
26	0.5976	0.3607	0.2198	0.1352	0.0839	0.0525	0.0331	0.0211	0.0135	0.0087
27	0.5859	0.3468	0.2074	0.1252	0.0763	0.0469	0.0291	0.0182	0.0115	0.0073
28	0.5744	0.3335	0.1956	0.1159	0.0693	0.0419	0.0255	0.0157	0.0097	0.0061
29	0.5631	0.3207	0.1846	0.1073	0.0630	0.0374	0.0224	0.0135	0.0082	0.0051
30	0.5521	0.3083	0.1741	0.0994	0.0573	0.0334	0.0196	0.0116	0.0070	0.0042
50	0.3715	0.1407	0.0543	0.0213	0.0085	0.0035	0.0014	0.0006	0.0003	0.0001

TABLE C
Future Value of an Ordinary Annuity of $1

n	Percent									
	2	4	6	8	10	12	14	16	18	20
1	1.0000	1.0000	1.0000	1.0000	1.0000	1.0000	1.0000	1.0000	1.0000	1.0000
2	2.0200	2.0400	2.0600	2.0800	2.1000	2.1200	2.1400	2.1600	2.1800	2.2000
3	3.0604	3.1216	3.1836	3.2464	3.3100	3.3744	3.4396	3.5056	3.5724	3.6400
4	4.1216	4.2465	4.3746	4.5061	4.6410	4.7793	4.9211	5.0665	5.2154	5.3680
5	5.2040	5.4163	5.6371	5.8666	6.1051	6.3528	6.6101	6.8771	7.1542	7.4416
6	6.3081	6.6330	6.9753	7.3359	7.7156	8.1152	8.5355	8.9775	9.4420	9.9299
7	7.4343	7.8983	8.3938	8.9228	9.4872	10.0890	10.7305	11.4139	12.1415	12.9159
8	8.5830	9.2142	9.8975	10.6366	11.4359	12.2997	13.2328	14.2401	15.3270	16.4991
9	9.7546	10.5828	11.4913	12.4876	13.5795	14.7757	16.0853	17.5185	19.0859	20.7989
10	10.9497	12.0061	13.1808	14.4866	15.9374	17.5487	19.3373	21.3215	23.5213	25.9587
11	12.1687	13.4864	14.9716	16.6455	18.5312	20.6546	23.0445	25.7329	28.7551	32.1504
12	13.4121	15.0258	16.8699	18.9771	21.3843	24.1331	27.2707	30.8502	34.9311	39.5805
13	14.6803	16.6268	18.8821	21.4953	24.5227	28.0291	32.0887	36.7862	42.2187	48.4966
14	15.9739	18.2919	21.0151	24.2149	27.9750	32.3926	37.5811	43.6720	50.8180	59.1959
15	17.2934	20.0236	23.2760	27.1521	31.7725	37.2797	43.8424	51.6595	60.9653	72.0351
16	18.6393	21.8245	25.6725	30.3243	35.9497	42.7533	50.9804	60.9250	72.9390	87.4421
17	20.0121	23.6975	28.2129	33.7502	40.5447	48.8837	59.1176	71.6730	87.0680	105.9306
18	21.4123	25.6454	30.9057	37.4502	45.5992	55.7497	68.3941	84.1407	103.7403	128.1167
19	22.8406	27.6712	33.7600	41.4463	51.1591	63.4397	78.9692	98.6032	123.4135	154.7400
20	24.2974	29.7781	36.7856	45.7620	57.2750	72.0524	91.0249	115.3797	146.6280	186.6880
21	25.7833	31.9692	39.9927	50.4229	64.0025	81.6987	104.7684	134.8405	174.0210	225.0256
22	27.2990	34.2480	43.3923	55.4568	71.4027	92.5026	120.4360	157.4150	206.3448	271.0307
23	28.8450	36.6179	46.9958	60.8933	79.5430	104.6029	138.2970	183.6014	244.4868	326.2369
24	30.4219	39.0826	50.8156	66.7648	88.4973	118.1552	158.6586	213.9776	289.4945	392.4842
25	32.0303	41.6459	54.8645	73.1059	98.3471	133.3339	181.8708	249.2140	342.6035	471.9811
26	33.6709	44.3117	59.1564	79.9544	109.1818	150.3339	208.3327	290.0883	405.2721	567.3773
27	35.3443	47.0842	63.7058	87.3508	121.0999	169.3740	238.4993	337.5024	479.2211	681.8528
28	37.0512	49.9676	68.5281	95.3388	134.2099	190.6989	272.8892	392.5028	566.4809	819.2233
29	38.7922	52.9663	73.6398	103.9659	148.6309	214.5828	312.0937	456.3032	669.4475	984.0680
30	40.5681	56.0849	79.0582	113.2832	164.4940	241.3327	356.7868	530.3117	790.9480	1181.8816
50	84.5794	152.6671	290.3359	573.7702	1163.9085	2400.0182	4994.5213	10435.6488	21813.0937	45497.1908

TABLE D
Present Value of an Ordinary Annuity of $1

n	Percent									
	2	4	6	8	10	12	14	16	18	20
1	0.9804	0.9615	0.9434	0.9259	0.9091	0.8929	0.8772	0.8621	0.8475	0.8333
2	1.9416	1.8861	1.8334	1.7833	1.7355	1.6901	1.6467	1.6052	1.5656	1.5278
3	2.8839	2.7751	2.6730	2.5771	2.4869	2.4018	2.3216	2.2459	2.1743	2.1065
4	3.8077	3.6299	3.4651	3.3121	3.1699	3.0373	2.9137	2.7982	2.6901	2.5887
5	4.7135	4.4518	4.2124	3.9927	3.7908	3.6048	3.4331	3.2743	3.1272	2.9906
6	5.6014	5.2421	4.9173	4.6229	4.3553	4.1114	3.8887	3.6847	3.4976	3.3255
7	6.4720	6.0021	5.5824	5.2064	4.8684	4.5638	4.2883	4.0386	3.8115	3.6046
8	7.3255	6.7327	6.2098	5.7466	5.3349	4.9676	4.6389	4.3436	4.0776	3.8372
9	8.1622	7.4353	6.8017	6.2469	5.7590	5.3282	4.9464	4.6065	4.3030	4.0310
10	8.9826	8.1109	7.3601	6.7101	6.1446	5.6502	5.2161	4.8332	4.4941	4.1925
11	9.7868	8.7605	7.8869	7.1390	6.4951	5.9377	5.4527	5.0286	4.6560	4.3271
12	10.5753	9.3851	8.3838	7.5361	6.8137	6.1944	5.6603	5.1971	4.7932	4.4392
13	11.3484	9.9856	8.8527	7.9038	7.1034	6.4235	5.8424	5.3423	4.9095	4.5327
14	12.1062	10.5631	9.2950	8.2442	7.3667	6.6282	6.0021	5.4675	5.0081	4.6106
15	12.8493	11.1184	9.7122	8.5595	7.6061	6.8109	6.1422	5.5755	5.0916	4.6755
16	13.5777	11.6523	10.1059	8.8514	7.8237	6.9740	6.2651	5.6685	5.1624	4.7296
17	14.2919	12.1657	10.4773	9.1216	8.0216	7.1196	6.3729	5.7487	5.2223	4.7746
18	14.9920	12.6593	10.8276	9.3719	8.2014	7.2497	6.4674	5.8178	5.2732	4.8122
19	15.6785	13.1339	11.1581	9.6036	8.3649	7.3658	6.5504	5.8775	5.3162	4.8435
20	16.3514	13.5903	11.4699	9.8181	8.5136	7.4694	6.6231	5.9288	5.3527	4.8696
21	17.0112	14.0292	11.7641	10.0168	8.6487	7.5620	6.6870	5.9731	5.3837	4.8913
22	17.6580	14.4511	12.0416	10.2007	8.7715	7.6446	6.7429	6.0113	5.4099	4.9094
23	18.2922	14.8568	12.3034	10.3711	8.8832	7.7184	6.7921	6.0442	5.4321	4.9245
24	18.9139	15.2470	12.5504	10.5288	8.9847	7.7843	6.8351	6.0726	5.4509	4.9371
25	19.5235	15.6221	12.7834	10.6748	9.0770	7.8431	6.8729	6.0971	5.4669	4.9476
26	20.1210	15.9828	13.0032	10.8100	9.1609	7.8957	6.9061	6.1182	5.4804	4.9563
27	20.7069	16.3296	13.2105	10.9352	9.2372	7.9426	6.9352	6.1364	5.4919	4.9636
28	21.2813	16.6631	13.4062	11.0511	9.3066	7.9844	6.9607	6.1520	5.5016	4.9697
29	21.8444	16.9837	13.5907	11.1584	9.3696	8.0218	6.9830	6.1656	5.5098	4.9747
30	22.3965	17.2920	13.7648	11.2578	9.4269	8.0552	7.0027	6.1772	5.5168	4.9789
50	31.4236	21.4822	15.7619	12.2335	9.9148	8.3045	7.1327	6.2463	5.5541	4.9995

TABLE E
Present Value of an Annuity Due of $1

					Percent					
n	2	4	6	8	10	12	14	16	18	20
1	1.0000	1.0000	1.0000	1.0000	1.0000	1.0000	1.0000	1.0000	1.0000	1.0000
2	1.9804	1.9615	1.9434	1.9259	1.9091	1.8929	1.8772	1.8621	1.8475	1.8333
3	2.9416	2.8861	2.8334	2.7833	2.7355	2.6901	2.6467	2.6052	2.5656	2.5278
4	3.8839	3.7751	3.6730	3.5771	3.4869	3.4018	3.3216	3.2459	3.1743	3.1065
5	4.8077	4.6299	4.4651	4.3121	4.1699	4.0373	3.9137	3.7982	3.6901	3.5887
6	5.7135	5.4518	5.2124	4.9927	4.7908	4.6048	4.4331	4.2743	4.1272	3.9906
7	6.6014	6.2421	5.9173	5.6229	5.3553	5.1114	4.8887	4.6847	4.4976	4.3255
8	7.4720	7.0021	6.5824	6.2064	5.8684	5.5638	5.2883	5.0386	4.8115	4.6046
9	8.3255	7.7327	7.2098	6.7466	6.3349	5.9676	5.6389	5.3436	5.0776	4.8372
10	9.1622	8.4353	7.8017	7.2469	6.7590	6.3282	5.9464	5.6065	5.3030	5.0310
11	9.9826	9.1109	8.3601	7.7101	7.1446	6.6502	6.2161	5.8332	5.4941	5.1925
12	10.7868	9.7605	8.8869	8.1390	7.4951	6.9377	6.4527	6.0286	5.6560	5.3271
13	11.5753	10.3851	9.3838	8.5361	7.8137	7.1944	6.6603	6.1971	5.7932	5.4392
14	12.3484	10.9856	9.8527	8.9038	8.1034	7.4235	6.8424	6.3423	5.9095	5.5327
15	13.1062	11.5631	10.2950	9.2442	8.3667	7.6282	7.0021	6.4675	6.0081	5.6106
16	13.8493	12.1184	10.7122	9.5595	8.6061	7.8109	7.1422	6.5755	6.0916	5.6755
17	14.5777	12.6523	11.1059	9.8514	8.8237	7.9740	7.2651	6.6685	6.1624	5.7296
18	15.2919	13.1657	11.4773	10.1216	9.0216	8.1196	7.3729	6.7487	6.2223	5.7746
19	15.9920	13.6593	11.8276	10.3719	9.2014	8.2497	7.4674	6.8178	6.2732	5.8122
20	16.6785	14.1339	12.1581	10.6036	9.3649	8.3658	7.5504	6.8775	6.3162	5.8435
21	17.3514	14.5903	12.4699	10.8181	9.5136	8.4694	7.6231	6.9288	6.3527	5.8696
22	18.0112	15.0292	12.7641	11.0168	9.6487	8.5620	7.6870	6.9731	6.3837	5.8913
23	18.6580	15.4511	13.0416	11.2007	9.7715	8.6446	7.7429	7.0113	6.4099	5.9094
24	19.2922	15.8568	13.3034	11.3711	9.8832	8.7184	7.7921	7.0442	6.4321	5.9245
25	19.9139	16.2470	13.5504	11.5288	9.9847	8.7843	7.8351	7.0726	6.4509	5.9371
26	20.5235	16.6221	13.7834	11.6748	10.0770	8.8431	7.8729	7.0971	6.4669	5.9476
27	21.1210	16.9828	14.0032	11.8100	10.1609	8.8957	7.9061	7.1182	6.4804	5.9563
28	21.7069	17.3296	14.2105	11.9352	10.2372	8.9426	7.9352	7.1364	6.4919	5.9636
29	22.2813	17.6631	14.4062	12.0511	10.3066	8.9844	7.9607	7.1520	6.5016	5.9697
30	22.8444	17.9837	14.5907	12.1584	10.3696	9.0218	7.9830	7.1656	6.5098	5.9747
50	32.0521	22.3415	16.7076	13.2122	10.9063	9.3010	8.1312	7.2457	6.5539	5.9993

Glossary

5 C's of credit   Character, capacity, capital, collateral, and conditions.

8-K   A report of unscheduled material events or corporate changes deemed of importance to the shareholders by the Securities and Exchange Commission.

10-K   A detailed audited annual report that must be submitted to the Securities and Exchange Commission (SEC), the listing exchange, and any shareholders who request it.

10-Q   A detailed unaudited quarterly report that must be submitted to the SEC and the listing exchange, and that may be sent to shareholders who request it.

A–B–C method   An ad hoc technique of monitoring inventories. *A* items are high value, whereas *C* items are low value.

Above-average financial risk   Greater financial leverage than may be prudent.

Absolute priority of claims principle   The bankruptcy principle that each class of liability claims is repaid in full before the next highest priority category can receive even a partial payment.

Absorbing state   As pertaining to accounts receivable analysis, it is a state in Markov chain analysis in which an account is either paid in full or declared delinquent.

Absorption costing (full costing)   A method of costing that assigns all manufacturing costs (variable and fixed) to units produced.

Accounting income   The excess of accounting revenues over all related accounting expenses for a given period. Also called earnings, income, or profit. See *Accrual accounting*.

Accounts payable   Liability representing money owed to suppliers. Normally a current liability.

Accounts receivable   Claim against customers for sales or services rendered. Normally a current asset.

Accrual accounting   A method of accounting in which revenue is recognized when earned and expenses are recognized when incurred without regard to the timing of cash receipts and expenditures. Contrast with *cash accounting*.

Accrued payables or income taxes   A current liability resulting from the passage of time but not yet due.

Accumulated benefits obligations   Calculation of an employee's pension benefits based on the average of her/his (say) five highest actual salaries received to date.

ACH   Automated clearinghouse, a corporation operated either by the Federal Reserve System or a group of private banks that electronically transfer funds from one bank account to another without the costly use of traditional check payment systems.

Acid test (quick ratio)   A measure of liquidity, defined as cash, marketable securities, and accounts receivable divided by current liabilities.

Activity ratios   Measures of efficiency of a firm's assets. The comparison is between the level of sales (activity) and the investment in some (or total) asset(s).

Actuarial gain or loss   Pension plan gains or losses resulting from changes in plan assumptions, changes in the amount of plan assets, and changes in the amount of the projected benefit obligation.

Additional paid-in-capital   An alternative title for either capital contributed in excess of par, capital surplus, or paid-in surplus.

Adjusted-earnings method   Similar to a pro forma statement of cash flows (cash breakeven analysis).

Aging of accounts receivable (aging schedule)   Process of classifying accounts by the amount of time they have been on the books. The schedule usually displays the percentage of current accounts receivable that are one month old, two months old, and so on.

Amortization   The process of allocating costs of assets or liabilities to the periods of benefit as expenses.

Annual report   A yearly report to shareholders and other interested parties containing a balance sheet, income statement, statement of cash flow, auditor's statement, and management's comments about events.

Annualized implicit cost (AIC)   The cost of forgoing cash discounts and paying at some date beyond the discount period.

Annuity   A level stream of cash flows for a limited number of time periods.

Annuity due   An annuity in which the first payment is immediate, not being one period delayed, as with an ordinary annuity.

Anticipation inventory   Inventory produced in anticipation of demand for it.

Asset-based financing   Borrowing using the firm's assets as collateral.

Asset-turnover ratios   See *Activity ratios*.

Asset-utilization ratios   See *Activity ratios*.

Assignment of accounts receivable   The transfer of legal ownership through sale; contrast with *Pledging*.

At the money   An option whose strike price is equal (or nearly so) to the current market price of the underlying asset.

Auditor's report   A letter from the auditor to the company and its shareholders in which the accounting firm certifies the propriety of the methods used to produce the firm's financial statements. Opinions are usually unqualified.

Authorized capital stock   Number of shares that can be issued by a corporation.

Automated clearinghouse   See *ACH*.

Average collection period   The average amount of time accounts receivable have been on the books.

Average cost (AC)   The total cost incurred per unit of output. Also known as average total cost, ATC.

Average-cost flow assumption   An inventory flow assumption that determines cost of units as the weighted average cost of beginning inventory and purchases.

Average physical product   A measure of the amount of output produced per input.

Average revenue   Measures revenue per unit of output; computed by dividing total revenue by the rate of output.

Average variable costs (AVC)   Is the amount of variable cost per unit of output.

Balance proportions   A monitoring technique for accounts receivable that relates the outstanding balance to the sale that generated the receivable.

Balance sheet   A financial statement that indicates what assets the firm owns, and how those assets are financed in the form of liabilities or ownership interest.

Banker's acceptance   A money market instrument that frequently is used in foreign trade. It is a draft or bill of exchange that is drawn on a bank that is obligated to ensure payment of the acceptance on presentation (sight draft) or at maturity (time draft).

Bankruptcy   A condition where a legal petition has been filed and accepted under the bankruptcy laws. The market value of a firm's assets are less than its liabilities, and the firm has a negative net worth. The firm is usually insolvent, but need not be.

Basis (commodity)   The difference between the cash (spot) and futures price of a commodity. In the equity market, the basis is often referred to as a premium or discount.

Basis point   One hundredth of one percentage point; primarily used with interest rates.

Basis risk   The risk that a commodity contract's basis will move adversely.

Baumol model   An economic order quantity (EOQ) model applied to cash management. Contrast with *Miller–Orr* and *Stone* models.

Bill of exchange   See *Draft.*

Blanket inventory liens   A secured borrowing arrangement in which the lender has a general claim against the inventory of the borrower.

Bond   A certificate showing evidence of debt. The par value is the face (principal) amount payable at maturity. The coupon rate is the interest rate payable in one year divided by the face amount.

Bond rating   An appraisal by a recognized financial organization of the soundness of a bond as an investment. Coupon rates are greatly influenced by a corporation's bond rating.

Book value   The value at which an item is reported in financial statements as an asset, liability, or owners' equity.

Borrowing from the future   Acceleration of later periods' revenues into the current period.

Breakeven analysis   A numerical and graphical technique that is used to determine at what point the firm will break even (revenue = cost) in terms of accounting profit. To compute the breakeven point, fixed costs are divided by (price minus variable cost per unit).

Budget   A financial plan (*pro forma*) that is used to estimate future operating results.

Business risk   Risk due to uncertainty about investment outlays, operating cash flows, and salvage values without regard to how investments are financed.

Call option   Option to buy an asset at a specified exercise price on or before a specified maturity date.

Capital asset pricing model (CAPM)   A model that relates the return of individual assets to market returns by incorporating risk.

Capital contributed in excess of par value   See *Additional paid-in capital.*

Capital gains taxes   Taxes on the excess of proceeds over cost from the sale of a capital asset as defined by the Internal Revenue Code. The Tax Reform Act of 1986 made the capital gains tax rate the same as the tax on other income.

Capital lease (financial lease)   A long-term, noncancelable lease that has many characteristics of debt. Under FASB 13, the lease obligation must be shown directly on the balance sheet.

Capital markets   Competitive markets for equity or debt securities with maturities or more than one year.

Capital surplus   See *Additional paid-in-capital.*

Capital structure   The composition of the liabilities and equities side of a company's balance sheet. The mix of funding sources a company uses to finance its operations.

Capitalization   The sum of all long-term sources of financing to the firm.

Capitalizing expenses   Placing current business expenses on the balance sheet and writing them off over time.

Cash accounting   A method of accounting in which changes in the condition of an organization are recognized only in response to the payment or receipt of cash. No matching of revenues and expenses is done to compute profits. Contrast with *Accrual accounting.*

Cash breakeven sales level   The sales level that is necessary to meet all cash needs. The calculation incorporates all sources and uses of funds, with operations providing the necessary balancing amount.

Cash budget   A schedule of expected cash receipts and disbursements, and the borrowing requirements, for a given period of time.

Cash concentration system   A system for transferring funds on deposit in regional banks to a central cash pool where they may be managed more efficiently.

Cash conversion cycle   It is the operating cycle less the accounts payable deferral period.

Cash flow   The amount of cash generated or consumed by an activity over a certain period of time.

Cash flow from financing activities   Cash flow, in the Statement of Cash Flows, that is generated (or reduced) from the sales or repurchase of securities or the payment of cash dividends.

Cash flow from investing activities   Cash flow, in the Statement of Cash Flows, that is generated (or reduced) from the sale or purchase of long-term securities or plant and equipment.

Cash flow from operations   Shown in the Statement of Cash Flows as cash generated or consumed by the productive activities of a firm over a period of time; defined as profit after tax plus noncash charges minus noncash receipts plus or minus changes in accounts receivable, inventories, prepaid expenses, accounts payable, accrued liabilities and deferred taxes.

Cash letter   Essentially the same as a deposit slip that lists attached checks.

Cash market   A (spot) market where physical commodities are traded for cash. See *Spot price*.

Collateral   Assets pledged by a borrower that will be transferred to the lender if the loan is not repaid.

Collection experience variance   This variance measures collection efficiency and is measured as the difference between actual receivables and revised budgeted receivables, given the actual sales realized.

Collection float   Checks written by customers that have not been received, deposited, and added to the company's available balance.

Collection period   A ratio measure of control of accounts receivable, defined as accounts receivable divided by credit sales per day.

Commercial paper   Short-term, low-risk negotiable promissory note that reputable large corporations issue to investors in order to finance cyclical needs. The minimum amount is usually $25,000 with maturity within nine months. It is sold at a discount from face value.

Common-size financial statements   Accounting statement expressed as a percentage of net sales and/or total assets to aid comparison.

Common stock   Securities representing an ownership interest in a firm. Holders have residual claim on the assets and earnings after debt and preferred shareholders' claims are satisfied.

Compensating balance   A bank requirement that business customers maintain a minimum non-interest-bearing average balance. It is used to compensate banks for bank loans or services and may be calculated as an absolute amount or as the daily average cash balance during the month. The borrower pays interest on these balances, thus raising the effective rate on the borrowed funds.

Concentration banking   System whereby customers make payments to a regional collection center. The collection center pays the funds into a regional bank account and surplus money is transferred to the company's principal bank.

Constant-dollar accounting   Process of inflation accounting in which historical-cost items are restated to adjust for changes in the general purchasing power of the currency. This information is no longer required to be shown in the firm's annual report. See *Current-dollar accounting*.

Constant purchasing power   The amount of a currency required over time to purchase a stable basket of physical assets.

Consumer price index (CPI)   An index measure of inflation equal to the sum of prices of a number of assets purchased by average consumers.

Contingent liability   A potential liability.

Contributed surplus   See *Additional paid-in capital*.

Contribution margin   Sales less all variable costs. Contribution margin ratio is calculated by dividing contribution margin by sales.

Controlled disbursing account   A cash disbursement technique in which a firm pays creditors with checks written on a bank located in a different region of the country from that of the creditor. The purpose is to increase the collection float. See *Remote disbursing account.*

Convertible debt   Debt that may be converted into common or preferred stock at the holder's option after specific criteria are met.

Correlation coefficient   Correlation is the degree to which yield or price fluctuations of one security or money market instrument are associated with those of another such security or money market instrument. A correlation of 1.0 implies a perfect 1-to-1 relationship between the instruments.

Correspondent banking relationship   A relationship whereby one bank keeps deposit balances in another bank in return for services such as check clearing, consulting, trust, and securities trading.

Cost minimization   A strategy of minimizing costs. It is the point where marginal cost equals average cost. It is not consistent with maximizing economic profit, other than in perfectly competitive markets.

Cost of capital   Return on new, average-risk investment that a company must expect in order to maintain share price. A weighted average of the cost to the firm of individual sources of capital.

Cost of debt   Yield to maturity on debt; frequently after tax, in which event it is one minus the tax rate times the yield to maturity.

Cost of equity   Return equity investors expect to earn by holding shares in a company. The expected return forgone by equity investors in the next best, equal-risk opportunity.

Cost of goods sold (cost of sales)   Inventoriable costs that are recognized in the income statement for goods sold.

Covenant   Clause in a loan agreement with legal validity.

Coverage ratio   Measure of financial leverage relating annual operating income to annual burden of debt.

Credit period   The time period within which a credit purchase is to be paid.

Credit policy   Company regulations concerning the minimum financial strength of firms that can purchase on credit, the terms of credit sales, and the collection efforts that will be used.

Credit scoring   A procedure for assigning scores to companies on the basis of the risk of default.

Credit standards   Criteria used to determine which customers receive credit. Usually encompasses an examination of the customer's credit rating, credit references, outstanding debt, and financial statements.

Credit terms   The repayment provisions that are part of a credit arrangement.

Creditor   Person or institution that holds the debt issued by a firm or individual.

Cross hedge   The buying or selling of futures contracts to protect the value of a cash position of a similar, but not identical, instrument or portfolio.

Current asset   Any asset that will turn into cash within the normal operating cycle of the firm.

Current-dollar accounting   System of inflation accounting in which historical-cost items are restated to adjust for changes in the price of specific items. No longer required to be shown in annual reports. See *Constant-dollar accounting.*

Current liability   Any liability that is payable within the firm's operating cycle.

Current ratio   A measure of liquidity, defined as current assets divided by current liabilities.

Days purchases outstanding   A method of monitoring accounts payable. It is equal to payables divided by average purchases per day.

Days sales outstanding   A method of monitoring trends in customer payment patterns. It is equal to total receivables divided by average credit sales per day.

Debenture   A long-term unsecured corporate bond backed by the general credit of the issuing corporation.

Debt capacity   The total amount of debt a company can prudently support, given its earnings expectations and equity base.

Debt-to-capital ratio   A measure of financial leverage, defined as debt divided by assets.

Debt-to-equity ratio   A measure of financial leverage, defined as debt divided by shareholders' equity.

Debtor   A borrower.

Default   Failure to make a payment when due.

Default risk   The risk of defaulting on an obligation.

Defensive interval   Measures the number of days of normal cash expenditures covered by quick assets.

Deferred tax liability   An indeterminate liability that results when pretax income shown on the tax return is less than that shown on the account statement.

Defined benefit plan   A type of qualified retirement plan under which eligible participants are promised specific benefits (such as 40 percent of salary) on retirement. The benefits are set according to a formula and the contributions are variable.

Defined contribution plan   A type of qualified retirement plan under which the participants are promised a certain contribution to the plan (such as 7 percent of salary or a percentage of profits to be allocated to compensation) but no particular benefit on retirement. The firm is committed to making contributions according to a fixed formula.

Degree of combined leverage   The percentage change in earnings per share is divided by the percentage change in sales at a given level of operation. It is a measure of the total combined effect of operating and financial leverage on earnings per share.

Degree of financial leverage   The percentage change in earnings per share is divided by the percentage change in earnings before interest and taxes at a given level of operation. It is a measure of the impact of debt on the earnings capability of the firm.

Degree of operating leverage   The percentage change in operating income is divided by the percentage change in volume at a given level of operation. It is a measure of the impact of fixed costs on the operating earnings of the firm.

Delivery month   Most contracts are posted every quarter for periods of two years. The delivery month is the calendar month during which these contracts mature. It is also called the *spot month*.

Demand curve   The relationship between the price at which a commodity is offered and the quantity demanded at that price. Usually shown as a downward sloping line.

Demand deposits   Bank deposits which may be withdrawn at any time by the account holder.

Depository transfer check   A check used solely for the purpose of transferring deposits from one of the firm's accounts to another. It is unsigned and nonnegotiable.

Depreciation   The reduction in the value of a long-lived asset from use or obsolescence.

Diminishing marginal returns   A point reached as additional units of a variable input are applied to fixed inputs, where total output increases at a diminishing rate as additional units of the variable input are applied to the fixed inputs.

Direct costing (variable costing)   A costing method that allocates only variable manufacturing costs to products and treats fixed manufacturing costs as period costs.

Direct sends   Bank bypasses the Federal Reserve Bank and sends a cash letter directly to the bank the check is drawn on.

Disbursement float   Funds available in the company's bank account until its payment check has cleared through the banking system. A decrease in book cash but no immediate change in bank cash, generated by checks written by the firm.

Discount rate   Interest rate used to convert future cash flows to present values.

Discounted loan   A loan in which the calculated interest payment is subtracted or discounted in advance. Because this lowers the amount of available funds, the effective interest rate is increased.

Discounting   Process of finding the present value of future cash flows.

Dividend payout ratio   A measure of the level of dividends distributed, defined as dividends divided by earnings.

Draft   A checklike instrument that may be payable on sight (sight draft) or at some future date (time draft).

Duration   A measure of the average life of a security, defined as the weighted average of the times until each payment is made, with weights proportional to the total present value of the payment.

Duration gap   Mismatch between the duration (maturities) of assets and liabilities.

Earnings   See *Accounting income*.

Earnings per share (EPS)   A measure of each common share's claim on earnings, defined as earnings available to common shareholders divided by the number of common share outstanding.

EBIT   Earnings before interest and taxes.

EBIT-EPS indifference point   The level of earnings before interest and taxes (EBIT) that equates earnings per share (EPS) between two different financing alternatives.

Economic order quantity (EOQ)   The traditional optimal inventory ordering quantity. The EOQ quantity minimizes the total ordering and carrying costs. It is being supplanted by just-in-time systems.

Economic profits   The excess of revenues over both explicit and implicit costs of the factors employed.

Economies of scale   Long-run average costs decline as output increases.

Efficient capital market   The prices of securities fully reflect available information. Investors buying securities in an efficient market should expect to earn an equilibrium rate of return.

Electronic funds transfer A system in which funds are moved between computer terminals without the use of written checks.

Equity The ownership interests of common and, possibly, preferred stockholders in a company; on a balance sheet, equity equals total assets less all liabilities.

Equity method Partially consolidating income and equity of affiliates which are 20 percent or more (but less than 50 percent) owned by the parent firm. The proportionate share of the earnings of the affiliate is debited to an investment account and credited to an income account as earned. Dividend received are debited to cash and credited to the investment account.

ERISA Employee Retirement Income Security Act.

Eurodollars U.S. dollars deposited in a U.S. bank branch or a foreign bank located outside the United States.

Exercise price The price of the underlying asset at which the option contract gives the owner the right to buy or sell the asset.

External reorganization A reorganization under the formal bankruptcy laws, in which a merger partner is found for the distressed firm.

Factor market Market in which a firm purchases its inputs for production.

Factoring Selling accounts receivable at a discount to a finance company or bank. The factor bears the risk of collection.

Fair market value Price determined at arms' length between a willing buyer and a willing seller, each acting in her or his own best interest.

Fed float Funds tied up during the time necessary for a deposited check to clear through the Federal Reserve banking system, and become usable funds to the company. See *Transit float*.

Fed funds Reserves member banks keep on account at the Federal Reserve Bank. See *Federal funds rate*.

Fed wire A computer system linking member banks to the Federal Reserve Bank used for making interbank payments of Federal Reserve funds and for making deliveries of and payment for Treasury and agency securities.

Federal funds rate The rate of interest at which Federal Reserve Bank funds are traded. This rate is currently pegged by the Federal Reserve through open-market operations.

Field warehousing financing agreement An inventory financing arrangement in which collateralized inventory is stored on the premises of the borrower but is controlled by an independent warehouse company.

FIFO First-in, first-out, a method of inventory accounting in which the oldest item in inventory is assumed to be sold first. Contrast with *Last-in, first-out* (LIFO).

Financial Accounting Standards Board (FASB) Official rule-making body in the accounting profession.

Financial asset Any asset having a value defined in unit of currency. Cash, accounts receivable, accounts payable, and debt are monetary items; inventories and plant and equipment are physical items. See *Monetary asset*.

Financial disclosure Presentation of financial information to the investment community.

Financial flexibility   The ability to raise sufficient capital to meet company needs under a wide variety of future contingencies.

Financial lease   See *Capital lease.*

Financial leverage   Use of debt to increase the expected return and the risk to equity.

Fixed-asset turnover   Sales divided by total fixed assets.

Fixed cost   Any cost that does not vary in the short run with changes in volume.

Float   The difference between the corporation's recorded ledger cash balance and the amount credited to the corporation by the bank.

Floating lien agreement   A legal contract in which a borrower gives a lender a general claim on the firm's entire inventory as collateral for a loan.

Foreign exchange rate   The relationship between the value of two or more currencies.

Foreign exchange risk   The possibility of a drop in revenue or an increase in cost in an international transaction due to a change in foreign exchange rates.

Forward contract   A contract that obligates the buyer to buy or the seller to sell a given commodity at a given price (the forward price) at a given point in time. There is no interim cash flow associated with a forward contract.

Forward market   A market in which participants agree to trade some commodity, security, or foreign exchange at a fixed price at some future date.

Fraudulent actions   Unlawful actions engaged in by management that misrepresent financial performance.

Full costing   See *Absorption costing.*

Funds   Generally means net working capital. Sometimes refers to cash or near cash. Along with cash flow, *funds* is one of the most frequently misused words in finance.

Futures contract   A standardized contract to buy or sell a commodity at some specified price in the future. It is generally traded on organized exchanges and is marked-to-market daily.

GAAP   Generally Accepted Accounting Principles, a set of accounting principles that are supposed to be followed in preparing accounting statements.

Gap   See *Duration gap.*

General creditor   A creditor whose loan is uncollateralized.

Going-concern value   The present value of a business' expected future after-tax cash flows.

Golden parachute   A very generous termination agreement that provides payments to current management in the event of a hostile takeover of the company.

Goodwill   An intangible asset that reflects value above that generally recognized in the tangible assets of the firm.

Gordon model   A widely known valuation model that is often used to determine the cost of equity. It is calculated as dividend yield plus expected growth.

Gross margin (gross profit)   Revenue minus cost of goods sold.

Hedge ratio   The number of units of a security (such as options, futures) that should be bought to hedge one unit of an underlying security, commodity, or exchange rate.

Hedging   To engage in a transaction that partially or fully reduces a prior risk exposure by taking a position that is the opposite of the initial position. A perfect hedge produces a riskless portfolio. See *Cross hedge*.

Historical cost   Initial acquisition cost.

Immunization   A strategy that matches durations of assets and liabilities so as to make net worth unaffected by interest rate movements.

Implicit costs   The opportunity costs of resources, both physical and financial.

Income   See *Accounting income*.

Income statement   A report of a company's revenues, associated expenses, and resulting income for a period of time.

Indeterminate debt   A liability lacking the criterion of being payable at a specific time.

Inflation   Upward movements of the average price level.

Insolvent   Insufficient liquid assets to meet currently due financial obligations. Assets may still exceed liabilities.

Insubstance debt defeasance   Borrower sets aside cash or bonds in an irrevocable trust that will generate future cash flows sufficient to service the borrower's debt. Both the borrower's debt and the offsetting cash or bonds are removed from the balance sheet.

Intangible asset   A nonphysical, noncurrent asset (such as a patent).

Interest rate risk   The risk that a rise in interest rates will take place, which will lead to a reduction in the market value of fixed-income securities.

Interest rate swap   A method to manage interest rate risk whereby parties trade the cash flows corresponding to different securities without actually exchanging securities directly.

In-the-money option   An option that would be worth exercising if it expired immediately.

Intrinsic value of an option   That portion of an option's price that reflects its value if immediately executed. For a call, intrinsic value is the market price of the underlying asset less the striking price, or zero if the difference is negative. For a put, the intrinsic value is the striking price less the stock price, or zero if the difference is negative.

Inventoriable costs   Costs that become part of the product's cost (asset) as opposed to a period cost (expense).

Inventory profits   Profits generated as a result of an inflationary economy, in which old inventory is sold at large profits because of increasing prices. This is particularly prevalent under FIFO accounting.

Inventory-turnover ratio   Cost of goods sold (or sometimes sales) divided by ending inventory. The ratio represents the number of times average inventory has been sold during the period.

Joint venture   A company in which two or more businesses participate with no one company owning more than 50 percent.

Junk bonds   Any bond rated BB or below by Standard & Poor's or Baa or below by Moody's. These bonds usually promise very high return but have substantial default risk.

Just-in-time inventory control   A production and management system in which inventory is cut down to a minimum through adjustments to the time and physical distance between the various production operations. The firm relies upon suppliers to furnish parts "just in time" for them to be assembled.

Lease   A contractual arrangement between the owner of equipment (lessor) and the user of equipment (lessee), which calls for the lessee to pay the lessor an established lease payment. There are two kinds of leases: financial (capital) leases and operating leases.

Less-than-conservative accounting   Management's selection of alternative GAAP that portray the company's financial condition and performance in a better light.

Letter of credit   A credit letter normally issued by an importer's bank, in which the bank promises to pay out the money for the merchandise when delivered.

Leverage   The use of fixed-charge items with the intent of magnifying the potential returns to the firm.

Leveraged buyout (LBO)   Purchase of a company financed in large part by company borrowings. The lender lends against the strength of the assets of the company being purchased and the future cash flow of the acquired business.

Liability   An obligation to pay an amount at a certain time in return for a current benefit.

LIBOR   London Interbank Offered Rate, an interbank rate applicable for large deposits in the London market. It is a benchmark rate, just like the prime interest rate in the United States. LIBOR is usually lower than the U.S. prime rate.

Lien   Lender's claims on specified assets.

Life cycle curve   A curve illustrating the growth phases of a firm.

LIFO   Last-in, first-out, a method of inventory accounting in which the newest item in inventory is assumed to be sold first. Contrast with *FIFO*.

LIFO reserve   Current or FIFO cost of ending inventory less historical cost. It is an unrealized holding gain in ending inventory.

Like-kind exchange   A nontaxable exchange of property that must be either trade or business property or property held for investment.

Line of credit   Prearranged agreement with a lender for short-term borrowings on demand under prespecified terms. There is no "legal" commitment on the part of the lender to provide the stated credit.

Liquid asset   Any asset that can be quickly converted to cash without significant loss of value. Generally includes cash, marketable securities and, maybe, accounts receivable.

Liquidation   The process of closing down a company, selling its assets, paying off its creditors, and distributing any remaining cash to owners. Priority of claims is important in a liquidation because it is unlikely that all parties will be fully satisfied in their demands.

Liquidation value   The cash generated by terminating a business and selling its assets individually. The liquidation value of equity is the proceeds of the asset sale less all company liabilities.

Liquidity   The extent to which a company has assets that are readily available to meet obligations as they come due.

Liquidity flow index   Ratio of expected operating cash inflows to the expected cash outflows.

Liquidity ratio   Any ratio used to estimate a company's liquidity.

Lockbox system   A form of concentration banking used to expedite cash inflows to a business. Customers mail their checks to a post office box in their geographic region, and a local bank picks up the checks and processes them for rapid collection. Funds are then wired to the corporate home office for immediate use.

Long position   The ownership of stocks of other securities; opposed to a short position, where one has sold securities that are not owned.

Lower of cost or market   A basis for inventory valuation where value is set at the lower of cost or market-replacement value, subject to a number of constraints.

Mail float   Funds tied up during the time that elapses from the moment a customer mails a remittance check until the firm begins to process it.

Margin call   A call by the broker requesting more capital be put up to maintain the investment. See *Mark-to-market*.

Margin of safety   Calculated as the difference between actual sales and breakeven sales, divided by actual sales.

Marginal cost (MC)   The change in total cost associated with producing an additional unit of output. Marginal costs equal average costs when average costs are at their minimum level and increase above average costs at higher levels of output.

Marginal factor cost   The additional cost incurred in purchasing the services of an additional unit of a productive input.

Marginal physical product (MPP)   The additional output that can be produced by one more unit of a particular input while holding all other inputs constant. It is usually assumed that an input's marginal productivity diminishes as additional units of the input are put into use while holding other inputs fixed.

Marginal revenue (MR)   The extra revenue produced for a firm by selling one more unit of output. For a perfectly competitive firm marginal revenue is equal to price. For economic profit maximization a firm must produce additional output until marginal revenue is equal to marginal cost; the cost incurred on the last unit of output just equals the additional revenues generated, but for each preceding unit, marginal revenue exceeds marginal cost.

Mark-to-market   Practice of recomputing profits or losses in a margin account (stock or futures) on a daily basis. See *Margin call*.

Markov chain analysis   As applied to accounts receivable, it is a probability model based on learned behavior about customers payment patterns.

Maturity date   The date on which the bond is retired and the principal (par value) is repaid to the lender.

Maturity factoring   Factoring arrangement that provides collection and insurance of accounts receivable. The factor does not advance funds on the uncollected receivables.

Miller–Orr model   A cash management control-limit model that allows irregular cash patterns. Contrast with the *Baumol model*.

Minority interest   An indeterminate liability showing the equity in a subsidiary company belonging to those who are not part of the controlling interest.

Mix variance   The difference between actual quantities and actual quantities restated in budgeted proportions, times budgeted prices. It is totally divorced from any price or quantity effects.

Monetary asset   See *Financial asset.*

Money markets   Competitive markets for securities with maturities of 270 days or less. The best examples of money market instruments are Treasury bills, commercial paper, and negotiable certificates of deposit.

Mortgage   A loan collaterized by property, particularly real estate. The lender is entitled to take possession of the property if the debt is not repaid in a timely manner.

Net income   Earnings after tax. See *Accounting income.*

Net monetary creditor   Economic agent having monetary assets in excess of liabilities.

Net monetary debtor   Economic agent having monetary assets less than liabilities.

Net present value (NPV)   Present value of all cash inflows and outflows at a given discount rate. The increase in wealth accruing to an investor when he or she undertakes an investment.

Net profit   See *Accounting income.*

Net sales   Total sales less returns and allowances and sales discounts.

Netting   The process of offsetting reciprocal liabilities between parties to arrive at a (reduced) net figure owed, or to be received, by each party.

Net working capital   The excess of current assets over current liabilities. Alternatively, the excess of shareholders' equity and long-term debt (including indeterminate debt) over fixed and intangible assets. Contrast with *Working capital.*

Net worth   See *Equity.*

Nonabsorbing state (transitional state)   As it applies to accounts receivable, it is a state in which the account is neither paid in full nor declared delinquent.

Noncash charge   An expense recorded by an accountant not matched by a cash outflow during the accounting period.

Nonmonetary items   All items not considered monetary.

Nonsub subsidiary   A venture in which another firm has played a significant role without taking an equity position at the outset.

Off-balance-sheet financing   Financing that is not shown as a liability in a company's balance sheet.

Old-line factoring   Factoring arrangement that provides collection, insurance, and finance for accounts receivable.

Oligopoly   A market in which several large firms control a large part of the industry's output; because the industry comprises so few firms, each firm must take into consideration the reactions of the other firms prior to deciding on its own course of action; mutually interdependent behavior of firms is the unique characteristic of this form of market structure.

One-time transaction   What accountants refer to as "extraordinary transactions."

Open interest   A figure that refers to the total number of contracts not offset or satisfied by a delivery for a given contract. The larger the number the more liquid the contract.

Operating cycle   The period of time between the acquisition of production inputs and the collection of sales receipts for the product manufactured with the inputs.

Operating lease   A short-term contractual commitment on the part of the firm leasing the asset (the lessee) to make a series of payments to the firm that actually owns the asset (the lessor) for use of the asset. The agreement is easily cancelable.

Operating leverage   Fixed operating costs that tend to increase the variation in profits. See *Degree of operating leverage.*

Opportunity cost   Expected return that is foregone by investing in a project rather than in comparable financial securities.

Optimal capital structure   A capital structure that has the best possible mix of debt, preferred stock, and common equity. The optimal mix should provide the lowest possible cost of capital to the firm.

Out-of-the-money option   An option that would not be worth exercising if it matured immediately.

Paid in capital   See *Additional paid-in-capital.*

Pass-through security   A security on which payment of interest and principal on the underlying securities are passed through to the security holder by an agent.

Payable period   A measure of a company's use of trade credit financing, defined as accounts payable divided by purchases per day.

Payment pattern approach   An approach that relates cash collections back to the sales that generates them.

Pension Benefit Guaranty Corporation (PBGC)   A federal corporation set up under Employee Retirement Income Security Act (ERISA); it provides insurance to pension participants in the event that a firm defaults on its pension obligations.

Pension fund   Assets held in trust to cover the costs of pension benefits to participants; not part of the firm's assets.

Pension liability   The present value of promised pension benefits.

Pension plan assets   The fair value of assets in the pension plan.

Percent-of-sales method   A method of determining future financial needs that is an alternative to the development of *pro forma* financial statements.

Perfect competition   The most widely used economic model, in which there are assumed to be a large number of buyers and sellers for any good and in which each agent is a price taker.

Permanent current assets   Current assets that are not reduced or converted to cash within the normal operating cycle of the firm.

Physical asset   Nonmonetary asset; real asset.

Pipeline inventory   Raw materials inventory in transit and work-in-process inventory.

Pledging receivables   Using accounts receivable as collateral for a loan. The firm usually may borrow 60 to 80 percent of the value of acceptable collateral.

Postemployment benefit (nonpension)   Retirement benefits provided to employees by employers, such as health care or health insurance, life insurance and disability benefits. Largely accounted for on a pay-as-you-go basis or cash basis.

Preauthorized checks (PACS)   A check that resembles the ordinary check but does not contain or require the signature of the person on whose account it is being drawn, although the individual's legal authorization is required.

Preauthorized debits (PADS)   Paperless transactions that require the customer's authorization for the seller to automatically transfer funds from the buyer's account to the seller's account.

Precautionary balances   Cash balances held as safety stock to absorb uncertainty in the cash flow stream.

Price variance   The difference between actual prices and budgeted prices, times actual quantity.

Prime rate   Rate at which banks lend to their most favored customers.

Prior service cost   Present value at a given time of a pension plan's unrecognized benefits assigned to employees for their service before that given time.

Pro forma **statement**   A financial statement prepared on the basis of some assumed future events.

Processing float   Funds tied up during the time required for the firm to process remittance checks before they can be deposited in the bank.

Product financing   The sale of a product to another party with the explicit understanding that the product will be repurchased in the future.

Production function   A conceptual mathematical function that records the relationship between a firm's inputs and its outputs.

Product market   The market where firms sell their production.

Profit   The excess of revenue over cost; accountants consider only the explicit costs incurred by a firm, while economists view total costs in terms of opportunity costs, which include both explicit and implicit costs.

Profit margin   The proportion of each sales dollar minus all expenses, divided by net sales.

Profitability ratios   A group of ratios that indicates the return on sales, total assets, and invested capital.

Project financing   When one or more companies invest in a venture without having to consolidate the venture with the investor companies. The equity method of accounting is used to record the investment.

Projected benefit obligation   Actuarial present value as of a date of all benefits attributed by the pension benefit formula to employee service rendered prior to that date.

Prospectus   A formal document that all companies offering new securities for public sale must file with the Securities and Exchange Commission. It details the financial position of the offering company, what the new funds will be used for, the qualifications of the corporate officers, and any other material information.

Proxy statement   Provides official notification to designated classes of shareholders of matters to be brought to a vote at a shareholders' meeting. Disclosures normally made via a proxy statement may in some cases be made using the 10-K.

Public warehousing   An inventory financing arrangement in which inventory, used as collateral, is stored with and controlled by an independent warehousing company.

Put option   Option to sell an asset at a specified exercise price on or before a specified date of maturity.

Quality of earnings   A relative concept that concerns company's conservatism in determining earnings. It addresses differences between accrual accounting and cash accounting.

Quantity variance   The difference between actual quantities restated in budgeted proportions and budgeted quantities, times budgeted price.

Quick ratio   See *Acid test ratio*.

Ratio analysis   Analysis of financial statements by means of ratios.

Reaching into the past   Reversal of expenses or reserves established in prior periods with the result that current period's profits are improved.

Real amount   Any quantity that has been adjusted for changes in the purchasing power of the currency due to inflation.

Real asset   Nonmonetary asset; physical asset.

Recourse   General claim of a lender against some party if collateral is insufficient to repay the debt of a "loan with recourse."

Relative liquidity index   The ratio of potential net cash flow sources divided by the uncertainty associated with those net cash flows.

Remote disbursing account   A disbursing account at a bank located at a point where check presentation times are long. See *Controlled disbursing account*.

Reorganization   An attempt to keep a company in continued operations by correcting its present financial structure.

Repo (repurchase agreement)   An investment in which a Treasury security is bought from a securities dealer with an agreement that the dealer will repurchase it at a specified price and date.

Residual income   Cash flow from operations less the dollar cost of capital employed.

Retained earnings   The amount of earnings retained and reinvested in a business and not distributed to stockholders as dividends.

Return on assets (ROA)   A measure of the productivity of assets, defined as income divided by total assets. A superior but less common definition adjusts for interest expense in the numerator.

Return on equity (ROE)   A measure of the productivity or efficiency with which shareholders' equity is employed, defined as income divided by equity.

Return on investment (ROI)   See *Return on assets*.

Revenues   Sales.

Revolving credit agreement   Legally assured line of credit with a bank.

Riding the depreciation curve   Management fails to make investments that at least equal the depreciation expense incurred.

Robert Morris Associates   An organization of bankers that compiles averages of financial ratios for various industry groups.

Sale and leaseback   Sale of an existing asset to an entity that then leases it back to the user for a specified period, under specified terms.

Secured creditor   A creditor whose obligation is backed by the pledge of some asset. In liquidation, the secured creditor receives the cash from the sale of the pledged asset to the extent of his or her loan.

Secured debt   See *Secured creditor*.

Securitization   Substituting tradable securities for privately negotiated instruments.

Sequential decision system   A cost/benefit analysis associated with examination of information.

Shareholder wealth maximization   Maximizing the wealth of the firm's shareholders through achieving the highest possible value for the firm in the marketplace. It is the overriding objective of the firm and should influence all decisions.

Shareholders' equity   See *Equity*.

Solvency   The state of being able to pay debts as they come due.

Sources and uses statement   A document that segregates all changes in balance-sheet accounts into those that provided resources and those that consumed resources.

Speculative balances   Cash balances held for purposes of speculating.

Speculator   A trader, in say futures contracts, who attempts to profit from anticipated price changes.

Spontaneous liability   Those liabilities such as accounts payable and accrued wages that arise automatically, without negotiation, in the course of doing business.

Spot price   The current cash market price of a security.

Staggered funding   Deposits of funds, on a forecasted basis, to cover checks to be presented against an account.

Standard cost   The forecasted cost of an item under assumed conditions for price, technology, and operational efficiency.

Statement of cash flow   A financial statement showing the sources and uses of cash for the period. The statement translates accrual-based net income into actual cash dollars.

Statement of changes in financial position   A financial statement showing the changes in net working capital for the period and the net working capital accounts themselves. Also called the funds statement.

Stone model   Control-limit cash management model.

Stretching payables   Failing to pay within the prescribed credit period. For example, under credit terms of 2/10, net 30, a firm would be stretching its payables if it paid on day 55 instead of on day 30.

Striking price (exercise price)   The fixed price for which a stock can be purchased in a call contract or sold in a put contract.

Sustainable growth rate   The rate of increase in sales a company can attain without changing its profit margin, assets-to-sales ratio, debt-to-equity ratio, or dividend payout ratio.

Swap   An arrangement whereby two companies lend to each other on different terms, for example, in different currencies, or one at a fixed interest rate and the other at a floating interest rate.

Take-or-pay contract   An agreement between a buyer and a seller for the buyer to pay a specified amount whether delivery of the product is taken or not.

Tangible assets   Physical assets such as plant and machinery.

Tax shield   The reduction in a company's tax bill caused by an increase in a tax-deductible expense, usually depreciation or interest. The tax shield equals the tax rate times the expense.

Technical insolvency   Inability of a firm to pay its bills as they come due. Although its assets may exceed its total liabilities, thereby indicating a positive net worth, the company simply does not have sufficient liquidity to pay its debts.

Term structure of interest rates   Relationship between interest rates on loans of similar default risk but having different maturities.

Terminal warehouse agreement   A security agreement in which the inventories pledged as collateral are transported to a public warehouse that is physically removed from the borrower's premises.

Through-put contract   Similar to "take-or-pay contracts" except for services.

Times interest earned   A coverage ratio measure of financial leverage, defined as earnings before interest and taxes divided by interest expense.

Total asset turnover   Sales divided by total assets.

Trade credit   Terms of credit whereby one business allows another business to buy from it in return for a promise to pay later.

Trade payables   See *Accounts payable*.

Transaction balances   Cash balances to satisfy operational needs.

Transaction exposure   Foreign exchange gains and losses resulting from actual international transactions. These may be hedged through the foreign exchange market, the money market, or the currency futures market.

Transit float   See *Fed float*.

Translation exposure   The foreign-located assets and liabilities of a multinational corporation, which are denominated in foreign currency units, and are exposed to losses and gains due to changing exchange rates. This is called *Accounting or translation exposure*.

Treasury bills   Government debt securities issued on a discount basis by the U.S. Treasury for periods of less than one year.

Trust receipt   An instrument acknowledging that the borrower holds the inventory and proceeds for sale in trust for the lender. Receipt for goods that are to be held in trust for the lender.

Unsecured debt   A loan that requires no assets as collateral but allows the bondholder a general claim against the corporation, rather than a lien against specific assets.

Value date   In the market for foreign exchange this term refers to the delivery date of funds traded. Normally it is on spot transactions two days after a transaction is agreed upon.

Variable cost   Any expense that varies with sales over the observation period.

Variable costing   See *Direct costing*.

Warrants   An option issued by the firm to purchase shares of the firm's stock.

Wealth-maximizing entity   A firm that enhances wealth of its shareholders. In an economic framework, it is where marginal revenue equals marginal cost.

Weighted average cost of capital   The weighted opportunity cost of all forms of financial capital employed by the firm as measured in market prices and market weights. It is only appropriate for non–risk-changing investments.

Window dressing   Making financial statements appear more favorable than they actually are.

Wire transfer   A means of effecting the immediate transferring of funds from one account at one bank to an account at another bank; instructions for this transfer are transmitted over one of two wire systems — one maintained by the Federal Reserve System and one maintained by a group of private banks.

Work-in-process-inventory   Inventory that is partially processed.

Working capital   Current assets. Contrast with *Net working capital*.

Yield curve   A graph of the relationship between the maturities of securities with comparable default risk and their yields.

Zero-balance account (ZBA)   A checking account in which a zero balance is maintained by transfers of funds from a master account in an amount only large enough to cover checks presented.

Z-score   An index derived from a multiple discriminant analysis model for ascertaining the category of an observation.

Selected Readings

Most of the readings cited here are in addition to those included in footnotes in the various chapters. An excellent source of readings pertaining to many of the topics discussed in this book is *Readings on Short-Term Financial Management*, 3rd edition, edited by K. V. Smith and G. W. Gallinger (St. Paul, MN: West Publishing Company, 1988).

Chapter 1
Introduction to Liquidity Management

Beranek, W. "Towards a Positive Theory of Working Capital," mimeo University of Georgia.

Doherty, N.A. *Corporate Risk Management: A Financial Perspective* (New York: McGraw-Hill, 1985).

Drucker, P. F. "The Delusion of 'Profits'," *Wall Street Journal* (February 5, 1975): 10.

Levasseur, M. G. "An Option Model Approach to Firm Liquidity Management," *Journal of Banking and Finance*, Vol. 1 (1977): 13–28.

Walker, E. W. "Towards a Theory of Working Capital," *Engineering Economist* (January-February 1964): 21–35.

Chapter 2
Economic Fundamentals for Analysis of Liquidity

Baskin, J. "Corporate Liquidity in Games of Monopoly Power," *The Review of Economics and Statistics* (May 1987): 312–19.

Black, F. "The Magic in Earnings: Economic Earnings Versus Accounting Earnings," *Financial Analysts Journal* (November-December 1980): 19–24.

Ross, S. A. "Accounting and Economics," *Accounting Review* (April 1983): 375–380.

Chapter 3
Cash Flow Analysis

Casey, C. J., and N. J. Bartezak. "Cash Flow is Not the Bottom Line," *Harvard Business Review* (July-August 1984): 61–66.

Senatra, P. "The New Statement of Cash Flows: The Basic Rules," *The Practical Accountant* (March 1988): 28–39.

Chapter 4
Traditional Financial Analysis: Some Shortcomings

Briloff, A. J. *The Truth about Corporate Accounting* (New York: Harper & Row, 1981).

Briloff, A. J. "Standards without Standards/Principles without Principles/Fairness without Fairness," *Advances in Accounting*, Vol. 3 (1986): 25–50.

Hawawini, G., C. Viallet, and A. Vora. "Industry Influence on Corporate Working Capital Decisions," *Sloan Management Review* (Summer 1986): 15–24.

Meonske, N. R., and H. Sprohge. "How to Apply the New Accounting Rules for Deferred Taxes," *The Practical Accountant* (June 1988): 15–50.

Siegel, J. G. *How to Analyze Businesses, Financial Statements, and the Quality of Earnings* (Englewood Cliffs, NJ: Prentice-Hall, Inc. 1982).

Chapter 5
Off-Balance Sheet Financing and Financial Analysis

Ang, J., and P. P. Peterson. "The Leasing Puzzle," *Journal of Finance* (September 1984): 1055–1065.

Briloff, A. J. *Unaccountable Accounting* (New York: Harper & Row, 1972).

Briloff, A. J. *More Debits than Credits* (New York: Harper & Row, 1976).

Donegan, J., and S. Sunder. "Contract Theoretic Analysis of Off-Balance Sheet Financing," *Journal of Accounting, Auditing & Finance* (Spring 1989): 203–216.

El-Gazzar, S., S. Lilien, and V. Pastena. "The Use of Off-Balance Sheet Financing to Circumvent Financial Covenant Restrictions," *Journal of Accounting, Auditing & Finance* (Spring 1989): 217–235.

Francis, J. R., and S. A. Reiter. "Determinants of Corporate Pension Funding Strategy," *Journal of Accounting and Economics* 9 (1987): 35–59.

Harper, R. M., W. G. Mister, and J. R. Strawser. "The Impact of New Pension Disclosure Rules on Perceptions of Debt," *Journal of Accounting Research* (Autumn 1987): 327–330.

Lovata, L. M., W. D. Nichols, K. L. Philipich. "Defeasing Discounted Debt: An Economic Analysis," *Financial Management* (Spring 1987): 41–45.

Mielke, D. E., and J. Seifert. "A Survey on the Effects of Defeasing Debt," *Journal of Accounting, Auditing & Finance* (Winter 1987): 65–78.

Searfoss, D. G., and N. Erickson. "The Big Unfunded Liability: Postretirement Healthcare Benefits," *Journal of Accountancy* (November 1988): 28–39.

Smith, C. W., Jr., and L. M. Wakeman. "Determinants of Corporate Leasing Policy," *Journal of Finance* (July 1985): 895–908.

Stewart, J. E., and B. S. Neuhausen. "Financial Instruments and Transactions: the CPA's newest Challenge," *Journal of Accountancy* (August 1986): 102–4.

Chapter 6
Indicators of Liquidity

Boyadjian, H. J., and J. F. Warren. *Risks: Reading Corporate Signals* (John Wiley & Sons, 1987).

Donaldson, G. *Managing Corporate Wealth: The Operation of a Comprehensive Financial Goals System* (New York: Praeger Publishers, 1984).

Emery, G. W. "Optimal Liquidity Policy: A Stochastic Process Approach, " *Journal of Financial Research* (Fall 1982): 273–283.

Emery, G. W. "Measuring Short-Term Liquidity," *Journal of Cash Management* (July/August 1984): 25–32.

O'Glove, T. L. *Quality of Earnings: The Investor's Guide to How Much Money a Company is Really Making* (New York: The Free Press, 1987).

Chapter 7
Overview of Cash Management

Driscoll, M. C. *Cash Management: Corporate Strategies for Profit* (New York: John Wiley & Sons, 1983).

Edmunds, J. C. "Working Capital Management in Multinational Companies: An Integrated Approach," *Management International Review*, Vol. 23, No. 3 (1983): 73–80.

Srinivasan, V. "Payments Netting in International Cash Management," *Journal of International Business Studies* (Summer 1985): 1–20.

Srinivasan, V., and Y. H. Kim. "Deterministic Cash Flow Management: State of the Art and Research Directions," *Omega*, Vol. 14, No. 2 (1986): 145–166.

Stone, B. K. "The Design of a Company's Banking System," *Journal of Finance* (May 1983): 373–385, 387–389.

Chapter 8
Minimizing Cash Balances

Daellenbach, H. "Are Cash Management Optimization Models Worthwhile?" *Journal of Financial and Quantitative Analysis* (September 1974): 607–626.

Emery, G. W. "Some Empirical Evidence on the Properties of Daily Cash Flow," *Financial Management* (Spring 1981): 21–28.

Stone, B. K., and T. W. Miller. "Daily Cash Forecasting with Multiplicative Models of Cash Flow Patterns," *Financial Management* (Winter 1987): 45–54.

Chapter 9
Duration Analysis and Hedging with Futures

Asset/Liability Management, edited by G. H. Troughton. The Institute of Chartered Financial Analysts (September 1985).

Casabona, P. A., F. J. Fabozzi, and J. C. Francis. "How to Apply Duration to Equity Analysis," *Journal of Portfolio Management* (Winter 1984): 52–58.

Kaufman, G. G. "Measuring and Managing Interest Rate Risk: A Primer," *Economic Perspectives* (Federal Reserve Bank of Chicago, January-February 1984): 16–29.

Kopprasch, R. W., and M. Pitts. *Hedging Short-Term Liabilities with Interest Rate Futures.* Solomon Brothers Inc. (April 1983).

Chapter 10
Hedging with Options, Options on Futures, and Interest-Rate Swaps

Adler, M., and J. B. Detemple. "On the Optimal Hedge of a Nontraded Cash Position," *Journal of Finance* (March 1988): 143–153.

Bhattacharya, A. K., and J. Breit. "Customized Interest Rate Risk Management," *Handbook of Fixed Income Securities,* 3rd edition. Hinsdale, IL: Dow Jones-Irwin (forthcoming).

Bicksler, J., and A. H. Chen. "An Economic Analysis of Interest Rate Swaps," *Journal of Finance.* (July 1986): 645–55.

Block, S. B., and T. J. Gallagher. "The Use of Interest Rate Futures and Options by Corporate Financial Managers," *Financial Management.* (Autumn 1986): 73–79.

Johnson, C. *An Introduction to Options,* Salomon Brothers Inc. (October 1987).

Wall, L. D., and J. J. Pringle. "Interest Rate Swaps: A Review of the Issues," *Federal Reserve Bank of Atlanta Economic Review* (December 1988): 22–40.

Chapter 11
Asset-Based Financing

Cumming, C. "The Economics of Securitization," *Federal Reserve Bank of New York Quarterly Review* (Autumn 1987): 11–23.

Estrella, A. "Corporate Use of Pension Overfunding," *Federal Reserve Bank of New York Quarterly Review* (Spring 1984): 17–25.

Hamdallah, A. E., and W. Ruland. "The Decision to Terminate Overfunded Pension Plans," *Journal of Accounting and Public Policy,* Vol. 5 (1986): 77–91.

Weil, P. H. *Asset-Based Lending: An Introductory Guide to Secured Financing* (New York, NY: Practising Law Institute, 1989).

Chapter 12
Credit Selection Models

Beranek, W., and W. Taylor. "Credit-Scoring Models and the Cut-Off Point — A Simplification," *Decision Sciences* (July 1976): 394–404.

Cyert, R. M., and G. L. Thompson. "Selecting a Portfolio of Credit Risks by Markov Chains," *Journal of Business* (January 1968): 39–46.

Mehta, D. "The Formulation of Credit Policy Models," *Management Science* (October 1968): B30–B50.

Stowe, J. D. "An Integer Programming Solution for the Optimal Investigation/Credit Granting Sequence," *Financial Management* (Summer 1985): 66–76.

Chapter 13
Analysis of Credit Policy

Beranek, W. "The Optimal Cash Discount," Mimeo, August 1989, University of Georgia.

Emery, G. W. "A Pure Financial Explanation for Trade Credit," *Journal of Financial and Quantitative Analysis* (September 1984): 271–285.

Emery, G. W. "Positive Theories of Trade Credit," *Advances in Working Capital Management*, Vol. 1: 115–130.

Lam, C. H., and A. H. Chen. "A Note of Optimal Credit and Pricing Policy Under Uncertainty: A Contingent-Claims Approach," *Journal of Finance* (December 1986): 1141–1148.

Monahan, J. P. "A Quantity Discount Model to Increase Vendor Profits," *Management Science* (June 1984): 720–726.

Smith, J. K. "Trade Credit and Information Asymmetry," *Journal of Finance* (September 1987): 863–872.

Chapter 14
Monitoring Trade Credit

Bukics, R. L., and W. T. Loven. *The Handbook of Credit and Accounts Receivable Management* (Chicago, IL: Probus, 1987).

Gallinger, G. W., and A. J. Ifflander. "Monitoring Accounts Receivable Using Variance Analysis," *Financial Management* (Winter 1986): 69–76.

Gentry, J. A., and J. De La Garza. "Monitoring Accounts Receivable: Revisited," *Financial Management* (Winter 1985): 28–38.

Lewellen, W. G., and R. W. Johnson. "Better Way to Monitor Accounts Receivable," *Harvard Business Review* (May-June 1972): 101–109.

Stone, B. K. "The Payments-Pattern Approach to the Forecasting and Control of Accounts Receivable," *Financial Management* (Autumn 1976): 65–82.

Chapter 15
Inventory Accounting and Cash Flow Effects

Granof, M. H., and D. G. Short. 'Why do Companies Reject LIFO?" *Journal of Accounting, Auditing & Finance* (Summer 1984): 323–333.

Chapter 16
Inventory Investment: How Much?

Kim Y. H., and K. H. Chung. "Inventory Management Under Uncertainty: A Financial Theory for the Transactions Motive," *Managerial and Decision Economics*, Vol. 10 (1989): 291–298.

Krajewski, L. J., B. E. King, and L. P. Ritzman. "Kanban, MRP, and Shaping the Manufacturing Environment," *Management Science* (January 1987): 39–57.

McDaniel, W. R. "The Economic Order Quantity and Wealth Maximization," *Financial Review* (November 1986): 527–536.

Zangwill, W. I. "From EOQ towards ZI (Zero Inventory)," *Management Science* (November 1987): 1209–23.

Chapter 17
Monitoring Inventory Balances

Schroeder, R. G., and R. Krishnan. "Return on Investment as a Criterion for Inventory Models," *Decision Sciences* (October 1976): 697–704.

Chapter 18
A Summary

Bhattacharya, A. K., and G. W. Gallinger. "The Relationship Between Liquidity, Capital Structure and Firm Value," *Advances in Working Capital Management* (forthcoming in Volume II, 1990).

Gilmer, R. "The Optimal Level of Liquid Assets: An Empirical Test," *Financial Management* (Winter 1985): 39–43.

Answers to Problems

Chapter 1

1. Residual income (RI) = $1388.40
2. RI = $1073
3. (a) RI = $647
   (b) RI = $1287
4. 63.3%
5. RI = $500
6. (a) NPV = $698.29
   (b) RI = $600
   (c) NPV = $7500
       RI = $600
7. RI = −$190.25
8. RI = $36.58

Chapter 2

1. (b) 20, 1.0
   (d) 56, 14, 2.8
2. Marginal cost for total output of 40 units = $1.88
3. Profit maximized at $522.50 sales
4. (a) Efficient output level = 147 units
   (b) Profit maximization = 147 units
   (c) Profit maximization = 105 units
5. (a) 1392 units
   (b) Current ratio = 2.78
   (c) Reduce current assets and liabilities by $540

Chapter 3

1. (a) 2   (g) 2
   (b) 1   (h) 3
   (c) 2   (i) 3
   (d) 2   (j) 1
   (e) 2   (k) 3
   (f) 2   (l) 1

2. (a) Disposal of fixed assets = $1959
   (b) Disposal of fixed assets = $1959
        Purchase of fixed assets = $2680

3. (a) Sale of fixed assets = $1000
   (b) Disposal of fixed assets = $1000
        Purchase of fixed assets = $1000

4. Cash flow from operations = $108,000

5. Cash flow from operations = $38,400

6. Profit after tax = $693
   Increase in cash = $2333

Chapter 4

1. Year 1990:
   Current ratio = 1.50
   Quick ratio = 0.83
   Defensive interval = 107 days
   Accounts receivable turnover = 4.44
   Inventory turnover = 2.13
   Net fixed-asset turnover = 2
   Total debt-equity = 0.90
   Fixed coverage = 1.09
   Simple interest coverage = 4.44
   Degree of financial leverage = 1.29
   Book value per share = $5.00
   Cash flow per share = $1.58
   Return on assets = 0.21 (using EBIT)
   Return on assets = 0.15 (using net income)
   Return on equity = 0.215
   Breakeven sales = $260.87
   Margin of safety = 0.37

3. Many different answers are possible.

4. Profit = $25.63
   Total assets = $358.75
   Total current assets = $172.77

5. $Z = 3.2252$

6. $Z = 2.8625$

7. $19x1$ Defensive interval = 63.5 days
        Current ratio = 2.70

8. 19x1 DOL = 1.68
   DFL = 1.25
   Estimated age of fixed assets = 6.6 years

9. 19x1 Breakeven = $524
   Margin of safety = 51.8%

10. Income tax expense = $513,381
    Income tax payable = $171,973
    Deferred income tax = $341,408

Chapter 5

1. (a) Unfunded liability = $2,115,691
   (b) Funding obligation = $859,691
   (c) Financial statement adjustment = $359,691

3. (a) Year 1's borrow option: net income = $24,900
       Year 2's capital lease: net income = $24,866
       Year 3's operating lease: net income = $25,439

4. (a) Rate = 12%
   (b) Present value = $30,198,158

5. Must capitalize; capitalized value equals market price.

6. Conventional ratio = 0.27; adjusted ratio = 0.31

7. $447,207.48

8. $97,991.02

9. (a) Operating lease cash outflow = $367,466.40
       Capital lease cash outflow = $411,562.00
   (b) Financial (capital) lease; $2782.68
   (c) IRR 9%–10%

11. (a)

	Current	After
$\dfrac{\text{Profit after tax}}{\text{Sales}}$ =	2.3%	5.7%
$\dfrac{\text{Quick assets}}{\text{Current Liabilities}}$ =	1.3	1.4

12. Segregate = $17,725,527.94; gain = $2,274,472.06

Chapter 6

1. ROA: no leverage = 10%, leverage = 10%
   ROE: no leverage = 10%, leverage = 15.2%

2. Last year, current assets = 0.105 of total assets
   Last year, profit = 0.098 of total sales

3. Last year, ROE = 0.198

4. $g_s = 0.265$; $g_a = 0.143$

5. Last year's cash conversion cycle = −52.6 days

6. Traditional breakeven (case 2 type) = $1,282,983
   Cash breakeven sales level = $2,307,409

8. 1990 current assets = 0.474 of total assets
   1990 net income = 0.107 of total sales

9. g_s = 0.024

10. 1990 cash conversion cycle = 219 days

11. 1990 cash breakeven sales level = $399.1

Chapter 7

2. (a) Deposits in transit = $5180
        Outstanding checks = $2200
   (b) Adjusted cash balance = $16,980

3. (a) $100,000
   (b) $120,000
   (c) $90,000

4. (a) $1,375,000
   (b) $705,000
   (c) $52,500
   (d) $32,100

5. (a) $497,333
   (b) $25,200
   (c) 5.07%
   (d) $24,533

6. (a) $1,133,333
   (b) $200,000
   (c) −$86,667

7. (a) Cash conversion cycle = 69.7 days
   (b) Net working capital = $8,451,000

8. (a) Ledger = −$200,000
   (b) $600,000 on day 4
   (c) Gain = $120,000

9. (a) Day 3 = $0
   (b) 3 days
   (c) −$1,200,000

10. Sales = $20,100,000

11. (a) Daily sales = $42,500
    (b) 21.5%

Chapter 8

1. (a) $60,000
   (b) $30,000

 (c) 33.33

 (d) $6000

 (e) $M^* = \$44,721.36$ and $\$70,710.68$

2. (a) $10,392.30

 (b) $5196.15

 (c) 41%

3. (a) $R = \$1004.15$; $h = \$3012.45$; average $= \$1338.87$

4. Total operating income $= \$14,202,000$
Total cash receipts $= \$20,087,000$
Total cash disbursements $= \$13,515,000$

5. August receipts minus disbursements $= -\$500$

6. June receipts minus disbursements $= \$41,750$

7. June receipts minus disbursements $= \$24,029$

8. July cumulative cash balance $= \$5$

9. Ending cash balance $= \$120,000$

10. Tuesday's $d_i^* = -0.002$

11. Day 3's budget $= -\$4137.93$

12. Buy $12,550 securities

13. (a) $10,200 securities bought on day 4

 (b) $25,200 securities bought on day 4

 (c) Residual income (forecast) $= \$210.98$

 (d) Residual income (no forecast) $= \$175.15$

14. Ending cash balance on day 3:
3-day forecast $= \$14,295$
No forecast $= \$27,405$

15. Forecast LFI $= 1.05$

16. (a) Budget RLI $= 2.77$

 (b) $39.72

Chapter 9

1. Micro duration $= 2$ years
Griggs duration $= 1.96$ years

2. Equity duration $= 1.4$ years

3. Equity to asset ratio decreases 4.5 percent

4. Table 3's discounted equity $= \$31.75$
Table 4's nondiscounted future equity $= -\$27.76$
Table 5's discounted equity $= \$4.57$

5. (a) Short hedge

 (b) Basis declines to $-0.10 = 0.05$ profit
Basis declines to $-.0.20 = 0.05$ loss

6. Profit $= \$146,312$

7. (a) $18/ounce loss
   (b) $15/ounce loss
8. (a) Long hedge
   (b) −0.25
   (c) −0.50
   (d) Profit = 0.25
9. 1.08 treasury bonds for each corporate bond
10. Buys 0.907 treasury bond for each corporate bond
11. Profit = $0.03 yen per dollar

Chapter 10

1. (a) $3
   (b) $1
2. Intrinsic value:
   March = 5/64
   June = 14/64
   September = 23/64
3. (a) Long hedge
   (b) Buy call options
   (c) Buy futures and buy put options
4. −$80
5. $1,750,000
6. −$16,500
8. BNI to FSC Nov. 1989 $1010
                Nov. 1990   265
                May 1991   1005
   FSC to BMI May 1990   545

Chapter 11

1. (a) 0.855
   (b) $58,480
   (c) $925.44
   (d) $467.04
   (e) Residual income if pledged = −$448.45
        Residual income if borrow = −$845.08
2. (a) $332,622.60
   (b) $369,531.42
   (c) 28% annually
3. (a) $3723.28
   (b) 13.75% annually
   (c) $386,734.07

4. (a) High: $3,863,399.22

   (b) Low: $145,430.61

5. Total cost = $141,562.50
   Annual effective rate = 18.88%

6. (a) $14,375

   (b) $11,250

   (c) $10,833

7. (a) Present total assets = $12,900,000
        Recasted total assets = $9,964,998

   (b) Recasted current ratio = 2.10
        Recasted debt-equity ratio = 1.53

   (c) Net cash outflow:
        Without leaseback = $217,756
        With leaseback = $328,870

8. (a) No

   (b) Year 2's before tax profit will be $19,034.83 higher by owning; after
        tax cash flows will be $71,593.10 higher in year 2 by leasing.

9. Debt-equity ratio:
   Loan = 4.33
   Lease = 2.33

10. Caves net gain is $15,000,000. It should accept the exchange.

Chapter 12

2. (a) Due date = 65%
        One month late = 69%
        Two months late = 74%

   (b) (i)   Due date = 70%
              One month late = 74.4%
              Two months late = 78.9%

        (ii) Due date = 65%
              One month late = 68%
              Two months late = 70.9%

        (iii) Due date = 65%
              One month late = 70.9%
              Two months late = 76.9%

        (iv) Due date = 65%
              One month late = 72.4%
              Two months late = 79.8%

3. (a) $45

   (b) 2 months

4. State 2's breakeven probabilities:
   State of $30 = 85%
   State of $85 = 74%
   State of $285 = 70%

5. (a) $Z = 1.2005C + 0.0783T$

6. (a) Index value for account $2 = -0.26$

   (b) Index value for firm $8 = -0.29$

7. (a) 30 days from point of sale for all sales levels

   (b) 30 days from point of sale for sales of \$50 and \$90; 60 days from point of sale for sales of \$145

8. Indifference value:
State $0 = 0.1520$
State $1 = 0.3859$
State $2 = 1.179$

Chapter 13

1. When terms are 3/15, n/45

   (a) 0.371

   (b) 0.441

2. For terms 1.5/20, n/36, AIC = 0.199

3. (a) 7.963

   (b) 0.276

   (c) 0.157

4. AIC = 0.80 for terms 4/15, n/30 and 30 days acceleration

5. (a) AIC = 0.1994

   (b) AIC = 0.2743

6. Residual income = \$164,750

7. Breakeven occurs between 40 and 50 days past the discount date.

8. Residual income

   (a) \$33,792

   (b) \$14,675

   (c) \$20,442

9. Turnover

   (a) 19.2

   (b) 24.0

   (c) 12.0

10. Breakeven sales = \$60,000

11. Breakeven sales increase

   (a) 1.1%

   (b) 10%

   (c) 52.5%

12. (a) Incremental profit = \$145.73

   (b) Days 11's cash flow = \$111.38
Days 26's cash flow = \$207.25

13. Residual income = \$3659.46

14. (a) $4018.20

    (b) 10%

15. Incremental DSO = 230 days
    Incremental investment = $1,170,000
    Residual income = $400,500
    Sybil Co. should change the credit standards.

16. DSO for new sales = 50 days
    Incremental investment = $133,333
    Residual income = $126,560
    Decision: Change the credit standards.

Chapter 14

1. (a) Collections in month 5 = $239
      Accounts receivable balance for month 5 = $387.75

    (b) Month 5, 90-days average = 44.56 DSO

2. April payment ratio = 0.896
    April DSO (based on 60 days sales) = 28.9

3. (b) April purchases discounted = 0.461

    (c) April cumulative payments: 0.461 by discount date; 0.563 by day 30; 0.929 by day 60

4. (a) Month 3 = $524

    (b) Month 3's aging schedule:
        30 days = 0.565
        60 days = 0.355
        90 days = 0.072
        120 days = 0.008

6. (a) May's aging schedule:
      Current = 0.82
      31–60 days = 0.12
      Over 60 days = 0.06

    (b) May's purchases discounted = 0.51

7. (a) June = $12,000

    (b) July, 30 days or less = 74.8%

    (c) May, 60-day average = 50.3 DSO

8. Collection experience variance = $5467.64, unfavorable
    Sales pattern variance = $732.36, unfavorable
    Sales quantity variance = $2494.66, unfavorable

9. Payment experience variance = $410,000, unfavorable
    Purchase mix variance = $12,000, unfavorable
    Purchase quantity variance = $378,000, unfavorable

10. Collection experience variance = $53.50, favorable
    Sales pattern variance = $19.50, unfavorable

11. Payment experience variance = $1562.20, unfavorable
    Purchase mix variance = $336.08, favorable
    Purchase quantity variance = $1548.88, unfavorable

Chapter 15

1. (a) Variable costing = $11,844.90
        Absorption costing = $12,816.90

    (b) $680.40

    (c) Net cash flow: Variable = $2402.28
                        Absorption = $2110.68

2. Item S: Original = $2700
          Present = $2890
          LCM = $2700

3. Year 3's gross margin (inventory at cost) = $100,000

4. (d) $2000 lower

5. (a) $6.30   (b) $9.00   (c) $8.40   (d) $9.00   (e) $8.10

6. (a) $3150

   (b) $4350

   (c) $5850

7. Year 1's profit after tax: Year 1's cash flow:
   Selling price = $1200   Selling price = −$10,800
   Conventional = −$600   Conventional = −$9600

8. (a) yes; no   (b) yes; no   (c) no; yes   (d) no; yes

   (e) no; yes   (f) yes; yes   (g) no; yes   (h) no; yes

   (i) no; yes   (j) no; yes   (k) no; yes   (l) no; yes

   (m) no; yes   (n) no; yes   (o) no; yes   (p) no; yes

   (q) no; yes   (r) yes; yes   (s) no; yes   (t) no; yes

   (u) no; no   (v) yes; no   (w) no; yes

9. March 31 inventory
   FIFO   1,600 units $18,000
   LIFO   1,600 $15,200

10. Cost of sales:
    Specific = $250
    FIFO = $245
    LIFO = $260

11. (a) Period 3's inventory value: FIFO = $54; LIFO = $60

    (b) Period 3's cost of sales: FIFO = $547; LIFO = $531

    (c) Profit difference, period 3: FIFO $16 less than LIFO

12. Cost of sales: LIFO = $41,200; FIFO = $39,900

Chapter 16

1. EOQ = 4000 units

2. Discount > 3.05%

3. EOQ = 1414.21
   Total investment cost = $1,000,707.10
   Average investment = $7071.05

4. 2-point average turnover ratio = 12
   13-point average turnover ration = 6.87

5. (a) 3333.33
   (b) $12,910
   (c) $6455
6. (a) $233,607
   (b) $250,000
7. (a) Last year end inventory level = $76,485
   (b) Next year end expected inventory level = $78,560
8. (a) 4.95
   (b) 0.202

Appendix B
1. (a) (i) EOQ = 1581
   (b) 5000 units
2. (a) 417 units
   (b) 277 units
   (c) 0 units
3. (a) $3,001,500
   (b) $299,900
   (c) 2.5
   (d) $1,350,800

Chapter 17
1. −$63,750
2. Price variance = $18,000, unfavorable
3. Total cost of sale price variance = $8750, unfavorable
4. Total price variance = $562.50, unfavorable
5. Total price variance = $20,000, unfavorable
6. (a) Gross margin price variance = $80, favorable
   (b) Gross margin cash flow variance = $172.50, favorable
7. Gross margin variance = $0
8. Sales volume variance = $50,000, unfavorable
9. Closing inventory price variance = $17,500, favorable
10. Gross margin volume variance = $44,500, unfavorable
11. Turnover volume variance = 0.1389, unfavorable

Appendix 1
1. (a) Element in row 1, column 1 = 1.78571
   (b) State 0 = 2.05 months
       State 1 = 2.27 months
       State 2 = 2.05 months

    (c) State 0 = 0.7%
          State 1 = 3.9%
          State 2 = 29.2%

    (d) Value of accounts receivable:
          State 0 = \$3571.42
          State 1 = \$681.82
          State 2 = \$129.87

    (e) Monthly cash flows = \$2097.40
          Monthly bad debts = \$25.97

2. Incremental receivables = \$805.43 at the new steady state.

Appendix 2

1. Partially secured receivables 69%
2. Unsecured creditors deficiency = \$51,000

Index